A CONCISE ENCYCLOPEDIA *of the* BAHÁ'Í FAITH

Other books in the series:

A Concise Encyclopedia of Christianity, Geoffrey Parrinder, ISBN 1–85168–174–4
A Concise Encyclopedia of Judaism, Dan Cohn-Sherbok, ISBN 1–85168–176–0
A Concise Encyclopedia of Hinduism, Klaus K. Klostermaier, ISBN 1–85168–175–2
A Concise Encyclopedia of Islam, Gordon D. Newby, ISBN 1–85168–295–3
A Concise Encyclopedia of Buddhism, John Powers, ISBN 1–85168–233–3

Other books on the Bahá'í Faith published by Oneworld:

The Gardeners of God: An Encounter with Five Million Bahá'ís, Colette Gouvion and Philippe Jouvion, ISBN 1–85168–052–7
The Hidden Words of Bahá'u'llah, ISBN 1–85168–007–1
Olya's Story: A Survivor's Dramatic Account of the Persecution of Bahá'ís in Revolutionary Iran, Olya Roohizadegan, ISBN 1–85168–073–X
The Seven Valleys of Bahá'u'llah, ISBN 1–85168–031–4
The Bahá'í Faith: A Short History, Peter Smith, ISBN 1–85168–208–2
The Bahá'í Faith: A Short Introduction, Moojan Momen, ISBN 1–85168–209–0
William Henry Randall: Disciple of 'Abdu'l Bahá, Bahíyyih Randall-Winckler with Mabel Garis, ISBN 1–85168–124–8

A CONCISE ENCYCLOPEDIA *of the* BAHÁ'Í FAITH

PETER SMITH

ONEWORLD
OXFORD

A CONCISE ENCYCLOPEDIA OF THE BAHÁ'Í FAITH

Oneworld Publications
(Sales and Editorial)
185 Banbury Road
Oxford OX2 7AR
England
www.oneworld-publications.com

Reprinted 2002

A CIP record for this book is available
from the British Library

ISBN 1–85168–184–1

Cover design by Design Deluxe
Typeset by LaserScript Ltd, Mitcham, Surrey
Printed in England by Clays Ltd, St Ives plc

To Philip and Parry Harvey and Betty Reed, and to the memory of Chattida Suwansathien ('Maew') (2509–2537 Buddhist Era/1966–94 CE*).*

'All that the sages and mystics have said or written have never exceeded, nor can they ever hope to exceed, the limitations to which man's finite mind hath been strictly subjected'.

Bahá'u'lláh (*Gleanings*, p. 316 no. 148).

'All human attainment moveth upon a lame ass, whilst Truth, riding upon the wind, darteth across space'.

Islamic tradition, cited by Bahá'u'lláh (*Kitáb-i-Íqán*, p. 120).

Contents

Maps

Preface

This book differs from its companion volumes in that the Bahá'í Faith is comparatively recent in its origins and, despite a growing body of academic studies, is not yet studied in the same detail and comprehensiveness as the other religions covered in the series. There are several earlier reference works – the most important in English being Wendi Momen's *A Basic Bahá'í Dictionary* (1989) (261 pp.) – but there is an obvious need for a more encyclopedic study. A large-scale 'Bahá'í Encyclopedia' project is at present under way in the United States, but its completion date is uncertain. In the interim, it is hoped that the present work will be of value to those who are seeking basic information about the Bahá'í Faith and the Bábí movement from which it emerged.

I am conscious of the limitations of this work. It is something of a pioneer effort, and no single writer can hope to have a comprehensive knowledge of all aspects of a religion – its history, doctrines, practices, and social embodiment in diverse cultures. Again, in some areas, there is as yet little primary research, so that my own remarks are necessarily highly provisional. I can aim only to provide a basic summary of our present knowledge, and to point readers in the direction of other works they might consult on particular topics.

I am solely responsible for such mistakes as the reader may discover. Writing an encyclopedia is a good way for any author to learn more about their area of research – and also to become more conscious of their own ignorance. In preparing this work, I have accumulated the following debts of gratitude: most particularly to Moojan Momen and Susan Maneck for having read through the entire manuscript and commenting on it; to Juan Cole, Graham Hassall, the National Spiritual Assembly of the Bahá'ís of Chile, Charles Nolley, Vaughan Smith, Robert Stauffer and Will van den Hoonaard for their responses to specific queries; to Jackson Armstrong-Ingram, Richard Hollinger, and

Moojan Momen for the provision of unpublished work; to Firouz Anaraki, Mozhdeh and Check Woo Foo, Victor Greenspoon, Virginia Harden, Sammi Smith and Dale Walton for their encouragement and assistance; and to those family members and friends who endured the considerable disruptions to everyday life caused by the writing of the book.

On language and names

The English language is implicitly 'sexist' (referring in the abstract to the third person singular, an author is forced to use 'he' or 'she'; many terms, such as 'mankind', contain gender references). Growing awareness of this reality has led many writers to question the use of what were formerly common turns of phrase. A 'non-sexist' English usage generally acceptable to most readers has yet to emerge, however. It is easy enough to substitute terms such as 'humanity' for 'mankind' (the latter is common in older Bahá'í texts), but other issues are more difficult to resolve, notably the third person singular, both regarding people and God. For the latter, I have followed contemporary Bahá'í usage – itself reflecting traditional biblical English – by referring to God as 'he', this despite the Bahá'í view that God is beyond gender, and is neither 'he' nor 'she'.

Traditional Persian, Arabic and Turkish names can be quite confusing for those who are not Middle Easterners. Prior to the twentieth century, there were no surnames, and individuals might be known by a variety of names and titles. A personal name might be bracketed by various titles (Mírzá *Taqí* Khán), or prefixed by a string of titles (Ḥájí Mírzá Sayyid *'Alí*), or an individual might become known by a religious or state title, or by a succession of such titles (Mírzá Taqí Khán is most commonly known as AMÍR KABÍR). Prefixes included Arabic religious titles, such as 'Ḥájí' (a man who has made the pilgrimage (*ḥáj*) to Mecca), 'Mullá' (an Islamic cleric), 'Sayyid' (a descendant of the Prophet Muḥammad), and 'Shaykh' (commonly a religious leader or teacher), as well as the secular 'Mírzá', which in 19th-century Iran had come to be used to indicate a respectable educated man. Suffixes included titles of social rank such as the Persian 'Khán' (originally a ruler or military chieftain, but by the early 20th century, 'sir') and 'Khánum' ('lady'), and their Turkish equivalents: 'Effendi' and 'Bagum'. The titles of social rank have also been subject to change over time. Other suffixes indicated place of origin ('Tihrání', one from Tehran), or, less commonly, occupation, and have often been the basis for the surnames adopted during the 20th century.

The format adopted here is to generally refer to individuals by whatever name or title they are most well known. Thus 'QUDDÚS', and not '(Mullá) Muḥammad-'Alí' or 'Bárfurúshí', and to provide cross-references where this seems helpful.

As the Bahá'í Faith developed in a 19th-century context in which all the major Middle Eastern languages were used, Bahá'í literature often melds Persian and Arabic (Bahá'í writings in Persian commonly include much Arabic vocabulary; Arabic writings may include Persian constructions). In the matter of names, however, I have generally sought to use personal names and technical terms in their original language.

References, transliteration and abbreviations

References to articles in the *Concise Encyclopedia of the Bahá'í Faith* are indicated by text in small capitals, e.g. PRAYER. The transliteration of Arabic and Persian follows an adapted version of that used by Bahá'ís, itself based on that of the Tenth International Congress of Orientalists (1894). Ottoman Turkish names are given in their modern Turkish form. Oriental names in common use are given without transliteration ('Tehran' not 'Ṭihrán'). Dates are given according to the Gregorian ('Common Era') calendar, but in some cases are preceded by the Muslim lunar date (e.g. AH 1260/1844). A list of abbreviations used in bibliographic references is given on pp. 11–12. Recommended reading on specific areas appears in a special font within or at the end of entries, e.g. *BKG* 11–12. As the book is intended for an English-language readership, few references are given to works in other languages.

A number of works of evident value arrived on my desk as I was finishing off the present manuscript (by Juan Cole (on BAHÁ'U'LLÁH); Charles Lerche (*Towards the Most Great Justice*); Diana Malouf (on the *HIDDEN WORDS*); Velda Metelmann (on Lua GETSINGER); and Moojan Momen (*Scripture and Revelation*)). I have included these in the bibliography, but was not able to use them in the preparation of this book.

Peter Smith, Bangkok

Introduction

The Bahá'í Faith centres on the person and teachings of Bahá'u'lláh (1817–92), the religion's prophet-founder. For Bahá'ís, Bahá'u'lláh is the latest in a succession of Manifestations of God, divine teachers who have revealed God's will to humankind over the millennia and have founded the world's great religions. From this perspective, all of these revelatory teachers – including Abraham, Moses, Zoroaster, the Buddha, Jesus and Muhammad – have contributed to a single process of progressive revelation, designed to lead humanity ever forward towards a future kingdom of God on Earth, which Bahá'u'lláh termed the 'Most Great Peace'. The Bahá'í teachings are regarded as the blueprint for that future global society and the Bahá'í community as a leaven for its accomplishment.

Bahá'u'lláh's religion of birth was the Shiʿi form of Islam, but while still a young man he announced his adherence to the religion of the Báb (1819–1850), a youthful merchant who was eventually to lay public claim to being the promised Mahdi. Those who followed the Báb – the Bábís – quickly became a significant element in Iranian religious life, and the new movement was violently persecuted, in large part at the instigation of the religious establishment, provoking what were regarded by their opponents as Bábí rebellions in various parts of Iran. The Báb himself was eventually executed (1850), and most of the Bábí leadership killed. For his part, Bahá'u'lláh was exiled to the Ottoman Empire, initially as a free man in Baghdad, but later as a prisoner, and finally consigned to Akka in Ottoman Syria. From exile, he was able to contact the Bábí remnant in Iran, reinvigorating the Bábís as a community through his writings, and subsequently gaining their allegiance for his claims to be the promised one foretold by the Báb (and indeed by the founders of all the religions). A vigorous campaign of Bahá'í missionary expansion followed, which under the guidance of Bahá'u'lláh's successors – his son, 'Abdu'l-Bahá (1844–1921), and great-grandson, Shoghi Effendi (1897–1957) – took on an increasingly global dimension. Thus, what had originally been seen as a religious movement amongst mostly Iranian Shi'i Muslims emerged as a world religion, with several million followers widely spread across the entire world, and comprising individuals from perhaps every religious background. A short summary of these historical developments is provided in the Chronology following this Introduction (pp. 1–10).

The Bahá'í teachings are derived from a corpus of canonical texts, mostly by Bahá'u'lláh, 'Abdu'l-Bahá and Shoghi Effendi, and to a lesser extent the Báb and the Universal House of Justice, an elected body which has led the Bahá'í world since 1963. Central beliefs include the idea of successive divine revelations (see above) and of a succession of authoritative and divinely sanctioned leaders of the Bahá'í Faith itself (the Covenant doctrine); the conviction that the purpose of human life is to know God, follow his teachings as given by his prophets, and to develop spiritual qualities; the belief that society as well as the individual can be reshaped according to the prescriptions of sacred law and the promulgation of a range of Bahá'í principles; the expectation that this reshaping of society will eventually lead to the development of a spiritualized and unified human race in a new World Order (the Biblical 'Kingdom of God on Earth'); and faith that the system of Bahá'í administration provides a divinely-sanctioned means for the expansion of the Bahá'í religion as well as a model for the organization of human society.

Specific teachings include the beliefs that:

(1) God in essence is unknowable, and that he can instead be best known through the Manifestations of God
(2) true religion is essential to human progress
(3) the major religions of the world share a common divine origin and 'fundamental unity' (religious diversity)
(4) reason and science are important sources of knowledge, and there is an essential harmony between true religion and science
(5) the progress of the individual soul involves the pursuit of the spiritual path
(6) the human race is one, God making no distinction between people on the basis of race
(7) human civilization depends on spiritual as well as material progress
(8) divine love is a powerful force

Important aspects of Bahá'í practice include the cultivation of prayer and meditation, fasting, the development of Bahá'í community and family life, consultation as a means of problem solving, the exercise of tolerance, freedom from prejudice, the non-use of alcohol and drugs, the value of work, particularly when performed in the spirit of service to others, the promotion of socio-economic development, and the endeavour of teaching the Bahá'í Faith and principles to others. Moral development is understood mostly in terms of the acquisition of spiritual qualities (including charity, chastity, detachment, the fear of God, trustworthiness, truthfulness, and wisdom).

Important Bahá'í social teachings deal with the topics of agriculture, economics, education, the environment, government, human rights, indigenous peoples, justice, the need for a universal language, social order, war and the advancement of women.

The Thematic Index at the end of the book (pp. 388–96) provides listings of entries on (1) 'The principle figures and periods of Bábí–Bahá'í history' – including listings of the major Bahá'í texts referred to; (2) 'Aspects of Bahá'í belief and practice' and (3) 'People and places' of significance.

Chronology

Research is gradually establishing a fairly reliable chronology for the Bábí and early Bahá'í period, but many obscurities still remain, and conflicting dates are given for a number of events. Cameron's *Bahá'í Chronology* makes a commendable attempt to bring together available dates. His neglect of the works by Amanat (*ARR*) and MacEoin represents a serious shortcoming for the early Bábí period, but his dating of Bahá'í developments is invaluable.

The early Bábí period, 1844–53

The emergence of the Bábí movement, centring on the Báb. The movement spreads to Iraq and much of Iran, generating increasing opposition and persecution. The Báb's claim to be the Mahdí/*Qá'im* (1848) and a growing radicalism on the part of many of his followers (Babi radicalism) leads to a more confrontational relationship with the authorities: armed conflicts break out (1848–53), and the movement is suppressed.

1843/4 Death of Sayyid Káẓim Rashtí (31 December/1/2 January). The search for a successor.

1844 The Báb's revelatory dream. His declaration of mission to Mullá Ḥusayn Bushrú'í (22–23 May), and composition of the *Qayyúmu'l-asmá'*. The conversion of the Letters of the Living. The Báb's pilgrimage to Mecca (beginning September) and declaration of mission there (December).

1845 Trial of Mullá 'Alí Basṭámí, the Báb's emissary in Iraq (13 January). The Báb cancels his plans to meet his followers in Karbalá, and after two months in Muscat (March–April) returns to Iran (15 May). In Shíráz, a group of Bábís is severely punished for adding the Báb's name to the Muslim call to prayer, and following his return to the city (early July) the Báb himself is arrested, interrogated and forced to make a public recantation. In Kirmán KARÍM KHÁN composes the first of his attacks on the Bábís (July). Secret propaganda continues, with the conversion of VAHÍD and ḤUJJAT. ṬÁHIRIH establishes Karbalá as an important Bábí centre.

1846 The Báb escapes from Shíráz (23 September) and proceeds to Iṣfáhán, where he is favourably received by the governor, MANÚCHIHR KHÁN.

1847 Following the death of Manúchihr Khán (21 February) the Báb is taken to Kulayn (March–April) and then to the fortress-prison of MÁKÚ (July). Ṭáhirih is expelled from Iraq (March), and eventually returns to Qazvín (July). The murder of Mullá MUḤAMMAD-TAQÍ BARAGHÁNÍ (August–September?) leads to Ṭáhirih's confinement, and persecution of the Qazvín Bábís. The first killings of Bábís occur. The Báb begins his composition of the *BAYÁN*.

1848 Mullá Ḥusayn journeys to see the Báb in Mákú, reaching there in March. He then visits QUDDÚS in Bárfurúsh, before returning to Mashhad. The Báb is transferred to the fortress of CHIHRÍQ (April–May). He is brought for trial in Tabríz, and makes public claim to be the *Qá'im* (July/August), and later denounces Ḥájí Mírzá ÁQÁSÍ. A group of Bábís gathers in BADASHT (June), Quddús is later arrested. Mullá Ḥusayn raises the BLACK STANDARD (July), and leads a growing band of followers from Khúrasán to Mázandarán. Following the death of MUḤAMMAD SHÁH (4 September) the conflict of Shaykh ṬABARSÍ begins (10 October–10 May 1849).

1849 The Ṭabarsí conflict ends (10 May). Quddús is taken to Bárfurúsh and killed (16 May).

1850 The SEVEN MARTYRS OF TEHRAN are executed (19/20 February). Vahíd's preaching in Yazd leads to disturbances (January–February). He goes to NAYRÍZ: an armed struggle between the Bábís and their opponents follows (27 May–21 June). An armed struggle also occurs in ZANJÁN (*c.* 13 May–

c. 2 January 1851). The Báb is executed at the instructions of AMÍR KABÍR (8/9 July).

1851 The Zanján conflict ends (January). Bahá'u'lláh leaves Iran for Karbalá at the urging of Amír Kabír (June(?)–April/May(?) 1852). Several Bábís are killed in Yazd and elsewhere.

1852 Amír Kabír is killed at the order of the king (January). One Bábí faction (headed by AẒÍM) makes an attempt on the life of NÁṢIRU'D-DÍN SHÁH (15 August). Many Bábís are killed, including Ṭáhirih. Bahá'u'lláh is arrested (16 August) and imprisoned in the SÍYÁH-CHÁL (August–December), where he experiences his initiatory vision.

1853 Renewed conflict in Nayríz (March–October).

The development of Bábism, 1853–66

The Bábí remnant in Iran maintains a more or less underground existence, and is divided into factions following different claimants to leadership, including DAYYÁN. Ṣubḥ-i-AZAL in BAGHDAD may have exercised an ineffective overall headship, but from 1856 onwards he is increasingly eclipsed by BAHÁ'U'LLÁH, who both revives and remodels Bábism.

1853 Bahá'u'lláh is exiled from Iran. He and his family journey from Tehran to Baghdad (12 January–8 April).

1854–6 Bahá'u'lláh leaves Baghdad for Kurdistan (10 April 1854–19 March 1856).

1856–63 Bahá'u'lláh gradually revivifies the Bábí community, and his writings, such as the *HIDDEN WORDS* (*c*. 1858) and *Kitáb-i-ÍQÁN* (1862), are widely circulated. He becomes the dominant Bábí leader. Ṣubḥ-i-Azal remains in hiding.

1863 Bahá'u'lláh stays in the garden of RIḌVÁN (22 April–3 May) prior to his journey to Istanbul (3 May–16 August). He remains in Istanbul until his journey to Edirne (1–12 December). Claims to divinely-bestowed authority become prominent in his writings.

1864 Major persecution of Bábís in Najafábád by Shaykh Muḥammad-Báqir (the 'WOLF').

c. 1865 Bahá'u'lláh is poisoned (by Azal), but survives. Western scholarly interest in Bábism begins with the publication of works by GOBINEAU and Mirza Kazem-Beg.

The emergence of the Bahá'í Faith, 1866–92

The development of the Bahá'í Faith as a new religion centring on Bahá'u'lláh.

1866 Bahá'u'lláh makes formal announcement to Azal to be HE WHOM GOD SHALL MAKE MANIFEST in the *Súri-yi-Amr* ('Chapter of Command'), and refers for the first time to his followers as 'the people of *Bahá*'. He withdraws to the house of Riḍá Big (10 March). The 'Most Great Separation' continues for two months, during which the Edirne Bábís are asked to choose between Bahá and Azal. Most follow Bahá'u'lláh. Bahá'í missionaries begin to convert the Bábí remnant in Iran, leading in some instances to confrontations between the Bahá'ís and the now-emergent Azali Bábís.

1867 Azal challenges Bahá'u'lláh to let God judge between them (*MUBÁHALA*), but does not attend the projected meeting. Bahá'u'lláh begins his proclamation to the RULERS. Execution of three Bahá'ís in Tabríz. Persecutions in various parts of Iran.

1868 Arrest of Bahá'ís in Egypt and Baghdad. Conversion of first Bahá'í of Christian background. Bahá'u'lláh is banished to AKKA under an order of life imprisonment (he and his companions leave Edirne on 12 August and reach Akka on 31 August). Azal and some others are sent to Famagusta (arr. 5 September).

1869 BADÍ' delivers Bahá'u'lláh's letter to Náṣiru'd-dín Sháh, and is tortured and killed.

1870 Death of Mírzá MIHDÍ (23 June). Bahá'u'lláh leaves the Akka barracks, and lives under house arrest in the city (from October).

1872 Three Azalis are murdered by Bahá'í hotheads in Akka (22 January).

1873 The new governor of Akka becomes sympathetic to the Bahá'ís. Bahá'u'lláh completes the *Kitáb-i-Aqdas*. 'Abdu'l-Bahá marries (8 March).

1875 'Abdu'l-Bahá writes the *Secret of Divine Civilization* (lithographed, 1882). Bahá'u'lláh sends Jamál Effendi to India as a missionary.

1876 Deposition of Sultan Abdulaziz (30 May).

1877 Bahá'u'lláh leaves Akka, and moves to Mazra'ih (June).

1879 Execution of the King and Beloved of Martyrs in Iṣfáhán (17 March). Bahá'u'lláh moves to Bahjí (September).

1889 Murder of a Bahá'í in Ashkhabad by Shí'ís (8 September) prompts Russian intervention. The Bahá'ís in Turkistan henceforth emerge as a separate religious community free of persecution.

1892 Death of Bahá'u'lláh (29 May). He designates 'Abdu'l-Bahá as head of the Faith.

The period of 'Abdu'l-Bahá's leadership (1892–1921)

'Abdu'l-Bahá becomes the leader of the Bahá'í movement; oversees its expansion to the West; and initiates administrative and other developments. He faces the persistent opposition of his half-brother Muḥammad-'Alí and other family members, which causes him to stress the doctrine of the Covenant, and to denounce his opponents as Covenant-breakers.

1894 Ibrahim Kheiralla begins Bahá'í teaching activity in Chicago. Conversion of the first American Bahá'ís.

1896 Assassination of Náṣiru'd-dín Sháh by a follower of Jamálu'd-dín 'al-Afghání' (1 May). 'Abdu'l-Bahá moves to the House of 'Abdu'lláh Páshá.

1897 Birth of Shoghi Effendi (1 March). Consultative council of Hands of the Cause in Tehran prepares for the formation of a Bahá'í assembly (1899).

1898 Tarbíyat Bahá'í school for boys established in Tehran. The first Western pilgrims arrive in Akka (December).

1899 Bahá'í activities begin in Paris and London. Kheiralla returns to America. A leadership crisis develops, finally marked by Kheiralla renouncing 'Abdu'l-Bahá (1900).

1902 Construction of the Bahá'í temple in Ashkhabad begins.

1905 Bahá'í activities begin in Germany. The Constitutional Revolution in Iran.

1908 The Young Turk Revolution transforms Ottoman government and releases political and religious prisoners. 'Abdu'l-Bahá is released from Ottoman confinement, and subsequently moves his family to Haifa (1909).

1909 The remains of the Báb are interred in a shrine on Mount Carmel (21 March). The BAHAI TEMPLE UNITY is established in Chicago.

1910 'Abdu'l-Bahá travels to Egypt (10 August). Establishment of a Bahá'í girls' school in Tehran.

1911 'Abdu'l-Bahá completes his first tour of Europe (August–December). A systematic teaching campaign is launched in India.

1912 'Abdu'l-Bahá begins his second Western tour (North America, 11 April–5 December; Europe, 13 December–13 June 1913). He returns to Haifa on 5 December.

1914 World War I begins. Bahá'í activity started in Japan.

1918 British take Palestine from the Turks, ensuring 'Abdu'l-Bahá's safety. World War I ends.

1919 The *Tablets of the Divine Plan* are ceremonially 'unveiled' in New York. Martha ROOT travels to Latin America to teach the Bahá'í Faith. 'Abdu'l-Bahá composes his *Tablet to The HAGUE*.

1920 Hyde and Clara DUNN arrive in Australia. Fanny KNOBLOCH arrives in South Africa. Work begins at the site of the proposed Bahá'í House of Worship at Wilmette, Illinois. The first All-India Bahá'í Convention is held. 'Abdu'l-Bahá is knighted by the British.

1921 Shí'is seek to gain possession of the House of Bahá'u'lláh in BAGHDAD (January; long-running legal dispute ensues, but

Bahá'ís lose possession (1922). Leonora Armstrong arrives in Brazil. The first Race Amity Conference is held in the USA. 'Abdu'l- Bahá dies (28 November).

The guardianship of Shoghi Effendi, 1922–57

Shoghi Effendi is head of the Faith. Process of administrative consolidation (*see* administration) begins (1922). Systematic planning becomes part of regular Bahá'í activity (from 1937) (*see* plans). Large-scale conversions of Bahá'ís in various parts of the 'Third World' begin in the 1950s (*see* expansion).

1922 Shoghi Effendi is publicly named as Guardian (January). He calls a conference of leading Bahá'ís to discuss the future of the Faith. His first general letter on Bahá'í administration is sent to the West (5 March).

1923 Shoghi Effendi's second general letter on administration (12 March). National assemblies are elected in Britain, Germany and India.

1925 The International Bahá'í Bureau is established in Geneva. A Bahá'í Esperanto magazine begins publication in Germany. An Egyptian court declares the Bahá'í Faith to be separate from Islam. Shoghi Effendi establishes definite qualifications for Bahá'í membership. Qájár rule in Iran formally comes to an end, and Reza Khan becomes Shah.

1926 Queen Marie of Romania meets Martha Root and pays public tribute to the Faith. Ruth White begins her campaign of opposition to the Bahá'í administration.

1927 The American national assembly adopts a Declaration of Trust preparatory to legal incorporation (May 1929).

1928 Persecution of the Bahá'ís in Soviet Asia. The case of Bahá'u'lláh's House in Baghdad is brought before the Permanent Mandates Commission of the League of Nations, which finds in favour of the Bahá'ís.

1929 New History Society founded by Ahmad Sohrab in New York. His *de facto* excommunication ensues. Shoghi Effendi obtains possession of the mansion at Bahjí, and begins work on the expansion of the SHRINE OF THE BÁB. He begins his 'WORLD ORDER' letters (until 1936).

1932 BAHIYYIH KHÁNUM dies (15 July). Shoghi Effendi publishes *DAWN-BREAKERS*.

1934 Bahá'í schools in Iran closed. Purge of Bahá'ís in government employment. Mounting campaign of official persecution (to 1941). National assembly established for Australia and New Zealand. The Egyptian assembly secures legal incorporation. Shoghi Effendi issues *The DISPENSATION OF BAHÁ'U'LLÁH* (8 February).

1937 Shoghi Effendi marries RÚḤIYYIH KHÁNUM (25 March). First American Seven Year Plan (to 1944) marks beginning of a systematic campaign to establish the Faith in Latin America. Other national PLANS follow (1938–53). The Bahá'í Faith is banned in Nazi Germany.

1938 Mass arrests and exile of Bahá'ís in Soviet Asia. The Ashkhabad temple is turned into an art gallery.

1939–45 World War II.

1944 Shoghi Effendi publishes *GOD PASSES BY*.

1946 Systematic campaign begins to establish the Bahá'í Faith throughout Western Europe.

1948 Establishment of the BAHÁ'Í INTERNATIONAL COMMUNITY (BIC) affiliated with the United Nations. The state of Israel comes into being. Construction of the superstructure of the Shrine of the Báb begins (to 1953).

1951 INTERNATIONAL BAHÁ'Í COUNCIL inaugurated. A systematic campaign to establish the Faith in Africa begins. Shoghi Effendi's first appointment of Hands of the Cause.

1953 TEN YEAR CRUSADE begins (to 1963). A series of intercontinental teaching CONFERENCES is held. The Bahá'í temple in Wilmette is dedicated for worship.

1954 Women become eligible to serve on Bahá'í ASSEMBLIES in Iran. Shoghi Effendi establishes the AUXILIARY BOARDS.

1955 Construction of the INTERNATIONAL ARCHIVES building begins (to 1957). National campaign of persecution against the Bahá'ís in Iran.

1957 Death of Shoghi Effendi in London (4 November). The Hands assume leadership of the Bahá'í world.

The custodianship of the Hands, 1957–63

An 'interregnum' between the death of Shoghi Effendi and the election of the Universal House of Justice during which the Hands seek to complete the Ten Year Crusade, and prepare for the election of the House.

1960 Mason REMEY makes claim to be the second Guardian, and is declared a Covenant-breaker. All Bahá'í activities in Egypt are banned by presidential decree (August).

1961 The Bahá'í temples in Kampala and Sydney are dedicated for worship. 'Mass teaching' begins in India. The International Bahá'í Council changes from an appointed to an elected body.

1962 Persecution of Bahá'ís in Morocco (to 1963). Bahá'í institutions are banned in Indonesia.

The Universal House of Justice, from 1963

The UNIVERSAL HOUSE OF JUSTICE becomes head of the Faith, and oversees its continued expansion and administrative development, as well as substantial developments at the BAHÁ'Í WORLD CENTRE. Political revolution in IRAN profoundly affects the Bahá'ís world-wide.

1963 Establishment of the Universal House of Justice (21–22 April). It announces that it knows of no way in which further Guardians can be appointed (6 October). First Bahá'í world congress held in London (28 April–2 May).

1964 The Bahá'í temple in Frankfurt is dedicated for worship. The Universal House of Justice declares that there is no way to appoint further Hands of the Cause. The Nine Year Plan begins (to 1973). Other international plans follow.

1967 Permanent BIC office established in New York. The Universal House of Justice issues *The Proclamation of Bahá'u'lláh* and presents copies to many world leaders. Global PROCLAMATION campaign begins.

1968 Establishment of the CONTINENTAL BOARDS OF COUNSELLORS.

1970 All Bahá'í institutions and activities are banned in Iraq. The BIC gains consultative status with the United Nations Economic and Social Council (ECOSOC).

1972 The Panama temple is dedicated for worship. The Universal House of Justice adopts its constitution.

1973 Establishment of the INTERNATIONAL TEACHING CENTRE.

1976 The Bahá'í Faith is banned in Vietnam. BIC is granted consultative status with the United Nations Children's Fund (UNICEF).

1977 First Bahá'í radio station established in Latin America (Ecuador). The first of a series of international Bahá'í women's conferences is held.

1979 Islamic revolution in Iran. Major persecution of Bahá'ís begins. The House of the Báb is destroyed.

1983 Seat of the Universal House of Justice comes into use. Office of Social and Economic Development established. The Bahá'í Faith is officially banned in Iran.

1984 Bahá'í temple in Apia dedicated for worship. International Bahá'í Refugee Office established.

1985 The Universal House of Justice issues its statement *The PROMISE OF WORLD PEACE*.

1986 The Bahá'í temple in New Delhi is dedicated for worship.

1989 The Bahá'í Office of the Environment is established as part of BIC. European Bahá'í Youth Council established. Collapse of communist rule in Eastern Europe.

1990 A special teaching plan for former Eastern Bloc countries is launched (to 1992).

1992 Second Bahá'í world congress in New York. Publication of the *Kitáb-i-AQDAS*. *ḤUQÚQU'LLÁH* becomes universally applicable. BIC Office for the Advancement of Women is established.

Abbreviations

AB	H.M. Balyuzi, *'Abdu'l-Bahá*
ADJ	Shoghi Effendi, *The Advent of Divine Justice*
ARR	A. Amanat, *Resurrection and Renewal*
BA	Shoghi Effendi, *Bahá'í Administration*
BFA	R.H. Stockman, *The Bahá'í Faith in America* (2 vols)
BFSH	Smith, *The Bahá'í Faith: A Short History*
BKG	H.M. Balyuzi, *Bahá'u'lláh: The King of Glory*
BW	*Bahá'í World* (19 vols to date)
BWNS	*Bahá'í World*, New Series (5 vols to date)
CC	Universal House of Justice, *Compilation of Compilations* (2 vols)
CF	Shoghi Effendi, *Citadel of Faith: Messages to America*
EB	H.M. Balyuzi, *Eminent Bahá'ís in the Time of Bahá'u'lláh*
EGBBF	H.M. Balyuzi, *Edward Granville Browne and the Bahá'í Faith*
EI2	*The Encyclopaedia of Islam*, 2nd edn.
ESW	Bahá'u'lláh, *Epistle to the Son of the Wolf*
Faith	Shoghi Effendi, *The Faith of Bahá'u'lláh, A World Religion*
GPB	Shoghi Effendi, *God Passes By*
GWB	Bahá'u'lláh, *Gleanings from the Writings of Bahá'u'lláh*
HW	Bahá'u'lláh, *The Hidden Words* (a=Arabic; p=Persian)
KA	Bahá'u'lláh, *The Kitáb-i-Aqdas: The Most Holy Book*
KI	Bahá'u'lláh, *The Kitáb-i-Íqán: The Book of Certitude*
LG	H. Hornby, *Lights of Guidance*
MBBR	M. Momen (ed.), *The Bábí and Bahá'í Religions, 1844–1944*
MBW	Shoghi Effendi, *Messages to the Bahá'í World, 1950–1957*
McR	D. MacEoin, *Rituals in Babism and Baha'ism*
McS	D. MacEoin, *The Sources for Early Babi Doctrine and History*
MF	'Abdu'l-Bahá, *Memorials of the Faithful*

MMS	M. Momen, unpublished manuscripts
MUHJ	Universal House of Justice, *Messages . . . , 1963–1986*
PDC	Shoghi Effendi, *The Promised Day is Come*
PM	Bahá'u'lláh, *Prayers and Meditations*
Proclamation	Bahá'u'lláh, *The Proclamation of Bahá'u'lláh*
PT	'Abdu'l-Bahá, *Paris Talks*
PUP	'Abdu'l-Bahá, *Promulgation of Universal Peace*
RB	A. Taherzadeh, *The Revelation of Bahá'u'lláh* (4 vols)
SAQ	'Abdu'l-Bahá, *Some Answered Questions*
SBBR	P. Smith, *The Babi and Baha'i Religions*
SDC	'Abdu'l-Bahá, *The Secret of Divine Civilization*
Star	*Star of the West*
'Survey'	P. Smith, and M. Momen, 'The Baha'i Faith 1957–1988: A survey of contemporary developments'
SV	Bahá'u'lláh, *Seven Valleys*
SWAB	'Abdu'l-Bahá, *Selections from the Writings of 'Abdu'l-Bahá*
TB	Bahá'u'lláh, *Tablets of Bába'u'lláh Revealed after the Kitáb-i-Aqdas*
TCB	A. Taherzadeh, *The Covenant of Bahá'u'lláh*
TDP	'Abdul'l-Bahá, *Tablets of the Divine Plan*
TJ	E.G. Browne, *The Táríkh-i-Jadíd*
TN	E.G. Browne, *A Traveller's Narrative*
UHJC	Universal House of Justice, *Constitution*
WEBW	O.Z. Whitehead, *Some Early Bahá'ís of the West*
Will	'Abdu'l-Bahá, *Will and Testament*
WOB	Shoghi Effendi, *The World Order of Bahá'u'lláh*
WSBR	O.Z. Whitehead, *Some Bahá'ís to Remember*

Other abbreviations

Ar.	Arabic
BSB	*Bahá'í Studies Bulletin*
CBC	Continental Board of Counsellors
ITC	International Teaching Centre
KSBBH	(Kalimát) *Studies in Bábí and Bahá'í History*
KSBBR	(Kalimát) *Studies in the Bábí and Bahá'í Religions*
NSA	national spiritual assembly
PA	Persianized Arabic
Pers.	Persian
UHJ	Universal House of Justice
UHJRD	Universal House of Justice, Research Department

A

'Abbás Núrí, Mírzá Buzurg (d. 1839)

The father of Bahá'u'lláh. 'Abbás came from an eminent family in the Iranian province of Mázandarán which traced its ancestry back to the last pre-Islamic Sassanian king of Iran, Yazdigird III. The family's ancestral lands were around the village of Tákur in the district of Núr. 'Abbás served as minister (*vazír*) to one of the sons of Fatḥ-'Alí Sháh (reg. 1797–1834) and later as a provincial governor for Burújird and Luristán. The enmity of the new chief minister, Ḥájí Mírzá Áqásí ('Abbás had been a friend of Áqásí's rival and predecessor), led to the loss of his political power in 1835 and to severe financial problems. *BKG* 11–12. (*See also* Núrí family.)

'Abbás Núrí (Mírzá Buzurg), father of Bahá'u'lláh

'Abbúd, Ilyás (d. 1878)

Christian merchant of Akka. Owner of the larger (seaward facing) part of what is now termed the house of 'Abbúd occupied by Bahá'u'lláh. (*See also* Akka.)

'Abduh, Shaykh Muḥammad (d. 1905)

Leading Muslim reformer whose ideas were influential throughout much of the Islamic world. Grand mufti of Egypt, 1889–1905. He met 'Abdu'l-Bahá in Beirut in 1878 and became his fervent admirer. *AB* 38; *EGBBF* 5; *GPB* 193

Abdulaziz (1830–76)

'Abdu'l-'Azíz, Ottoman sultan, 1861–76, who advanced the Tanzimat reforms, but opposed liberalism; the first sultan to visit Western Europe. He was deposed in 1876 (30 May), and shortly after either committed suicide or was murdered. It was during his reign that the successive exiles of Bahá'u'lláh within the Ottoman empire took place. After receiving the order of banishment to Edirne, Bahá'u'lláh sent him a strongly worded tablet in which the sultan's ministers were censured (*see* ÂLI PAŞA; FUAT PAŞA). He later addressed the sultan in the *Súra of the* KINGS, calling upon him not to entrust the affairs of state into the hands of corrupt and godless ministers, but himself to rule with justice and fear God. He was God's 'shadow on earth' (a traditional royal title), and as such should be detached from the world and ensure the well-being of his subjects. Bahá'u'lláh also deplored the extremes of wealth and poverty he witnessed in ISTANBUL, and protested his own innocence of any wrongdoing that would have merited his banishment. The sultan's downfall was prophesied in Bahá'u'lláh's tablet to Fuat Paşa. *GPB* 158–60, 172–3, 195–6; *PDC* 11, 37–40, 61–3, 66, 71; *RB2*: 312–15.

'Abdu'l-Bahá (Ar., 'Servant of Bahá') (1844–1921)

Title of Bahá'u'lláh's eldest son and successor.

'Abdu'l Bahá as a young man in Edirne

TITLES AND APPOINTMENT

His given name was 'Abbás, but his father also referred to him as the 'Master' (*Áqá*) and the 'Most Great (or Mighty) Branch' (*ghuṣn-i-a'ẓam*), the 'Mystery of God' (*sirru'lláh*), the 'Limb of the Law of God' who 'encompassed the whole of creation', and the apple of his eye. During the period of his leadership (1892–1921), he preferred to be known as 'Abdu'l-Bahá, and it is by this title that he is now generally known. Bahá'u'lláh explicitly named him as his successor in his will, the *Book of the* COVENANT, but prior to this had implicitly directed that after his own death, his followers should turn to 'Abdu'l-Bahá as their leader and as the interpreter of his writings (*KA* 63 k121, 82 k174). In the *Tablet of the* BRANCH, a letter to an individual Bahá'í, composed in the 1860s when 'Abdu'l-Bahá was only in his twenties, Bahá'u'lláh had also stated that those who had turned towards 'Abdu'l-Bahá had turned towards God, and that those who rejected him had repudiated Bahá'u'lláh and transgressed against him (*WOB* 135).

EARLY LIFE

According to tradition 'Abdu'l-Bahá was born on the very night of the BÁB's declaration (23 May 1844). His mother was Bahá'u'lláh's first wife, NAVVÁB. As a boy he experienced the shocks of his father's arrest in 1852, the subsequent exile to Iraq (he himself suffered from frost-bite during the journey in the bitter cold), and Bahá'u'lláh's withdrawal to the mountains of Kurdistan (1854–6). Greatly attached to his father, he began to assist him whilst still in his teens, increasingly taking responsibility for the practical affairs of the family and acting as one of his father's secretaries. By the time of the move to Akka (1868) he had become effectively responsible for the whole exile community (Bahá'u'lláh's family and disciples) and its relations with Ottoman officialdom. Although never attending any school he evidently read widely and became well known and respected amongst Ottoman officials and reformers, including several of the provincial governors in their various places of exile and figures such as Midhat Pasha and the Egyptian Shaykh Muḥammad 'Abduh. After his father moved out of Akka (1877) he continued to live in the city, increasingly gaining acceptance as a local notable despite continuing to live under the government's order of banishment. Giving alms to the poor and regularly attending the local mosque, he came to be seen by the local population as a pious, albeit heterodox Muslim leader rather than as the son of the founder of a new religion. In 1873, he married Munírih Nahrí (1847–1938), a girl from a prominent Iṣfáhání Bahá'í merchant family. The couple had four daughters who survived to adulthood, in addition to two sons and three daughters who died in childhood (*see* Núrí family). Unlike his father, grandfather and uncles, all of whom followed the contemporary upper-class Muslim practice of having several wives, 'Abdu'l-Bahá remained monogamous.

ministry (1892–1921)

'Abdu'l-Bahá's ministry can be divided into three phases:

(1) 1892–1908

The first phase was one of persistent difficulty and danger. Although most of the Bahá'ís readily accepted Bahá'u'lláh's clear appointment of 'Abdu'l-Bahá, and gave him their devotion, members of Bahá'u'lláh's extended family, led by 'Abdu'l-Bahá's half-brother, Muḥammad-'Alí, rejected his authority, and began an at first covert and then open campaign to discredit him (*see* Covenant-breakers). Of the family, only his sister (Bahiyyih Khánum), wife and daughters, together with a surviving uncle and his family, remained loyal. Unable to shake the allegiance of the mass of the Bahá'ís, this campaign led to recurrent problems for 'Abdu'l-Bahá with the Turkish authorities, including the reimposition of confinement in Akka (1901) and the appointment of two official commissions of enquiry, the second of which (1907–8) was expected to cause his exile to North Africa. This prolonged opposition caused 'Abdu'l-Bahá to give great emphasis to the doctrine that there was a sacred Covenant which ensured the preservation of Bahá'í unity through obedience to the properly appointed leaders of the Faith. Those who broke this covenant, such as Muḥammad-'Alí and his associates, were denounced as 'Covenant-breakers' and were ultimately excommunicated.

During this period 'Abdu'l-Bahá sought to ensure that the Faith would remain co-ordinated and protected from his opponents even if something were to happen to him, writing his Will and Testament, in which he appointed his eldest grandson, Shoghi Effendi – then still a child – to be the Guardian of the Faith after him; outlining the system to be employed for the election of the Universal House of Justice referred to by Bahá'u'lláh; and excluding Muḥammad-'Alí from succession on account of his Covenant-breaking. He also began to encourage the formation of locally elected Bahá'í councils (assemblies) in various parts of the Bahá'í world, as well as of several 'national' bodies.

Other developments of this period were the composition of 'Abdu'l-Bahá's *Treatise on Politics* (1892–3), written as a guide for the Iranian Bahá'ís at a time of growing political instability; the emergence of Bahá'í groups in North America and Europe, and the first pilgrimage visit from Western Bahá'ís to Akka (1898–9); 'Abdu'l-Bahá's encouragement of educational, medical and economic development among the Eastern Bahá'ís; the beginning of the construction of the first Bahá'í house of worship in the city of ASHKHABAD in Russian Turkestan; and the construction of the SHRINE OF THE BÁB on Mount Carmel.

(2) 1908–14

In 1908 the Young Turk revolution led to the freeing of Ottoman political prisoners, and the dangers that had faced 'Abdu'l-Bahá in Akka came to an end. In 1910 he moved across the bay from Akka to the newly developing city of HAIFA, which thenceforth was to remain the headquarters of the Faith. The Báb's remains were interred in the completed Shrine there on 21 March 1909, giving Haifa additional spiritual importance for Bahá'ís.

Taking advantage of his new freedom of movement 'Abdu'l-Bahá, now in his late sixties and far from well, moved to Egypt in 1910, and then embarked on a three-month journey to visit the new Bahá'ís of England and France (September–December 1911) (*see* p. 17). Resting for the winter in Egypt, he made a longer second journey to visit the Western Bahá'ís (March 1912–June 1913). After fourteen months of extensive travelling in the United States and Canada, during which he visited thirty-eight cities, he returned to Europe, where he visited Britain, France, Germany, and Austria-Hungary. He returned to Egypt (June 1913) and to Haifa (December) in a state of exhaustion.

The journeys were of major importance: (1) they contributed to the consolidation of the fledgling Western Bahá'í communities, giving the Bahá'ís a wider vision of their faith and encouraging them to greater action; (2) they attracted considerable public attention – including extensive sympathetic newspaper coverage – so that many people heard of the Bahá'í teachings for the first time; (3) 'Abdu'l-Bahá met many eminent people (including churchmen such as Archdeacon Wilberforce and T.K. Cheyne in England; academics such as the comparative religionist J. Estlin Carpenter, David Starr Jordan of

'Abdu'l Bahá in Paris

Itinerary of 'Abdu'l-Bahá: Egypt and the journeys to the West

EGYPT

1910 Leaves Haifa, ? Aug.
Port Said
Alexandria (Ramlih), to 11 Aug. 1911

THE FIRST VISIT TO EUROPE

1911 London, 4–23 Sept.
Bristol, 23–25 Sept.
London, 25 Sept.–3 Oct.
Paris, 3 Oct.–2 Dec.
Returns to Egypt

NORTH AMERICA

THE EAST COAST

1912 Leaves Alexandria, 25 March
New York, 11–20 April
Washington DC, 20–28 April
Chicago, 29 April–6 May
Cleveland, OH, 6–7 May
Pittsburgh, 7–8 May
Washington DC, 8–11 May
New York, 11–14 May (Montclair, NJ, 12 May)
Lake Mohonk, NY, 14–16 May
New York, 16–22 May
Boston, 22–26 May (Worcester, MA, 23 May)
New York, 26–31 May
Fanwood, NJ, 31 May–1 June
New York, 1–3 June
Milford, PA, 3 June
New York, 4–8 June
Philadelphia, 8–10 June
New York, 10–20 June
Montclair, NJ, 20–25 June
New York, 25–29 June
West Englewood, NJ, 29–30 June
Morristown, NJ, 30 June
New York, 30 June-23 July (West Englewood, NJ, 14 July)
Boston, 23–24 July
Dublin, NH, 24 July–16 Aug.
Greenacre, nr Eliot, ME, 16–23 Aug.
Malden, MA, 23–29 Aug.
Montreal, Quebec, 30 Aug.-9 Sept.
Buffalo, NY, 9–12 Sept.

THE MID-WEST

Chicago, 12–15 Sept.
Kenosha, WI, 15–16 Sept.
Chicago, 16 Sept.
Minneapolis, 16–21 Sept.

THE WEST

Omaha, NB, 21 Sept.
Lincoln, NB, 23 Sept.
Denver, CO, 24–27 Sept.
Glenwood Springs, CO, 28 Sept.
Salt Lake City, UT, 29–30 Sept.
San Francisco, 1–13 Oct.
Pleasanton, CA, 13–16 Oct.
San Francisco, 16–18 Oct.
Los Angeles, 18–21 Oct.
San Francisco, 21–25 Oct.
Sacramento, 25–26 Oct.
Denver, 28–29 Oct.

BACK TO THE EAST

Chicago, 31 Oct.–3 Nov.
Cincinnati, OH, 5–6 Nov.
Washington, DC, 6–11 Nov.
Baltimore, 11 Nov.
Philadelphia, 11 Nov.
New York, 12 Nov.–5 Dec.

THE SECOND VISIT TO EUROPE

BRITAIN

Liverpool, England, 13–16 Dec.
London, 16 Dec.–6 Jan. 1913 (Oxford, 31 Dec.)

1913 Edinburgh, 6–11 Jan.
London, 11–15 Jan.
Bristol, 15–16 Jan.
London, 16–21 Jan. (Woking, 18 Jan.)

CONTINENTAL EUROPE

Paris, 22 Jan.–30 March
Stuttgart, 1–8 April (Bad Mergentheim, 7–8 April)
Vienna, 8 April
Budapest, 9–19 April
Vienna, 19–24 April
Stuttgart, 25 April–1 May
Paris, 2 May–12 June
Marseilles, 12–13 June

EGYPT AGAIN

Port Said, 17 June–11 July
Ismá'iliyyah, 11–17 July
Alexandria (Ramlih), 17 July–2 Dec.
Returns to Haifa, 5 Dec.

Stanford University, the orientalist Arminius Vambery, and the philosophers John Dewey and Henri Bergson; the suffragette leader Emmeline Pankhurst; Annie Besant, the president of the Theosophical Society; and the author Kahlil Gibran) and addressed members of sympathetic organizations such as peace societies and the Esperantists; and (4) 'Abdu'l-Bahá's public addresses were an important addition to the corpus of Bahá'í scripture. Apart from specific religious issues, he addressed a number of social issues, including PEACE and RACE. He also made a point of visiting the poor. Given his status as an Iranian exile and former Ottoman prisoner, his reception in the United States by the Turkish ambassador and the Iranian *chargé d'affaires* (at that time ALI-KULI KHAN, a Bahá'í) were particularly significant.

(3) 1914–21

The onset of World War I (1914–18) prevented any further travel, and led to new threats against 'Abdu'l-Bahá's life (from the Turkish army chief, Cemal (Jamál) Paşa. This danger ended with the collapse of Turkish rule and the establishment of the British mandate. The war years and their immediate aftermath also brought famine to Palestine, 'Abdu'l-Bahá averting local catastrophe through the supply of grain stocks. He gained the respect of the newly established British authorities who secured him the award of a knighthood (1920). The post-war years were spent attending to the work of directing the affairs of the Faith. In addition to being a prominent and widely respected local notable, 'Abdu'l-Bahá was now clearly recognized as the head of an international religious movement. He died peacefully on 28 November 1921, his funeral being marked by the great number and religious diversity of its mourners. He was survived by his sister, wife, and daughters and their families. Shoghi Effendi succeeded him as head of the Faith.

Funeral procession of 'Abdu'l Bahá, 1921

PERSONALITY

For Bahá'ís 'Abdu'l-Bahá is the perfect exemplar of their faith, and stories about him are commonly presented as representing the ideal of Bahá'í behaviour. Many non-Bahá'ís also referred to him as a powerful and impressive personality, as did E.G. Browne, who wrote of his eloquence, wide religious knowledge, and 'majestic' and 'genial' bearing (*TN* xxxvi). He was both a commanding presence and intensely approachable, with a ready sense of humour. He sought to avoid religious disputation, but was uncompromising on matters of principle, as when he very deliberately scandalized social convention in Washington DC in order to demonstrate the Bahá'í belief in racial equality by insisting that a leading black Bahá'í (Louis GREGORY) should sit next to him at a prestigious dinner. Many Western Bahá'ís were inclined to see him in Christ-like terms as the personification of love and compassion.

THEOLOGICAL STATUS

Whilst stressing the Covenant doctrine and his authority as Bahá'u'lláh's successor and interpreter, 'Abdu'l-Bahá otherwise insisted that his station was one of servitude to his father, and strongly discouraged both Iranian and American Bahá'ís from describing him in exalted terms.

The definitive official statement of his status was given by Shoghi Effendi, who identified 'Abdu'l-Bahá as the third of the three 'Central Figures' of the Faith (after Bahá'u'lláh and the Báb): he was 'the Center and Pivot' of Bahá'u'lláh's covenant; his vicegerent on earth; the executive of his authority; the shepherd of his flock; the stainless mirror of his light; Bahá'u'lláh's 'most exalted handiwork'; the perfect exemplar of his teachings; the unerring interpreter of his mind and word; the embodiment of every Bahá'í ideal; the incarnation of every Bahá'í virtue; the 'Mainspring' of the oneness of humanity; the 'Architect' of Bahá'u'lláh's WORLD ORDER; and the 'Ensign' of the 'Most Great Peace' (*GPB* 245; *WOB* 134). 'Abdu'l-Bahá reflected 'the glory and power' of the MANIFESTATIONS OF GOD to a degree that no other human being could rival. In his person 'the incompatible characteristics of a human nature and superhuman knowledge and perfection' had been blended and 'completely harmonized' (*WOB* 134). He was not a Manifestation, however. Like a perfect mirror, he reflected 'the rays of Bahá'u'lláh's glory', and he derived his light, inspiration and sustenance from that source. His words possessed 'an equal validity' with those of Bahá'u'lláh, but they were not equal in rank (*WOB* 139). Contrary to the beliefs of various Bahá'ís in the early part of the century, 'Abdu'l-Bahá's

'Abdu'l Bahá as an older man – an image frequently displayed in Bahá'í homes

station was not identical or in some way equivalent to that of his father. Nor was there any 'mystic unity' between 'Abdu'l-Bahá and his father. Nor was 'Abdu'l-Bahá the return of Jesus Christ (*WOB* 138–9). Such beliefs were impious and heretical. His function was unique, not only in relationship to the Bahá'í dispensation, but in the entire field of religious history. No other figure had ever occupied a comparable station (*WOB* 131–2).

AB; see also *GPB* 237–32; Khursheed; *MBBR* 315–50; Muhájir, *Mystery of God*; NSA of Canada; *BFSH* 74–87; Ward. Memoirs include Blomfield; Blomfield and Shoghi Effendi; Brown; Chase; Gail, *Sheltering Branch*; Goodall and Cooper; Grundy; Hammond; Ives; Maxwell; Parsons; Phelps; Sohrab, *Abdul Baha in Egypt*; Thompson; Wilhelm *et al*; Winckler. On 'Abdu'l-Bahá as exemplar see Honnold. On his 'station' see *WOB* 131–9.

'Abdu'l-Bahá's writings and talks

Bahá'ís regard 'Abdu'l-Bahá as the authoritative interpreter of his father's writings. The corpus of his writings and authenticated talks thus form a major part to the Bahá'í 'canon' of sacred literature. In addition to several books, over 27,000 of his letters have survived. There is also a substantial body of unauthenticated 'PILGRIMS' NOTES' of conversations with him, but these are specifically excluded from the canon and have no binding authority.

Most of 'Abdu'l-Bahá's writings date from after his accession to leadership in 1892, but during his father's lifetime he had written a treatise on the 'modernization' of Iran (*SECRET OF DIVINE CIVILIZATION*, 1875), as well as a short history of the Bábí and Bahá'í religions (*TRAVELLER'S NARRATIVE*, 1886) and his *COMMENTARY ON 'I WAS A HIDDEN TREASURE'*. The first two of these at least have been accorded the same canonical status as his later writings. Later works include his *Treatise on* POLITICS (1892/3), the *Tablet of* ONE THOUSAND VERSES (1897/8), the *TABLETS OF THE DIVINE PLAN* (1916–17), the *Tablets* to the HAGUE (1919) and to Dr. FOREL (1921), and his *WILL AND TESTAMENT*. 'Abdu'l-Bahá wrote mostly in Persian, but also in Arabic, and a small number of items in Ottoman Turkish are extant. Many of his letters to Western Bahá'ís were published in English translation in the *Star of the West* (*see* PERIODICALS) and *Tablets of Abdul Baha Abbas*. A small compilation of his writings is also available (*Selections from the Writings of 'Abdu'l-Bahá*). In addition to individual texts, there is also a collection of his writings in Persian (*Makatíb-i-'Abdu'l-Bahá*, 8 vols.). Collins, *Bibliography*, 9–17, lists titles under his name in English.

Of his authenticated recorded oral teachings, the most important works in English are *SOME ANSWERED QUESTIONS* (1904–6) and *MEMORIALS OF THE FAITHFUL* (1915). There are several volumes recording 'Abdu'l-Bahá's talks in the West (1911–13). These mostly represent transcripts or reconstituted notes of the oral translation in English or French made by 'Abdu'l-Bahá's various interpreters, and have not yet been systematically checked against the Persian transcripts or notes which were made at the time by 'Abdu'l-Bahá's secretaries. Although no doubt generally accurate, they can not be regarded in their present form as completely authoritative or scriptural. The best known of these works are *'Abdu'l-Bahá in London* (Hammond); *Paris Talks*; and *Promulgation of Universal Peace*. All three of these are widely used by Bahá'ís as sources of doctrine, despite the caveat regarding their authoritativeness noted above. Notes on 'Abdu'l-Bahá's talks during his second visit to Paris are given in Chamberlain.

Abdulhamit II (1842–1918)

'Abdu'l-Ḥamíd, Ottoman sultan, 1876–1909. Initially approving a constitution and parliament, he became increasingly autocratic in his rule, arresting opponents and establishing an extensive network of spies. He lost power following the Young Turk Revolution (July 1908), and was deposed on 27 April 1909, following the failure of an attempted counterrevolution. Late in his reign, Ottoman commissions of enquiry were sent to investigate 'Abdu'l-Bahá. His overthrow led to the freeing of prisoners of state, including 'Abdu'l-Bahá. (*See also* OTTOMANS).

'Abdu'lláh Páshá

Governor of AKKA, 1819–31, and holder of extensive lands in the area. The building he had used as his governorate in the city ('the House of 'Abdu'lláh Páshá') was later rented by 'Abdu'l-Bahá, as also was the mansion of Mazra'ih. The original (1821) structure of BAHJÍ was built by him. Ruhe 205–6.

abjad

Traditional system of giving numerical values to the letters of the Arabic alphabet. Individual words could thus be represented by numbers equalling the sum of their component letters (thus *bahá'* ('glory') has a numerical value of 9, with ب b=2, ه h=5, ا á=1, ء '=1). The system was still much in use in 19th-century Iran, and was employed by both the Báb and Bahá'u'lláh to make linkages between concepts, and to 'convert' the names of their prominent followers into titles which might honour the individuals involved at the same time as sometimes concealing their true identities in correspondence ('Muḥammad' becomes 'Nabíl'; 'Yaḥyá' becomes 'Vaḥíd'; etc.). The importance attached to the numbers 9 and 19 is also partly derived on the basis of this system. MacEoin, 'Hierarchy' 109; *LG* 414. (*See also* NUMBERS).

ablutions (Ar.: *wudú'*)

In the *Kitáb-i-AQDAS* Bahá'u'lláh prescribed the performance of ritual ablutions (the washing of hands and face) both before saying obligatory PRAYERS and the repetition of the GREATEST NAME and of the special verse to be said by menstruating women. They should be performed even if one has just bathed. Fresh ablutions should be performed for each devotional act unless several prayers are being offered at the same time. If no water is available, or if its use

The abjad numbering system

a,á,'	b	j	d	h	v,ú	z	ḥ	ṭ	y,í
ا ء	ب	ج	د	ه	و	ز	ح	ط	ى
1	2	3	4	5	6	7	8	9	10

k	l	m	n	s	'	f	ṣ
ك	ل	م	ن	س	ع	ف	ص
20	30	40	50	60	70	80	90

q	r	sh	t	th	kh	dh	ḍ	ẓ	gh
ق	ر	ش	ت	ث	خ	ذ	ض	ظ	غ
100	200	300	400	500	600	700	800	900	1000

would be harmful to the hands or face, the believer should instead repeat the words 'In the Name of God, the Most Pure, the Most Pure' five times before prayer. Warm water may be used if the weather is cold. *KA* 23 k10, k13, 26 k18, 98–9, 112–3 q18, 122 q51, 125 q62, 126 q66, 129 q77, 132 q86, 146–7, 171–2 n16, 180–1 n34; *LG* 468.

abortion

For Bahá'ís the human soul appears at conception. Abortion merely to prevent the birth of an unwanted child is therefore forbidden. Abortion for medical reasons is permitted, however, after due reflection on the ethical issues by those concerned. In practice, all such matters are left up to the judgement of the parents. *LG* 344.

Mírzá Abu'l Faḍl, eminent Bahá'í scholar and teacher

Abraham

Biblical patriarch and Quranic prophet recognized as a MANIFESTATION OF GOD by Bahá'ís, and as the originator of monotheistic religion. In Islamic and Bahá'í texts he is often referred to as 'the Friend of God'. Through his son Isaac he is regarded as the father of the Jewish people, and through his son Ishmael (Ismá'íl) as the progenitor of the Arabs. His descendants included the Jewish prophets, Muḥammad, the Báb and (through his third wife, Katurah) Bahá'u'lláh. 'Abdu'l-Bahá compared Bahá'u'lláh's exile to that of Abraham's in terms of its historical consequences and religious impact. Heggie 3–6; *SAQ* 12–3.

Abu'l-Faḍl Gulpáygání, Mírzá Muḥammad (1844–1914)

Leading Iranian Bahá'í scholar and teacher. Abu'l-Faḍl ('the Father of Virtue') was his adopted epithet, but 'Abdu'l-Bahá often referred to him as Abu'l-Faḍá'il ('the Father of All Virtues'). Born into a prominent clerical family, his own clerical education was wide ranging, including rational and gnostic philosophy as well as the mainstream Islamic sciences. His intellectual interests included European science and Buddhism. He taught speculative theology (*kalám*) at one of the religious colleges in Tehran. In about 1876 he met a number of Bahá'ís and converted following the fulfilment of Bahá'u'lláh's prophecies regarding the fall of Sultan ABDULAZIZ. Openly talking about his new faith, he was dismissed from his post and imprisoned for some months. Altogether he was imprisoned for his Bahá'í activities for almost four out the next ten years. He then began to travel within Iran, teaching the Faith and attracting many new Bahá'ís, including a number of Jews and two Qájár princes in Hamadán. In 1889 he went to ASHKHABAD, where he became a focal point in the developing Bahá'í community, making journeys to Samarqand and Bukhara to promote the Faith. In 1894 he journeyed to Akka and after ten months there proceeded to EGYPT, where he gained recognition as an Islamic scholar at al-Azhar University and succeeded in converting some of his students, including 'Abdu'l-Jalíl SA'D. For the first time the Bahá'í community came to include a number of native Egyptians. In Egypt he also wrote extensively. In 1901 at 'Abdu'l-Bahá's instruction he went to the United States in order to combat the influence of Ibrahim KHEIRALLA and deepen the knowledge of the Bahá'ís. En route he also visited the Paris Bahá'ís. In 1904 he returned to Egypt, which remained his base until his death. 'Abdu'l-Bahá named one of the doors of the SHRINE OF THE BÁB in his honour. Shoghi Effendi named him as one of the APOSTLES OF BAHÁ'U'LLÁH.

Abu'l-Faḍl wrote a number of important works in both Persian and Arabic. Some of these deal with historical and doctrinal questions, others are concerned with prophetic proofs of Bahá'u'lláh's mission, and yet others are responses to criticisms of the Faith by various clerics. His work includes some of the first presentations of Bahá'í ideas for Jewish, Christian and Zoroastrian readers. Those of his writings that have been translated into English include: *al-Ḥujaju'l-Bahá'iyyih* (*The Behai Proofs*, trans. 1902); *ad-Duraru'l-Bahiyyih* ('The Shining Pearls', trans. as *Miracles and Metaphors*); and a collection of *Letters and Essays*. The front matter of these books contains information about his life. *EB* 263–5.

action and merit

For those who are detached, good deeds are regarded as their own reward, but all actions also bring existential consequences, such that good deeds will be rewarded by God, whether in the individual's present life or in the afterlife (TB 189).

Adam

Biblical and Quranic figure regarded as the father of humankind. Regarded by Bahá'ís as the first *known* MANIFESTATION OF GOD, preceded by others in a preliterate world. The story of Adam and Eve is seen as symbolic: Eve represents Adam's soul, and the serpent attachment to the human world (i.e. SIN). Ever since Adam's 'fall', humans had lived with the consciousness of good and evil. That all human beings were regarded as descended from Adam indicated their essential unity. The 'Adamic Cycle', starting with Adam, and dating back about six thousand years, was the period of known religious history; it had been consummated by Bahá'u'lláh's revelation (*see* TIME). Heggie 6–9; *SAQ* 122–26.

Adíb, Mírzá (Muḥammad-) Ḥasan (1848–1919)

Iranian HAND OF THE CAUSE. He was born into a prominent clerical family in Ṭalaqán and received a clerical education. He worked with the Qájár princes I'tidádu's-salṭanih and Mu'tamidu'd-dawlih on their literary works, and for a time was a teacher and leader of the Friday prayers at the Dáru'l-Funún college. He was also an accomplished poet, and was given the title *Adíbu'l-'ulamá* (litterateur of the 'ulamá). He became a Bahá'í in about 1889 after prolonged conversations with NABÍL-I-AKBAR, and was named a Hand of the Cause by Bahá'u'lláh shortly after this. He travelled within Iran, and also to India and Burma, in part with the American Bahá'í Sydney Sprague, author of the book *A Year With the Bahais in India and Burma* (1908). Shoghi Effendi named him as one of the APOSTLES OF BAHÁ'U'LLÁH. *EB* 272–3; Harper 17–18; *RB4*: 312–14.

administration

The current organization of the Bahá'í Faith is often referred to as the 'Administrative Order'. As it developed it increasingly replaced the more personalized and informal patterns of local leadership and organization that had previously prevailed. *SBBR* 120–8, 132–5.

EARLY ORGANIZATION

As they grow religious movements need to develop some system of organization if they are to remain cohesive in doctrine and structure. In the case of Bábism, key elements were the importance of clerical leadership (often of a highly charismatic kind), at both a local and national level, and of itinerant couriers, these providing effective internal communications (and hence cohesion) within the movement, a need given particular significance by the Báb's separation in imprisoned exile from the mass of his followers. Given that Iran was then a traditionalistic society with a very low level of literacy, the prominence of clerics in the movement is not surprising. It was natural for such individuals to assume positions of leadership and for the laity to defer to them. Indeed, in some cases – notably Ḥujjat in Zanján and Vaḥíd in Nayríz – the local Bábís followed their traditional leader into the new religion (Smith and Momen, 'Bábí movement' 56–62). Both these elements – local clerical leadership and interlinking by couriers – reappeared in the early development of the Bahá'í Faith. With Bahá'u'lláh removed to various and remote parts of the Ottoman empire and the mass of his followers in Iran, the need for effective internally organized communications was again crucial (only with the expansion of the Bahá'í Faith into areas where it was not subject to persecution could public systems of communication be relied on). In the case of local leadership there was a change, however. Whilst most 19th-century Bahá'í leaders (including the Hands of the Cause appointed by Bahá'u'lláh) were still clerics, who had normally completed a traditional Islamic education prior to their conversion, prominent Bahá'í merchants, such as the Afnáns and, in Iṣfáhán, the Nahrí family, also assumed positions of importance. Bahá'u'lláh's reference to future elected houses of justice also promised the development of a quite different form of organization.

THE DEVELOPMENT OF THE ADMINISTRATIVE ORDER

Bahá'u'lláh had appointed certain prominent Bahá'ís as Hands of the Cause, and referred to future houses of justice. 'Abdu'l-Bahá in turn encouraged the formation of various locally elected Bahá'í counsels, and in his *Will and Testament*, outlined a comprehensive administrative system under the joint headship of a succession of Guardians (guardianship) and the elected Universal House of Justice. The establishment and elaboration of that system developed during the period of Shoghi Effendi's guardianship (in two separate phases), and was subsequently augmented by the Universal House of Justice.

THE 1920s

Shoghi Effendi regularized and extended the system of elected spiritual assemblies. The basic elements were laid out in 1922–3. All Bahá'í groups in which there were at least nine adult Bahá'ís (twenty-one years old and above) were called upon to form their own local spiritual assemblies, each assembly superintending all Bahá'í activities in its locality. In all 'national' communities in which there was a sufficient number of Bahá'ís, national spiritual assemblies were to be elected by a delegate convention. Both local and national assemblies were to establish their own funds and necessary committees to help them in their work of promoting Bahá'í teaching endeavour; publishing; and organizing the community life of the Bahá'ís. There were subsequent elaborations of detail, but in its key aspects the system has not changed to the present day. Other administrative developments from the 1920s included the delineation of specific requirements for voting membership of the Bahá'í community (*see* ELECTIONS); the establishment of national administrative centres (*ḤAẒÍRATU'L-QUDS*), each overseen by the elected secretary of the relevant national spiritual assembly, the secretaryship in some cases becoming a full-time occupation; and the introduction of membership rolls, of enrolment cards to record professions of faith, and of credential cards or letters to validate membership. The regular nineteen day FEASTS were also strongly emphasized and came to include a period of consultation on local Bahá'í activities and assembly directives. Wherever possible, the national and local assemblies secured some form of legal identity, enabling them to own property (*see* INCORPORATION). The overall effects of these developments were to create a far more tightly organized network of Bahá'í communities. Organization came to be a central element in Bahá'í community life and was invested with spiritual and moral importance. Levels of administrative functioning varied of course, but by the 1930s a generally efficient system was in place, the establishment of local and national spiritual assemblies coming to provide one of the major goals of Bahá'í activity as well as a significant measure of Bahá'í expansion PLANS.

THE 1950s

Three administrative institutions were newly created or reanimated during this period.

(1) The INTERNATIONAL BAHÁ'Í COUNCIL (1950/51–63), an initially appointed body, charged with assisting Shoghi Effendi in his work in Haifa. It was also seen as the precursor of the future Universal House of Justice.

(2) The HANDS OF THE CAUSE OF GOD, revived in 1951 as a functioning group of senior Bahá'ís, responsible for assisting the national spiritual assemblies achieve their goals, and later with the protection of the Faith from external and internal attacks. An initial group of twelve was increased to twenty-seven by 1957, comprising individuals in all continents and including several members of the first International Council. Organized by continent, the Hands provided the Bahá'ís with a system of transnational co-ordination, as well as a form of leadership quite different from that of the assemblies. They also unexpectedly came to exercise overall headship of the Bahá'ís during the 'interregnum' between the death of Shoghi Effendi and the establishment of the Universal House of Justice (1957–63).

(3) The AUXILIARY BOARDS, whose members were to act as the 'deputies, assistants and advisors' to the Hands. Two Boards were established, each organized on a continental level: one concerned with the propagation and expansion of the Faith (1954), and a second with its protection (1957).

THE ESTABLISHMENT OF THE UNIVERSAL HOUSE OF JUSTICE

The formation of the House of Justice in 1963 marked a major transition in Bahá'í administration, as overall leadership of the Faith for the first time became vested in an elected body. The House confirmed its own authority as 'the supreme institution' of the Administrative Order in its *Constitution* (1972). It had earlier stated that it was not possible to appoint further Guardians (October 1963) (*MUHJ* 14 no. 5), so there was no longer a living Guardianship. Administrative developments since 1963 may be summarized as follows:

(1) The House's ruling that it was no longer possible to appoint Hands of the Cause (November 1964) (*MUHJ* 44 no. 20.4), and the subsequent development of new institutions to fulfil their functions: the CONTINENTAL BOARDS OF COUNSELLORS (1968) and the INTERNATIONAL TEACHING CENTRE (1973).

(2) Responses to the need for administration to cope with the growing extent and complexity of the Bahá'í community. Thus the enormous increase in the number of Auxiliary Board members (from 72 in 1957 to 846 in 1991); the introduction of ASSISTANTS to the Board members (1973); and, in certain countries, the establishment of REGIONAL BAHÁ'Í COUNCILS (first tried experimentally from 1986 onwards, formalized in 1997), intermediate bodies between the national and local assemblies.

Present structure of Bahá'í administration

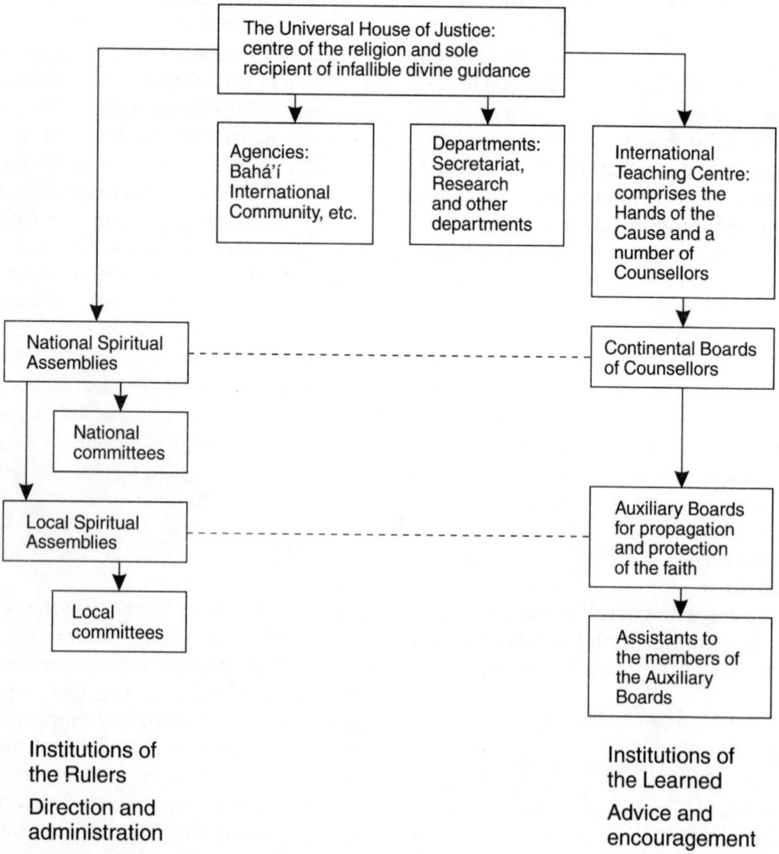

Key: —, formal authority; - - -, consultive relationship

(3) The introduction of various specialist committees and agencies: the Continental Pioneer Committees (1965) (*MUHJ* 47–50 no. 22) to organize the movement of PIONEERS; the various bodies linked to the BAHÁ'Í INTERNATIONAL COMMUNITY, including a Haifa-based Office of Public Information; and a network of *ḤUQÚQU'LLÁH* deputies and representatives.
(4) A massive increase in the number of staff working at the BAHÁ'Í WORLD CENTRE in Haifa–Akka.

THE RULERS AND THE LEARNED

Most Bábí and early Bahá'í leaders were Islamic clerics, 'the learned' (*'ULAMÁ*). The role of such individuals became transformed with the passage of time, however. Executive authority came to rest with elected bodies, leaving Bahá'í 'learned' with responsibilities for TEACHING and providing moral leadership. Those 'learned' who yearned for power analogous to many of their Shí'í counterparts were out of place, as perhaps evidenced by the 'rebellions' of JAMÁL BURÚJIRDÍ and 'Abdu'l-Ḥusayn ÁVÁRIH. In terms of their relationship to the Administrative Order, a distinction is thus now made between the 'rulers' and the 'learned' of the Faith, the former being the members of the Universal House of Justice and national and local assemblies, and the latter, the Hands, Counsellors, Board members, and their assistants, all of whom perform an educative and inspirational role. Other eminent Bahá'í teachers are also implicitly included in this second category (*MUHJ* 214–17). See 'LEARNED'.

PURPOSE, SPIRIT AND FORM

Shoghi Effendi linked the Administrative Order to the emergence of Bahá'u'lláh's promised WORLD ORDER, describing it as the 'nucleus' and 'Charter' of that Order, and the basis for the future 'Bahá'í World Commonwealth' (*GPB* 324–5; *WOB* 144). At the same time he emphasized its evolutionary nature, and warned the Bahá'ís not to reify their present institutions or procedures. The administration was an instrument of the Faith, not a substitute for it. Bahá'í administrators, in particular, should exercise great care to gain the support, respect and affection of Bahá'ís. This was only possible through 'extreme humility' and selfless devotion on their part, together with loving CONSULTATION with the mass of the Bahá'ís. The 'right' of individual self-expression was fundamental. The assemblies should not over-administer, or get bogged down in matters of detail that obscured the vision of the Faith and dampened its spirit (*BA* 63–4, 103; *WOB* 9).

He also emphasized the distinctiveness of the Administrative Order. Unlike the organizational forms that had developed in other divine religions, it was directly rooted in the writings of the Faith's founder and his appointed successor (i.e. Bahá'u'lláh and 'Abdu'l-Bahá). Nor was it like any of the various organizational systems human beings had created: instead, it blended the beneficent elements of several systems. Its supreme institutions (the guardianship and the Universal House of Justice) were assured of divine guidance and protection, but the Bahá'í system was unlike any former theocracy: it had no PRIESTHOOD; the Guardians did not have the absolutist powers of the popes or IMÁMS. It was 'non-autocratic' and inclined towards 'democratic methods', with elected houses of justice/assemblies (at the local level by universal suffrage), but whilst the members of these houses were bound to acquaint themselves with the conditions of the Bahá'í community, they did not draw their mandate from 'the people': they were answerable to their own consciences and not to the feelings of the mass of the Bahá'ís (thus avoiding the dangers of demagogy). It upheld the 'hereditary principle' (through the guardianship), but it was not a system of aristocracy (*GPB* 324–7; *WOB* 144–7, 152–7).

WOMEN

With the exception of the Universal House of Justice and the guardianship all Bahá'í administrative institutions are now open to both women and men. Unremarkable as this may be in the West, it has been of major significance in the Middle East and those parts of the 'Third World' in which women have traditionally occupied a subordinate social role (*see* WOMEN).

OPPOSITION TO THE ADMINISTRATION

Whilst accepted by the majority of Bahá'ís, Shoghi Effendi's emphasis on administrative development initially encountered some opposition, notably from Ruth WHITE and Ahmad SOHRAB.

administrative rights

Membership of the Bahá'í community confers rights, particularly in relationship to administrative participation: e.g. to attend the nineteen day FEAST; to contribute to the Bahá'í FUND; to vote in Bahá'í elections; to serve on Bahá'í ASSEMBLIES and committees; to represent the Faith publicly (as a speaker at a public meeting, etc.); and to be married according to Bahá'í law. Flagrant breach of certain Bahá'í laws may lead to the loss of some or all of these rights. In such cases, it is the responsibility of the relevant national spiritual assembly to investigate the matter properly, and if necessary deprive the offending individual of their rights. This action is considered as extremely severe, and should only be taken as a last resort. Offenders should first be lovingly counselled and given sufficient time to change their behaviour. Each case should be considered on its own merits. *LG* 50–62.

Offences that may entail loss of administrative rights are:

(1) Flagrant immorality (drinking, active HOMOSEXUALITY, companionate MARRIAGE, sexual impropriety, etc.). In cases of immorality the assembly should be compassionate towards human frailty. If the offence is not widely known, it is not flagrant. It is only if the behaviour in question is in blatant and public disregard of Bahá'í law, particularly if it is a cause of public scandal, that the assembly should act. In these circumstances the assembly should lovingly offer advice, encourage the individual to rectify their conduct, and ultimately warn them of the consequences of their actions. Only if repeated warnings go unheeded should the assembly then deprive the individual of their rights.

(2) Breach of Bahá'í marriage laws (marriage without a Bahá'í ceremony or without parental consent; marrying a third party before the 'year of patience' required for a Bahá'í DIVORCE is completed). If possible, the situation should be rectified. If not, rights should be removed.

(3) Public dissimulation of faith (e.g. making a promise to raise one's children in another religion; going through the marriage ceremony of another religion *as if* one was actually an adherent of that religion; holding religious office in another religion). As (2).

(4) Persistent political involvement (refusal to dissociate oneself from political activity or office; membership of a secret society). As (2), but prompt action on the part of the assembly may be necessary in order to protect the Faith.

(5) Severe forms of mental illness which debar the individual from normal social involvement. Extreme care should be taken in such cases, and

deprivation of rights is not to be regarded as a sanction, but as a recognition of the individual's incapacity.

(6) Criminal activities that seriously injure the reputation of the Faith. The assembly needs to exercise great discretion in such cases. Criminality of itself does not automatically debar an individual from participation in the Bahá'í community.

Adrianople

See EDIRNE.

adultery and fornication

(Ar.: *ziná*)

Bahá'ís recognize MARRIAGE as the only legitimate basis for a sexual relationship. Pre- and extra-marital relationships are therefore forbidden under Bahá'í law. They are regarded as retarding the progress of the soul. In the *Kitáb-i-Aqdas* Bahá'u'lláh prescribes that adulterers should pay a fine to the HOUSE OF JUSTICE (9 *mithqáls* (32.775 grams) of gold for the first offence, and progressively doubled thereafter) and states that they would suffer a 'humiliating torment' in the afterlife. More detailed legislation would be determined by the house of justice. *KA* 26 k19, 37 k49, 114 q23, 121 q49, 181 n36, 200 n77; *LG* 344–5.

Advent of Divine Justice

Book-length letter from Shoghi Effendi to the North American Bahá'ís, dated 25 December 1938. Written shortly after the beginning of the first American Seven Year Plan (1937–44) (*see* PLANS), the letter focuses on three major themes.

THE IMPORTANCE OF AMERICA

At a time of widespread social disruption, when the Bahá'ís in IRAN, Central Asia and Germany faced restriction, the North American Bahá'ís had become the 'chief remaining citadel' of the Faith. The Bahá'í prophecy of a special role for the AMERICAS was emphasized.

THE 'SPIRITUAL PREREQUISITES' FOR THE ACCOMPLISHMENT OF THE PLAN

These were: (1) moral rectitude (JUSTICE, honesty, TRUSTWORTHINESS, etc.), especially by members of local and national spiritual ASSEMBLIES, but also by all Bahá'ís in their business and professional dealings, private lives, and the conduct of all Bahá'í activities; (2) absolute CHASTITY, especially by Bahá'í YOUTH; and (3) complete freedom from PREJUDICE regarding RACE, class or creed. A 'double crusade' was called for: to regenerate the inner life of the Bahá'í community by adhering to these principles, and to attack certain long-standing evils of American society, with its widespread deceit, corruption, moral laxity and licentiousness, and racial prejudice. The Bahá'ís should not be surprised when they encountered OPPOSITION in this endeavour.

THE REQUIREMENTS OF THE TEACHING CAMPAIGN

It was the duty of every individual believer to support the Plan, working with the Bahá'í administrative institutions, but not waiting for any specific appeal or initiative. Teaching should become the 'all-pervading concern' in the life of every Bahá'í. Each should consider every approach available to them, seeking out those who might become interested in the Faith, attracting them to the Faith, and subsequently nursing them into full maturity as Bahá'ís. In so doing, the teachers should be sensitive to the hearer's degree of receptivity, and also ensure that the dignity of the Faith was preserved. By way of preparation, they should (1) thoroughly study the history and teachings of the Bahá'í Faith; (2) gain a sound knowledge of ISLAM; and (3) acquire a basic knowledge of the languages and cultures of the peoples they would contact in their teaching endeavours (in this case, of the Latin Americans). PIONEERS and travelling Bahá'í teachers were needed. Translations and literature needed to be prepared. The Bahá'ís should also seek to increase the racial diversity of their community.

Afghání, al-

See JAMÁLU'D-DÍN, SAYYID.

Afnán (Ar., 'Twigs' of the sacred lote-tree)

Title given to the maternal relatives of the Báb by Bahá'u'lláh, and adopted as a surname by their descendants. During the late 19th-century the family built up an extensive trading empire based in Shíráz and Yazd, with offices in Bombay, Hong Kong, ASHKHABAD, and Beirut. Some of the first Bahá'í printed literature was produced on their printing press in Bombay. *ARR* 121–4; *BKG* 388–9, (*see also* BÁB, FAMILY OF).

ages (of the Bahá'í Era)

See TIME.

Aghṣán (Ar., 'Branches'; sing. *ghuṣn*)

The generic title for the male descendants of Bahá'u'lláh, including 'ABDU'L-BAHÁ, the 'Most Great Branch' (*ghuṣn-i-a'ẓam*); MUḤAMMAD-'ALÍ, the 'Greater Branch' (*ghuṣn-i-akbar*); and Mírzá MIHDÍ, the 'Purest Branch' (*ghuṣn-i-aṭhar*). Bahá'u'lláh bade the Bahá'ís to show kindness to his 'kindred', but denied his descendants any right 'to the property of others', though they were made responsible for charitable endowments prior to the election of the Universal House of Justice (this is in contrast to Shí'í Islam, in which *sayyids* were given special financial rights on a permanent basis) *KA* 35 k42, 41 k61, 203 n85; *TB* 222. 'Abdu'l-Bahá directed that the GUARDIANSHIP should be confined to the *Aghṣán* (*Will* 12). (*See also* NÚRÍ FAMILY.)

agriculture

In his *Tablet of the* WORLD, Bahá'u'lláh refers to five 'fundamental principles' for the administration of human affairs and the advancement of the world, the most important of which was the promotion of agriculture. He deplored its neglect in IRAN and noted the attention given to it elsewhere (*TB* 89–90). 'Abdu'l-Bahá identified agriculture as the 'fundamental basis' of the community, and in a context in which farmers comprised the majority of the population, as the basis for the economic system (*LG* 547; *PUP* 217). He also praised study of 'the science of agriculture', describing devotion to such study as an act of worship (*SWAB* 144–5). Village communities should organize their own affairs under the control of a board of 'wise men', and establish a 'general storehouse' designed to fund local community development, fulfil financial obligations to the state, and support the local poor. This would be funded by graduated local taxes, treasure trove, and voluntary contributions (*LG* 547–48). *CC1*: 81.

'Ahd, Kitáb-i-

See COVENANT, BOOK OF.

Aḥmad, Tablets of

Two tablets of Bahá'u'lláh, both composed in Edirne for men named Aḥmad.

(1) The more well known of the two tablets is in Arabic and was revealed in about 1282 AH/1865. It is regarded by Bahá'ís as having a special potency, and is frequently used at times of difficulty or distress. In it Bahá'u'lláh describes himself as 'the Nightingale of Paradise', whose song guides the lovers of God to 'this resplendent Beauty', foretold in the holy books and through whom 'truth shall be distinguished from error'. Those who turned away from him had also turned away from the

divine messengers of the past. The recipient, a Bábí and former dervish, was counselled to remember Bahá'u'lláh's distress and banishment; to be 'steadfast in My love' in the face of persecution; and not be troubled if he encountered affliction in 'My path'. This Aḥmad then returned to Iran, where he became one of the leading figures in gaining the allegiance of the remaining Bábís for Bahá'u'lláh. He died in 1902 at an extremely advanced age. *RB2* 107–16, 119–20. This tablet is found in most Bahá'í prayer books.

(2) The second tablet, in Persian, was addressed to Ḥájí Mírzá Aḥmad of Káshán, half-brother of the Bábí chronicler Ḥájí Mírzá Jání and of DHABÍḤ of Káshán. One of Bahá'u'lláh's companions in Edirne, this second Aḥmad rejected Bahá'u'lláh's claims and became a partisan of Ṣubḥ-i-AZAL. The tablet to him states that Bahá'u'lláh's revelation is like a fathomless and surging ocean which is closer to the individual than his 'life-vein', and warns of the need to protect 'the flame of the love of God', so that 'the evil whisperings of the ungodly' do not extinguish it in the believer's heart. The believer should regard the world as a vain and empty show which only had 'the semblance of reality', and should not set his affections on it. *GWB* nos. clii, cliii; *RB2*: 137–40.

Aḥmad al-Aḥsá'í, Shaykh (1753–1826)

Founder of the Shaykhí school of Shí'í Islam. He was born in the Ḥasá region of eastern Arabia. He migrated to the Shí'í shrine cities in Iraq in the early 1790s, quickly gaining a reputation for piety and learning, and attracting a growing following. In 1806 he moved to Iran, where he gained the support of many members of the QÁJÁR family, including the reigning monarch, Fatḥ-'Alí Sháh. In about 1822 he was accused of heresy by Ḥájí Mullá MUḤAMMAD-TAQÍ BARAGHÁNÍ, one of the leading clerics in Qazvín. He returned to Iraq (1822), but encountered such resentment from some other clerics that after a few years he determined to migrate to Mecca. He died en route and was buried at Medina. He was succeeded by his chief disciple, Sayyid KÁẒIM RASHTÍ, as leader of what had now become a distinctive sect within SHÍ'ISM. Shaykh Aḥmad's teachings were complex, and he often resorted to the Shí'í practice of pious dissimulation (*taqiyya*) to conceal his more controversial ideas from his opponents. He emphasized the mystical dimension of religious faith and claimed to unveil deeper esoteric truths. He believed that he had a special relationship with the IMÁMS, whom he encountered in visionary experiences and from whom he derived his authority. (*See also* SHAYKHISM.)

Ákhúnd, Ḥájí (*c.* 1842–1910)

Ḥájí Mullá 'Alí-Akbar Shahmírzádí, Iranian HAND OF THE CAUSE. In the writings of Bahá'u'lláh and 'Abdu'l-Bahá he is addressed as ''Alí qabl-i-Akbar'. His father was a village cleric in Shahmírzád (near Simnán) who had at one time been active as a Bábí. Ḥájí Ákhúnd himself became a Bábí in about 1861 after reading Bahá'u'lláh's *Kitáb-i-Íqán* and meeting with the Bábís. He was at that time a seminary student in Mashhad and his open efforts to convert his fellow students enraged the local religious authorities. Returning to Shahmírzád he debated religion with local clerics until forced to flee to Tehran, where he was subjected to the first of a series of imprisonments for his religious activities (1868). He soon became one of the focal points within the Tehran Bahá'í community, and was appointed as one of the Hands of the Cause by Bahá'u'lláh in the late 1880s. At one point he acted as custodian of the remains of the Báb, then hidden in Tehran. Shoghi Effendi named him as one of the Apostles of Bahá'u'lláh. *EB* 265–6; Harper 3–8; *MF* 9–12; *RB4*: 294–301.

Akka (Ar., *'Akká*; Heb., *Acco*)

An ancient port city now part of the state of Israel, and one of the main sites of Bahá'u'lláh's exile. During the crusades Westerners called it St Jean d'Acre. In the late 19th century, it was part of Ottoman Syria, and had become a political and economic backwater, a walled city used as a place of exile and imprisonment (Bahá'u'lláh called the city his 'Most Great Prison'). Bahá'ís cite various biblical verses and Islamic traditions (*hadíths*) to indicate its prophetic importance. Bahá'u'lláh arrived in Akka on the afternoon of 31 August 1868 and remained within the city walls until June 1877 (i.e. for almost nine years). 'Abdu'l-Bahá continued to live in the city until August 1910 (i.e. for forty-two years). For Bahá'ís the city is thus redolent with historical associations. Ruhe 16–104, 123–9; *BW18*: 77–80; *GPB* 183–4.

Important Bahá'í sites

Within the city

The barracks

Bahá'u'lláh and his family were initially imprisoned there (1868–70). The cell occupied by Bahá'u'lláh is of particular importance.

The Houses of 'Údí Khammár and 'Abbúd

After Bahá'u'lláh left the barracks (4 November 1870), he lived in a succession of houses in various parts of the city (the houses of Malik, Khawwám and Rábi'a) before moving into a house belonging to 'Údí Khammár, a Christian merchant (also the owner of the mansion of Bahjí) in September 1871. It was here that 'Abdu'l-Bahá was married and the *Kitáb-i-Aqdas* revealed. The larger adjoining house of 'Abbúd was later rented and openings made to join the two houses together, the whole complex becoming known as the House of 'Abbúd. 'Abdu'l-Bahá and his family remained resident until about October 1896. The room of Bahá'u'lláh became a place of pilgrimage during his lifetime.

The House of 'Abdu'lláh Páshá

With the marriages of 'Abdu'l-Bahá's daughters (1896 onwards) the House of 'Abbúd was no longer adequate for the growing family, and parts of the complex of buildings known as the House of 'Abdu'lláh Páshá were rented. This is where Shoghi Effendi was born (March 1897) and the early Western pilgrims met 'Abdu'l-Bahá (from December 1898). After 'Abdu'l-Bahá moved to Haifa the house was no longer in Bahá'í hands, and eventually fell into disrepair. It was purchased by the Bahá'ís in 1975, and after extensive restoration was opened to Bahá'í pilgrimage in 1983.

Other places associated with the Faith include the Khán al-'Umdán (Ar. 'Inn of the Pillars', also known as the Khán-i-'Avámíd), a caravanserai in which many Bahá'í residents and pilgrims were lodged; and two Muslim cemeteries just outside the city in which about thirty-four Bahá'ís are buried.

In the neighbourhood of the city

The mansion of Mazra'ih

When Bahá'u'lláh first moved out of Akka, he lived at Mazra'ih, about four miles north of Akka (June 1877–September 1879). The property was recognized as a Bahá'í holy place by the Israeli authorities in 1950 and leased by the Bahá'ís. It was finally purchased in 1973.

House of ‘Abbúd

House of ‘Abdu’lláh Páshá

Aerial view of Akka showing the barracks in the foreground

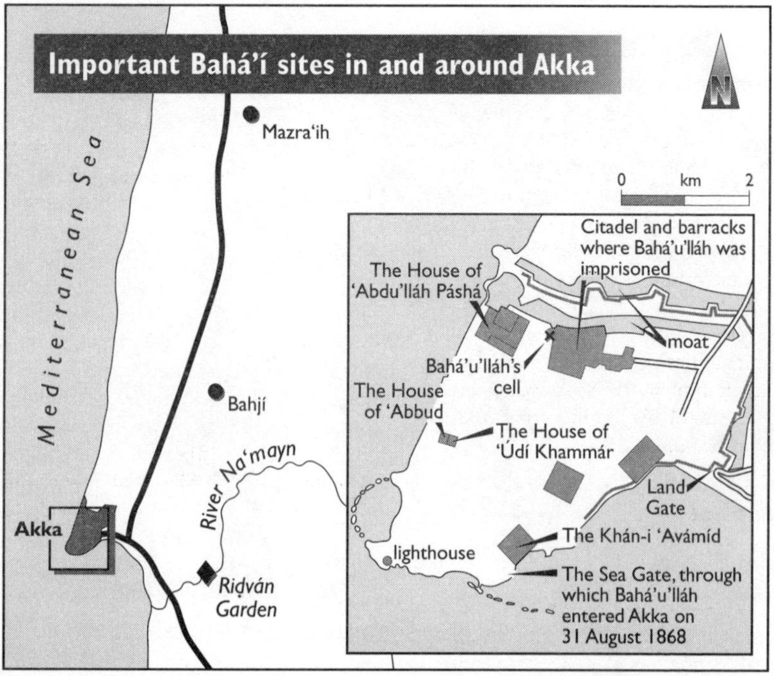

The Riḍván garden at the Na'mayn River

This island garden was rented by 'Abdu'l-Bahá in 1875 and visited by Bahá'u'lláh from 1877 onwards. He loved its beauty and named it *Riḍván* (Paradise), after the original RIḌVÁN Garden near Baghdad, and 'Our Verdant Isle'. It was the site of Bahá'u'lláh's vision of Trustworthiness (*TB* 37–8). Iranian Bahá'ís brought seedlings to grow in it. Two other Bahá'í gardens (Firdaws and Ashraf) are nearby.

The mansion of Bahjí and the Shrine of Bahá'u'lláh

See BAHJÍ.

'Alá'í, Shu'a'u'llah (1889–1984)

Iranian HAND OF THE CAUSE. He was born in Tehran into a prominent family: his father was set to become a cleric, but had converted to the Bahá'í Faith, subsequently becoming physician to the royal household. He himself studied accountancy, after which he pursued a distinguished career in various fields of government service, becoming chief controller of army finances (with the rank of general). He was elected on to the Tehran Bahá'í assembly in 1913, and the newly formed Iranian Bahá'í national assembly in 1934, often serving as its chairman. Shoghi Effendi appointed him as one of the first group of Hands in 1952, and thereafter he travelled extensively, visiting Bahá'í communities in many parts of the world. He left Iran in 1978, spending the last few years of his life in France and then Arizona. Harper 335–8.

alcohol

Bahá'ís are prohibited from drinking any form of alcohol (unless prescribed by a physician) on the grounds that intoxicants lead the mind astray and weaken the body: God has endowed humans beings with reason, and intoxicants take it away. Neither should Bahá'ís consume alcohol-flavoured foods or serve alcohol to non-Bahá'í guests in formal Bahá'í contexts. In ambiguous situations they should be guided by their own conscience or consult with a spiritual ASSEMBLY. It is preferable not to work in occupations involving the manufacture of alcohol or its large-scale sale. In the case of those Bahá'ís who are persistent drinkers, assemblies should first lovingly exhort them to stop. Later, if these exhortations are unheeded, they may warn them, and finally deprive them of their ADMINISTRATIVE RIGHTS. Bahá'ís who are alcoholics should seek the help of doctors or organizations such as Alcoholics Anonymous. *KA* 62 k119, 226–7 n144; *LG* 349–52. (*See also* WINE).

Alexander, Agnes Baldwin (1875–1971)

American HAND OF THE CAUSE. Born into a Hawaiian Christian missionary family, she became a Bahá'í during a visit to Italy in 1900. She returned to Hawaii in December 1901 as the first Bahá'í on the islands, becoming instrumental in the growth of a Bahá'í community there. After the deaths of her parents she moved to the American mainland, and then, at the request of 'Abdu'l-Bahá, moved to Japan. Reaching there in November 1914, she worked with George AUGUR and his wife to establish a Bahá'í community, spending much of the rest of her life in the country. She was also the first to present the Bahá'í teachings in Korea (1921). She was appointed a Hand on 27 March 1957. She died in Hawaii. Alexander, *History; Personal Recollections*; *BW15*: 423–30; Harper 145–55.

Alexander II (1818–81)

Russian tsar, 1855–81 ('the Liberator'). He emancipated the serfs in 1861, but later became increasingly reactionary. He was assassinated by nihilists. Bahá'u'lláh wrote to him from Akka, summoning him to listen to the voice of God and himself call the nations unto God. He should beware that nothing deter him from this and that he did not barter away the 'sublime station' he occupied by dint of the offer of refuge given to Bahá'u'lláh by the Russian minister when he had been released from the SÍYÁH-CHÁL. The tsar's prayer – according to one account to make his forces victorious against the Ottomans – had been heard and answered. *ESW* 56–9; *PDC* 32–4, 57; *RB3*: 118–23.

'Alí, Ḥájí Mírzá Sayyid (d. 1850)

A leading merchant of Shíráz and the Báb's maternal uncle and guardian. He was one of the first after the LETTERS OF THE LIVING to accept his nephew's claims. He was executed as a Bábí in 1850. (*See also* BÁB, FAMILY OF; SEVEN MARTYRS OF TEHRAN.)

'Alí Basṭámí, Mullá (d. 1845)

One of the Báb's first group of disciples (LETTERS OF THE LIVING), and formerly one of the leading students of Sayyid KÁẒIM RASHTÍ, who joined Mullá ḤUSAYN BUSHRÚ'Í in religious retreat following the Káẓim's death, and subsequently joined him in Shíráz, where he became the 'second who believed'. The Báb identified him with the Imám 'Alí, and sent him to the Shí'í shrine cities of Iraq (particularly Najaf and KARBALÁ) to proclaim the Báb's advent. Arriving in August/September 1844, Basṭámí appears initially to have gained the support of most of the local Shaykhís. Distributing extracts from the *QAYYÚ-MU'L-ASMÁ* and presenting Bábí claims directly to Shaykh Muḥammad-Ḥasan Najafí, one of the pre-eminent Shí'í clerics of the day, he provoked both widespread millenarian fervour and strident opposition. Denounced as a heretic, he was arrested, and eventually tried before a joint tribunal of Sunní and Shí'í *'ulamá* in January 1845 – an unprecedented event. The tribunal was unanimous in condemning the as yet unnamed author of the *Qayyúmu'l-asmá* as an unbeliever, but disagreed as to the fate of the messenger. Finally, in April, on instructions from the Ottoman government, Basṭámí was transferred to Istanbul, where he was sentenced to hard labour in the naval dockyard, and died shortly thereafter. *ARR* 175–6, 211–37; *TJ* 401; *TN* 248–9; *MBBR* 83–90; Momen, 'Trial of Mullá 'Alí Basṭámí'; Nabil 66–9, 88–92.

Ali-Kuli Khan (*c.* 1879–1966)

Also known as *Nabílu'd-dawlih*. Eminent Iranian Bahá'í. He served briefly as 'Abdu'l-Bahá's English-language secretary (1899–1901) and was subsequently sent to America where he translated several Bahá'í books into English as well as continuing to translate 'Abdu'l-Bahá's correspondence with the American Bahá'ís. He was appointed Iranian *chargé d'affaires* in Washington in 1910 and later served in various high-ranking diplomatic posts. His marriage to Florence Breed (1875–1950) in 1904 was praised by 'Abdu'l-Bahá as the first between East and West. Their daughter, Marzieh Gail (1908–93), also became an eminent Bahá'í translator. *BW12*: 703–4; *BW14*: 351–3; Gail, *Arches of the Years*; Gail, *Summon up Remembrance*. On Gail see *Baha'i Studies Review* 6 (1996): 135–9.

Âli Paşa, Mehmet Emin (1815–1871)

'Alí Páshá, OTTOMAN statesman and reformer who was grand vizier during the 1850s and again from 1867 to 1871 under Sultan ABDULAZIZ. As such, Bahá'u'lláh held him responsible for the order of banishment to Akka, and reproved his actions in the two Tablets of RA'ÍS and the tablet to FUAT PAŞA, predicting his downfall. *GPB* 160, 196.

'Alí Turshízí, Mullá Shaykh

See Aẓím.

'All Food', Tablet of

(PA: *Lawḥ-i-Kullu'ṭ-ṭa'ám*)

Arabic tablet of Bahá'u'lláh composed during the first period of his stay in Baghdad (1853–4).

It was addressed to Ḥájí Mírzá Kamálu'd-dín Naráqí (d. c.1881) in commentary on a Quranic verse ('All food was allowed to the children of Israel except what Israel made unlawful for itself'). In it Bahá'u'lláh stated that the verse had infinite meanings in the various worlds of God, each word in it being multivalent (e.g. 'food' as 'knowledge', as recognition of the Manifestation of God, etc.). He also lamented his own sufferings and referred to the greatness of Quddús. The tablet was significant in the developing tension between Bahá'u'lláh and Ṣubḥ-i-Azal: Naráqí had first requested Azal to comment on the verse, but was so disappointed with his answer that he became disillusioned with his leadership. Bahá'u'lláh's commentary, by contrast, won his admiration, and he became a devotee. Cole, 'Bahá'u'lláh and the Naqshbandí Sufis' 12–13; *GPB* 116–17; Lambden, 'A tablet'; *RB1*: 55–60.

Americas

In the *Kitáb-i-Aqdas* Bahá'u'lláh addressed the rulers of the American republics, announcing that he was God's promised one to whom they should turn, and counselling them to 'adorn the temple of dominion' with the ornament of justice, the fear of God and divine remembrance. They should bind 'the broken' with 'the hands of justice', and 'crush the oppressor' with the rod of divine commandments (*KA* 52 k88). 'Abdu'l-Bahá referred to the Americas as the home of the righteous and the gathering place of the free. In them God's light would be revealed. Their aboriginal inhabitants were likened to the ancient Arabians who had become so enkindled by the 'Muḥammadan Light' that they had illumined the world (*TDP* 32–3, 59–60). The Bahá'ís of the United States and Canada were given a special mission to take the Bahá'í teachings to the rest of the world. Under Shoghi Effendi's direction the North American Bahá'ís began to realize this mission in their first Seven Year Plan (1937–44). Shoghi Effendi also described the American Bahá'í community as the 'cradle' and 'stronghold' of the future Bahá'í World Order, and as the 'prime mover and pattern' of Bahá'í communities in the rest of the Americas. They were the spiritual descendants of the Bábís, and their sacrificial services in the administrative and teaching work of the Faith were much praised (*ADJ* 5–9). As to the United States of America, Shoghi Effendi noted in December 1938 its inevitable role in the developing world crisis, and predicted that it would rise to fulfil its destiny – to 'lay the corner-stone of a universal and enduring peace', proclaim the solidarity of the human race, and establish righteousness on earth – after involvement in a second world war (*ADJ* 72–7).

Amín, Ḥájí (*c.* 1831–1928)

Ḥájí Abu'l-Ḥasan Ardikání, prominent Iranian Bahá'í, also known as *Amín-i-Iláhí* (the trustee of God). He became a Bábí in about 1851, and after accepting Bahá'u'lláh's claims converted many Bábí families to the Bahá'í Faith. He later became the assistant to Ḥájí Sháh-Muḥammad Manshádí (*Amínu'l-Bayán*), who had been appointed by Bahá'u'lláh as collector of *Ḥuqúqu'lláh* and, after his death in 1880, succeeded him in that position. These tasks involved him in lengthy journeys during which he would visit Bahá'u'lláh in Akka to deliver money and letters from Bahá'ís and then visit various parts of Iran distributing

Bahá'u'lláh's letters to the Bahá'ís. He first visited Akka in AH1286/1869, and was able to bring back the news to the Iranian Bahá'ís that Bahá'u'lláh was safe. He was one of the prominent Bahá'ís imprisoned in 1891–3. He travelled less as he got older and eventually chose Ḥájí Ghulám-Riḍá as his assistant, gradually delegating his functions to him. He died in his nineties. 'Abdu'l-Bahá named one of the doors of the SHRINE OF THE BÁB in his honour. Shoghi Effendi posthumously named him as one of the HANDS OF THE CAUSE and listed him among the APOSTLES OF BAHÁ'U'LLÁH. Harper 53–6.

Amír Kabír, Mírzá Taqí Khán (1807/8–52)

First of NÁṢIRU'D-DÍN SHÁH's prime ministers, 19 October 1848–13 November 1851. He was subsequently killed (bled to death) on the shah's order. He is now best remembered for his efforts to introduce government reform and his establishment of the Dáru'l-Funún college. Determined and capable, he regarded the Bábís as a serious threat to civil order and repressed them. He was instrumental in the suppression of the Bábí upheavals of 1848–51 and personally ordered the execution of the SEVEN MARTYRS OF TEHRAN and of the Báb, in this last case entrusting his brother, Mírzá Ḥasan Khán, the *vazír-niẓám* (army commander in Azerbaiján), with the task of superintending the execution. He credited Bahá'u'lláh with having given decisive support to the Bábís at ṬABARSÍ and induced him to retire to the Shí'í shrines in Iraq in 1851. 'Abdu'l-Bahá referred to him as the greatest of the Faith's oppressors but also acknowledged his significance as a government reformer. *MBBR* 160–5.

Amír Kabír, chief minister of Náṣiru'd dín Sháh

Andalíb ('Nightingale'), Áqá 'Alí-Ashraf (d. 1920)

Prominent Iranian Bahá'í teacher famed as a poet. *EB* 60–74.

angels

Spiritual beings, traditionally believed to be attendant upon God, who serve as messengers or executors of the divine will. The concept is found in several religions. In the *Kitáb-i-ÍQÁN* Bahá'u'lláh referred to angels as those people who have consumed 'all human traits and limitations' with 'the fire of the love of God', and have 'clothed themselves' with angelic qualities and become 'endowed with the attributes of the spiritual' (*KI* 50–1). 'Abdu'l-Bahá stated that 'angels' are both 'the confirmations of God and His celestial powers' by which certain holy people were supported, and those 'blessed beings', who have 'severed all ties with the nether world' and 'been released from the chains of self', and become the 'revealers of God's abounding grace' (*SWAB* 81, 166, 287–8). There are also references to an angelic host – the 'Concourse on high' – who aid those who serve the Bahá'í Cause, and to celestial figures, notably the MAID OF HEAVEN of Bahá'u'lláh's visions.

animals

Cruelty to animals is condemned. 'Abdu'l-Bahá taught that Bahá'ís should treat animals with loving-kindness and compassion, and should train their children to care for animals. Cruelty to animals is unjust: they can experience pain in the same way as human beings can but unlike humans cannot complain to the authorities about their oppressors. Again, they are innocent whilst humans are sinful. The only exception is those animals that are dangerous to people and other animals: to deal with these is to protect those they might attack (*SWAB* 58–60). Vivisection for research purposes is regarded as permissible as long as the animal is anaesthetized and does not suffer (*LG* 292–3 no. 993–5). Bahá'u'lláh stated that no one should burden an animal with more than it can bear (*KA* 87 k187).

VEGETARIANISM

For 'Abdu'l-Bahá eating animals was 'somewhat contrary' to compassion. He taught that whilst a vegetarian DIET is commendable, and would become increasingly favoured by people in the future, there is no requirement to adopt it (*LG* 295). It is also necessary to remember that, with every breath of air or drink of water, humans swallow a multitude of microscopic animal life: they too are part of the web of life (*SWAB* 157).

HUNTING

Bahá'u'lláh stated that hunting was lawful, but should not be excessive. In response to the complex of Islamic laws regarding the lawfulness of eating animals that had been hunted, he prohibited eating those creatures that had been found dead in snares or traps, but permitted eating those that had been shot, or caught using beasts or birds of prey. In this latter case, the hunter should invoke God's name when they sent out their hunting animal. *KA* 40 k60, 115 q24, 203 n83–4.

antichrist (Ar.: *dajjál*)

Expected figure in Christian and Islamic apocalypticism. Shoghi Effendi identified Ḥájí Mírzá ÁQÁSÍ as the antichrist of the Bábí dispensation for having turned MUḤAMMAD SHÁH against the Báb, and Sayyid MUḤAMMAD IṢFÁHÁNÍ as the antichrist of the Bahá'í dispensation for having misled Ṣubḥ-i-AZAL (*GPB* 164). In both cases, the antichrist had manipulated a weak person who was in a position of influence in order to oppose God's Cause. For the Bábís, KARÍM KHÁN KIRMÁNÍ assumed a similar oppositional role (*SBBR* 18). *TN* 304–6.

apocalypticism

See CALAMITY; MILLENARIANISM.

apologetics

That branch of theology concerned with the rational justification of a religion. Bahá'ís commonly believe that religious truth can be 'proved', and that INDEPENDENT INVESTIGATION OF TRUTH will invariably lead the seeker who is pure in heart to acceptance of the Bahá'í Faith.

PROOF

For Bahá'ís the validity of each of the MANIFESTATIONS OF GOD is shown by the following:

(1) The compelling power of the WORD OF GOD: those who recognized its truth were transformed, obeying the Prophets' teachings and laws (e.g. fasting, going on pilgrimage, abandoning wrongdoing), even when this involved inconvenience; being brought together in unity, thereby

overcoming pre-existing divisions (Jew and Gentile, black and white, etc.); and being ready to die for the sake of their convictions. Ultimately, a new civilization developed from the impetus the Prophets gave to their followers.

(2) The REVELATION of divine verses: particularly emphasized by both the Báb and Bahá'u'lláh as the primary proof of their mission. Correspondingly, Bahá'u'lláh challenged Ṣubḥ-i-AZAL to produce a single verse if he wished to prove that he possessed divinely inspired knowledge (*TB* 75–6).

(3) The characteristics of the Manifestation himself: the integrity of his life and teachings, his willingness to suffer for the sake of the truth, his endurance and steadfastness in the face of opposition, and his innate knowledge.

(4) PROPHECY: the latest Manifestation both fulfilled the prophecies of those who preceded him and foretold the future.

(5) The Prophet's teachings, which were attractive, challenging and appropriate to the age to which he came.

(6) The defeat of those who opposed divine truth, often expressed in specific DIVINE JUDGEMENT.

MIRACLES are not generally regarded as an adequate proof of divine mission, though Shoghi Effendi included the 'marvelous happenings' that had heralded the Báb's advent and the 'miraculous tragedy' of his martyrdom as amongst the 'sufficient evidence' for the validity of his claim (along with the dramatic circumstances of his life, and the 'magic' of the influence he had exerted on the most eminent and powerful among his countrymen) (*WOB* 124). Lample.

APOLOGETIC LITERATURE

Both the Báb (*SEVEN PROOFS*) and Bahá'u'lláh (*Kitáb-i-ÍQÁN*) presented 'proofs' of their religion, the *Íqán* remaining a primary proof text for Bahá'ís. 'Abdu'l-Bahá often offered proofs of his father's mission during his talks in the West (1911–13). Of other Bahá'í apologists, the most important was Mírzá ABU'L-FAḌL, who wrote books in support of Bahá'í claims addressed to Muslims, Iranian Jews and Western Christians. Given the Bahá'í acceptance of other religions as true (*see* RELIGIOUS DIVERSITY), there is a growing body of Bahá'í apologetic literature addressed to the members of the various world religions (in English, mostly CHRISTIANITY, but also BUDDHISM; Hinduism (*see* INDIAN RELIGIONS); INDIGENOUS RELIGIONS; and ISLAM), as well as more 'secular' works (such as Huddleston, *Earth*).

apostasy

Abandonment of one's religious faith. Regarded as a cardinal sin by the early Christians and theoretically (and sometimes in practice) punished with death in Islam. The Bahá'í belief in the INDEPENDENT INVESTIGATION OF TRUTH entails freedom of religious belief, so that those who no longer accept the Bahá'í Faith as true are free to leave. National ASSEMBLIES generally ask for formal letters or statements of resignation before officially accepting a person's withdrawal from the Faith. The term 'apostate' is not used except to refer to those former Bahá'ís, such as the Iranian historian ÁVÁRIH, who volubly attack the Faith and its institutions.

Apostles of Bahá'u'lláh

Honorific designation by Shoghi Effendi for nineteen prominent early Bahá'ís (*BW3:* 80–1). They are also termed 'Pillars of the Faith' (cf. DISCIPLES OF 'ABDU'L-BAHÁ). The list comprises:

(1) Mírzá MÚSÁ, Bahá'u'lláh's 'only true brother'

The Apostles of Bahá'u'lláh (see text for key)

(2) Mírzá Buzurg BADÍ', 'youthful martyr', the bearer of Bahá'u'lláh's letter to NÁSIRU'D-DÍN SHÁH
(3) Sayyid Ḥasan, the KING OF MARTYRS
(4) Mullá Abu'l-Ḥasan Ardikání, surnamed AMÍN, 'faithful steward' of Bahá'u'lláh and 'Abdu'l-Bahá
(5) Mírzá ABU'L-FAḌL Gulpáygání
(6) Mírzá 'Alí-Muḥammad VARQÁ, 'poet, teacher, and martyr'
(7) Mírzá Maḥmúd FURÚGHÍ, 'an indomitable spirit and jealous defender of the Faith'
(8) Mullá 'Alí-Akbar Shahmírzádí, also known as Ḥájí ÁKHÚND, 'a flame of zeal and devotion'
(9) Mullá Muḥammad Qá'iní, NABÍL-I-AKBAR, 'learned and steadfast exponent of the Bahá'í Revelation'
(10) Ḥájí Mírzá MUḤAMMAD-TAQÍ, *Vakílu'd-dawlih*, '*Kabír-i-Afnán*', 'chief builder' of the *Mashriqu'l-Adhkár* of Ashkhabad
(11) Ḥájí Mírzá Muḥammad-Taqí Abharí, IBN-I-ABHAR, 'prominent teacher'
(12) Mullá Muḥammad Zarandí, NABÍL-I-A'ẒAM, 'poet, historian, and teacher of the Faith'
(13) Shaykh Káẓim SAMANDAR, 'a flame of the love of God, favored of Bahá'u'lláh'
(14) Mírzá MUḤAMMAD MUṢṬAFÁ al-Baghdádí, 'brave and vigilant custodian and bearer of the remains of the Báb'
(15) Mírzá Ḥusayn MISHKIN-QALAM, calligrapher and Bahá'u'lláh's companion-in-exile
(16) Mírzá Ḥasan, ADÍB, 'devoted teacher of the Cause'
(17) Shaykh MUḤAMMAD-'ALÍ QÁ'INÍ, 'eloquent and learned champion of the Faith in Russian Turkistán'
(18) Mullá Zaynu'l-'Ábidín, ZAYNU'L-MUQARRABÍN, 'noted scribe' and chief among the exiles of Mosul
(19) Mírzá 'Alí-Muḥammad, IBN-I-AṢDAQ, 'zealous advocate' of the Covenant.

appeals

Individuals may appeal against decisions of their local or national ASSEMBLIES, in the first instance to the assembly itself, and subsequently to a higher authority (to the respective national assembly and the Universal House of Justice). Differences between local assemblies that cannot be amicably resolved between themselves should be addressed to the respective national assembly. *LG* 62–4; *UHJC* no. viii.

Áqá Ján Káshání, Mírzá (*c.* 1837–1901)

Secretary of Bahá'u'lláh. Born into a merchant family, he became a Bábí as a youth. He was still only sixteen when he first met Bahá'u'lláh in Karbalá in 1853 and became his fervent disciple, being accorded the status of being 'the first to believe' in him. Some time after Bahá'u'lláh's return from Kurdistan, Áqá Ján became his attendant and chief secretary, subsequently accompanying him on the various stages of his exile. Bahá'u'lláh called him *Khádimu'lláh* ('servant of God'). Towards the end of Bahá'u'lláh's life Áqá Ján fell into some disfavour with him, and after Bahá'u'lláh's passing Áqá Ján joined the partisans of MUḤAMMAD-'ALÍ and was declared a COVENANT-BREAKER by 'Abdu'l-Bahá. *BKG* 109–12; *TCB* 181–92. (*See also* REVELATION.)

Áqá Khán-i-Núrí, Mírzá (Naṣru'lláh) (d. 1865)

Second of NÁṢIRU'D-DÍN SHÁH's prime ministers (1851–8), successor of AMÍR KABÍR, whose downfall he helped engineer. He oversaw the execution of Bábís in the aftermath of the attempt on the life of the shah. He was distantly related to Bahá'u'lláh. *MBBR* 135–6, 165–7.

Áqásí, Ḥájí Mírzá (*c.* 1783–1849)

Chief minister of MUḤAMMAD SHÁH, 1835–48. He dominated his master, in part through his role as his religious guide. He became greatly opposed to the BÁB, presumably seeing him as a potential threat to his own position, and successfully endeavoured to ensure that he was never received by the shah. After the death of MANÚCHIHR KHÁN, Áqásí had the Báb imprisoned in MÁKÚ, a village under his influence. He later had him transferred to CHIHRÍQ and arranged for him to be tried in Tabríz in 1848. The Báb wrote a number of letters to Áqásí and also addressed him in various of his writings. Finally, when Áqásí's enmity was clearly evident, he referred to him as Satan and condemned him unreservedly in the *Khuṭbi-yi-Qahriyyih* ('Sermon of Wrath'). Áqásí fell from power with the death of his master in 1848 and had to flee from Tehran to escape his many enemies. Shoghi Effendi stigmatized him as the ANTICHRIST of the 'Bábí Revelation' (*GPB* 164). *MBBR* 154–6.

Aqdas, Kitáb-i-

(PA, '*The Most Holy Book*')

Bahá'u'lláh's book of holy law. He composed it in Arabic, and completed it around 1873 whilst he was still in the city of Akka. It was supplemented by various later writings (*TB*), and by Bahá'u'lláh's replies to a series of questions about it posed by one of his secretaries, ZAYNU'L-MUQARRABÍN, himself an expert in Islamic law. It was first published in Bombay in 1890/1. Bahá'u'lláh stated that it was revealed in response to repeated requests from his followers for laws to follow (*KA* 55–6 k98).

For Bahá'u'lláh, the *Aqdas* is God's proof 'unto all who are in heaven and all who are on earth' (*KA* 3). It is also his 'unerring Balance', whereby all the peoples of the world are tested (*KA* 56 k99). Its ordinances are 'the mightiest stronghold for the protection of the world'. True belief in God and his messenger is only complete by acceptance of what he has revealed and observance of his law (*KA* 19 k1; *TB* 50). This is not a 'mere code of laws', but a 'choice Wine' (*KA* 21 k5). The laws are 'the breath of life' for 'all created things' (*GPB* 215), and 'the highest means for the maintenance of order in the world and the security of its peoples' (*KA* 19 k2). Acceptance of God's messenger requires also acceptance of his laws. They should be followed out of love for his 'beauty', and for the 'sweetness' of their taste (*KA* 20 k3, 4), and even if they cause 'the heaven of every religion to be cleft asunder' (*KA* 21 k7). They are God's laws. Conscious breach of them indicates heedlessness, and both God and Bahá'u'lláh would 'be clear of such a one' (*TB* 188–9). 'True liberty' consists in obedience to these laws (*KA* 63 k125). They suffuse the heart of the true believer with light, and should be obeyed with 'joy and gladness' (*KA* 73 k148). Shoghi Effendi described the *Aqdas* as the 'Mother Book' of the Bahá'í dispensation; the 'brightest emanation of the mind of Bahá'u'lláh'; and the charter of his 'New World Order', foretold in the Bible in such phrases as the promised 'new heaven' and 'new earth' (*GPB* 213).

The laws themselves partly follow the pattern of the Islamic and Bábí holy law, and include:

(1) personal obligations towards God (obligatory PRAYER, FASTING, PILGRIMAGE, *ZAKÁT*, *ḤUQÚQU'LLÁH*, daily repetition of God's name (*see* DEVOTIONALISM));
(2) the regulation of personal status and contracts (MARRIAGE, DIVORCE, the age of MATURITY; INHERITANCE; WILLS, endowments);
(3) community life (CALENDAR, certain HOLY DAYS, the HOUSES OF JUSTICE, the *MASHRIQU'L-ADHKÁR*, EDUCATION, BURIAL);

(4) prohibitions (against ADULTERY, pederasty, ALCOHOL, DRUGS, ASCETICISM, MONASTICISM, BEGGING, GAMBLING, CONFESSION OF SINS, the kissing of hands, sedition, the SLAVE TRADE, the use of insanitary Iranian public baths, overburdening ANIMALS);
(5) exhortations (to goodly deeds CLEANLINESS, DETACHMENT, TRUSTWORTHINESS, WORK, SOCIAL ORDER, to associate amicably with the followers of all religions, to promote the development of countries and cities, to adopt a single world LANGUAGE); and
(6) punishments for CRIME and breaches of certain social laws.

Bahá'u'lláh also

- abrogated Islamic teachings of ritual impurity, the Islamic prohibitions against MUSIC and the use of vessels of gold and silver, and the Bábí prohibition against marrying non-believers;
- called upon the KINGS of the world to recognize him;
- addressed specific RULERS (*see also* FRANZ-JOSEPH, WILHELM I), the presidents of the American republics (*see* AMERICAS), the inhabitants of ISTANBUL and TEHRAN;
- emphasized the INFALLIBILITY of the MANIFESTATIONS OF GOD;
- warned against pride and perverse interpretation of God's laws;
- warned RELIGIOUS LEADERS not to evaluate the *Aqdas* by their own criteria or to prevent the people from recognizing Bahá'u'lláh;
- warned the Bábís not to reject him;
- directed the Bahá'ís to follow 'Him Whom God hath purposed' amongst his sons after his death (*see* COVENANT); and
- stated that there would be no further Manifestation of God for a thousand years.

An English translation was made in about 1900 and circulated amongst the early American Bahá'ís, and a literalistic non-Bahá'í translation was published in 1961. An official Bahá'í translation was long delayed, however, and it was not until 1973 that the Universal House of Justice published a *Synopsis and Codification* of the text, and 1992 that a full translation was made available. Accompanied by the supplementary questions and answers, and by copious notes, this edition was designed to help readers from a non-Islamic background understand aspects of the book that would have otherwise seemed strange or obscure to them. *GPB* 213–16; *KA*; *MUHJ* 67–9 no. 27, 231 no. 125, 272–3 no. 145, 277–9 no. 147, 447–51 no. 251; *RB3*: 275–399; *BFSH* 71–3; UHJ, *Synopsis*; Walbridge, *Sacred* 248–52.

Aqdas, Lawḥ-i-

(PA, '*The Most Holy Tablet*')

Arabic tablet of Bahá'u'lláh revealed in Akka, sometimes also referred to as the *Tablet to the Christians*. The recipient was possibly Fáris Effendi, a Bahá'í of Syrian Christian background (*BKG* 267–78; *RB3* 5–11). The tablet addresses all Christians; proclaims that Bahá'u'lláh is the promised Spirit of Truth who has come to guide them to all truth; and asks them not to be like the Jewish Pharisees who awaited the advent of the Messiah but were unable to recognize Jesus when he came. The leaders of society were now pleased to call themselves Christians, but when Jesus came the most learned of his own people condemned him to death, whilst he was recognized by a humble fisherman. Present Christian leaders were specifically summoned: the priests should leave their churches and proclaim Bahá'u'lláh's Cause and the monks become the 'heirs of My Kingdom'. The fall of bishops ('the stars of the heaven of My knowledge') was stated to be by divine justice. *TB* 7–17; Sours, *Study*; *RB4*: 227–35. (*See also* CHRISTIANITY.)

Arc, buildings of

In his *Tablet of* CARMEL Bahá'u'lláh stated that God would 'sail His Ark' upon the mountain, a prophecy which Shoghi Effendi interpreted to refer to the future establishment of the Universal House of Justice. More widely, it was linked to the evolution of a number of 'world-shaking' administrative institutions which would be sited on Mount Carmel, the focal centre of which was the grave of BAHIYYIH KHÁNUM (*see also* HAIFA). These institutions would be built along an 'Arc' which Shoghi Effendi traced along the flank of the mountain above the grave. The completion of these buildings is regarded by Bahá'ís as being linked to the onset of the Lesser PEACE. The first of the buildings to be constructed for these institutions was that for the INTERNATIONAL ARCHIVES, its stately, classical style setting a model for the rest.

In 1972 the Universal House of Justice announced that it would initiate planning for its own Seat, the second of the buildings of the Arc. Its choice of architect, Husayn Amanat, was announced in 1973. Work started in 1975 and was completed in 1982. The building was formally occupied in 1983. The Seat, located at the apex of the Arc, is a large building comprising five-and-a-half storeys. In addition to the council chamber of the House of Justice and considerable office space, it includes a reception concourse, banquet room, reference library and storage vaults. The exterior is constructed in classical style, with a colonnade of Corinthian columns, and is topped by a low dome.

The decision to construct two further buildings of the Arc was announced by the Universal House of Justice in 1987:

(1) the seat of the INTERNATIONAL TEACHING CENTRE.
(2) the Centre for the Study of the Texts, an institution of scholars which would assist the House of Justice in consulting the Bahá'í sacred writings and prepare translations and commentaries. It would represent the

A model of the buildings of the Arc. In the centre is the Seat of the Universal House of Justice; on the left is the International Library and the Seat of the International Teaching Centre; on the right is the Centre for the Study of the Sacred Texts and the International Archives Building.

> 'efflorescence' of the Research Department of the BAHÁ'Í WORLD CENTRE.

Work on these was delayed pending the collection of sufficient funding, finally beginning in 1992. It is now in an advanced state. The architect was again Husayn Amanat. The buildings are located on either side of the Seat of the Universal House of Justice. At the same time, a large underground extension to the International Archives building and the terraces above and below the SHRINE OF THE BÁB are being constructed. The architect for the terraces is Fariborz Sahba.

A final building is projected for construction at some point in the next century: an International Bahá'í Library. This will extend the activities of the present Bahá'í World Centre Library, and is to serve both as the central depository of all literature on the Bahá'í Faith and as a resource centre on subjects relating to the Faith and the conditions of humanity. It is intended to become a centre of knowledge in all fields and give rise to institutions of scientific discovery. It is to be located at the far end of the Arc from the Archives building. *BW18*: 465–72; *BWNS* 1992–3: 169–76; 1993–4: 67–75; 1994–5: 65–73; 1995–6: 55–64; Ruhe 172–4.

architecture

There is no distinctive style of Bahá'í architecture. The various Bahá'í 'temples' (See *MASHRIQU'L-ADHKÁR*) conform to the same basic pattern; they are nine-sided buildings with domes, but are otherwise extremely diverse in style. Several incorporate indigenous elements and motifs (notably the Kampala, Panama, Apia, and New Delhi temples). The Wilmette and New Delhi temples have attracted considerable interest among architects for their originality of construction. Shoghi Effendi's artistic taste has been a major influence on the design of many of the

Some major Bahá'í edifices

BUILDING	PERIOD OF CONSTRUCTION	ARCHITECT
Inner Shrine of the Báb	1899/1900–7	
Ashkhabad temple	1902–8 (Outer decoration completed in 1919)	Ustád 'Alí-Akbar Banná/Volkov
Wilmette temple	1920–53	Louis Bourgeois
Outer Shrine of the Báb	1948/9–53	Sutherland Maxwell
International Archives	1955–7	Andrea Rocca/Shoghi Effendi
Kampala temple	1958–61	Mason Remey
Sydney temple	1958–61	Mason Remey
Langenhain temple	1960–4	Teuto Rocholl
Panama temple	1967–72	Peter Tillotson
Seat of the Universal House of Justice	1975–83	Husayn Amanat
New Delhi temple	1977–86	Fariborz Sahba
Apia temple	1980–4	Husayn Amanat
Arc buildings	1992–	Husayn Amanat
Mt. Carmel terraces	1992–	Fariborz Sahba

most important Bahá'í buildings in the world, notably those of the ARC at the BAHÁ'Í WORLD CENTRE, and several of the temples. The buildings of the Arc follow a general classical style established by Shoghi Effendi in the design for the INTERNATIONAL ARCHIVES building. His view was that classical Greek buildings were not only beautiful and dignified (both qualities he wanted in the structure), but had also proved to be of enduring value. Much modern architecture, by contrast, he regarded as ugly and experimental (and therefore transient), and he vetoed the original design for the Kampala temple on this basis. (*BW13*: 705; Rabbani, *Priceless Pearl* 264, 359). National and local Bahá'í centres and other Bahá'í buildings in various parts of the world conform to no particular style.

archives

Bahá'í archival collections comprise both historical documents and relics. Shoghi Effendi emphasized the importance of individual, local and national Bahá'í archives, and himself built up the extensive INTERNATIONAL ARCHIVES, which were eventually housed in a stately building in Haifa (1957). He also published copies of much original documentation relating to Bahá'í history in the series *BAHÁ'Í WORLD*. He urged ASSEMBLIES to be cautious in the disposal of their papers as these might be of unexpected value to future historians, and directed that such disposal should be checked by an appointed committee rather than being entrusted to an individual. At the BAHÁ'Í WORLD CENTRE there are now well-established programmes to collect, classify and preserve documents and relics as part of the work of the archives office. Similar departments have also been established by the American Bahá'í national assembly. *LG* 95–7.

armaments

Bahá'u'lláh desired that war weapons be converted into 'instruments of reconstruction' so that conflict might cease (*TB* 23). If the world's rulers established PEACE between the nations, then the need for armaments would disappear, apart from the limited quantities required for defence and to maintain internal order in each country (*Proclamation* 13; *TB* 165). Similarly, 'Abdu'l-Bahá deplored the economic burden that armament development placed on the hapless masses who were required to pay for it. He taught that internationally agreed and enforced limits should be placed on the extent of each nation's armaments. This would obviate the 'crazed competition' to develop new weapons and increase the size of armed forces which itself aroused the suspicions of others (*SDC* 61–2, 65–6; Esslemont A 148–9/B 157; *see also* WAR).

Armstrong, Leonora Stirling (née Holsapple) (1895–1980)

American PIONEER to Brazil (1921–80) and first Bahá'í resident in South America. She translated Bahá'í literature into Portuguese and Spanish, and during a short visit to Spain (1930) formed the first Bahá'í group in that country. She was appointed to the CONTINENTAL BOARD OF COUNSELLORS in 1973. The Universal House of Justice described her as the 'spiritual mother' of South America. *BW18*: 733–8.

art

Bahá'u'lláh praised CRAFTSMANSHIP; it reflects God's name, 'the Fashioner'. As with other types of WORK it is a form of worship, and those who follow a particular craft or art should attain the greatest proficiency in it, for God loves 'the highest perfection'. Shoghi Effendi noted that the spirit of every religion had come to be expressed in art. What

Bahá'í artists and architects had so far produced was only the first rays of the dawn. There was as yet no 'Bahá'í art' (or music, literature, and architecture), as this would be the flower of a future Bahá'í civilization. Then, when Bahá'í played a larger role in society, its spirit would find fuller expression in the work of artists and would act to ennoble peoples' sentiments and attract them to the Faith. *CC1*: 1–8.

Bahá'ís are not permitted to portray any MANIFESTATION OF GOD in any of the visual or dramatic arts. Such portrayals in past religions include great works made in a spirit of reverence and love, but according to the Bahá'í view, greater human maturity should now engender a higher sense of reverence. *LG* 97–100.

Of the visual arts, CALLIGRAPHY occupies an honoured place in the Iranian cultural tradition, and there have been a number of eminent Bahá'ís who were gifted calligraphers, notably MISHKÍN-QALAM. Amongst Western Bahá'ís, the potter Bernard LEACH and the painter Mark TOBEY achieved international renown. Also increasingly well known is the South African painter Reginald Turvey. The South African Bahá'í community has now established a Bahá'í association for the arts, and holds an annual art exhibition. An international Bahá'í Association for Arts was formed in 1986 based in the Netherlands. A Canadian Bahá'í arts council was started in 1988. Fitzgerald; *BWNS* 1994–5: 243–72.

artificial fertilization

Childless couples can use artificial insemination and in-vitro fertilization methods as long as it is the husband's own sperm that fertilizes the wife's own ovum. Surrogate motherhood is not permitted on account of its complex spiritual and social implications. *LG* 288 nos. 973–5, 348 no. 1168.

Asadu'lláh Khu'í, Mullá

See DAYYÁN.

asceticism

Bahá'u'lláh taught the importance of DETACHMENT and piety, but forbade asceticism (*TB* 71). God created the bounties of the world for human beings to enjoy, and ascetic practices such as those of some Sufis (e.g. seclusion in mountain caves and graveyards) and Hindus were not the means of approaching God (*KA* 31 k36). Again, whilst the pious deeds of Christian monks were to be praised, they should now abandon seclusion and live in the 'open world'. (*See also* MONASTICISM).

Ashkhabad (Pers.: 'Ishqábád)

Capital of Turkmenistan, and of the former imperial Russian governorate of Turkestan. The city is close to the Iranian border, and received large numbers of Iranian immigrants from the 1880s onwards. These included Bahá'ís, many of them merchants and builders, who were seeking both economic opportunity and the chance to escape persecution in their homeland. Their numbers soon rose to about four hundred. The Bahá'í presence led to growing anti-Bahá'í sentiment amongst the Iranian Shí'í settlers, culminating in the brutal public murder of a prominent Bahá'í (Ḥájí Muḥammad-Riḍá Iṣfáhání) on 8 September 1889, preliminary to a projected general attack on the Bahá'ís. To the assailants' surprise, however, the Russian authorities intervened to protect the Bahá'ís, and arrested the murderers and their backers, sentencing several to death or internal exile, the severer sentences only being commuted at the request of the Bahá'ís. The trial served to mark off the Bahá'ís as a separate religious community recognized and protected by the government – a situation unique at the time. Ashkhabad thenceforth attracted more Bahá'í immigrants, and the community rapidly developed into a model of the Bahá'í ideal, establishing a 'Spiritual Board of Counsel' (1895–6, possibly the first Bahá'í ASSEMBLY in the world), and constructing a travellers' hospice; dispensary and clinic; schools for boys (1894) and girls (1897); cemetery; kindergartens (1917–18); and reading room and library. Of particular significance was the building of the first Bahá'í House of Worship (*MASHRIQU'L-ADHKÁR*) (1902–7), the foundation stone of which was laid by the Russian governor-general, General Subotich, in 1904. In accordance with Russian law, there was no attempt to gain ethnic Russian converts. The situation changed following the two Russian revolutions of 1917. Initially the Bahá'ís were able to teach their religion openly, but opposition from the Communist Party organizations mounted, and in 1928 the temple was confiscated. The closure of the schools and the arrest of some of the Bahá'ís followed. The community – now consisting of about 1,400 families – was effectively destroyed in 1938, with the arrest and exile of many of the men, and the deportation of the women and children and the remainder of the men to Iran. When conditions in the Soviet Union were finally relaxed, the Ashkhabad Bahá'í assembly was the first to reform (1989). Lee, 'Rise'; *MBBR* 296–300, 473; Momen, 'Baha'i community'; *SBBR* 91, 173.

Ashraf

Name of two Bahá'í martyrs in Iran.

(1) SAYYID ('ALÍ-)ASHRAF OF ZANJÁN

He was also called *Ashrafu'sh-shuhadá* (the 'Noblest of Martyrs'). A son of one of the martyrs of ZANJÁN, he became a Bahá'í, and travelled to EDIRNE to meet Bahá'u'lláh. Returning to Zanján, he succeeded in converting many of the Bábís. Fearing a reanimation of Bábism, the local *'ULAMÁ* ordered his execution, along with that of his fellow Bahá'í Áqá Naqd-'Alí (born blind, but named *Abú-Baṣír* (the 'Father of Insight') by Bahá'u'lláh). Ashraf's refusal to recant – he was related to one of the leading clerics of the city who sought to intervene on his behalf – and the constancy of his mother, Umm Ashraf, were praised by Bahá'u'lláh. He was also the recipient of an Arabic tablet from Bahá'u'lláh (the *Lawḥ-i-Ashraf*, see *GWB* no. 52). *RB2*: 223–35; *EB* 24–5.

(2) MÍRZÁ ASHRAF OF ÁBÁDIH

A respected elderly Bahá'í of clerical background, he was executed in Iṣfáhán on 23 October 1888 and his body subjected to various barbarities by order of Áqá Najafí (the Son of the WOLF). *MBBR* 277–80; *EB* 25, 29–32; *RB4*: 385–6.

Aṣl-i-Kullu'l-Khayr

See WORDS OF WISDOM.

assemblies ('spiritual assemblies', PA sing. *maḥfil-i-rawḥání*)

Elected Bahá'í administrative councils at local and national level. *BW18*: 456–7, 536–45, 554–67; *CC2*: 29–60, 83–136; *GPB* 330–6; *UHJC* nos. ii-iv. (*See also* ADMINISTRATION; CONVENTION; REGIONAL BAHÁ'Í COUNCILS.)

Bahá'u'lláh called for the establishment of HOUSES OF JUSTICE in every city to administer Bahá'í affairs, calling upon their members to be 'the trusted ones of the Merciful', and to meet together as if in the presence of God (*KA* 29 k30). At 'Abdu'l-Bahá's direction or with his encouragement, a variety of local councils in various parts of the world were formed from the 1890s onwards. These included assemblies at ASHKHABAD (from 1895/6) and Tehran (from 1897/9); and 'Council Boards' and other bodies in several American cities (1899–1900). (*BFA1*: 112, 169–70, 174; *BFA2*: 11–15, 67–8, 323, 394–6; *EB* 175, 268, 272; *GPB* 260; *BFSH* 91–4; Smith,

'American Bahá'í community' 137–43.) These bodies varied in their names, manner of formation and number of members. Those in the West came to have members of both sexes, whilst those in Iran were confined to men. There was also an evident need for more 'national' bodies to superintend activities in their respective countries. This was met by the Tehran and Ashkhabad ('Central') assemblies coming to assume a more general directive role, and the formation of the North American BAHAI TEMPLE UNITY (1909), elected by delegates from the various local communities. The concept of national ('secondary') houses of justice was formally introduced by 'Abdu'l-Bahá.

The present system of spiritual assemblies (as the forebears of future houses of Justice) was standardized and developed by SHOGHI EFFENDI at the very onset of his ministry in two general letters to the Western Bahá'ís, dated 5 March 1922 and 12 March 1923 (*BA* 17–25, 34–43). Local spiritual assemblies were to be established forthwith wherever there were nine or more adult Bahá'ís (aged twenty-one or above). They would be directly elected by the local adult Bahá'ís (ELECTIONS), and have authority over all local Bahá'í activities. National spiritual assemblies were to be established in all the larger communities (Britain, 1923; Germany, 1923; India and Burma, 1923; Egypt (with the Sudan), 1924; Turkistan, 1925; and the Caucasus, 1925); and the executive committee of the American Bahai Temple Unity transformed into a similar body. These would be elected indirectly by an electoral college of locally elected delegates, and would have authority over national Bahá'í activities, including the local assemblies under their jurisdiction. They were also to keep in regular contact with the BAHÁ'Í WORLD CENTRE. Both types of assembly would be re-elected annually; have nine members; use the principles of PRAYER and CONSULTATION in their decision making; establish their own FUNDS; and elect their own officers (chairman or president, vice-chairman, secretary, treasurer). With modification of details, this has remained the main element in Bahá'í ADMINISTRATION until the present day.

Shoghi Effendi also outlined the 'most outstanding obligations' of the spiritual assemblies: (1) directing the TEACHING work; (2) protecting the Bahá'í Faith from its enemies; (3) promoting amity amongst the Bahá'ís and their active service to the Faith; (4) assisting the poor, sick, disabled, orphaned and widowed, 'irrespective of colour, caste and creed'; (5) promoting the material and spiritual enlightenment of youth and child education; (6) maintaining regular correspondence with Bahá'í centres throughout the world and sharing news of their activities; (7) stimulating the development of Bahá'í PERIODICALS; (8) arranging regular Bahá'í meetings (*see* FEAST; HOLY DAYS), together with gatherings to promote 'the social, intellectual and spiritual interests of their fellow-men'; and (9) REVIEW of all Bahá'í publications and translations (whilst the Faith was 'still in its infancy'), and provision for their distribution to the public (*BA* 37–8). Another responsibility was superintending the application of Bahá'í LAW where this was applicable. Where necessary, the assemblies should delegate particular areas of activity to appointed committees. They were strictly to eschew any political involvement (*BA* 24).

In a letter to the Eastern Bahá'ís (1926) he noted the 'basic' and 'inescapable' responsibilities of assembly members: they should embody SPIRITUAL QUALITIES, such as TRUSTWORTHINESS, TRUTHFULNESS, DETACHMENT, courage, kindliness and purity of motive; develop self-reliance; exercise MODERATION; be efficient in the management of the assemblies' affairs; serve the general interests of the people; study the Bahá'í texts and apply their guidance to the needs of modern society, working to improve morals; spread learning and enlightenment (making 'detailed inquiry' into contemporary arts and sciences); support and revere scholars and the exponents of arts and sciences; eradicate ignorance and prejudice; uphold the right of freedom of conscience; support agricultural and industrial development; and promote the emancipation and advancement of women, compulsory education for both sexes, mutual assistance and co-operation, and 'the principles of consultation among all classes'. They must be sincerely obedient to the laws of the country; strictly avoid entanglement in political and theological controversies; and abstain from criticizing the beliefs and customs of other individuals and peoples (*CC2*: 347–9).

Both Shoghi Effendi and the Universal House of Justice have written extensively on the importance of assemblies and their manner of functioning; emphasized the responsibilities of membership; stressed the need for the assemblies to gain 'the confidence and affection of those whom it is their privilege to serve' (*BA* 143); encouraged assemblies to gain legal status (commonly requiring the adoption of a constitution consisting of a declaration of trust and by-laws (*see* CONSTITUTIONS; INCORPORATION)), facilitating the holding of land and property; warned of the dangers of personalistic leadership and of over-administration (excessive rule making and regulation is to be avoided); and encouraged flexibility in 'secondary matters', whilst strictly adhering to basic principles. Individual Bahá'ís are advised to consult their respective assembly regarding the course of action in Bahá'í activities and obey it (*BA* 21). They also have the right to consult assemblies on matters of concern, and to appeal against decisions they consider to be wrong (including appeal to a higher administrative body).

There has been a vast increase in the number of assemblies over the past 75 years. By May 1994 there was a total of 172 national assemblies or their regional equivalents and 17,780 local assemblies (*BWNS* 1994–5: 317; *see also* EXPANSION). Individual assemblies clearly vary in their 'style' of functioning, as well as their efficiency and maturity in applying Bahá'í principles. Several national assemblies have produced their own administrative manuals (e.g. NSA of the Bahá'ís of the United Kingdom, *Principles*).

assistants

Institution created by the Universal House of Justice in June 1973 to provide assistance to the members of the AUXILIARY BOARDS. Given the rapid EXPANSION of the Faith, the work load of individual Board members in some parts of the world had enormously increased, and it was no longer possible for them to discharge all their duties adequately: to encourage (and where necessary activate) *all* the local spiritual ASSEMBLIES and communities in their area; conduct DEEPENING classes for the Bahá'ís; stimulate TEACHING etc. Therefore, subject to the approval of the relevant CONTINENTAL BOARD OF COUNSELLORS, individual Board members were encouraged to appoint assistants for specific tasks or to be responsible for particular areas. Subsequent experience also indicated their value in promoting specific qualitative goals, such as increasing the role of WOMEN in Bahá'í administration. The assistants could include young people (*see* YOUTH), and they could continue to serve as elected assembly members. The Board members would be responsible for training the assistants and supervising their activities. CBC in Europe 135–49; *LG* 332–4; *MUHJ* 255–6 no. 137, 359–60 no. 189.2.

astrology

The Bahá'í teachings reject astrology as imagination and, in large part, superstition. Bahá'ís should not regard the stars and planets as guiding their lives or influencing their health or wealth. They should be patient and tolerant with those who do believe in such things, however. *LG* 516–17 nos. 1746–52; *SAQ* 245–7.

Augur, George (1853–1927) and Ruth (d. 1936)

Prominent early Hawaiian Bahá'ís, who converted around 1906. George was the first Bahá'í to live in Japan (1914–19), where he was later joined by his wife and by Agnes ALEXANDER. Shoghi Effendi named him as one of the DISCIPLES OF 'ABDU'L-BAHÁ. *WSBR* 187–98.

Auxiliary Boards

Institution created by Shoghi Effendi to provide assistance to the HANDS OF THE CAUSE. These Boards were first appointed by the Hands in April (RIḌVÁN) 1954. The members of each Board were to act as the deputies, assistants and advisers of the Hands in the work of the TEN YEAR CRUSADE. They were organized on a continental basis (initially nine members each in Africa, the Americas and Europe; seven in Asia; and two in Australasia), and were responsible to the Hands in their respective continents. Continental FUNDS were established to support their work. The appointment of a second set of Boards was called for in October 1957. These were to be responsible for the security of the Faith ('Protection', i.e. safeguarding the unity of the Bahá'í community and responding to attacks by COVENANT-BREAKERS and non-Bahá'í opponents), whilst the original Boards focused their attention on the TEACHING work ('Propagation'). The individual members became responsible for specific geographical areas, and each area came under the purview of both a member of the propagation and protection Boards. The work of the Boards has expanded since 1963 with the further EXPANSION of the Bahá'í community world-wide. Under the Universal House of Justice, Board members have been freed from membership of national assemblies so that they can concentrate on their own tasks (1963); responsibility for the work of the Boards has been transferred to the more recently formed CONTINENTAL BOARDS OF COUNSELLORS (1968); the Board members are empowered to appoint ASSISTANTS to help them in their work (1973); five-year (reappointable) terms of service to the Boards have been set (from November 1986); and the total number of possible Board members enormously increased: to 270 in 1973, 378 in 1976, 756 in 1986, and 846 in 1991. The House has stressed the division of responsibility between the two arms of the Bahá'í ADMINISTRATION, noting that it was the function of the Board members to help arouse and release the energies of the Bahá'ís to accomplish the goals of the Faith, and not to impinge on the local ASSEMBLIES' administrative work. They were to reinforce the work of the assemblies and committees; consolidate local communities; enthuse the Bahá'ís; and deepen their understanding of the Faith. *LG* 328–38; *MBW* 44, 58–9, 63, 128; *MUHJ* 24 no. 11 132 no. 59.5, 150–3 no. 72, 255–6 no. 137, 323–5 no. 170, 350 no. 182.7, 367 no. 194, 622 no. 394.3; *UHJC* no. x.

Ávárih, Mírzá 'Abdu'l-Ḥusayn Taftí (1290/1873–1953),

Former cleric, also known as Áyatí, who became one of the most prominent Iranian Bahá'ís. He wrote what was regarded at the time as a particularly authoritative history of the Bábí and Bahá'í religions, *al-Kawákib ad-duriyya fí ma'áthir al-Bahá'iyya* (2 vols. Cairo, 1342/1923). Frustrated in his apparent desire for a position of leadership (1924), he withdrew from the Faith and later wrote extensively to try to discredit it (*Kashfu'l-hiyal*, 'The Uncovering of Trickery', 3 vols. Tehran). *BA* 137–9; *McS* 174; Miller 275; *TCB* 334–42.

Ayyám-i-Há (PA, 'the days of *Há*')

Intercalary days introduced into the Badí' CALENDAR (of 19 × 19 months (=361 days)), to make it equivalent to a solar year. In ordinary years there are four days, and in leap years five (the Arabic letter *Há* has a numerical equivalent of 5). Bahá'u'lláh specified that these days occur immediately before the month of FASTING. They should be a period of celebration, charity, hospitality and gift giving. *KA* 25 k16, 178–9 n27–9; Walbridge, *Sacred* 216.

Azal, Ṣubḥ-i-

(PA, 'Morn of Eternity')

Religious title of Mírzá Yaḥyá (1831/2–1912), son of Mírzá 'ABBÁS by Kúchik Khánum, one of his concubines (*see* NÚRÍ FAMILY). He was a younger half-brother of Bahá'u'lláh, and was raised by him following their father's death (1839). He was presumably introduced to the Bábí religion by his brother. His exact status within the Bábí community is a matter of considerable controversy. The Báb bestowed various exalted titles on him – 'Everlasting Mirror' (*Mir'átu'l-azaliyya*), 'Name of Eternity' (*Ismu'l-azal*), and 'Fruit of the Bayán' (*Thamara-i-Bayán*) – and in about 1849, despite Azal's youth (he was then about seventeen), appointed him to 'preserve what hath been revealed in the *Bayán*', 'for verily thou art a Great Way of Truth' (*EGBBF* 38–9; Browne, *Selections* 302–3; *TJ* 426–7), an appointment 'Abdu'l-Bahá regarded as a stratagem to divert attention away from Bahá'u'lláh (*TN* 62–3). Although later understood by Azal's followers as a clear appointment of succession, his position within the Bábí community following the Báb's execution (1850) seems vague, with strong centrifugal forces, including a large number of separate claims to special spiritual authority, threatening to tear the movement apart. At some point he became the 'recognized chief of the community' (*GPB* 163), but his headship seems to have been to little effect. In 1852 he was associated with AẒÍM – an older Bábí cleric of considerable repute, who had become the leader of the militant faction of the Bábís – and sought to ferment an uprising in Tákur, seemingly to coincide with the attempt on the life of the shah (*BKG* 90–1). After this he fled in disguise, later joining Bahá'u'lláh in Baghdad, where he maintained a semi-secret existence, secluding himself from most of the Bábís. In 1856 he ordered the killing of DAYYÁN, perhaps the most important of those claiming leadership of the fragmented Bábí remnant. Bahá'í sources accuse him of increasing jealousy towards Bahá'u'lláh, whose growing pre-eminence he resented. Azal accompanied his brother to Edirne, and there began to conspire against him, eventually trying to poison him (again according to the Bahá'í account). A definite separation between the two brothers then occurred, and Bahá'u'lláh made open claim to be HE WHOM GOD SHALL MAKE MANIFEST, the great majority of the Bábís eventually becoming his followers as Bahá'ís, whilst a small minority continued to acknowledge Azal as their leader (*see* AZALIS). Meanwhile, accusations that Azal and Sayyid MUḤAMMAD IṢFÁHÁNÍ had made to the Ottoman authorities against Bahá'u'lláh led to a further order of exile, Bahá'u'lláh and most of his companions being sent to Akka, whilst Azal and a few others were sent to Famagusta in Cyprus. His order of exile ended in 1881, when the British acquired Cyprus. Azal remained on the island as a British pensioner until his death (29 April

1912). Although continuing to write a great deal, Azal was reclusive, and does not appear to have maintained close contact with his followers in Iran. In Cyprus itself he came to be regarded as a Muslim holy man, receiving a Muslim burial, and his grave being regarded as Muslim shrine. Contrary to the supposition of E.G. BROWNE, he was never one of the LETTERS OF THE LIVING. Variant Azali and Bahá'í accounts make it difficult to reconstruct an 'objective' account of the dispute between the two groups. *BKG*; Blomfield 48–52; Browne, *Materials* 311–14; *EGBBF*; *GPB* 112–17, 124–5, 163–70, 179, 233; *SBBR* 59–62, 66–9.

FAMILY

Azal had a number of wives during his lifetime (eleven, twelve, fourteen, or seventeen, according to different sources), including four whom he married in Iran, and at least five in Baghdad. He briefly married the second wife of the Báb (*see* BÁB, FAMILY OF). There were perhaps twenty-five children in all. Some of his descendants remained as Azalis, a few established contact with the Bahá'ís, and some became Christians, but in Cyprus at least, most seem eventually to have become *de facto* Muslims. Momen, 'Cyprus exiles'.

Azalis

Those Bábís who follow Ṣubḥ-i-AZAL and deny Bahá'u'lláh's claim to be HE WHOM GOD SHALL MAKE MANIFEST. During the 1860s and 1870s the great majority of the Bábís became Bahá'ís, leaving a minority of 'Azali' Bábís in several cities. Over the years their numbers diminished, some becoming Bahá'ís and others Muslims. Azal had originally intended one of his sons to be his successor, but following a family dispute he appointed HÁDÍ DAWLATÁBÁDÍ in his stead. By the 1970s there were perhaps only 500–5,000 Azalis left in Iran, seemingly with no formal leadership. One of Azal's grandsons, Jalal Azal (d. 1971), was involved in an attempt to bring together the various groups of 'COVENANT-BREAKERS' during the 1950s. Despite their small numbers the Azalis have included several prominent Iranian political and literary figures, notably Shaykh Aḥmad Rúḥí and Mírzá Áqá Khán Kirmání, both sons-in-law of Azal, as well as supporters of Sayyid JAMÁL-U'D-DÍN 'al-Afghání', and both executed following the assassination of NÁṢIRU'D-DÍN SHÁH (1896). *EGBBF*; Momen, 'Cyprus exiles', see Bayat on Kirmání.

Aẓím (Ar., 'Great')

Title of the Bábí leader Mullá Shaykh 'Alí Turshízí (d. 1852). Formerly a leading Shaykhí cleric, he came to prominence as a Bábí during the period of the Báb's imprisonment in Azerbaiján, acting as his chief agent and leader of the growing number of Bábís in the region. He was the recipient of the Báb's proclamatory sermon in which the open claim to be the *QÁ'IM* was finally made, copies of which he distributed extensively. He also made efforts to present the Báb's claims to government leaders; and in 1849, and again in 1852, was organizing conspiracies to overthrow the government. Living in Tehran, he became the leader of those Bábí who favoured militancy. He was arrested and executed following the unsuccessful attempt on the life of NÁṢIRU'D-DÍN SHÁH (1852), for which he claimed responsibility. *ARR* 280–1, 375–7, 383; *BKG* 74, 101–11; *McS* 16–17, 82; Nabil 313, 599; *TJ* 240, 353, 368–9, 388, 392–3, 420–5, 434–41; *TN* 53n, 184–5, 191, 261, 276, 329, 374.

B

Báb (Ar., 'Gate')

Religious title assumed by Sayyid 'Alí-Muḥammad Shírází (1819–50), the prophet-founder of the Bábí religion. Among Iranian Bahá'ís he is commonly referred to as *Haḍrat-i-a'lá* ('His Holiness the Exalted One') or *Haḍrat-i-rabb-i-a'lá* ('His Holiness the Most Exalted Lord'). *ARR*; Balyuzi, *Báb*; *GPB* 3–36, 49–60; Kazem-Beg; Lambden, 'Episode'; Nabil; MacEoin, 'From Shaykhism'; *MBBR* 69–82; *SBBR* 13–29; *BFSH* 19–47; *TJ*; *TN*; *WOB* 123–8. For popular Bahá'í accounts see Perkins and Sears, *Release the Sun*. (*See also* Báb, writings of; Shíráz: House of the Báb.)

EARLY LIFE

The Báb was born into a family of traders and merchants in the southern Iranian city of Shíráz on 1 Muḥarram 1235/20 October 1819. His father, Sayyid Muḥammad-Riḍá, died when he was still a child (*c.* 1826), and he grew up with his mother, Fáṭima Bagum, and under the guardianship of one of her brothers, Ḥájí Mírzá Sayyid 'Alí (*see* Báb, Family of). He had no brothers or sisters. Little is known about his early years. As a child he attended a local Quranic school and received an elementary education. He also gained the commercial training necessary to join the trading operations run by members of his mother's family. In 1835 he began to work as a merchant in the port city of Bushire, at first in his uncle's business and then independently.

Later accounts emphasize 'Alí-Muḥammad's extreme piety as a youth, and religious concerns eventually impelled him to close his office in Bushire (1840) and embark on an extended pilgrimage to the Shí'í shrine cities in Iraq, remaining there for about a year. During this time he attended some of the classes of the Shaykhí leader Sayyid Káẓim Rashtí (*see also* Shaykhism), and attracted the attention of some of the Sayyid's disciples by his great piety. He did not embark on any formal course of religious training, however, and eventually returned to Shíráz where he married a cousin, Khadíjih Bagum, in August 1842, and established a household. The young couple had one son, Aḥmad, who died in infancy (1843).

During these years in Shíráz the fervent devotionalism of 'Alí- Muḥammad's childhood and youth continued, but he now experienced a number of visionary dreams, in the most dramatic of which he later described how he saw the severed head of the Imám Ḥusayn, whose blood he drank, and from the grace of which he felt that his breast had been filled with 'convincing verses and mighty prayers' (MacEoin, 'From Shaykhism' 141). The spirit of God having 'permeated and taken possession of My soul', 'the mysteries of His Revelation were unfolded before my eyes in all their glory' (Nabil 253). He began to write what, by the early months of 1844 if not earlier, he regarded as divinely inspired verses. He also apparently began to gain a reputation as a holy ascetic, blessed with the grace of the Hidden Imám (*see* IMÁMS), and miracles may have been attributed to him (Kazem-Beg 7/339).

DECLARATION AND EARLY MINISTRY (MAY 1844–MARCH 1847)

The development of a distinct religious movement centring on 'Alí-Muḥammad is traditionally dated to the night of 22 May 1844, with the conversion of Mullá ḤUSAYN BUSHRÚ'Í as the first of his inner circle of disciples, the LETTERS OF THE LIVING, and the beginning of the composition of the *QAYYÚMU'L-ASMÁ'*, effectively the Báb's own declaration of mission. Occurring within the context of the Shaykhí succession crisis following the death of Sayyid Káẓim, these developments marked the Báb as the promised messianic leader expected by many Shaykhís. Announcing the near advent of the RESURRECTION, and making claims to divinely appointed authority, the Báb also potentially addressed the entire Muslim world, and was soon widely understood to be claiming to be the 'gate' (*Báb*) to the Hidden Imám: thus the title 'Báb' and the description of his followers as 'Bábís' came into general use (See 'The Báb's claims' below).

The room where the Báb declared his mission in 1844

Directing his disciples to announce his cause (but without divulging his name), the Báb himself, together with his disciple QUDDÚS, and his servant, Mubárak, left Shíráz (September 1844) and set out for Mecca to make a public proclamation of his mission. This act was in deliberate fulfilment of Islamic prophecy regarding the time of the return of the Imám MAHDÍ. From Mecca, he intended to join his followers in Iraq, again in fulfilment of messianic prophecy. In the event, his proclamation during his stay in Mecca (12 December 1844–7 January 1845) went largely unheeded and his chief emissary to the shrine cities of Iraq, Mullá 'ALÍ BASṬÁMÍ, met with concerted opposition from the Shí'í clerics, and was eventually imprisoned by the Ottoman authorities. In consequence of this the Báb announced a change in the divine decree (*BADÁ*), and returned to Bushire. His emissaries in Shíráz had, however, caused such a stir (by adding the Báb's name to the Muslim call to prayer) that the governor of Shíráz, Ḥusayn Khán, sent a detachment of troops to arrest the Báb en route from Bushire. The Báb then returned to Shíráz (early July 1845) to face a stormy interview at the court of the governor, after which he was released to the charge of his uncle, and required to make a public recantation of the claim to be the *Báb* of the Imám.

Writing extensively, and covertly receiving visitors, including Sayyid Yaḥyá Dárábí (Vaḥíd), and a representative of Mullá Muḥammad Zanjání (Ḥujjat) – prominent clerics who converted to his cause – the Báb was now the identified leader of a heterodox religious movement. In September 1846 the Báb was arrested again, but, in the chaotic conditions in Shíráz that followed an outbreak of cholera, he left Shíráz, and moved to Iṣfáhán. There he remained until March 1847, as a guest of its governor, Manúchihr Khán, whose sympathetic support seemed to promise a possible meeting with Muḥammad Sháh, so that the Báb could proclaim his claims directly to the king.

THE BÁB'S LATER MINISTRY (MARCH 1847–JULY 1850)

Manúchihr Khán's death in February 1847 marked a major turn in the Báb's fortunes. Muḥammad Sháh appears to have been sympathetic towards the Báb at this stage, but Ḥájí Mírzá Áqásí, the shah's chief minister, undoubtedly saw in the Báb's growing popularity as a religious leader a potential threat to his own position. At Áqásí's order then, the Báb was made an effective prisoner of state and transferred to the remote fortress of Mákú in Azerbaiján (July 1847–April 1848) and later to the fortress of Chihríq (April 1848–June 1850).

The period of the Báb's captivity in Azerbaiján was one in which both the Bábí movement and its relationship with Iranian society were profoundly transformed. The Báb himself, early in 1848, made open claim to his followers to be the Mahdí, and as such declared the abrogation of Islamic holy law. This was to be replaced by a new order, which he delineated in his book, the *Bayán*. The Báb also denounced the shah and his chief minister in letters which he sent to them. The radical break with Shí'i Islam was reinforced in July 1848 with two events that occurred almost simultaneously: in Tabríz, the provincial capital of Azerbaiján, the Báb was brought before a tribunal of clerics presided over by the crown prince (the future Náṣiru'd-Dín Sháh) and made public claim to be the Mahdí (in response to which he received the bastinado in the house of one of the leading clerics). Meanwhile, a gathering of leading Bábís at Badasht announced the termination of the Islamic era and the inauguration of a new dispensation (*see* Babi radicalism).

By this time the increasing fervour of the Báb's followers and the consolidation of clerical opposition had already led to a number of confrontations between the Bábís and their opponents. Then, after the death of Muḥammad Sháh (September 1848), an armed struggle broke out at Ṭabarsí, in which government troops eventually extirpated the Bábí combatants. Other conflicts ensued in 1850, convincing the new chief minister, Mírzá Taqí Khán, Amír Kabír, that the whole Bábí movement was a threat to public order, which could best be ended by depriving it of its central focus. Accordingly, the Báb was brought again to Tabríz, and executed in public by a firing squad on 27/28 Sha'bán 1266/8–9 July 1850. With him died one of his dedicated followers, Mírzá Muḥammad 'Alí Zunúzí (*Anís*). The events of the execution – the first (Christian) regiment missed, leaving the Báb unscathed, and had to be replaced by a second Muslim regiment which completed the task – ensured that an aura of the miraculous accompanied the Báb to his death.

The remains of the Báb and his companion were later secured by the Bábís and kept hidden in various locations until they were finally transferred to the Holy Land in 1899 at the instruction of 'Abdu'l-Bahá. They were interred on Mount Carmel in 1909 (*see* Shrine of the Báb).

THE BÁB'S CLAIMS

The exact nature of the Báb's claims at different stages of his mission is complicated, and sometimes veiled by his allusive and esoteric language. There is an overt progression of claims, with the Báb first claiming in Shíráz to be the 'Remembrance' (*dhikr*) and 'Gate' (*báb*) of God and of the Hidden Imám, whilst in Azerbaiján he laid claim to be the Mahdí (i.e. the Hidden Imám himself) and beyond that to be a MANIFESTATION OF GOD, empowered to abrogate Islamic holy law and replace it with his own (thus deviating radically from Shí'í expectations of the role of the Mahdí). He also referred to himself as the 'Primal Point' (*nuqti-yi-úlá*) from which all things have been created, and foretold the coming of a further messianic figure, HE WHOM GOD SHALL MAKE MANIFEST – again in obvious divergence from traditional Shí'í expectations regarding the resurrection.

Whether these changes represent the prudential unveiling of implicit claims (as modern Bahá'ís believe) or the development of the Báb's own self-understanding is not easy to establish. However, whilst in SHÍ'ISM the title *Báb* refers in the first instance to the four men who successively claimed to be the 'gates' (*abwáb*) of the Hidden Imám, and it was in this sense that many understood the Báb's early claims, the *Qayyúmu'l-asmá'* itself is presented as the 'descent' of divine verses, and was written in the style of the Quran – a radical gesture noted by the Báb's clerical opponents, whilst from the outset the Báb laid claim to being the recipient of some form of divine revelation, and to have supreme authority from God. Again, the term 'Gate of God' could also be given wider interpretation, having been used to refer to divine PROPHETS, Imáms and saints (Lawson, 'Remembrance' 23–42).

THE BAHÁ'Í VIEW OF THE BÁB

For Bahá'ís the Báb was both an independent Manifestation of God, and the forerunner of Bahá'u'lláh, 'Abdu'l-Bahá declaring that this was one of the foundations of Bahá'í belief (*Will* 19). The Báb's exact doctrinal status was delineated by Shoghi Effendi: (1) His twofold station was 'the most distinctive feature of the Bahá'í Dispensation', adding to its strength and its 'mysterious power and authority'. (2) His primary role and the major source of his greatness was his rank as a self-sufficient Manifestation of God. In this role, Bahá'u'lláh described him as one whose rank excelled that of all previous prophets. (3) As forerunner, he was allied with Bahá'u'lláh (though subordinate in rank), and with him presided over the destinies of the Bahá'í 'Dispensation'. It was the inauguration of the Báb's mission that in fact constituted 'the founding of the Faith of Bahá'u'lláh'. (4) He had inaugurated a new universal prophetic cycle (*see* TIME), and the 'creative energies' released at the hour of the birth of his revelation and the spiritual impact of his mission and martyrdom had endowed mankind with the potentialities of the attainment of maturity, and were now deranging the existing equilibrium of human society so as to prepare it for its future unity. (5) His greatness was not affected by the 'short duration of His Dispensation' (i.e. the very brief period of time that elapsed before Bahá'u'lláh, as the next Manifestation of God, replaced the Báb as central religious focus) or by the 'restricted range' within which his laws were ever able to operate. (6) The Báb was the object and fulfilment of all the prophets who had gone before him. He was the 'Úshidar-Máh' referred to in Zoroastrian scriptures, the return of Elijah for Jews, the return of John the Baptist for Christians, the 'second woe' referred to in the book of Revelation, and the *QÁ'IM* and Mahdí expected by Muslims. (7) Contrary to common Western Bahá'í views in the 1930s, he was 'not to be regarded merely as an inspired Precursor of the Bahá'í Revelation' (Shoghi Effendi stated that his 'chief motive' in editing and translating *The* DAWN-BREAKERS had been to enable the Western Bahá'ís both 'to better understand and more readily grasp the tremendous implications of (the Báb's) exalted station' and 'to more ardently admire and love Him'). *CF* 80–3; *GPB* 57–8; *WOB* 97, 123–4.

Báb, family of

The Báb was born into a merchant family in Shíráz. Following the death of his father, he came under the guardianship of one of his mother's brothers, later joining his maternal family in business. He married one of his mother's cousins (1842), by whom he had one son, Aḥmad, who died in infancy. He married a second wife in Iṣfáhán, but had no children by her. During his own lifetime, out of his family, only his wives and guardian accepted his religious claims, other family members opposing him or remaining neutral. Later, many of his maternal relatives – his uncles and the siblings of his first wife – became Bahá'ís, and were given the title AFNÁN by Bahá'u'lláh. For a genealogical table of the maternal family see Nabil lix (facing table). For a table of part of the paternal family see *BKG* 404. See also *ARR* 112.

THE MATERNAL FAMILY

The Báb's mother, Fáṭimih Bagum, had three brothers: (1) Ḥájí Mírzá Sayyid Muḥammad (d. 1876), *Khál-i-akbar* (the 'Greatest Uncle'), the recipient of the *Kitáb-i-Íqán*, who became a believer after his receipt of this book; (2) Ḥájí Mírzá Sayyid 'Alí, known as *Khál-i-a'ẓam* (the 'Most Great Uncle'), the Báb's guardian following his father's death, the first male member of the family to accept his nephew's claims, and subsequently one of the SEVEN MARTYRS OF TEHRAN (1850); and (3) Ḥájí Mírzá Ḥasan-'Alí, *Khál-i-aṣghar* (the 'Younger Uncle'). Muḥammad's son, Ḥájí Mírzá MUḤAMMAD-TAQÍ, the *Vakílu'd-dawlih*, was the chief builder of the Bahá'í House of Worship in ASHKHABAD.

The Báb's first wife, KHADÍJIH BAGUM, the niece of his mother's father, had two brothers and a sister. The brothers were Ḥájí Mírzá Abu'l-Qásim (1811–87), *Saqqá-khání*, and Ḥájí Mírzá Sayyid Ḥasan (d. 1892), *Afnán-i-kabír* (the 'Great Afnán'), both of whom had sons who married daughters of 'Abdu'l-Bahá (Mírzá Hádí, who married Ḍiyá'iyyih, and was the father of SHOGHI EFFENDI, and Mírzá Muḥsin, who married Ṭúbá, and was the father of RÚḤÍ AFNÁN (*see also* NÚRÍ FAMILY). Another son of Ḥasan, Ḥájí Mírzá Sayyid 'Alí, married Bahá'u'lláh's daughter, Furúghiyyih. Khadíjih's sister, Zahrá Bagum (d. 1889), married Mírzá Zaynu'l-'Ábidín, a cousin of the Báb's father.

THE PATERNAL FAMILY

Details of the family of the Báb's father, Mír Muḥammad-Riḍá, are less readily available: most did not become Bahá'ís. Two of his father's cousins were eminent Shí'í clerics, Mírzá-yi-SHÍRÁZÍ (1815–95), the leading *MUJTAHID* of his time, and Ḥájí Sayyid Javád (d. 1870/1), the leader of the Friday prayers (*imám-jum'a*) in Kirmán. Both are said to have been secret Bábís/Bahá'ís, and to have protected Bábís and Bahá'ís from persecution (*ARR* 118–19; *BKG* 403–4). Other cousins of the Báb's were Mírzá 'Alí-Akbar, a close associate of the Bábí leader DAYYÁN, and Ḥájí Mírzá Zaynu'l-Ábidín, who married Zahrá Bagum, the sister of the Báb's wife. The son of Zaynu'l-Ábidín, Áqá Mírzá Áqá (1842–1903), became a Bábí (the second male member of the Báb's family to do so) in his teens, and was later an active Bahá'í teacher, responsible for the conversion of other members of his extended family.

He was honoured by Bahá'u'lláh with the title *Núru'd-dín* ('Light of Faith'), and was the recipient of the *Tablet of the* WORLD. Bahá'u'lláh appointed the descendants of Zahrá to be the hereditary custodians of the House of the Báb (*BKG* 403–6, 410; *EB* 216–36).

Whilst he was in Iṣfáhán (1846–7), the Báb married a second wife, Fáṭimih (d. 1916), the sister of Mullá Rajab-'Alí (*Qahír*). Despite the Báb's instructions that his wives should remain unmarried after his death, Ṣubḥ-i-AZAL briefly married the second wife (for one month), but then divorced her and married her instead to Sayyid MUḤAMMAD IṢFAHÁNÍ (*EGBBF* 34–5n; *BKG* 418).

Báb, house of

See SHIRAZ: THE HOUSE OF THE BÁB.

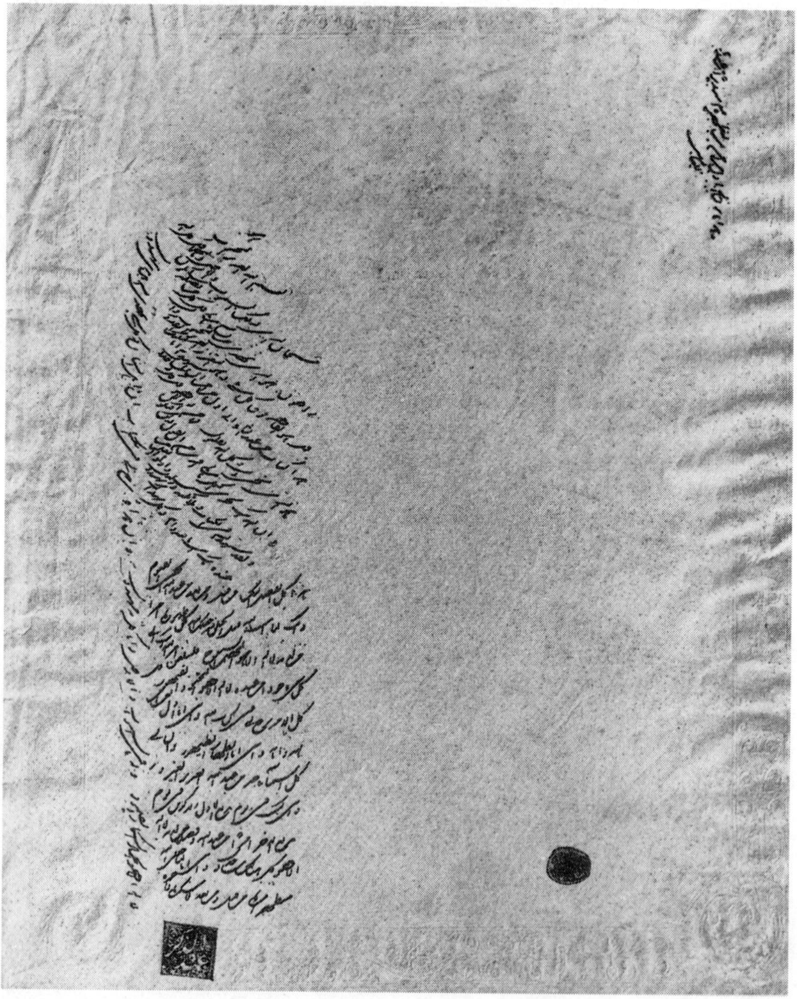

Facsimile of the Báb's Tablet to the first Letter of the Living

Báb, Shrine of

See SHRINE OF THE BÁB.

Báb, writings of

The Báb wrote extensively, either in his own hand – mostly during the early stage of his mission – or dictated to his companion and secretary, Sayyid Ḥusayn Yazdí ('Azíz'), one of the LETTERS OF THE LIVING. He himself refers to having composed 500,000 verses (by 1848 – i.e. the equivalent of eighty books the size of the Quran), one-fifth of which had been disseminated. Although the suppression of Bábism led to the loss of a considerable quantity of his writings, widespread copying has ensured the survival of many manuscripts. Little of this is as yet generally accessible – even in the original Arabic and Persian, let alone European languages (there is one volume of selected extracts published in English, and three titles in French). Five works are known from prior to his initial declaration of mission in May 1844, including a Quran commentary, a treatise on 'right behaviour', and a pilgrimage prayer in honour of Muḥammad, his daughter Fáṭima, and the IMÁMS (tablets of VISITATION). The first work of his mission was the *QAYYÚMU'L-ASMÁ'* (May–June 1844). Subsequent works composed up until the Báb's departure for Iṣfáhán (September 1846) include eleven more commentaries on Quranic verses or Islamic traditions, the best known being on the Chapter of Kawthar, composed for VAḤÍD; thirteen treatises on theological and legal issues, including elements of specifically Bábí ritual; homilies; and collections of prayers. Works composed in Iṣfáhán (September 1846–March 1847) include a commentary on the Quranic *súra* of Wa'l-'asr, written for the *imám-jum'a* (Friday prayer leader), Sayyid Muḥammad, and a treatise on the 'specific prophethood' (*nubuwwa kháṣṣa*) of Muḥammad for the city governor, MANÚCHIHR KHÁN. Of the Báb's works written after his departure from Iṣfáhán (mostly during the period of his confinement in Azerbaijan), the most important is his book of laws, the *Persian* BAYÁN and its companion Arabic volume. Others include the *SEVEN PROOFS*; the *Book of NAMES*; a further nine commentaries on the whole Quran; and the *Kitáb-i-panj sha'n* – a book of the '*Five Grades*' in which the Báb wrote, i.e. Quranic-style verses in Arabic, prayers, homilies, commentaries, and Persian-language writing. Throughout his ministry the Báb composed numerous letters, including letters to MUḤAMMAD SHÁH, Ḥájí Mírzá ÁQÁSÍ, and to all the leading clerics in Iran. In addition to his writings the Báb also fashioned many TALISMANS. Browne, *Selections* 198–239; *GPB* 22–7; *McS* 11–103.

Bábí and Bahá'í Studies

Academic study of the Bábí and Bahá'í religions. The term 'Bahá'í Studies' has also come to have a wider usage (*see* below; *see also* SCHOLARSHIP).

TRADITIONAL BAHÁ'Í SCHOLARSHIP

Many of the prominent early Iranian Bahá'ís were former Shí'í *'ULAMÁ*. As part of their service to the Bahá'í Faith, several of these men wrote apologias for their religion and made compilations of Bahá'í writings and historical documents which were widely circulated amongst the Bahá'ís. Although scholarly and enormously erudite, their work differs from the modern Western field of religious studies in its unambiguous faith commitment: the underlying purpose of their scholarship was to help advance the Bahá'í religion. The only early Bahá'í scholar whose work has been translated into English is Mírzá ABU'L-FAḌL GULPÁYGÁNÍ. Others whose work is highly regarded include FÁḌIL MÁZANDARÁNÍ and 'Abdu'l-Ḥamíd ISHRÁQ-KHÁVARÍ. The more recent work of Muḥammad 'Alí Faizí, 'Azízu'lláh Sulaymání, and (in English) of Hasan Balyuzi continue this tradition.

EARLY ACADEMIC STUDIES

Critical academic studies of Bábí and Bahá'í texts, doctrines and history began with the work of European orientalists in the late 19th and early 20th centuries. The most important of these scholars was E.G. Browne. Others of note were A.L.M. Nicolas, Victor Rosen, Alexander Tumanski and Hermann Roemer. The work of the Comte de Gobineau must also be mentioned, not for its scholarship, but because of its early date (1865) and its inspiration of subsequent studies. The major works of Browne on the subject date from 1889–1910. *MBBR* 17–52.

THE MODERN PERIOD

A new phase in Bábí and Bahá'í Studies began in the 1970s. Although overlapping, two distinct trends may be identified.

INSTITUTIONAL

There have been a number of developments sponsored by the Bahá'í community. '[A]nimated by the spirit of inquiry into the limitless meaning of the Divine Teachings', these have sought both to present the Bahá'í Faith and its ideals to a wider intellectual audience and explore the implications of the Bahá'í teachings in all aspects of human life. This approach to 'Bahá'í Studies' was effectively begun with the establishment of The Canadian Association for Studies on the Bahá'í Faith in 1975, in response to a call by the Universal House of Justice. This body aimed to promote lectures and conferences relating to the Bahá'í Faith at Canadian universities. Reflecting international interest, the organization was renamed the Association for Bahá'í Studies (ABS) in 1981. It also published a series of *Bahá'í Studies* volumes (mostly monographs), and *The Journal of Bahá'í Studies* (from 1988) (*BW17*: 197–201; 18: 194–200; Danesh). Regarding all Bahá'ís as potential scholars, it has promoted a wide range of activities within the Bahá'í community, including in the arts and health (a Bahá'í International Health Agency was formed under its sponsorship in 1982). A large number of national or regional affiliate associations have now been established (twenty-two by 1995, including eight in the Americas, six in Europe, three each in Africa and Asia, and two in Australasia). Activities of these associations range from academic study of aspects of Bahá'í history and belief to studies of the possible application of the Bahá'í teachings to varied aspects of human life (including moral education and the search for a global ethic) and Bahá'í deepening. Various publications of seminars and the like have been produced, of very variable quality. In some places the traditional Bahá'í summer schools have become more rigorous, as in Australia, where a three-year Certificate Programme in Bahá'í Studies was introduced in 1995. Other institutional developments have included the establishment of the first Bahá'í University (Universidad Núr) in Santa Cruz, Bolivia in 1984, and of Bahá'í-sponsored Chairs at the Universities of Maryland in the United States and Indore in India in 1990. The UK-based ABS affiliate for English-speaking Europe produces the scholarly *Bahá'í Studies Review* (from 1990). *BWNS* 1994–5: 89–95, 321–4.

INDEPENDENT

At the same time there has been renewed interest in the more focused academic study of the Bábí and Bahá'í religions. Although most of those involved in this movement have been Bahá'ís or former Bahá'ís they have sought to employ the tools of modern critical scholarship to advance understanding for its own sake rather than to promote particular faith positions. This approach has sometimes engendered tensions with more traditional Bahá'ís. Instances of this approach include several series of academic seminars on Bahá'í Studies in Britain and the United States, including at the University of Lancaster in England (1977–80) (*BW18*: 204–5) and at the American Academy of Religion (from 1984) and Middle East Studies Association (from *c*.1992); Moojan Momen's collection of source materials, *The Bábí and Bahá'í Religions* (*MBBR*, 1981); new translations of works by Mírzá Abu'l-Faḍl (1981, 1985); the Kalimat Press series *Studies in Bábí and Bahá'í History* (from 1982); the scholarly journal *Bahá'í Studies Bulletin* (from 1982); the George Ronald series *Bahá'í Studies* (from 1996); the internet discussion forum 'H-Bahai' (from 1997) (one of the H-Net humanities list sites); and a flurry of doctoral and other dissertations on Bahá'í-related topics from the mid-1970s onwards (Collins, *Bibliography*, 303–10), some of which have since found their way into print (Amanat (*ARR*); MacEoin (*McS*); Smith (*SBBR*)).

For a review of English-language sources up to 1985 see *SBBR* 225–38.

Bábí radicalism

In a traditional Islamic society, such as 19th-century Iran, religious dissent was readily seen as a threat to social order and could easily assume political dimensions. This was most particularly the case with the intense messianic expectations associated with the appearance of the Mahdí. Bábism from the beginning, then, represented a major challenge to religious and by implication secular authority, whilst the rising tide of Persecution served to alienate many Bábís from the existing social order.

Both in theological and socio-political terms, the Bábí movement changed dramatically in 1847/8. Theologically, Bábism became radicalized by the Báb's open claim to be the *Qá'im* (1848) – as made most dramatically during his trial in Tabríz – and his replacement of Islamic law by his own holy law in the *Bayán*. This was reflected in the proceedings at Badasht, and in the antinomian tendencies that were expressed by some of the Bábís thereafter. Meanwhile, the relationship between the Bábís and the surrounding society was rapidly deteriorating.

The murder of Mullá Muḥammad-Taqí Baraghání (late 1847) – and the laying of the blame for the act on the Bábís (notably his niece Ṭáhirih, the leading representative of radical Bábism) – marked a particular catalyst, leading to the killing of a number of Bábís and a hardening of attitudes on all sides. The subsequent 'Bábí upheaval' at Ṭabarsí (1848–9) and the urban conflicts in Nayríz and Zanján, together with the confused disturbances in Yazd (1850), have been portrayed in various ways – both the Bábís' opponents and some modern writers (e.g. Ivanov; Greussing) seeing the Bábís as insurrectionaries, whilst modern Bahá'ís emphasize the defensive nature of the struggles. The reality is undoubtedly complex: the predominance of clerics among the Bábís at Ṭabarsí makes it unlikely that these were simply 'primitive rebels', albeit that the Bábís may well have wished to see the establishment of a Bábí state, and instead points to the importance of symbolic acts and the motif of sacrificial martyrdom in the karbalá tradition. The urban conflicts, by contrast, whatever wider implications they had, must also be seen in terms of existing tensions involving local notables and neighbourhoods. It is only after the martyrdom of the Báb that we can identify a clearly insurrectionary trend, with the formation of an ultra-radical Bábí faction headed by Aẓím. It was individuals from this group who attempted to assassinate Náṣiru'd-dín Sháh in August 1852, thus precipitating a bloody pogrom against the remaining Bábís. Whilst the radical tradition was continued to some extent by Ṣubḥ-i-Azal, the rise of Bahá'u'lláh as pre-eminent Bábí leader led to a marked change in perspective. This was made explicit in Bahá'u'lláh's Riḍván declaration and in subsequent writings, in which he forbade his followers to engage in holy war and sedition, or to respond to persecution with violence. The secular radicalism of some Azali intellectuals in late 19th-century Iran represents a variant expression of the earlier Bábí concerns. Bayat; MacEoin, 'Babi concept'; 'From Babism to Baha'ism'; *SBBR* 21–8, 51–6, 97–9; Smith and Momen, 'Babi movement'; Walbridge, 'Babi uprising'.

backbiting

The Bahá'í teachings condemn backbiting categorically, Bahá'u'lláh teaching that backbiting extinguished 'the life of the soul', and 'Abdu'l-Bahá describing it as 'the most great sin' and the most hateful human characteristic. It is a cause of divine wrath: the backbiter is accursed. In their conversations, then, Bahá'ís should endeavour never to speak of the faults of others in their absence, or to gossip about them. They might speak of their praiseworthy qualities, but rather than even think of the imperfections of others, they should remember their own faults and seek to root those out. Each individual is responsible for their own life and perfecting their own character. Bahá'ís should show love and patience towards others, encouraging rather than criticizing them, being understanding of human weakness, and seeking to conciliate. Love and tact can overcome jealousy and pettiness.

The difficulty of following this teaching is recognized, 'Abdu'l-Bahá and Shoghi Effendi accepting that backbiting was probably the major cause of disunity amongst Bahá'ís (as amongst human beings in general) and of withdrawal from Bahá'í activities. If one Bahá'í begins to backbite about another, then their hearers should stop them from continuing. This should be done with tact and friendship, but also with firmness: it is essential. Otherwise the hearer is guilty of complicity. As to those cases in which an individual's behaviour might seem to be harmful to the Faith or contravenes Bahá'í law, then others might discuss the matter with them directly, but without adopting a condemnatory attitude. If this is not effective, the issue should be reported to the local spiritual assembly. *LG* 88–94.

badá (Ar., 'alteration of God's will')

Shí'í doctrine subject to various interpretations. In the stronger (and more heterodox) form, God's will is believed to be alterable in response to changed circumstances: thus those who truly repent are spared destruction; the succession of the Imáms was changed; and God's command to Abraham to sacrifice his son was rescinded. The Báb seems to have understood the cancellation of his own projected proclamation in Karbalá (1845) as *badá*. God had 'suspended the appearance of His signs' because of the perversity of those who had rejected his call (*ARR* 250, 252–4; Nabil 158). The cessation of a living guardianship following Shoghi Effendi's unexpected death (1957) is also popularly explained in these terms. In perhaps similar vein Bahá'u'lláh, in his *Kitáb-i-Íqán*, stressed that God tested the sincerity of those who sought to believe in him by not fulfilling their expectations (*KI* 5–6, 32–3).

Badasht

Hamlet on the borders of eastern Mázandarán off the road to Khurásán, close to Sháhrúd. It was the site of a three-week conference of eighty-one Bábís in June–July 1848, including Ṭáhirih and Quddús. Details are unclear, but the conference marked a major step in the 'radicalization' of

Bábism. Initial tensions between Ṭáhirih, proclaiming the advent of a new age and the abrogation of Islamic holy law, and Quddús, stressing caution, were resolved in favour of the former. To dramatize her position Ṭáhirih appeared unveiled, proclaiming that she was 'the Word' which the *QÁ'IM* was to utter on the day of judgement, and on another occasion brandished a sword. The more conservative Bábís in attendance were so shocked that several abandoned the movement and one attempted suicide. According to Bahá'í accounts the meeting was organized and financed by Bahá'u'lláh, who effected the reconciliation between the two principals and 'revealed' tablets for each of those present. Plans for securing the Báb's release from his captivity may also have been discussed. Reports of the proceedings scandalized many (including Mullá ḤUSAYN BUSHRÚ'Í), and the Bábís were afterwards dispersed following an attack by Muslim villagers. *ARR* 324–8; *GPB* 31–4; Nabil 288–300; *TJ* 281–2, 355–60, 377; *TN* 176.

Badí‘ (*c.* 1852–69)

Áqá (or Mírzá) Buzurg Khurásání, Iranian Bahá'í youth who delivered Bahá'u'lláh's letter to NÁṢIRU'D-DÍN SHÁH in 1869. He was the son of Ḥájí 'Abdu'l-Majíd Nishápúrí, one of the Bábí survivors from the conflict at Shaykh ṬABARSÍ. Initially indifferent to Bábism, Áqá Buzurg later became a fervent believer and set out to visit Bahá'u'lláh in Edirne. En route he stayed for a time in Baghdad, where he volunteered to act as water-carrier for the House of Bahá'u'lláh in place of Áqá 'Abdu'r-Rasúl Qumí who had recently been murdered by Muslim zealots. Áqá Buzurg was himself repeatedly attacked as he performed this task. In 1869 he went to Akka where, as a teenage youth dressed as a poor water-carrier, he was able to pass the guards and enter the city, becoming one of the first Bahá'ís from outside to be able to meet Bahá'u'lláh there. Bahá'u'lláh entrusted him with his letter to the shah and instructed him to return to Iran alone to deliver it, warning that he could easily face death when he had completed his task. Áqá Buzurg approached the Shah whilst the latter was on a hunting trip and delivered the letter to members of the entourage. He was then tortured and killed. Bahá'u'lláh named him *Badí‘* ('wondrous', 'unique', 'new') and the 'Pride of Martyrs' (*Fakhru'sh-shuhadá'*). Shoghi Effendi named him as one of the APOSTLES OF BAHÁ'U'LLÁH. *BKG* 294–309; *RB3*: 176–91.

Badí‘, Bahá'u'lláh's messenger to the Shah

Bagdadi, Zia 'Mabsut'
(1884–1937)

Prominent American Bahá'í. His father was MUḤAMMAD MUṢṬAFÁ AL-BAGHDÁDÍ. He was born in Beirut and moved to Chicago in 1909 to complete his medical studies. He came to play a leading role in the American Bahá'í community, translating letters from 'Abdu'l-Bahá, editing the *Star of the West* magazine, and assuming various local and national administrative responsibilities. *BW7*: 535–9.

Baghdad (Baghdád)

Capital both of the Abbasid empire and caliphate and of modern IRAQ. Effectively autonomous in the 18th century, it was restored to direct Ottoman control in 1831. As provincial capital it was the site of the trial of Mullá 'ALÍ BASṬÁMÍ (1845), and the place of ṬÁHIRIH's house arrest (1847). It was also Bahá'u'lláh's place of exile from 8 April 1853 until 3 May 1863, apart from a month spent in the nearby Shí'í shrine city of Káẓimayn after his initial arrival in Iraq, and his two-year retreat in Kurdistan (10 April 1854–19 March 1856). From 1856 Bahá'u'lláh increasingly became the predominant figure in the Bábí movement, many Bábís from Iran visiting his house in Baghdad. He also gained the respect of many of the local people and the provincial governor during this time, and wrote a number of his most influential writings there. His initial declaration of mission was made in the nearby garden of RIḌVÁN immediately prior to his departure for Istanbul. Bahá'u'lláh called Baghdad the 'City of God', and designated it a centre of pilgrimage (*GPB* 110). Shoghi Effendi designated it the 'third holiest city' in the Bahá'í world, and wished to have the 1963 Bahá'í world congress there (*MBW* 43, 166).

Baghdad: the House of Bahá'u'lláh

Referred to as 'The Most Great House' (*Bayt-i-a'ẓam*) of God. Located in the Karkh district in the west of the city, the house is a large but simple mud brick structure of two to three storeys surrounding a central courtyard. It was at first rented by Mírzá MÚSÁ, whilst Bahá'u'lláh was in Kurdistan. Bahá'u'lláh lived in the house from his return on 19 March 1856 until his departure for the RIḌVÁN garden on 22 April 1863, and at some point purchased it. It was here that he both wrote most of his early writings and received the increasing throng of visitors who recognized his role as the premier Bábí leader. He later named it as a place of Bahá'í pilgrimage, the 'Throne of His Glory', and the 'Lamp of Salvation between earth and heaven'. Specific rites of pilgrimage were detailed.

Bahá'u'lláh prophesied that the house would later be so abased by the infidels as to cause tears to flow, but that God would eventually exalt it, causing it to become 'the Standard of His Kingdom'. Bahá'ís interpret subsequent events in the light of these statements.

After Bahá'u'lláh's departure from Baghdad the house was held in the name of various custodians and allowed to fall into a state of disrepair. At the time of the establishment of the British mandate over Iraq (1920) 'Abdu'l-Bahá authorized extensive restoration work under the supervision of Ḥájí Maḥmúd QAṢṢÁBCHÍ. This activity attracted the hostile attention of local Shí'ís, and after the death of the old custodian they sued for possession (January 1921). In the absence of proper deeds the Shí'í religious court found against the Bahá'ís. A lengthy and complex legal struggle then ensued, which took the case through the Iraqi courts and then, through the work of Mountfort MILLS, to the Permanent Mandates Commission and Council of the League of Nations. The upshot was twofold: (1) the Iraqi authorities first took possession of the house (February 1922) and subsequently handed it over to the Shí'ís (November 1925), who have remained in possession to the present day (it is now used as a place to commemorate the sufferings and martyrdom of the Imám Ḥusayn); (2) enormous international publicity and sympathy was generated for the Bahá'ís, who were regarded as having suffered a considerable injustice by the League authorities. With the attainment of Iraqi independence in 1932, international interest in the case dropped. *BW2*: 33–4; *3*: 50–5, 198–209; *4*: 97–8, 237–47; *5*: 31–3, 351–9; *GPB* 110, 356–60; *GWB* 111–14 no. 57; Walbridge, Sacred 140–3.

Bahá'í Faith

TERM

The term Bahá'ís most commonly use to describe their own religion in English. The terms 'Cause of God' (Ar. *amru'lláh*), 'the Cause' and 'the Faith' are also used. During the earlier part of this century the term 'Bahá'í Movement' was common, reflecting a more inclusivist understanding of their religion by Bahá'ís (*SBBR* 109–14, 145–6; *see also* Bahá'í Faith and other religions).

STATUS

For Shoghi Effendi the Bahá'í Faith was unquestionably a world religion, by dint of the nature of Bahá'u'lláh's claims; the religion's growth in all continents; and its possession of its own distinctive laws and administration. It was supranational, non-partisan, and non-sectarian (*WOB* 196–201; *see* Fazel, 'Is the Baha'i Faith a world religion').

PURPOSE

The purpose of Bahá'u'lláh's revelation was 'the rehabilitation of the world and its nations', such that it might be administered through love and 'the power of utterance' rather than armed might, and its peoples live together in harmony (*CC2*: 332). He had come to adorn every individual 'with the ornament of holy and goodly deeds' and the 'mantle of a saintly character'. He summoned all peoples to acquire spiritual qualities (*ADJ* 24). At a societal level, he had come to bring the 'Most Great peace' and to establish world unity and a new World Order.

DEVELOPMENT

Shoghi Effendi regarded Bábí–Bahá'í history as constituting a single evolutionary process in which internal maturation, external expansion and a series of crises (*see* opposition; Covenant-breakers) interacted to impel the Faith towards its destined goal. The potentialities of the Faith were gradually revealed, expressing in the visible world the spiritual forces of divine revelation. Crises, despite the immediate problems they engendered, caused the added release of divine power leading to the 'further unfoldment' of the Faith (*GPB* xiii, 409–10). What had originally been 'a heterodox and seemingly negligible offshoot' of Shaykhism, itself a sectarian development within Shí'ism, had become a world religion (*GPB* xii). The future progress of the Faith would see it develop through the successive stages of: (1) unmitigated obscurity; (2) active repression; (3) complete emancipation; (4) recognition as an independent religion accorded the status of full equality with other faiths; (5) establishment as a state religion; (6) the formation of a Bahá'í state; and (7) the emergence of a worldwide Bahá'í commonwealth 'animated wholly by the spirit, and operating solely in direct conformity with the laws and principles of Bahá'u'lláh'. *ADJ* 12; *GPB* xvii; *MBW* 155.

Bahá'í Faith and other religions

Bahá'u'lláh and 'Abdu'l-Bahá taught that all divine religions come from the same source (*see* RELIGIOUS DIVERSITY); emphasized the necessity for religious TOLERANCE; and lamented the consequences of religious hatred and fanaticism. Shoghi Effendi insisted that the Bahá'í Faith upheld the 'eternal verities' enshrined in previous religions, and did not belittle their value, distort their teachings, or deny their 'God-given authority'. It did, however, regard religious truth as relative rather than absolute, and sought to incorporate the world's religions into a single schema of PROGRESSIVE REVELATION (*GPB* 100; *WOB* 57–9, 114–15; *see also* INTERFAITH DIALOGUE).

BAHÁ'Í MEMBERSHIP

In many cultures multiple religious identity is regarded as normal, but in others membership of a religious group is seen as excluding other memberships. There has been a significant historical change in Bahá'í practice in this regard. The great majority of Bábís and early Bahá'ís were drawn from the milieu of Iranian Shí'ism and, despite the distinctive nature of their own Bahá'í beliefs, retained much of their traditional religious identity and world-view. Because of the realities of persecution, many also kept their Bahá'í identity relatively secret (*see* WISDOM). Those who had previously been Islamic clerics often continued to function at least partially in that role. 'Abdu'l-Bahá himself continued to attend the mosque whilst he lived in Akka. Issues of communal identity raised by the conversion of religious minority group members in Iran were initially met by the retention of semi-separate identities as 'Muslim-', 'Jewish-', and 'Zoroastrian-' Bahá'ís. Thus marriage networks remained mostly separate, and a separate 'Israelitish' Bahá'í assembly even functioned for a while in Tehran in the early years of the 20th century. Similarly, many early Western Bahá'ís retained their former Christian identity, and in some cases their previous church memberships, long after they became Bahá'ís. (This included the future HANDS OF THE CAUSE Horace HOLLEY and George TOWNSHEND. Thus Holley, then American national spiritual assembly secretary, remained closely associated with the Episcopal Church until 1933 and Townshend remained an archdeacon in the Church of Ireland until 1947. Townshend was the highest ranking of a number of Bahá'ís who were also ordained Christian ministers. Others included T.K. CHEYNE and Howard Colby IVES.) This retention of multiple religious identity in the West reflected a view that the Bahá'í Cause was an 'inclusive Movement' and a 'spiritual attitude' rather than a separate religion. Shoghi Effendi advanced a more exclusivist conception of Bahá'í identity, however, emphasizing that Bahá'í was a distinct religion 'divorced from every ecclesiastical system', and instructing Bahá'ís to sever any affiliations they had with other religious groups. Whilst the Bahá'í Faith sought to instil in its adherents a new love for all the world's religions and an appreciation of their interrelatedness, it was itself an independent world religion, with its own distinctive laws and administration, and Bahá'ís could thus not subscribe to the 'obsolescent observances and doctrines' of other religions. They should of course continue to associate with the followers of other religions in a spirit of friendliness and love (*LG* 52 no. 183, 159–63, 420–6; *WOB* 196–201). This change was linked to the conception of the Bahá'í Faith as going through a series of stages of development, one of which was its recognition as an independent religion. SBBR 95, 109–10, 113, 145–6. (*See also* BAHÁ'Í FAITH, 'development'; PUBLIC RECOGNITION.)

Bahá'í International Community (BIC)

Term that first came into use to describe Bahá'í representation at the United Nations as a non-governmental organization (NGO). It is now used more generally in any context in which the Bahá'í Faith is functioning as an NGO in relationship to international or government bodies or to other NGOs, as for example in Bahá'í SOCIO-ECONOMIC DEVELOPMENT projects. It encompasses all Bahá'ís in the world. All national spiritual ASSEMBLIES are its affiliates.

HISTORY

The BIC first came into existence in 1948 as the representative agency at the UN for the eight national assemblies then extant. It functioned under the aegis of the American assembly, with Mrs Mildred Mottahedeh as its accredited observer in New York. A full-time Bahá'í representative, Dr Victor de Araujo, directly responsible to the Universal House of Justice, was appointed in 1967, and BIC involvement with the UN significantly increased. Consultative status was granted with the UN Economic and Social Council (ECOSOC) in 1970, and with the UN Children's Fund (UNICEF) in 1976. With subsequent growth, the BIC now has administrative offices in Haifa and New York; a United Nations Office in New York and Geneva; an Office of Public Information in Haifa (est. 1985), with branches in Paris and London; and specialist Offices of the Environment (1989) and for the Advancement of Women (1992) in New York. It also has representation at regional United Nations offices in Addis Ababa, Bangkok, Nairobi, Rome, Santiago and Vienna. It is headed by a secretary-general based in New York.

ACTIVITIES

BIC involvement in UN commissions, committees, conferences and working groups has been extensive, frequently involving the presentation of Bahá'í statements on such issues as human rights, the status of women, education, literacy, racial discrimination, narcotic drugs, the environment and social development. Special statements include *The Prosperity of Mankind* (1995), dealing with the concept of global prosperity in the context of the Bahá'í teachings. Since 1989 it has published a quarterly newsletter, *One Country* (1country@bic.org), which reports on Bahá'í activities and issues of global concern. The original English-language edition has now been augmented by French, Chinese, Russian, Spanish and German editions. Other activities have included being a founding member of 'Advocates for African Food Security: Lessening the Burden for Women' (1988), and the BAHÁ'Í-UNIFEM PROJECT (1991–). The BIC has also been a major channel for making appeals to the international community for support in instances of persecution of Bahá'ís, most notably of those in IRAN – criticism in the UN or in the UN Commission on Human Rights acting as a powerful brake on action against the Bahá'ís (*see also* OPPOSITION). *BW12*: 597–615; *13*: 785–802; *14*: 277–90; *15*: 358–77; *16*: 327–51; *17*: 229–44; *18*: 393–425; *19*: 378–97; *NS* 1993–4: 131–8, 295–316; 1994–5: 37–46, 139–50, 273–96, 305–10, 321–4.

'Bahá'í principles'

In his public talks in the West (1911–13) 'Abdu'l-Bahá frequently presented a list of Bahá'í principles (9, 10, 11, 12, 14 – the number varied; there is no definitive list). This listing of principles thenceforth became a common element in Bahá'í literature (the *Tablet to The* HAGUE (1919) provides a good example). The principles listed included the following: (1) Each individual should independently investigate TRUTH, putting aside historic prejudices. Thus would they find the one reality which is common to all. (2) All divine religions are one, expressions of a single reality. The teachings of Bahá'u'lláh best represented the 'universal religion' needed at the present time (*see also* RELIGION). (3) Genuine religion is a powerful support for social stability: without it crime and irreligion flourish. (4) For all its fruits, material CIVILIZATION by itself is not sufficient to promote human progress. Only when combined with 'divine civilization' and empowered by the holy spirit will it be the cause of genuine advance. (5) Religion should be the cause of love and unity. If a particular religion only produces hatred and division then it is no longer an expression of true religion and should be abandoned. (6) Religion must be in conformity with SCIENCE and reason; if it is not then it is only ignorant superstition. (7) Bahá'u'lláh had come to establish the Most Great PEACE. An international tribunal should be instituted to adjudicate disputes between nations. (8) The whole HUMAN RACE is one, all human beings are equally the children of God, the only differences between them being those of education and spiritual health. (9) Religious, racial, political, national and class PREJUDICES are destructive and based on ignorance, they cause strife and impede moral progress. (10) Human progress can not occur as long as people are still forced to struggle for their daily existence (*see* ECONOMIC TEACHINGS). (11) Extremes of wealth and more especially of poverty should be abolished; all must have access to the necessities of life. (12) All individuals must be equal before the LAW, and JUSTICE must be securely established in society. (13) WOMEN are the equals of men and should have equality of rights, particularly of educational opportunity. Without such equality the progress of both sexes is impeded. (14) All children must receive EDUCATION. (15) There should be an international auxiliary LANGUAGE.

Although derived in large part from the principles delineated by Bahá'u'lláh, these listings and the talks in which particular principles were developed in more detail show significant differences in emphasis from them. This is most obvious in the advocacy of the emancipation and equality of women, a principle that appears to have received little more than passing reference from Bahá'u'lláh, but which was discussed at length by 'Abdu'l-Bahá. Again, 'Abdu'l-Bahá dealt with economic questions, education, the critique of materialistic philosophies, and the principle of racial equality in far more detail than his father had. Listings of teachings are also found in several of Bahá'u'lláh's writings – notably BISHÁRÁT – but a number of these are distinctively different from those given by 'Abdu'l-Bahá.

Bahai Temple Unity

The first representative national Bahá'í administrative body. It was established by the North American Bahá'ís in 1909 to oversee the project to construct a Bahá'í *MASHRIQU'L-ADHKÁR* in the Chicago area, and consisted of an annual assembly of delegates representing the various local Bahá'í communities. The Temple Unity in turn selected a nine-member Executive Board to superintend the routine progress of the work. Both the Temple Unity and the Board became concerned with wider issues of national Bahá'í activity, and came to provide national organization and leadership. The Executive Board developed into the American national spiritual assembly during the early 1920s. *BFA2*: 299, 306–14; Smith, 'American Baha'i community' 143–50.

Bahá'í–UNIFEM project

Working with the United Nations Development Fund for Women (UNIFEM), the BAHÁ'Í INTERNATIONAL COMMUNITY developed a project ('Traditional Media as Change Agent', begun in 1991) to promote socio-economic development by changing attitudes in local communities towards the status of women through a combination of locally based CONSULTATION and traditional song, dance and drama. Initially organized in three test sites (Bolivia, Cameroon and Malaysia), the project indicated the effectiveness of change generated at the 'grass-roots' level, and has since been emulated elsewhere. As with many other Bahá'í development projects, the focus was on the community as a whole and not just the local Bahá'í minority. There is a video of the project: *Two Wings*. *BWNS* 1993–4: 259–63.

Bahá'í Vocational Institute for Rural Women, Indore

Indian rural development institute established in 1983. It aims to improve the lives of rural women through training in literacy, health and income-generating skills. Its activities are directed to the community as a whole and not just to Bahá'ís, and it has received support from the Indian government and other external bodies. It emphasizes the importance of Bahá'í moral teachings and the abandonment of caste prejudices. *BWNS* 1993–4: 255–7, 258.

Bahá'í World

Series of books recording Bahá'í activities world-wide. The first volume appeared as a *Bahá'í Year Book* for 1925–6, with subsequent volumes covering varying time spans up to the 1990s. The material in many of the earlier volumes in particular is an invaluable historical resource, including international surveys of current Bahá'í activities; copies of significant documents; directories of Bahá'í assemblies and lists of Bahá'í centres world-wide; bibliographies; and articles on particular Bahá'í events. The books are illustrated with numerous photographs. Much of the work on the earlier volumes represents a collaboration between Shoghi Effendi and the American national assembly secretary, Horace HOLLEY. A new series of shorter one-year volumes under the same title was started in 1992–3. The years covered in each volume of the original series are as follows:

1 (1925–6)	11 (1946–50)
2 (1926–8)	12 (1950–4)
3 (1928–30)	13 (1954–63)
4 (1930–2)	14 (1963–8)
5 (1932–4)	15 (1968–73)
6 (1934–6)	16 (1973–6)
7 (1936–8)	17 (1976–9)
8 (1938–40)	18 (1979–83)
9 (1940–4)	19 (1983–6)
10 (1944–6)	

Bahá'í World Centre

The spiritual and administrative centre of the Bahá'í Faith, consisting of the Shrine of Bahá'u'lláh at BAHJÍ (the Bahá'í *QIBLAH*); the SHRINE OF THE BÁB in HAIFA (which includes the Shrine of 'Abdu'l-Bahá); and the various buildings associated with the Faith in the Haifa–AKKA area in northern Israel.

1868–1921

Bahá'u'lláh's arrival in Akka (31 August 1868), then part of Ottoman Syria, occurred shortly after the emergence of a distinctive Bahá'í community. Lines of communication were soon established with the Bahá'ís in Iran and elsewhere, with special couriers conveying correspondence between Bahá'u'lláh and his followers. Akka became the directive centre of an expanding network of Bahá'í groups in the Middle East, India and Central Asia. As conditions of confinement eased an increasing number of pilgrims also made the long journey to see Bahá'u'lláh, Bahá'í 'agents' in Beirut and other staging posts assisting them in their journeys. With the introduction of *ḤUQÚQU'LLÁH* (1878), its trustees made regular journeys to deliver contributions from the Bahá'ís. Akka was also given a wider importance by dint of its location in a land hallowed both by the Judaeo-Christian Bible and Islam, Bahá'u'lláh himself regarding his arrival in the city as a sign of divine providence in fulfilment of PROPHECY. Mount CARMEL, across the bay from Akka, was also given prophetic significance for the future. This situation continued under 'Abdu'l-Bahá, with three major changes: the establishment of Bahá'í centres in the West – and hence an increase in correspondence; the placement of the Báb's remains in the newly constructed Shrine on Carmel in 1909; and the transfer of 'Abdu'l-Bahá's residence from Akka to Haifa, thenceforth the administrative headquarters of the Faith, in 1910. The increasing flow of correspondence necessitated employment of a number of secretaries, some fluent in Western languages. The flow of pilgrims led to the provision of a pilgrim house in Haifa.

1922–63

Under Shoghi Effendi's direction, there was considerable development involving a number of separate projects. In the Akka area he obtained the mansion of Bahá'u'lláh at Bahjí in 1929 and began an extensive renovation. Later, during the 1950s, he secured legal possession of the surrounding lands and created a number of gardens and installed ornamental lighting. He also renovated the house in which Bahá'u'lláh had spent most of his years in Akka (the House of 'Abbúd), and obtained possession of other sites associated with Bahá'u'lláh. In Haifa he extended the shrine complex in which the Báb and 'Abdu'l-Bahá were interred (1929), and had an elaborate golden-domed superstructure constructed to envelop the shrine (1948–53). He also purchased the surrounding lands and created gardens, again with ornamental lighting. Above the shrine, he had the Parthenon-like INTERNATIONAL ARCHIVES building constructed to house Bahá'í relics and scriptures (1955–7), the two buildings together with the gardens becoming a major Haifa landmark. He also enjoyed an entirely different public status from that of 'Abdu'l-Bahá. Although coming to be regarded as a important local notable, 'Abdu'l-Bahá had been a prisoner or under threat of renewed incarceration almost to the end of his life. By contrast, both under the British Mandate (1920–48) and the newly established state of Israel (from 1948), Shoghi Effendi was accorded the status of the head of an independent religion. In the earliest days of his ministry members of his family and the Bahá'í spiritual assembly in Haifa had functioned as a secretariat. This took a more institutionalized form in 1950, with the establishment of the INTERNATIONAL BAHÁ'Í COUNCIL.

SINCE 1963

Like Shoghi Effendi the Universal House of Justice has worked to secure ownership of sites associated with the central figures of the Faith – such as the house in which 'Abdu'l-Bahá lived in Akka (the House of 'Abdu'lláh Páshá) – and to extend and beautify the gardens surrounding the Bahá'í shrines in Haifa and Bahjí. Most dramatic has been its construction of a large stately building to serve as its own seat in Haifa (1975–83) and the extensive project (begun in 1992) to construct the buildings of the ARC on Mount Carmel and complete the terraces of the Báb's Shrine. The Bahá'í administrative staff have enormously increased in numbers – to several hundred, reflecting both the growth of the Faith internationally and the increasing range of work undertaken at the Bahá'í World Centre, both by the House of Justice's own specialized departments (secretariat, finance, research, archives, statistics, maintenance (of the gardens and buildings), etc.), and those of other bodies, such as the INTERNATIONAL TEACHING CENTRE and the Office for Socio-Economic Development.

Bahá'u'lláh (Ar., the 'Splendour' or 'Glory of God'), (1817–92)

The religious title of Mírzá Ḥusayn-'Alí Núrí, the prophet-founder of the Bahá'í Faith.

LIFE

IRAN BEFORE 1853

Bahá'u'lláh was born on 12 November 1817 in Tehran, the son of Mírzá 'Abbás, a landowning notable from Núr in Mázandarán (*see* Núrí family), whose family traced its origins back to the ancient Sassanian kings of Iran. Bahá'ís also believe that he was a descendant of the prophets Abraham (through his wife Katurah) and Zoroaster (*see* Zoroastrianism). His father was a rising government official until forced out of office in 1835 and ruined by Ḥájí Mírzá Áqásí. Bahá'u'lláh himself subsequently refused all official appointments, and later recalled a childhood memory of a puppet play of a royal court, in which he saw the transience of worldly grandeur revealed when the puppets and their finery were taken from the stage and put away in their box. As a youth he showed strong religious and mystical tendencies, and in 1844 became a Bábí, promulgating the new religion among his kinsfolk and in his native province. He married his first wife, Ásíyih (Navváb), in 1835, and his second, Fáṭimih (Mahd-i-'Ulyá), in 1849. His three eldest children ('Abdu'l-Bahá, Bahiyyih Khánum, Mírzá Mihdí) were all born in Tehran.

One of the most socially eminent of the Bábís, he began to assume an increasing prominence within the religion – one of the few non-clerics to do so – organizing Ṭáhirih's escape from Qazvín in 1847, and in 1848 he was one of the principal figures at the Badasht conference, where he took the name *Bahá*. Attempting to join the Bábís at Ṭabarsí, he was arrested, and taken to Ámul, where he was bastinadoed. Following the death of so many of the leading Bábís at Ṭabarsí, a new pattern of Bábí leadership developed, with the Báb in correspondence with various of his followers, including Bahá'u'lláh and his young half-brother, Mírzá Yaḥyá Ṣubḥ-i-Azal, the latter being appointed by the Báb to 'preserve' his religion (according to the Bahá'í account, to shield Bahá'u'lláh). It was Bahá'u'lláh, however, who was seen by the new chief minister, Amír Kabír, as the major directive force behind the remaining Bábís, and who at his urging left Iran for Karbalá in June 1851, only returning (April/May 1852) after Amír Kabír's fall from power, and at the invitation of his replacement, Mírzá Áqá Khán Núrí, himself distantly related to Bahá'u'lláh. Following the attempt on the life of Náṣiru'd-Dín Sháh by the militant Bábí faction headed by Aẓím (15 August 1852), all prominent Bábís, including many who were not involved in the plot, were arrested. This included Bahá'u'lláh, who had been staying with the chief minister's brother at the time. Any hopes he may have had for a rapprochement with the new government were ended, and he was thrown into the Síyáh-Chál dungeon (August). Despite his proven innocence, he was threatened with life imprisonment. However, following representations by his family and the Russian envoy he was finally released after four months (December) and banished from Iran, leaving Tehran on 12 January 1853. During his imprisonment, heavily chained and suffering great privations, he had undergone a series of mystical experiences, in one of which he had had a vision of a heavenly maiden (*see* Maid of Heaven) who assured him of his divine mission, and rejoiced his soul with the promise of divine assistance – an event regarded by Bahá'ís as marking the birth of the Bahá'í revelation.

The táj hat of Bahá'u'lláh

IRAQ, 1853–63

Accompanied by his family (his wives, eldest two children, and brothers, Mírzá MÚSÁ and Mírzá MUḤAMMAD-QULÍ) Bahá'u'lláh made the difficult winter journey over the mountains to Ottoman Iraq, arriving in BAGHDAD on 8 April 1853. Here they were later joined by Azal, who had gone into hiding following the attempt on the life of the shah. What happened next is difficult to establish in detail, and is coloured by the later partisan accounts of Bahá'ís and AZALIS, but in essence it would seem that Bahá'u'lláh began to eclipse Azal as a leader (e.g. see *Tablet of 'ALL FOOD'*), a development increasingly resented by the latter, who yet insisted on maintaining a hidden existence from most of the Bábís for his own protection. The tensions were such that Bahá'u'lláh finally decided to abandon the city to pursue the life of a solitary mystic in the mountains of Kurdistan, leaving his family in the care of Mírzá Músá. He left Baghdad on 10 April 1854, accompanied by a single servant, later writing that his 'withdrawal contemplated no return' (*KI* 160). Initially living as a hermit in a cave in the mountains at Sar-Galú, he 'communed with [his] spirit' oblivious of the world. Later he came into contact with Sufi leaders in the regional centre of Sulaymániyya, where he came to be regarded highly as a mystic and spiritual teacher, and wrote the *ODE OF THE DOVE*. After two years he returned to Baghdad (19 March 1856), to find the Bábí remnant in sorry disarray; dispirited and divided into factions, with Azal unable to provide effective leadership and continuing a policy of militancy rejected by Bahá'u'lláh (e.g. *see* DAYYÁN). Bahá'u'lláh now began to work to revive the Bábí community, both in Iraq and, through correspondence, in Iran, attracting a band of dedicated personal disciples. Writing extensively, he began to give the Bábís a new understanding of their religion. Of particular importance were the *HIDDEN WORDS* (*c.*1858) and *Kitáb-i-ÍQÁN* (1862), in which he emphasized the importance of the 'SPIRITUAL PATH', and outlined the practical, ethical and

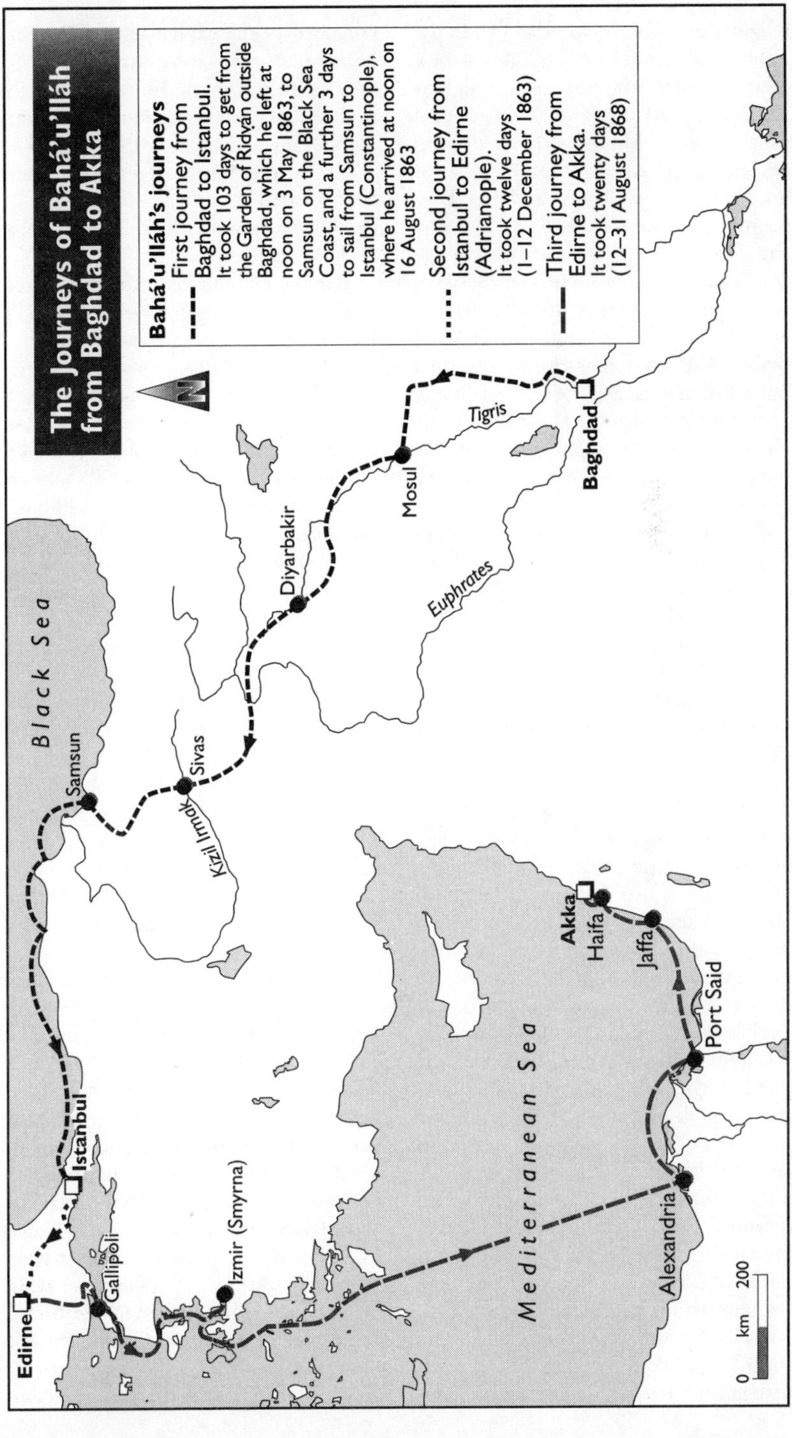
The Journeys of Bahá'u'lláh
from Baghdad to Akka
Bahá'u'lláh's journeys
First journey from Baghdad to Istanbul.
It took 103 days to get from the Garden of Riḍván outside Baghdad, which he left at noon on 3 May 1863, to Samsun on the Black Sea Coast, and a further 3 days to sail from Samsun to Istanbul (Constantinople), where he arrived at noon on 16 August 1863
Second journey from Istanbul to Edirne (Adrianople).
It took twelve days (1–12 December 1863)
Third journey from Edirne to Akka.
It took twenty days (12–31 August 1868)
N
Black Sea
Mediterranean Sea
Edirne
Istanbul
Gallipoli
Izmir (Smyrna)
Samsun
Sivas
Kizil Irmak
Diyarbakir
Mosul
Tigris
Euphrates
Baghdad
Akka
Haifa
Jaffa
Port Said
Alexandria
0
km
200

religious goals of the spiritual life. In the *Íqán* he also provided the Bábís with a clear account of their own religious doctrines, particularly the concept of a progression of MANIFESTATIONS OF GOD and the fulfilment of prophecy. Also of note are his writings addressed to prominent Sufis – the *FOUR VALLEYS* and *SEVEN VALLEYS* – dealing with the concerns of Islamic mysticism (SUFISM); his frequent reference to and evident knowledge of the Judaeo-Christian BIBLE; and his references to his own intense religious experiences, including continuing visions of the MAID OF HEAVEN. He was soon recognized as the pre-eminent Bábí leader, both by the Bábís and by the Iranian and Ottoman authorities. Outside the Bábí community he also gained increasing sympathy from both residents and visitors in Baghdad, including Ottoman officials, Iranian notables, and even Sunní and Shí'í clerics, and was widely regarded as an important personage. He married a third wife (Gawhar) whilst in Baghdad, but the date is unknown.

RUMELIA, 1863–8

Fearing a revival of Bábism, the Iranian government requested that the Ottoman authorities return Bahá'u'lláh to Iran. Refusing, the Ottomans instead invited Bahá'u'lláh – now an Ottoman citizen – to Istanbul. Immediately prior to his departure from Baghdad he stayed for twelve days in a garden outside the city which he named RIḌVÁN ('Paradise') (22 April–3 May 1863). Here he bade farewell to well-wishers, and made known to some of his immediate disciples his claim to be the Bábí promised one. He also commanded them strictly to avoid sedition. Then, dressed as a Sufi leader, he together with his family and companions – some seventy or so persons in all – made the long overland journey to Samsun on the Black Sea, and from thence continued to ISTANBUL by boat, arriving on 16 August (*see* map). They remained in the capital until 1 December, when they were transferred to EDIRNE, in European Turkey, seemingly as a result of pressure from the Iranian ambassador, Mírzá ḤUSAYN KHÁN. Whereas previously Bahá'u'lláh had been treated as an honoured guest of the Ottoman authorities, he was now evidently an exile.

Bahá'u'lláh and his entourage stayed in Edirne for four-and-a-half years (12 December 1863–12 August 1868). During this period the tensions between Bahá'u'lláh and Azal came to a head, probably because the gradual circulation of Bahá'u'lláh's claims to be the Bábí promised one undermined Azal's authority and intensified his jealousy. Although not included in the Ottoman invitation, Azal had joined the Bábí exiles during the journey from Baghdad, initially concealing his identity. In Edirne, according to the Bahá'í account, he began to plot against Bahá'u'lláh, finally making an attempt to poison him (*c.*1865; Azali sources make the counter-accusation that Bahá'u'lláh tried to poison Azal but consumed the poison himself by accident. Whatever the case, Bahá'u'lláh became very sick, and the effects of the poison were felt for the rest of his life: his hair turned white and he could no longer write without his hand shaking).

Following this, Bahá'u'lláh laid open claim to be HE WHOM GOD SHALL MAKE MANIFEST, and began to refer to his own followers as the 'people of Bahá' (i.e. Bahá'ís) (*c.* March 1866). He then isolated himself from the Bábís in Edirne for a two-month period (the 'Most Great Separation'), instructing them to choose whether to follow Azal or himself. Almost all chose Bahá'u'lláh, as also increasingly did the Bábís in Iran. A great outflow of writings from Bahá'u'lláh followed, including the beginning of his proclamation to the RULERS (specifically the *Súra of the KINGS* (*c.*1867) and the first tablet to

NAPOLEON III. Bahá'u'lláh's ascendency over Azal was further reinforced in September 1867, when Azal challenged him to *MUBÁHALA* – to appear together at a local mosque and await God's judgement to decide between them – but then declined to attend the arranged meeting. Thereafter the Azali group sought to discredit Bahá'u'lláh with the Ottoman authorities, accusing him of sedition. The resultant investigation cleared Bahá'u'lláh of these charges, but alerted the authorities to the fact that both Bahá'u'lláh and Azal were making and propagating religious claims. This, it was decided, represented a potential source of disorder and merited the further exile of the 'Bábí' leaders. Accordingly, a royal command was issued (26 July 1868) condemning them to perpetual banishment, imprisonment and isolation. Bahá'u'lláh's property in Baghdad was also confiscated at this time, and the leading Bábís/ Bahá'ís of Baghdad arrested and exiled to Mosul.

SYRIA, 1868–92

The Ottomans decided to exile Bahá'u'lláh and his entourage to AKKA in the province of Syria, and Azal and a few others to Famagusta in Cyprus. The whole group departed from Edirne on 12 August 1868 under armed escort, and was taken first to Gallipoli, and thence by sea to their respective destinations, the ship going by way of Egypt. The Akka group arrived in the city on 31 August, and were confined in the barracks-citadel. They were sixty-seven in number: Bahá'u'lláh, his brothers, and their families, servants, other Bahá'ís, and two Azalis, the latter no doubt intended to serve as spies on the rest. Living conditions were at first appalling, with everyone becoming sick, and three of the exiles dying. Bahá'u'lláh's son Mírzá Mihdí also died, following a fall (23 June 1870). Conditions improved after they left the barracks (4 November 1870), although the exiles were still confined to the city. A major crisis occurred in 1872, when a few Bahá'í

The barracks block in Akka where Bahá'u'lláh was imprisoned

hotheads finally murdered the resident Azalis who had been making difficulties for them (22 January). This action was strongly condemned by Bahá'u'lláh. Thereafter, however, relations between the Bahá'ís and the local authorities and inhabitants eased, Bahá'u'lláh's eldest son, the future 'Abdu'l-Bahá, in particular acting as an effective go-between. Finally, following the overthrow of Sultan ABDULAZIZ (30 May 1876), it became possible for Bahá'u'lláh to leave the city. Initially residing in the mansion of Mazra'ih (from June 1877), Bahá'u'lláh subsequently moved to BAHJÍ (September 1879), remaining there, apart from visits to Mount CARMEL, for the remainder of his life. He died at Bahjí on 29 May 1892 following a slight fever, and was buried in a room in an adjoining house. He was then aged seventy-four. He appointed 'Abdu'l-Bahá to be his successor (*Book of the* COVENANT).

During this final twenty-four years of his exile the distinctive features of the Bahá'í Faith as a religious movement were developed. An effective system of communications was established between Bahá'u'lláh and his immediate entourage (specifically his chief secretary, Mírzá ÁQÁ JÁN, and 'Abdu'l-Bahá, who acted as his father's principal assistant) and the Bahá'ís in IRAN; the Iranian Bahá'ís themselves became coordinated and developed a sense of cohesion as a distinct religious community; and EXPANSION of the community to India and Asiatic Russia was accomplished. With much of the practical management of the movement in the hands of 'Abdu'l-Bahá, Bahá'u'lláh was able to spend much of his time in 'the revelation of verses' and, from 1877, in the enjoyment of nature. His writings during this period include his proclamatory letters to the rulers; his book of laws, the *Kitáb-i-*AQDAS (*c.*1873) (*see also* LAW); and a series of letters in which he called for the establishment of just GOVERNMENT and world PEACE, and outlined various 'social' teachings, such as the need for a world LANGUAGE and the development of AGRICULTURE. Themes from his earlier writings are also continued, as in the emphasis on the need for piety and ethical action on the part of his followers (*see* DEVOTIONALISM; PRAYER; SPIRITUAL QUALITIES); the announcement that this is the 'day of God'; and his references to the immediacy of the relationship he felt with the Godhead (*BFSII* 64–73).

PERSONALITY

The great devotion and love that his followers felt for Bahá'u'lláh makes it difficult for us to gain an impression of what he was actually like. Thus their accounts of Bahá'u'lláh emphasize his overwhelming and ineffable presence, one writer stating that it was almost impossible for anyone to look into his eyes or utter a complete sentence in his presence. The English orientalist E.G. BROWNE, who had had an audience with him in 1890, described him as 'a wondrous and venerable figure', whose face he could neither describe nor forget, and whose piercing eyes 'seemed to read one's very soul'. Though his face was deeply lined with age, his 'ample brow' emanated power and authority. He wore both his hair and beard long (the beard almost to his waist) and dyed them jet-black. In addition to his robes he wore a tall dervish hat, round the base of which was wound a small white turban (*TN* xxxix–xl).

THEOLOGICAL STATUS

Bahá'ís regard Bahá'u'lláh as the Manifestation of God for the present age; the promised messianic figure of all previous religions; and the inaugurator of a new universal religious cycle (*see* TIME), who has come to establish the millennial Most Great Peace, unify the human race, and found a new WORLD ORDER and civilization. All the former books of God referred to him and extolled his glory. For Jews he was the 'Everlasting Father', the 'Lord of Hosts' come down 'with ten thousands of saints'; for Christians Christ returned 'in the glory of the Father'; for Shí'í Muslims the return of the Imám Ḥusayn; for Sunnís the descent of Jesus, the 'Spirit of God'; for Zoroastrians, Sháh-Bahrám; for Hindus the reincarnation of Krishna; and for Buddhists the fifth Buddha (*GPB* 94). For the Bábís he was He whom God shall make manifest. As the divine messenger for the present day, knowledge of God and attainment of the divine presence could now only be reached through him. Through his potency all hidden truths were now unveiled (*TB* 50). He was the guiding light that illumined the way, and all should seek him and none other, lest they be bereft of all things (*TB* 169). He was the 'Fountain-Head' of God's wisdom and utterance; the revealer of God's oneness, who had been invested with divine sovereignty, power and glory; the lawgiver and redeemer of the entire human race; the 'Day-Star of the Universe'; the 'Eternal Truth'; the 'Lord of all men'; the 'Lord of the Day of Reckoning'; the 'mighty Trumpet' whose blast was to signal the resurrection of all humanity; God's lamp, light, voice, testimony and proof; the river of life; the refuge of the fearful; the 'True Physician'; the 'Beloved' and 'Desire' of the world; the 'Most Great Ocean'; and the 'Sifter of Men' (*GPB* 94; Rabbani, *Desire of the World* 175–86). He shared with the other Manifestations of God the dual station of having a human life whilst acting as a divine agent. Thus Bahá'u'lláh described himself as having been 'a man like others' until the 'breezes' of God were 'wafted' over him, and taught him 'the knowledge of all that hath been'. He spoke because God had commanded him to speak, and not of his own choosing (*ESW* 11–12). At the same time, however, in many of his writings he expressed his sense of exaltation and identity with the divine presence: he was the bearer of God's Greatest Name (*Bahá*), 'the Speaker on Sinai' – the voice that called from the Burning Bush – who was now seated upon 'the throne of Revelation' (*TB* 107); 'the Unconditioned', who had come in 'clouds of light' to 'quicken all created things with the breezes of his Name' (*ESW* 46); the 'Face of God', the revealer of God's own self, and the manifestation of his essence (Rabbani, *Desire*, 176). Yet he denied accusations that he had laid claim to divinity (*TB* 49) – a question that appears to have generated discussion amongst his followers (*RB1*: 303), and Shoghi Effendi was insistent that whilst Bahá'u'lláh had spoken with the voice of God, this was not to be misconceived or misinterpreted: he was a great Being, and incarnated the names and attributes of God to an extraordinary degree, but his 'human temple' remained 'entirely distinguished' from that 'eternal Essence of Essences' that was God. This was a major Bahá'í belief and should never be obscured or compromised (*WOB* 112–14). (See *GPB* 93–102; Lambden, 'Sinaitic mysteries'.) *ARR* 361–6; *BKG*; Cole, 'Bahá'u'lláh and the Naqshbandí Sufis'; Cole, 'Iranian millenarianism'; *EB*; Furútan, *Stories*; *GPB* 66–72, 89–224; Ḥaydar-'Alí; *MBBR* 177–240; Nabil; *RB*; Salmání; *SBBR* 57–70; *BFSH* 51–62; *TN*.

Bahá'u'lláh, House of

See Baghdad: the House of Bahá'u'lláh.

Bahá'u'lláh, Shrine of

See Bahjí.

Bahá'u'lláh, writings of

Bahá'u'lláh wrote extensively. Some 15,000 'tablets' by him have been identified so far (*see* lawḥ). Many of these are short letters to Bahá'ís, but they also include major works dealing with religious doctrine; the proclamation of Bahá'u'lláh's claims; Bahá'í law; and social and moral teachings, in addition to prayers, ecstatic poems, and visionary accounts of Bahá'u'lláh's religious experiences. All are regarded by Bahá'ís as divine revelations, including those written prior to the announcement of Bahá'u'lláh's prophetic claims. The writings can be subdivided by time period into those composed ('revealed') in Iran (up to 1853); Iraq (Baghdad/Kurdistan, 1853–63); Rumelia (Istanbul/Edirne, 1863–8); and Ottoman Syria (Akka/Mazra'ih/Bahjí, 1868–92). Only a fraction of this material has been translated into English as yet, albeit that the writings that have been translated include many of the most important. *BW18*: 833–4 provides a partial listing of titles. For summaries of some of the works see Browne, *Selections* 248–88; *GPB* 116–17, 120–1, 123, 137–41, 170–6, 205–20; *RB*.

The following is a summary of some of Bahá'u'lláh's better-known works, with dates of composition where known. (Abbreviations used: AkE early Akka, in the barracks; AUK in the house of 'Údí Khammár; EB Baghdad II, early; LB Baghdad II, late; *see relevant entry in this volume.)

TEHRAN

Rashḥ-i-'Amá ('The Sprinkling of the Cloud'). Short poem of exaltation composed in the Síyáh-Chál. Cole, 'Bahá'u'lláh and the Naqshbandí Sufis', 10–11; *RB1*: 45–6.

THE IRAQI PERIOD

BAGHDAD I, 1853–4

Lawḥ-i-Kullu'ṭ-ṭa'ám ('*Tablet of "All Food"*'). Arabic. Addressed to Ḥájí Mírzá Kamálu'd-dín Naráqí in commentary on a verse of the Quran.*

KURDISTAN, 1854–6

Qaṣída al-Warqá'iyyah (Pers. *Qaṣídi-yi-Varqá'iyyih*) ('Ode of the Dove'). Arabic mystical work.*

Sáqí az ghayb-i-baqá ('The Cup-bearer from the Eternal Unseen'). Persian ode. *RB1*: 64.

BAGHDAD II, 1856–63

Az bágh-i-iláhí ('From the Divine Garden'). LB. Persian and Arabic. Ecstatic poem, in which Bahá'u'lláh announces the advent of the Day of God. *RB1*: 218–9.

Four Valleys (*Chahár vádí*). EB. Persian. Mystical work addressed to Shaykh 'Abdu'r-Raḥmán Tálabání, a Qádirí Sufi leader.*

Halih-halih yá bishárat ('Jubilation! Glad Tidings!'). LB. Persian. Ecstatic poem announcing the Day of God and Bahá'u'lláh's station. *RB1*: 219–20.

Hidden Words (*Kalimát-i-maknúnih*). *c.*1858. Persian and Arabic. A collection of counsels on the spiritual and ethical life.*

Ḥurúfát-i-'állín ('The Exalted Letters'). Arabic and Persian. Written in honour of Bahá'u'lláh's deceased cousin, Mírzá Muḥammad Vazír, and to console Maryam and Ḥavvá, the man's sister and wife. It describes God's bounties to the human soul, the soul's immortality, and the reality of physical death. *RB1*: 122–5; Walbridge, *Sacred* 267–8.

Ḥúr-i-'uját ('The Wondrous Maiden'). LB. Arabic. Refers to the unveiling of Bahá'u'lláh's station. *RB1*: 218.

Javáhiru'l-asrár ('The Essence of Mysteries'). *c.*1860–1. Arabic. Written for Ḥájí Sayyid Muḥammad Iṣfáhání, a prominent Shí'í cleric who became a Bábí following receipt of the tablet. It describes the stages of the spiritual quest, comments on biblical prophecies and Quranic verses related to the coming of the Mahdí, and discusses various theological concepts. In some of its themes it prefigures the *Kitáb-i-Íqán*. *RB1*: 149–52.

Kitáb-i-Íqán (*The Book of Certitude*). 1862. Persian. Bahá'u'lláh's foremost theological work.*

Lawḥ-i-Áyi-yi-núr ('Tablet of the Verse of Light'). Also known as the *Tafsír-i-Ḥurúfát-i-muqaṭṭa'ah* ('Commentary on the Isolated Letters'). Arabic. Interpretation of a particular verse of the Quran, and of the letters which appear at the beginning of many of its chapters. Written for Mírzá Áqá Rikáb-Sáz. *RB1*: 125–6.

Lawḥ-i-Bulbulu'l-firáq ('Tablet of the Nightingale of Separation'). LB. Announces that the 'nightingale of paradise' (himself) is now about to establish a new nest, and warns his followers of the 'birds of night'. *RB1*: 244–5.

Lawḥ-i-Fitnah ('Tablet of the Test'). Arabic. Possibly written in the Edirne period. Written for Shams-i-Jihán, a Qájár princess who became a Bahá'í. It declares that the whole of creation is tested at the coming of a new Manifestation of God, such that the faithful and faithless may be distinguished. Many religious leaders – the stars of the heaven of knowledge – will fall. *RB1*: 128–37.

Lawḥ-i-Ghulámu'l-khuld ('The Tablet of the Deathless Youth'). ?1863. Arabic and Persian. Written to commemorate the anniversary of the declaration of the Báb ('the deathless youth'). *RB1*: 213–14; Walbridge, *Sacred* 161–3.

Lawḥ-i-Ḥúriyyah ('Tablet of the Maiden'). Arabic. Recounts a visionary meeting between Bahá'u'lláh and the Maid of Heaven. *RB1* 125; Walbridge, *Sacred* 160–1.

Lawḥ-i-Malláḥu'l-quds (*Tablet of the Holy Mariner*). 1863. Arabic and Persian. Visionary rhymed prose concerning the dwellers of the 'ark' of God's cause. Regarded by Bahá'ís as prophetic. *RB1*: 228–44; Walbridge, *Sacred* 163–5.

Madínatu'r-riḍá ('City of Radiant Acquiescence'). Arabic. Counsels that contentment requires detachment and humility. *RB1*: 108–9.

Madínatu't-tawḥíd ('City of Unity'). Arabic. Discusses the nature of God and the Manifestations of God. It was written for Shaykh Salmán, the courier of Bahá'u'lláh's letters. *RB1*: 109–18.

Ṣaḥífi-yi-Shaṭṭiyyih ('Book of the River'). Persian. Compares the power of God's cause to that of an irresistible river which overcomes all obstructions to its progress. *RB1*: 105–8.

Seven Valleys (*Haft vádí*). EB. Persian. Bahá'u'lláh's best-known mystical work, written in reply to Shaykh Muḥiyu'd-dín, a Qádirí Sufi.*

Shikkar shikan shavand ('They Shall Crack Sugar'). Persian. Addressed to a prominent Iranian (variously identified), who had suggested that Bahá'u'lláh leave Baghdad for his own safety. The tablet announces the imminence of persecution, but states that no calamity can lessen Bahá'u'lláh's ardour in God's path, or defeat God's power. *BKG* 149, 446; *RB1*: 147–9.

Subḥána rabbíya'l-a'lá ('Praise be my Lord, the most exalted'). Arabic. Written for Ḥájí Mírzá Músá Javáhirí, the owner of Bahá'u'lláh's house in Baghdad. It announces the advent of the Day of God and warns the faithful to expect tests of their faithfulness. *RB1*: 211–13.

Súratu'lláh ('The Chapter of God'). LB or Edirne. Announces Bahá'u'lláh's station to the Bábís and rebukes those who oppose him. *RB1*: 245.

Súri-yi-Nuṣḥ ('Chapter of Exhortation'). Written for Sayyid Ja'far Yazdí, one of the survivors of the Nayríz conflict. It refers to the various prophets of God; their sufferings at the hands of the religious leaders of their day; and their ultimate victory. Shaykh 'Abdu'l-Ḥusayn Ṭihrání, a Shí'í cleric who sought to persecute Bahá'u'lláh and the Bábís in Baghdad, is condemned as one who 'drew the sword of his self against the face of God'. *GPB* 141; *RB1*: 137–47.

Súri-yi-Qadír ('Chapter of the Omnipotent'). Declares that the revelation of this tablet has caused the release of divine power and might into the world. *RB1*: 119–22.

Súri-yi-Sabr ('Chapter of Patience'). Also known as the *Lawḥ-i-Ayyúb* ('Tablet of Job'). 1863. Arabic. Written for Ḥájí Muḥammad-Taqí, one of the survivors of the NAYRÍZ conflict. In it Bahá'u'lláh praises the Bábís at Nayríz, portrays their sufferings, and condemns their persecutors. Further, he details the sufferings of the biblical Job; extols fortitude and patience in the face of suffering; and notes the continuity of divine revelation. *RB1*: 263–73.

FROM BAGHDAD TO ISTANBUL

Lawḥ-i-Hawdaj ('Tablet of the Howdah'). Arabic. Revealed at Samsun on sighting the Black Sea. Linked to the *Tablet of the Holy Mariner*, it warned of 'grievous and tormenting mischief' which would assail the companions. *RB2*: 6–7.

THE RUMELIAN PERIOD

ISTANBUL, 1863

Lawḥ-i-'Abdu'l-azíz va vukalá. Tablet to Sultan ABDULAZIZ and his ministers. Lengthy letter revealed on receipt of the order of banishment to Edirne and sent to ÂLI PAŞA condemning the ministers for this action. No extant copy has as yet been discovered. *GPB* 160.

Lawḥ-i-Náqús ('Tablet of the Bell'). Also called *Subḥánika-yá-hú* ('Praise be to Him!'). Arabic. Revealed on 18 October (on the eve of the anniversary of the Báb's declaration). Its pulsating rhythm lends itself to ecstatic chanting. It declares that 'the Day of God' has now come. *RB2*: 18–20.

Mathnaví-yi-mubárak ('The great poem'). Persian poem. Refers to the advent of the day of God, and to the 'Day-star of truth' which illumines all created things, but which only those with new (spiritual) eyes are able to see. *RB2*: 29–31.

EDIRNE, 1863–8

Kitáb-i-Badí' ('The Wondrous Book'). Mostly in Persian. Lengthy apologia for Bahá'u'lláh, written in reply to a letter from Mírzá Mihdí Gílání, one of the Bábís who rejected his claims, to Áqá Muḥammad-'Alí, one of Bahá'u'lláh's close companions. The book emphasizes the importance of the Bábí messianic figure of HE WHOM GOD SHALL MAKE MANIFEST; proclaims Bahá'u'lláh's fulfilment of this promise, and the outpouring of divine verses from his pen; and counters the arguments of those who would support Ṣubḥ-i-AZAL. Mihdí himself is condemned as 'he who contends with God' and warned of divine wrath. *RB2*: 370–81.

Lawḥ-i-AḤMAD (2). Two tablets, one each in Arabic and Persian, for two separate men.*

Lawḥ-i-Ashraf. Tablet for ASHRAF (no. 1). *RB2*: 230–2.*

Lawḥ-i-Bahá ('Tablet of Glory'). Arabic and Persian. Revealed for Khátún Ján Farhádí of Qazvín. In it, Bahá'u'lláh lamented the attacks made on him by his (Azali) opponents, stigmatizing them as the hosts of Satan. He compared his sufferings to those of Abraham and Joseph, and referred to his followers as the 'people of Bahá' (i.e. Bahá'ís rather than Bábís). *RB2*: 171, 178–80.

Lawḥ-i-Khalíl. Tablet to Ḥájí Muḥammad-Ibráhím of Qazvín, '*Khalíl*' ('Friend'), responding to the confusion caused by Mírzá MUḤAMMAD-'ALÍ's distribution of Arabic verses which he claimed were from God. In it Bahá'u'lláh stated that as long as his sons believed in him and obeyed his commandments, they remained members of his family and the mercy of God would be revealed through them. RB2: 259–61.

Lawḥ-i-Laylatu'l-quds ('Tablet of the Holy Night'). Written for Ṣidq-'Alí the dervish. It calls on Bahá'u'lláh's followers to be united and detached from worldly things. A second tablet by the same title was revealed in Akka. RB2: 188–9.

Lawḥ-i-Mubáhilih ('Tablet of the Challenge'). Tablet revealed at the time of the MUBÁHALA challenge with Ṣubḥ-i-Azal. RB2: 293.

Lawḥ-i-Nápulyún I. The first tablet to NAPOLEON III.*

Lawḥ-i-Naṣír. Persian. Tablet for Hájí Muḥammad-Naṣír of Qazvín (martyred in 1888), who was praised for his steadfastness. It announces the excellence of the present Day when the 'Celestial Youth' (Bahá'u'lláh) had come; calls on the Bábís to tear asunder the veils that had prevented them from recognizing him in the face; and reveals the exalted station of the true believer. Browne, *Selections* 255–60; RB2: 245–55.

Lawḥ-i-Rúḥ ('Tablet of the Spirit'). Arabic. It proclaims Bahá'u'lláh's mission; states that the value of one's faith in God is today dependent on recognizing him; predicts the triumph of his cause; calls upon his followers to be united through the love of God; and laments the treachery of Azal and his followers. RB2: 181–2, 186–8.

Lawḥ-i-Salmán I. Tablet for Bahá'u'lláh's messenger, Shaykh Salmán. In it Bahá'u'lláh bids him to journey with steadfastness, detachment and the love of God; complains of his own sufferings at the hands of Ṣubḥ-i-Azal; exalts the station of the true believer; comments on the Islamic phrase 'There is no god but God'; and explains the meaning of a line of poetry by Rúmí. RB2: 263–4, 283–9.

Lawḥ-i-Sayyáḥ. Tablet to '*Sayyáḥ*' ('Traveller'), Mullá Ádí-Guzal (Mírzá 'Alí), the Báb's courier. In it Bahá'u'lláh stated that he was the 'Ancient Beauty' through whose command the whole of creation came into being; declared that if the peoples of the world wish to hear the voice of God, they should listen to his verses; and warned that this is the day of tests on which the deeds of all human beings will be weighed with justice. RB2: 210–15.

Lawḥ-i-Siráj. Tablet to Mullá 'Alí-Muḥammad-i-Siráj of Iṣfáhán, brother of the Báb's second wife, and a supporter of Ṣubḥ-i-Azal. It announces Bahá'u'lláh's cause; laments Azal's behaviour; and explains why Azal should now be denounced despite his former high religious station. RB2: 262–3, 268–9.

*Lawḥ-i-*SULṬÁN ('Tablet of the King'). Arabic and Persian. To NÁṢIRU'D-DÍN SHÁH.*

Munáját-há-yi-Síyám ('Prayers for Fasting').

Súri-yi-Amr ('Chapter of Command'). *c.* March 1866. Statement of Bahá'u'lláh's status as a divine revealer, read aloud at his order to Ṣubḥ-i-Azal by Mírzá ÁQÁ JÁN, and shortly followed by the 'Most Great Separation', and the split between the Bahá'ís and the Azalis. RB2: 161–5.

Súri-yi-Aṣḥáb ('Chapter of the Companions'). Arabic. Lengthy tablet addressed to Mírzá Áqá Muníb (Munír), '*Ḥabíb*' ('Friend') – Bahá'u'lláh's companion and lantern-bearer on the journey from Baghdad to Istanbul – proclaiming Bahá'u'lláh's status as a divine revealer; warning the Bábís not to reject his claims; and calling upon Muníb to awaken the Bábís to his call. It played a significant role in the subsequent conversion of the majority of the Bábís. RB2: 65, 72–7, 84, 91.

Súri-yi-Damm ('Chapter of Blood'). Arabic. Tablet addressed to NABÍL-I-A'ẒAM, telling him to teach the Bábís in Iran about Bahá'u'lláh, but flee from those who show enmity; and to be resigned and submissive in the face of oppression. RB2: 236–40.

Súri-yi-Ghusn ('*Tablet of the* BRANCH'). Arabic.*

Súri-yi-Ḥajj I & II ('Chapters of Pilgrimage'). Tablets detailing the rites of pilgrimage to the House of the Báb in Shíráz and the House of Bahá'u'lláh in Baghdad. These were sent to Nabíl-i-A'ẓam, who became the first person to perform the rites. RB2: 240.

Súri-yi-'Ibád ('Chapter of the Servants'). Arabic. Tablet for Sayyid Mihdí Dahají, the caretaker of Bahá'u'lláh's house in Baghdad, who subsequently became a prominent Bahá'í teacher, and later a follower of Muḥammad-'Alí. It urges him to live a pious life, detached from the world, his own self and all created things. It recounts the details of Bahá'u'lláh's journey to Edirne and calls upon all the believers to be steadfast and united. RB2: 272–4.

Súri-yi-Mulúk (*Súra of the* KINGS). Arabic. *c.*1867.*

FROM EDIRNE TO AKKA

Súri-yi-Ra'ís ('Chapter of the Chief'). Arabic. 1868. Tablet to Ḥájí Muḥammad-Ismá'íl Káshání, DHABÍḤ, it includes an address to Âli Paşa ('The Chief'). Written on the journey to Gallipoli. See *Tablets of* RA'ÍS.*

THE SYRIAN PERIOD

EARLY AKKA, 1868–73

*Kitáb-i-*AQDAS ('The Most Holy Book'). Arabic. *c.*1873. Bahá'u'lláh's book of laws.*

Lawḥ-i-Aḥbáb ('Tablet of the Friends'). *c.*1870. Arabic. Counsels addressed to the Bahá'ís to be detached from all else but God, and united amongst themselves; to live their lives in accordance with his commandments; and to teach the Faith with wisdom. RB3: 258–9.

Lawḥ-i-Fu'ád. Composed following the death of the Ottoman minister FUAT PAŞA (1869). It rebukes Fuat for the wrongs he had inflicted upon Bahá'u'lláh; states that God had taken his life as a punishment; and predicts the downfall of Âli Paşa and Sultan Abdulaziz. It was addressed to Shaykh Káẓim SAMANDAR. The sultan's downfall (1876) and the fulfilment of the prophecy was instrumental in the conversion of Mírzá ABU'L-FAḌL. RB3: 87–8, 91–2, 99–102.

Lawḥ-i-Haft pursish ('Tablet of the Seven Questions'). Tablet to one of the early Zoroastrian Bahá'ís, Ustád Javán-mard, '*Shír-mard*'. It is written in 'pure' Persian without any Arabic admixture. It includes an appeal to the Zoroastrian priests to investigate Bahá'u'lláh's cause. RB3: 272–3.

Lawḥ-i-Hirtík. AUK. Arabic. Tablet for David Hardegg (Hirtík), the leader of the TEMPLE SOCIETY in Haifa. In it Bahá'u'lláh states that people were kept back from recognizing truth in this day by their own idle imaginings, just as in the days of Christ, when simple fishermen were the first to recognize him, whilst the learned denied him. RB3: 28–31.

Lawḥ-i-Malikih. Arabic. Tablet to Queen VICTORIA.*

Lawḥ-i-Malik-i-Rús. Arabic. Tablet to Tsar ALEXANDER II.*

Lawḥ-i-Mánikchí Ṣáhib. Tablet to the Indian Zoroastrian representative in Iran, Mánikchí. It is written in 'pure' Persian without any Arabic admixture. It invites the people of the world to 'drink' from the 'springs' of his knowledge, and refers to Bahá'u'lláh as the 'All-Knowing Physician' who has his finger on the pulse of mankind. RB3: 270–1.

Lawḥ-i-Nápulyún II. 1869. Arabic. Second tablet to Napoleon III, which predicts his downfall.*

Lawḥ-i-Páp. *c.*1869. Arabic. Tablet to Pope PIUS IX.*

Lawḥ-i-Pisar-'amm ('Tablet of the Cousin'). AkE. Written for Mírzá Ḥasan Mázandarání, a paternal cousin of Bahá'u'lláh who was also a believer. It celebrates the ties of kinship when reinforced by religious faith, and exhorts Ḥasan to good deeds. *RB3*: 216–18.

Lawḥ-i-Qad iḥtaraqa'l-mukhliṣún ('Tablet of "Indeed the hearts of the sincere are consumed..."'). Generally known as 'The Fire Tablet'. *c.*1871. Arabic. Written for Ḥájí Sayyid 'Alí-Akbar Dahají. A dialogue between Bahá'u'lláh, who complains of his sufferings, and God, who comforts and reassures him. Its rhymed verse has a powerful invocatory quality even in English translation. Bahá'u'lláh, *Writings* 697–701; *RB3*: 226–9.

Lawḥ-i-Ra'ís. AkE. Persian. Second of the Tablets of Ra'ís, addressed to Âli Paşa, the Ottoman minister.*

Lawḥ-i-Ru'yá ('Tablet of the Vision'). 1873, AUK. Arabic. Portrays a vision of the Maid of Heaven, and alludes to Bahá'u'lláh's own death. *RB3*: 223–4; Walbridge, *Sacred* 161.

Lawḥ-i-Salmán II. AkE. Another tablet composed for Bahá'u'lláh's messenger, Shaykh Salmán. It counsels resignation to the will of God and acceptance of trials in his path. *RB3*: 25–6.

Lawḥ-i-Ṭibb ('*Tablet of* MEDICINE').*

Súratu'l-Haykal ('Chapter of the Temple'). Arabic. First composed in Edirne, and subsequently revised in Akka (*c.*1869). A symbolic tablet in which Bahá'u'lláh, speaking with the voice of God, addresses Bahá'u'lláh as the promised biblical 'Temple of God', and expresses his sense of identity with God. He also refers to his sufferings at the hands of Azal and his followers, and to the transformative power of divine creation. Bahá'u'lláh ordered this tablet to be copied together with his letters to Pius IX, Napoleon III, Alexander II, Victoria, and Náṣiru'd-dín Sháh in the form of a pentacle symbolizing the 'human temple'. *GPB* 212–13; *PDC* 47–8; *RB3*: 133–7, 140–6; Walbridge, *Sacred* 165–9.

LATE AKKA, MAZRA'IH AND BAHJÍ, 1873–92

Aṣl-i-kullu'l-khayr ('WORDS OF WISDOM').*

BISHÁRÁT ('Glad-tidings').*

ISHRÁQÁT ('Splendours').*

Kalimát-i-Firdawsiyyih ('WORDS OF PARADISE'). *c.*1890.*

Lawḥ-i-Arḍ-i-bá ('Tablet of the Land of "B" [Beirut]'). 1879. Composed on the occasion of 'Abdu'l-Bahá's visit to Beirut, it expresses Bahá'u'lláh's regard for his eldest son 'round Whom all names revolve'. *RB4* 240–1; *TB* 227–8.

*Lawḥ-i-*AQDAS ('The Most Holy Tablet'). Bahá'u'lláh's tablet to the Christians.*

*Lawḥ-i-*BURHÁN ('Tablet of the Proof'). 1879.*

Lawḥ-i-Dunyá ('*Tablet of the* WORLD'). 1891.*

*Lawḥ-i-*ḤIKMAT ('Tablet of Wisdom'). 1873/4.*

Lawḥ-i-Ittiḥád ('Tablet of Unity'). Addressed to Sayyid Asadu'lláh, it describes different forms of unity: the unity of a common faith; unity of speech; unity of deeds; the unity of peoples; and the unity of earthly possession (advocating generosity and self-sacrifice on behalf of others). *RB4* 191–5.

*Lawḥ-i-*MAQṢÚD. Tablet to Maqṣúd.*

Lawḥ-i-Sayyid Mihdí Dahají. A tablet to Sayyid MIHDÍ, by this time one of the most prominent Bahá'í teachers. *RB4* 236–8; *TB* 195–201.*

Lawḥ-i-Times ('Tablet to *The Times*'). 1891. Composed after the killing of the first 'Seven Martyrs of Yazd' (19 May 1891). It includes an address to *The Times* of London (the 'dawning place of news') calling for the paper, and newspapers throughout the world, to concern themselves with the plight of the persecuted Bahá'ís in Iran. RB4 348–50.

Lawḥ-i-Karmil ('*Tablet of* CARMEL'). 1891.*

Lawḥ-i-Ibn-i-dhi'b ('EPISTLE TO THE SON OF THE WOLF'). 1891/2.*

*Súri-yi-*VAFÁ. Tablet in honour of Shaykh Muḥammad-Ḥusayn, '*Vafá*'.*

TAJALLÍYÁT ('Effulgences'). *c*.1885/6.*

ṬARÁZÁT ('Ornaments'). *c*.1889.*

Bahiyyih Khánum (1846–1932)

Eldest daughter of Bahá'u'lláh by his first wife, NAVVÁB, and 'Abdu'l-Bahá's full sister. She was devoted to Bahá'u'lláh, 'Abdu'l-Bahá and Shoghi Effendi, and on several occasions acted as head of the Faith. She was only six or seven years old when her father was imprisoned in the SÍYÁH-CHÁL in 1852, and thereafter shared the poverty, exile and sufferings of Bahá'u'lláh's family. Dedicated to serving her father, she renounced the idea of marriage. In Akka (1868–1909/10) she managed the affairs of the household; attended to her father's daily needs; and cultivated social relationships with the wives of local notables and officials which might shield her father and brother. In the aftermath of Bahá'u'lláh's passing she led the minority of family members who supported 'Abdu'l-Bahá against the 'machinations' of MUḤAMMAD-'ALÍ and his associates. With the end of the government's restrictions on the family (1908) – though already in poor health – she received the increasing number of Bahá'í pilgrims from both East and West, and during 'Abdu'l-Bahá's Western tours (1911–13) she assumed management of Bahá'í affairs in the Holy Land. During World War I (1914–18) she superintended with her brother the distribution of considerable amounts of food, clothing and medical aid to a local population suffering both from maladministration and potential starvation. After 'Abdu'l-Bahá's death (1921) she supported and advised the youthful Shoghi Effendi during the early years of his guardianship, and during his several prolonged absences from Haifa acted as head of the Faith. In the late 1920s her health suffered further decline. She died at the age of eighty-six, one hour after midnight on 15 July 1932, from respiratory failure, and was buried on Mount Carmel near the joint shrine of the Báb and 'Abdu'l-Bahá (*see* HAIFA). Her funeral was massively attended by the general public, and was reminiscent of that of 'Abdu'l-Bahá in the prestige and religious diversity of the mourners.

Bahiyyih Khánum with Shoghi Effendi before he left to study in England

Shoghi Effendi was devastated by her death, recalling her resignation, serenity, cheerfulness and love for all, and praying that she would intercede for him and for 'the toiling masses of thy ardent lovers'. He quickly had constructed a domed, pillared, Carrara marble monument to mark her grave, this later coming to mark the focal centre for the administrative buildings of the 'ARC'. He praised her heavenly qualities, describing her as a 'pure angelic soul', and attributed to her the power of intercession for all humankind: she was in direct communion with God, and watched over the Bahá'ís and sent them her blessings. For their part, Bahá'ís should take her as a model of how they should live a spiritual life of self-abnegation and service. He compared her station to that of the heroines of previous religions: Sarah, wife of Abraham; Ásíya, the wife of Pharaoh who sought to intercede for Moses; the Virgin Mary; Fáṭima, the daughter of Muḥammad and wife of the Imám 'Alí; and the Bábí leader ṬÁHIRIH. *BA 187–96; GPB 347; UHJRD, Bahíyyih Khánum.*

Bahjí (Ar., 'Delight')

Mansion north of Akka occupied by Bahá'u'lláh from September 1879 until his death in 1892. The present structure was built by 'Údí Khammár, the Christian merchant whose house in AKKA had earlier been occupied by Bahá'u'lláh, and was completed in 1870. It was here that Bahá'u'lláh wrote most of his later writings, and also received the English orientalist E.G. BROWNE. When Bahá'u'lláh died he was interred in a room in one of the surrounding buildings occupied by his daughter Furúghiyyih Khánum and her husband, Sayyid 'Alí Afnán. That room became the Shrine of Bahá'u'lláh, and is regarded by Bahá'ís as the most sacred place on earth. It is the *QIBLAH* to which Bahá'ís turn in prayer.

Many members of Bahá'u'lláh's family had lived with him at Bahjí, in the mansion itself or in a number of smaller buildings surrounding it. 'Abdu'l-Bahá and his family had continued to live in Akka. After Bahá'u'lláh's passing a complex situation developed, in which 'Abdu'l-Bahá was the majority (two-thirds) owner of the mansion, but the actual occupants were his half-brothers, headed by MUḤAMMAD-'ALÍ, together with their families and supporters. Given the increasingly open animosity displayed by this group towards 'Abdu'l-Bahá (*see* COVENANT-BREAKERS), visits to the Shrine of Bahá'u'lláh subsequently became fraught, 'Abdu'l-Bahá obtaining a small 'tea-house' in the vicinity so that he could visit his father's Shrine in greater serenity. He also rented an adjoining building to serve as a pilgrim house. A Bahá'í loyal to 'Abdu'l-Bahá was appointed caretaker of the Shrine itself. After 'Abdu'l-Bahá's death Muḥammad-'Alí made legal claim to become the custodian of the Shrine, forcing the issue by having the keys seized (30 January 1922). The British authorities then intervened and retained the keys until February 1923 when they decided the case in Shoghi Effendi's favour. Thenceforth the Shrine remained in uncontested Bahá'í possession. The mansion meanwhile was falling into increasing disrepair, until Muḥammad-'Alí was finally forced to abandon it in November 1929. Shoghi Effendi straightaway began to have the building restored, furnishing it as a Bahá'í museum and place of pilgrimage (by 1932). Complete ownership of the building was only secured in 1957, however.

THE GARDENS

With possession of the mansion, Shoghi Effendi began to beautify the small amount of land that by then still remained with the building. In 1952 he was able to acquire more land (over 145,000 sq.m.) and to begin an extensive project to surround the Shrine and

Aerial view showing the complex of buildings at Bahjí.

The interior of Bahá'u'lláh's room at Bahjí

mansion with ornamental gardens, personally supervising the construction of the *Ḥaram-i-Aqdas* (the Most Holy Precincts or Sanctuary), comprising the north-western quadrant next to the Shrine itself. He was also able to appropriate and begin the demolition of houses adjoining the mansion which had been occupied by Covenant-breakers. The last of these, a large two-storey structure immediately to the north of the mansion, was demolished shortly after his death, this action being regarded as a final 'cleansing' of the site. The material from these demolitions was used to construct terraces within the gardens. Further land acquisitions have been made by the Universal House of Justice, and the remaining three quadrants completed. Ruhe 105–22; Rabbani, *Priceless Pearl*, 53–4, 71, 231–4; Giachery 123–47.

Baker, Dorothy B. (1898–1954)

American HAND OF THE CAUSE of New England Protestant background. Her paternal grandmother, 'Mother (Ellen Tuller) Beecher', was a well-known early American Bahá'í. Dorothy became active as a Bahá'í public speaker during the 1930s, and became heavily involved in local and national Bahá'í administration. In 1937 she was elected on to the American national spiritual assembly. She also wrote Bahá'í pamphlets and radio scripts. During the 1940s she travelled extensively in Latin America and Europe to promote the Faith. She was appointed a Hand of the Cause by Shoghi Effendi in December 1951. She died in an air crash in January 1954. *BW12*: 670–4; Freeman; Harper 191–201.

Baker, Richard St. Barbe (1889–1982)

English environmentalist and pioneer of 'social forestry'. Concerned with the problems of deforestation in colonial Kenya, he appealed for help from the Kikuyu people and in 1922 established

Richard St. Barbe Baker, pioneer social forester

with them an organization to protect the trees. This subsequently became an international organization ('The Men of the Trees', later the International Tree Foundation. HRH the Prince of Wales is the foundation's patron), and Baker became involved in conservation and reforestation projects in various parts of the world. He was also a prolific author. He became a Bahá'í in London around 1924. Shoghi Effendi became the first life member of the Men of the Trees. *BW18*: 802–5. (*See also* ENVIRONMENT.)

Balyuzi, Hasan M. (1908–1980)

Iranian-born HAND OF THE CAUSE and leading Bahá'í scholar who spent most of his life in Britain. His father was governor of the Persian Gulf ports and later Iranian minister of the interior. Although a descendant of the Báb's family on both sides of his family (i.e. an AFNÁN), the young Balyuzi remained a Muslim until he met Shoghi Effendi in 1925 and became a devoted Bahá'í. In 1932 he proceeded to Britain to study for a Master's degree in diplomatic history at the London School of Economics. His hopes of completing a doctorate were dashed by the onset of

Hasan M. Balyuzi, Iranian–British Bahá'í scholar and Hand of the Cause, c. 1951

World War II, and he subsequently became a senior member of the BBC's newly established Persian section.

Balyuzi's arrival in Britain contributed towards a revival in Bahá'í activities there, and he was elected on to the national spiritual ASSEMBLY in 1933 – he was only twenty-four – remaining on that body until ill-health forced his retirement in 1960. He was appointed a Hand of the Cause by Shoghi Effendi in October 1957, and acted as one of the translators at the Conclaves of the Hands. Increasingly, health problems prevented him from travelling to visit the Bahá'ís and he turned to scholarly research (*see* BÁBÍ AND BAHÁ'Í STUDIES). A string of books followed: detailed studies of the lives of the central figures of the Faith – on *'Abdu'l-Bahá* (1971), *The Báb* (1973), and *Bahá'u'lláh* (1980); a monograph, *Edward Granville Browne and the Bahá'í Faith* (1970); and a study of Islam, *Muḥammad and the Course of Islam* (1976). Two further books were published posthumously: *Khadíjih Bagum* (1981), and *Eminent Bahá'ís in the Time of Bahá'u'lláh* (1985). *BW18*: 635–51; Harper 411–25; Momen, 'Hasan M. Balyuzi'.

Banani, Musa (1886–1971)

Iranian HAND OF THE CAUSE of Jewish background. He became a Bahá'í in 1913. In 1951, accompanied by his wife, daughter and her family, he became a Bahá'í PIONEER in Uganda. Shoghi Effendi referred to him as the 'spiritual conqueror' of Africa, and appointed him as a Hand of the Cause in February 1952. He oversaw many of the subsequent developments of the Faith in Uganda, and also did much to coordinate activities in the continent as a whole. *BW15*: 421–3; Harper 339–48.

baptism

Christian practice. 'Abdu'l-Bahá regarded (adult) baptism as having been a physical symbol of purification from SIN. The true 'baptism' was spiritual, and required genuine REPENTANCE. The practice had now become little more than a cultural trait, and was not followed by Bahá'ís (or Muslims). Infant baptism was an empty ceremony which entailed no spiritual benefit for the child, i.e. of itself it led neither to religious faith nor spiritual awakening. *SAQ* 91–6.

Bárfurúsh

(Bábul; 1868 pop. est. 10,000)

Town in the northern Iranian province of Mázandarán, close to the Caspian Sea. It was the birthplace of QUDDÚS and his place of martyrdom. The shrine of Shaykh ṬABARSÍ is nearby.

Bárfurúshí, Mullá Muḥammad-'Alí

See QUDDÚS.

Basṭámí, Mullá 'Alí

See 'ALÍ BASṬÁMÍ.

Bausani, Alessandro (1921–88)

Prominent Italian academic and Bahá'í. He had wide-ranging scholarly interests in the fields of linguistics, Islamic studies and comparative religion. Academic positions included professor of Persian language and literature at the Oriental Institute in Naples (1956–71) and of Islamic Studies at the University of Rome (1971–88). He became a Bahá'í in 1950 and served on the Italo-Swiss and Italian national spiritual ASSEMBLIES for most of the period from 1953 to 1984. His publications include *Persia Religiosa: Da Zaratustra a Bahá'u'lláh* (Milan, 1959), one of the few studies to treat the Bahá'í Faith as an important and integral part of Iranian religious history.

Bayán

(Ar., 'Exposition', 'Explanation')

Title of two works of the Báb, a longer one in Persian written whilst he was a prisoner in MÁKÚ (1847–8), and a shorter one in Arabic from the same period. Both books were left incomplete: they were envisaged as consisting of nineteen 'unities' (*váḥids*), each of nineteen chapters (i.e. 19 × 19 = 361), this having numerological significance (*see* NUMBERS), but stop in their ninth and eleventh 'unity' respectively, the Báb leaving their completion to the prophetic figure HE WHOM GOD SHALL MAKE MANIFEST (*Man-yuẓhiruhu'lláh*; Bahá'ís regard Bahá'u'lláh's *Kitáb-i-Í*QÁN as the completion). The major contents of the book are the elements of Bábí religious LAW; discussion of various religious concepts; and glorification of the expected *Man-yuẓhiruhu'lláh*. Shoghi Effendi regarded it primarily as 'a eulogy of the Promised One', which had at the same time abrogated the laws of Islam; proclaimed the advent of the Day (of RESURRECTION); and prophesied the future rise of the Bahá'í WORLD ORDER (*GPB* 24–6). There are French translations of both works (by Nicolas), and an abstract and index of the *Persian Bayán* by Browne (*Selections* 316–406; *Kitáb-i-Nuqṭatu'l-Káf* liv–xcv). English translations of selected extracts are in Báb, *Selections* 77–113. *ARR* 409–10; Browne, *Selections* 224–39; *McS* 83–5; *SBBR* 34–5; Wilson, 'Bayan'.

begging

Bahá'u'lláh forbade begging, referring to beggars as the most despised of men in God's sight.

In what appears to be a reference to a future more ideal society, it was also forbidden to give to beggars (certainly, 'Abdu'l-Bahá gave food to beggars in Akka in the absence of any effective poor relief (*AB* 351)). The Bahá'í view is that everyone should work for a living and that it is wrong to waste one's time in idleness and sloth. Those who are unable to work or in dire poverty should be given adequate provision by the relevant authorities (the HOUSES OF JUSTICE) and by the rich. Ideally, it is believed, mendicancy should be totally abolished in the future. *KA* 30 k13, 72 k147, 192–3 n56, 235 n162; *LG* 120; *TB* 26. (*See also* CHARITY; ECONOMIC TEACHINGS; WORK.)

Benke, (George) Adam

(1878–1932)

Prominent European Bahá'í. Born into a German-speaking family in Russia, he migrated to Germany with his wife at the end of World War I. There they became Bahá'ís. During 1931 and 1932 Benke was energetically involved in promoting the Faith in Bulgaria, particularly amongst Esperantists. He died unexpectedly whilst still in Bulgaria, and Shoghi Effendi subsequently accorded him the spiritual status of being the first European martyr for the Faith in recognition of his dedication (*see also* MARTYRDOM). *BW5*: 416–18.

Bible

Collection of Jewish and Christian scriptures. Bahá'ís regard the Bible as a holy book 'in substance', recognizing that not every word is necessarily the authentic sayings of the Prophets, and believing that some sections – such as the Genesis creation account – are to be taken figuratively rather than literally (*LG* 494 nos. 1658–60; *see* INTERPRETATION). 'Abdu'l-Bahá described it as celestially inspired; the mystery and light of God's kingdom; the sign of his guidance; the book of salvation; and a divine bounty (*AB* 145). Because they embody the teachings of MOSES and JESUS respectively, the Torah (Pentateuch) and Gospels are regarded as the WORD OF GOD. Reference to competent Bible scholars should be made for further understanding. For a discussion of the Bible from a Bahá'í perspective, see the works of Michael Sours. (*See also* CHRISTIANITY; JUDAISM.)

Bahá'u'lláh's evident knowledge of the Bible (as indicated in such works as the *Kitáb-i-Íqán*) is highly unusual in a 19th-century Muslim context. He also evidenced sympathy for Christianity in general, and rejected the common Muslim belief that the Jews and Christians had perverted their scriptures so as to expunge prophetic references to Muḥammad: those who loved their sacred writings would not knowingly mutilate them. RELIGIOUS LEADERS (such as those rabbis who opposed Muḥammad) would interpret their scriptures according to their own prejudices, however, and it was this that was referred to in the relevant Quranic verses (*KI* 54–58).

birth control

For Bahá'ís the primary purpose of MARRIAGE is the procreation of children. Thus whilst Bahá'í couples may use contraception (or abstain from sex) to limit the total number of children they have, they should not use it to avoid having children completely, unless for medical reasons. Birth-control methods involving the ABORTION of the fertilized egg or the permanent sterilization of either partner are not permitted, again unless for medical reasons (e.g. a threat to the mother's health; the risk of severe genetic defects). In such matters, couples should make their own judgement on the basis of the Bahá'í teachings and competent medical advice. *LG* 344–9, nos. 1155–70.

Bishárát (Pers., '*Glad-Tidings*')

Persian tablet of Bahá'u'lláh revealed at Bahjí. It is also called the *Tablet of the Call* (*Lawḥ-i-Nidá*). In it Bahá'u'lláh announces fifteen 'glad-tidings'. These comprise:

(1) The abolition of various Islamic and Bábí laws and practices: of HOLY WAR (no. 1); of restrictions on association between believers and those of other religions (no. 2); of how they should DRESS and wear their hair (no. 7); and what subjects they might study (no. 11; *See also* KNOWLEDGE); of the (Bábí) law regarding the destruction of books (no. 10); of the Shí'í encouragement to make special journeys to visit the graves of the dead (other than formal PILGRIMAGE) (no. 14).

(2) Instructions to Bahá'ís regarding their relations to secular powers: Bahá'ís should love and serve any king who protects their community (no. 4); wherever they reside, they should be loyal, honest and truthful in their behaviour towards the government (no. 5).

(3) The statement that the government of human affairs was entrusted to the (Universal) House of Justice, whilst acts of worship were to be observed according to the God's book (i.e. the AQDAS) (no. 13).

(4) Instructions to the world's rulers: - that they choose a single LANGUAGE and script to be taught universally to all schoolchildren (no. 3); conversion of weapons of war into instruments of reconstruction (no. 5); the

establishment of the Lesser PEACE (no. 6); that the ideal form of government was a combination of republicanism with kingship (i.e. as in a constitutional monarchy) (no. 15); that they enforce holy LAW (*TB* 29).

(5) Various injunctions: to associate with the followers of other religions 'in a spirit of friendliness and fellowship' (no. 2; *see also* TOLERANCE); that all the peoples of the world should aid Bahá'u'lláh's Cause (no. 5); that Christian monks and priests should abandon seclusion and live in the 'open world', working, marrying and having children (no. 8); that CONFESSION OF SINS should be made to God, and not to other people (no. 9); that every person should have an occupation, their WORK being a form of worship; and the condemnation of idleness and BEGGING (no. 12). *RB4* 160–7; *TB* 19–29.

Black Standard

Islamic messianic symbol. The Prophet Muḥammad is reported to have said that one of the signs of the advent of the MAHDÍ would be 'Black Standards' proceeding from the north-eastern Iranian province of Khurásán. In accordance with this prophecy, and at the Báb's instructions, Mullá ḤUSAYN BUSHRÚ'Í left Mashhad with his followers and raised a Black Standard for his proclamatory westward journey (21 July 1848). It flew over the Bábí 'fortress' at ṬABARSÍ. Nabil 325, 351.

Blomfield, Lady Sara Louisa
(1859–1939)

Prominent British Bahá'í, named Sitárih ('star') Khánum by 'Abdu'l-Bahá. Of mixed Catholic–Protestant Irish background, she became part of London high society, marrying the architect Sir Arthur William Blomfield, a son of the bishop of London. After her husband's death in 1899 she became increasingly interested in movements such as Theosophy, and in 1907 encountered the Bahá'ís in Paris. Her home (97 Cadogan Gardens) was 'Abdu'l-Bahá's base during his visits to Britain (1911, 1912–13). She and her daughters also attended 'Abdu'l-Bahá in Paris and published their notes on his talks (*Talks by Abdul Baha Given In Paris*, 1912; later retitled *Paris Talks*). After World War I she became involved in the work of the Save the Children Fund and sought to promote the Bahá'í teachings within League of Nations circles. She accompanied Shoghi Effendi back to Haifa after 'Abdu'l-Bahá's death and wrote with him the memorial booklet *The Passing of 'Abdu'l-Bahá* (1922). She was amongst the group of prominent Western Bahá'ís who consulted with Shoghi Effendi about the future progress of the Faith in 1922, and was subsequently involved with the development of the Bahá'í administration in Britain. During lengthy stays in Haifa she gathered notes on Bahá'í history – many of them from the sister, wife and one of the daughters

Lady Sara Louisa Blomfield, prominent early British Bahá'í

of 'Abdu'l-Bahá. These were subsequently published as *The Chosen Highway* (1940). BW8: 651–6; WEBW 101–10.

Bourgeois, Jean-Baptiste Louis (1856–1930)

French-Canadian designer of the Wilmette House of Worship (*Mashriqu'l-Adhkár*). Born in rural Quebec, he left Canada following the death of his first wife. He later established himself as an architect-designer in the United States, working in various cities. He and his second wife, Alice (daughter of the painter Paul deLongpre), encountered Bahá'ís in the early 1900s. His basic design for Wilmette was accepted in 1920 by the Bahai Temple Unity, and he continued to work on detailed drawings for the building during the years before his death. The artist's studio he had constructed close to the site of the future Temple later became the residence of the secretary of the American national spiritual assembly.

Branch, Tablet of the (Ar.: *Súri-yi-Ghuṣn*)

Arabic tablet of Bahá'u'lláh composed during the Edirne period (1864–8). It is addressed to Mírzá 'Alí-Riḍá Mustawfí, *Mustasháru'd-dawlih* (*EB* 52–5), and concerns the station of 'Abdu'l-Bahá, identified only as the 'Branch' (*ghuṣn*, pl. Aghṣán), and then in his twenties. This was 'the branch of command' which encompassed all existence. The people should seek its shelter and taste the fruits of its knowledge and wisdom. Those who did not would perish. Bahá'ís were bidden to teach their religion and avoid disputation and corruption. The tablet is regarded as an important textual source for the Covenant doctrine, and several English translations were made during the early years of the century. Shoghi Effendi was dissatisfied with the available translation, regarding it as doctrinally misleading, and making his own translations of certain passages (*WOB* 135, 137). RB2: 388–9. The text of the earlier translation is available in *Covenant of Bahá'u'lláh* 49–53 and Forghani 159–62.

Brauns, Artur (d. 1925) and Marta (1888–1948)

Prominent German Bahá'ís. Artur was a doctor, and was seemingly honoured by Shoghi Effendi as one of the Disciples of 'Abdu'l-Bahá. Marta was Swiss by birth (the daughter of August Forel) and, after her husband's early death in a canoeing accident, became a major promoter of the Faith as well as of various social causes in Germany. BW11: 481–3.

Breakwell, Thomas (*c.*1872–1902)

Young Englishman who became a Bahá'í in Paris in 1901. His fervour and detachment attracted much admiration from other Bahá'ís, including 'Abdu'l-Bahá, who composed a eulogy in his honour following his early death. Shoghi Effendi later referred to him as a 'luminary' of the Faith. AB 74–80; WEBW 65–72.

Brittingham, Isabella D. (1852–1924)

Prominent early American Bahá'í. She became a Bahá'í in 1898 in New York, and soon became one of the most energetic teachers of the Faith, lecturing extensively in many cities. She also wrote one of the most popular early introductory books, *The Revelation of Bahä-ulläh in a Sequence of Four Lessons* (1902). Shoghi Effendi honoured her as one of the Disciples of 'Abdu'l-Bahá. WEBW 131–8.

Browne, Edward Granville (1862–1926)

English orientalist who wrote extensively on the Bábí and Bahá'í religions.

He was Sir Thomas Adam's Professor of Arabic at the University of Cambridge from 1902, and is well known for his pioneering work on Persian literature and his support for the Iranian Constitutional Revolution of 1905–9. He first made contact with Bahá'ís and Azalis during his visit to Iran in 1887–8 (his experiences are described in *A Year Amongst the Persians* (1893)), and in 1890 visited both Ṣubḥ-i-Azal in Cyprus and Bahá'u'lláh at Bahjí (his well-known description of his first meeting with Bahá'u'lláh is in *TN* xxxix–xli). He collected a large number of manuscripts, publishing some and providing summaries of others. His major publications in this area were: (1) text and translation of 'Abdu'l-Bahá's TRAVELLER'S NARRATIVE, together with extensive notes (1891); (2) translation of *The Táríkh-i-Jadíd or New History of Mírzá 'Alí Muḥammad the Báb*, again with extensive notes (1893); (3) Persian text of the *Kitáb-i-Nuqṭatu'l-Káf*, together with a lengthy introduction in English (the Persian introduction was almost certainly not by him) (1910); (4) *Materials for the Study of the Bábí Religion* (1918). Other published materials relating to the Faith are in Browne, *Selections*. His position on the Bahá'í–Azali split is the subject of considerable controversy. *EGBBF; MBBR* 29–36. (*See also* BÁBÍ AND BAHÁ'Í STUDIES.)

E. G. Browne as a young man in Persian costume

Buddhism

Both 'Abdu'l-Bahá and Shoghi Effendi referred to Buddhism, and included the Buddha in the succession of MANIFESTATIONS OF GOD. Buddhism was regarded as one of nine known revealed religions, and its scriptures as predictive of Bahá'u'lláh (identified as the messianic 'Fifth Buddha' Maitreya). Much of the original teachings of the Buddha had been lost, however, and the authenticity of the present Buddhist canon of scripture was regarded as uncertain. Not all present-day Buddhist beliefs and practices were necessarily in accord with the Buddha's teachings (*CC1*: 15–23).

Interest in Buddhism amongst Bahá'ís has increased in recent years, and there are a growing number of Bahá'ís of Buddhist background. Given the very different religious concepts characteristic of Buddhism and the Semitic tradition (of which Bahá'í forms a part: *see* RELIGION), the inclusion of Buddhism in the list of Bahá'í revealed religions poses questions for Bahá'í religious scholarship. Two quite different responses to these questions are offered by Jamshed Fozdar (*The God of Buddha*; *Buddha Maitrya-Amitabha has Appeared*) and Moojan Momen (*Buddhism and the Bahá'í Faith*), with Fozdar seeking to establish the reality in Buddhist terms of an unknowable reality equivalent to the concept of God and presenting the Bahá'í Faith as the prophetic fulfilment of Buddhism, whilst Momen details the considerable similarities of ethical teachings between Theravadan Buddhism and Bahá'í, and argues that metaphysical differences between the two reflect culture-bound terminologies. He notes also that both religions emphasize religious practice and regard many metaphysical issues as being unknowable.

Burhán, Lawḥ-i-

(PA, *Tablet of the Proof*)

A tablet of Bahá'u'lláh composed in 1879 shortly after the execution of the King and Beloved of Martyrs. It is addressed to Shaykh Muḥammad-Báqir – stigmatized by Bahá'u'lláh as the Wolf (*Dhi'b*) – one of the two Iṣfáhání clerics responsible for the deaths. Bahá'u'lláh rebukes him for his tyranny and injustice, and compares him to those Jewish leaders who were responsible for the crucifixion of Christ, but assures him that he neither fears his cruelty nor hates him for his falsity and folly. He was like one of 'the last traces of sunlight upon the mountain-top', and would soon fade away. He and those like him had subverted Islam. Nevertheless, repentance would evoke divine forgiveness. The second cleric involved in the executions – and the prime mover – Mírzá Muḥammad-Ḥusayn, is referred to as the She-Serpent (*Raqshá*), who had stung the children of the Prophet (The martyrs were both *sayyids*). He had acted out of a desire for material gain, but his possessions would not avail him: he would shortly encounter divine chastisement and his fire would be quenched (*TB* 203–16; *RB4*: 91–102). Muḥammad-Ḥusayn's subsequent disgrace and awful death are regarded by Bahá'ís as vivid fulfilment of the prophecy.

burial

Bahá'ís bury their dead, regarding this as being in accord with the natural process of decomposition. Cremation, by contrast, is seen as unnatural. Bahá'í law stipulates that burial should not be at a place more than one hour's journey from the place of death (a contrast with the 19th-century Shí'í practice of transporting bodies for burial at distant shrines), and should be preceded by the recitation of a specific prayer. Other provisions – which at present are only widely practised by Middle Eastern Bahá'ís – include first washing the corpse and shrouding it in silk or cotton cloth; placing a ring on its finger, with a specially inscribed verse ('I came forth from God, and return unto Him, detached from all save Him, holding fast to His name, the Merciful, the Compassionate'); using a coffin of durable wood, stone, or crystal (so as to show respect for the body as the former 'temple of the spirit'); and burying the body with its feet facing towards the Bahá'í *Qiblah* (i.e. Bahjí). The special prayer and the placement of the ring are applicable only if the deceased has reached the age of maturity (i.e. fifteen). Several of these provisions follow Bábí law. Additionally, the body should be buried as soon as possible after death; it should not be embalmed; ideally, it should not be buried at sea. Bodies can be left for medical research, as long as it is stipulated that they will eventually be buried. The bodies of foetuses should also be treated with respect. Bahá'ís should not let burials become ritualistic; they should pray for the dead; and state in their Wills that they wish to be buried according to Bahá'í law. The Bahá'í form of burial can be followed for non-Bahá'ís if their families so wish, and non-Bahá'ís can be buried in Bahá'í cemeteries. *CC1*: 9–13; *KA* 64–6 k128–30, 101–2, 111–12 q16, 123 q56, 127 q70, 228–30 n149, 151–2; *LG* 194–202; *McR* 31–2, 60–1; Walbridge, *Sacred* 77–82. (*See also* DEATH.)

Búshihr (Bushire; 1868 pop. est. 18,000)

Southern Iranian port on the Persian Gulf. The Báb began his merchant career there, and it was his port of embarkation and return when he made the pilgrimage to Mecca.

Bushrú'í, Mullá Ḥusayn

See ḤUSAYN BUSHRÚ'Í, MULLÁ.

business and professional organizations

In recent years an increasing number of Bahá'í-based business and professional organizations have been formed. One of the best known is the European Bahá'í Business Forum (established in 1990), which provides a forum for the discussion of Bahá'í approaches to business matters; holds seminars on raising the standards of business ethics; and has established contacts with educational centres in several countries, including Albania, Bulgaria and Rumania. Other associations have been established in Australia and Hong Kong (*BWNS* 1994–5: 124). There are a number of organizations for Bahá'ís involved in medicine and health care (*see* HEALTH AND HEALING).

Buzurg, Mírzá

See 'ABBÁS NÚRÍ.

C

calamity

Bahá'u'lláh referred to 'an unforeseen calamity' and 'grievous retribution' which would befall 'the peoples of the world' (*HWp* no. 63), and to calamities and commotions which would afflict the world as a consequence of its failure to heed the divine summons (*TB* 166). At 'the appointed hour' there would 'suddenly appear' that which would 'cause the limbs of mankind to quake', after which 'the Divine Standard' would be unfurled (*GWB* 118 no. lxi). God's 'wrathful anger' would 'cleanse the earth' from the defilement of those who had corrupted it, and give it to those who were 'nigh unto Him' (*ADJ* 68–9). These apocalyptic prophecies were combined with a millennial vision of a future 'the Most Great PEACE'. Shoghi Effendi reiterated these warnings, and placed them in the context of what he saw as a titanic spiritual struggle between the forces of construction and disintegration, in part connected to the rise of the Faith and OPPOSITION to it. Outworn institutions incompatible with the new age were being swept away. The promised new WORLD ORDER was likely only to be attained through 'a period of intense turmoil and wide-spread suffering'. SECULARISM, increasingly prevalent in the world, eroded both the power of established religions and the basis for social morality. Economic problems, wars and international instability threatened the world, but also underlined the need for the principle of collective security outlined by Bahá'u'lláh and 'Abdu'l-Bahá (*ADJ* 6809; *WOB* 161–2, 170–1, 180–91). Speculation as to the nature and timing of the expected calamity has periodically become a focus of popular Bahá'í concern. Shoghi Effendi and the Universal House of Justice have called upon Bahá'ís not to dwell on such issues, however, nor to despair in the face of the world's sufferings. They should rather increase their efforts to spread their religion and exemplify the love and unity that it inculcated. The main cause of SUFFERING at the societal level was the corruption of human morals, and this could only be rectified by the spiritual rejuvenation of humanity which the Bahá'í were trying to accomplish. *LG* 126–37; *MUHJ* 153–4 no. 73, 281 no. 149, 282–3 no. 151, 434–5 no. 246.2–4, 451–2 no. 252. (*See also* MILLENARIANISM.)

calendar

The Báb established a new '*Badí*'' (wondrous) calendar, which Bahá'u'lláh subsequently amended slightly as the form of a distinctive Bahá'í calendar. Beginning on the ancient Iranian new year (*NAW-RÚZ*) at the spring equinox – normally 21 March – the year is divided into nineteen months of nineteen days,

The Bahá'í calendar

The names of the months are as follows, together with their English equivalents and first days:

1.	*Bahá*	Splendour	21 March
2.	*Jalál*	Glory	9 April
3.	*Jamál*	Beauty	28 April
4.	*'Aẓamat*	Grandeur	17 May
5.	*Núr*	Light	5 June
6.	*Raḥmat*	Mercy	24 June
7.	*Kalimát*	Words	13 July
8.	*Kamál*	Perfection	1 August
9.	*Asmá'*	Names	20 August
10.	*'Izzat*	Might	8 September
11.	*Mashíyyat*	Will	27 September
12.	*'Ilm*	Knowledge	16 October
13.	*Qudrat*	Power	4 November
14.	*Qawl*	Speech	23 November
15.	*Masá'il*	Questions	12 December
16.	*Sharaf*	Honour	31 December
17.	*Sulṭán*	Sovereignty	19 January
18.	*Mulk*	Dominion	7 February
19.	*'Alá'*	Loftiness	2 March

The nineteen day feast is usually held on the first day of each month.

Days are named both as days of the week and as days of the month. In this latter case the days are named in the same way as the months (e.g. the fourteenth day of the month is *Qawl*). The weekday names are:

1.	*Jalál*	Glory	Saturday
2.	*Jamál*	Beauty	Sunday
3.	*Kamál*	Perfection	Monday
4.	*Fiḍál*	Grace	Tuesday
5.	*'Idál*	Justice	Wednesday
6.	*Istijlál*	Majesty	Thursday
7.	*Istiqlál*	Independence	Friday

The day begins at sunset (21 April begins at sunset on the previous day). The first day of the week is Saturday (*Jalál*). Friday (*Istiqál*) is the day of rest.

Years are named as follows:

1.	*Alif*	A	11.	*Bahháj*	Delightful
2.	*Bá'*	B	12.	*Javáb*	Answer
3.	*Ab*	Father	13.	*Aḥad*	Single
4.	*Dál*	D	14.	*Vahháb*	Bountiful
5.	*Báb*	Gate	15.	*Vidád*	Affection
6.	*Váv*	V	16.	*Badí'*	Beginning
7.	*Abad*	Eternity	17.	*Bahí*	Luminous
8.	*Jád*	Generosity	18.	*Abhá*	Most luminous
9.	*Bahá*	Splendour	19.	*Váḥid*	Unity
10.	*Ḥubb*	Love			

The name of each year has a numerical value equal to the number of the year (see ABJAD). The cycle of 19 years is called a *váḥid* ('unity' =19), that of 361 years a *kull-i-shay'* ('all things' =361).

with four intercalary days (five in a leap year) being added to make up a full solar year of 365 days (19 × 19 = 361). The months are named after attributes of God. The first year of the calendar is 1844, the year of the Báb's declaration (the *Badí'* year 156 begins at *Naw-Rúz* 1999). The days of the month and week are also named, and the years are grouped into cycles of 19 and 361 (19 × 19) years. At the present time only the monthly divisions are in common use, as these fix the dates of the regular nineteen day FEASTS held in local Bahá'í communities. The *Badí'* year numbers are also sometimes used. The intercalary days (*AYYÁM-I-HÁ*) are placed between the eighteenth and nineteenth months. The last month ('Alá') is the Bahá'í month of FASTING. *KA* 64 k127, 177–8 n26–7; *BW* 18: 598–601; Walbridge, *Sacred* 181–205. Walbridge discusses the significance of the names of the various months, days and years. (*See also* HOLY DAYS.)

caliphate

Islamic institution established after the death of the Prophet Muḥammad. The caliph (*khalífa*) came to be regarded as the viceregent of God and the Prophet. He was 'Commander of the Faithful', i.e. theoretically the leader of all Muslims everywhere. By the 19th century, the title rested with the OTTOMAN rulers. Bahá'ís follow the Shí'í position and consider the rightful successors to Muḥammad to have been the IMÁMS, and the caliphate therefore to have been illegitimate. The abolition of the caliphate by the new Turkish republic (3 March 1924) was regarded by Shoghi Effendi as a 'retributive act' directed against the 'arch-enemy' of the Bahá'í Faith, and as a 'catastrophic fall' of the 'mightiest institution' of Islam, which had 'irretrievably shattered' its unity. *GPB* 228, 407; *PDC* 98–102; *WOB* 178. (*See also* DIVINE JUDGEMENT; SULTANATE.)

calligraphy

In the Iranian cultural tradition calligraphy is highly regarded as an art form, reflecting both the Islamic emphasis on the importance of the word of God and its prohibition of the visual representation of humans and animals. This high regard for calligraphy is also expressed in the Bábí–Iranian Bahá'í tradition. Thus both the Báb and Bahá'u'lláh were famed for the beauty of their handwriting and praised calligraphic skill. There have been a number of eminent Iranian Bahá'ís who were gifted calligraphers, notably MISHKÍN-QALAM.

canonical texts

The most important category of Bahá'í LITERATURE is what we may term the religion's 'canonical texts'. These comprise the writings of the Báb, Bahá'u'lláh, 'Abdu'l-Bahá, Shoghi Effendi and the Universal House of Justice, together with the authenticated talks of 'Abdu'l-Bahá. Of these, the writings of the Báb and Bahá'u'lláh are regarded as divine REVELATION; the writings and talks of 'Abdu'l-Bahá and the writings of Shoghi Effendi as authoritative INTERPRETATION; and those of the Universal House of Justice as authoritative legislation (LAW) and elucidation. In all cases some measure of divine guidance is assumed. The authenticated writings of secretaries written on behalf of the principals are included, in so far as these were either dictated or read and approved by the principal. The terms 'SCRIPTURE' or 'sacred texts' can be applied to the writings of the Báb, Bahá'u'lláh and 'Abdu'l-Bahá. (*See also* 'ABDU'L-BAHÁ, WRITINGS AND TALKS OF; BÁB, WRITINGS OF; BAHÁ'U'LLÁH, WRITINGS OF; SHOGHI EFFENDI, WRITINGS OF.)

NON-AUTHORITATIVE TEXTS

Transcripts of the extempore oral translations of 'Abdu'l-Bahá's talks into Western languages (e.g. *Paris Talks*;

Promulgation of Universal Peace) occupy an ambiguous status: officially they are excluded from the scriptural canon, but are popularly accorded authoritative status by many Bahá'ís. Little work has yet been done to compare these Western transcripts with authenticated texts in the original Persian where these exist. 'PILGRIMS' NOTES' record the memories of individual Bahá'ís of the words spoken by an authoritative leader, particularly 'Abdu'l-Bahá and Shoghi Effendi (i.e. they are the equivalent of the Islamic traditions (*HADÍTH*)). They are not regarded as canonical.

BELIEF AND PRACTICE

The canonical texts have different levels of importance: (1) Those of Bahá'u'lláh, 'Abdu'l-Bahá and Shoghi Effendi are normative for Bahá'í practice and belief; they are sources of law and doctrine. (2) Those of the Báb are important doctrinally, and as a source of inspiration, but they are not binding in terms of practice, the laws of the *BAYÁN* having been superseded by those of the *Kitáb-i-AQDAS*. (3) Those of the House of Justice are concerned with the leadership of the Bahá'í community and the supplementary legislation necessary for a particular time in its development. They are not a source of doctrine.

Carmel, Mount

A range of hills in northern Israel associated with the biblical prophet Elijah (9th century BCE). The main ridge runs some 12 miles inland from the sea at HAIFA and reaches a height of about 1,740 feet. Jews, Christians, Muslims and Druze regard particular places on the mountain as holy places. Bahá'u'lláh visited the mountain during his trips to Haifa, and during a lengthy visit in 1891 pitched his tent on the mountainside, close to the Carmelite monastery at the upper Cave of Elijah. It was here that he revealed the *Tablet of CARMEL*. Shoghi Effendi applies biblical references to the 'mountain of the Lord' and God's 'Vineyard' to Carmel; refers to Bahá'u'lláh as the 'Lord of the Vineyard'; and identifies the Báb as the returned Elijah, his entombment on Carmel (*see* SHRINE OF THE BÁB) thus assuming particular significance. *GPB* 58, 194, 276–7; Ruhe 133–6, 183–8.

Carmel, Tablet of

(PA: *Lawḥ-i-Karmil*)

Short Arabic tablet revealed by Bahá'u'lláh during a visit to Mount CARMEL, almost certainly in 1891. It takes the form of a dialogue between Bahá'u'lláh and the personified mountain, in which Bahá'u'lláh bids Carmel rejoice that God 'hath in this Day established upon thee His throne'. The tablet is exultant in tone, and is regarded as a prophetic foretelling of the building of the SHRINE OF THE BÁB and the establishment of the BAHÁ'Í WORLD CENTRE and of the Universal House of Justice (God's 'Ark'). *TB* 1–5; *RB4*: 351–67; Giachery 209–11; Ruhe 170–2.

'Central Figures'

Term commonly used to refer to the Báb, Bahá'u'lláh and 'Abdu'l-Bahá, and meaning the Centres of the Faith.

Centre for the Study of the Texts

See ARC, BUILDINGS OF.

charity

Bahá'u'lláh praised charity, making it an obligation on the rich to help support those in dire need (*KA* 72 k147; *TB* 71). More generally, Bahá'ís should bring 'good cheer' to the poor and needy during the intercalary days (*AYYÁM-I-HÁ*) (*KA* 25 k16). The future HOUSE OF JUSTICE would be a shelter for the needy (*KA* 37 k48). 'Abdu'l-Bahá engaged in considerable charity, regularly feeding many of the poor of Akka, and on occasion personally nursing some of them. He also distributed money and goods to poor people during his Western tours. During World War I he was able to organize extensive food distribution in the Galilee region which helped avert a famine (*AB* 98–101, 176–8, 196, 239, 351, 418–19, 435, 459). Shoghi Effendi specified that one of the duties of every local Bahá'í ASSEMBLY was to endeavour to help the poor, the sick, the disabled, orphans and widows 'irrespective of color, caste and creed' (*BA* 38), and that in the future the Bahá'í temple complex (*MASHRIQU'L-ADHKÁR*) would afford 'sustenance to the poor', including free schooling and medical services (*KA* 191 n53, *LG* 121 no. 411). For the present, Bahá'ís – at least in countries with numerous governmental and private bodies already assisting the poor – should temper their charitable concerns with the realization that they were the only ones who could contribute to the Bahá'í FUNDS, by means of which the Faith would be enabled to create the spiritual basis for a new social order freed from many of the sufferings and injustices now prevalent in the world. The Universal House of Justice has stressed the value of Bahá'ís entering professions in which they can help other people, and encouraged the initiation of SOCIO-ECONOMIC DEVELOPMENT projects which can alleviate the material and social conditions causing poverty and other social ills. *LG* 120–5. (*See also* ECONOMIC TEACHINGS.)

Chase, (James Brown) Thornton (1847–1912)

One of Ibrahim KHEIRALLA's first group of four students of the Bahá'í teachings (1894), and the only one to remain a Bahá'í after 1900. 'Abdu'l-Bahá named him *Thábit* ('Steadfast'), and accorded him the status of the first American

Thornton Chase, 'the first American Bahá'í'

Bahá'í. He played a key role in the organization of the Chicago Bahá'ís, and was a prominent teacher of the Faith. An insurance salesman, he travelled extensively, visiting Bahá'ís as he went. Through an extensive correspondence he was one of the focal points of the developing American Bahá'í community. He visited 'Abdu'l-Bahá in Akka in 1907, recording his impressions in *In Galilee*. He also wrote a short introduction to the Bahá'í teachings (1909). He died in Los Angeles, 'Abdu'l-Bahá making a special point of visiting his grave. Shoghi Effendi honoured him as one of the DISCIPLES OF 'ABDU'L-BAHÁ. *BFA1*: 33–6, 95; *BFA2*; *GPB* 257; *WEBW* 1–12.

chastity

Bahá'u'lláh called upon his followers to lead chaste and holy lives, escaping from their own 'evil and corrupt desires', so that neither a valley of pure gold nor the most comely of women would distract them from their spiritual path. Those who follow their lusts are of the lost, and dissipate their efforts. Shoghi

Effendi sketched the elements of such a sanctified life: modesty, purity, temperance, decency and clean-mindedness; moderation in dress, language, amusements, and all artistic and literary pursuits; daily vigilance in the control of one's carnal desires; the abandonment of frivolous conduct; and total abstinence from all DRUGS, including ALCOHOL. In the face of the declining standards of a decadent age Bahá'ís should purge themselves and their community from all moral laxity. There can be no compromise: promiscuity, easy familiarity, sexual vices, infidelity in marital relationships, companionate marriage, nudism and the prostitution of art and literature are all to be condemned. At the same time, however, Bahá'ís are to avoid ASCETICISM or an 'excessive and bigoted puritanism': God had created the good things of the world, and these should be enjoyed.

The Universal House of Justice has emphasized the importance of individuals using their own judgement and conscience in following these teachings, and has refused to issue detailed instructions. Individuals should by all means turn for guidance to their parents and the Bahá'í institutions, but what is needed is a prayerful life, oriented towards service to Bahá'u'lláh, and not a set of rigid regulations of behaviour. The present life consists of a series of spiritual struggles and tests, the development of self-control being an important element in character building as well preparing the individual soul for the next life. To become a slave to one's animal impulses brings no lasting happiness. The teachings on chastity are of particular relevance to Bahá'í YOUTH. *ADJ* 24–8; *LG* 358–64. (*See also* ADULTERY; SEX.)

Cheyne, Thomas K. (1841–1915)

Prominent British biblical scholar (Oriel Professor of the Interpretation of Holy Scripture at the University of Oxford, 1885–1908) who became a Bahá'í. 'Abdu'l-Bahá visited him in Oxford in 1912. He was the author of *The Reconciliation of Races and Religions*.

The castle of Chihríq, near the Turkish and Iraqi borders, where the Báb was imprisoned, 1848–50

Chihríq

Fortress in north-western Iran (Azerbaiján), in the region of Urúmiyyih, in which the Báb was imprisoned for two years prior to his execution (April 1848–June 1850). The Báb was transferred to Chihríq from MÁKÚ. The Báb called it the 'Grievous Mountain' (*Jabal-i-shadíd*), to differentiate it from Mákú (the 'Open Mountain'), although the pattern of imprisonment was similar, with initial strictness eventually giving way to comparative freedom, as the warden, Yaḥyá Khán, became devoted to his prisoner. Even more than at Mákú the Báb received large numbers of visitors. Incidents of note during this period include the conversion of DAYYÁN; the popular enthusiasm that greeted the Báb's arrival in Urúmiyyih (including the taking of the water in the public bath after he had used it because the water was thus assumed to have acquired holiness); and the despatch of the Báb's 'Sermon of Wrath' (*Khuṭbi-yi-qahriyyih*) for Ḥájí Mírzá ÁQÁSÍ, following the Tabríz trial (July 1848). *ARR* 380–1; Balyuzi, *Báb* 134–9, 147; *MBBR* 73–4; *McS* 16–17, 88–95; Nabil 301–11.

children

See EDUCATION; FAMILY LIFE.

Chinese religion

Traditional Chinese religion represents a synthesis of elements from Confucianism, Daoism and BUDDHISM. There are very few references in the Bahá'í writings to these traditions: 'Abdu'l-Bahá described Confucius as a blessed soul who had 'renewed morals and ancient virtues', and become 'the cause of civilisation, advancement and prosperity' for the Chinese. Present-day Confucian rites and beliefs were not in accordance with his teachings, however. Shoghi Effendi explicitly excluded Confucius and Lao-tse from the list of MANIFESTATIONS OF GOD recognized by Bahá'ís: Confucius had been a great moral reformer, but not a prophet (*CC1*: 15–16, 20, 21). Parallels between Chinese and Bahá'í beliefs and moral concepts have been examined in a recent book by Phyllis Chew, *The Chinese Religion and the Bahá'í Faith*.

Christ

See JESUS.

Christianity

Bahá'ís regard Christianity as one of the nine known revealed religions and include JESUS in their list of MANIFESTATIONS OF GOD. The divine origin of Christianity and the Gospels (*see* BIBLE), and the divinity and sonship of Jesus Christ, are all acknowledged, as are his immaculate conception (i.e. the belief that Jesus' conception was through the intervention of the Holy Spirit whilst Mary was still a virgin), and the primacy of Peter as 'the Prince of the Apostles' (*PDC* 113–14). Christianity is regarded as the prophetic fulfilment of JUDAISM, and the harbinger of ISLAM. 'Abdu'l-Bahá frequently referred to Christian history in his writings and talks, praising in particular the early Christians. Persecuted outcasts, they had propagated Jesus' cause far and wide. Their nobility of spirit and action had attracted the praise of non-Christian philosophers such as Galen. They had founded hospitals, schools and other philanthropic institutions. Later, however, control over Christian affairs passed into the hands of unenlightened ecclesiastics. These had rejected MUḤAMMAD. During the following centuries Europe languished in its Dark Ages, much of its later civilization being gained from the influence of Islamic civilization by way of Islamic Spain and through its impact on the crusaders. In the 16th century the Protestant Reformation successfully challenged the authority of the pope, in part because Luther's views on various issues were 'demonstrably correct'. In more recent times the dedication of Christian missionaries had led to world-wide conversions and the establishment of schools amongst formerly pagan peoples (*SDC* 41–3, 80–7, 90–4). Christian doctrines and institutions discussed in the Bahá'í writings include BAPTISM, CONFESSION OF SINS; MIRACLES; MONASTICISM; PRIESTHOOD; RESURRECTION. Fazel, ''Abdu'l-Bahá'; Heggie 40–2; *LG* 489–94; *SAQ* 16–17, 83–137.

Bahá'ís believe that the Báb was the spiritual RETURN of John the Baptist, and Bahá'u'lláh Christ returned 'in the glory of the Father' (*GPB* 58, 94), and view the future of Christianity as depending on Christians' response to Bahá'u'lláh's call. In various tablets Bahá'u'lláh addressed Christian leaders – including Pope PIUS IX – calling upon them to hearken to the 'Everlasting Father' and 'King of the Day of Reckoning' who had now come (*PDC* 104–7; *see also Lawḥ-i-AQDAS*). For Shoghi Effendi organized Christianity was now experiencing the impact of this divine summons, beginning with the papacy's loss of temporal power (1870). Christian institutions were being assailed by the forces of SECULARISM, becoming riven by division, watering down their creeds, and losing their hold on human conduct. Numerous obscure cults had emerged, reflecting 'the confused aspirations of the disillusioned masses': a situation similar to that in the Roman empire at the time of the expansion of Christianity. The fratricidal nature of the fighting in Europe during World War II offered yet further proof of the failure of the contemporary Christian churches. *PDC* 107–11; *WOB* 180–6. (*See also* RELIGIOUS LEADERS.)

The first Christian to become a Bahá'í was probably a Syrian doctor named Fáris, resident in Egypt, taught by NABÍL-I-A'ẒAM whilst in prison in Alexandria in 1868. He was probably the recipient of the *Lawḥ-i-AQDAS* (Bahá'u'lláh's 'Tablet to the Christians') (*RB3*: 5–11). The Christian minorities in Iran did not respond to the Bahá'í teachings (unlike the Jews and Zoroastrians), but a number of Levantine Christians became Bahá'ís, including Ibrahim KHEIRALLA, who became the pioneer Bahá'í teacher in the United States (from 1894). Most of the Westerners who initially became Bahá'ís were of Christian background, including some who were deeply knowledgeable in their religion and were able to present the Bahá'í teachings in a 'language' adapted to Christian hearers. Several clergymen also converted. Bahá'í EXPANSION into Latin America, Africa and the Pacific has also involved the conversion of Christians. *SBBR* 83–4, 93–6, 188.

There are a number of secondary works (of very uneven quality) on the relationship between the Bahá'í Faith and Christianity. Those by Bahá'ís include studies by Backwell, Sours and Townshend. Moffett, Riggs and Sears are particularly concerned with Christian prophecy. Stephens presents Bahá'í in relationship to the Latter-day Saints (Mormons).

cinema and film

For Shoghi Effendi any films about Bahá'í history or teachings should be of the highest quality. Acting in and watching movies was permissible, but he deplored the excessive corruption that prevailed in the industry and thus discouraged movie acting as a career (*LG* 99–100). Unlike other areas of the arts, film acting seems to have attracted few Bahá'ís. The 1930s film star Carole Lombard (1908–42) is probably the best known (*BW9*: 635–7).

circumcision

Male circumcision is a requirement of Jewish law, and has become a universal Islamic practice. Many Bahá'ís of Jewish or Muslim background continue the practice, but it is neither encouraged nor forbidden in Bahá'í law.

civilization

For all its benefits, Bahá'ís regard material civilization by itself as insufficient to promote human progress. Only when combined with 'divine civilization' and empowered by the holy spirit will it be the cause of genuine advance. Bahá'u'lláh stated that whatever passed beyond the bounds of MODERATION will cease to exert a beneficial influence. Thus, carried to excess, material civilization – as embodied by the technological advances of the WEST – has become pernicious in its influence, producing terrible weapons of destruction (*GWB* 341–2; *TB* 69, 169). A true and 'ever-advancing' civilization is based on the development of virtues which enhance human dignity (*GWB* 214 no. 109). 'Abdu'l-Bahá emphasized that human success and prosperity depend on the combination of material progress (including wise laws; just government; the promotion of the arts and sciences; discovery; the expansion of trade; the development of industry; and the beautification of the country) with spiritual and moral guidance. By itself, material civilization also gives birth to forces of destruction, and has been conjoined to barbarism (*CC1*: 6 no. 22; *SWAB* 283–5, 303). He also held that moral behaviour and SPIRITUAL QUALITIES have been established amongst peoples in the past as a result of divine teachings, 'even the minutest details of civilized life' deriving from the grace of the PROPHETS of God. Through their influence individuals can put aside their own interests for the sake of the common good (*SDC* 95–7). JUDAISM, CHRISTIANITY, and ISLAM all provide clear examples of the way in which divine revelation has initiated a process that leads to the growth of both spiritual and material civilization. (*See also* *SECRET OF DIVINE CIVILIZATION*.)

cleanliness

Bahá'u'lláh emphasized the importance of extreme cleanliness and refinement (*liṭáfat*), instructing Bahá'ís to bathe regularly (at least once a week) and pare their nails, to wash their feet (daily in summer, every three days in winter), and to endeavour that no trace of dirt be seen on their garments. The water used for bathing and cleaning should be pure, and the fetid water of Iranian public bath houses and courtyard pools should specifically be avoided. Warm water was preferable. Rose-water and other pure perfumes should also be used. Bahá'ís should also try to renew their household furnishings once every nineteen years. 'Abdu'l-Bahá noted that physical cleanliness was conducive to spirituality, and discouraged SMOKING, in part because of its uncleanliness. There is no concept of ritual impurity. *KA* 46–7 k74, k76, 57–8 k106, 74–5 k151–2, 135 q97, 162, 199 n74, 212 n104–5, 222 n131–2, 236–7 n166–7; Walbridge, *Sacred* 63–7. (*See also* PURITY.)

clergy

See PRIESTHOOD.

Collins, Amelia ('Milly') E.
(1873–1962)

American HAND OF THE CAUSE of Lutheran background. She became a Bahá'í in 1919 and was elected onto the American national spiritual ASSEMBLY in 1924, serving on that body for over twenty years. Wealthy as a result of her marriage, she was able to make large donations to various Bahá'í projects, including the Western Pilgrim House in HAIFA, the buildings for the original Geyserville SUMMER SCHOOL in the USA, the superstructure of the SHRINE OF THE BÁB, the land for the future Bahá'í Temple on Mount Carmel, and the INTERNATIONAL ARCHIVES building. She travelled extensively in Latin America and Europe to promote the Faith, and

Amelia Collins, leading American Bahá'í and Hand of the Cause

in January 1951 was appointed as Vice-President of the newly established INTERNATIONAL BAHÁ'Í COUNCIL. Already privately named as a Hand of the Cause in 1947 by Shoghi Effendi, she was publicly appointed to this rank in December 1951. *BW13*: 834–41; Faizi; Harper 202–10.

Commentary on 'I was a Hidden Treasure'

(PA.: *Tafsír-i-Kuntu kanzan makhfíyan*)

Commentary on an Islamic tradition ('I was a hidden treasure and loved to be known. Therefore I created the creation that I might be known') by 'Abdu'l-Bahá, composed in Baghdad at the request of Âli Şevket Paşa ('Alí Shawkat Páshá). It is concerned with various themes related to Islamic mystical philosophy, including the stages of divine love and the unknowability of God. 'Abdu'l-Bahá also addressed the traditional argument between those who believed that archetypal forms were eternal and pre-existed with God and those who believed that they were created. Both viewpoints could be supported by logical argument, and for 'Abdu'l-Bahá the difference between the two rested with the mystical state of their respective proponents rather than the characteristics of what they were trying to describe. Momen, ''Abdu'l-Bahá's commentary'; Momen, 'Relativism'.

Commentary on the Súra of the Sun (Ar.: *Tafsír súrat wa'sh-shams*)

Arabic Tablet of Bahá'u'lláh, probably composed during the Akka period, partly in commentary on *súra* 91 of the Quran. In it Bahá'u'lláh states that the meaning of the word of God could never be exhausted. Only those who were God's appointed representatives could comprehend its 'manifold wisdom', however. They were the root of knowledge, and all others should cleave to them, freeing themselves from the exponents of human learning (*GWB* 175–6 no. 89). Quranic commentary required that the reader harmonize the literal and metaphorical meanings of scripture. Those who clung only to the outward sense of the words were ignorant, whilst those who ignored the obvious meaning in favour of esoteric exegesis (*ta'wíl*) were heedless. Thus, in this *súra*, 'the sun' refers to the physical sun; God's messengers, who are 'the suns' of God's names and attributes, and illumined human beings with their divine knowledge; and the 'friends and lovers of God', who diffuse his light in the gloomy world. Cole, 'Commentary'.

communism

Several early Western commentators interpreted Bábism as a form of revolutionary communism (*MBBR* 6, 16), a view echoed by some historians (Ivanov; Greussing), who emphasized the elements of social protest expressed in Bábism from about 1848 onwards. Without denying the importance of social discontent in the development of the movement, such characterizations are misleading, even for the later radical stage of the movement (*see* BÁBÍ RADICALISM), and in the case of the early accounts reflected concerns about increasing contemporary radicalism in Europe.

Bahá'u'lláh and 'Abdu'l-Bahá advocated the economic restructuring of society so as to end the scourge of poverty (*see* ECONOMIC TEACHINGS), and emphasized the dignity and legal rights of all human beings regardless of gender or social station, but they also upheld the validity of social status differences, and 'Abdu'l-Bahá stated unambiguously that economic equality was impossible to maintain: even if it was ever attained, it would lead to social disorder and 'universal disappointment' (*PT* 157; *SAQ* 274). In 1920 'Abdu'l-Bahá predicted that the 'movement of the left' would acquire great importance in the future, and its influence spread (*WOB* 30). The subsequent expansion and later collapse of communist states are thus both regarded as having been foretold (Matthews 66–9). Shoghi Effendi regarded communism as one of the 'attendant evils' of the 'excessive growth of industrialism', and noted its inability to create a genuinely egalitarian society (*WOB* 182, 190); characterized it as one of the three 'false gods' of SECULARISM, which rather than creating a just society tolerated the dominance of one privileged group over the rest of society and, along with militant NATIONALISM, convulsed society and engendered war (*PDC* 117–18); and condemned it – together with American capitalism – for its materialistic philosophy and its neglect of 'those spiritual values and eternal verities', which alone provided the basis for a stable CIVILIZATION (*CF* 125).

Given the policies of 'militant atheism' adopted by most communist governments, the Bahá'ís – along with other religious groups – have suffered persecution in several communist states, including the effective suppression of the once flourishing Bahá'í community of ASHKHABAD by the Soviet authorities during the 1930s.

community

Bahá'ís commonly refer to their local congregations and national memberships as 'communities'. They also sometimes refer to the 'world-wide Bahá'í community'. This usage reflects the ideal of Bahá'í collective life, i.e. Bahá'ís are encouraged to develop a strong sense of shared identity, expressed in mutual concern and care, and not just common attendance at the formal succession of Bahá'í meetings. The extent to which this ideal is attained evidently varies greatly from one Bahá'í 'community' to another: it is easier to develop a sense of communal solidarity in large Bahá'í congregations in Third World villages than among a small scattering of Bahá'ís in a large city. Such practices as communal dawn prayers are intended to enhance this solidarity (*MUHJ* 269 no. 142.14, 311 no. 162.37). All Bahá'ís are urged to build up unity within their own communities; to learn to overlook the faults of others with a 'sin-covering eye'; to be loving, forbearing, patient and merciful; to resolutely abstain from gossip and BACKBITING (described by 'Abdu'l-Bahá as 'the most great sin' and as the cause of divine wrath); to overcome personal differences and petty preoccupations; to use CONSULTATION to solve problems; to take responsibility for their own lives rather than focusing on the faults of others; to avoid criticizing others and using harsh language against them (*LG* 88–94). Bahá'ís should daily strive to become more united and loving ('as one being and one soul') (*SWAB* 203; *see also* LOVE). For an account of possible interpersonal problems in a Bahá'í community see Nerenberg.

conferences and congresses, international

International contacts between Bahá'ís have been an important part of Bahá'í life since the expansion of the Faith beyond its original Islamic milieu, reflecting the self-consciously global sense of identity felt by many Bahá'ís. Since the 1950s one major factor encouraging this sense of wider identity has been the holding of a number of international Bahá'í conferences, commonly organized in groups on a continental basis. The first of these were organized by Shoghi Effendi in 1953 at the beginning of the Ten Year PLAN, with one conference each for Africa, the Americas, Asia and Europe. Including those held in 1953 there have been a total of thirty-eight such conferences held to date (see below), in addition to two world congresses: London, 1963, to celebrate the ending of the Ten Year Plan; and New York, 1992, as part of the HOLY YEAR commemorations. In addition to the formal programmes of these meetings (talks, musical entertainments, etc.), they provide a setting for Bahá'ís of different backgrounds to meet, socialize and discuss matters of common concern. With improvements in communications technology, link-ups between conferences have now become common, further enhancing the sense of the Bahá'ís as members of a single global community. Of note, as an indication of Bahá'í growth, is the increase in the number of participants at the two congresses: about 6,000 in London and 27,000 in New York. In addition there have been various conferences concerned with specific issues and interests (e.g. collaboration between national assemblies, MUSIC festivals, EDUCATION), or catering for particular groups (e.g. WOMEN, YOUTH).

The 1963 Congress in progress in the Royal Albert Hall, London

INTERNATIONAL CONFERENCES AND CONGRESSES

1953	4 conferences: Kampala, Uganda; Chicago, USA; New Delhi, India; Stockholm, Sweden
1958	5 conferences: Kampala; Wilmette, USA; Singapore (as replacement for a proposed conference in Jakarta); Sydney, Australia; Frankfurt, Germany
1963	London World Congress, United Kingdom
1967	6 conferences: Kampala; Chicago/Wilmette; Panama City, Panama; New Delhi; Sydney; Frankfurt
1968–72	*Series of 10 conferences:*
1968	(1) Palermo, Italy, followed by mass pilgrimage to the Bahá'í World Centre
1970	(2) Rose Hill, Mauritius; La Paz, Bolivia
1971	(6) Monrovia, Liberia; Kingston, Jamaica; Singapore; Sapparo, Japan; Suva, Fiji; Reykjavik, Iceland
1972	(1) Panama City, including Temple dedication
1976–7	*Series of 8 conferences:*
1976	(5) Nairobi, Kenya; Anchorage, Alaska; Hong Kong; Helsinki, Finland; Paris, France
1977	(3) Bahia, Brazil; Merida, Mexico; Auckland, New Zealand
1982	5 conferences: Lagos, Nigeria; Montreal, Canada; Quito, Ecuador; Canberra, Australia; Dublin, Ireland
1992	New York World Congress

confession of sins

Bahá'u'lláh forbade the practice of confession of sins to another human being (as it occurs in the Roman Catholic sacrament of penance), stating that this causes humiliation. The sinner should instead seek detachment and beg forgiveness from God (*KA* 30 k34, 194 n58; *TB* 24–5). Various prayers imploring forgiveness were given. Bahá'u'lláh counselled his followers to bring themselves 'to account' each day 'ere thou art summoned to a reckoning; for death, unheralded, shall come upon thee and thou shalt be called to give account for thy deeds' (*HWa* no. 31).

conscience

Bahá'ís emphasize the importance of the individual acquiring a sense of right and wrong. Human beings have FREE WILL, and can choose to develop good or bad qualities in themselves. Accordingly, it is essential for them to develop a moral sense. This is an essential element in the EDUCATION of a child, and a basic purpose of RELIGION. Fear of worldly punishment might make people outwardly avoid wrongdoing, but only with moral education and the growth of conscience will people abstain from wrongdoing of their own accord (*see* CRIME AND PUNISHMENT). Bahá'í moral teachings often emphasize general principles rather than giving detailed instructions for behaviour. In applying these principles Bahá'ís should use their own consciences in the particular contexts of their lives.

consolidation

The process of Bahá'í community development. This has assumed major importance following the great EXPANSION in Bahá'í numbers that began in various parts of the world in the 1950s and 1960s, the Universal House of Justice indicating that it was of coequal importance with TEACHING in its contribution to Bahá'í growth. Without it growth could not be maintained. By its means new Bahá'ís would become spiritually transformed, united and devoted to the Faith, and continue the work of teaching and administrative development for themselves. It comprises the establishment of Bahá'í administrative institutions; DEEPENING of Bahá'ís in the Faith's 'fundamental verities', spiritual principles, administration and 'prime purpose' of establishing human unity; and instruction in the behavioural standards of Bahá'í life (particularly of daily PRAYER, the EDUCATION of children, observance of the MARRIAGE laws; abstention from POLITICS, the obligation to contribute to the FUND; the practice of equality between men and WOMEN); and encouragement of local spiritual ASSEMBLIES to discharge their primary duties. National assemblies should promote it through sending deepened Bahá'ís to visit new communities; organizing SUMMER SCHOOLS, INSTITUTES, correspondence courses, etc.; disseminating literature; and holding training courses for local assembly members. Where appropriate, the use of RADIO and other mass media could be highly effective. *MUHJ* 9 no. 2.7, 80–1 no. 34.13, 301 no. 162.5, 304–5 no. 162.14–15, 485 no. 280.4–7, 487 no. 280.13, 623 no. 394.7.

Constantinople

See ISTANBUL.

constitutions

Fundamental principles governing the regulation of a state or organization, normally embodied in a specific document. The prototype of all national Bahá'í constitutions was the Declaration of Trust and its associated by-laws adopted by the National Spiritual Assembly of the Bahá'ís of the United States and Canada in 1927, and the prototype of all local constitutions was the similar document adopted by the New York local assembly in November 1931. The Universal House of Justice adopted its constitution on 26 November 1972. *BW3*: 95–104; 4: 159–65; *GPB* 335–6; *LG* 64–6; *UHJC*.

consultation

Discussion in order to reach decisions or gain advice. It is much emphasized in Bahá'í writings, particularly with regard to all levels of Bahá'í administration, but also in relation to GOVERNMENT, community affairs, business, family life and individual decision making. Bahá'u'lláh taught that consultation enhances understanding, awareness and certitude. It is a light in the heaven of divine wisdom and a prerequisite of human well-being. 'Abdu'l-Bahá regarded it as a potent means of advancing any project, great or small. It is better to seek the views of many than just to have the views of one. It leads to fresh insights. Consultation does not consist of the mere voicing of personal views, however. This can lead to altercation and useless quibbling, which are always destructive to truth (he attended a meeting of the French senate, which he criticized on these grounds). Those who consult together need to have a sense of mutual fellowship and unity. They should carefully consider the views expressed by others, and express their own views with the utmost courtesy, dignity, care and moderation. They should search out the truth, weighing all the views expressed with calmness and composure. If the views expressed by someone else seem better than their own, they should support those, and not wilfully cling to their own opinions. All should be able to express their views with 'absolute freedom'. No one should belittle the thoughts of another, or feel hurt if others oppose their own views. Only if matters are fully discussed will the right way be found, and the 'shining spark of truth' emerge out of the 'clash of differing opinions'. It is important therefore to avoid feelings of ill-will and discord, and if these develop the discussions should straightaway be stopped, and postponed until a more propitious time. When a decision has been reached it should be followed. True consultation (as between the members of a Bahá'í ASSEMBLY) should be a 'spiritual conference' characterized by love and harmony between those consulting. These should be sincere, pure in their motives, spiritually radiant, attracted to God and detached from all else, humble, patient and devoted to service. They should discuss matters so thoroughly that a unanimity of views will emerge. If it does not then a majority vote should prevail, all supporting that decision. Whatever is arranged with harmony, love and purity of motive will attract divine assistance, and result in light. Shoghi Effendi described consultation as the 'bedrock' of the Bahá'í administrative order. Assembly members should not only consult amongst themselves, but consult as much as possible with the wider community they represent. The Universal House of Justice has stated that there was no one set way of dealing with personal problems and decisions: the individual can use PRAYER, consult with an assembly, or anyone they chose. *CC1*: 93–110; *LG* 176–80. See also Kolstoe, *Consultation*; Kolstoe, *Developing Genius*.

Continental Boards of Counsellors

Institution created by the Universal House of Justice in 1968 to perpetuate the functions of the HANDS OF THE CAUSE, specifically the protection and propagation of the Faith. They were made responsible for overseeing the work of the AUXILIARY BOARDS; consulting and collaborating with the national spiritual ASSEMBLIES; and informing the Hands and the House of Justice of developments in their areas. One Counsellor on each Board was appointed as trustee of their respective continental fund. The Hands were thus freed from many routine responsibilities, and were able to concentrate their energies on more general tasks. At first the Hands in Haifa acted as liaison between the House of Justice and the Boards. In 1973 the INTERNATIONAL TEACHING CENTRE assumed responsibility for the direction of the Boards. Initially, eleven Boards were formed (three each in Africa, the Americas and Asia; one each for Australasia and Europe) with a total of thirty-six Counsellors. The Board areas were subsequently changed (in 1973 they were increased to twelve, and in 1980 reduced to five: one per continent), and the number of Counsellors increased (to fifty-seven in 1973, and seventy-two in 1985). The term of appointment was set at five years, beginning in 1980. The Counsellors' rank is lower than that of the Hands, whose functions they took over. The Boards outrank the national assemblies, but their role is only advisory: administrative authority rests with the assemblies (*see* ADMINISTRATION). Since 1985–6, a number of international conferences have been held in Haifa for all Counsellors. *MUHJ* 130–4 nos. 58–60, 149 no. 70, 246–53 no. 132, 323–4 no. 170, 345 no. 180, 373 no. 200, 464–6 no. 267, 583 no. 366, 606 no. 382, 696–8 no. 439; *LG* 324–7.

contraception

See BIRTH CONTROL.

convention

A type of electoral gathering. At the present time there are three main forms of Bahá'í convention:

(1) Unit conventions: local or regional meetings to elect delegates for national convention. They are normally held once a year at a time specified by the national spiritual assembly, which also determines the number and location of the electoral units. All adult Bahá'ís of good standing resident in the unit may participate as electors. This has become the standard system for electing delegates world-wide since 1985 (*see* ELECTIONS).

(2) National conventions: meetings of delegates to elect the members of their national spiritual assembly (*see* ASSEMBLIES). They are normally held once a year during the RIḌVÁN period (21 April–2 May). The total number of delegates is determined by the centre of the Faith (now the Universal House of Justice) in rough proportion to the numerical size of the national Bahá'í community. The format was established by Shoghi Effendi during the 1920s and 1930s.
(3) International convention: meeting of the members of all national spiritual assemblies to elect the members of the UNIVERSAL HOUSE OF JUSTICE. At present, this is held once every five years (the first in 1963).

In some national communities, sub-unit and state conventions may also be held. *LG* 14–23.

All these conventions have two functions: the election of their respective delegates, assembly or House members; and as consultative bodies (*see* CONSULTATION). If circumstances necessitate it the election may be conducted by postal vote. The role of the national conventions was described by Shoghi Effendi as that of a temporary advisory body to the national assembly. The delegates had the 'vital duty' to consult fully and freely with the assembly (they should 'unburden their hearts' and 'state their grievances'), whilst the assembly's duty was to 'give earnest, prompt and prayerful consideration' to the delegates' views (*LG* 18 no. 59). Although the assembly remained the supreme administrative body for its Bahá'í community, the proceedings of the convention were to be entirely under its own control, and the assembly should not interfere. Thus the delegates elected their own officers, and might invite whom they wished to address them. The convention was not a permanent body akin to a parliament, however. Only for the short period of time during which it was in session (a weekend in many countries) was it an advisory body. For the rest of the year, the normal means by which the community could make its views known to the national assembly was through local assemblies and nineteen day FEASTS. *CC2*: 98–105.

conversion

The process of changing one's religion. Bahá'ís are of a multitude of religious and non-religious backgrounds, and there is no single way of being or becoming a Bahá'í. Fundamental to Bahá'í identity is the personal spiritual bond of acceptance of Bahá'u'lláh as a MANIFESTATION OF GOD. Beyond this, social recognition as a Bahá'í requires acceptance into a particular Bahá'í COMMUNITY (*see* also MEMBERSHIP). The factors that have attracted different people to the Bahá'í Faith vary widely. Bábí and early Bahá'í conversion accounts from the Middle East include many that emphasize the transforming impact of witnessing the REVELATION of verses by the Báb or Bahá'u'lláh, or of reading them or hearing them recited (*see* WORD OF GOD). The sacrificial heroism displayed by martyrs was also a factor for some. In the early Western Bahá'í communities the charismatic figure of 'Abdu'l-Bahá appears to have been a frequent factor of appeal. Other accounts, both in the 19th century and in various parts of the world today, refer to the perceived fulfilment of PROPHECY or to 'logical proofs' (APOLOGETICS); the 'modernism' of the Bahá'í social teachings; the attractive nature of the Bahá'í community, particularly its unity and freedom from religious or racial PREJUDICE, and its loving welcome; and the lay rather than priestly nature of Bahá'í decision making and communal authority (*SBBR* 39–40, 93–7, 188–90). There are references to some Western Bahá'í conversions in Ebaugh and Vaughn, and

Ullman. Gottlieb and Gottlieb provide a diverse selection of autobiographical 'conversion' accounts by North American Bahá'ís. There has as yet been no study of 'withdrawals' (i.e. 'deconversions') from the Faith.

Covenant (Ar.: *'ahd*)

An agreement between parties which binds them together and carries mutually recognized obligations. For Bahá'ís there are two specific forms of covenant which operate within religious history: (1) The 'Greater Covenant' between each MANIFESTATION OF GOD and his followers regarding the promise of the next Manifestation. This is expressed in PROPHECY. Thus, in the Western tradition, each Manifestation in the series ABRAHAM, MOSES, JESUS, MUḤAMMAD, the BÁB and BAHÁ'U'LLÁH prophesied the appearance of the next, and their respective followers were duty bound to investigate the claims of the following Manifestation.

(2) The 'Lesser Covenant' which a Manifestation of God makes concerning his immediate successor to whom his followers should turn and obey, as per the appointment of the apostle Peter by Jesus, the Imám 'Alí by Muḥammad, and 'Abdu'l-Bahá by Bahá'u'lláh. In the case of Peter and 'Alí, their covenants of appointment were neither written nor sufficiently explicit for them to gain universal acceptance, with the result that both Christianity and Islam became riven by contending sects. By contrast, the Bahá'í Lesser Covenant was both explicit and in written form. Thus Bahá'u'lláh appointed 'Abdu'l-Bahá as centre of his covenant in his *Book of the* COVENANT, and 'Abdu'l-Bahá in his *WILL AND TESTAMENT* directed the Bahá'ís to follow SHOGHI EFFENDI, and at the same time made a promise of divine guidance and protection for the as yet unelected UNIVERSAL HOUSE OF JUSTICE. Those who reject any of the links in this chain of succession are regarded as COVENANT-BREAKERS, and as having rejected Bahá'u'lláh. 'Abdu'l-Bahá described the Covenant doctrine as 'the most great characteristic' of Bahá'u'lláh's religion. Through it the unity of the Bahá'í Faith was assured and schism prevented. It was 'the pivot of the oneness of mankind', and its light educated hearts and souls. It was a fortress to protect the Bahá'ís, and all Bahá'ís were called to make their steps firm in its path. Thus would they become the recipients of divine confirmations. Shoghi Effendi emphasized the particular importance of Bahá'ís gaining a proper understanding of this doctrine.
CC1: 111–29; *Covenant of Bahá'u'lláh*; LG 181–3; *TCB*.

There is also reference to a more general covenant by which God bestows his bounties on humanity and in return demands recognition of his messengers and obedience to his laws. Faithfulness to this covenant on the part of the individual requires a distinctive pattern of behaviour marked by morality and piety.

Covenant, Book of the (PA: *Kitáb-i-'Ahd*, also known as *Kitáb-i-'Ahdí*, 'The Book of my Covenant')

Bahá'u'lláh's last testament, written in Arabic in his own handwriting, and given to 'Abdu'l-Bahá during his final illness (May 1892). The document was read both to a select group of witnesses and to a large gathering of Bahá'ís on the ninth day after Bahá'u'lláh's passing. It explicitly appoints 'Abdu'l-Bahá (the *ghuṣn-i-a'ẓam*, the Most Great (or Mighty) Branch) as Bahá'u'lláh's successor, and directs his family and the AFNÁN relatives of the Báb to turn to him. Other provisions were: Bahá'u'lláh's second surviving son, Mírzá MUḤAMMAD-'ALÍ (the *ghuṣn-i-akbar*, the Greatest Branch) was subordinate to 'Abdu'l-Bahá; the Bahá'ís should love Bahá'u'lláh's sons (the *Aghṣán*), but the sons had no rights over the property of others; all should respect the Afnán; the Aghṣán, the Afnán and other members of Bahá'u'lláh's family were to fear God and perform praiseworthy deeds; Bahá'u'lláh's purpose in revealing verses had been to establish concord and tranquillity; God's religion should not be made a cause of enmity; conflict was forbidden; God's domain was the hearts of men: rulership was entrusted to the kings, themselves the manifestations of divine power; the rulers (*umará*) and learned (*'ULAMÁ*) among the Bahá'ís were Bahá'u'lláh's trustees. *TB* 217–23; *GPB* 237–9.

Covenant-breakers

(*Ar.: náqiḍín*)

Bahá'í term for those Bahá'ís who have broken (*naqḍ*) the COVENANT, by which the official succession of Centres of the Faith was established, i.e. denial of the legitimacy of 'Abdu'l-Bahá, Shoghi Effendi or the Universal House of Justice, or wilful opposition to their authority. The term is also used to refer to AZALI Bábís. It does not apply to those who have simply left the Faith because they no longer believe in it (*see* APOSTASY). 'Abdu'l-Bahá likened Covenant-breakers to the carriers of a spiritual disease, and instructed that they were to be avoided by others because of the danger of infection. Bahá'ís therefore avoid association with declared Covenant-breakers, even when such individuals are family members. Only the Centres of the Faith, or those appointed by them – specifically the HANDS OF THE CAUSE – are entitled to declare someone a Covenant-breaker, thereby excommunicating them from the Faith. The Counsellors and members of the AUXILIARY BOARDS have a particular responsibility to watch out for 'internal opposition' to the Centres of the Faith, and to report such activity. *LG* 183–90.

HISTORY

As the appointed centre of his father's Covenant, 'Abdu'l-Bahá regarded the actions of his half-brother, Mírzá MUḤAMMAD-'ALÍ, as a rebellion against God, and not simply as insubordination to him personally. He therefore declared Muḥammad-'Alí and his followers to be Covenant-breakers, thus expelling the larger part of Bahá'u'lláh's family from the Faith, as well as such prominent Bahá'ís as Jamál BURÚJIRDÍ and Ibrahim KHEIRALLA. He also finally expelled Dr Ameen U. Fareed (Amínu'lláh Faríd), his wife's nephew, who had used his position as one of 'Abdu'l-Bahá's entourage to extract money from some of the American Bahá'ís, and who later returned to America in breach of 'Abdu'l-Bahá's explicit instructions (*TCB* 341).

Following the passing of 'Abdu'l-Bahá (1921) there was almost universal acceptance of Shoghi Effendi as Guardian, 'Abdu'l-Bahá's emphatic insistence in his *WILL AND TESTAMENT* on his successor's authority making effective opposition to Shoghi Effendi extremely difficult to mount in Bahá'í terms. Thus the only immediate opposition came from Muḥammad-'Alí and his followers, who asserted his claims to leadership on the basis of Bahá'u'lláh's will (the *Book of the COVENANT*). Given Muḥammad-'Alí's existing separation from the Bahá'í community, this claim was universally rejected by the Bahá'ís. Opposition to Shoghi Effendi's leadership from recognized Bahá'ís did emerge, however, most notably in response to his emphasis on the development of Bahá'í ADMINISTRATION, which some Bahá'ís saw as a deviation from 'Abdu'l-Bahá's policies. The frustrated desire for leadership also appears to have been a factor in some cases. This opposition took its most organized form in the United States, where it came to centre on the activities of Ruth WHITE (who also had followers in Germany) and Ahmad Sohrab. There was also a short-lived opposition movement in Egypt, whilst in Iran one of the most prominent Bahá'ís, Ávárih, apostatized and began to attack the Faith in his writings. In a separate series of events Shoghi Effendi expelled a widening circle of his relatives from the Faith, primarily because of the marriages that several contracted with existing Covenant-breaking members of Bahá'u'lláh's family. (*See also* Núrí family; Rúḥí Afnán.)

After the death of Shoghi Effendi (1957) the only significant oppositional movement was that led by the veteran American Bahá'í C.M. Remey, who claimed to be the second Guardian. The movement subsequently splintered, some groups remaining active (*see* Remeyite groups and organizations). Some attempts were made during the 1950s and 1960s to bring together the disparate groups of Covenant-breakers, but these had little effect. Globally, the Bahá'í community has maintained its unity. *TCB*.

craftsmanship

Bahá'u'lláh and 'Abdu'l-Bahá praised craftsmanship, and equated such work with worship. God, himself, 'the Fashioner', loves craftsmanship. Craftsmen should be treated with deference, and not looked down on and abused as has been their lot in the past. They should endeavour to achieve excellence in their work. *CC1*: 1–6.

creation

In Graeco-Islamic philosophy, the Aristotelian view of the eternity of the world conflicted with the orthodox understanding of the world as created by God. Bahá'u'lláh held that both views could be regarded as correct: the material universe has always existed, albeit in different form, but its generating impulse was the Word of God. Nature is the expression of God's will in the contingent world. It will not decay (*TB* 140–2). Thus, creation as a whole has neither beginning nor end, though individual objects within it (e.g. the planet earth; an individual human body) will come into being at a particular moment in time, and subsequently cease to exist, breaking down into their component elements (*SAQ* 180–3, 203–4). Bahá'ís also believe that creation is not confined to the material universe: there are many 'worlds of God'. (*See also* metaphysics.)

cremation

Bahá'í law stipulates burial of the dead, and forbids cremation. 'Abdu'l-Bahá taught that just as the human body has been formed gradually, so should it decompose slowly and naturally. Bahá'ís who leave their bodies for medical research should stipulate that they want their remains to be eventually buried and not cremated. *LG* 200–2.

crime and punishment

'Abdu'l-Bahá stated that society has the right to impose punishments on criminals in order to protect its members. The individual who has been wronged by the criminal does not have the right to take revenge, which is despised by God, but does have the right of self-defence. The purpose of civil punishment is social protection and not vengeance. Some individuals are like 'bloodthirsty wolves', and the community has to protect itself from them. Community life depends on justice, not forgiveness. In the long run, however, communities need to educate their citizens in morality, so that conscience deters crime. Passing penal laws and building prisons are not in themselves the solution to crime. Punishment is necessary, but it also serves to further pervert the morality and character of the criminal. *KA* 203; *SAQ* 268–72.

Bahá'í law specifies general punishments for a number of criminal offences.

In the *Kitáb-i-Aqdas* Bahá'u'lláh prescribed the death penalty both for intentional arson and murder, with life imprisonment as an alternative punishment. In the case of unintentional killing (manslaughter) the killer should pay the family of the deceased an indemnity of 100 *mithqáls* (=364 grams) of gold. Theft was to be punished with exile and imprisonment, with a mark being placed on the forehead of the thief at the third offence, so that they could be publicly identified. Details (degrees of offence; mitigating circumstances; which punishment was to be applied in which circumstance; the manner of application; liability of the criminally insane; etc.) are left for the future decision of the Universal House of Justice. *KA* 35–6 k45, 41 k62, 87–8 k188, 121 q49, 198 n70–1, 203–5 n86–7; *LG* 357, no. 1199.

Bahá'u'lláh counselled that these punishments had been ordained by a merciful and compassionate God in order to protect and elevate human beings. They should not be neglected out of a sense of compassion: Bahá'u'lláh was schooling his followers with 'the rod of wisdom'. Shoghi Effendi commented that concern for the innocent who might occasionally be punished by mistake should not cause a salutary law to be abandoned: in the case of the death penalty, God would compensate a man who was wrongly executed 'a thousandfold' (*KA* 36, 204). He also stated that in a more evolved society – the future Bahá'í society in which Bahá'í law would actually be enforced – the mere threat of such punishments would be sufficient to deter (*LG* 357, no. 1198).

At the present time Bahá'í assemblies do not enforce criminal law, although they do concern themselves with the legal aspects of matters of personal status, such as marriage and divorce. They may also deprive individuals who have breached aspects of Bahá'í law of their Bahá'í administrative rights. Bahá'ís who have been convicted of criminal offences do not automatically lose their Bahá'í rights, however (*LG* 356, no. 1194–5).

Custodians

Those Hands of the Cause who exercised a collective leadership of the Bahá'í Faith from the passing of Shoghi Effendi in November 1957 until the election of the Universal House of Justice in April 1963. Nine Custodians (the term is a legal one) were selected at the first conclave of the Hands in November 1957. Two were later unable to continue their residence in Haifa, one was expelled from the Faith, and one died; all four were replaced by other Hands. The Hands initially selected were: Hasan Balyuzi (replaced by John Ferraby, November 1959); Amelia Collins (d. 1962; temporarily replaced by Hasan Balyuzi); 'Alí-Akbar Furútan; Paul Haney; Leroy Ioas; Jalál Kházeh; Adelbert Mühlschlegel (shortly replaced by A.Q. Faizí); Charles Mason Remey (replaced by Horace Holley, November 1959; Holley himself died in 1960, and was replaced by William Sears); and Rúḥiyyih Khánum. Other Hands acted as substitute Custodians at various times. UHJ, *Ministry of the Custodians*.

D

Dalá'il-i-sab'ih

See SEVEN PROOFS.

dancing

There is nothing in the Bahá'í teachings against dancing, but Shoghi Effendi emphasized that it should conform to the Bahá'í standards of modesty and chastity. Bahá'ís should never be vulgar in their actions or indecently clad. Classical dancing was seen as harmless, but the atmosphere of smoking, drinking and promiscuity common in modern (1952) dance halls was harmful. *LG* 98. (*See also* DRAMA AND DANCE.)

Dawn-Breakers

Shoghi Effendi's translation of an early narrative of Bábí history, the *Táríkh-i-Nabíl* (*Nabíl's Narrative*), composed by NABÍL-I-A'ẒAM in AH1305/1887–8. Although written long after the events it describes, the book relies heavily on the memoirs of surviving early Bábís (including the author), and is thus an important source. The publication of the English translation in 1932 had an enormous impact on Western Bahá'ís' understanding of their religion, firmly linking it to Bábism, and to the heroic acts and martyrdoms of the Bábís. Shoghi Effendi specifically intended the book to inspire the reader to greater dedication and self-sacrifice. As yet the work is only available in edited translation, the Persian original being in manuscript only. The introduction to the English edition is by George TOWNSHEND. *McS* 166–9; *CC1*: 216, nos. 463–4; Rabbani, *Priceless Pearl* 217–18.

Dayyán (Ar., 'Judge')

Bábí title of Mullá (or Mírzá) Asadu'lláh Khu'í (d. 1856) of Khuy in western Azerbaiján. He converted during the period of the Báb's exile in the province, and soon gained the Báb's praise for a learned apologia he wrote for the new faith. He was unusual for the range of his learning, which included knowledge of Syriac and Hebrew. He was the recipient of the Báb's *Lawḥ-i-Ḥurúfát* ('Tablet of the Letters'). In the confused period of the early 1850s he was one of those who laid claim to Bábí leadership, and gained a following. He was finally murdered in Baghdad, seemingly at the instigation of Ṣubḥ-i-AZAL, who had denounced him as the 'father of iniquities', and questioned why his followers did not 'transfix him with their spears', or 'rend his bowels with their hands'. *ARR* 383, 384; *EGBBF* 43–4; *BKG* 123–4; Browne, *Materials* 218–19; *GPB* 124–5; *McS* 23–24 n77, 88–90; Nabil 303–4.

death and the afterlife

Bahá'ís are instructed to bury their dead (*see* BURIAL), and to write a WILL. SUICIDE is condemned.

For Bahá'ís the death and decomposition of the body are a natural part of human life. We may lament the death of those we love, but for the individual death represents a potential liberation whereby the eternal SOUL is freed from the fetters of material existence and progresses towards God's presence throughout eternity. Thus death can be seen as a 'messenger of joy' (*HWa* no. 32). 'Abdu'l-Bahá compared the afterlife of the soul to the birth of a child. Just as for the child whose uterine existence is a preparation for its life after birth, so is the present life a period of preparation for the soul before it enters its eternal environment. In both cases the period of preparation is of vital importance, but it does not stand by itself. Only if the soul has become purified from worldly attachment will it be able to breathe 'the sweet scents of holiness' in the afterlife (*SWAB* 184–5). The actual nature of the afterlife is beyond the understanding of those who are still living, just as the present world would be to the unborn foetus (*LG* 204, 208–9). The soul is immortal, and spiritual progress in the afterlife without limit (*SAQ* 233–7). Infants who die are under the mercy and bounty of God (*SAQ* 240). The doctrine of REINCARNATION is rejected.

After death souls retain their individuality and consciousness. They are able to recognize and commune spiritually with other souls, including former marriage partners on the basis of 'profound friendship of spirit'. The souls of those who are close to God are able to intercede on behalf of the living, but those who are far from God have no impact on the living: they are spiritually as dead, and have no power. There are no 'earth-bound souls' or ghosts (*see* EVIL SPIRITS). *LG* 206–7; *SAQ* 231.

INTERCESSION

Charitable donations and good deeds done in the name of the dead are approved, and are regarded as helpful to the development of the soul in the afterlife. Children should implore pardon and forgiveness before God for their deceased parents. All may pray for the spiritual progress of the dead. The wealthy may perhaps gain merit before God if they bequeath wealth to the poor. *LG* 204; *SAQ* 231–2, 240.

deepening

The Bahá'í term for the process by which individuals deepen their knowledge and understanding of the Bahá'í Faith through study, discussion and MEDITATION. Bahá'u'lláh bade his followers to 'immerse' themselves in 'the ocean' of his words so that they might discover 'the pearls of wisdom' that lay hidden in its depths. They should read his verses every morning and evening to uplift their souls; reflect and meditate on what they read; and strive to translate it into action. True understanding depends on purity of heart, and not acquired learning (*KA* 73 k149, 85 k182; *CC1*: 187–93). 'Abdu'l-Bahá called on the Bahá'ís to seek KNOWLEDGE and WISDOM, increasing their knowledge of scripture and their ability to present the 'divine proofs', and holding meetings for this purpose. They should both memorize Bahá'u'lláh's writings (such as the *HIDDEN WORDS*) and pray fervently that they might be enabled to live their lives in accordance with his counsels (*CC1*: 193–204). Shoghi Effendi directed Bahá'ís to deepen the 'Spirit' of the Cause in their own lives and exemplify it in their conduct. They should study the 'fundamentals of the Faith', its history, administration, COVENANT, and spiritual, ethical and social teachings; constantly endeavour to understand better 'the significance' of Bahá'u'lláh's revelation; and widen their vision. To study was a 'sacred obligation'. Without deepening, the TEACHING work would be ineffective, and new Bahá'ís would not become firmly committed to the Faith. Bahá'ís should study the actual writings of Bahá'u'lláh and 'Abdu'l-Bahá, and not rely unduly on accounts of the writings given by others. They should also study the DAWN-BREAKERS and the QURAN. SUMMER SCHOOLS and similar institutions are intended as means of helping Bahá'ís to deepen. There is no limit to the study of the Faith. SCHOLARSHIP is also needed (*CC1*: 204–34). The Universal House of Justice has stated that deepening is more a matter of developing a spiritual attitude, devotion and selflessness than of acquiring information as such (important though that is). Bahá'ís should ask themselves: what is God's purpose (through Bahá'u'lláh) for the human race? What are the profound changes that he will bring about? What is the goal of a new WORLD ORDER? And why did the Báb, Bahá'u'lláh, 'Abdu'l-Bahá and Shoghi Effendi submit themselves to the sufferings that were heaped upon them? (*MUHJ* 106–7 no. 42.22–6, 499 no. 289.4, 571 no. 353). (*See also* CONSOLIDATION.)

detachment

Bahá'u'lláh taught that the world, its vanities and glories are worthless, more contemptible than 'dust and ashes' (*ADJ* 25). Worldly possessions and dominion are transient. They should not become the cause of exultation. The whole world should be seen as no more valuable than the black in the eye of a dead ant. The tombs of the proud are an object lesson for the beholder, who should flee the world and turn to God's kingdom (*ESW* 56). The 'glamour' of the world is deceptive. The world itself is impermanent. What now is left of the rich and powerful of past ages, or of their treasures and palaces? The faithful believer should not let such trappings cut them off from 'God's enduring bestowals' and 'spiritual sustenance'. They should rather place their 'whole reliance' on him (*CC2*: 333). Even if they pass through cities of gold and silver, they should not deign to look at them, nor be seduced by their allure (*CC2*: 330). Worldly attachment causes people to follow their own covetous desires, and hinders them from entering God's 'straight and glorious path' (*ADJ* 26). At the same time, God ordained the good things of the world for those who believe in him. Thus, so long as believers do not let 'the ornaments of the earth' become a barrier, they can adorn themselves with them and partake of their benefits, and no harm will befall them (*ADJ* 28). Detachment applies not only to earthly delights, but to the desire for paradise, pride in one's knowledge or attainments, and attachment to the self (*RB2*: 35–44).

development of the Faith

See BAHÁ'Í FAITH.

development, social and economic

See SOCIO-ECONOMIC DEVELOPMENT.

devil

See EVIL; SATAN.

devotionalism

Consciousness of God should pervade the thoughts and actions of the believer's daily life. Religion is not to be regarded as a separate sphere of life. As regular devotions, Bahá'ís should perform daily obligatory PRAYER; read from the writings of Bahá'u'lláh every morning and evening, contemplating on what they read; and invoke God by his GREATEST NAME (*Bahá*) ninety-five times each day. Additional use of prayer as the individual wishes is encouraged, but Bahá'ís are bidden to link devotionalism to action (*see* SPIRITUAL PATH). Devotional practices ordained by the Báb were detailed and extensive, such that the believer would be 'in an almost constant state of remembrance of God' (Walbridge, *Sacred* 42–5).

The daily readings from the writings are regarded as obligatory, failure to do so being regarded as a lack of faithfulness to God's COVENANT. Their purpose is to draw the believer closer to God. To this end, it is better to read one verse 'with joy and radiance' than to read 'all the Holy Books' with lassitude. The soul should be uplifted not wearied. Nor should anyone pride themselves on their piety (*KA* 73–4 k149, 127 q68, 236 n165).

Dhabíḥ (Ar., 'Sacrifice')

Name given by Bahá'u'lláh to two of his followers.

(1) SAYYID ISMÁ'ÍL ZAVÁRIHÍ

An early Bábí who became a devotee of Bahá'u'lláh when the latter was in Baghdad. As a gesture of humility he undertook the menial task of sweeping the approach to Bahá'u'lláh's house. Overcome by his feelings of religious intoxication he became unable to eat or drink, and after a forty-day fast cut his own throat. Bahá'u'lláh extolled the purity of the blood thus shed, and also named him 'King and Beloved of Martyrs'. *RB1*: 101–5.

(2) ḤÁJÍ MUḤAMMAD-ISMÁ'ÍL KÁSHÁNÍ

Also named *Anís* (Companion). One of his brothers was the Bábí chronicler Ḥájí Mírzá Jání. He became a devoted follower of Bahá'u'lláh, and was imprisoned in Tehran for his efforts to teach the Bahá'í Faith. He died of natural causes, but was given the spiritual station of a martyr by Bahá'u'lláh. The *Súratu'l-Ra'ís* was revealed in his honour. *RB2*: 411–13. (*See also Tablets of* RA'ÍS.)

diet

There are no dietary restrictions in the Bahá'í Faith other than prohibitions on consuming ALCOHOL and on eating meat from an animal found dead in a trap or snare (*KA* 40 k60, 115 q24). Thus, in contrast to Islamic practice, Bahá'ís can eat pork and the meat of animals that have been shot during a hunt.

Bahá'u'lláh advocated simplicity of diet and recommended herbal cures for diseases (*see Tablet of* MEDICINE). Similarly, for 'Abdu'l-Bahá one of the principal causes of disease was chemical imbalance in the body. This imbalance could be corrected by drugs, but natural curing by diet was better. The elements needed by the body were found in plants, and eating specific foods would correct deficiencies of particular nutrients. This is what animals did when they sought particular foodstuffs when their bodies were in imbalance, and for the most part, they suffered from the same maladies as humans. By eating meals with a complex mixture of ingredients, human beings place extra strains on their physical health. A diet of simple foods was better. Future medical research would reveal the best diets to follow. Specifically, abstinence from alcohol, DRUGS and tobacco SMOKING greatly contributed to health and vigour. 'Abdu'l-Bahá also regarded a vegetarian diet as desirable, except for people with a weak constitution or the sick who might need meat. The health of strictly vegetarian Brahmins in India indicated that it was entirely possible to survive without meat. There was no requirement for Bahá'ís to become vegetarians, but in the future people would gradually adopt a diet of fruit and grains. Killing ANIMALS for food was also considered somewhat contrary to compassion. Shoghi Effendi and the Universal House of Justice have stated that these teachings did not constitute a specific Bahá'í dietary regimen. Bahá'ís are entirely free to eat as they choose, and should be tolerant of those who eat differently from them. They should be guided by the growing body of scientific knowledge about diet. *CC1*: 459–88; *LG* 294–8. (*See also* HEALTH AND HEALING.)

Disciples of 'Abdu'l-Bahá

Group of nineteen or twenty early Western Bahá'ís identified by Shoghi Effendi. He also termed them 'Heralds of the Covenant' (*BW3* : 84–5; 4: 118–19). The identity of the German Bahá'í so honoured is unclear. In *BW3* he is named as Arthur Brauns, but in *BW4* as Albert Schwarz. The list comprises:

(1) Dr J.G. AUGUR, 'pioneer of the Faith in the Pacific Islands'
(2) Dr Arthur BRAUNS, 'pioneer worker for the Faith in Germany'
(3) Mrs Isabella BRITTINGHAM, 'trusted and energetic sower of the Seed'
(4) Mr Thornton CHASE, 'first Bahá'í in America'
(5) Mr Arthur P. DODGE, 'staunch advocate of the Cause'
(6) M. Hippolyte DREYFUS-BARNEY, 'author, translator, and international promoter of the Faith'
(7) Dr John E. ESSLEMONT, 'distinguished Bahá'í author'
(8) Miss Sarah FARMER, 'founder of Green Acre'
(9) Mr Charles GREENLEAF, 'firm supporter of the Faith'
(10) Mrs Helen S. GOODALL, 'ardent establisher of the Cause in America'
(11) Mrs Lua M. GETSINGER, 'renowned and devoted international Bahá'í teacher'
(12) Mr Joseph HANNEN, 'indefatigable servant of the Cause'
(13) Mr William H. HOAR, 'prominent Bahá'í teacher'
(14) Miss Lillian KAPPES, 'noted teacher of the Tarbíyat School, Ṭihrán'
(15) Mr Howard MACNUTT, 'noted Bahá'í teacher'
(16) Mrs Mary Virginia THORNBURGH-CROPPER, 'a pioneer of the Faith in England'
(17) Mr William Henry ('Harry') RANDALL, 'eloquent upholder of the Bahá'í Cause in America'
(18) Consul Albert SCHWARZ, 'pioneer worker for the Faith in Germany'
(19) Mr C.I. THATCHER, 'zealous Bahá'í worker'
(20) Mr Robert TURNER, 'first Bahá'í of the Negro race in America'

dispensation

Term of Christian origin used by Shoghi Effendi to refer to the period associated with each successive MANIFESTATION OF GOD. (*See also* TIME.)

Dispensation of Bahá'u'lláh

Major letter of Shoghi Effendi to the Western Bahá'ís, dated 8 February 1934. It is a doctrinal statement in which Shoghi Effendi delineates the religious 'stations' of the central figures of the Bahá'í Faith (Bahá'u'lláh, the Báb and 'Abdu'l-Bahá) as well as the role of the guardianship and the Universal House of Justice as the primary institutions of the Bahá'í Administrative Order (*see* ADMINISTRATION). *WOB* 97–157.

divine judgement

Major OPPOSITION to God's Cause (and in particular PERSECUTION) is believed to incur divine wrath, often expressed during the lifetime of the offender. Bahá'u'lláh stated that whilst his mercy had 'encompassed all created things', the fierceness of his anger against the wicked could be terrible, such that they might receive grievous chastisement (*GWB* 324 no. 153). God did not blink at the tyranny of the oppressor, and his vengeance would be visited on every tyrant (*GPB* 224). Similarly, Shoghi Effendi referred to the 'rod of Divine chastisement' which had afflicted those who had assailed the Bábí and Bahá'í religions, or, in some instances, those who had failed to respond to its summons. Thus the early deaths of MUḤAMMAD SHÁH, and of Sultan ABDULAZIZ and his ministers, ÂLI PAŞA and FUAT PAŞA; the execution or violent deaths of AMÍR KABÍR, his brother, Mírzá Ḥasan Khán, and of the members of the execution regiment who had between them encompassed the death of the Báb; the disgrace and impoverishment of Ḥájí Mírzá ÁQÁSÍ, of the governor of Shíráz who had persecuted the Báb, and of various other Iranian and Ottoman officials; the foul diseases and awful deaths that afflicted the clerics responsible for the torture and killing of QUDDÚS, applying the bastinado to the Báb, and the deaths of the KING AND BELOVED OF MARTYRS; the sufferings of the Iranian people as a whole during the 19th century; and the sudden loss of power of NAPOLEON III and Pope PIUS IX. More generally, the decline in the fortunes of monarchy and ecclesiastical influence was related to their neglect of Bahá'u'lláh's call (*see* proclamation to the RULERS), as in particular with the collapse of the OTTOMAN and QÁJÁR regimes, and the consequent secularization of Islamic institutions in Turkey and Iran (including the CALIPHATE) (*GPB* 81–5, 224–33, 317–20, 407–9). Shoghi Effendi also described the Roman destruction of Jerusalem (70 CE) as a divine response to the persecution of Jesus (*WOB* 176).

divorce (Ar.: *ṭaláq*)

Divorce is permitted by Bahá'í law, but strongly discouraged and condemned. Bahá'ís should regard MARRIAGE as a sacred tie, which is only to be severed in extreme circumstances and as a last resort. The common practice of divorce in contemporary society is regarded as an indication of the decline of religion, and as a major factor leading to societal breakdown.

There are no specific grounds for divorce in Bahá'í law other than antipathy between the partners. If antagonism arises between husband and wife they should seek to resolve their problems through consultation, both between themselves, and jointly with others who might be of assistance, such as Bahá'í ASSEMBLIES and marriage-guidance counsellors. They should be patient with each other and avoid anger, aiming to find some way of overcoming their differences. If such endeavour is unavailing, the couple jointly or one partner alone may ask the relevant Bahá'í assembly to set the 'year of waiting' or 'year of patience' necessary for a Bahá'í divorce to be recognized. The assembly also endeavours to secure reconciliation between the couple. During the year, the couple live separately and do not engage in sexual relations. If they become reconciled during the year then their marriage continues. If at the end the year one or both remain unreconciled, they are considered divorced according to Bahá'í law. They must also follow whatever procedures are necessary to secure a divorce according to the laws of the country in which they live. It is against the spirit of Bahá'í law to court a new partner during the year of waiting.

Bahá'u'lláh specified that the husband should support the wife financially during the year of waiting. The Universal House of Justice has noted that individual cases may occur in which the wife was formerly the family breadwinner, and that in such a case, the couple might decide upon a different arrangement (*LG* 396 no. 1323). In all cases it is the responsibility of the assembly involved to encourage and assist the divorcing couple to work out the financial details of their future lives between themselves. They should similarly determine suitable arrangements for the custody of children, including recognition of the continuing role of the non-custodial partner as a parent.

Specific circumstances referred to in the *Kitáb-i-Aqdas* are: the prohibition of the Islamic practice of a divorced woman having to marry another man before she can remarry her first husband; there is no need for a year of waiting if the couple decide to divorce before the marriage is consummated (normally assumed to have taken place within twenty-four hours of the marriage ceremony); if differences arise between a couple whilst they are travelling, the husband must ensure that his wife is safely returned to her home in addition to paying her expenses for the journey and the forthcoming year; if the husband disappears, the wife must wait for a year before remarrying; and a wife who is divorced as a consequence of infidelity forfeits her right to receive maintenance during the year of waiting.
KA 42–5 k67–70, 105–6 q4, 110 q11–12, 113 q19, 119 q38, q40, 128 q73, 135–6 q98, 152–3, 209–212 n96–102; *CC1*: 235–44; *CC2*: 441–59; *LG* 390–402.

Dodge, Arthur Pillsbury
(1849–1915)

Prominent early American Bahá'í. A lawyer, magazine publisher, and inventor, he became a Bahá'í in 1897. His home in New York City became the meeting place for the newly established Bahá'í community, and he was chosen as its first president (1898). Shoghi Effendi named him as one of the Disciples of 'Abdu'l-Bahá. *BFA1*; *BFA2*; *WSBR* 1–16.

dogma

There are various statements of official Bahá'í belief, notably Shoghi Effendi's *Dispensation of Bahá'u'lláh* (1934) and *The Faith of Bahá'u'lláh* (1947), the latter prepared as a summary of Bahá'í beliefs for the United Nations Special Committee on Palestine. The various listings of 'Bahá'í principles' also summarize aspects of Bahá'í belief. Beyond this there is a strong anti-dogmatic element in the Bahá'í teachings. 'Abdu'l-Bahá stated that the 'foundation' of Bahá'í belief was acceptance of the Báb and Bahá'u'lláh as Manifestations of God (*Will* 19), and stressed the necessity for Bahá'ís to be firm in the Covenant (i.e. to accept the official line of leadership succession), and Bahá'í identity focuses more on this common adhesion than on any doctrinal statements as such. In any case, human understanding of religious truth is regarded as limited and relative in nature (Momen, 'Relativism') and certain key concepts – God; the Manifestations of God; the soul; the afterlife (*see* death) – as being beyond human definition. Thus a variety of individual understandings is regarded as normal, and is accepted as long as there is no attempt by the individual to impose their own interpretation on others. Again, whilst Bahá'u'lláh stated that acceptance of him as a Manifestation of God was inseparably linked to obedience to his laws (*KA* 19 k1), much of Bahá'í law is operable at the level of individual conscience rather than communally enforced orthopraxy as in Islam.

Dolgorukov, Prince Dmitri Ivanovitch (d. 1867)

Russian minister in Tehran from January 1846 until May 1854. His diplomatic dispatches make reference to the Báb and the emergence of Bábism. A Persian text, purporting to be a translation of his 'Political Confessions', was published in 1943 in Mashhad, seemingly in an attempt to discredit the Bábí and Bahá'í religions by 'proving' that Bábism had been established as part of a Russian conspiracy to weaken Iran. Although long since shown to be a forgery, the book has found widespread currency in Iran and the Arab world, and has contributed to the prevalent negative and hostile view of the religions. *MBBR*; *McS* 170–1.

drama and dance

'Abdu'l-Bahá referred to the educational potential of drama, and gave one of the Bahá'ís an outline of a religious play ('The Drama of the Kingdom', *AB* 497–502). Shoghi Effendi noted the value of stage productions in awakening noble sentiments among the mass of the people and attracting them to the Faith. Such productions could include Bahá'í historical episodes, but there could be no portrayal of any MANIFESTATION OF GOD, as this would be irreverent. The same applied to films. *LG* 97–100.

Drama and dance performances have become an increasingly common element in Bahá'í conferences in recent years, most notably at the 1992 Bahá'í World Congress in New York. Bahá'í dance groups have proliferated in various parts of the world, mostly made up of enthusiastic amateurs and inspired by local dance traditions. There is at least one semi-professional group, Ballet Shayda in Canada (started in the 1980s). There are several Bahá'í theatre groups, including Afrika Bikonda in the Ivory Coast (started in the mid-1980s). Some of this dance and drama is employed to present Bahá'í ideas to a wider audience (*BWNS* 1994–5: 251–9). A dramatic pop video, Doug Cameron's *Mona and the Children*, was made about a group of young women who were executed as Bahá'ís in Iran in 1983. (*See also* GRINEVSKAYA.)

dreams and visions

In his writings Bahá'u'lláh referred to a number of his own powerful visionary experiences (*see* MAID OF HEAVEN) and emphasized the reality of the dream world as a source of foreknowledge and as 'the most mysterious of the signs of God amongst men' (*SV* 32–3; *TB* 187–8). However, both 'Abdu'l-Bahá and Shoghi Effendi cautioned that visionary experiences that corresponded with reality were very rare. Visions might seem real to the individual experiencing them, but simply be the product of the subconscious mind. Dreams and visions are always coloured by the mind of the dreamer; bad feelings or evil motives warp and distort genuine inspiration. Only by freeing oneself from prejudice and desire can one make one's dreams (as well as conscious thoughts) pure and true. Dreams should be checked against the revealed word to see if they were in harmony with it. Too much significance should not be given to them, and they should never be regarded as being an infallible source of guidance, even for the individual experiencing them. This is particularly the case when an individual believes that they are receiving messages from Bahá'u'lláh or 'Abdu'l-Bahá. These holy beings had the channels of the Cause through which to guide the Bahá'ís, and had no need to go outside these to send individual revelations. Most of the experiences of those who claim communication with the spirits are 'pure imaginations', have no reality, and yielded no result in terms of human discovery or action. *SAQ* 251–3; *LG* 514–15. (*See also* PSYCHIC POWERS.)

dress

There is no distinctive Bahá'í form of dress. In contrast to Islamic and to a lesser extent Bábí law, Bahá'u'lláh abolished any restrictions on the style and type of dress his followers might adopt, with the proviso that they should not make themselves 'playthings of the ignorant'. Men could also cut their beards as they wished, but were neither to shave their heads nor to let their hair 'pass beyond the limit of the ears' (the precise meaning of this instruction has yet to be clarified, but includes not following the 19th-century Iranian custom of wearing long sidelocks (*zulf*)) (*KA* 22 k9, 35 k44, 76–7 k159, 109 q10, 197–8 n68–9, 241–2 n174–5; *TB*

23). The need for 'utmost' CLEANLINESS was emphasized (*KA* 47 k76). Shoghi Effendi instructed the Bahá'ís to be modest and moderate in their dress, and condemned nudism (*ADJ* 25). During the 19th century, some of Bahá'u'lláh's followers followed the Bábí practice of wearing white (Browne, *Selections* 159–60; *TN* xxxi).

Dreyfus-Barney, Hippolyte (1873–1928)

Prominent early French Bahá'í and scholar. An advocate at the Paris Court of Appeal, he became a Bahá'í in 1900, and soon had mastered Persian and Arabic so as to be able to translate Bahá'í writings into French. A stream of publications followed (from 1904), such that by 1913 French readers had available to them a substantial portion of Bahá'u'lláh's major works. He also published an introductory work, *Essai sur le behaisme* (1908), which remains in use. He married Laura Barney in 1911, and together they travelled widely to promote the Faith. They were amongst the group of prominent Western Bahá'ís whom Shoghi Effendi consulted regarding the future of the Faith in 1922. Shoghi Effendi referred to Hippolyte as one of the DISCIPLES OF 'ABDU'L-BAHA. *BW3*: 210–11.

Hippolyte and Laura Dreyfus-Barney, prominent early Bahá'ís in France

Dreyfus-Barney, Laura Clifford (1879–1974)

Prominent expatriate American Bahá'í who lived for most of her life in France. She came from a well-known liberal artistic family established in Paris and became a Bahá'í there around 1900 after meeting May Bolles (MAXWELL). She made a number of prolonged visits to see 'Abdu'l-Bahá in Akka, and from 1904 onwards began carefully to compile 'Abdu'l-Bahá's answers to her questions. These were published in English, Persian and French editions in 1908 (*see* SOME ANSWERED QUESTIONS). She married Hippolyte Dreyfus in 1911, and until his death in 1928 worked closely with him. Later she was greatly involved with activities associated with the League of Nations and the International Council of Women. She was honoured by the French government. *BW16*: 535–38.

drugs

The use of opium, or of any other substance that induces torpor and sluggishness, or which damages the body, is explicitly forbidden in the *Kitáb-i-Aqdas*. 'Abdu'l-Bahá described opium smoking as a hideous act which destroys both the mind and conscience, and as a plague that should be opposed by force. All other habit forming drugs (hashish, marijuana, heroin, hallucinogens such as LSD and peyote, ALCOHOL, etc.) are also forbidden, except when prescribed by a physician. Dealing in any of these drugs is also forbidden. The renunciation of intoxicants increases health, strength and beauty. Those who seek spiritual experience in drugs are mistaken, and should turn instead to Bahá'u'lláh. *KA* 75 k155, 88 k190, 238–9 n170; *LG* 353–4.

Dunn, Clara (1869–1960)

Australian HAND OF THE CAUSE of British background. She became a Bahá'í in Washington around 1907, and accompanied her husband, J.H. Hyde Dunn, to Australia in 1920. She was appointed a Hand of the Cause by Shoghi Effendi in February 1952. *BW13*: 859–62; Harper 349–61.

Clara and Hyde Dunn, pioneer Bahá'í teachers to Australia, and later Hands of the Cause

Dunn, (John Henry) Hyde (1855–1941)

English-American Bahá'í who, with his wife, Clara, was responsible for the introduction of the Faith to Australia. He became a Bahá'í around 1905 in Seattle, and was an active promoter of the Faith. He married Clara in 1917, and the couple moved to Australia in 1920 in response to 'Abdu'l-Bahá's call in the *TABLETS OF THE DIVINE PLAN*. Already in his sixties, Hyde became a travelling salesman, using his mobility as a means of presenting the Faith throughout Australia. Shoghi Effendi named him as Australia's 'spiritual conqueror', and in 1952 posthumously designated him a HAND OF THE CAUSE. *BW9*: 593–7; Harper 60–71.

E

economic teachings

The Bahá'í teachings value economic activity. Each individual should work to support themselves and their families, such work counting as a form of worship, particularly when performed in a spirit of service to others. It should be a means of expressing one's piety and TRUSTWORTHINESS (stressed as a vital quality for economic success). It is not a barrier to service to God (*CC2*: 341). (*See also* AGRICULTURE; CHARITY; GAMBLING; *ḤUQÚQU'LLÁH*; WORK.)

POVERTY

Bahá'u'lláh regarded the poor as a divine trust (*HW*p no. 54), and reaffirmed the Islamic practice of *ZAKÁT*, in part a tax-levy to be paid to the poor. He also stated that God did not despise people for being poor. Those who were steadfast in patience are exalted (*CC1*: 496 no. 1123).

'Abdu'l-Bahá saw the struggle for physical existence as 'the fountain-head of all calamities' and 'the supreme affliction' (*SWAB* 302). Poverty degrades and demoralizes people, and in its extreme forms is indicative of tyranny. It is against God's law (*PT* 159). Every human being has a right to such necessities of life as food, adequate clothing, and rest from labour (*PT* 134).

WEALTH

Bahá'u'lláh bade the rich to heed 'the midnight sighing of the poor', so that they themselves would not follow 'the path of destruction'. They should be generous, as this reflects the divine quality of generosity, and cleanse themselves from 'the defilement of riches'. The poor are a divine trust, who should be protected by the rich. No one should be proud of their wealth. Wealth itself is a 'mighty barrier' between the seeker and God, and most rich people will thus fail to attain 'the court of His presence'. On the other hand, those who are rich, but who are not hindered thereby from the eternal kingdom, were eulogized, and their spiritual splendour compared to the illumination of the sun (*CC1*: 496 no. 1123; *HW*p no. 49, 53–5). He also stated that earthly riches bring with them fear and peril (*TB* 219), and could be held but fleetingly: 'tonight they are yours, tomorrow others will possess them' (*KA* 33–4 k40). The seeker should aim for DETACHMENT from worldly things. Those who spend their lives merely seeking to amass wealth waste their lives (*CC1*: 505 no. 1145).

'Abdu'l-Bahá noted that whilst detachment from worldly things is a virtue, wealth is not evil in itself. Under certain circumstances it might be praiseworthy, specifically if it was acquired through an individual's own efforts; is expended to help the mass of the people (through the promotion of education, social welfare and development); and is not possessed by only a few whilst the remainder of the population was impoverished (*SDC* 24–5). Ultimately, wealth is an illusion, and he condemned those who lusted after it as evil, predicting that they would be 'plunged into confusion and despair' (*CC2*: 343).

THE ABOLITION OF EXTREMES

'Abdu'l-Bahá taught that it was necessary to abolish the extremes of both poverty and wealth. To let starvation and destitution continue whilst the rich are 'overburdened' with wealth is morally wrong. Effective legislation and the voluntary sharing of their wealth by the rich are both necessary. At the same time, absolute equality is unobtainable, and any forced attempt to achieve it would be both futile – as people vary in their abilities and would soon create new inequalities – and destructive of SOCIAL ORDER (*PT* 156–9; *SAQ* 273–4; *SWAB* 115, 302. *See* COMMUNISM). Shoghi Effendi bade the writers of WILLS to remember the 'social function' of wealth, and the need to avoid its 'over-accumulation and concentration in a few individuals or groups of individuals' (*KA* 182 n38).

RECIPROCITY

'Abdu'l-Bahá noted the reciprocal nature of human life. Human beings are social beings who live together and rely upon each other for their survival. The recognition of this reciprocity is necessary for a just and compassionate society. Thus there should be both mutual concern and legal protection to ensure the welfare of all. This is a single world, and its inhabitants should be like a single family in which the existence of destitution is unacceptable to others (NSA of Canada 31–6).

PROPERTY OWNERSHIP AND ECONOMIC INSTITUTIONS

Bahá'u'lláh legitimized individual property ownership; the right to deed property to others as one wished; and the charging of moderate rates of interest (in contradistinction to Islam, in which all forms of interest on loans is forbidden as usury). It should be remembered that all ultimately belongs to God, however (*KA* 127 q69; *TB* 133–4). 'Abdu'l-Bahá advocated the establishment of institutions to ensure protection of the poor, including communal village storehouses, funded in part through a graduated income tax, and responsible for the welfare of all in the village (including orphans and the poor, elderly and incapacitated); adequate wages or benefits to ensure that workers would not be destitute as a result of sickness or old age; and industrial profit sharing, so that workers would have a stake in the company in addition to their wages (NSA of Canada 33–4; *SAQ* 274–5).

INDUSTRIAL RELATIONS

'Abdu'l-Bahá regarded strikes as harmful to the common good, and attributed them to economic injustice in society, as well as to the greed of either the employers or the workers. Governments should certainly interfere to prevent labour disputes, because society is affected by the breakdown of economic life. Thus, they should establish industrial courts with power to establish and enforce just relations between the two sides. *SAQ* 273, 276.

Edirne

Ancient city in what is now European Turkey, about 200 kilometres north-west of ISTANBUL. Europeans commonly used to call it by its old Roman name, Adrianople. Bahá'u'lláh and his companions were exiled there by the OTTOMAN authorities in 1863, arriving there on

12 December. They remained until 12 August 1868. During this period the definitive break between Bahá'u'lláh and Ṣubḥ-i-Azal occurred, and Bahá'u'lláh began the proclamations of his claims. In his writings he often referred to the city as 'the Land of Mystery' (*arḍ-i-sirr*), *sirr* having the same numerical value as Edirne according to the *abjad* system. The city suffered greatly during the Russian occupation of 1878 and much territory to the north was lost, events regarded by Bahá'ís as a fulfilment of Bahá'u'lláh's prophecies in the *Súratu'l-Ra'ís* (*see* Tablets of *ra'ís*). One of the houses occupied by Bahá'u'lláh during his stay (the house of Riḍá Beg) survives and has become a place of pilgrimage. The other houses no longer exist.

education

Bahá'ís emphasize the importance of education in both its religious and 'secular' aspects, seeing it as a major element in the spiritual and material development of the individual and society as a whole. *CC1*: 245–313. (*See also* knowledge; schools; science.)

DIVINE EDUCATION

Bahá'u'lláh taught that the spiritual essence and latent perfections of each human being can only be realized through education in religious principles: one of God's names is 'the Educator', and his purpose in sending Prophets was to guide and educate humanity, so that society might advance, and each individual at the hour of death ascend 'with absolute detachment' to the divine presence. Bahá'ís are responsible for educating the peoples of the world. Human nature is such that without spiritual education the individual would be overwhelmed by lusts and attachment to the world. The fear of God is a primary factor in education (*CC1*: 245–51). Holy law was given as a form of education, so as to elevate the individual's station, and protect them from that which is harmful (*KA* 36 k45). Thus, parents should teach their children to be God-fearing and staunch in faith; and schools train them in the principles of religion – but without making them ignorantly fanatical or bigoted. It is necessary for children to learn to distinguish right from wrong, and follow the divine commandments. They should learn sacred scripture and develop spiritual qualities (*CC1*; *TB* 68; *see* reward and punishment). 'Abdu'l-Bahá stressed that human dignity and good behaviour are only possible as a result of moral education (*SDC* 97–8). Children should be carefully trained from infancy in morality so as to abhor wrongdoing: beyond puberty, their characters are largely set. The role of the mother as the child's first educator is particularly important (*CC1*: 262–71).

'SECULAR' EDUCATION

Bahá'u'lláh emphasized literacy and the moral and social importance of work. To this end, a father has the obligation to ensure that his children (daughters and sons) learn how to read and write (as well as learning about Bahá'u'lláh's teachings). If he does not do this, the responsibility devolves upon the houses of justice (*KA* 37 k48, 138 q105; *TB* 128). Similarly, children have the obligation of 'to exert themselves to the utmost' in becoming literate (*CC1*: 249 no. 569). All workers, men and women, should contribute financially to the education and training of children (*TB* 90). It is not necessary for all children to achieve the same level of education: for some a basic education, followed by practical skills training, would be sufficient. In whatever the child does, however, it should seek perfection (*CC1*: 249 no. 569). Children should also study a universal language, and those arts and sciences that are conducive to human progress (*ESW*

138; *TB* 168). 'Abdu'l-Bahá stressed the need for comprehensive education: the 'first attribute of perfection' is learning and 'the cultural attainments of the mind' (*SDC* 35). Children should be taught the various branches of learning; training for a profession or trade; and also CLEANLINESS, health education, MUSIC, kindness to ANIMALS and courtesy. Particular attention should be given to the education of girls – as future mothers and hence the first educators of their children, their education is more important than that of boys – and of orphans, who had hitherto been neglected. Children should be praised and encouraged: beating them perverts their characters. Schools should be well organized, and established in every town and village (*CC1*: 275–90, 310–13; *CC2*: 372–8; *KA* 199–200 n76).

SOCIETAL ASPECTS

'Abdu'l-Bahá regarded education as an urgent requirement for both SOCIO-ECONOMIC DEVELOPMENT and the reform of GOVERNMENT. Ignorance is the principal reason for national decline and an underlying cause of social injustice. Only if the common people are well educated will they be able to appeal against unjust governance and secure their rights. Otherwise, most people lack 'even the vocabulary to explain what they want' (*SDC* 18). The masses long for happiness but, knowing nothing of the world, are unable to attain it. Education would release the dynamic power latent in the people (*SDC* 109–12). Education should be systematic and well organized. It should focus on those subjects that are of value to society. Subjects that are of trivial importance or based on supposition should not receive undue attention. Public opinion should be directed towards the important issues of the day (*SDC* 105–6).

EDUCATIONAL INVOLVEMENT

'Abdu'l-Bahá encouraged Bahá'ís in Iran and ASHKHABAD to establish SCHOOLS which would combine moral and the best 'secular' education. These developed particularly from the 1890s (there were some earlier pioneer efforts), and were open to children of all religions. In recent years an increasing number of Bahá'í schools, colleges, and pre-schools in various parts of the world have been set up, including both official Bahá'í institutions, such as the New Era and Rabbani Schools in India, and institutions established by groups of Bahá'ís incorporating Bahá'í principles, such as the Universidad Núr and the Private Technical University of Santa Cruz (both in Bolivia).

As Bahá'í communities in many countries have become larger and more visible there has been increasing involvement in wider educational debates and training courses concerned with moral and religious education (e.g. Bahá'í proposals for national educational reform submitted to the government authorities in Cameroon). School textbooks for religious education courses are also now more likely to include references or sections on the Faith, and in some places Bahá'í is now included as part of the religious education syllabus (e.g. the London borough of Wandsworth). Bahá'í commitment to education has gained public recognition in the Marshall Islands, where in 1993–4 the government placed seven elementary schools under Bahá'í supervision for the purpose of upgrading their quality (*BWNS* 1994–5: 118–23, 128, 131). For examples of Bahá'í educational thinking see Nikjoo and Vickers; Rost, *Brilliant Stars*.

Egypt

An early centre of Bahá'í activity in the Middle East. The first Bahá'ís in the country were mostly Iranian merchants who settled in the country during the

1860s. Action by the local Iranian consul in 1868 led to the arrest of several of these, and the exile of some of them to Khartoum in Sudan (*MBBR* 257–64). NABÍL-I-A'ZAM was sent by Bahá'u'lláh to make an appeal to the khedive on behalf of the captives, but was himself arrested. During his imprisonment in Alexandria he succeeded in converting Fáris Effendi, possibly the first Bahá'í of Christian background (*BKG* 265–8; *RB3*: 5–11). From the 1870s a Bahá'í community emerged, including both expatriate Iranians and Egyptian converts of Sunní Muslim and Christian background. Ibrahim KHEIRALLA, a pioneer Bahá'í teacher in the United States, converted in the early 1890s. The Bahá'í scholar Mírzá ABU'L-FAḌL GULPÁYGÁNÍ came to Egypt in 1895, and established himself at al-Aẓhar University. He later publicly identified himself as a Bahá'í, and published various articles and books. The number of local converts increased. 'Abdu'l-Bahá also visited Egypt, staying there for many months before, between and after his Western tours (1910–13). During these visits, he met many local notables, including the khedive ('Abbás Ḥilmí Páshá) and chief mufti. As the Bahá'ís became more organized – forming ASSEMBLIES, publishing, trying to establish new groups – so opposition from conservative Muslim elements increased, leading, in 1925, to a legal judgement nationally declaring the Bahá'ís to be non-Muslims, a statement hailed by Shoghi Effendi as a means of gaining recognition of the independence of the Faith from Islam (*GPB* 364–9). A national Bahá'í assembly was established in 1924, which was legally incorporated in 1934. Internationally, Egyptian Bahá'ís helped establish Bahá'í communities in various parts of Africa, mostly in the 1950s. In 1960 all Bahá'í institutions in Egypt were banned by presidential decree and a number of Bahá'ís arrested. The banning order remains in effect. (*See also* Shaykh Muḥammad 'ABDUH; Muḥammad-Taqí IṢFÁHÁNÍ; 'Abdu'l-Jalíl Bey SA'D.

elections

The members of Bahá'í local and national spiritual ASSEMBLIES, the UNIVERSAL HOUSE OF JUSTICE and some REGIONAL BAHÁ'Í COUNCILS are elected, either directly (local assemblies), or indirectly by elected delegates at a CONVENTION. All such elections are carried out by secret ballot by the eligible electors. Nominations, canvassing and all other forms of electioneering are prohibited. There should be no discussion of personalities before the election. Instead, each individual elector should prayerfully follow the dictates of his or her own conscience in determining whom to vote for. In countries where universal literacy prevails the electors write down the names of those they wish to vote for, and appointed tellers then count up the votes. Those with the most votes are elected if eligible to serve. There are procedures for resolving tie votes. Individual Bahá'ís bear a spiritual responsibility to vote, familiarize themselves with the qualities required of elected members, and learn about their fellow Bahá'ís (whom they may wish to vote for) through direct personal experience rather than the opinions of others. Assemblies and committees elect their own officers, but those elected must gain the votes of an absolute majority of the members. *CC1*: 315–18; *LG* 9–13, 23–8.

emotions

Different emotional states have different spiritual and physical consequences. Contentment and happiness are a cause of health, whilst anxiety and depression are afflictions which lay the body open to disease. Contentment can be developed through DETACHMENT from material concerns and reliance upon God and receipt of his bounties. Envy and hate are barriers to spiritual development, and envy and rage are physically destructive to the individual experiencing them. They should be avoided. Fananapazir and Lambden 40–3; *HWp* nos. 6, 42.

environment

Although several individual Bahá'ís have had a long and distinguished record of involvement in environmental issues, Bahá'í community interest is comparatively recent, with a particular impetus coming in 1987, when the BAHÁ'Í INTERNATIONAL COMMUNITY (BIC) joined the Network on Conservation and Religion of the World Wide Fund for Nature, and again in 1989, with the BIC's establishment of a separate Office of the Environment, and its revival of the World Forestry Charter Gatherings first convened by the pioneer promoter of 'social forestry', Richard St Barbe BAKER, in 1945. Also in 1989 the Research Department of the Universal House of Justice issued a compilation of Bahá'í writings on '*Conservation of the Earth's Resources*' (*CC1*: 65–91). Bahá'ís have since become increasingly involved in promoting environmental awareness and working with non-governmental organizations concerned with environmental issues, including in the United Nations Conference on Environment and Development (UNCED, 'the Earth Summit') in Rio de Janeiro in 1992, and in various follow-up activities. Bahá'í 'environmental philosophy' is based on the beliefs that all of nature expresses God's 'names and attributes'; human life is dependent on nature; the world is one, its component parts interdependent, and its problems require a global vision if they are to be successfully addressed (*see* WORLD UNITY); co-operation and reciprocity are fundamental to existence; diversity in nature is a source of beauty and a divine bestowal; material CIVILIZATION is by itself inadequate and potentially harmful, and needs to be melded with spirituality and moral purpose; human beings are able to improve their environment and society by the application of rationality and SCIENCE; natural resources are a divine gift and should be both protected and developed for human use; and human beings should exercise MODERATION. (*See also* AGRICULTURE; ANIMALS.) Baha'i International Community, *World Citizenship*; *BWNS* 1994–5: 112–16, 142–3, 147–9; *CC1*: 65–91; *Dahl Eco Principle*; "World Order".

Epistle to the Son of the Wolf
(PA: *Lawḥ-i-Ibn-i-Dhi'b*)

Bahá'u'lláh's last major work (*c.*1891), also known as the *Lawḥ-i-Shaykh* ('Tablet to the Shaykh'). It was composed at BAHJÍ, and addressed to Shaykh Muḥammad-Taqí Isfahání (Áqá Najafí), named by Bahá'u'lláh 'the Son of the WOLF', a prominent Iranian cleric who persecuted the Bahá'ís. Bahá'u'lláh called on the shaykh to repent of his wrongdoing and beseech God's forgiveness; declared his own mission to be God's cause; summarized some of his own teachings and cited passages from his own earlier works; noted the transforming effect he had had on the Bábís (turning them away from sedition to goodly deeds); called for protection for his followers from religious persecution and martyrdom; presented biblical prophecies fulfilled by his coming; lamented the behaviour of Ṣubḥ-i-AZAL and his followers; and called on the Bábí leader, HÁDÍ DAWLATÁBÁDÍ, to investigate his cause. *ESW*; *RB4*: 368–412.

eschatology

Beliefs concerning 'last things', typically the end of the world and the final condition of human existence. In Christianity and Islam traditional belief expects the world to end in the RESURRECTION of the dead and a final judgement, and for individual souls to be assigned to HEAVEN or hell. By contrast,

Bahá'ís believe that the CREATION has neither beginning nor end (though the earth itself may cease to exist in the future). Instead, human TIME is marked by a series of revelational and 'universal' cycles. The coming of each MANIFESTATION OF GOD marks a day of judgement for the adherents of previous religions, who may choose to enter either the 'heaven' of belief or the 'hell' of denial in relationship to the new divine messenger. The present age marks the beginning of the fulfilment of the prophecies of previous religions. As such it is the promised Day of Resurrection. The spiritual progress of each individual marks their state of SOUL, 'heaven' and 'hell' being regarded as symbolic terms for nearness to or distance from God, approach towards whom is the ultimate objective of individual existence. The objective of the human race as a whole is to progress towards the 'Most Great PEACE', the 'kingdom of God on Earth'.

esotericism

The concern with occult knowledge, a major theme in Bábism. Both the Shaykhí leaders and the Báb believed themselves to have access to hidden esoteric knowledge. This was gained both directly from God or through spiritual intercourse with the IMÁMS, and through mastery of the occult sciences of the day (especially TALISMANS, gematria and alchemy). The Bahá'í teachings, by contrast, greatly de-emphasize the esoteric elements of the Bábí tradition (stressing rationality instead). Esotericism was again briefly important during the initial EXPANSION of the Faith in the West, many of the early Western Bahá'ís being drawn from the 'cultic milieu'. *SBBR* 35–8, 84–5, 111–12, 154–5; Smith, 'American Bahá'í community', 161–70; Smith, '*Reality* magazine'.

With regard to the Western occult tradition, Shoghi Effendi was dismissive: for the most part it was a 'pseudo-science', made up of 'non-sensical' superstitions. The Bahá'ís should be patient with those who believed in it, gradually weaning them away from reliance on such things. They should themselves attach no importance to astrology or horoscopes, nor seek guidance from numerology, or identify it with the teachings of the Faith. (*See also* DREAMS AND VISIONS; MAGIC; PSYCHIC POWERS.) *LG* 516–22.

Esperanto

Artificial language created by Dr Ludwik Zamenhof (1859–1917) to promote inter-ethnic and international understanding. Following publication of the language in 1887 an Esperanto movement developed. The common commitment to the need for an international LANGUAGE and for amity between all peoples created an obvious 'elective affinity' between Esperantists and Bahá'ís, and there were contacts between the two movements from an early date – including an Esperanto booklet on Bahá'í published in London in 1907. 'Abdu'l-Bahá praised Esperanto and encouraged Bahá'ís in both West and East to learn it. Zamenhof similarly expressed his admiration for 'Abdu'l-Bahá and the Bahá'í movement. Prominent early Bahá'ís who were also active Esperantists included Agnes ALEXANDER and J.E. ESSLEMONT. Bahá'í–Esperanto contacts were particularly strong in the 1920s and 1930s: Hermann GROSSMANN published a monthly Bahá'í Esperanto magazine (*La Nova Tago*, 1925–36) and established a network of Bahá'í Esperanto groups in Germany; Martha ROOT utilized Esperanto contacts in her worldwide travels and began the practice of having Bahá'í representation at the annual world Esperanto congresses (from 1925); Lidia ZAMENHOF (Ludwik's daughter) became a Bahá'í (1926) and translated Bahá'í literature into Esperanto; and Muḥammad Labíb began a bilingual Esperanto newsletter in Iran

(1926; the introduction of Esperanto into Iran was almost entirely the work of Bahá'ís). There has been some revival of Bahá'í Esperanto activities since the 1970s, with the formation of a Bahá'í Esperanto League (*Bahaa Esperanto-Ligo*) in 1973. Whilst encouraging Bahá'ís to learn Esperanto, both Shoghi Effendi and the Universal House of Justice have emphasized that there is no official Bahá'í endorsement of Esperanto as a future world language.

Esslemont, John E. (1874–1925)

Prominent British Bahá'í, best known for his book *Bahá'u'lláh and the New Era* (1923), which even now remains one of the most widely available introductions to the Bahá'í teachings. Both 'Abdu'l-Bahá and Shoghi Effendi supported his work. He first encountered the Faith in 1914 and was a major figure in its early development in Britain. He became a close friend and confidant of Shoghi Effendi, who invited him to come to Haifa to serve as his English-language secretary in 1924. He was posthumously designated a HAND OF THE CAUSE, and was named as one of the DISCIPLES OF 'ABDU'L-BAHA. *BW1*: 133–6; Harper 72–84; Momen, *Esslemont*.

John E. Esslemont, distinguished early Scottish Bahá'í and author

ethics

Good character is a source of human glory. Bahá'ís should under all circumstances behave in a manner that is 'seemly', acting in accordance with God's desire. They should be fair-minded, pious and upright (*TB* 36–7). They should never be a cause of grief to another, or curse them, or be a cause of strife (*TB* 129). Courtesy is the 'prince of virtues' (*TB* 88). (*See also* SPIRITUAL QUALITIES.)

evil

Evil has no objective reality other than in the negative and destructive behaviour of individual human beings and animals. Individuals are subject to temptation from the lower aspect of their own HUMAN NATURE. Bahá'ís should guard themselves against such influences by turning towards God, deepening themselves in the Bahá'í teachings, and seeking the guidance and protection of the holy spirit. They should also be on their guard against the negative influences of others, and seek to replace that evil with good. If this proves impossible and they are unable to exert any positive influence, they should shun the company of such evil ones. *LG* 512–13.

evil spirits

The belief in evil spirits (demons, ghosts and the like) which can harm or exert some form of negative influence on human beings (e.g. through demonic possession) is rejected as superstitious in the Bahá'í writings, which emphasize the goodly nature of God's creation and the responsibility of individuals for any evil acts they might commit (*see* EVIL; FREE WILL). Individuals who commit evil may have an enormous influence in this world, but their own souls cease to have any influence after they die and they have no power over the living. There are no non-human evil spirits which human beings should fear or seek to placate. When the New Testament refers to people as being 'possessed' by devils, it is purely symbolic: the individuals concerned have yielded to the 'dark forces' of their own passions and baser natures. *LG* 512–13, 521–2.

evolution

'Abdu'l-Bahá emphasized the radical difference between animals and human beings. Animals are captives of the world of nature: they act according to their instincts, possess no power of ideation, and lack 'spiritual susceptibilities'. Humans, by contrast, possess intelligence, moral FREE WILL and the capacities to discover and control the workings of nature and to know and love God (*PUP* 177–8). He thus rejected the philosophical MATERIALISM that underlies the Darwinian theory of human evolution. The human physical form has changed over the millennia – just as the form of the individual changes from that of an embryo to an adult human being – and become more perfect, but the human spirit was always distinctive (*SAQ* 177–99). (*See also* SOCIAL EVOLUTION.)

excellence

Bahá'u'lláh called on his followers to display 'such deeds and character' that 'all mankind' would profit by their example. They should be the 'lump that would leaven the peoples of the world'. Bahá'ís should strive to acquire both inner and outer perfections – both moral virtues (*see* SPIRITUAL QUALITIES) and knowledge and skills. Their deeds should not differ from their words; each day they should seek to be better than the day before. 'Abdu'l-Bahá appealed to Bahá'ís to attain such distinction that

A group of Bahá'ís from around the world outside the Seat of the Universal House of Justice

they would be recognized as Bahá'ís by their virtues. Whatever work they did, they should strive that it was of the highest standard. From childhood they should be inspired to undertake studies that would benefit humanity. They should exert all their efforts to acquire EDUCATION. Bahá'ís should become famous in all branches of knowledge. For Shoghi Effendi to be a 'true' Bahá'í it was necessary to struggle against both the evils that prevailed in the world and the weaknesses, prejudices and selfishness of one's own character. When the Bahá'ís did this they would exert a great influence on others, and many would become Bahá'ís by the force of their example. *CC1*: 367–84; *MUHJ* no. 303.

expansion

There has been a strong missionary emphasis in both the Bábí and Bahá'í religions (*see* TEACHING), with a determined effort to increase the number of adherents; the geographical range of their locations; and, in the Bahá'í case, their religious and cultural diversity. This is reflected in the present global diffusion of the Bahá'í Faith: by 1995 it was established in 190 countries and 45 dependent territories, and in many parts of the world had succeeded also in gaining or at least settling followers in every major town and island, no matter how remote; over 2,000 tribes and ethnic groups were represented by the 1980s.

THE PATTERN OF EXPANSION

Geographical and numerical expansion of Bahá'í and its religio-cultural diversification have been closely interlinked, notably in a series of 'geo-cultural breakthroughs' whereby Bahá'í communities have been established in an ever more diverse range of religious and cultural milieux. Three stages and three 'worlds' of Bábí–Bahá'í expansion can be identified: (1) an initial 'Islamic' stage (1844–*c*.1892), in which Bábism and the early Bahá'í movement were largely confined to the environing culture and society of the Islamic Middle East; (2) an 'international' stage (*c*.1892–*c*.1953), during which Bahá'í missionary expansion succeeded in transcending the religion's Islamic roots, in particular by gaining a small but intensely active Western following; and (3) the present 'global' stage (from *c*.1953), in which the Faith has begun to assume the characteristics of a world religion, and large numbers of adherents have been gained in the 'Third World'. The recent collapse of the communist regimes of the Soviet Union and its former satellites, and the consequent opening up of these countries to organized activity by religious groups, has enabled Bahá'ís finally to establish themselves in every country in the world (with the possible exception of North Korea).

THE 'ISLAMIC PERIOD', 1844–*c*.1892

Bábism began as a sectarian movement within SHAYKHISM (*GPB* xii), in the particular context of the succession crisis following the death of Sayyid KÁẒIM. The LETTERS OF THE LIVING were Shaykhís, and the initial expansion of the movement was largely confined within the existing network of Shaykhí communities. Some transcendence of the Shaykhí milieu later occurred, both because the Báb exercised a wider appeal at a popular level in terms of his messianic claims and as a perceived Islamic holy man, and as a result of conversions such as ḤUJJAT and VAḤÍD, prominent non-Shaykhí clerics, whose followers also became Bábís – making ZANJÁN and NAYRÍZ major Bábí strongholds. Nevertheless, the Bábís remained part of the world of sectarian Shí'ism.

Whether or not Bábism in its original form could ever have expanded more widely is unknown – it was all but obliterated as a movement by 1852 – but when it re-emerged in the late 1850s under the direction of BAHÁ'U'LLÁH in Baghdad, it was something different. Reviving the Bábí movement, he simultaneously transformed it, laying the basis for expansion beyond the Bábí community by addressing Sufi and Judaeo-Christian themes, and presenting Bábí beliefs in a style that could appeal directly to literate Iranian Muslims and which did not need to be mediated through clerical leaders. Later – from the 1870s onwards – the basis of Bahá'í appeal was further widened as Bahá'u'lláh presented a vision of sociopolitical reconstruction (Western ideas of constitutionalism; a new international world order), whilst 'Abdu'l-Bahá circulated a proposal for the 'modernization' of Iran (*see* SECRET OF DIVINE CIVILIZATION), and Mírzá ABU'L-FAḌL and others developed Bahá'í apologetics addressed specifically to the Jews, Christians and Zoroastrians.

Correspondingly, when the newly emerged Bahá'í Faith began to expand (from the 1860s), its 'target' population was much wider than that addressed by the Bábís. Most of the new Bahá'ís were still Iranian Muslims, but they were joined by small numbers of Sunní Muslims in the Ottoman empire and Egypt; Jews and Zoroastrians in Iran; and Levantine Christians. There was also wider geographical expansion. The Bábís had been confined to Iran and Iraq, but there were Bahá'ís among the Shí'í population of Russian Caucasia, Iranian migrants in Russian Turkistan, and Muslims and Zoroastrians in India and Burma. Small groups of Iranian Bahá'ís also established themselves in Iraq, Turkey, Lebanon and Egypt.

By 1892, the year of Bahá'u'lláh's passing and 'Abdu'l-Bahá's accession to leadership, a distinctive Bahá'í religion had come into being. The total number of Bahá'ís by this date may have been in the region of 100,000 (Smith, 'Bábí and Bahá'í numbers').

'INTERNATIONALIZATION', *c.*1892–*c.*1953

During 'Abdu'l-Bahá's leadership (1892–1921) a major change occurred in the nature of the Bahá'í community as it broke out of the cultural confines of its traditional Islamic milieu and became a truly international religious movement. This process continued under Shoghi Effendi, so that by 1952 there were Bahá'ís in some 116 countries and major colonial territories (including quite remote areas such as Greenland and the Bismarck Archipelago of New Guinea). The total number of Bahá'ís remained small, however (*c.*200,000), and the majority – over 90 per cent – were still Iranian. Nevertheless, the cultural adaptability of the Faith and its potential to attract a wide diversity of peoples had been vividly demonstrated, and the basis for more global expansion following the start of the TEN YEAR CRUSADE (1953) established.

The Faith in the West

Of key importance in this transformation was the establishment of the Faith in the West (from 1894; see below). Although small numbers of non-Muslims had already become Bahá'ís in the Middle East, they had done so in an Islamic cultural environment, many of the values of which they themselves shared. By contrast, in the West, the Bahá'í Faith was something alien. A cultural gap had to be bridged if the Faith was going to gain followers. Significantly, the pioneer Bahá'í teacher in the United States was a recently converted Syrian Christian (Ibrahim KHEIRALLA), who was able to express his own version of the Bahá'í teachings in a way that appealed to Christian sentiment. Subsequently, the newly converted American Bahá'ís (followed by a smaller number of Europeans) played a major role in reformulating the Bahá'í teachings in Western and Christian terms: composing their own introductions to the Faith (often quoting extensively from the Bible), and continuing to use Christian devotional styles (Armstrong-Ingram, *Music*). In much of this they were supported by 'Abdu'l-Bahá, who took an active role in the process of reformulation: addressing Western religious and social concerns in Bahá'í terms in his conversations with Western pilgrims, his letters to the Western Bahá'ís, and his talks during his tours of Europe and North America in 1911–13. 'Abdu'l-Bahá's own personal presence and the enormous devotion he received from so many of his Western followers also acted to consolidate and dynamize the fledgling Western Bahá'í communities. Initially, the identification (adamantly repudiated by 'Abdu'l-Bahá) that many early American Bahá'ís made between 'Abdu'l-Bahá and Jesus Christ also acted as an important cultural 'bridge'.

Administration and planning

The other major changes linked to expansion were the twin developments of the system of Bahá'í ADMINISTRATION (begun in 1922) – elected spiritual ASSEMBLIES becoming the directive agencies for organized Bahá'í activities – and systematic planning (from 1937; *see* PLANS). Both of these were rooted in earlier periods of Bahá'í history, but were given fresh emphasis and form by Shoghi Effendi. The Western Bahá'ís, particularly those of the United States, took the lead in both developments. Unlike the Bahá'ís of the Middle East they enjoyed conditions of religious freedom and material opportunity which enabled them to accomplish Shoghi Effendi's objectives with relative ease, although often also with much personal sacrifice.

Shoghi Effendi's expansion plans called for an extension of Bahá'í TEACHING activities; the settlement of PIONEERS in those territories in which there were as yet no Bahá'ís; the establishment of local and national assemblies; the acquisition of properties (temple sites and administrative headquarters); the translation of Bahá'í literature into an increasing range of languages; and the gradual completion of the Bahá'í House of Worship in Wilmette.

Initially, the plans were assigned individually to each national spiritual assembly (eight by the late 1930s, eleven by 1951), aiming for the expansion of each community's 'home front' (in size and geographical extent) as well as following a strategy of global expansion: North American Bahá'ís being required to establish the Faith in Latin America and the Caribbean (1937–53), and later in those areas of post-war Western Europe in which there were few or no Bahá'ís (1946–53); those of India and Burma being directed to South-east Asia (1946–53); the Iranians to Afghanistan and the Arab world (1946–50); the Egyptians to North Africa (1949–53); and the British, in concert with all the above, to Africa (1951–3). The success of this collaborative inter-assembly 'Africa project' heralded the launching of the Ten Year Crusade (1953–63), which by the extent and magnitude of its accomplishments marked the beginning of a new stage in Bahá'í growth (see below). In terms of geographical diffusion and administrative expansion the results of the plans were impressive: in 1935 Bahá'ís resided in 1,034 places in the world (139 with local spiritual assemblies); by 1952 these figures had risen to 2,425 and 611 respectively (*SBBR* 161).

GLOBAL EXPANSION, FROM 1953

It is only from the 1950s onwards that the Bahá'í Faith has begun to fulfil the vision of its founders and become a world religion, albeit still small in scale.

(1) In absolute numbers, the total number of Bahá'ís in the world has increased from 200,000 or so in the early 1950s to about 5 million by

the early 1990s. Again, whilst in the 1950s the number of Bahá'ís in most countries was minute (Iran and the USA being the only communities of substantial size), many national Bahá'í communities are now quite large, and in several places (notably some of the Pacific Island nations) they have come to form a significant component in the wider population. More generally, local Bahá'í communities have become more widely diffused, and in many areas strong local roots have been put down, the Bahá'ís coming to form an integral part of the environing culture.

(2) The social composition of many communities has also radically changed: in 1950, most Bahá'ís outside Iran, were drawn from the educated and middle classes, even in countries such as those of Latin America where such social groups were a tiny minority. Now the majority are drawn from the rural and, to a lesser extent, urban masses in the 'Third World' (i.e. Latin America, the Caribbean, sub-Saharan Africa and monsoon Asia). Even the North American Bahá'í communities now comprise people from a much wider range of social backgrounds, including large numbers of ethnic minority group members.

(3) The cultural diversity of the Bahá'ís is now much greater, in terms both of the number of ethnic groups represented within it and the range of cultural expressions of 'being Bahá'í'. There is no longer the dominance of Iranian or Western cultural styles that characterized earlier stages in the development of the Faith (for an example see Garlington on the 'Bahá'í *bhajans*' of India).

Large-scale enrolment

This transformational expansion has reflected a fundamental shift in the focus of Bahá'í teaching work. Thus, whilst up to the 1950s Bahá'ís commonly concentrated their attention on urban, educated audiences – often utilizing newspaper publicity and public meetings as a major part of their activities – in much of the world they have since adopted 'mass teaching' methods: learning to teach large numbers of often illiterate people directly, and making much greater use of music. Significant contacts with rural populations in several parts of the 'Third World' (Uganda, Bolivia, the Mentawai Islands of Indonesia and the Malwa area of India) began during the Ten Year Crusade, and have subsequently been expanded to many other countries, often with the same results: the influx of hundreds or even thousands of new Bahá'ís. Although this sometimes places severe logistical strains on the local and national Bahá'í administrations involved, increasing experience has led to the use of more effective methods of integrating the new Bahá'ís into the community and of deepening their knowledge and commitment to the Faith.

The large-scale influx of new Bahá'ís – often poorly educated, lacking in material means, and remote from the main centres of population – has prompted the development of new means of communication within the Bahá'í communities involved (e.g. teaching institutes, Bahá'í RADIO stations) as well as increasing concern with LITERACY programmes, schooling, self-help rural development schemes, and the promotion of indigenous cultural activities (see SOCIO-ECONOMIC DEVELOPMENT).

Planning and administrative expansion

Since 1953 Bahá'í expansion has been channelled by a series of global plans (Shoghi Effendi's Ten Year Crusade (1953–63), and the Nine (1964–73), Five (1974–9), Seven (1979–86), Six (1986–92), Three (1993–6), and Four (1996–2000) Year Plans directed by the Universal House of Justice).

One major focus of these plans has been administrative expansion (*see* Table 1). There had already been substantial increase, but this was dramatically overshadowed by later developments: since 1953 the number of localities has increased to over 120,000, of local assemblies to over 17,000 and of national assemblies to 174.

Community Developments

Since 1953 certain aspects of change within the Bahá'í community have been increasingly emphasized, notably the establishment of Bahá'í SCHOOLS; the promotion of SOCIO-ECONOMIC DEVELOPMENT projects (particularly LITERACY and primary health care); and the enhanced role of WOMEN and YOUTH. The schools and development projects both indicate the increasingly well-established nature of particular Bahá'í communities and, as normally they are made available to non-Bahá'ís as well as to Bahá'ís, have an impact on the wider societies of which these communities form part. Although not designed as a means of propagating the Faith, they have often had that effect. The emphasis on the role of women has caused Bahá'ís to think more deeply about the role of women in Bahá'í administration and community life (of major significance in those societies in which male domination is taken for granted); increased the number of those actively involved in Bahá'í teaching work; and promoted a stronger 'familialization' of Bahá'í communities, and hence more effective religious socialization of Bahá'í children (*SBBR* 92–3). The enhanced role of youth (from the 1960s onwards) gave young people, with their abundant energy and relative freedom from constraining social ties, a leading role in Bahá'í activity, particularly the teaching work. It has also had a major impact on Bahá'í cultural styles, as with the much greater emphasis now given to music in Western communities.

Table 1: Administrative expansion of the Bahá'í Faith 1928–95

	NSAs	LSAs	Localities
1928	9	102	579
1935	10	135	1,034
1944	7	482	1,880
1953	12	670	2,700
1963	56	4,437	14,437
1977	123	17,415	77,451
1992	165	20,435	120,046
1995	174	17,148	121,058

Notes: The 1928 figure for LSAs includes 5 in Germany, undifferentiated in the 1928 directory but assumed to have existed at that time (see the 1930 directory, *BW3*: 218, 222), and 17 for Iran, which represents the total number of 'administrative divisions' rather than of LSAs, for which at that early stage of administrative development in the East figures are unobtainable.

Sources: 1928 and 1935 figures calculated from *BW2*: 189–91 and *BW6*: 505–24; 1944–77 figures from Universal House of Justice, Department of Statistics, memorandum, 15 May 1988; 1992 figures from Universal House of Justice, *Six Year Plan*, pp. 111, 114; 1995 figures from *BWNS*, 1995–6: 317.

DISTRIBUTION OF THE FAITH

These periods of expansion have been closely linked in changes in the overall distribution and composition of the Bahá'í community world-wide. Thus, up until the early 1890s almost all Bahá'ís were Iranians, and lived in what might be termed the religion's 'Islamic heartland' (Iran, the Middle East, Egypt, the Caucasus, Central Asia). Then, between the 1890s and 1950s, a small but significant minority of Westerners became Bahá'ís, coming to play a disproportionate role in the further geographical expansion of the Faith as well as in its administration and public presentation (*SBBR* 171–2). Only since the 1950s has the Bahá'í Faith succeeded in attracting large numbers from the 'Third World', these Bahá'ís now constituting the majority of the global Bahá'í population.

Some indication of the changing distribution of Bahá'ís in the world is given in Table 2. In 1954 over 90 per cent of Bahá'í's lived in Iran, and there were probably fewer than 10,000 Bahá'ís in the West and no more than 3,000 in the whole of Africa, Asia (excluding the Middle East), Latin America, the Caribbean and Oceania combined. Indian Bahá'ís then constituted less than 1 per cent of the world total. This situation began to change from the late 1950s onwards with the large-scale influx of people in many parts of the Bahá'í 'Third World' (East Asia is an obvious exception), and by 1988 Middle Eastern and Western Bahá'ís probably constituted respectively less than 7 and 5 per cent of the world total. South Asia (mostly India) (42 per cent), sub-Saharan Africa (22 per cent), and Latin America and the Caribbean (16 per cent) were now the areas of greatest numerical strength.

A similar picture emerges from figures for the number of local spiritual assemblies and localities in which Bahá'ís reside (see Table 3). In 1949 one-third of all localities and over half of all assemblies were in the Faith's 'Islamic heartland' (mostly in Iran);

Table 2: Estimated Bahá'í populations

	1954 (000s)	(%)	1988 (000s)	(%)
1. The 'Islamic Heartland'	200	93.6	300	6.7
2. The West	10	4.7	200	4.5
3. The Bahá'í 'Third World':				
– South Asia	1	0.5	1,900	42.9
– sub-Saharan Africa	>2 (combined)	0.9 (combined)	1,000	22.3
– Latin America and the Caribbean			700	15.6
– South East Asia			300	6.7
– East Asia			20	0.4
– Oceania (excl. the 'Anglo-Pacific')			70	1.6
Totals	213		4,490	

The division of the world into 'cultural areas' is adapted from *SBBR* 165–71. The 'Anglo-Pacific' comprises Australia, New Zealand and Hawaii.

Source: Adapted from 'Survey' 72.

Table 3: Local Spiritual Assemblies (LSAs) and localities in which Bahá'ís reside: 1949, 1964 and 1992

Geographical Areas	1949		1964		1992	
	LSAs	Localities	LSAs	Localities	LSAs	Localities
The Islamic Heartland	304 (51.0)[a]	777 (33.8)	594 (13.1)	1,679 (11.1)	162 (0.8)	1,396 (1.2)
Iran	281 (47.1)	709 (30.8)	530 (11.6)	1,503 (9.9)	0 (0.0)[b]	709 (0.6)
Middle East and North Africa (excl. Iran)	22 (3.7)	66 (2.9)	52 (1.1)	136 (0.9)	88 (0.4)	349 (0.3)
Central Asia, Caucasus and Turkey	1 (0.2)	2 (0.1)	12 (0.3)	40 (0.3)	74 (0.4)	338 (0.3)
The West	222 (37.2)	1,352 (58.8)	637 (13.9)	2,959 (19.5)	2,979 (14.6)	13,133 (10.8)
North America	171 (28.7)	1,207 (52.5)	414 (9.0)	2,044 (13.5)	1,890 (9.3)	8,530 (7.1)
Anglo-Pacific	12 (2.0)	19 (0.8)	39 (0.9)	176 (1.2)	255 (1.2)	530 (0.4)
Western Europe	39 (6.5)	125 (5.4)	182 (4.0)	726 (4.8)	708 (3.5)	3,273 (2.7)
The Balkans, Eastern Europe and Russia	0 (0.0)	1 (0.0)	2 (0.0)	13 (0.1)	126 (0.6)	800 (0.7)
The Bahá'í Third World	70 (11.7)	171 (7.4)	3,347 (73.1)	10,547 (695)	17,287 (84.6)	105, 508 (87.9)
Sub-Saharan Africa	1 (0.2)	8 (0.3)	1,327 (29.0)	3,173 (20.9)	5,877 (28.8)	33,040 (27.5)
Latin America and the Caribbean	35 (5.9)	70 (3.0)	294 (6.4)	1,456 (9.6)	3,501 (17.1)	18,940 (15.8)
South Asia	28 (4.7)	69 (3.0)	1,111 (24.3)	4,651 (30.6)	5,676 (27.8)	37,086 (30.9)
South East Asia	5 (0.8)	15 (0.7)	543 (11.9)	905 (6.0)	1,426 (7.0)	11,671 (9.7)
East Asia	1 (0.2)	7 (0.3)	29 (0.6)	126 (0.8)	193 (0.9)	1,207 (1.0)
Oceania	0 (0.0)	2 (0.1)	43 (0.9)	236 (1.6)	614 (3.0)	3,564 (3.0)
World Totals	**596**	**2,300**	**4,578**	**15,185**	**20,428**	**120,037**

Notes:
a Figures in parentheses represent the percentage of the world total.
b Bahá'í institutions in Iran were disbanded by government order in 1983.

Sources: Calculated from *BW11*: 519–74; *BW14*: 124–35; Universal House of Justice, Department of Statistics, 'Statistical Table, Six Year Plan Final Figures, 20 April 1992' mimeographed.

almost 60 per cent of localities and 37 per cent of assemblies were in the West (mostly the USA); and only 7 per cent of localities and 12 per cent of assemblies in the rest of the world. By 1964 (after the completion of the Ten Year Crusade) the situation had changed dramatically. Not only had there been a marked increase in the number of localities (×6.6) and assemblies (×7.6), but the Islamic heartland and the West were now overshadowed by the Bahá'í 'Third World' (with 70 per cent of localities and 73 per cent of assemblies, as compared with 11 per cent and 13 per cent for the Islamic heartland and 19 per cent and 14 per cent for the West respectively). Within this 'Third World', South Asia (mostly India) and sub-Saharan Africa stood out in particular (with respectively 31 per cent and 21 per cent of the localities and 24 per cent and 29 per cent of the assemblies).

This 'Third World' dominance has continued to the present day, with 88 per cent of the total localities and 85 per cent of the assemblies in 1992, as against 11 per cent and 15 per cent for the West and the astonishing figure of 1 per cent for both in the Islamic heartland, this latter drop being largely caused by the banning of Bahá'í institutions in Iran. Africa and South Asia continue to stand out as the regions with the greatest numbers of localities (28 per cent and 31 per cent) and assemblies (29 per cent and 28 per cent), followed by Latin America and the Caribbean, South East Asia and North America (respectively 16 per cent, 10 per cent and 7 per cent of localities, and 17 per cent, 7 per cent and 9 per cent of assemblies). By contrast, the Pacific (Anglo-Pacific and Oceania), Europe and the countries of the former Soviet Union, the Middle East, North Africa and Central Asia, and East Asia are all areas with comparatively small numbers of assemblies and localities.

This is only part of the picture, however. The relative size of 'host' populations also needs to be considered. A general measure of this is provided by the quotient for the number of local spiritual assemblies per million population. Thus, in relation to total population figures the greatest density of Bahá'í localities and assemblies in the world is in the Pacific, both 'Oceania' (76 assemblies per million) and the 'Anglo-Pacific' (Australia, New Zealand and Hawaii, with 12 assemblies per million). This is followed by Africa (10); the Americas (7 for both North America and Latin America and the Caribbean); South Asia (4); South East Asia (2.4); and Western Europe (1.8). The Islamic heartland; the Balkans and Eastern Europe; and East Asia all have figures of less than 1 per million.

THE 'ISLAMIC HEARTLAND'

Iran

The Bábís succeeded in establishing a widespread network of adherents in Iran during the 1840s (Smith and Momen, 'Bábí movement'), the Bahá'ís later building on that base, eventually embarking on a systematic campaign to establish Bahá'í groups and assemblies throughout the length and breadth of the country. During the late 19th century Bahá'í conversions were gained amongst the Iranian Jewish and Zoroastrian minorities (but significantly not amongst the Christians: Stiles; *SBBR* 93–6), thus decisively broadening the religious base of the Bahá'í community.

As the majority of Iranian Bábís became Bahá'ís, the present Bahá'í community has effectively been in existence for 150 years. During this period a distinctive sense of communal identity has developed, supported by the development of a variety of Bahá'í social, educational and administrative bodies and by the tendency of Iranian Bahá'ís to marry their co-religionists and the resultant 'familialization' of the Faith.

Communal identity and a tremendous sense of sacrificial dedication on the part of the most active Bahá'ís has also been increased by the intermittent outbreaks of persecution and martyrdom that have befallen the Iranian Bahá'ís throughout this period, reaching their greatest intensity under the present revolutionary Islamic regime (from 1979). The Bahá'ís now possibly constitute a minority of between 0.5 and 1 per cent of the Iranian population (Smith, 'Bábí and Bahá'í Numbers'), which is probably a lower figure than in the past (*SBBR* 175–8).

INTERNATIONAL ROLE: The Iranian Bahá'ís have played a massive role in the global expansion of the Faith (up until the 1960s the majority of Bahá'ís in the world were Iranians or of Iranian origin). The Iranian Bahá'í diaspora now reaches to almost every country in the world, and a significant proportion of these expatriates are active Bahá'í pioneers. In recent years young Westernized Iranian professionals (doctors, engineers, etc.) have come to play a very important role in the development of many Third World Bahá'í communities. Iranian Bahá'ís have also played a major part in the international leadership of the Faith: of thirty-two Hands of the Cause appointed to office by Shoghi Effendi in the 1950s, eleven were Iranians, several of them overseas pioneers; of the sixteen members of the Universal House of Justice elected to date, five have been Iranian. Again, the sad persecution of Iranian Bahá'ís since 1979 has also had a global impact, gaining the Bahá'ís world-wide sympathy and the public support of many governments and organizations.

The Middle East and North Africa

A network of Bahá'í groups was established in Ottoman IRAQ, Syria, Lebanon and Palestine, as well as in EGYPT and (briefly) Sudan, during the late 19th century. These groups were initially mostly composed of Iranian Bahá'í émigrés, however. There were few conversions of Arabs, both because most Arabs are Sunnís, suspicious of Bahá'í's Iranian Shí'í origins (though Sunní and Christian converts were gained in Egypt), and because of persistent constraints on Bahá'í missionary expansion, including extreme caution on the part of the Bahá'ís themselves. It was not possible for Bahá'ís to conduct an open campaign of teaching and proclamation of their Faith, or even always to defend themselves publicly against attack. A modest programme of activity was mounted in Egypt and Iraq (with national assemblies being established in 1924 and 1931 respectively), but this sparked opposition from conservative Islamic groups, leading to the seizure of Bahá'u'lláh's house in BAGHDAD (1922), and a significant legal case in Egypt, in which the Bahá'ís were nationally proclaimed to be unbelievers (1925).

There was an increase in the spread and numerical base of Bahá'ís in the Arab world during the 1940s as a result of pioneer moves by Iranian Bahá'ís to various Arab countries. National assemblies were established from the 1950s onwards, but Bahá'ís in the Arab world have also experienced a number of major reverses, including a presidential banning order against the Bahá'ís in Egypt in 1960. Since then the Bahá'í Faith has been banned in several other Arab countries and Bahá'ís imprisoned in Egypt, Iraq and, for a while, in Morocco (1962). In such circumstances it is not possible for the Bahá'ís to organize public activities, although an Arabic-language Bahá'í publishing trust was established in Lebanon.

Central Asia, the Caucasus and Turkey

Bahá'í groups were established in Turkey, and the provinces of Asiatic Russia adjoining Iran during the lifetime of Bahá'u'lláh.

The communities of the Caucasus and Turkistan rapidly became some of the most important centres of Bahá'í activity in the Bahá'í world, and the Ashkhabad community in particular achieved great prominence, expressed by its choice as the first site for the construction of a Bahá'í House of Worship. The Bahá'ís of these areas were initially mostly expatriate Iranians or culturally related Azeri Shí'í Turks, but with the greater religious freedoms initially gained after the Russian revolutions of 1917, opportunities for expansion beyond these groups increased dramatically. The former central assemblies for Turkistan and the Caucasus (some of the earliest Bahá'í administrative institutions in the world) were also recast as national assemblies in 1925. As communist power was consolidated, however, restrictions on religious activities were imposed, and the Bahá'í communities of Soviet Asia crushed during the 1930s, only re-emerging during the recent period of liberalization in the Soviet Union and the emergence of independent republics. A network of Bahá'í communities has now been established throughout the region, and national assemblies formed in each of the republics (1992/4).

The early Bahá'í groups in Turkey consisted largely of expatriate Iranians, and it was not until the establishment of an independent Turkish nation out of the ruins of the Ottoman empire that a genuinely Turkish Bahá'í community slowly developed. Since World War II it has come to resemble the Bahá'í communities of Europe, experiencing slow, consistent growth since the 1950s. A national assembly was formed in 1959, and Turkey now has the greatest number of local assemblies of any country in the Islamic heartland.

THE WEST

'The West' here includes Europe, North America and the 'Anglo-Pacific' (Australia, New Zealand and Hawaii). All these areas share a European Christian inheritance, the cultures and social and political institutions of North America and the Anglo-Pacific having been largely shaped by European migrants. Excluding Russia and the formerly Communist countries of Eastern Europe, there is a common pattern of Bahá'í development throughout much of this area (although also significant differences in responsiveness: Smith, 'Bahá'í Faith in the West').

North America

The most important area of Bahá'í expansion in the West has always been North America, the United States in particular. Bahá'í expansion in the West began in America (in Chicago in 1894), and the initial rapid spread of the movement was at first largely confined to the United States. Thus by 1900 there were some 1,500 American Bahá'ís, scattered across 60 localities in 25 states, and by 1916 the number of Bahá'ís was approaching 3,000. By contrast, although a number of Bahá'í groups were established in Canada and Europe during this period, they remained few in number and small in size. It was also the American Bahá'ís who played the major role in the early production of Bahá'í literature in the West; initiated the mammoth project of constructing a Bahá'í temple (in the Chicago suburb of Wilmette); developed the earliest Western Bahá'í administrative bodies; and played the major role in the early introduction of the Faith to other parts of the West.

All these activities became more systematic during the period of Shoghi Effendi's guardianship. Numerical expansion was slow (by 1947 there were still only in the region of five thousand Bahá'ís in North America as a whole, but sustained effort led to the creation of a well-organized network of spiritual assemblies; the completion of the Wilmette temple (finally dedicated for worship in 1953); and the dispatch of pioneers to establish the Faith throughout Latin America (from 1937), and to consolidate it in post-World War II Europe.

During the Ten Year Crusade there was a marked increase in the number of Bahá'ís – to perhaps around 19,000 for the whole of North America by 1963, as well as further significant internal diffusion and world-wide pioneering activity. Even more dramatic growth occurred during the late 1960s and early 1970s, with a large influx of young people, and successful 'mass teaching' amongst the rural black population in the south-eastern states of the USA. Conversions of members of other minority groups were also made. As a result, the total number of Bahá'ís increased to an estimated 105,000 by 1973 and 179,000 by 1988 (all figures cited in Smith, 'Bahá'í Faith in the West').

Significant growth in Canada began in the 1940s, with the establishment of a separate Canadian national assembly in 1948 (the Canadian and American Bahá'ís had shared a common national administration since 1909). The community was early distinguished by its inclusion of many Native Americans. Outside the contiguous USA, the Alaskan (1957) and Hawaiian (1964) Bahá'ís also formed their own separate national assemblies and increased their numbers.

North American Bahá'ís have played a major role in the international leadership of the Faith: of thirty-two Hands of the Cause appointed to office by Shoghi Effendi between 1951 and 1957, thirteen were North Americans, including three overseas pioneers. Of the sixteen members of the Universal House of Justice, seven have been Americans, and one Canadian.

Europe

Bahá'í expansion in Europe began within a few years of the establishment of the Faith in North America. The earliest groups formed were in Paris and London, but by the time of 'Abdu'l-Bahá's visits to the continent in 1911 and 1913 there was a network of Bahá'ís in all the major European countries as well as in several of the minor ones. Germany had become the major centre for Bahá'í activity, and remained so after the disruptions of World War I (1914–18). During the inter-war years the establishment of the International Bahá'í Bureau in Geneva (1925) came to provide an effective focus for communication for European Bahá'ís, and a number of visiting Bahá'ís from North America (e.g. Martha Root) together with the work of European Bahá'ís led to further expansion. Esperanto conferences proved to be an important means of contacting sympathetic non-Bahá'ís. The conversion of the dowager Queen Marie of Romania also occurred in this period, and there was translation of Bahá'í literature into many of the European languages, as well as a considerable amount of original literature produced by Bahá'ís in Britain, France and Germany.

The European Bahá'í situation changed markedly with the rise of the Nazis, and the subsequent outbreak of World War II (1939–45). The German Bahá'í community, thitherto the strongest in Europe, was severely persecuted, and forced to disband its administrative institutions (1937), and Bahá'í activities in much of Europe came to a halt for the duration of the war. The notable exception to this was Britain, which from the mid-1930s onwards became a major centre of Bahá'í activity.

After the war most of Europe was in ruins. The task of helping to re-establish Bahá'í activity was entrusted to the American Bahá'ís under their Second Seven Year Plan (1946–53). Meanwhile, Britain took a different course and, from the two-year Africa Plan (1951–3) onwards, became increasingly involved with Bahá'í expansion outside Europe. Strong but small Bahá'í communities were soon established in all of Western Europe, but the total number of Bahá'ís remained small. As late as 1952 there were still only about 1,400 Bahá'ís in the whole of Europe, and even by 1963 there were fewer than 5,000. No activity was possible in the Soviet Union or the newly communized states of Eastern Europe and the Balkans. The 1960s also saw the dedication of the European House of Worship in Frankfurt (1964). As in North America the late 1960s and early 1970s saw an influx of youth, who often added a new dynamism to the various Bahá'í communities. Compared to America the overall growth remained small, however, the total number of Bahá'ís by the late 1980s being in the region of 25,000.

Of major recent importance has been the collapse of communism in the Soviet Union and most of Eastern Europe (1989–91). This has created conditions of unexpected religious freedom which the Bahá'ís as well as many other religious groups have sought to utilize. A special two-year plan (1990–2) was accordingly devised, and extensive expansion of the Faith in this region has taken place so that, by 1992, there were a total of 112 assemblies and 757 localities in the former Eastern Bloc countries excluding the former East Germany.

The size of the various European Bahá'í communities varies considerably, with the largest being Germany, Britain, France, Italy, Spain, and the recently established communities in Romania and Albania. There are now thirty-four national spiritual assemblies in Europe. The oldest of these were those of the British Isles (the United Kingdom and Ireland) and Germany and Austria, both established in 1923. National assemblies began to be formed in other European countries from the 1950s onwards (fifteen by 1962).

Despite their limited numbers the European Bahá'ís have made a major contribution to the overall progress of the Faith. Early European Bahá'ís such as Hippolyte DREYFUS and J.E. ESSLEMONT wrote works of lasting importance to Bahá'í literature. Between 1951 and 1957 six of the Hands appointed were Europeans or resident in Europe. Of the membership of the first Universal House of Justice, two were Europeans (British). Many European pioneers have played an important role in the expansion of the Faith in other parts of the world, particularly Africa. European Bahá'í publishing and authorship is of major importance.

The 'Anglo-Pacific'

The expansion of the Faith into the Pacific began with Agnes ALEXANDER's return to Hawaii in 1901. The first Bahá'ís were established in New Zealand and Australia in 1912 and 1920 respectively. The growth of the Faith in all three territories was slow, and the number of Bahá'ís remained small: by the early 1950s there were 400 or so, and by 1963, in the region of 1,000. Institutional growth was also slow, and it was not until 1934 that a joint national assembly for Australia and New Zealand was formed. Separate assemblies for the two countries were established in 1957 and for Hawaii in 1964. A steady increase in Bahá'í numbers was achieved from the late 1960s onwards – as in other parts of the West spearheaded by youth – and by the late 1980s there were some 10,000 Bahá'ís in the region. By 1992 there were 255 local assemblies and Bahá'ís resided in 530 localities. Although only few in number, the Bahá'ís of the three territories have played an active role in the overall progress of the Faith. Pioneering work by Hawaiian Bahá'ís in Japan began as early as 1914, and from the 1950s there have been pioneers from all three 'countries', particularly within the Pacific region. The New Zealand and Australian Bahá'ís also initiated the international Bahá'í magazine *Herald of the South* in 1925. Two Hands were appointed from the region in the 1950s: Clara DUNN and Collis FEATHERSTONE, both in Australia. A Bahá'í House of Worship was dedicated in Sydney in 1961.

THE BAHÁ'Í 'THIRD WORLD'

Africa

BEFORE THE 1950S: Bahá'í expansion into non-Arab Africa was at first extremely limited. There were Bahá'ís in Southern Africa from at least as early as 1912, but their numbers remained extremely limited, despite the efforts of various Western Bahá'ís, notably Fanny KNOBLOCH, who arrived in the region in 1920, and Martha Root, who visited the area in the 1920s. A short-lived local assembly came into being in Pretoria (1925–31), but thereafter organized Bahá'í activities effectively ceased until the 1950s. A second early focus of activity was Abyssinia (Ethiopia) where an Egyptian Bahá'í pioneer, Sabri Elias, settled during the early 1930s. Again the results appear to have been meagre, and it was not until the late 1940s that a local assembly was established in Addis Ababa. Elsewhere there was no sustained endeavour to teach the Faith in Africa, although a small number of individual Bahá'ís came to live in various parts of the continent. Shoghi Effendi himself visited non-Arab Africa twice: the first time by himself in 1929, when he transversed the continent from Cape Town to Cairo, and the second when he made a somewhat similar journey with Rúḥiyyih Khánum in 1940 (Rabbani, *Priceless Pearl* 180–1).

THE AFRICA CAMPAIGN, 1951–3: The beginning of systematic Bahá'í teaching work in Africa began with the 'Africa campaign' of 1951–3. Coming to involve the British, American, Egyptian, Persian and Indian national assemblies, and co-ordinated by the British, the campaign was intended to lay the structural basis of the Bahá'í administration in the continent. The results far exceeded the initial goals, and by 1953 there were Bahá'ís in nineteen territories of sub-Saharan Africa; seventeen new local assemblies had been formed; and translations into six languages had been made, with at least another eight in progress. The area of greatest receptivity was Uganda (with almost 300 Bahá'ís drawn from twenty different tribal groups by early 1953), which Shoghi Effendi designated as the 'heart' of the continent, and selected as the venue for the first ever African Teaching Conference (February 1953), the first ever intercontinental Bahá'í conference. Uganda was also the residence of Africa's first Hand of the Cause, the Iranian pioneer Musa BANANI (1952).

THE TEN YEAR CRUSADE, 1953–63: Growth accelerated during the Crusade, and by 1963 there were probably in excess of 50,000 Bahá'ís in the continent, with Bahá'ís resident in 2,655 localities, some 1,076 of which had local assemblies; Bahá'í literature had been translated into 94 African languages; and 348 African tribal groups were represented in the Faith (*BW13*: 290, 463, 465–7). This was an impressive achievement for essentially twelve years of Bahá'í activity. Significantly, pioneers included newly converted Africans. The Crusade also saw the formation of four large regional spiritual assemblies to cover the entire continent in 1956; the construction of the Bahá'í Houses of Worship at Kampala, the 'mother temple of Africa' (dedicated in January 1961); and the appointment of three more Hands of the Cause in Africa in October 1957: two North American pioneers – John ROBARTS and William SEARS – and a Ugandan, Enoch OLINGA, the only native African so honoured.

DEVELOPMENTS SINCE 1963: The overall pattern of development since 1963 has been one of impressive growth. Thus the total number of localities has increased from over 3,000 in 1964 to over 33,000 in 1992 and the number of local spiritual assemblies from 1,327 to 5,877. There has been considerable variation in the success of Bahá'í endeavour as between different countries, but large-scale enrolments of new Bahá'ís have occurred in many areas. In many countries the Bahá'í communities have also been able to gain favourable public attention and government recognition, a tendency strengthened by the increasing emphasis on socio-economic development projects. In a few countries, war and civil disorder have disrupted Bahá'í activity. The number of national assemblies had increased to forty-four in 1992, and considerable administrative consolidation achieved. The advancement of women within the Bahá'í community and the promotion of literacy have become increasingly important themes.

Latin America and the Caribbean

UP TO THE 1950s: In his *TABLETS OF THE DIVINE PLAN* 'Abdu'l-Bahá called for North American Bahá'ís to travel to Latin America and the Caribbean to teach the Faith, emphasizing in particular the importance of contacting the Amerindian peoples and of visiting Bahia in Brazil (because of the resemblance of its name to 'Bahá'í') and Panama (because of its location) (*TDP* 32–3, 95–6). The initial response to this was largely confined to the activities of two women: Martha Root, who made a three-month voyage in 1919, during which she visited seven Latin American countries, contacting newspapers, placing Bahá'í literature in libraries and English clubs, and giving talks to groups such as the Esperantists and Theosophists (Garis 87–110; Zinky and Baram 39–74), and Leonora Holsapple ARMSTRONG, who settled in Brazil in 1921, attracting sympathizers and translating Bahá'í literature. A number of Bahá'ís visited the region in the mid-1930s, but it was only with the first American Seven Year Plan (1937–44) that a sustained campaign of activity was launched, with pioneers dispatched to all the independent republics of Latin America (1939–41); an inter-America committee appointed to co-ordinate activities; and an inter-America bulletin produced to give news of activities. The results were very encouraging, the first local assembly of the Plan (Mexico City) being formed in 1938, and by 1943 there were nineteen assemblies in the whole region, and Bahá'ís were living in fifty-seven localities in twenty-two countries and territories (*BW9*: 652–9). All the independent republics had been opened to the Faith, as also had Jamaica and Puerto Rico. Many of the new groups were also extremely active, sending teachers to open new localities; organizing Bahá'í radio programmes; translating Bahá'í writings (eventually including such heavyweight volumes as the *Dawn-Breakers*); publishing their own newsletters and pamphlets and holding children's classes. Most teaching effort was directed towards the urban and educated population. The first Latin American Bahá'í congress was subsequently held in Panama (1945) with native Bahá'ís from ten of the countries in attendance. Expansion continued during the second Seven Year Plan (1946–53), and by 1953 Bahá'ís were living in a total of 124 localities in the region, 40 of which had local spiritual assemblies. Co-ordination of Bahá'í activities was transferred from North to Latin American hands in 1947, with the establishment of two regional teaching committees (for Central and South America respectively), and in 1951 these were replaced by regional national spiritual assemblies.

THE TEN YEAR CRUSADE, 1953–63: During this period the regional assemblies were replaced by new national assemblies in all twenty independent states of the region (1961), with an additional assembly in Jamaica as a bonus. Large-scale conversions of Amerindians also began, most dramatically in Bolivia (from 1956) where, by 1963, there were an estimated 8,000 Bahá'ís and 98 assemblies (*BW13*: 258–69). A similar breakthrough occurred in Panama (from *c.*1961), and more limited conversions occurred in several other countries. Given the largely middle-class, educated Latino background of most of the early Latin American Bahá'ís this was a major shift in community membership. Other achievements of the Plan included the settlement of Bahá'ís on several of the islands of the Caribbean, as well as on other islands such as Easter Island and the Falklands; the formation of assemblies in several Caribbean territories; the translation of Bahá'í literature into a number of Amerindian languages; the establishment of institutes for the Amerindians of Bolivia and Ecuador; and the formation of Bahá'í publishing trusts in Buenos Aires (Spanish) and Rio de Janeiro (Portuguese).

THE RECENT PERIOD, FROM 1963: Since 1963 there has been a massive increase in the number of Bahá'ís in the region, such that there may now be in excess of 700,000, with 3,501 local assemblies established by 1992, and Bahá'ís residing in almost 19,000 localities. This growth represents the successful extension of 'mass teaching' probably to most territories of the region, involving both Amerindians and those of African and East Indian descent. National spiritual assemblies have also been established in the newly independent states of the Caribbean; the first Bahá'í temple of Latin America constructed in Panama (dedicated in 1972); and six Bahá'í RADIO stations set up. Activity designed to foster indigenous culture has also been emphasized, including holding Bahá'í conferences in Quechua for the Andean countries; using Bahá'í radio stations to promote local cultural events; and the development of the Guaymi cultural centre in Panama. Given the despised and disadvantaged status of the American Indians in many countries, this promotion has considerable significance. Cultural promotion has also been used as a means of proclaiming the Faith regionally and internationally, as in the Inter-American 'Trail of Light', involving Amerindian Bahá'ís from all the Americas, and the folk-singing group 'El Viento Canta' ('The Wind Sings'). Rúḥiyyih Khánum's South American journey, 'The Green Light Expedition' (1975), and the film of it that she produced have also had wide international coverage, including a showing on Chinese television.

South Asia

South Asia consists of the Indian subcontinent and its surrounding islands.

UP TO 1960: A small number of Indian Muslims became Bábís, but there is no evidence that the Bábí religion ever became established in the subcontinent. Indian Bahá'í history begins with the missionary journeys of JAMÁL EFFENDI in the 1870s. A small number of converts were gained, including Siyyid Mustafa RUMI. Other Bahá'í teachers followed, and by the early 1900s Bahá'í groups had been established in a number of towns, and some Bahá'í literature published in Urdu and English. Most of the Bahá'ís were former Muslims or Zoroastrians, but there were also others, most prominently Pritam SINGH, a Sikh, and Narayanrao VAKIL, a high-caste Hindu. A national Bahá'í teaching plan was launched in 1910, and in 1911 a national teaching council formed to coordinate activities. The first All-India Bahá'í Convention was held in Bombay in 1920, leading to the formation of a national spiritual assembly for India and Burma in 1923. The first summer school was held in 1938. There was also a succession of teaching plans (1938–53), and Bahá'í literature was translated into a number of major Indian languages. Although these activities served to increase the number of Bahá'ís, groups and assemblies, the total number of Bahá'ís remained small (less than 900 in India itself by 1961). The core of the community remained largely 'Persianate'; Hindu-background Bahá'ís were a minority; and the style of teaching was generally 'élitist' in orientation (lecture tours; contact with universities) and concentrated in urban areas, with little contact with the mass of the population. International contributions included the publication of the first Bahá'í books (in Persian and Arabic) from the 1880s, and the dispatch of Bahá'í pioneers to South East Asia from the 1940s. Separate national assemblies were formed in Pakistan (1957), India (1959), Burma (1959) and Sri Lanka (then Ceylon, 1962).

SINCE *c.*1960: The Bahá'í situation in India changed dramatically in 1960–1 when, with the encouragement of Raḥmatu'lláh MUHÁJIR, the first sustained teaching campaigns were mounted in Indian villages. Later adopted also in Pakistan and Bangladesh (amongst the non-Muslim minorities), these led to large-scale influxes of mainly poor, rural and often illiterate peoples, including many who came from scheduled castes and tribal groups. As 'mass teaching' was extended to more areas of the country, the numbers of Bahá'ís steadily increased: by 1973 there were close on 400,000 Indian Bahá'ís; and by 1993 India had the largest Bahá'í community in the world, with more than 2.2 million members (living in over 30,000 localities, some 3,674 of which had local assemblies). The nature of the Bahá'í community was utterly transformed: approaches to teaching and DEEPENING were designed to cater for a largely illiterate audience (including the use of visual aids and music and the establishment of 'tutorial SCHOOLS'), and began to refer to Hindu cultural themes. Other major developments include the construction of a Bahá'í House of Worship in New Delhi (finished in 1986), which attracts thousands of overseas visitors every day (apparently more than the Taj Mahal); and the development of REGIONAL ('State') BAHÁ'Í COUNCILS (from 1986) to devolve Bahá'í administrative work in a country of enormous size and cultural complexity. National assemblies were established in Sikkim (1967–92), Nepal (1972), Bangladesh (1972), and the Andaman and Nicobar Islands (1984). (*See also* INDIAN RELIGIONS.)

South East Asia

UP TO WORLD WAR II: Bahá'í expansion into South East Asia began in 1878 with the visit of Jamál Effendi and Siyyid Mustafa Rumi to Burma. Going first to Rangoon and later to Mandalay, they taught the Faith quietly amongst the Muslim trading community, itself largely of Indian origin. The response was far greater than in India, and after two years more than 200 new Bahá'ís had been converted. Rumi later settled in Rangoon and was instrumental in the mass conversion of the villagers of Daidanaw. He also learnt Burmese and published the first Burmese-language Bahá'í book (*c.*1907) as well as translations of Bahá'í scripture. A strong Burmese Bahá'í community came into being, and by the 1930s there were four local spiritual assemblies. Elsewhere in South East Asia, Jamál and Rumi also visited Singapore and a number of the islands of what was then the Dutch East Indies (now Indonesia), gaining converts amongst the native elite of Sulawesi. Rumi also visited Penang on the Malay

Peninsula. In the absence of further visits by Bahá'í teachers, these efforts did not lead to the formation of permanent Bahá'í groups. Even by the 1930s there were only a few isolated individual Bahá'ís living in the other countries of the region.

SINCE WORLD WAR II: The Burmese Bahá'í community was severely disrupted by the chaotic conditions that prevailed during World War II, and Rumi was murdered (1942). With help from the Indian Bahá'ís a fairly rapid recovery was made after the war, however, with local assemblies being reformed and Bahá'í activities resumed. Significant expansion began in the Ten Year Crusade (1953–63), the total number of assemblies in 1964 reaching eleven, and of localities, twenty-six. A national spiritual assembly was established in 1959.

Sustained Bahá'í activity also now began in the rest of South East Asia, with the Four-and-a-Half Year Plan of the Indian Bahá'ís (1946–50) and the settlement of pioneers in Singapore, Indonesia and Thailand. Progress was at first slow, but during the Ten Year Crusade increasing endeavour, supported by the arrival of more pioneers, saw the beginning of sustained growth. Expansion into the remaining countries of the region was also started. The results were generally impressive, especially in Vietnam (195 local spiritual assemblies by 1964), the Philippines (150), Malaysia (97) and Indonesia (63), in all of which there were large-scale enrolments of new Bahá'ís. In several instances it is of note that the new Bahá'ís included members of the various 'aboriginal' peoples of the region, as amongst the Iban of Sarawak and the Mentawai islanders of Indonesia. A regional spiritual assembly was formed in 1957, most of the component countries establishing their own national assemblies in 1964. Since 1964 the Bahá'í communities of the region have undergone a diversity of experiences, restrictions on religious activities being introduced in some countries, but with more or less sustained expansion elsewhere.

East Asia

The Bahá'í history of East Asia began with the settlement of Iranian Bahá'í merchants in Shanghai, the earliest in the 1860s, but there seems to have been little sustained Bahá'í activity in the region until 1914, with the arrival of Hawaiian Bahá'í pioneers in Japan (George AUGUR and Agnes ALEXANDER) and of more Iranian Bahá'ís in Shanghai (notably Husayn Uskuli (d. 1956) and his family). International teachers included Martha Root, who visited the region four times in the 1920s and 1930s, speaking extensively in universities and colleges, and meeting dignitaries. Some eminent people became Bahá'ís – notably Dr Y.S. Tsao, the president of Tsing Hua (Xinhua) University – and translations of Bahá'í literature were made, but the overall response to these efforts was extremely meagre. Very few Chinese or Japanese became Bahá'ís, and by 1933 there were only two local spiritual assemblies (both in Japan) and eight localities where Bahá'ís resided in the whole region. Thereafter a prolonged period of warfare, devastation and internal political struggles made any Bahá'í activities difficult.

Bahá'í activities in Japan resumed after the end of World War II in 1945, and were aided by the arrival of American and Iranian Bahá'ís. Activities in South Korea and Taiwan began in the 1950s. Given the strong anti-religious policies adopted in the new communist states, there were no Bahá'í activities in Mongolia or the People's Republic of China until the 1990s. Dramatic political changes in Mongolia coincided with the settlement of the first Bahá'í in the country in 1988, and there has since been some modest growth. In China meanwhile there has been some liberalization of official policies regarding religion and there are now a small number of Bahá'ís, but no formal Bahá'í organization. As far as is known, North Korea remains the only country in the world (apart from the Vatican) in which there are no Bahá'ís. A regional spiritual assembly for North East Asia was formed in 1957, based in Japan, and separate assemblies for Korea, Taiwan, Hong Kong, Japan, Macau and Mongolia have since been formed. The number of Bahá'ís in the region remains small.

Oceania

There were a few Bahá'í settlers and visitors to the region during the 1920s and 1930s (notably in Tahiti) but, excluding the 'Anglo-Pacific' (see above), sustained and systematic Bahá'í activity in Australasia only began during the 1950s, mostly in connection with the Ten Year Crusade (1953–63), during which Bahá'í pioneers settled in many of the island groups. Overall progress was at first slow, with the exception of the Gilbert Islands (Kiribati), but by 1964 there were forty-three local spiritual assemblies in the whole region. A regional assembly of the South Pacific was established in 1959. Translations of Bahá'í literature into several local languages were made during this early period. In some islands opposition from the established churches was encountered, sometimes amounting to actual persecution of newly declared Bahá'ís. Friendliness by white pioneers towards the indigenous population also attracted the opposition of colonial authorities in some instances.

Since 1963 there has been a marked increase in the extent and success of Bahá'í activities throughout most of the region. Large numbers of converts have been gained, such that a significant proportion of the population of some island groups is now Bahá'í (above 5 per cent in several island groups, and perhaps almost 20 per cent in Kiribati). The Bahá'ís generally now enjoy good relations with the various governments and churches of the region. By 1992 the total number of localities in which Bahá'ís resided in the region was over 3,500, of which 614 had local assemblies. Fourteen national assemblies had been formed. There are also a number of Bahá'í schools in the region as well as numerous socio-economic development projects. Other developments of note include the conversion of Malietoa TANUMAFILI II (1968), the head of state of Western Samoa; and the construction of the first *Mashriqu'l-Adhkár* in the region at Apia in Western Samoa (dedicated in 1984).

Braun, *From Strength*; *BW*; *SBBR*; *BFSH* 88–97, 129–50; 'Survey'. North America: Armstrong-Ingram, *Music, Devotions*; *BFA*; Hollinger; Morrison; Smith, 'American Bahá'í community'; Van den Hoonaard 'Development', *Origins*. Europe: Phillip Smith; Szanto-Felbermann; Warburg; Weinberg. Anglo-Pacific: Alexander, *Personal Recollections*; Hassall, 'Outpost'. Africa: Bramson-Lerche, 'Baha'i Faith in Nigeria'; Williams. South Asia: Garlington 'Bahá'í bhajans'; 'Bahá'í Conversions'; Bahá'í Faith'; Garrigues; Khianra; Sprague. South East Asia: Muhájir, *Blazing Years*; Seow. East Asia: Alexander, *History*; Seow; Sims *Japan*; 'Traces'. Oceania: Hassall, 'Baha'i Faith'.

F

Fáḍil (Fazel) Mázandarání, Mírzá Asadu'lláh (?1880–1957)

Eminent Iranian Bahá'í scholar and teacher. 'Abdu'l-Bahá and Shoghi Effendi both entrusted him with important missions, including visits to Iraq, North America and India. He prepared a voluminous history of the Bábí and Bahá'í religions (*Ẓuhúru'l-Ḥaqq*, 'The Manifestation of Truth') – only a limited part of which has ever been published – and a five-volume dictionary of the two religions (*Asráru'l-áthár*). He also served on the Bahá'í assemblies of Iran and Tehran. BW14: 334–6; McS 174–5.

faith

For Bahá'u'lláh the 'essence' of faith was 'fewness of words and abundance of deeds' (*TB* 156). 'True belief' in God requires acceptance and observance of whatever he has revealed, whilst steadfastness in God's Cause rests upon faith that 'He doeth whatsoever He willeth', i.e. a complete acceptance of God's authority as revealed through the MANIFESTATION OF GOD. Ultimately no one can fathom 'the manifold exigencies of God's consummate wisdom'. Thus if the Manifestation were to pronounce earth to be heaven then no one has the right to question his authority (*TB* 50–1). 'Abdu'l-Bahá taught that the SOUL needs both faith and knowledge to acquire divine perfections. Faith can entail both public obedience and 'unconscious obedience to the will of God', only rarely does it constitute that 'discerning faith' based on a true knowledge of God and comprehension of his words (*Bahá'í World Faith* 364, 382). Faith is only possible when compatible with REASON (*PUP* 181).

Faizí, Abu'l-Qásim (1906–80)

Iranian HAND OF THE CAUSE. Following studies at the American University in Beirut, he taught Bahá'í children in the

Abu'l-Qásim Faizí, pioneer Bahá'í teacher in Arabia and later Hand of the Cause

village of Najafábád after the closure of their school by the government authorities (1930s). In 1939 he married Gloria 'Alá'í. In 1941, the couple moved to Iraq, and in the following year to Bahrain as Bahá'í PIONEERS. Shoghi Effendi designated Faizí as 'spiritual conqueror' of Arabia, and appointed him a Hand of the Cause in October 1957. After Shoghi Effendi's death Faizí generally served as translator between the Persian- and English-speaking Hands and was one of those chosen to remain in Haifa as one of the CUSTODIANS of the Faith. After the election of the Universal House of Justice in 1963 he travelled extensively, visiting Bahá'í communities. He also published a number of essays and translations in both Persian and English. *BW18*: 659–65; Harper 426–33.

family life

The Bahá'í teachings emphasize the importance and sanctity of MARRIAGE and family life. Bahá'u'lláh taught that parents should raise their children to be religious (but not fanatical), God fearing, and moral; and praised parenthood (both natural and adoptive), equating raising one's own son or the son of another with raising one of his own sons (*TB* 128). The father is responsible for ensuring that both his daughters and sons become literate and learn about the Bahá'í teachings (*see* EDUCATION). Children have a duty to obey their parents. Such service is equated with obeying God, and takes precedence over service to Bahá'u'lláh. 'Abdu'l-Bahá stressed the importance of love, unity and CONSULTATION between family members; stated that each member had his or her rights and prerogatives which should be respected; called on Bahá'ís to make their homes centres 'for the diffusion of the light of divine guidance' (*CC1*: 392); and equated a mother's education of her child with worship, regarding her as the child's first teacher, who normally sets the pattern of its moral and religious life (*CC1*: 286–8). Shoghi Effendi counselled Bahá'ís to balance their desire to serve the Faith with their responsibilities towards their parents, spouses and children, if necessary limiting their Bahá'í activities so as to preserve family unity. This is particularly important in those cases where the spouse is not a Bahá'í. He also deplored the weakening of parental control and the rising tide of divorce in American society, seeing them as evidences of moral laxity and irresponsibility (*PDC* 119). The Universal House of Justice has noted that whilst the Bahá'í teachings emphasize gender equality (*see* WOMEN), this does not imply identity of function within the family: the circumstances of individual families vary greatly, but in general a mother has the primary obligation to nurture her child and a corresponding right to receive material support from her husband. The husband in turn would normally be considered the 'head' of the family, although this implies no overriding authority or right of domination. All forms of family injustice and violence are to be condemned. *CC1*: 385–416.

There was extensive Bahá'í activity as part of the United Nations International Year of the Family (1994), including a symposium on violence-free families sponsored by the BAHÁ'Í INTERNATIONAL COMMUNITY (*BWNS* 1994–5: 47–63, 140–2). Bahá'í reflections on family life include works by Furútan; Ghaznavi; Hellaby; Khavari and Khavari; Nakhjavání; and Wilcox.

Farmer, Sarah (1847–1916)

Early American Bahá'í of New England Transcendentalist background. In 1894 she was the driving force in the establishment of the GREEN ACRE conference centre at Eliot, Maine. She became a Bahá'í in 1900. She suffered from bouts of ill-health which later led to her being confined in a mental asylum. Her mental state became the focus of a bitter custody battle. *BFA2*: 142–5; Martin, 'Life and Work of Sarah Jane Farmer'; Richardson.

fasting

The Báb ordained a nineteen-day fast for his followers during the Bábí month of 'Alá'. In the *Kitáb-i-Aqdas* Bahá'u'lláh confirmed both the fast and the calendar, fixing the month of fasting as intermediate between the intercalary days and the new-year festival of Naw-Rúz, i.e. normally 2–20 March. During this month Bahá'ís between the ages of fifteen and seventy are required to fast, abstaining from food, drink and smoking between sunrise and sunset. Exemptions are granted to the sick, pregnant and menstruating women, nursing mothers, and those who are engaged in heavy labour or are travelling. The exemption for travellers is defined as covering journeys of nine hours or more (or two hours by foot), and to include a period of rest if away from home. Those who are excused from fasting on account of their work are encouraged to eat frugally and in private to show respect for the fast. If those Bahá'í holy days that were determined by the lunar calendar occur during the fast, then fasting is not obligatory on those days. Those who wish to make religious vows to fast during additional periods of time outside the month of fasting (a Muslim and Bábí practice) can do so, but they are advised that vows that benefit mankind are better in the sight of God. Together with obligatory prayer, the fast is one of the pillars of divine law, drawing the believer closer to God. It is intended to be a period of meditation and prayer, during which the individual abstains from selfish desire and seeks to reorient his or her life to reinvigorate the inner spiritual forces of the soul. Fasting is an individual spiritual obligation and responsibility, and Bahá'í institutions have no right to enforce it. In high latitudes the times for fasting are fixed by the clock. *KA* 22–5 k10, k13, k16–17, 114 q22, 118 q36, 127–8 q71, 129 q75–6, 134 q93, 148–9, 171 n14, 176–7 n25–6, 179 n30–2, 225 n138; *LG* 233–5.

fate

'Abdu'l-Bahá taught that human beings should both rely on God's will and at the same time take all wise precautions against adversity (*PUP* 46–8; *SAQ* 244). Such final eventualities as death could not be avoided, and should be accepted as a natural part of existence, but the individual should seek protection from the calamities of human existence if possible. Shoghi Effendi commented that whilst illness and poverty might be irrevocable, they could often be avoided. No one knows what their future holds, or to what degree they are spoiling or creating it. One should do one's daily best and let the future take care of itself (*LG* 515 no. 1744, 516 no. 1750). Again, God's will is not regarded as immutable (*see* badá), and whilst prophecy reflects divine foreknowledge it does not cause the events it foreshadows, any more than astronomic calculations cause a predicted eclipse (*SAQ* 138–9).

fear

Bahá'ís should be God-fearing (*see* fear of God), but should seek not to be overwhelmed by earthly fears. To overcome their own fears they should rely upon God for guidance and help, trust in Him, and serve the Faith. This will give them greater strength. They should turn away from ideas that weaken the soul, such as fear of future wars and of death. No one knows what the future holds in their present life, but faith in an afterlife lessens fear. *LG* 236–8.

fear of God

Bahá'u'lláh taught that the fear of God is the main deterrent against human wrongdoing and hence a protection for humankind. Only a minority of people possess an inner agency – a sense of shame – which deters them from wrongdoing (*TB* 63). Fear of punishment leads to outward conformity to the law, but the fear of God also leads to inward observance (*TB* 93). It encompasses all things and leads to praiseworthy behaviour (*TB* 126). Children should be taught to be God-fearing. We should fear God because he is just and we are sinful: though God's mercy exceeds his justice, we should still fear his righteous anger at our wrongdoing. Few can be disciplined by love alone (*LG* 236–8). (*See also* REWARD AND PUNISHMENT.)

feast, nineteen day

(Pers.: *ḍíyáfat-i-navazdah-rúzih*)

The Báb instructed his followers to offer hospitality once in nineteen days, and Bahá'u'lláh confirmed this practice in the *Kitáb-i-*AQDAS. The purpose was to 'bind hearts together' through both material and heavenly means. The feast itself might be simple – even consisting of only the serving of water. It was not obligatory. 'Abdu'l-Bahá developed this feast into a communal institution as a regular monthly meeting at which the Bahá'ís came together to pray and eat together. For Western Bahá'ís of Christian background, the analogy with the Lord's Supper was explicitly made. The present format of the feast was established by Shoghi Effendi, who introduced consultation between the local Bahá'í community and its spiritual ASSEMBLY as an additional element. The feast should thus consist of three distinct sections: an initial devotional, mainly consisting of prayers and other writings from Bahá'u'lláh, 'Abdu'l-Bahá and the Báb; an administrative period for community consultation and reports from the assembly; and a final social section with fellowship between the Bahá'ís. Music is also permitted. The feast should be held on the first day of each Bahá'í month if possible, and all Bahá'ís are encouraged to attend. To ensure freedom of discussion during the consultative portion of the feast, only recognized Bahá'ís may attend. The local assembly of the area is responsible for arranging the feast. *KA* 40 k57, 121 q48, 202 n82; *LG* 239–46; Walbridge, *Sacred* 206–11.

Featherstone, (Howard) Collis (1913–90)

Australian HAND OF THE CAUSE. An engineer and businessman from the Adelaide area, Collis and his wife, Madge, became Bahá'ís in 1944, their home becoming a centre for Bahá'í activity. He served on the Australian national spiritual ASSEMBLY from 1949 until 1962, often as its chairman, and in 1954 was appointed as one of two AUXILIARY BOARD members for Australasia. He was appointed a Hand of the Cause by Shoghi Effendi in October 1957, subsequently travelling extensively to encourage Bahá'í activity, particularly in the Pacific region and parts of Asia. He died in Kathmandu during a visit to the Bahá'ís of Nepal (14 September 1990). Harper 434–48.

Ferraby, John (1914–73)

British HAND OF THE CAUSE of Liberal Jewish background. He became a Bahá'í in 1941, and in 1946 was elected as secretary of the British national spiritual ASSEMBLY, remaining in that position until he moved to Haifa in 1959. In 1957 he published what remains one of the most comprehensive introductory books on Bahá'í, *All Things Made New*. In October of the same year Shoghi Effendi appointed him as a Hand of the Cause. He served as one of the custodial Hands at the Bahá'í World Centre from 1959 until 1963. *BW16*: 511–12; Harper 449–54.

finances, Bahá'í

See FUNDS; ḤUQÚQU'LLÁH; ZAKÁT.

fireside

Informal meeting for the purpose of TEACHING enquirers about the Bahá'í Faith. It is commonly held in an individual's house on a regular basis. Shoghi Effendi encouraged all Bahá'ís to hold such a meeting at least once in every Bahá'í month (i.e. every nineteen days), and regarded this method of teaching to be far more effective in gaining new Bahá'ís than advertising and public lectures. The term 'fireside' in this context appears to be of American origin. *LG* 247–8.

Forel, August (1848–1931)

Swiss psychiatrist, entomologist and social reformer who became a Bahá'í in 1921. A letter to 'Abdu'l-Bahá asking how he could combine Bahá'í belief with his own agnostic and monist philosophical position elicited the *Tablet to Dr Forel*, in which 'Abdu'l-Bahá discussed the existence of God and the spiritual nature of human beings. Mühlschlegel; Vader.

Four Valleys (Pers: *Chahár Vádí*)

Short mystical work by Bahá'u'lláh composed in Baghdad some time after his return from Kurdistan (1856). It is addressed to Shaykh 'Abdu'r-Raḥmán Tálabání of Kirkúk, leader of the Kurdish Qádirí Sufis, with whom Bahá'u'lláh had been in contact in Sulaymániyya (*GPB* 122). It describes four 'stations' the mystic might attain in relationship to God, each corresponding to a particular aspect of the divine: 'the self that is well pleasing to God'; attainment of the true standard of knowledge; seeing the inner reality of the divine; and 'the realm of full awareness [and] utter self-effacement', which is 'free of all the attributes of [the] earth'. Bahá'u'lláh writes with great authority, implying perhaps a station greater than that of a Sufi teacher. *SV* 44–62; *RB1*: 104; Walbridge, *Sacred* 157–8.

Fozdar, Shirin (1905–92)

Indian Bahá'í of Iranian Zoroastrian background who achieved prominence as an advocate of women's rights and as a promoter of the Bahá'í Faith in South East Asia. She became a member of the executive committee of the All-Asian Women's Conference in the early 1930s and represented this body at the League of Nations to press for a Universal Declaration of Women's Rights. In 1936 she became the first woman elected on to the Indian Bahá'í national ASSEMBLY. In 1940 she and her husband, Dr K.M. Fozdar (d. 1958), the first Bahá'í of native Parsi Indian background, went as Bahá'í PIONEERS to Singapore. She established the Singapore Council of Women of which she became secretary-general. She was active in promoting Bahá'í in other parts of South East Asia, notably Thailand where she lived from 1961 to 1971. *BW13*: 892–3; Chew, 'Singapore Council'.

Franz-Joseph (1830–1916)

Hapsburg emperor of Austria-Hungary, 1848–1916. Bahá'u'lláh addressed him in the *Kitáb-i-Aqdas*, reproving him for not having enquired about Bahá'u'lláh during a visit the emperor had made to Jerusalem in 1869. Bahá'u'lláh stated that he was with the emperor 'at all times', and appealed to him to open his eyes so that he would see the promised one. Shoghi Effendi noted the repeated tragedies of his reign, and implied that the eventual collapse of the empire at the end of World War I represented a consequence of the emperor's failure to heed Bahá'u'lláh's summons. *KA* 50–1 k85, 216 n116; *PDC* 59–60.

free will

'Abdu'l-Bahá taught that human beings have free will. They can choose to commit good or evil actions, to be just or unjust, to praise God, practise philanthropy, etc. They are responsible for their moral actions. On the other hand, they are not responsible for those aspects of their lives over which they have no control, such as unavoidable illness or misfortune. They also have to endure such inevitabilities of human existence as sleep and death. Under all circumstances, they are dependent upon God. (*See also* FATE.) SAQ 248–50.

Fuat Paşa (Fu'ád Páshá) (1815–69)

OTTOMAN statesman and reformer under Sultan ABDULAZIZ. He was grand vizier almost continuously from 1861 until 1866 and also at various times foreign minister. He worked closely with ÂLI PAŞA. Bahá'u'lláh regarded him as sharing responsibility for the exile of the Bahá'ís from Edirne to Akka, and rebuked him in the *Lawḥ-i- Fu'ád*, written shortly after Fuat's death, stating that his life had been taken by God, whose wrath he now faced. The tablet also prophesied the imminent downfall of Âli Paşa and Abdulaziz; the subsequent death of Âli (1871) followed by the sultan's deposition and probable murder (1876) being regarded by Bahá'ís as a vivid example of DIVINE JUDGEMENT. *RB3*: 87–8.

funds

The activities of the Bahá'í Faith are financed by the voluntary contributions of Bahá'ís. No solicitation of contributions is allowed other than general appeals for donations. Only donations from Bahá'ís are accepted for support of the propagation work of the Faith, but outside assistance is allowed in funding charitable and SOCIO-ECONOMIC DEVELOPMENT projects.

ORIGINS

Although the Báb referred to donations being made to himself and to the future HE WHOM GOD SHALL MAKE MANIFEST (Walbridge, *Sacred* 95–6), no organized funding system ever seems to have developed amongst the Bábís. By contrast, Bahá'u'lláh noted that 'the progress and promotion of the cause of God depend on material means' (*CC1*: 489), and called upon his followers voluntarily to contribute a specified proportion of their wealth. This was the *ḤUQÚQU'LLÁH* (established *c*.1873, implemented 1878). He also referred to the future establishment of an alms-tax (*ZAKÁT*). The *Ḥuqúq* was payable at first to Bahá'u'lláh, and later to his successors as centres of the Faith, and was used for such purposes as the support of Bahá'í teachers. Its payment remained largely confined to Middle Eastern Bahá'ís until 1992. In addition to the *Ḥuqúq*, early Bahá'ís also made gifts to Bahá'u'lláh and later to 'Abdu'l-Bahá, and expended resources on particular projects which they considered important, such as the building of local Bahá'í centres and the ASHKHABAD temple (*MASHRIQU'L-ADHKÁR*). The early Western Bahá'ís did not pay *Ḥuqúq*, but they followed the example of their Middle Eastern co-religionists in making donations and supporting local projects such as publishing and the planned temple near Chicago (*see* BAHAI TEMPLE UNITY).

LOCAL AND NATIONAL FUNDS

The overall system of funding was regularized by Shoghi Effendi. In 1923 he directed that all local and national ASSEMBLIES should establish their own funds. These would be under their exclusive control, and should be expended as they saw fit to promote the interests of the Faith (e.g. for TEACHING campaigns; help for the needy; EDUCATION). The funds would be administered by the assemblies' elected treasurers. The flow of contributions represented the 'life-blood' of these institutions. All Bahá'ís are encouraged to support the funds 'freely and generously', and in a spirit of sacrifice. This is a source of spiritual blessings. Giving is a means whereby individuals can test the extent of their own devotion and spiritual progress. There is no limit; it is the extent of the sacrifice not the actual amount that is important. They should be 'undeterred by thoughts of poverty' and reliant on God's bounty, but also wise and not incur debts or cause suffering to others in order to donate. Local assemblies as well as individuals should support their respective national funds. All donations should be entirely voluntary, and no one should ever be psychologically pressurized into giving. It is a personal matter, and each individual should follow the dictates of his or her own conscience. They are free to make their contributions anonymously or to receive a receipt from the treasurer. They are also free to earmark donations for specific purposes. Monies for philanthropic and strictly Bahá'í administrative and teaching purposes should be differentiated, with only Bahá'ís being allowed to contribute to the latter (those Bahá'ís who have been deprived of their ADMINISTRATIVE RIGHTS were not allowed the 'bounty' of contributing to the funds). The monies available to Bahá'ís are limited in extent, and the assemblies should ensure that the funds under their control are expended wisely and carefully. Heavy budgets should not be imposed on weak Bahá'í communities. *CC1*: 529–50.

Since 1963 the Universal House of Justice has specified various matters of detail regarding fund-raising and disbursement (e.g. ruling that raffles and 'garage sales' were inappropriate means), and has stated that governmental and other public funds could be applied for to support Bahá'í humanitarian ventures. It has also appealed for 'universal participation' in giving; prepared guidelines for treasurers and study materials on TRUSTWORTHINESS; and directed that assemblies adopt proper measures of auditing and expenditure control. *LG* 249–65; *MUHJ* 10 no. 2.11, 26–7 no. 13, 650–2 no. 419, 676–9 no. 435.

OTHER FUNDS

Shoghi Effendi designated the monies under his control as head of the Faith as the International Fund. This was used for the international projects of the Faith, including the programme of building and land acquisition at the BAHÁ'Í WORLD CENTRE, international CONFERENCES, and the subsidy of activities and property acquisitions in poorer parts of the Bahá'í world. Individuals and local and national assemblies were all encouraged to contribute to it. In 1954 he instituted five continental funds to support the work of the HANDS OF THE CAUSE and the newly established AUXILIARY BOARDS (*MBW* 59, 63). Under the Universal House of Justice the demands on the international fund have increased enormously (almost doubled from 1963 to 1967 alone), both because of the increasing range of activities and projects at the World Centre and the EXPANSION of Bahá'í communities in poorer countries which needed subsidy. All local and national communities have been urged to become self-supporting, but this is evidently all but impossible in some poorer countries. A number of crises have therefore developed, the most serious in the wake of the Islamic revolution in Iran (1979), when the sufferings of the Iranian Bahá'í community drastically reduced what had hitherto been the major source of international funding. Nevertheless, these crises have been overcome, and an ever-increasing range of activities undertaken. The House has also established an International Deputization Fund to support PIONEERING (1965) and an Arc Fund to fund the extensive building projects of the ARC. *MUHJ* 26–7 no. 13, 62 no. 24.11, 97–8 no. 40, 178–9 no. 87, 412 no. 223.

Furúghí, Mírzá Maḥmúd
(d. 1927/8)

Prominent Iranian Bahá'í. He was born in the Khurásání village of Dúghábád, itself called *Furúgh* ('Splendour', 'Light') by Bahá'u'lláh. His father was Mullá Mírzá Muḥammad, an influential cleric who became a Bábí and was one of the survivors of the Shaykh ṬABARSÍ struggle. Furúghí became a staunch Bahá'í whose zeal agitated orthodox Muslim clerics, but impressed several members of the Qájár administration. He was subject to several imprisonments, beatings and attempts on his life before being finally poisoned. In addition to promoting the Faith in Iran he travelled to Ashkhabad and Egypt, as well as visiting 'Abdu'l-Bahá. He took a leading part in opposing the influence of COVENANT-BREAKERS such as JAMÁL BURÚJIRDÍ, and was able to have an extended interview with Muẓaffaru'd-dín Sháh, to assure him of the loyalty of the Bahá'ís. Shoghi Effendi named him as one of the APOSTLES OF BAHÁ'U'LLÁH. *EB* 156–70.

Furútan, 'Alí-Akbar (b. 1905)

Iranian HAND OF THE CAUSE. In the face of sustained persecution, Furútan's family left their native city of Sabzivár in Khurásán in 1914 and settled in Ashkhabad across the Russian border. The young Furútan became an active member of the local Bahá'í community and, whilst still in his teens, became a teacher in its school. In 1926 he won a scholarship to the University of Moscow to study education and child psychology. In 1930 he was expelled from the Soviet Union on account of his Bahá'í activities

'Alí-Akbar Furútan, prominent Iranian Bahá'í and Hand of the Cause

and returned to Iran, where he established a school for Bahá'ís in one of the villages. In 1934 he was elected on to the newly formed Iranian national spiritual ASSEMBLY and served as its secretary until the death of Shoghi Effendi. He was also appointed as principal of the Tarbíyat school for boys (*see* SCHOOLS) until its closure, and wrote study books for Bahá'í children's classes which are still in use. He was appointed a Hand of the Cause by Shoghi Effendi in the first contingent in December 1951. In 1957 he became one of the custodial Hands in Haifa. His Persian publications are extensive, and several have been translated into English. Furútan, *Story of my Heart*; Harper 211–22.

G

gambling

Gambling is forbidden in the *Kitáb-i-Aqdas*, but the Universal House of Justice has yet to specify exactly what activities are to be included in this prohibition, instead advising Bahá'ís to determine their own actions on the basis of individual conscience, and not to make gambling an issue within the community. They note 'Abdu'l-Bahá's description of betting on horse races as a 'pernicious disease' that causes enormous distress, and have ruled that funds for the Faith should not be raised through lotteries, raffles and games of chance. *KA* 75 k155, 237–8 n169; *LG* 357–8.

gender equality

See WOMEN.

Getsinger, Edward (1866–1935) and Louisa ('Lua') Aurora Moore (1871–1916)

Prominent early American Bahá'ís, who converted and married in 1897, soon assuming a leading role as teachers of the Faith. It was they who introduced Phoebe HEARST to the new religion, and they accompanied her in the first group of Western pilgrims to visit 'Abdu'l-Bahá (1898–9). The first of the Americans to arrive, they remained for five months, again making lengthy visits in 1900 and 1901. Edward was prominent in the growing conflict associated with Ibrahim KHEIRALLA's defection. Both were sent by 'Abdu'l-Bahá as Bahá'í teachers to India in 1914, but it was Lua who achieved particular renown as an international Bahá'í teacher. 'Abdu'l-Bahá called her '*Livá*' ('Banner'), and entrusted her with a special mission to present a petition for the protection of the Iranian Bahá'ís to Muẓaffaru'd-dín Sháh whilst the latter was visiting Paris. She died in Cairo. Shoghi Effendi honoured her as one of the DISCIPLES OF 'ABDU'L-BAHÁ and as 'mother teacher of the West'. *BW6*: 493–6; *GPB* 257; Metelmann; Sears and Quigley; *Star* 7/4: 29–30.

Giachery, Ugo (1896–1989)

Italian HAND OF THE CAUSE. Born into an aristocratic family in Palermo, he received a doctoral degree in chemistry. After World War I he migrated to the United States, where he met and married his wife, Angeline Westergren, and became a Bahá'í (*c*.1926). The couple moved to Italy in 1947 as PIONEER Bahá'í teachers in the second American Seven Year PLAN, establishing themselves in Rome. Ugo completed the translation of a large number of Bahá'í books into Italian. From 1948 onwards he became heavily involved in securing the marble and various building supplies for the construction of the superstructure of the SHRINE OF THE BÁB and the INTERNA-

Ugo Giachery, prominent Italian Bahá'í and Hand of the Cause, 1973

TIONAL ARCHIVES building in Haifa. One of the doors of the Shrine was later named after him. Shoghi Effendi appointed him as a Hand of the Cause in December 1951, and as a member-at-large of the INTERNATIONAL BAHÁ'Í COUNCIL in March 1952. He was elected chairman of the newly formed national spiritual ASSEMBLY of Italy and Switzerland in 1953. As a Hand he travelled extensively world-wide. In Western Samoa he was able to present the Bahá'í teachings to the head of state, the Malietoa TANUMAFILI II, who subsequently became a Bahá'í. Giachery himself died during a later visit to the island and is buried there. Giachery; Harper 223–42.

Gillespie, (John Birkes) 'Dizzy' (1917–93)

Leading jazz trumpeter who became a Bahá'í in 1968. With Charlie Parker he created and developed the 'bebop' style in the 1940s. (See cover image.)

Gobineau, Joseph Arthur, Comte de (1816–82)

French diplomat and writer, who is perhaps now best known for his racist philosophy (*Essai sur l'inégalité des races humaines*, 1854). He was appointed to various posts in Iran (1854–8, 1862–3; this last as ambassador) during which he learned of the Bábí movement, later giving vivid accounts of Bábí heroism in his *Religions et philosophies dans l'asie centrale* (1865). This book proved enormously influential in attracting attention to the religion amongst educated Europeans, and specifically prompted both E.G. BROWNE and A.L.M. NICOLAS to begin their studies of Bábism. Some of the historical and doctrinal details in the book are inaccurate. *MBBR* 17–26, 502.

God

For Bahá'ís God in essence is unknowable, being exalted above human attributes and understanding (*KI* 63). Human conceptions of God are mere imaginations, which some individuals mistake for reality (*SWAB* 53–4 no. 24). It is impossible to even hint at the nature of God's essence (*GWB* 3–4 no. 1). Knowledge of God is therefore primarily to be achieved by way of the MANIFESTATIONS OF GOD, who act as God's messengers and reflect 'his' attributes. More generally, every created thing in the universe is a 'sign' of God's sovereignty, and a 'door' leading to knowledge of him (*GWB* 160 no. 82). All existence reflects his image (*GWB* 165 no. 84). His 'signs' – his attributes – are revealed most particularly in human beings (*see* HUMAN NATURE). Thus seekers who turn their gaze to their own selves will find God (*HWa* no. 13). Shoghi Effendi described God as one, personal, unknowable, inaccessible, eternal, omniscient, omnipresent and almighty (*GPB* 139), and as being 'invisible yet rational' (*WOB* 112); a supreme reality

(*LG* 477 no. 1574). He rejected incarnationist, pantheistic and anthropomorphic conceptions of God (*WOB* 112–13).

The Bahá'í writings abound with the names and attributes of God. These include: Almighty; All-Knowing; All-Sufficing; All-Loving; Most Compassionate; Ever-Forgiving; Ever-Faithful; Lord of all being; Lord of grace abounding; King of the realms of justice; Shaper of all the nations; Source of all Sources; Cause of all Causes; Chastiser; Inspirer; Help in Peril; Eternal Truth; central Orb of the universe, its Essence and ultimate Purpose; Fountain-Head of all Revelations; and Well-Spring of all Lights. Rabbani, *Desire of the World* 164–74.

'Abdu'l-Bahá presented various proofs for the existence of God: there must be an ultimate cause; composition of elements cannot be the result of accident or inherent properties; human qualities such as volition are exceptional in nature and suggest a creator with similar qualities. *Bahá'í Revelation* 224–9; Savi 24–6. (*See also* METAPHYSICS.)

God Passes By

Historical work by Shoghi Effendi, published in 1944, and describing the first hundred years of the 'Bahá'í Era' and 'Cycle' (i.e. incorporating the Bábí as well as the Bahá'í 'Dispensations'; (*see* TIME). It was not intended to be a 'detailed history' and, whilst evidently drawing on extensive research, does not include the academic apparatus of notes, references and bibliography. Rather, it presented the Bahá'ís with a review and interpretation of their religion, and its transformation from 'a heterodox and seemingly negligible offshoot of the Shaykhí school of the Ithná-'Asharíyyih [Twelver] sect of Shí'ah Islám' into a world religion (p. xii). It describes Bábí–Bahá'í history in terms of four distinct periods, centring respectively on the missions of the Báb, Bahá'u'lláh and 'Abdu'l-Bahá, and on the rise of the Bahá'í ADMINISTRATION, these together forming a single indivisible divine drama and evolutionary process. It summarizes the main events, and the writings and teachings of the Bahá'í CENTRAL FIGURES; provides characterizations of the main participants – believers and their opponents; details the prophetic role of the Báb and Bahá'u'lláh, and the implementation of the Bahá'í COVENANT; and instances examples of DIVINE JUDGEMENT on those who had attacked the Faith. Its major importance for Bahá'ís lies less in its presentation of historical detail than in its vision of the onward progress of the Faith in the face of opposition and tribulation, and the doctrinal significance it gives to the events and processes it describes. Shoghi Effendi also composed a shorter Persian-language version, the *Lawḥ-i-Qarn*. *GPB*; Rabbani, *Priceless Pearl* 222–5.

golden rule

The ethical rule that we should treat others as we would wish to be treated. It is found in most religions, including the Bahá'í Faith. Thus Bahá'u'lláh taught that the individual should 'choose ... for thy neighbour that which thou choosest for thyself' (*TB* 64), and not wish for others 'what ye wish not for yourselves' (*KA* 73 k148), and 'ascribe not to any soul that which thou wouldst not have ascribed to thee' (*HWa* no. 29). Rost, *Golden Rule*.

Goodall, Helen S. (1847–1922)

Leading early Bahá'í in the San Francisco area. She and her daughter, Ella Cooper (1870–1951), began to study the Bahá'í Faith in 1898, and subsequently became the focus of Bahá'í activities in California. Ella joined the first Western pilgrimage group to Akka (1899). Mother and daughter also visited Akka in 1908. Shoghi Effendi honoured Helen as one of the DISCIPLES OF 'ABDU'L-BAHÁ, and Ella as a 'herald' of the Covenant. *BW12*: 681–4; CF 162; *Star* 13/8: 203–7; *WEBW* 21–34.

government

JUSTICE

Bahá'u'lláh emphasized the need for JUSTICE in government: God has committed government into the hands of rulers that they might rule with justice over their people, safeguarding the rights of the downtrodden, caring for the poor and punishing wrongdoers. If they do not do this they are in grievous error, and will be judged by God (*GWB* 246 no. 116, 250–1 no. 118). Those guilty of tyranny, injustice and oppression are answerable to God (*HWp* no. 64). Governments are obliged to acquaint themselves with the conditions of those whom they govern; confer office on the basis of merit; and ensure that those who are appointed are not unjust (*TB* 127). The rulers should regard the people as their treasure, for by them they rule, subsist, and conquer. Yet absolutist regimes disdain them (the people), robbing them in order to build palaces and burdening them in order to pursue their own extravagances. The 19th-century rulers, who held their peoples at their mercy, were 'so drunk with pride' that they could not even discern their own best advantage. Even at their best, their motives were their own gain (*PDC* 26). Those rulers who governed with justice and wisdom are blessed by God (*TB* 164). The persecution of religious minorities, such as Jews in certain European countries (*TB* 170) and Bahá'ís in the Middle East (*GWB* 123–5 no. 65), was unjust, and was condemned ('Abdu'l-Bahá also cited the existence of extreme poverty and starvation as evidence of tyranny (*PT* 159)). A just society also requires that there be equality before the LAW. SOCIAL ORDER depends on there being just government.

FORM OF GOVERNMENT

Bahá'u'lláh praised constitutional monarchy as a form of government. Republican government by itself profits 'all the peoples of the world', but it is better when combined with 'the majesty of kingship' (as one of 'the signs of God' (*see* KINGS)) (*TB* 28). The British system of representative government was particularly referred to in this context (PDC 35; TB 93; *see* VICTORIA). Such views were radical in a 19th-century Middle Eastern context (Cole, 'Iranian millenarianism'), as was the Bahá'í advocacy of a separation of church and state and liberty of conscience (Bayat 130; *TN* 160–5; *see also Treatise on* POLITICS). 'Abdu'l-Bahá also held that there should be a separation of legislative and executive powers in Iran (*SDC* 37); viewed constitutional monarchy as having a continuity and stability lacking in republican regimes; spoke against a hereditary aristocracy (Esslemont A 123–4); and regarded centralization of government as promoting despotism, predicting that federalism would become the future pattern of government (*PUP* 167).

CORRUPTION

'Abdu'l-Bahá argued that not until government officials at all levels were free from corruption could Iran (and by extension any other country) be properly administered. Good and orderly government was essential if national development was to occur. Establishing consultative assemblies elected by universal suffrage is the 'bedrock' of government. But these assemblies can only be effective if ministers and the elected representatives are righteous and uncorrupt. If the elected representatives are ignorant and corrupt there will just be more people demanding bribes. National EDUCATION is necessary so that the common people can check governmental injustice (*SDC* 16–21, 23–4).

OTHER

Bahá'u'lláh linked national political development to the achievement of international PEACE and to the lessening of the tax burden consequent upon the reduction of ARMAMENTS procurements. Both he and 'Abdu'l-Bahá also linked it to economic development (*see* AGRICULTURE; *SECRET OF DIVINE CIVILIZATION*). He also stated that those who were members of constitutional assemblies (specifically the British Parliament) should take counsel together and seek that which would profit the condition of humanity, entering the assembly for the sake of God, and praying for divine assistance in that which would cause the affairs of the people to prosper (*ESW* 61–2). Contemporary advocacy of Bahá'í ideas regarding government has included contributions to the national debate in the process of preparing new national constitutions (Ethiopia, 1994); commentary on general foreign policy (Canada, 1994; Ireland, 1994); and assistance in re-establishing a parliamentary group for world government (UK, 1994) (*BWNS* 1994–5: 123–4).

government, Bahá'í attitude towards

The growth of BÁBÍ RADICALISM was linked to increasingly militant attitudes which contributed to the conflicts with Qájár state, and later led a small group of Bábís to make an attempt on the life of NÁṢIRU'D-DÍN SHÁH. Bahá'u'lláh, by contrast, opposed militancy from an early date, and later abrogated the Islamic–Bábí laws of HOLY WAR (1863), and insisted that his followers strictly avoid sedition. Bahá'ís were to be loyal, honest and truthful in their dealings with the government of whichever country they inhabited (*TB* 22–3). None should contend with those in lawful authority (*KA* 54 k95). Similarly, 'Abdu'l-Bahá instructed the Bahá'ís to be the well-wishers of governments; obey just kings, and regard disloyalty to them as disloyalty towards God; and not meddle in political affairs (*SWAB* 293–4, 319; *Will* 8). Bahá'ís in public employ should be exemplary in their honesty, integrity, trustworthiness, justice and service (*CC2*: 341–5; *LG* 452–4). Shoghi Effendi forbade any party-political involvement on the part of the Bahá'ís (*see* POLITICS), and insisted that Bahá'ís obey the laws and government of any state, even if they personally regard them as unjust, as long as these do not necessitate them denying their basic religious beliefs as Bahá'ís. If this obedience requires the dismantling of the Bahá'í ADMINISTRATION, then Bahá'ís should accept that consequence, and not compromise with the principle (*see also* PERSECUTION) (*LG* 445–52).

greatest name

According to Islamic belief GOD has ninety-nine names (compassionate, merciful, etc.). In esoteric tradition it is believed that there is also a hundredth name – the greatest – which has special potency. For Bahá'ís this 'greatest name' (*ism-i-a'ẓam*) is *bahá* ('glory', 'splendour'), as used in the religious title of their own founder, *Bahá'u'lláh*. 'Abdu'l-Bahá referred to it as a name of comfort and protection. Expressions using this name or derivatives of it are commonly used by Bahá'ís. Thus the invocation,

The 'Greatest Name', in the calligraphy of Mishkín-Qalam

alláhu'abhá ('Alláh-u-Abhá', 'God is Most Glorious'), which Bahá'ís are bidden to repeat ninety-five times each day as a devotional act, and which is widely used as a greeting; the phrase *yá bahá'u'l-abhá* ('O Glory of the Most Glorious'), which appears in a calligraphic device designed by MISHKÍN-QALAM, which many Bahá'ís use as a wall hanging; and the 'ringstone symbol', with a configuration of the Arabic letters 'b' and 'h', which is featured on Bahá'í rings. It should be used with proper dignity and reverence (not used on stationery or as a car sticker, for example); neither should it be used on gravestones). According to the *ABJAD* system, *bahá* has a numerical equivalence of 9, hence the frequent use of that number in Bahá'í symbolism. *KA* 26 k18, 38 k51, 64 k127, 180 n33, 224 n137; *LG* 266–70; Walbridge, *Sacred* 263–4.

Green Acre ('Greenacre')

Conference facility at Eliot, Maine, first opened by Sarah FARMER in 1894. Initially it featured a variety of summer courses on subjects such as Transcendentalism, evolution, comparative religion and the 'Metaphysical Movement' then in vogue (New Thought, etc.). Following Farmer's conversion in 1900 Bahá'í speakers were increasingly in evidence, including ABU'L-FAḌL (1902) and 'Abdu'l-Bahá (1912). The centre came under Bahá'í control in 1913, and the wide-ranging eclecticism of the early years was increasingly replaced by a curriculum focused on the Bahá'í Faith. It was formally converted into a summer school facility in 1929, and became the prototype of Bahá'í SUMMER SCHOOLS world-wide. *BFA2*: 143–6, 217–18; *SBBR* 104; Smith, 'American Bahá'í community' 125–26. Richardson provides a hostile account of the Baha'i role at Green Acre.

Greenleaf, Charles (1856/7–1920) and Elizabeth (1863–1941)

Prominent early American Bahá'ís. They converted in 1897. Charles became a member of Chicago's first Bahá'í administrative body, the Board of Council (1900), and was later named by Shoghi Effendi as one of the DISCIPLES OF 'ABDU'L-BAHÁ. After her husband's death Elizabeth became one of the leading teachers of the Bahá'í Faith in North America, being instrumental in its growth in Canada and Florida. *BW9*: 608; *WSBR* 97–117.

Gregory, Louis C. (1874–1951)

Prominent African-American Bahá'í. Born of slave parents in South Carolina, he later graduated from Howard University with a degree in law. He became a Bahá'í in Washington DC in 1909. Already an advocate of racial equality, Gregory challenged *de facto* segregation in the local Bahá'í community. In this he

Louis Gregory, prominent early African–American Bahá'í

was supported by 'Abdu'l-Bahá, who during his own visit to Washington DC (1912) deliberately sat Gregory next to him at a formal luncheon in clear disregard of social convention. 'Abdu'l-Bahá also encouraged him to marry Louisa Mathew (1866–1956), a white Englishwoman, this being the first black–white marriage in the American Bahá'í community, and an act requiring considerable courage in the social conditions of the time. Gregory undertook extensive travels to promote the Faith, particularly in the southern states. He played a leading role in the advocacy of racial equality by the Bahá'ís, and for a number of years was the only black Bahá'í on the American national spiritual assembly. Shoghi Effendi posthumously named him as a HAND OF THE CAUSE. Louisa was prominent in Bahá'í teaching activities in the Balkans. *BW12*: 666–70; *13*: 876–8; Harper 85–98; Morrison.

Grinevskaya, Izabella Arkadevna (1864–1944)

Russian Bahá'í, dramatist and writer. Her dramatic poem *Bab* – presenting the Báb's life and teachings – was published in St Petersburg in 1903 and performed on stage the following January, receiving enormous acclaim from literary figures, including Leo TOLSTOY. A second dramatic poem, *Bekha-Ulla* (Bahá'u'lláh) was written in 1912, again being well reviewed. Grinevskaya also lectured on the Báb and Bahá'u'lláh to academic societies. She met Abdu'l-Bahá in Egypt in 1910. *BW6*: 707–12; *MBBR* 50–1.

Grossmann, Hermann (1899–1968)

German HAND OF THE CAUSE. Born in Argentina, he moved with his family to Germany in 1909. In 1920 he both became a Bahá'í and met his future wife, Anna Hartmuth. He was able to promote the Bahá'í Faith in various parts of Germany and later served on the newly formed national spiritual ASSEMBLY. He was particularly active in Bahá'í child education and the Bahá'í ESPERANTO movement, which he organized in Germany. He also wrote a number of books on the Faith (in German) and translated Bahá'í literature. After the banning of the Bahá'í Faith by the Nazi regime in May 1937 he suffered intermittent persecution, including the confiscation and destruction of much of his Bahá'í library and archives and a six-month period of imprisonment. In June 1945 he was able to start reorganizing the Bahá'í communities in the American zone of occupation in south-western Germany. He was among the first contingent of those appointed Hands of the Cause by Shoghi Effendi in December 1951. As a Hand he made several extended visits to promote the Faith in South America. *BW15*: 416–21; Harper 243–52.

guardianship

Institution created by 'Abdu'l-Bahá to provide a line of future heads of the Faith. In many respects it is reminiscent of the Shí'í imamate (*see* IMÁMS).

In his *WILL AND TESTAMENT* 'Abdu'l-Bahá appointed SHOGHI EFFENDI as his successor, naming him as Guardian of the Cause of God (*Valí amru'lláh*), and the first in a projected line of Guardians. As such he was 'expounder of the words of God', and under the protection of Bahá'u'lláh and the Báb. Obedience to him was obligatory on all Bahá'ís (*see* COVENANT). The line of Guardians would follow on amongst the male descendants of Bahá'u'lláh (*AGHṢÁN*), ideally through the firstborn of the lineal descendants (i.e. according to the principle of primogeniture). It was incumbent upon each Guardian to appoint his successor during his own lifetime so that differences amongst the Bahá'ís would not arise after his death. In this, he should ensure that his successor had the necessary goodly character (that the child was the 'secret essence' of its sire; the qualities required of the appointed Guardians were detachment from worldly things, purity, the fear of God, knowledge, wisdom and learning). The approval of his choice by the elected representative HANDS OF THE CAUSE was also required.

The Guardian would be the sacred head of the UNIVERSAL HOUSE OF JUSTICE following its establishment, and a lifelong member. He was authorized to expel any of its members who committed a sin 'injurious to the common weal'. He would also be responsible for the receipt of the *ḤUQÚQU'LLÁH*, and appoint the Hands of the Cause and direct them in their work. All were to be submissive and subordinate to him.

Commenting on the institution of the guardianship in the *DISPENSATION OF BAHÁ'U'LLÁH* (1934), Shoghi Effendi noted that each Guardian was empowered to be able 'to reveal the purport and disclose the implications' of the utterances of Bahá'u'lláh and 'Abdu'l-Bahá. Such interpretations were 'authoritative and binding'. Together with the Universal House of Justice, the guardianship was also to function to ensure the continuity of divinely appointed authority within the Faith; safeguard the unity of its followers; maintain the integrity and flexibility of its teachings; administer and co-ordinate its activities; promote its interests; execute its laws; and defend its subsidiary institutions. In this the two institutions were complementary. Each had its own specific sphere of jurisdiction. Thus the Guardians could only interpret what had already been revealed, and could only legislate in their capacity as members of the House of Justice. They could insist that a particular legislative decision be reconsidered, but not dictate the activities and procedures of the House. Shoghi Effendi stressed the essential nature of the guardianship (without the guardianship, the Bahá'í world order would be mutilated, affecting the Faith's stability and prestige; only the Guardians would be able to take a long and uninterrupted view of developments and define the House's sphere of legislative action). He also emphasized the distinction between the spiritual station of the Guardians and that of 'Abdu'l-Bahá: the distance between them was greater than that which separated the rank of 'Abdu'l-Bahá from that of his father; unlike 'Abdu'l-Bahá, no Guardian would ever be a perfect exemplar of Bahá'u'lláh's teachings. It would be wrong, therefore, for any Bahá'í to address the Guardian as lord, seek his benediction, or commemorate events associated with his life (*WOB* 132, 147–52). Elsewhere he stressed that his own INFALLIBILITY only extended to matters relating to the Faith, and not to subjects such as economics and science (*LG* 309–13).

Shoghi Effendi did not have any children, and during the course of his own lifetime expelled his brothers and cousins from the Faith as COVENANT-BREAKERS. By the 1950s there were none among the male descendants of Bahá'u'lláh who remained loyal. Presumably for this reason Shoghi Effendi felt himself unable to appoint a successor, and in the event left no will. Apart from the practical issue of succession (*see* HANDS OF THE CAUSE), his death in 1957 therefore created theoretical problems for the Bahá'ís. The newly formed Universal House of Justice declared in October 1963 that no further Guardians could be appointed. In subsequent letters they made it clear that their own legislative functioning was unaffected by the absence of a Guardian. Moreover, they were also assured of divine protection and guidance by 'Abdu'l-Bahá, and were thus able to assume the function of head of the Faith (i.e. the Covenant was secure). In their legislation they were also able to turn to the great mass of interpretation left by Shoghi Effendi. No new authoritative interpretation would be available, however (*MUHJ* 14 no. 5, 83–90 no. 35, 156–61 no. 75).

H

Hádí Dawlatábádí, Mírzá
(d. 1908)

Well-known Iṣfáhání cleric who became a Bábí and later a supporter of Ṣubḥ-i-Azal, who appointed him his representative in Iran and his successor. After the martyrdom of Mírzá Ashraf (2) of Ábádih (October 1888), the leading cleric Áqá Najafí (the 'Son of the Wolf') denounced Hádí as a Bábí and demanded his death. Hádí thereupon made a public recantation although he remained an Azali leader in secret, an act of duplicity for which he was condemned by Bahá'u'lláh (*ESW* 86–8; *TB* 42). After Hádí's death Azal appointed the man's son, Ḥájí Mírzá Yaḥyá, as future head of the *Azalis*, but he had little involvement with them (*McS* 38n).

hadíth

Islamic traditional saying attributed to the Prophet Muḥammad or (for Shí'ís) to one of the *Imáms*. *Hadíths* vary greatly in their reliability, and many are now supposed to be forgeries. Both Bahá'u'lláh and 'Abdu'l-Bahá cite *hadíths* in their writings.

Hague, Tablet to The

Letter of 'Abdu'l-Bahá to the executive committee of the Central Organization for a Durable Peace (based at The Hague), dated 17 December 1919. It is an important statement of the Bahá'í principles. In it 'Abdu'l-Bahá placed the attainment of international peace within the context of the need for wider political, economic and cultural change, and stated that the newly created League of Nations was too restricted to realize such an objective. *Baha'i Revelation* 208–19; *SWAB* 296–308; *AB* 438–40.

Haifa (1995 pop. 252,300)

Modern port city in northern Israel, located on the slopes of Mount Carmel. The town was quite small in the 19th century, but began to grow more rapidly after it became a stopping point on the railway from Damascus to the Hijaz (1905). Growth was even more marked from the 1920s onwards when, first, the British made Haifa into an oil port and naval base, and, later, the city became a major place of settlement for immigrant Jews. In 1914 'Abdu'l-Bahá predicted that the city would become a major port and metropolis, and would expand to join up to Akka. Bahá'ís note the accuracy of this prophecy. Ruhe 133–6, 145–67, 174–83.

BAHÁ'Í HISTORY

Bahá'u'lláh and his companions in exile were briefly in Haifa in 1868 (31 August) when they transhipped from the steamer that had brought them from

Alexandria to a sailing boat which took them to Akka. After Bahá'u'lláh's release from the prison city he visited Haifa three times (1883, 1890 and 1891), the final visit lasting for several months, during which he indicated to 'Abdu'l-Bahá the site for the future Shrine of the Báb and revealed his *Tablet of* CARMEL. 'Abdu'l-Bahá organized the building of the Shrine of the Báb (1899–1907) whilst he was still resident in Akka. At the same time, with the assistance of Laura Clifford DREYFUS-BARNEY, he purchased land lower down the mountain and had a house built near to the German TEMPLE SOCIETY colony. From February 1907 he began to transfer members of his family from Akka to Haifa, and moved there himself in August 1910, making Haifa his official residence. The remains of the Báb were formally interred in the Shrine on 21 March 1909, as later also were those of 'Abdu'l-Bahá himself (29 November 1921). The city has since remained the administrative centre of the Bahá'í Faith (*see* BAHÁ'Í WORLD CENTRE), as well as the site of some of the most important Bahá'í sacred places.

BAHÁ'Í SITES IN HAIFA

These are numerous. The most important are the SHRINE OF THE BÁB; the INTERNATIONAL ARCHIVES building; and the Seat of the Universal House of Justice and the other buildings of the ARC. Other significant sites include:

THE HOUSE OF 'ABDU'L-BAHÁ

Later the residence of Shoghi Effendi, and now of his widow, RÚḤIYYIH KHÁNUM. In the early 1920s Shoghi Effendi had an apartment constructed on the roof to serve as his quarters. Rooms on the ground floor associated with 'Abdu'l-Bahá are visited by pilgrims.

THE PILGRIM HOUSE

Built in 1909 in the vicinity of the Shrine of the Báb by one of the Bahá'ís from Ashkhabad, Mírzá Ja'far Raḥmání, it became the residence of visiting Bahá'í pilgrims from the East (*see* PILGRIMAGE). An annex was constructed in 1935. By 1969, with the increase in their numbers, it was no longer possible to accommodate pilgrims, and the main part of the building was converted into a pilgrim centre, with a library, tearoom, administrative office, etc. Other parts of the complex are used as residences for the custodian of the Shrine and other staff.

THE FORMER WESTERN PILGRIM HOUSE

Built in the early 1920s with funds provided by William Harry RANDALL and Amelia COLLINS, it is close to the House of 'Abdu'l-Bahá and was intended to accommodate the Western pilgrims. In 1951 it became the seat of the INTERNATIONAL BAHÁ'Í COUNCIL, and later of the Universal House of Justice (1963–82) and then of the INTERNATIONAL TEACHING CENTRE (from 1982).

THE BAHÁ'Í CEMETERY

A six-acre plot close to the lower Cave of Elijah on Mount Carmel, the site was purchased on 'Abdu'l-Bahá's instructions. Those buried there include a number of eminent Bahá'ís. The earliest recorded burial was of the Báb's cousin, Mírzá MUḤAMMAD-TAQÍ Afnán, *Vakílu'd-dawlih*, in August 1911.

THE MONUMENT GARDENS

Shoghi Effendi constructed a series of monuments to the various members of 'Abdu'l-Bahá's family on the hillside above the Shrine of the Báb. These are now surrounded by gardens. The first to be built was a columned and domed monument at the grave of 'Abdu'l-Bahá's sister, BAHIYYIH KHÁNUM (d. 1932). Smaller monuments were later constructed at the graves of 'Abdu'l-Bahá's wife, MUNÍRIH KHÁNUM (d. 1938), and of his mother and brother, NAVVÁB and Mírzá MIHDÍ, whose

The House of 'Abdu'l-Bahá in Haifa

The Pilgrim House in Haifa, built in 1909, and now a centre of pilgrimage activities

The tombs of Bahá'u'lláh's first wife, Navváb, and her son, Mírzá Mihdí, in the Monument Gardens, Haifa

The obelisk which marks the site of the the future Mashriqu'l-Adhkár, Haifa

remains Shoghi Effendi had moved from their original graves in Akka in December 1939 (Rabbani, *Priceless Pearl* 259–63). Shoghi Effendi designated Bahiyyih Khánum's grave as the focal point of the future institutions of the Arc.

THE SITE OF THE *MASHRIQU'L-ADHKÁR*

An area at the head of Mount Carmel chosen by Shoghi Effendi as the site for a future Bahá'í House of Worship. The site is above the upper Cave of Elijah, in the vicinity of which Bahá'u'lláh revealed the *Tablet of Carmel*. In April 1955 Shoghi Effendi announced the acquisition of an area of 36,000 sq.m. for the site. He also commissioned an obelisk to be built in Italy to mark the site. This was finally erected in August 1971 following lengthy negotiations to gain planning permission from the Israeli authorities (Giachery 170–4).

Hands of the Cause of God

(Ar.: *Ayádí Amru'lláh*)

Institution of prominent Bahá'ís appointed by the Centre of the Faith. Also used as an HONORIFIC TITLE. Harper; UHJ, *Ministry of the Custodians*.

THE EARLY HANDS

The institution was first established by Bahá'u'lláh, and he named four individuals to this rank between 1887 and about 1890 (see list below). This group served as one of the channels of communication between Bahá'u'lláh and the Bahá'ís in Iran. They later played a key role in consolidating support for the succession of 'Abdu'l-Bahá and, under his direction, formed the nucleus for the Tehran Bahá'í ASSEMBLY, established in 1899. 'Abdu'l-Bahá did not appoint any further individuals to this rank, but later posthumously designated a number of prominent Bahá'ís as Hands, in this way using the term as an honorific.

APPOINTED BY BAHÁ'U'LLÁH

(1) Mírzá Ḥasan-i-ADÍB (Mírzá Muḥammad-Ḥasan Adíbu'l-'Ulamá)
(2) Ḥájí ÁKHÚND (Ḥájí Mullá 'Alí-Akbar Shahmírzádí)
(3) Mirzá 'Alí-Muḥammad, IBN-I-AṢDAQ
(4) Ḥájí Mírzá Muḥammad-Taqí Abharí IBN-I-ABHAR

NAMED BY 'ABDU'L-BAHÁ (This list is not necessarily exhaustive)

(1) MUḤAMMAD-RIḌÁ Muḥammad-Ábádí Yazdí, Mullá
(2) NABÍL-I-AKBAR, Shaykh Muḥammad Qá'iní
(3) Mullá ṢÁDIQ Khurásání, '*Muqaddas*', *Ismu'lláhu'l-Aṣdaq*
(4) Mírzá 'Alí-Muḥammad VARQÁ, the martyr

In his WILL AND TESTAMENT, 'Abdu'l-Bahá gave authority to the future Guardian of the Faith to appoint Hands of the Cause. The Hands were to be under his direction and shadow. They were also to elect nine of their number to work in his service, and, in secret ballot, give approval to his choice of successor (*see* GUARDIANSHIP). Their obligations were to 'diffuse the Divine Fragrances', 'edify the souls of men', 'promote learning', 'improve the character of all men', and be always 'sanctified and detached from earthly things' (*Will* 12–13).

DURING THE MINISTRY OF SHOGHI EFFENDI

Between 1925 and 1952, Shoghi Effendi honoured several Bahá'ís as Hands posthumously (see list below). In 1951, he began to appoint functioning Hands with an initial group of twelve (24 December 1951), soon raised to nineteen (29 February 1952). A further five individuals were appointed between 1952 and 1957 to replace Hands who had died (in two cases, replacing parents). The total number of Hands was raised again to twenty-seven in October 1957, shortly before Shoghi Effendi's death. Most of those appointed were assigned responsibilities in the continents in which they resided, notably to assist in the achievement of teaching PLAN goals. Five were appointed from or as members of the newly formed INTERNATIONAL BAHÁ'Í COUNCIL (created 1950). The Hands were also later given responsibility to protect the Faith by exercising vigilance against attacks from its external and internal enemies (*see* OPPOSITION). To assist them in their work they were authorized to appoint AUXILIARY BOARDS (from 1954).

NAMED POSTHUMOUSLY BY SHOGHI EFFENDI
(dates named appear in parentheses)

(1) John E. ESSLEMONT (30 Nov. 1925)
(2) Ḥájí AMÍN, Ḥájí Abu'l-Ḥasan Ardikání (July 1928)
(3) Keith RANSOM-KEHLER (28 Oct. 1933)
(4) Martha ROOT (2 Oct. 1939)
(5) 'Abdu'l-Jalíl Bey SA'D (25 June 1942)
(6) Siyyid Mustafa RUMI (14 July 1945)
(7) Muḥammad-Taqí IṢFÁHÁNÍ (15 Dec. 1946)
(8) Louis C. GREGORY (5 Aug. 1951)
(9) Roy C. WILHELM (23 Dec. 1951)
(10) John Henry Hyde DUNN (26 Apr. 1952)

APPOINTED BY SHOGHI EFFENDI, 1951–7

First contingent, 24 December 1951

(1) Dorothy B. BAKER (1898–1954)
(2) Amelia E. COLLINS (1873–1962)
(3) 'Alí-Akbar FURÚTAN (b. 1905)
(4) Ugo GIACHERY (1896–1989)
(5) Hermann GROSSMANN (1899–1968)
(6) Horace HOLLEY (1887–1960)
(7) Leroy IOAS (1896–1965)
(8) William Sutherland MAXWELL (1874–1952)
(9) Charles Mason REMEY (1874–1974)
(10) Ṭarázu'lláh SAMANDARÍ (1874–1968)
(11) George TOWNSHEND (1876–1957)
(12) Valíyu'lláh VARQÁ (1884–1955)

Second contingent, 29 February 1952

(13) Shu'á'u'lláh 'ALÁ'Í (1889–1984)
(14) Musa BANÁNÍ (1886–1971)
(15) Clara DUNN (1869–1960)
(16) Zikrullah KHADEM (1904–1986)
(17) Adelbert MÜHLSCHLEGEL (1897–1980)
(18) Siegfried SCHOPFLOCHER (1877–1953)
(19) Corinne TRUE (1861–1961)

Appointed individually

(20) RÚḤIYYIH KHÁNUM, Amatu'l-Bahá (b. 1910), 26 March 1952
(21) Jalál KHÁZEH (1897–1990), 7 December 1953
(22) Paul E. HANEY (1909–82), 19 March 1954
(23) 'Alí-Muḥammad VARQÁ (b. 1911), 15 November 1955
(24) Agnes Baldwin ALEXANDER (1875–1971), 27 March 1957

Third contingent, October 1957

(25) Hasan BALYUZI (1908–80)
(26) Abu'l-Qásim FAIZÍ (1906–80)
(27) Collis FEATHERSTONE (1913–90)
(28) John FERRABY (1914–73)
(29) Raḥmatu'lláh MUHÁJIR (1923–79)
(30) Enoch OLINGA (1926–79)
(31) John ROBARTS (1901–91)
(32) William SEARS (1911–92)

THE 'INTERREGNUM', 1957–63

Shoghi Effendi's death (4 November 1957) came as an unexpected blow to Bahá'ís. Gathering together in Haifa (18–25 November), the Hands discovered that Shoghi had left no will or any instructions as to what was to be done regarding the future leadership of the Bahá'ís. However, in his last general letter to the Bahá'ís he had referred to the Hands as the 'Chief Stewards' of the Faith, and it was in this capacity that they now acted, assuming temporary headship of the Bahá'ís, and electing nine of their number to serve as 'Custodians' in Haifa to oversee the continued progress of Shoghi Effendi's plans. They received the worldwide support of the Bahá'ís. Meeting in annual conclave, the Hands determined that the best response to the absence of a Guardian was the rapid establishment of the UNIVERSAL HOUSE OF JUSTICE, a body guaranteed divine guidance and protection by 'Abdu'l-Bahá in his *WILL AND TESTMENT.* To this end, they called for the International Council to become an elected body in 1961, and for the House itself to be elected in April 1963. They asked that they themselves should not be voted for. Support for this policy from the Bahá'ís was almost universal, the main opposition coming from the veteran American Hand C.M. Remey, President of the existing Council, who laid claim to be the second Guardian (1960), a claim that was rejected by all but a small number of Bahá'ís. The Hands retained their headship until 1963 and the elections for the first Universal House of Justice.

SINCE 1963

The Hands have served the Universal House of Justice since its formation. The House determined that it was not possible to appoint any further Hands (1964), and sought ways of both relieving the Hands from unnecessary administrative work so that they could devote themselves to inspiring Bahá'ís throughout the world and of creating new institutions to continue the Hands' functions of the propagation and protection of the Faith into the future. The new institutions created were the CONTINENTAL BOARDS OF COUNSELLORS (1968) and the INTERNATIONAL TEACHING CENTRE (1973). Meanwhile, the passing years greatly reduced the number of Hands, such that by the end of 1998 only three remained.

Haney, Paul E. (1909–82)

American HAND OF THE CAUSE of Bahá'í parentage. He was active in American

The Hands of the Cause of God at their Plenary Meeting, April 1963

Bahá'í administration, and was a member of the national spiritual assembly from 1946 until 1957. He was appointed a Hand of the Cause by Shoghi Effendi in on 19 March 1954, and became one of the custodial Hands living in Haifa after Shoghi Effendi's death. *BW18*: 613–18; Harper 156–63.

Hannen, Joseph (d. 1920) and Pauline (d. 1939)

Prominent early American Bahá'ís from Washington DC. They played a major role in promoting racial unity in the Bahá'í community. Shoghi Effendi honoured Joseph as one of the DISCIPLES OF 'ABDU'L-BAHÁ (*BW8*: 660–1; *Star* 10/19 345–6).

Ḥaydar-'Alí Iṣfáhání, Ḥájí Mírzá (d. 1920)

Eminent Iranian Bahá'í. He became a Bábí in Iṣfáhán, and subsequently became a learned and effective Bahá'í teacher, travelling widely in Iran and the Ottoman empire. He was arrested by the Iranian consul-general in Egypt (1867), and with other Bahá'ís exiled to Sudan in conditions of enormous hardship. They were eventually released by General Gordon (1877). He later settled in Akka/Haifa (1903). Extracts from his memoirs, *Bihjatu'ṣ-ṣudúr* (*The Delight of Hearts*), have been published in English. *EB* 237–50; *RB2*: 438–50.

Hayden, Robert E. (1913–80)

African-American poet of considerable repute who became a Bahá'í in 1943. His poetry attracted international attention and he became the first black American to be appointed as consultant in poetry to the Library of Congress (1976–8), the equivalent of poet laureate. J.S. Hatcher; Auroral Darkness; *BW18*: 715–17.

Ḥaẓíratu'l-Quds

(Ar., 'Sacred Fold')

Bahá'í administrative headquarters. National *Ḥaẓíratu'l-Quds* began to be established in the 1940s at Shoghi Effendi's direction, all national spiritual ASSEMBLIES eventually being directed to obtain one. These were to be the seats of their respective assemblies, and so would provide office space for the national secretariat and treasury, and a meeting room for the assembly. They should also include an archives, library, publishing office, assembly hall and pilgrims' hostel. If there was no other place available they might also serve as a meeting place for the local Bahá'í community, its assembly and committees. They should embody the Bahá'í ideal of service, both to the Faith and humanity in general. Although essentially administrative buildings, they could also be used for social occasions such as weddings and funerals. Dancing was not to be permitted in them, however. In the future the *Ḥaẓíratu'l-Quds* would be located in the environs of the *MASHRIQU'L-ADHKÁR*, the two institutions being complementary in their functions. Bahá'í assembly and committee members would then gather for dawn prayers at the *Mashriqu'l-Adhkár* before beginning their day's work. In larger Bahá'í communities it has become increasingly common for there to be local or regional *Ḥaẓíratu'l-Quds*. *GPB* 339–40; *LG* 271–4.

health and healing

The Bahá'í writings praise medicine as the noblest of sciences (*see Tablet of* MEDICINE), and encourage its study. Medical work, offered in a spirit of service, is regarded as a means of praising God. Those who are sick should consult competent physicians and follow their instructions (even if they are physicians themselves). They should also turn to God, and a number of Bahá'í healing prayers are provided for Bahá'ís to use. The individual's spiritual and emotional state (*see* EMOTIONS) is regarded as affecting their physical health. 'Abdu'l-Bahá taught that ill health can result from both physical and spiritual causes, and accordingly can be treated by both material and spiritual healing. He said that a major cause of physical ill health was chemical imbalances in the body caused by poor DIET: dietary and herbal remedies were the appropriate response to these maladies (moderation and simplicity in eating were advised). Some illnesses result from emotional shocks, fear, and the experience of SUFFERING; these should be treated spiritually. In general, a person's spirit has a great effect on their physical condition. It is therefore important for doctors to bring comfort and joy to their patients, even if it involves not telling the truth about the nature of their condition (the only circumstance in which this is permitted: *see* TRUTHFULNESS). Similarly, everyone should visit the sick, showing them kindness, and seeking to bring them love and happiness; giving medicine to treat a physical ailment is only part of the cure. Specific forms of spiritual healing include turning to God, PRAYER, and the healer concentrating his mind on a sick person who has faith that this will effect a cure. This latter method requires a cordial relationship between the two. Sometimes a healer laying his or her hands on a patient might also have an effect. Healing can also be effected through the power of the Holy Spirit, and a Bahá'í doctor should turn to Bahá'u'lláh for power and guidance in effecting a cure. Responding to questions, Shoghi Effendi noted the complementarity of spiritual and material healing methods, and stressed that spiritual healing should not be regarded as a substitute for material healing, and that those who practise it should not regard themselves as 'Bahá'í healers', as there is no such thing. He also stressed the importance of getting sufficient sleep, and taking care of one's health. Again, he noted that psychiatric medicine was as yet in its infancy – psychiatrists were neither always wise nor always right – and refused to comment on a variety of issues, including the value of Freudian psychoanalysis or chiropractic. If an individual Bahá'í found some particular method beneficial, they were welcome to use it and recommend it to others. The Universal House of Justice has stated that although mental illness may impede an individual's striving for spiritual progress, it is not in itself a spiritual malady. It has also suggested that in some cases of such illness, prayer, study, work and involvement in Bahá'í activities may aid the sufferer to recover (*LG* 283–4). *CC1*: 459–88; *LG* 275–94.

OTHER MEDICAL ISSUES

CHILD CARE

'Abdu'l-Bahá emphasized the importance of proper child care: from birth, each infant should be provided with whatever is conducive to its health; unless impossible, this should include the mother's breast milk as this is best suited to the child. Children should also receive physical education to ensure their strength and growth (*CC1*: 461 no. 1026; *LG* 293–4 nos. 998–1000).

EUTHANASIA

There is as yet no Bahá'í policy on euthanasia or the removal of life support in certain medical situations. Bahá'ís are reminded that God is the giver of life, and that he alone can dispose of it as he deems best, but the decision is left to the consciences of the individuals involved (*LG* 290–1 no. 985, no. 987).

ORGAN DONATION

This is commended, but the donor's body and organs should be treated with respect as the former 'temple' of the human spirit (*LG* 290–1 no. 984, no. 986).

HEALTH-CARE PROFESSIONALS

Given the great importance given to medicine in the Bahá'í writings, it is not surprising that many Bahá'ís have become doctors or other health-care professionals. Health care has also become an important part of Bahá'í SOCIO-ECONOMIC DEVELOPMENT work. This has involved numerous medical projects, including many temporary medical camps organized in poorer countries or districts to provide free or reduced-cost medical services by groups of doctors and other health professionals.

A number of Bahá'í medical associations and health agencies have recently been established, notably the Bahá'í International Health Agency (BIHA, 1982), and also organizations in Britain, Canada, France, India and the United States, as well as European continental associations (including one for Bahá'í dentists). *BW18*: 201; *NS* 1994–5: 116–18. (*See also* ABORTION; ARTIFICIAL FERTILIZATION; BIRTH CONTROL; CIRCUMCISION.)

Hearst, Phoebe (1842–1919)

Millionaire widow of Senator George Hearst. She became a Bahá'í after meeting Edward and Lua GETSINGER (1898), and subsequently invited the Getsingers, several of her relatives and employees, together with I.G. KHEIRALLA and his wife, to join her in a trip to the Middle East, including a visit to 'Abdu'l-Bahá in Akka which constituted the first Western Bahá'í pilgrimage (1898–9). After her return to the United States she played an important role in holding the fledgling Bahá'í community together during the time of Kheiralla's defection. She subsequently became alienated from the community after a few Bahá'ís had sought to importune money from her. She retained her regard for 'Abdu'l-Bahá, whom she hosted during his visit to San Francisco (1912). *BFA1*: 139–45, 155, 168–9; *WEBW* 13–19.

heaven and hell

For Bahá'ís heaven and hell are states of the SOUL, which may be entered both in the present life and the afterlife (*see* DEATH). The purpose of human existence is to know and love God. To come closer to God fulfils this purpose and raises the individual to a heavenly state: one attains 'eternal life' and enters the 'Kingdom of God'. To turn away from God and become immersed in worldly attachments is to rebel against the divine purpose, and will ultimately lead to degradation and despair. Each individual has FREE WILL, by which they can choose to develop the heavenly qualities that are their natural potential, or adopt qualities that are satanic (*see* HUMAN NATURE). After death those who are near to God rejoice, whilst those who are distant from him lament. The soul is a non-material reality, and heaven and hell are not physical places (*ESW* 132; *SAQ* 241–3; *see* METAPHYSICS). The coming of each MANIFESTATION OF GOD also separates the faithful from the unbelievers or, metaphorically, the living from the dead. Acceptance of God's messenger is equivalent to 'life', 'paradise', and 'resurrection'; rejection to 'death' and 'hell' (*KI* 72–9).

He whom God shall make manifest (Ar.: *Man-yuẓhiruhu'lláh*)

Bábí messianic figure repeatedly referred to by the Báb in the *BAYÁN*. This personage was said to be the origin of all divine names and attributes; his command was equivalent to God's command. All should seek refuge in him. Not to believe in him would be to cease to be a believer. A thousand perusals of the *Bayán* were not equal to reading one of his verses. The *Bayán* was itself a gift to him, and revolved around his word. The day of his advent was known only to God, but would certainly occur. It was impossible for anyone to falsely claim to be him. He would be known by his own self, and not by the *Bayán*. In the meantime, all must rise on hearing his name and in every meeting a vacant place was to be left for him.

After the Báb's execution (1850) and the crushing of Bábism as an organized movement (1852), several Bábís claimed high-ranking spiritual stations, including that of *Man-yuẓhiruhu'lláh*. Bahá'u'lláh himself eventually laid claim to be the Bábí promised one in the 1860s. The AZALIS objected to Bahá'u'lláh's claim, on the ground that the Báb had stated that the promised one would come before the number of '*mustagháth*' ('the Beseeched', a divine attribute; the word is numerically equivalent to 2,001 years), or '*aghyath*'/'*ghiyáth*' ('the Most Succouring', =1,511 years), i.e. in the distant future. The Bahá'ís countered by stressing that the Báb had also said that the promised *Man-yuẓhiruhu'lláh* would arise suddenly at a time known only to God, after 'a while' (*ḥin*, =68, i.e. 1268 AH/1851–2 CE), and had stressed the significance of the 'year nine' (i.e. of his own dispensation, =1269/1852–3), the year of Bahá'u'lláh's arrival in Baghdad. *EGBBF* 39–40; MacEoin, 'Hierarchy' 123–35.

Hidden Words

(PA: *Kalimát-i-Maknúnih*)

Collection of Arabic and Persian verses by Bahá'u'lláh composed in Baghdad in 1274 AH/1857–8 CE. Identified by Bahá'u'lláh with the 'Hidden Book of Fáṭima', which in Shí'í tradition had been addressed to the Prophet's daughter to console her after her father's death. It is presented as the 'inner essence' of what had been revealed by the prophets of the past, 'as a token of grace unto the righteous', that they might be faithful to God's Covenant, live according to his trust, and obtain 'the gem of Divine virtue'. Shoghi Effendi described it as Bahá'u'lláh's pre-eminent ethical work (*GPB* 140). In it Bahá'u'lláh assures the reader of God's love. God has made human beings noble, and they should cleanse their hearts so that they might find the divine light within themselves. The human heart is God's home and the human spirit his place of revelation. This is their natural station, but human beings busy themselves with the world ('that which perisheth'), and thus lose sight of their true natures. Instead, they should commune with God and free themselves from the 'prison' of self and the 'fetters' of worldly attachments. They should bring themselves to account each day; sorrow only at their separation from God; not fear death; follow divine law; submit themselves to God; accept trials for God's sake; ready themselves for martyrdom; neither fear abasement nor rejoice in prosperity; not vaunt themselves over the poor (who are God's trust), but rather bestow God's wealth upon them; not breathe the sins of others, nor exalt themselves over others, nor commit iniquity; eschew covetousness, envy and malice; be forbearing with others; avoid fellowship with the ungodly; distinguish themselves by their deeds; plant only 'the rose of love' in the garden of the heart; and work to support themselves. They should know that a 'new garden' had appeared, inhabited by heavenly beings. They should seek to learn the mysteries of its love and wisdom. God is always close to them, but they heedlessly ignore him. They should seize their chance before the 'fleeting moment' of their lives is ended. *HW*; Malouf; *RB1*: 71–83.

Ḥikmat, Lawḥ-i-

(PA, *Tablet of Wisdom*)

Early Akka-period tablet of Bahá'u'lláh composed in 1873/4 and addressed to NABÍL-I-AKBAR, a distinguished Bahá'í, well versed in Islamic philosophy. It discusses a number of topics, including:

CREATION, the Word of GOD; PHILOSOPHY; and the importance of TEACHING, which it presents as encompassing the SPIRITUAL PATH. *TB* 135–52; Cole, 'Problems of chronology'; *33–49.*

Hinduism

See INDIAN RELIGIONS.

Hoar, William H. (1856–1922)

Prominent early American Bahá'í. He converted in Chicago in 1895/6, and subsequently became one of the leading Bahá'ís of New York. Shoghi Effendi honoured him as one of the DISCIPLES OF 'ABDU'L-BAHÁ. *Star* 12/19 (1922): 311.

Holley, Horace H. (1887–1960)

American HAND OF THE CAUSE of New England background. Holley first encountered the Bahá'í teachings in 1909 en route to Europe. He later established himself in New York, and in 1923 was elected to the American national spiritual ASSEMBLY, serving as its secretary almost continuously from 1924 to 1959. In this role he played a crucial part in the development of the Bahá'í ADMINISTRATION in North America. He also was Shoghi Effendi's closest collaborator in the production of the *BAHÁ'Í WORLD* volumes. He was among the first contingent of Hands of the Cause appointed by Shoghi Effendi in December 1951. He later became one of the custodial Hands in Haifa. *BW13*: 849–58; Harper 253–64.

Horace Holley, prominent American Bahá'í and Hand of the Cause

holy days

In the *Kitáb-i-AQDAS*, Bahá'u'lláh ordained two 'Most Great Festivals' for the Bahá'ís to celebrate: the anniversaries of the Báb's declaration of mission in 1844 (when God 'shed upon the whole of creation the effulgent glory of His most excellent Names') and Bahá'u'lláh's own declaration in the RIḌVÁN Garden in 1863, 'the King of Festivals'. He also identified *NAW-RÚZ* (New Year) and the birthdays of the Báb and himself as holy days, and directed that these 'Twin Birthdays' (they occur on the first and second days of the Muslim month of Muḥarram respectively) be accounted as one. During Bahá'u'lláh's lifetime Bahá'ís also commemorated the anniversary of the martyrdom of the Báb. The anniversary of Bahá'u'lláh's passing was subsequently commemorated as a holy day. 'Abdu'l-Bahá did not wish Bahá'ís to celebrate his own birthday (it coincided with the anniversary of the Báb's declaration). Instead, he allowed them to celebrate the Bahá'í covenant of leadership and his own accession, but appointed a date for this 180 days after Bahá'u'lláh's passing. The anniversary of his own passing was also later commemorated. Shoghi Effendi did not permit any dates connected to his life to be marked as holy days.

The dates of commemoration of the major Bahá'í holy days are as follows:

- *Naw-Rúz*, 21 March
- The Riḍván Festival, 21 April–2 May, with the first, ninth, and twelfth days (21, 29 April, 2 May) being specifically marked as holy days (these commemorate the arrival of Bahá'u'lláh at the Garden, the arrival of his family, and his final departure). The celebration of the first day of Riḍván should be at 3 o'clock in the afternoon, marking the time of Bahá'u'lláh's arrival
- Declaration of the Báb, 22/23 May. Commemorated at about two hours after sunset on the twenty-second
- Ascension of Bahá'u'lláh, 29 May Commemorated at 3 o'clock in the morning
- Martyrdom of the Báb, 9 July. Commemorated at noon
- Birth of the Báb, 20 October
- Birth of Bahá'u'lláh, 12 November

Bahá'ís should abstain from work on the three special days of Riḍván and on the other major holy days. At present, the 'twin birthdays' are celebrated according to the Islamic lunar calendar in the Middle East, but according to the Gregorian calendar elsewhere. There is no set format for these various commemorations, and Bahá'í communities organize their own meetings for them as they see fit. Devotional programmes of prayers and specific writings for the holy day – particularly Bahá'u'lláh's tablet of VISITATION for the day of his passing and for the martyrdom of the Báb – are commonly organized. Public celebrations and communal dinners are often held on *Naw-Rúz* and the birthday of Bahá'u'lláh.

The two minor holy days on which work is not suspended are:

- Day of the Covenant, 26 November
- Passing of 'Abdu'l-Bahá, 28 November. Commemorated at about 1 o'clock in the morning

Again, there is no set format for these days, and Bahá'í communities organize their own meetings.

Shoghi Effendi emphasized the importance of Bahá'ís abstaining from work on the major Bahá'í holy days, unless this was specifically disallowed under the terms of their employment. Such abstention was an important means of gaining PUBLIC RECOGNITION of the Faith. Bahá'í parents should similarly seek to gain permission for their children not to attend school on these days. He also encouraged the Bahá'ís not to celebrate the holy days of other religions among themselves. *KA* 59–60 k110–12, 105 q1–2, 224–6 n138–40; *LG* 299–303; Forghani; Walbridge, *Sacred* 183–4, 213–47.

holy war

In Islam, holy war (*jihád*) against unbelievers has been regarded as a means of expanding and defending the Islamic realm. War against apostates and dissenters has also been legitimized. The messianic figure of the MAHDÍ is expected to lead a final *jihád* against the forces of unbelief. The Báb's major references to the subject occur in his *QAYYÚM'L-ASMÁ'*, written during the early 'Islamic' phase of his mission. There, in keeping with traditional Islamic expectations, he bade his followers prepare for 'the day of slaughter' that would accompany the advent of the predicted Mahdí, and promised the descent of angels to help them slay the unbelievers. In his later writings the Báb made it clear that the *jihád* could only be called by the Mahdí. However, following his own open claim to that station, no such call was ever issued, and the Báb instead instructed future Bábí kings to bring the peoples of the world to the Bábí religion and not to allow unbelievers – with the exception of traders – to live in their territories. The manner in which the Bábí 'upheavals' (*see* BÁBÍ RADICALISM) involved concepts of holy war remains controversial. Certainly the Bábí fighters saw themselves engaged in a holy struggle against unbelievers, but no declarations of *jihád* ever appear to have been made, even though at Ṭabarsí, both Quddús and Mullá Ḥusayn were accorded messianic status, and as such could have taken the role of the Mahdí in leading a *jihád*. The struggles may perhaps be seen as 'defensive *jihads*', in which the paradigm of martyrdom at the hands of the ungodly coexisted with the use of the sword as a means of proving God's truth. MacEoin, 'Bábí concept of holy war'; *SBBR* 21–2, 27, 44–5; Walbridge, 'Bábí uprising'.

In marked contrast to Bábism and Islam, the Bahá'í Faith explicitly rejects the concept of *jihád*. One of the statements made by Bahá'u'lláh at the time of his Riḍván declaration (1863) was to forbid holy war, a command later reiterated in his writings (*RB1* 278; *TB* 21, 28, 91; *SBBR* 79). Instead, Bahá'ís should teach the Bahá'í cause with moral example and peaceful persuasion (*see* teaching). If they were persecuted for this, they should be willing to accept martyrdom. It is of note, however, that 'military' imagery remains common in Bahá'í references to the teaching work. Thus 'Abdu'l-Bahá referred to Bahá'ís as the 'armies of God' who, supported by 'the cohorts of the Supreme Concourse', would defeat the 'hosts' and 'legions' of the nations and become the 'conquerors' of East and West (*TDP* 47–9), and Shoghi Effendi called upon them to 'mount the steed of steadfastness, unfurl the banner of renunciation, don the armor of utter consecration to God's Cause, gird themselves with the girdle of a chaste and holy life, [and] unsheathe the sword of Bahá'u'lláh's utterance' (MBW 49). Again, the first international teaching plan was designated as a 'Global Crusade', and its pioneers as 'Knights of Bahá'u'lláh'.

holy years

Shoghi Effendi declared 1952–3 (from October to October) to be a holy year, commemorating the centenary of the 'birth' of Bahá'u'lláh's revelatory mission in the Síyáh-Chál. It was marked by the first series of international Bahá'í conferences; the start of the Ten Year Crusade; and the dedication to public worship of the Bahá'í temple at Wilmette (*BW12*: 115–88). The Universal House of Justice declared the period from Riḍván 1992 to Riḍván 1993 to be a second holy year, marking the centenary of Bahá'u'lláh's passing and the inauguration of his Covenant. Events of the year included an international gathering of Bahá'ís at the Bahá'í World Centre (27–30 May 1992), at which a scroll with the names of the pioneers of the Ten Year Crusade (the Knights of Bahá'u'lláh) was ceremonially interred at the Shrine of Bahá'u'lláh, and the holding of the second Bahá'í World Congress in New York City (23–26 November). The authorized English-language translation of the *Kitáb-i-Aqdas* was also published during the year, and the law of *Ḥuqúqu'lláh* came into general effect (*BWNS* 1992: 19–46, 95–102).

homosexuality

In the *Kitáb-i-Aqdas* Bahá'u'lláh forbade pederasty. Shoghi Effendi interpreted this to imply a general prohibition on all forms of homosexual activity, regarding it as 'spiritually condemned'. Love between two people of the same sex may be very devoted, but to express this love in a sexual relationship is considered wrong. Homosexuality is an affliction, and a Bahá'í who is homosexual should struggle against his or her condition, if necessary seeking medical advice. Such a struggle may be very hard, but will lead to spiritual growth. Daily spiritual struggle to conform to God's standard is something all devoted Bahá'ís strive for, as with the unmarried heterosexual who seeks to remain chaste. Bahá'í institutions should offer loving counsel to homosexuals, and only consider administrative sanctions in the case of public scandal. *KA* 58 k107, 223 n134; *LG* 364–8. (*See also* SEX.)

honorific titles

The Báb gave various of his followers honorific religious titles. The best known of these are the LETTERS OF THE LIVING. Others were named 'Mirrors'. Individuals were also given specific religious names: QUDDÚS ('Holy'), ṬÁHIRIH ('Pure'), VAḤÍD ('Unique'), etc. Similarly, Bahá'u'lláh gave a number of his early followers titles, including some recognizing various names of God (*Ismu'l-lláh*, the 'Name of God'). These included Mullá ṢÁDIQ Khurásání (*Ismu'lláhu'l-Aṣdaq*, the 'name of God, the most truthful') and Sayyid MIHDÍ DAHAJÍ (*Ismu'lláhu'l-Mihdí*). He also appointed four of his followers as HANDS OF THE CAUSE OF GOD, a title that was both a rank and came to entail an administrative function. 'Abdu'l-Bahá posthumously identified a number of individuals as Hands. He also gave some of his Western followers Persian names indicative of spiritual qualities and referred to some as 'Handmaiden of Bahá' (*Amatu'l-Bahá*) or 'Handmaiden of the Most High' (*Amatu'l-A'lá*). Shoghi Effendi named various early Bahá'ís as APOSTLES OF BAHÁ'U'LLÁH and DISCIPLES OF 'ABDU'L-BAHÁ. He also named a number of Bahá'ís as Hands, and gave PIONEERS during the TEN YEAR CRUSADE the title of 'KNIGHTS OF BAHÁ'U'LLÁH'.

House of the Báb

See SHÍRÁZ: HOUSE OF THE BÁB.

House of Bahá'u'lláh

See BAGHDAD: HOUSE OF BAHÁ'U'LLÁH.

House of Worship

See MASHRIQU'L-ADHKÁR.

houses of justice

Bahá'u'lláh called for the future establishment of 'houses of justice' in each city to administer Bahá'í affairs (*KA* 29 k30), the present 'local spiritual ASSEMBLIES' being regarded as precursors of these. He also envisaged the establishment of what is now referred to as the UNIVERSAL HOUSE OF JUSTICE, as the ruling body of the Faith (*KA* 35 k42). In some instances it is not clear which of these bodies is being referred to; some responsibilities – EDUCATION and care for the poor – perhaps being assigned to both (*KA* 37 k48, 72 k147, 185 n42). 'Abdu'l-Bahá introduced the concept of 'secondary' or national houses of justice (the present 'national spiritual assemblies') to act as the electors of the Universal House of Justice (*CC1*: 322, 325).

Húd

Quranic prophet referred to by Bahá'u'lláh (*KI* 6–7).

Ḥujjat (Ar., 'Proof')

Religious title of the Bábí leader in ZANJÁN, Mullá Muḥammad-'Alí Zanjání (1812/3–50). Ḥujjat was already a leading clerical figure in his home town when he received a copy of some of the Báb's writings, and his conversion was followed by that of several thousand of his fellow townsmen. He was a controversial figure prior to his conversion, adhering to the minority Akhbárí school of Shí'ism, and was summoned to Tehran on several occasions after accusations were made against him by other clerics in Zanján. Greatly revered by his followers, he became the focal point of the lengthy struggle between the local Bábís and government forces. His death (?29 December 1850) precipitated the surrender of the remaining Bábís. *ARR* 101–2; Browne, 'Personal reminiscences'; *GPB* 12; *MBBR* 114–23; McS 116–17; Nabil 178–9, 529–73; *TJ* 135–70, 371–3; TN 9–10; Walbridge, 'Bábí uprising'.

human life, purpose of

Bahá'ís believe that the purpose of life is for the individual to know, love and worship God and to contribute to the onward progress of humanity. To these ends, all human beings are called upon to recognize the MANIFESTATION OF GOD (i.e. at the present time, Bahá'u'lláh); to follow his laws and teachings; to seek to develop SPIRITUAL QUALITIES, so that they draw closer to God, receive his grace and realize their own spiritual potential; and to work for the betterment of the world, through both TEACHING the Bahá'í Faith and spreading and implementing the BAHÁ'Í PRINCIPLES (EDUCATION, racial and gender equality, etc.). *GWB* 65 no. 27, 214 no. 109; *KA* 19 k1, 100–1.

human nature

For Bahá'u'lláh human beings are created because of divine love, and in order that they might in turn love God (*HWa* nos. 3, 4). Uniquely, the human reality (*see* SOUL) is able to mirror all of GOD's names and attributes: howsoever imperfectly they might do this, humans have been made in the 'image' of God (*GWB* 65 no. 27; *HWa* no. 3). They are 'as a mine rich in gems of inestimable value'. But these treasures can only be revealed, and individuals achieve their potential, if the human 'mirror' is cleansed 'from the dross of earthly defilements', and this in turn is to be achieved through divine grace and the spiritual EDUCATION expressed through the MANIFESTATION(s) OF GOD and their scriptures (*GWB* 65 no. 27, 261–2 no. 124; *TB* 161–2). God has given humans FREE WILL, however, and it is thus first necessary for the individual to decide to turn to God (*GWB* 148 no. 77). If people only realize the greatness of their own station, they will manifest goodly conduct (*TB* 172).

Similarly, 'Abdu'l-Bahá referred to human beings as having both an angelic and an animal nature: if they choose, they are able to advance towards moral perfection, ultimately becoming heavenly beings (ANGELS), but they can also turn to degradation, acquire 'satanic qualities', and become viler than the most savage beast. They can acquire spiritual characteristics, or they can accustom themselves to wrongdoing, thus perverting their natural potential (*SAQ* 214, 235–7; *SWAB* 287–8). Divine education is essential. Self-love is 'kneaded' into the human clay. It is mistaken to believe that there is 'an innate sense of human dignity' which prevents the individual from committing evil and ensures the attainment of perfection. Infants display signs of aggression and lawlessness, and if they do not receive the instruction of a teacher their undesirable qualities increase. Through the force of divine RELIGION human beings are able to overcome their innate selfishness and express SPIRITUAL QUALITIES in their lives (*SDC* 96–9). Individuals differ in their innate, inherited characteristics, but whatever these are, they can be transformed, both as a result of education and the capacities the individual acquires for good or evil through the life they lead (*CC1*: 257–60; *SAQ* 212–16).

human race

UNITY

Bahá'u'lláh taught that the human race is one indivisible whole: 'the fruits of one tree, and the leaves of one branch' (*TB* 164). The earth is a single homeland, and people should work for the well-being of all humankind. Glory lies in upright conduct, not in nationality or rank (*TB* 67–8). The vision of the Bahá'ís should be world embracing. They should love the whole world and not just their own nation (*TB* 87–8, 127). SERVICE to the entire human race and promotion of its best interests is called for (*TB* 167). Unity would be promoted by TOLERANCE and the adoption of a universal LANGUAGE, and most of all by the union of all the world's peoples in one common faith, religion being a 'binding force' which unites people of different beliefs, creeds and temperaments (*KI* 72–3). 'Abdu'l-Bahá compared the human race to a flower garden, made beautiful by its diversity of colour and form (*SWAB* 290–2). Shoghi Effendi identified the principle of the oneness of mankind as the pivotal teaching of the Bahá'í Faith (*WOB* 42–3). (*See also* PEACE; RACE; SOCIAL EVOLUTION; WORLD ORDER; WORLD UNITY.)

MATURITY

Bahá'u'lláh stated that the adoption of a universal language; the ability to transmute elements; and the refusal by individuals to accept the burden of kingship would all be signs of the maturity of the human race (*KA* 88 k189, 250–1 n194).

human rights

HUMAN RIGHTS AND OBLIGATIONS

The Bahá'í view of human rights is based on conceptions of divinely revealed standards of social justice and of the responsibilities of human beings towards each other and towards God. Human responsibilities include both those of individuals and those of governments. Specific teachings include:

(1) *Economic* Individuals have the right to life, food, clothing, adequate wages and rest from labour, private property and familial inheritance; as well as freedom from both chattel and economic slavery (*see* ECONOMIC TEACHINGS; SLAVE TRADE). Governments have a responsibility to care for the poor, to institute equitable systems of taxation, to intervene in industrial disputes, and to promote AGRICULTURE and economic development. The rich have a moral responsibility to help the poor. Everyone has a responsibility to WORK. Everyone has a right to receive a basic EDUCATION and to become literate (*see* LITERACY), and parents and the community have a responsibility to ensure that all children are educated.

(2) *Political* A GOVERNMENT has the responsibility to rule with JUSTICE, and to combat CRIME. Arbitrary rule is to be condemned, and should be checked by the existence of consultative assemblies, an educated populace and a free press. Individuals have the right to be treated equally before the LAW, and only to be sentenced after due legal process. NEWSPAPERS have a responsibility to report with 'fair speech and truthfulness'. Bahá'ís have an obligation to be loyal to government.

(3) *International and moral order* Governments have a responsibility to work for PEACE and international accord, and to promote RELIGION.

(4) *Human equality* In the estimation of God all human beings are equal, and 'an equal standard of human rights must be recognized and adopted' (*PUP* 182). WOMEN have equal rights with men (education, work, political participation). All have a responsibility to counter racism (*see* RACE). Special consideration should be given to MINORITIES.

(5) *Family* Individuals have the right to choose their own MARRIAGE partner subject to parental consent, and to determine the number of children they have (*see* BIRTH CONTROL). Everyone within a FAMILY has rights and responsibilities. No one has the right to domination.

The BAHÁ'Í INTERNATIONAL COMMUNITY has issued a number of statements relating to various aspects of human rights. These include *Religious Intolerance* (1995) and *Violence Against Women* (1995) (*BW* NS 1994–5: 297–303).

RELIGIOUS LIBERALISM AND RELIGIOUS AUTHORITY

Bahá'ís are enjoined to 'consort with the followers of all religions in a spirit of friendliness and fellowship' (*TB* 22); religious intolerance and persecution are condemned; the principle of the INDEPENDENT INVESTIGATION OF TRUTH is upheld; and Bahá'í children are free, if they wish, to choose their own religion (*LG* 153–6 no. 512, 519–23); Again, within the Bahá'í community 'the undoubted right of the individual to self-expression, his freedom to declare his conscience and set forth his views' is stated to be at 'the very root of the Cause' (*BA* 63). In seeming contrast to these 'liberal' teachings, however, Bahá'ís also have a strong belief in the vital importance of religious authority. The most important expressions of this are in the claims of the successive Bahá'í leaders (Bahá'u'lláh, 'Abdu'l-Bahá, Shoghi Effendi and the Universal House of Justice) to various forms of divinely bestowed authority and infallible guidance (*see* INFALLIBILITY), and in the concept of the Bahá'í COVENANT, the belief that there is a clear chain of authoritative succession that links these leaders together. Those Bahá'ís who reject the authority claims of some of these centres of the Faith whilst claiming to accept the authority of others are deemed to have broken this Covenant and are expelled from the religion as COVENANT-BREAKERS. Other expressions of the concern with authority are the emphasis on obedience to the Bahá'í ADMINISTRATION; the deprivation of ADMINISTRATIVE RIGHTS of those who seriously breach Bahá'í moral and certain social teachings; and the system of official REVIEW of Bahá'í literature.

For the great majority of Bahá'ís the coexistence of these 'liberal' and 'authoritarian' elements within their Faith has probably been unproblematic: the two elements are seen as component parts of a single religious system. Some Bahá'ís, however, have experienced difficulty with the assertion of authority within their religion. Given that Western liberal ideas are most firmly established as part of popular consciousness in the West, it is not surprising that it has been in the Western Bahá'í communities, particularly that of the United States of America, that issues of authority have led to difficulties. Thus divergent attitudes towards authority and organization can be traced within the American community from the turn of the century through to the late 1920s and early 1930s (*SBBR* 122–26). The contradiction between Western liberalism and the Bahá'í insistence on religious authority has again become an issue in the American Bahá'í community in recent years, as is evidenced by the statement of the Universal House of Justice to the American Bahá'ís, on *Individual Rights and Freedoms* (29 December 1988).

THE BAHÁ'Í CRITIQUE OF WESTERN LIBERALISM

Part of the distinctiveness of the Bahá'í position on issues of freedom and authority derives from the complex attitude that Bahá'u'lláh and 'Abdu'l-Bahá took towards Western civilization in general: they condemned tyranny and oppressive governments and praised the democratic rights and freedoms of the West, but were also extremely critical of what they saw as the excesses of the WEST, particularly its MATERIALISM and immorality. For them true civilization could only develop on the basis of true religion ('the highest means for the maintenance of order in the world and the security of its peoples' (*KA* 19 k2; cf. *ESW* 28, *TB* 63–4)) and the FEAR OF GOD. Again, Bahá'u'lláh wrote that he approved of LIBERTY in certain circumstances, but refused to sanction it in others. Absolute liberty was licence. True liberty consisted 'in man's submission unto My commandments' (*KA* 63 k122–5). Similarly, the Universal House of Justice regards liberty as having been carried to excess in the modern world. Its promotion originally emerged in the struggle against social oppression and injustice, but it has become a wide-ranging philosophy which promotes the interests of the individual even to the detriment of wider society, leading to the rejection of all forms of authority and social institutions, whether of government, religion or marriage (UHJ, *Individual Rights* 11). Civilized life depends upon 'the utmost degree of understanding and cooperation between society and the individual'. There has to be a correct balance between the rights of the individual and the integrity of the social group. The progress and viability of society depends on the development of individual potential and the exercise of individual initiative. It is, therefore, one of the responsibilities of Bahá'í institutions to safeguard the rights of the individual. At the same time, 'the subordination of the individual will to that of society' is a basic principle of Bahá'u'lláh's world order (UHJ, *Individual Rights* 20).

Ḥuqúqu'lláh

(Ar., 'the Right of God')

Monetary payment to be made to the head of the Faith by all Bahá'ís able to afford it. It was established in the *Kitáb-i-Aqdas* by Bahá'u'lláh, who described payment as a spiritual bounty which brings the individual closer to God and purifies their possessions. Payment is an individual spiritual obligation, and no Bahá'í is to be solicited for it. It should be offered in a spirit of joy. It is to be paid when a person's property exceeds 19 *mithqáls* of gold (2.2 troy ounces) in value. It then amounts to 19 percent of the value of all wealth other than one's residence, place of business and household furnishings. The payment is to be made only once on any particular amount, and subsequent payments become payable on further increments of wealth after necessary expenses have been deducted. Payment of *Ḥuqúq* should precede division of a deceased's estate, but after the settlement of funeral expenses and debts. Those who are unable to pay are exempt. Payment also precedes donations to other Bahá'í funds. The payment is made to the Centre of the Faith, who determines how it is to be disbursed. Expenditures may be used for such purposes as the promotion of the Bahá'í religion; the upkeep of its properties; and general charity. *KA* 28 k28, 55 k97, 108–9 q8–9, 120–1 q42, q44–5, 132–3 q89–90, 135 q95, 137–8 q102, 187–8 n47, 218–19 n125; *CC1*: 489–527; *LG* 304–8; Walbridge, *Sacred* 98–101.

HISTORY

Bahá'u'lláh promulgated the law of *Ḥuqúq* in 1873, but initially declined to accept payments. In 1878, however, he appointed Ḥájí Sháh-Muḥammad Manshádí, *Amínu'l-Bayán* (trustee of the *Bayán*) as the first Trustee of the *Ḥuqúqu'lláh*, charged with collecting the *Ḥuqúq* from the Bahá'ís in Iran. Payments were also made via Zaynu'l-Muqarrabín in Mosul. The successive trustees following Manshádí's death in 1881 were: Ḥájí Amín (Abdu'l-Ḥasan Ardikání), *Amín-i-Iláhí* ('trustee of God'; 1881–1928); Ḥájí Ghulám- Riḍá, *Amín-i-Amín* ('trustee of the trustee'; 1928–38); Valíyu'lláh Varqá (1938–55); and 'Alí-Muḥammad Varqá (from 1955). Ḥájí Amín was posthumously named as a Hand of the Cause, and the two Varqás (father and son) were appointed to this rank directly. After Bahá'u'lláh's death in 1892 the successive Centres of the Faith have been the recipients of the *Ḥuqúq*, expending it largely for the promotion and practical needs of the religion as it expanded world-wide. Payment of *Ḥuqúq* was at first mostly confined to the Bahá'ís of the Middle East, this being one of a number of laws (*see* LAW) that were deliberately not applied universally throughout the Bahá'í world. Information about the *Ḥuqúq* was made freely available to Bahá'ís elsewhere in 1985 (increasing the potential number who might pay if they wished), but the law was not made universally applicable until 1992. As the number of Bahá'ís paying *Ḥuqúq* has increased, a network of deputies and representatives has been appointed to receive the payments. A central office of *Ḥuqúqu'lláh* was established in Haifa in 1991. *Ḥuqúq* resembles the Shí'í payment of *khums*, 'the fifth' of gained wealth, in part payable to the representatives of the IMÁMS. The term also occurs in the *BAYÁN*. *MUHJ* 637–8 no. 404, 670 no. 430; Walbridge, *Sacred* 93–8.

Ḥusayn (626–80)

Third of the Shí'í IMÁMS; killed at KARBALÁ. Having refused to pledge his allegiance to the Umayyad caliph Yazíd, Ḥusayn, with a small group of supporters, was confronted by the Ummayad forces. All the fighting men were killed, apart from Ḥusayn's son 'Alí, the future Fourth Imám, and the women and children captured. Ḥusayn's death is regarded by Shí'ís as sacrificial MARTYRDOM for the cause of truth against the forces of impiety. It is annually commemorated with great emotional fervour by Shí'ís during the holy month of Muḥarram and continues to inspire Shí'ís to sacrificial action. Ḥusayn is expected to return following the advent of the MAHDÍ. Bahá'u'lláh eulogized Ḥusayn, claimed to be his RETURN and identified himself with him, and promised that God would soon 'torment' those who had waged war against him (a prophecy that Bahá'ís associate with the downfall of the OTTOMAN sultans and the CALIPHATE). Shoghi Effendi referred to Ḥusayn's uniqueness, and stated that he had been endowed with a special 'grace and power' amongst the Imáms. Heggie 86–8; *LG* 496, 498; Momen, *Shi'i Islam* 28–33, 288–9.

Ḥusayn Bushrú'í, Mullá (*c.*1814–49)

The first of the Báb's disciples (*see* LETTERS OF THE LIVING), and called by him the *Bábu'l-báb* ('Gate of the Gate'). He was born in the hamlet of Zírak near the small town of Bushrúyih in the north-eastern Iranian province of Khurásán. His father appears to have been a wealthy cloth dyer who was also a local cleric. His mother was a respected poet. He furthered his own religious studies in Mashhad and Iṣfáhán, and then went to Karbalá as one of the students of the Shaykhí leader Sayyid KÁẒIM RASHTÍ, becoming so highly respected that some thought that he might be his successor. He was sent as Rashtí's representative to defend Shaykhí views before Mullá Muḥammad-Báqir Shaftí, the pre-eminent Shí'í cleric of his age. Returning to Karbalá shortly after Rashtí's death (31 December 1843/1 January 1844), he became leader of a group of younger Shaykhís who held messianic expectations. After a period of religious retreat he travelled to SHÍRÁZ, perhaps intending to travel on to Kirmán to meet KARÍM KHÁN, one of the claimants to Shaykhí leadership. Instead, he met the BÁB and, after a period of hesitation (doubting that a non-cleric could have a station of leadership), accepted his claims, the night of his acceptance (22 May) effectively marking the start of Bábism as a religious movement. Others of his companions followed his lead, including his brother and nephew. He then journeyed to Iṣfáhán, Káshán and Tehran (where he forwarded a letter from the Báb to MUḤAMMAD SHÁH and Ḥájí Mírzá ÁQÁSÍ), gaining converts in each (including Mullá ṢÁDIQ Khurásání and BAHÁ'U'LLÁH), before returning to his home province, where he established himself in Mashhad, making it a focal point for Bábí mission. He travelled extensively, including visiting the Báb again in Shíráz and MÁKÚ. In July 1848, at the Báb's instructions, he left Mashhad at the head of a group of followers, carrying the messianic symbol of the BLACK STANDARD. Eventually reaching Bárfurúsh, the party was attacked, leading to the Shaykh ṬABARSÍ 'upheaval', during which Mullá Ḥusayn was killed (2 February 1849). Accounts of this conflict note his physical frailty, and contrast his former life as a scholar to his new life as a fearless and much-feared warrior. *ARR* 155–74, 261–3, 266–73; Mehrabkhani; Nabil 19–24, 47–67, 85–7, 97–108, 123–8, 159–61, 170, 254–67, 288–91, 324–68, 379–83; *TJ* 32–9, 43–55, 67–71, 93–5, 106–8, 335–6, 344–5, 359–63; *TN* 240–1.

The Bábís accorded Mullá Ḥusayn an exalted station. He was the 'gate' to the Báb, acting as his deputy; 'the first to believe'; and the 'primal mirror'. He was also regarded by some as the 'RETURN' of the Prophet Muḥammad and of the Imám Ḥusayn, as well as the *QÁ'IM* of Khurásán. The Báb's eulogies and prayers for him amount to three times the volume of the Quran. Bahá'u'lláh stated that if it had not been for him God 'would not have ... ascended the throne of eternal glory'. *GPB* 7, 50; MacEoin, 'Hierarchy' 105–8.

Ḥusayn Khán, Mírzá, *Mushíru'd-dawlih*

(Ar., 'Counsellor of state') (d. 1881)

As Iranian minister in Istanbul, 1859–70, he was responsible for discussions with the Ottoman authorities regarding the exiles of Bahá'u'lláh. He became NÁṢIRU'D-DÍN SHÁH's chief minister in 1871, and embarked on an energetic campaign of government reform. Opposition to his policies led to his dismissal in 1873. He remained an influential political figure for a few more years, but was then increasingly marginalized. He died under mysterious circumstances – poisoned by order of the shah according to some. Bahá'u'lláh held him responsible for his own exile to Akka, but praised his honesty and dedication to his country, and asked for divine forgiveness for him (*ESW* 68–9). Bakhash 77–132; *Cambridge History of Iran 7*: 184–90.

I

Ibn-i-Abhar (1853/4–1917)

Ḥájí Mírzá Muḥammad-Taqí Abharí, Iranian HAND OF THE CAUSE. He was born into a family of respected *'ULAMÁ* in the village of Abhar (between Qazvín and Zanján). His father became a Bábí in 1847 and later a Bahá'í. After the murder of his father in 1874 and threats to his own life, Ibn-i-Abhar moved to Zanján and brought the large Bábí community there to an acceptance of Bahá'u'lláh. He travelled extensively in Iran, consolidating the network of Bahá'í communities and teaching the Faith. Bahá'u'lláh appointed him a Hand of the Cause in about 1886. He was imprisoned for his Bahá'í activities in 1878–9 and again between 1890 and 1894. He was one of a group that travelled to India to promote the Faith in 1907, and also visited Turkistan and the Caucasus. His wife, Munírih Khánum (d. 1957), daughter of Ḥájí ÁKHÚND, was involved in the establishment of a Bahá'í school for girls in Tehran, and both she and her husband were members of a Bahá'í committee for the advancement of women formed in 1909 (*see* WOMEN). Shoghi Effendi named him one of the APOSTLES OF BAHÁ'U'LLÁH.

EB 268; Harper 13–16; *RB4*: 304–12.

Ibn-i-Aṣdaq, (*c.*1850–1928)

Mirzá 'Alí-Muḥammad, Iranian HAND OF THE CAUSE. He was the son of the revered Bábí and Bahá'í teacher Mullá ṢÁDIQ KHURÁSÁNÍ (*Muqaddas*). Ibn-i-Aṣdaq visited Bahá'u'lláh in Baghdad with his father in 1861–3, and father and son were imprisoned together as Bahá'ís shortly after their return to Iran. He longed to attain the station of a martyr for the Faith and wrote to Bahá'u'lláh to supplicate for this. Bahá'u'lláh replied (in 1880) that what was called for was service to the Cause, and in particular TEACHING it with wisdom. Such endeavour might have the status of MARTYRDOM even though no blood was shed. In 1882 Bahá'u'lláh gave Ibn-i-Aṣdaq the title of 'Martyr, son of a martyr' (*Shahíd ibn-i-shahíd*). Meanwhile Ibn-i-Aṣdaq had begun to devote himself to extensive

Ibn-i-Aṣdaq, one of the Hands of the Cause appointed by Bahá'u'lláh

travels within Iran to promote the Faith. In 1887 he was designated a Hand of the Cause by Bahá'u'lláh and he was involved in the subsequent work of that body in Tehran. Through his marriage to 'Udhrá Khánum (d. 1923), a member of the QÁJÁR nobility, he was able to contact members of the ruling stratum and inform them about the Faith. He was also able to deliver 'Abdu'l-Bahá's 'Treatise on POLITICS' (*Risáli-yi-Siyásiyyih*) to the shah. He later travelled widely in India, Burma, the Caucasus and Russian Turkistan. In 1919, together with Aḥmad Yazdání, he delivered 'Abdu'l-Bahá's letter to the Central Organization for a Durable Peace in The Hague (*see Tablet to the* HAGUE). Shoghi Effendi named him as one of the APOSTLES OF BAHÁ'U'LLÁH. *EB* 171–6; Harper 9–12; *RB4*: 301–4.

iconography

There is little in the way of a distinctive Bahá'í iconography. Calligraphic representations of the GREATEST NAME in Arabic are commonly found as wall hangings and on the covers of some older Bahá'í books. Many Bahá'ís place photographs of 'Abdu'l-Bahá in their homes (but never those of Bahá'u'lláh, as a mark of respect for his sanctity). Much Bahá'í ARCHITECTURE at the BAHÁ'Í WORLD CENTRE is classical (largely Greek) in inspiration, but other buildings, particularly the Houses of Worship (*MASHRIQU'L-ADHKÁR*) reflect the indigenous styles of their localities. The Houses of Worship do not contain any figurative representations. Nine-pointed stars (*see* NUMBERS) are sometimes used as a decorative motif. (*See also* ART; CALLIGRAPHY.)

Imáms

In general, Islamic religious leaders (Ar.: *imám*, lit. 'one who stands in front'), including the leader of the Friday communal prayers (*imám-jum'a*).

In Twelver SHÍ'ISM the term designates specifically the succession of twelve legitimate leaders after the Prophet Muḥammad. Denied their rightful role as rulers of the Islamic community, they guided their followers in the path of true faith. They were the signs of God on earth. Created from divine light, they received inspiration from God. They were the best of men, immune from sin and error. It was the duty of every person to recognize the Imám of the age: those who did not were not true believers. Each received the specific designation (*naṣṣ*) of his predecessor. The Twelver succession is as follows (other Shí'í groups having different lists):

(1) 'Alí ibn Abí Ṭálib. The cousin and son-in-law of Muḥammad. Briefly caliph, 656–61. His shrine is at Najaf in Iraq.
(2) Ḥasan (d. 669). Eldest son of 'Alí by his wife (Muḥammad's daughter) Fáṭima. He was buried in Medina.
(3) ḤUSAYN (626–80). Second son of 'Alí and Fáṭima. Killed at KARBALÁ.
(4) 'Alí, Zaynu'l-'Ábidín (658–712/3). Son of the Imám Ḥusayn by Shahrbánú, daughter of the last Sassanian ruler of Iran. He was buried in Medina.
(5) Muḥammad al-Báqir (676–?735). Son of the Fourth Imám and a daughter of the Imám Ḥasan. He was buried in Medina. His half-brother, Zayd, revolted against Ummayad rule in 740, and was the originator of Zaydí Shí'ism.
(6) Ja'far aṣ-Ṣádiq (d. 765). Son of the Fifth Imám and of a great-granddaughter of the first caliph, Abú Bakr. The Ismá'ílí Shí'í Imáms traced their descent from his eldest son, Ismá'íl, who predeceased his father.
(7) Músá al-Káẓim (d. 799). Son of the Sixth Imám and a Berber slave. Poisoned by order of the Abbasid

caliph Hárún ar-Rashíd. His shrine is in what became the Káẓimayn suburb of Baghdad.

(8) 'Alí ar-Riḍá (765–818). Son of the Seventh Imám and a slave. He died in Khurásán, and his shrine is in what is now the Iranian city of MASHHAD. The shrine of his sister, Fáṭima, is in the Iranian city of Qum.

(9) Muḥammad at-Taqí (810–33). Son of the Eighth Imám and a Nubian slave. He was buried in what is now Káẓimayn.

(10) 'Alí al-Hádí (827/9–68). Son of the Ninth Imám and a Moroccan slave. He spent most of his adult life under house arrest in the Iraqi city of Sámarrá.

(11) Ḥasan al-'Askarí (?846–73/4). Son of the Tenth Imám and a slave. He spent most of his life in detention at Sámarrá.

(12) Muḥammad al-Mahdí. Supposed son of the Eleventh Imám and a slave. At the time of the Eleventh Imám's death, the Shí'ís disagreed as to whether he had had a son, and if he had, whether this son had survived him, and what he was called. According to the Twelver Shí'ís there was a son, and he disappeared into mysterious occultation (*see* SHÍ'ISM). Momen, *Shi'i Islam* 23–45.

Bahá'ís accept the validity of the imamate, Bahá'u'lláh referring to the Imáms as 'lights of divine guidance' and 'lamps of certitude' (*KI* 92, 98), and Shoghi Effendi describing the imamate as a 'divinely-appointed institution' which was 'the chosen recipient' of divine guidance for some 260 years after the passing of Muḥammad, and was (with the Quran) one of the two 'most precious legacies' of Islam (*WOB* 102). Bahá'ís do not believe that there was a Twelfth Imám, however. The Bahá'í doctrine of COVENANT, with its emphasis on designated succession, and the institution of GUARDIANSHIP have obvious similarities to the imamate.

Imbrie, Major Robert

(d. 18 July 1924)

Recently appointed American vice-consul in Tehran, who was murdered by a mob on the mistaken suspicion that he was a Bahá'í. The incident attracted enormous attention in the United States, and indicated the continued force of anti-Bahá'í sentiment in Iran. It had significant diplomatic consequences and prompted the departure of resident American Bahá'ís from Tehran. (*See also* MOODY) *MBBR* 462–5.

incorporation

Constitution of an organization as a separate legal entity. It is used by many national and local ASSEMBLIES as a means of gaining a definite legal status, enabling them to enter into contracts, hold property and receive bequests. The first national assembly to gain this status was that of the United States and Canada in May 1929, and the first local assembly that of Chicago in February 1932, in each case following the adoption of their respective CONSTITUTIONS. Numerous other assemblies around the world have since followed their example. Apart from legal advantages, incorporation has been regarded as a means of securing PUBLIC RECOGNITION. *GPB* 335–6.

independent investigation of truth

Basic Bahá'í principle, repeatedly stressed by 'Abdu'l-Bahá. Everyone should investigate truth for themselves rather than following tradition and the beliefs of others. They should depend on their own perceptions and be guided by their own consciences. They should use the power of REASON, itself a divine creation and gift. In the investigation of

RELIGION they should seek divine assistance for themselves. As reality is one, such investigation will lead to religious unity and human solidarity. It was the blind following of the past that led to the rejection of the successive MANIFESTATIONS OF GOD. Unthinking imitation of the past stunts the mind. Independent enquiry frees society from endlessly repeating the mistakes of the past (*PT* 131; *PUP* 62–3, 105–6, 169, 180, 221–2, 274, 291–4, 312–13, 327, 372, 433, 443–6, 454; *SWAB* 29, 248, 298). There is an implicit contrast here with the Shí'í principle of *taqlíd* (imitation), whereby it is considered necessary for the ordinary believer to follow a learned specialist in matters of religious law (Momen, *Shi'i Islam* 175–6). 'Abdu'l-Bahá was rejecting *taqlíd* and the clerical status of certain 'ULAMÁ (the *mujtahids*) which rested on it.

Indian religions

A complex variety of religious traditions coexist in India, many of them included within the overarching framework of Hinduism. Separate and distinctive religious traditions include BUDDHISM, Jainism and Sikhism. The Bahá'í writings contain few explicit references to any of these religions (*see* RELIGION). Such references as there are – mostly from Shoghi Effendi – recognize Krishna as a MANIFESTATION OF GOD and Hinduism as one of nine recognized revealed religions; doubt the origins and authenticity of the Hindu scriptures; and claim that Bahá'u'lláh was the prophetic 'tenth avatar' in succession to Krishna. *CC1*: 15–22; Cole, 'Bahá'u'lláh on Hinduism and Zoroastrianism'.

The very rapid expansion of the Bahá'í community in India from the 1960s onwards has in part rested on a successful presentation of the Bahá'í Faith in popular Hindu terms, and specifically de-emphasizing Islamic terminology (Garlington, 'Bahá'í *bhajans*'). Scholarly studies relating the two religions are as yet few. Mishra; Momen, *Hinduism*.

indigenous peoples

Bahá'ís believe in the unity and oneness of the human race, but also value the diversity of culture and thought (*WOB* 41–2), in part because this demonstrates the universality of the Faith. Thus ethnic diversity has come to be valued as a characteristic of the world Bahá'í community, Shoghi Effendi noting with pleasure the conversion of representatives of an increasing number of ethnic groups during the course of Bahá'í EXPANSION (leaving aside the question of what exactly constitutes an 'ethnic group', a total of 2,112 such groups are now (May 1994) said to be represented in the Faith (*BWNS* 1994–5: 317)). This diversity was well illustrated in the Bahá'í World Congresses of 1963 and 1992 (*see* CONFERENCES), with Bahá'ís in indigenous dress from around the world.

In a number of national Bahá'í communities indigenous peoples have become a significant presence, and community life has evolved to reflect their concerns, as with the establishment of Bahá'í RADIO stations in Latin America catering for local needs and promoting Amerindian culture. Members of indigenous groups have also sometimes played an international role, as with Native American Bahá'í musical and cultural groups which have toured parts of Europe and Asia promoting the Faith, and contacts made by traditional leaders among the Bahá'ís of various Pacific nations with their counterparts in other parts of the Pacific. Again, Bahá'ís have participated in such events as the United Nations International Year for the World's Indigenous Peoples (1993) and International Decade for Indigenous Peoples (launched in December 1994); the 'Spiritual Gathering of the Tribes' bringing together indigenous peoples from Siberia and North America; and the Australian Aboriginal Reconciliation Council (*BWNS* 1994–5: 85–8). (*See also* MINORITIES; PREJUDICE; RACE.)

indigenous religions

Although now increasingly overlain or replaced by more universal religious systems, such as Buddhism, Christianity or Islam, localized religions traditionally provided an important basis for the sense of identity of 'tribal' and other peoples. Such 'indigenous religions' vary greatly in their beliefs and practices. They commonly stress a particular pattern of moral and community life, specify techniques for approaching or utilizing sacred power, and provide an overarching explanation for the way the world is. Animistic and magical elements are often prominent, as they are also in the folk versions of the universal religions.

Specific references to other religions in the Bahá'í writings focus on the 'historic' religions, particularly Islam and Christianity, but it is also believed that God has communicated his will to all the world's peoples, 'Abdu'l-Bahá explicitly stating that God's call had undoubtedly been raised in the Americas in the past. Combined with the Bahá'í belief in the common humanity of all peoples, this belief has provided a potential point of contact between Bahá'ís and indigenous groups in various parts of the world: rather than condemning traditional beliefs as 'pagan' – as is sometimes done by the missionaries of other religions – Bahá'ís are often able to accept at least elements of traditional religious culture as compatible with Bahá'í membership. Native American or Native Australian Bahá'ís, for example, may thus be able to regard Bahá'í as a fulfilment of their own traditional beliefs. This is particularly relevant when the native tradition contains millenarian elements which can be interpreted in Bahá'í terms. Buck, 'Native messengers'; Osei; Weixelman; Willoya and Brown.

individual

For Shoghi Effendi the role of the individual in the progress of the Faith was primary. The fate of the entire Bahá'í community depends on its individual members. Only through the support of the 'rank and file' can the Bahá'í ADMINISTRATION function effectively, and the Faith's expansion PLANS be accomplished (*CF* 130–1). TEACHING is dependent on individual effort (*CC2*: 320 no. 1991, 324 no. 2004). Again, ultimately the only factor that will secure the 'triumph' of the Cause is the extent to which the 'inner life' of individual Bahá'ís mirrors forth Bahá'u'lláh's principles (*BA* 66). He also stressed that the right of individual self-expression (in relationship to the administration) lies 'at the very root of the Cause' (*BA* 63). Similarly, the Universal House of Justice has repeatedly stressed the importance of the individual in accomplishing all Bahá'í plans, stating that through 'universal participation', both the individual and the whole body of believers would be empowered. Each person has their own 'talents and faculties' which they are able to contribute. All can teach, pray, 'fight their own spiritual battles', deepen their knowledge of the Faith, and contribute to the Bahá'í FUND (*MUHJ* 33 no. 14.7, 42–3 no. 19).

infallibility

Being incapable of error, particularly in terms of doctrinal statements. The term used in the Bahá'í writings – *'isma* – means both sinless and infallible, and is of Islamic origin (according to Shí'í belief Muḥammad, Fáṭima and the Twelve Imáms all possessed *'isma*). Bahá'ís distinguish between two kinds of infallibility.

THE 'MOST GREAT INFALLIBILITY'

Bahá'u'lláh taught that this was the possession of the MANIFESTATIONS OF GOD alone, whereby they were both sanctified from error, and constituted in themselves the standard of truth which others were to follow. Thus they were not limited by human standards: if they pronounced water to be wine, or heaven to be earth, it was the truth. It was incumbent on others to adhere to what they ordained (*KA* 36–7 k47; *TB* 108–10). Some other individuals might also be guarded from sin, but this was a lesser infallibility. 'Abdu'l-Bahá commented that the Manifestations' infallibility was essential to themselves and inseparable from them. Thus, whatever emanated from them was identical with the truth. Whatever they said was the word of God. Whatever they did was an upright action. No one had the right to criticize. If their words and actions were not understood by people, this was because of human ignorance (*SAQ* 171–4).

'CONFERRED' OR 'ACQUIRED' INFALLIBILITY

This is granted by God to those who are the mediators of grace and guidance between God and human beings. By this God protects and preserves many 'holy beings' from error, so that they may act as guides to other humans. Such acquired infallibility would not be inherent in their persons, however. 'Abdu'l-Bahá stated that it would be granted to the as yet unelected UNIVERSAL HOUSE OF JUSTICE as a body, but not to its individual members (*SAQ* 172–3); as Guardian of the Bahá'í Faith, Shoghi Effendi would also be under God's unerring guidance (*see* GUARDIANSHIP); whilst as appointed interpreter 'Abdu'l-Bahá himself voiced 'the very truth', and whatever his pen recorded was correct (*SWAB* 214; *MUHJ* 545). Shoghi Effendi defined his own infallibility as being confined to the INTERPRETATION and application of SCRIPTURE and to the protection of the Bahá'í Faith. It did not extend to economics, science or technical matters. Unlike the Manifestations of God he was not 'omniscient at will'. When he stated that something was for the protection of the Faith he should be obeyed, but if he merely gave advice to an individual, then this was not binding (*LG* 311 no. 1050, 313 no. 1055; *MUHJ* 546n). He also distinguished his own position from that of 'Abdu'l-Bahá, in whose person human nature and 'superhuman knowledge and perfection' had been blended (*WOB* 134, 151).

inheritance

Bahá'u'lláh instructed his followers to write WILLS, and specified that they had complete freedom to dispose of their property as they wished. In cases of intestacy, however, he provided a detailed schedule of inheritance adapted from the provisions set out by the Báb in the BAYÁN. According to the Bahá'í schema it is necessary first to ensure that the funeral and burial expenses of the deceased have been paid, then any other outstanding debts, and then the ḤUQÚQU'LLÁH. After this the estate is to be divided among seven categories of heirs (the equivalent of three-sevenths to the children, with progressively smaller shares for the spouse, father, mother, brothers, sisters and teachers). In the absence of all or some of these categories the son's children (not the daughter's), nephews and nieces, uncles and aunts, cousins, and the local HOUSE OF JUSTICE may inherit specified portions of the estate. In the absence of any of these relatives the entire estate passes to the house of justice. The deceased's principal house passes to the eldest son, who also has the responsibility to support his widowed mother. Clothing and personal effects generally pass to the same-sex offspring. The proportions allotted to sons are greater than those allotted to daughters.

'Abdu'l-Bahá upheld the principle of primogeniture, emphasizing the 'extraordinary distinctions' given to the eldest son in most religions, not only in matters of material inheritance, but also in religious leadership (KA 186; *WOB* 148). Both the Shí'í imamate (*see* IMÁMS) and the Bahá'í GUARDIANSHIP are based on the idea of primogeniture. *KA* 26–8 k20–8, 106–9 q5–7, q9, 115–17 q28, q33–4, 118 q37, 119–20 q41, 122–3 q53–5, 127 q69, 128 q72, 129–30 q78, 130 q80, 136–7 q100, 153–6, 182–8 n38–47; Walbridge, *Sacred* 83–93.

institutes

Bahá'í educational and DEEPENING facility. With the large-scale EXPANSION of the Bahá'í Faith into the 'Third World' from the late 1950s onwards, new approaches to deepening the large number of new and often illiterate rural Bahá'ís were necessary: it was not feasible to expect the new Bahá'ís to journey to often distant SUMMER SCHOOLS and follow their traditional book-based curriculums. One response increasingly adopted during the 1960s was rural-based 'teaching institutes', held in the areas where the new Bahá'ís lived, and often utilizing modest buildings constructed to serve as village Bahá'í centres. Visiting or local tutors would then present courses covering the basic rudiments of Bahá'í belief and practice and designed to prepare the new Bahá'ís for active involvement in the ongoing TEACHING campaigns. The institute buildings were also readily used as a venue for LITERACY classes and simple 'tutorial SCHOOLS'. With increasing experience, the institute concept has been expanded to include various aspects of human resource development, based on local needs and the Bahá'í ideal of service to the community (e.g. training courses for teachers and Bahá'í administrators). Permanent institutes have now been established in many countries, the Ruhi Institute in Puerto Tejada, Columbia (established 1976), and the Bahá'í Academy in Panchgani, India (1982) being particularly well known. *CC1*: 42–4; *LG* 563–4.

intellect

The capacity for KNOWLEDGE, understanding and thinking. 'Abdu'l-Bahá regarded it as God's greatest gift to humanity: it is a wonderful power, born of divine light, which enables human beings to comprehend the material creation. It distinguishes human beings from all other creatures. Through it, human beings are able to develop their science and technology by which they understand and to some extent gain control over nature. Its divine purpose is the promotion of human CIVILIZATION, but it can also be misused to create means of war and destruction (*PT* 32–3, 65). With WISDOM, it is one of the two most luminous lights in creation (*SDC* 1). Human beings vary in their intellectual capacity, but intellectual development requires EDUCATION, and through it the ignorant become learned (*SAQ* 212–14). The intellectual faculty is viewed as unlimited, and the source of discoveries, arts, crafts and sciences. No subject should be excluded from its purview. (*PUP* 63–4, 287).

intercalary days

See AYYÁM-I-HÁ.

intercession

See DEATH.

interfaith dialogue

Bahá'ís regard all divine religions as expressions of the same God-given truths (*see* RELIGIOUS DIVERSITY). Non-disputatious interfaith dialogue is implicitly encouraged, Bahá'ís offering their support to organizations such as the World Fellowship of Faiths and the World Conference on Religion and Peace, and initiating or supporting interreligious conferences concerned with such topics as the promotion of religious tolerance or the contribution of religion to peace and justice. American

Bahá'ís began celebrating World Religion Day (held on the third Sunday in January) in 1950. It is now celebrated world-wide, and in some countries has generated considerable interest, attracting the support of various religious leaders and other dignitaries. Its format varies, commonly featuring speakers from various religious traditions, but its essential purpose is to express the need for a single world religion (*LG* 507 no. 1710). *BWNS* 1994–5: 93–4, 128–30; W. Momen, *Baha'i Dictionary* 242.

International Archives

The international archives of the Faith comprise a variety of items, including personal effects of the Báb, Bahá'u'lláh and 'Abdu'l-Bahá (clothes, pen-cases, rings, watches, etc.), relics such as locks of their hair, a photograph of Bahá'u'lláh and a portrait of the Báb, original manuscripts, and other objects of historical interest such as Mullá Ḥusayn's sword. Shoghi Effendi wanted to display these in a way in which they could be viewed reverentially by visiting Bahá'ís. The three new rooms Shoghi Effendi had added on to the Shrine of the Báb (1929) were at first used for this purpose, becoming the first 'international Bahá'í Archives'. A second 'minor' archives was later established in a building close to what is now the Monument Gardens.

These arrangements were not adequate, and in 1952 Shoghi Effendi announced his decision to construct a purpose-built archives building. Work began in 1954 and was completed in 1957. The building itself is in the style of the Parthenon in Athens, with a colonnade of fifty Italian marble columns and a green-tiled roof. It measures 32 × 14 metres and is 12 metres high. The interior consists of a large display hall with a surrounding balcony. Shoghi Effendi referred to the building as the first of the 'stately' edifices of the Bahá'í world administrative centre. A large extension connected to the basement of the original building has been constructed as part of the present development of the Arc. Ruhe 168–70; Rabbani, *Priceless Pearl* 263–6; Giachery 148–69.

The International Archives Building, Haifa

International Bahá'í Bureau

Office established by Mrs Jean Stannard in Geneva in 1925 following consultations with Shoghi Effendi. It served to promote Bahá'í teaching activities in Europe, and also as a communications centre between Bahá'í groups internationally. It organized meetings, distributed Bahá'í literature, maintained contacts with the League of Nations as a recognized international organization, and produced various publications and translations, including a trilingual (English, French, German) bulletin. It functioned as an auxiliary to the Bahá'í administrative centre in Haifa. Its public relations activities were greatly reduced in the worsening political situation of the 1930s. Much of its work was taken over by the Bahá'í International Community from 1948 onwards. The Bureau closed following the formation of the national spiritual assembly of Switzerland in 1957. *BW4*: 257–61, 6: 130–5; *GPB* 380.

International Bahá'í Council

Institution created in November 1950 by Shoghi Effendi, and formally announced to the Bahá'í world in January 1951 as a forerunner of the Universal House of Justice. Its initial functions were to forge links with the Israeli authorities and to conduct negotiations regarding matters of personal status with them (i.e. regarding the possibilities of establishing a Bahá'í court), and to assist Shoghi Effendi in the work of completing the superstructure of the Shrine of the Báb. It also served as an international Bahá'í secretariat. The Council was to be evolutionary in nature. Eight members were initially appointed, and a ninth added in 1955. Five were also appointed as Hands of the Cause. After Shoghi Effendi's death in 1957 the Council operated under the direction of the Custodial Hands in Haifa. The original appointed Council was reformed as an elected body in Riḍván 1961. The election was by postal ballot by the members of all national and regional spiritual assemblies formed at Riḍván 1960; all adult Bahá'ís except for the Hands were eligible for election. The Council ceased to exist with the election of the Universal House of Justice in 1963. All five of its then male members were elected onto the House. *BW12*: 378–90, *13*: 395–401; *MBW* 7–8, 22, 86; Rabbani, *Priceless Pearl* 92–94, 249–53.

International Bahá'í Library

Projected future building on the Arc. There is at present a Bahá'í World Centre library which serves as a library of deposit for all Bahá'í publications.

International Teaching Centre

Bahá'í institution established in Haifa by the Universal House of Justice in June 1973, primarily in order to extend into the future the functions of the Hands of the Cause resident at the Bahá'í World Centre. Its original duties were: (1) to direct and co-ordinate the work of the Continental Boards of Counsellors and to act as liaison between these Boards and the Universal House of Justice; (2) to be fully informed of the situation of the Faith in all parts of the world, and on the basis of that knowledge make recommendations to the House of Justice and advise the Continental Counsellors; (3) to be alert to the possibilities for the extension of Bahá'í teaching activity; (4) to determine and anticipate needs for literature, pioneers, and travelling teachers (*see* teaching), and to work out regional and global teaching plans for approval by the House of Justice. It directs the work of the Continental Pioneer Committees. It is directly responsible to the House of Justice. A building to serve as the permanent seat of the International

Members and office-bearers of the IBC

	Appointed	Elected	
Rúḥiyyih Khánum	1950–61 LSE/Hand		
Amelia Collins	1950–61 VP/Hand		
Charles Mason Remey	1950–61 P/Hand		
Lotfullah Hakim	1950–61 AS-E	1961–3	(→ UHJ)
Jessie Revel	1950–61 Tr	1961–3	
Ethel Revel	1950–61 AS-W	1961–3	
Ben Weeden	1950–1		
Gladys Weeden	1950–1		
Leroy Ioas	1952–61 SG/Hand		
Ugo Giachery	1952–61 MaL/Hand		
Sylvia Ioas	1955–61	1961–3 VP	
Ali Nakhjavani		1961–3 P	(→ UHJ)
Charles Wolcott		1961–3 SG	(→ UHJ)
Ian Semple		1961–3 AS	(→ UHJ)
Mildred Mottahedeh		1961–3	
Borrah Kavelin		1961–3 MaL	(→ UHJ)

AS	assistant secretary	SG	secretary-general
AS-E	Eastern assistant secretary	Tr	treasurer
AS-W	Western assistant secretary	VP	vice-president
LSE	liaison with Shoghi Effendi	→ UHJ	subsequently elected as a member of the Universal House of Justice
MaL	member-at-large		
P	president		

Teaching Centre is at present under construction (*see* Arc). *BW16*: 411–14.

Its original working nucleus comprised the four Hands resident in Haifa (Rúḥiyyih Khánum, A.A. Furútan, P. Haney and A-Q. Faizí), together with three newly appointed International Counsellors (see list below). All other Hands were members. The remaining Hands were freed from regular involvement with the work of the Centre in May 1988, maintaining only an advisory role (only three Hands are now still alive, all based in Haifa). The number of Counsellor members was raised to four in 1979, to seven in 1983, and to nine in 1988. A five-year (reappointable) term of service was introduced in 1983, and a requirement that a quorum of five should always be present at the Bahá'í World Centre in 1988.

COUNSELLOR MEMBERS

Mr Hooper Dunbar	1973–88 (→ UHJ)
Mrs Florence Mayberry	1973–83 (retired)
Mr Aziz Yazdi	1973–88 (retired)
Miss Anneliese Bopp	1979–88 (retired)
Dr Magdalene Carney	1983–91 (d.)
Mr Masud Khamsi	1983–93
Dr Peter Khan	1983–7 (→ UHJ)
Mrs Isobel Sabri	1983–92 (d.)
Dr Farzam Arbab	1988–93 (→ UHJ)
Mr Hartmut Grossmann	1988–
Mrs Lauretta King	1988–
Mr Donald Rogers	1988–98
Mrs Joy Stevenson	1988–98
Mr Peter Vuyiya	1988–93
Mr Kaiser Barnes	1993–
Mrs Joan Lincoln	1993–
Mr Shapoor Moadjem	1993–8
Mr Fred Schechter	1993–8
Mrs Kimiko Schwerin	1993–8

Mr Rolf von Czékus	1998–
Mrs Violett Haake	1998–
Dr Firaydoun Javaheri	1998–
Dr Payman Mohajer	1998–
Dr Penny Walker	1998–

interpretation

Bahá'ís recognize two different kinds of interpretation of their own canonical LITERATURE.

AUTHORITATIVE

Both 'Abdu'l-Bahá and Shoghi Effendi were explicitly appointed as authoritative interpreters of the Bahá'í writings (*WOB* 133, 134, 136, 148–50), and their interpretations are regarded by Bahá'ís as infallible (*LG* 311 no. 1050, 313 nos. 1055–6; *see* INFALLIBILITY). Since the death of Shoghi Effendi in 1957, and the consequent loss of a living GUARDIANSHIP, there is no Bahá'í institution empowered to give authoritative interpretation (*LG* 310 no. 1049). The Universal House of Justice explicitly refrains from interpretation (*MUHJ* 87 no. 35.12). The interpretations of 'Abdu'l-Bahá and Shoghi Effendi remain a major source of guidance.

INDIVIDUAL

In studying the writings, each individual arrives at his or her own understanding of the Bahá'í teachings. The House of Justice states that such interpretation is to be seen as the fruit of human REASON, and should not be suppressed. What should be avoided is disputation amongst the Bahá'ís regarding the teachings, or any insistence that one's own understanding is the only correct one. Individuals should make it clear that their views are merely their own and not press them on their fellows. Again, they should learn to listen to the views of others without being either overawed or shaken in their faith. They should remember that individual understandings continually change through the process of DEEPENING. (Taken with the ending of authoritative interpretation, this implies that a single 'correct' view of the Bahá'í Faith is not possible at the present time: cf. 'Abdu'l-Bahá's statement regarding the limitation of scriptural tradition as a source of KNOWLEDGE.) In previous religions believers had sought to encompass the divine message within the framework of their own limited understanding, defining as doctrines matters that were beyond easy simple definition. This tendency had to be avoided (*MUHJ* 87–8 no. 35.11–13).

INTERPRETATION OF THE SCRIPTURES OF OTHER RELIGIONS

All three of the Bahá'í 'Central Figures' (the Báb, Bahá'u'lláh and 'Abdu'l-Bahá) wrote commentaries on Quranic verses. Bahá'u'lláh and 'Abdu'l-Bahá also commented on biblical verses. In the *Kitáb-i-Íqán* Bahá'u'lláh states that God's messengers use both straightforward and concealed language. PROPHECY is often metaphorical, and to interpret it always in a literalistic fashion leads not only to a loss of understanding, but to the failure to recognize future promised messengers – as in the Jews' failure to recognize Jesus, and the Christian failure to recognize Muḥammad (*KI* 17, 51–2, 162–3). (*See* COMMENTARY ON THE SÚRA OF THE SUN). There is a growing secondary literature concerned with presenting the Bahá'í Faith as the prophetic fulfilment of other religions (*see* APOLOGETICS).

Ioas, Leroy (1896–1965)

American HAND OF THE CAUSE. Both his parents were of German Lutheran background and became Bahá'ís in the 1890s. He played a major role in the development of systematic Bahá'í teaching plans in North America, and was elected onto the national spiritual ASSEMBLY in 1932. Shoghi Effendi appointed him a Hand of the Cause in

Leroy Ioas, prominent American Bahá'í and Hand of the Cause

December 1951 and invited him to Haifa, where he became both secretary-general of the INTERNATIONAL BAHÁ'Í COUNCIL and an assistant secretary to Shoghi Effendi. The octagon door of the SHRINE OF THE BÁB was named after him.
BW14: 291–300; Harper 265–75.

Íqán, Kitáb-i-
(PA, *Book of Certitude*)

The most important and influential of Bahá'u'lláh's early writings, regarded by Shoghi Effendi as his outstanding doctrinal work (and as the basis for unity between the religions of the world). Composed in Persian in Baghdad in 1278AH/1861–2 CE in response to questions by one of the as yet unconverted maternal uncles of the Báb, Ḥájí Mírzá Sayyid Muḥammad, it was soon widely circulated among the Bábís in Iran. It was also one of the first Bahá'í books to be printed (by lithography in India), perhaps as early as 1882. The first English translation was published in 1900. The present official translation by Shoghi Effendi was published in 1931.

Asked to reconcile the Báb's claim to be the *QÁ'IM* with traditional Shí'í expectations, Bahá'u'lláh noted that the contemporary rejection of the Báb echoed similar rejections of the past. In every age, people had expected God's messenger (*see* MANIFESTATION OF GOD), but had opposed him when he came. RELIGIOUS LEADERS had ignored the truth, either through ignorance – judging the messengers' claims by their own limited understanding – or because they feared what they saw as a threat to their own leadership. Most other people then blindly followed their religious leaders in opposition rather than investigating truth for themselves. One persistent 'veil' was literalistic INTERPRETATION of scripture (e.g. of biblical verses regarding 'stars' falling from heaven and the promised one coming in the 'clouds of heaven' (Matthew 24:29–31)), much of which was to be understood metaphorically. Again, God was not bound by human expectations: he chose MOSES, a murderer, and JESUS, with no known father, as messengers, and directed MUḤAMMAD to change the *QIBLAH* – to the consternation of his followers. God tested the people. True understanding was only possible to those who had put their trust in God and did not use human standards as a measure of God and his prophets. Repeatedly the reader was called upon to 'cleanse' his heart from worldly standards. The essential proof of any of God's messengers was his own self and the divine word revealed in his scripture. Other signs were his constancy in proclaiming his cause in the face of opposition; the transforming influence he had on his followers; the willingness of those followers to give their lives for his cause (*see* MARTYRDOM); and the fulfilment of PROPHECY. All these evidences the Báb had. People expected the messengers to exercise worldly sovereignty (as Shí'ís did of the *Qá'im*), but the messengers' true sovereignty was a spiritual ascendancy which they exercised over all in heaven and on earth. During their lives they suffered from opposition and persecution, and it was only later, when the religions they founded had grown, that peoples bowed before their names. The life of the Imám Ḥusayn was a vivid example of the sufferings of God's chosen ones. Bahá'u'lláh also referred to knowledge; the spiritual path; and the future Bábí messianic figure of He whom God shall make manifest, perhaps making cryptic reference to his own claims, shortly to be made explicit (1863). He hoped that the Bábí learned would not treat this personage in the same way as the messengers of the past had been treated. The book is of interest in indicating Bahá'u'lláh's knowledge of the Bible, and his sympathy for Christianity, both unusual in a 19th-century Islamic context.

The *Íqán* became an important element in attracting Bábís and others to Bahá'u'lláh (including the uncle for whom it was written). A factor in its appeal was its straightforward Persian prose style, which contrasted markedly with such Bábí writings then extant, and which made it extremely accessible to ordinary Iranians who had not received a clerical education. Although written prior to Bahá'u'lláh's open claim to prophetic status, it was readily accorded the status of divine revelation by Bahá'ís *KI*; Buck, *Symbol*; *GPB* 138–40; *RB1*: 153–97.

Iran

Birthplace of the Bábí religion and, until the 1960s, homeland of the majority of the world's Bahá'ís. *MBBR*; Rafati, 'Bahai community'; *SBBR* 48–56, 86–99, 175–80.

GEOGRAPHY AND HISTORY

Ancient Iranian empires extended their control over large areas of the Middle East and Central Asia, and embraced Zoroastrianism as their state religion. The Arab conquest (from 637) gradually led to the conversion of most Iranians to Islam, but did not destroy a sense of separate Persian identity. The establishment of Shí'ism as the state religion under the Safavid dynasty (1501–1722) served further to distinguish Iran from its Arab, Turkish and Central Asian neighbours, and laid the basis for modern Iranian nationalism. The country's present borders were established during the rule of the Qájár dynasty (1794–1925). The country's size (three times the size of France) and geography (large areas of semi-desert and mountainous terrain) have favoured regionalism, and it has only been with the development of modern transport and communications that a centralized, unitary state has been able to develop.

Although the majority of the population in modern times have been Persian-speaking Shí'ís, there are significant minorities of Azeris and other Turkic speakers, together with Arabs, Kurds and Baluchis. There are also Sunní Muslims, and Christian, Jewish and Zoroastrian minorities. Until recently the great majority of the population were poor peasant farmers, dominated both by the local urban elites and the nomadic and semi-nomadic tribal groups (such as the Turkoman Qájárs) who provided the country's main military forces until the development of a modern army.

Iran's relative isolation meant that Western influence only became a major influence on Iranian economic and political life in the second half of the 19th-century. This precipitated a lengthy period of crisis and instability which culminated in the rise to power of the cavalry leader Reza (Riḍá) Khán, who proclaimed himself shah in 1925 (with the dynastic name Pahlaví), and embarked on a campaign of modernization (until 1941). These policies were

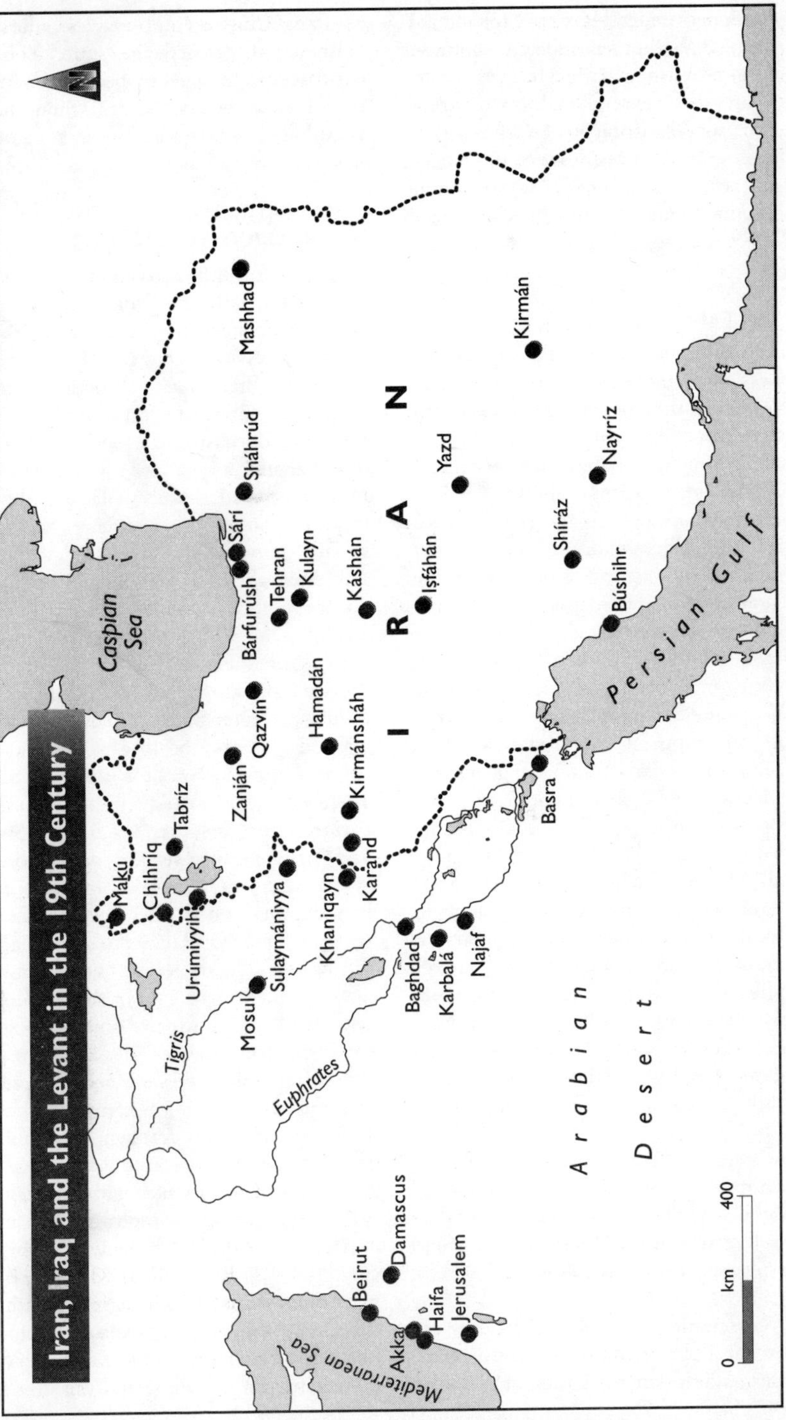

Iran, Iraq and the Levant in the 19th Century

continued under his son, Mohammad-Reza Sháh, but engendered enormous cultural tensions within Iranian society. These were exacerbated by economic and social problems in the 1970s, leading to the overthrow of the regime, and the establishment of an Islamic Republic under Áyatu'lláh Khomeini in 1979. *Cambridge History of Iran*; Keddie, *Roots of Revolution*; Issawi.

THE BÁBÍS

As a movement within Shí'ism, SHAYKHISM drew most of its support from Iranians, although its centre of operations for many years was in Ottoman IRAQ. Similarly, Bábism was essentially a movement within Shí'ism, and its membership was largely Iranian. Effective Bábí missionary endeavour succeeded in gaining converts widely amongst the settled population, particularly in the towns (with perhaps 100,000 adherents the Bábís may have constituted some 2.5 per cent of the non-nomadic population). Persecution of the Bábís in Iran began after the return of the Báb from his pilgrimage to Mecca (1845). Early opposition to the Bábís came primarily from the Islamic learned (*'ULAMÁ*) acting as defenders of an Islamic orthodoxy from which the Bábís clearly diverged. Support from local governors was at first limited, and motivated by the desire to maintain public order which they saw threatened by Bábí fervour. Strong action by a governor in support of the Bábís (as with MANÚCHIHR KHÁN in Iṣfáhán) was sufficient to contain clerical opposition. The situation changed with the development of BÁBÍ RADICALISM: by proclaiming himself the *QÁ'IM*, the Báb laid implicit claim to absolute temporal as well as spiritual authority within a Shí'í universe, whilst his followers' growing readiness to respond to attack made confrontation ever more likely. Attacks on the Bábís then led to armed struggles, and the stigmatization of the Bábís as dangerous revolutionaries whose existence threatened the state. Their extirpation subsequently became a matter of state policy. Several thousand were killed. *ARR*; Smith and Momen, 'Babi movement'.

BAHÁ'Í DEVELOPMENT DURING THE QÁJÁR PERIOD (TO 1925)

Bahá'u'lláh both revived and transformed the Bábí movement following its near collapse in the early 1850s. Bahá'í EXPANSION (from the 1860s) was correspondingly much broader than that of the Bábís, encompassing Iranian Jews and Zoroastrians as well as Shí'ís (the Bahá'ís' acceptance of non-Muslims contrasted sharply with the Shí'í treatment of these people as being ritually impure, and was a factor in attracting them to the Bahá'í Faith), and the reformist nature of the Bahá'í teachings appealing to some of those who wanted to see Iran modernized. Bahá'u'lláh sought to dissociate his followers from Bábí extremism, and insisted that they be loyal to GOVERNMENT. Although NÁṢIRU'D-DÍN SHÁH (r. 1848–96) remained antagonistic towards the Bahá'ís, his successors and many local governors were more sympathetic – or at least indifferent. Persecutions continued, however, and several hundred Bahá'ís were killed during the Qájár period. Opposition again came primarily from the *'ulamá*, who were able to use their judicial role to issue sentences of death against Bahá'ís as unbelievers as well as summoning up bands of strong-armed followers and mob action to occasion their death and to intimidate local governors. The situation varied widely from region to region depending on the power and attitudes of local governors and clerics. Persecution was not always motivated by religious hatred alone. Declaring a Bahá'í an unbeliever meant that his property and womenfolk could be taken with impunity, and this could provide mobs with additional cause to follow the anti-Bahá'í urgings of clerics. At a more sophisticated level, the killing of the KING AND BELOVED OF MARTYRS (1879) was evidently to the pecuniary advantage of the clerics involved. Again, a wily politician such as ẒILLU'S-SULṬÁN could use persecution of Bahá'ís for his own political ends. Periods of political unrest also became times when Bahá'ís (and other minority groups) could be made scapegoats for the people's discontents and frustrations. Persecution neither deterred Bahá'í missionary endeavour nor the consolidation of the community (with the establishment of Bahá'í SCHOOLS (from *c*.1870s), children's classes (from 1898), local councils (ASSEMBLIES; from 1899), a Bahá'í FUND (1907) and a children's savings fund (1917)). At 'Abdu'l-Bahá's instruction most Bahá'ís remained uninvolved in the political movements that buffeted Iranian society at the turn of the century.

THE BAHÁ'ÍS DURING THE PAHLAVÍ PERIOD, 1921/5–79

The establishment of a centralizing, modernizing regime initially seemed to promise a better situation for the Bahá'ís, and an end to the clerically inspired persecution of the past. Thus during the early years of Pahlaví rule the Bahá'ís were able to expand their activities, and for the first time to hold large public meetings, sometimes attended by government officials. They also established modern public baths, and were able to organize a national elective system, culminating in the election of the first national spiritual assembly in 1934, and to consolidate local spiritual assembly administration throughout the country. A campaign of government repression (1932–41) ensued, however, seemingly as part of an endeavour to cow all potentially independent groups in Iranian society. Thus, Bahá'í schools were closed; Bahá'í meetings prohibited; a number of

Senior Iranian military officers under the Pahlaví government attacking the National Bahá'í Centre, Tehran, 1955

Bahá'ís dismissed from government employ; and Bahá'ís imprisoned for contracting Bahá'í marriages. The official campaign ended only with the overthrow of Reza Sháh by the British and Russians during World War II (1941), but was followed by a partial breakdown of public order, and a recrudescence of locally inspired attacks (clerical and political) on Bahá'ís. Internal development of the Bahá'í community continued, with the establishment of a Bahá'í-linked hospital and orphanage in 1940. It was also at this time that Iranian Bahá'ís began to send PIONEERS to neighbouring countries and to implement systematic expansion PLANS. A special plan for the advancement of Bahá'í women was also adopted (1946–50), and women became eligible to serve on Bahá'í assemblies for the first time in 1954. Major advances in female literacy were also made. A new wave of attacks was mounted against the Bahá'ís in 1951 and 1955 (probably as a government sop to Muslim religious extremists). Thereafter, the situation eased – in part to protect Iran's public image abroad – until the rising turmoil that presaged the Islamic Revolution. However, Bahá'ís were still not allowed to contract legal marriages (leading their opponents to accuse them of immorality); publish literature other than by lithography; or combat the activities of various anti-Bahá'í groups which were able to operate freely and widely disseminate a distorted and intensely hate-filled propaganda against them, accusing them of political manipulation, acting as agents of foreign powers, and immorality. The development of a 'culture of hatred' resulted. There has been no proper study of Iranian Bahá'í demographics, but the impression is of gradual growth to perhaps 350,000 by 1979. However, this growth seems to have been mainly the result of natural increase rather than new conversions: the proportion of Bahá'ís in the total population appears to have declined since the early years of the century (Smith, 'Bábí and Bahá'í numbers'). The Bahá'í birth rate has probably been lower than the Muslim rate (Jensen).

THE ISLAMIC REPUBLIC, FROM 1979

In the early years of the republic there was a massive campaign of persecution against the Bahá'ís, exacerbated by the activities of one of the anti-Bahá'í groups (the *Ḥujjatiyyih* or *Tablíghát-i-Islámí*) which for a while enjoyed political influence. Thus there was a systematic endeavour to destroy all Bahá'í organization (including the judicial murder of many Bahá'í leaders), as well as to pressurize the rank-and-file to apostatize: Bahá'ís were arrested; dismissed from their jobs; and not allowed to attend school or university. Bahá'í sacred sites and burial grounds were also destroyed. More than two hundred Bahá'ís were killed or have disappeared and are presumed dead. The Faith was officially banned in 1983, and membership of Bahá'í administrative bodies made a criminal offence (the Bahá'ís subsequently disbanded all their assemblies). There was widespread international condemnation and enormous publicity, which may have contributed to some easing of the situation since the mid-1980s. Persecution continues, however, and the economic plight of many Bahá'ís remains dire, with Bahá'ís being disbarred from higher education and many forms of employment. Bahá'ís may not legally inherit property, and it is difficult for them to obtain passports or exit visas. Their marriages and divorces are not recognized. Bahá'í graves continue to be desecrated, and Bahá'ís receive little or no protection from the law, as indicated by the case of two Muslims who killed a Bahá'í, but were subsequently released from prison because their victim was 'an unprotected infidel'. The situation apparently varies from one part of the country to another, but an official document of 1991 indicated that it was then government policy to stifle any further development of the Bahá'í community, and, if possible, to uproot its cultural foundations. International condemnation of human rights abuses in Iran, specifically mentioning the Bahá'ís, continues. Ironically, the single most important factor in attracting international attention to the Bahá'í Faith has probably been its persecution in the land of its birth. Bahá'í International Community, *Baha'is of Iran*; *BW18* 291–4; *NS* 1994–5: 133–8; Cooper; Ghanea-Hercock; Labib; MacEoin, 'Bahai persecutions'; D. Martin, *Persecution*; *MBBR*; *SBBR* 89, 173–80; Warburg, *Iranske dokumenter.*

THE BAHÁ'Í FAITH AND IRAN

Iran remains a sacred land for Bahá'ís, both as the birthplace of their Faith and as the site of numerous Bahá'í holy places. Until the 1960s the largest single Bahá'í community in the world was that of Iran, and the majority of Bahá'ís in the world were Iranians (including expatriates). Correspondingly, a large proportion of prominent Bahá'ís have been Iranian (including eleven out of the thirty-two HANDS OF THE CAUSE appointed by Shoghi Effendi between 1951 and 1957), and up to the present time Iranian Bahá'ís have continued to play a major role as pioneers and in the administration of the Faith world-wide. Since the 1960s, however, the enormous growth of the Faith in the 'Third World' (*see* EXPANSION) has greatly lessened the proportion of Bahá'ís who are Iranian (perhaps to 6–7 per cent). Prior to the Islamic Revolution the Bahá'ís of Iran were the main contributors to Bahá'í international funds, but this is no longer possible.

IRANIAN BAHA'Í DIASPORA

The largest and most recent dispersion of Iranian Bahá'ís has occurred in the aftermath of the Islamic Revolution in Iran, with many thousand Bahá'ís fleeing Iran to escape actual or possible persecution. Some of these émigrés have become pioneers, using their own hardship as a vehicle for Bahá'í activity. For others religious motivation has been less important, and they have gathered in large 'enclave communities' in various Western cities. In some instances this influx initially created tensions within the receiving Bahá'í communities, with linguistic and cultural barriers emerging between the incoming Iranians and the indigenous Bahá'ís, but such evidence as there is (from Britain and Italy) suggests that successful integration may have occurred quite rapidly, with the newcomers soon taking part in the Bahá'í administration in their adopted homes, and a high level of intermarriage between Iranian and Western Bahá'ís (a third of all Bahá'í marriages in Britain in 1984–6) (Momen, 'Integration'; Saint-Blancat).

Iraq

Iraq has a special significance in SHÍ'ISM as the burial place of six of the IMÁMS: 'Alí (the First Imám) at Najaf; ḤUSAYN (the Third Imám) at KARBALÁ; Músá al-Káẓim (the Seventh Imám) and Muḥammad at-Taqí (the Ninth Imám) at Káẓimayn ((the place of) the two Káẓims); and 'Alí al-Hádí (the Tenth Imám) and Ḥasan al-'Askarí (the Eleventh Imám) at Sámarrá. Sámarrá was also the place of the disappearance ('occultation') of the Twelfth Imám. Collectively these shrine-cities are known as the 'thresholds' (*'atabát*), and have assumed a special significance, both as revered places of Shí'í pilgrimage, residence and burial, and as centres of Shí'í learning, focused on the leading *'ULAMÁ* who lived there (thus Sayyid KÁẒIM RASHTÍ made Karbalá the centre of Shaykhism). During the 19th-century, the shrine cities assumed particular importance, because they allowed leading Shí'í clerics to function outside Iranian government control (*SBBR* 7).

Karbalá was briefly a centre of Bábí activity, and BAGHDAD assumed importance during the period of Bahá'u'lláh's exile there (1853–63), whilst his two-year retreat to the mountains of Iraqi Kurdistan led to important contacts with Sufi leaders. A small number of Bábís remained in Baghdad after his departure, and these subsequently became Bahá'ís. Shí'ís murdered one of them in 1868, and the conversion of the son of a prominent Sunní cleric in the same year led to public uproar, and to the exile of thirty or forty leading Bahá'ís to the northern city of Mosul (*MBBR* 265–7), which for a while became an important staging post for Iranian Bahá'ís journeying to see Bahá'u'lláh. Bahá'í communities developed in various parts of Iraq, gaining a small but significant number of converts. Local assemblies formed from the 1920s, and a national assembly was established in 1931. Also during the 1920s local Shí'ís expropriated the House of Bahá'u'lláh in Baghdad. The lengthy and unsuccessful litigation by the Bahá'ís to try to recover the building brought the Bahá'í situation to the attention of the League of Nations. Official action against Bahá'ís began in 1965, and since 1970 all Bahá'í activities have been banned.

Iṣfáhán (1868 pop. est. 60,000)

Central Iranian provincial capital, formerly seat of the Safavid dynasty (1501–1732) and an important centre of Bábí and Bahá'í activity. The Báb found refuge there under the governorship of MANÚCHIHR KHÁN. A number of Bahá'ís were martyred in the city and region during the governorship of *ẒILLU'S-SULṬÁN*.

Iṣfahání, Muḥammad-Taqí (*c.*1860–1946)

Prominent Egyptian Bahá'í who migrated from Iran some time after 1878. A merchant by profession, he became a centre of Bahá'í activities in Egypt, and was posthumously named a HAND OF THE CAUSE by Shoghi Effendi.
BW11: 500–2; Harper 110–11.

Ishráqát (*Splendours*)

Late Syrian-period tablet of Bahá'u'lláh composed in Arabic and Persian for Jalíl-i-Khú'í, a Bahá'í coppersmith from the province of Azerbaiján. In it Bahá'u'lláh addresses the Bábís (the 'people of the *Bayán*'), calling upon them to recognize him and not to be misled by their 'vain imaginings'; proclaims his own coming 'invested with power and sovereignty'; asserts the INFALLIBILITY of the MANIFESTATIONS OF GOD; reveals a long prayer in which the supplicant is to praise God and ask for his mercy, and which sorrows over the behaviour of Ṣubḥ-i-AZAL towards Bahá'u'lláh; proclaims the fulfilment of prophecies regarding the promised one; summons the Bahá'ís to piety and the development of praiseworthy characters; laments the behaviour of some of his followers; recalls his vision of TRUSTWORTHINESS; complains of the oppressive actions of a recent governor of Akka; and permits the charging of moderate interest on loans (in contradistinction to Islamic law). The tablet also includes nine 'splendours' from Bahá'u'lláh's teachings: (1) RELIGION is a stronghold for social order and must be supported by those in authority. (2) KINGS are a manifestation of God's power and should uphold the Lesser PEACE. (3) God's LAW brings life to the world. (4) That which best promotes Bahá'u'lláh's Cause is the praiseworthy deeds of the Bahá'ís, and these are led by the FEAR OF GOD. (5) A GOVERNMENT has responsibilities towards its citizenry. (6) The unity of the HUMAN RACE is stressed, and the need for a universal LANGUAGE to promote that unity. (7) The importance of parenthood (*see* FAMILY LIFE) and EDUCATION are emphasized. (8) The responsibilities of the House of Justice and aspects of Bahá'í ethics are enumerated. (9) The purpose of religion is to establish unity. *TB* 99–134; *RB4*: 145–60.

Ishráq-Khávarí, 'Abdu'l-Ḥamíd (1902–72)

Prominent Iranian Bahá'í teacher and scholar. He received an Islamic clerical education in Mashhad and was beginning to gain a reputation as an Islamic teacher when he converted to the Bahá'í Faith in 1927. He devoted the rest of his life to Bahá'í activities: taught in one of the Bahá'í schools until their closure in 1934, travelled extensively to promote the Faith, and produced an enormous body of compilations of Bahá'í writings, commentaries, apologetic works and historical studies. *BW15*: 518–20.

Islam

Bahá'ís uphold the divine origin and independent status of Islam, regarding it as one of the nine known revealed religions, and Muḥammad as a Manifestation of God. They follow what is an essentially Shí'í interpretation of the rightful succession following the death of Muḥammad, i.e. accepting the validity of the imamate as a divinely appointed institution which continued to be 'the chosen recipient' of divine guidance after the death of the Prophet and was 'one of the two most precious legacies of Islam' (i.e. along with the Quran; *WOB* 102; see Imáms; Shí'ism). Bahá'u'lláh referred to Muḥammad's exalted station, and blessed his kindred and companions who had established the religion of God in the world. The enemies of God had finally caused 'the banner of Islám to be reversed amongst all peoples', however (*TB* 162–3). Specifically, the *'ulamá* had subverted Islam, opposed those who sought to exalt it, and caused the people to become abased (*TB* 213). 'Abdu'l-Bahá stressed the transforming impact of early Islam on the formerly brutish tribes of Arabia, who had thereby become the founders of a brilliant and enlightened civilization, which had in turn exerted enormous influence on the civilization of Christian Europe (*SDC* 87–9). He deplored the ignorance and prejudice of many Western writers on Islam, as well as the fanaticism of many Muslims. For Shoghi Effendi Islam was 'the source and background' of the Bahá'í Faith, and a study of Islam was 'absolutely indispensable' for Bahá'ís if they were to gain a sound understanding of their own religion. Western Bahá'ís were therefore encouraged to study the Quran; the rise of Islamic civilization; and the particular institutions and circumstances out of which Bahá'í emerged. He noted that the public acknowledgement of the validity of Islam by Bahá'ís of non-Muslim background (prominently Queen Marie of Romania) represented powerful evidence of Bahá'í support for true Islam, and countered the claims of those Muslims who thought that Bahá'í was anti-Islamic (*ADJ* 41; Heggie 91–4; *LG* 494–8, 561 nos. 1903–4; *PDC* 112–14).

There is as yet no proper study of the Islamic roots of the Bahá'í Faith. Bahá'í shares with Islam the belief in a series of divine messengers – generally referred to as prophets in Islam, and as Manifestation of God by Bahá'ís – but diverges from it in denying that the line of messengers has ended. Specifically, the Quranic statement that Muḥammad was the 'Seal of the Prophets' (*khátam an-nabiyyín*; 33: 40) is interpreted to mean that he was the last in the cycle of prophets preparing the way for the present Day of Resurrection, not that he was the last of God's messengers (popularly, a distinction is made between the terms *nabí* ('prophet') and *rasúl* ('messenger')). The Báb and Bahá'u'lláh are thus regarded as having fulfilled Islamic messianic expectations (for Sunnís as the Mahdí and the descent of Jesus (the 'Spirit of God') respectively; for Shí'ís, as the *QÁ'IM* and the return of the Imám Ḥusayn (*GPB* 57–8, 94, 96-7)), whilst at the same time functioning as sources of divine revelation and the initiators of the latest expression of God's eternal religion (i.e. Islam; this divergence reflects a quite different understanding of TIME: Bahá'ís do not regard the resurrection as marking the end of time). Bahá'í also shares with Islam the concept of Holy LAW as a necessary guide for human action, and many aspects of Bahá'í law bear a clear relationship to the corresponding elements of Islamic law, although the emphasis in observance is more on individual conscience than communal enforcement. Again, elements of Bahá'í PHILOSOPHY and METAPHYSICS are rooted in parts of the Islamic tradition, particularly Mu'tazilite rationalism and Ishráqí ('Illuminationist') Neoplatonism.

As a religious movement Bábism can only be understood in the context of Iranian Shi'ism, and it never transcended that milieu (*see* EXPANSION). Bahá'u'lláh's teachings represent a significant departure from that context, but the great majority of early Bahá'ís were still former Muslims (mostly Iranian Shí'í), and even the small numbers of non-Muslims who converted during his lifetime were heavily imbued with the religion's culture of origin. It was only with the conversion of Westerners and others from the 1890s onwards that the Bahá'í Faith began to transcend its Islamic origins. Within the Middle East Bahá'ís have been extremely cautious in their TEACHING endeavours, but even outside the region, conversions of Sunní Muslims have been relatively few.

Bahá'í apologetics directed at Muslims commonly focus on passages in the Quran and Traditions (*HADÍTH*) which Bahá'ís regard as prophetic of their own religion. Several such works exist in Persian and Arabic, but there is little material in English. Exceptions are Áfáqí and Muṣṭafá. On Bahá'í and Islam in general, see Moayyad.

Istanbul (1856 pop. est. 430,000)

The city of Constantine, the former Eastern Roman/Byzantine capital known as Constantinople. It fell to the OTTOMANS in 1453, and remained their imperial capital until the formal end of their empire in 1922. The new Turkish republic relocated the capital to Ankara (1923). During the Ottoman period it was the 'Great City', the seat of the SULTANATE and CALIPHATE, and the premier city of the Muslim world. Bahá'u'lláh and his companions arrived in Istanbul as guests of the Ottoman government on 16 August 1863 and remained until 1 December 1863, when they were sent as exiles to EDIRNE, this change in his political status marking the key event of the sojourn. Bahá'u'lláh's eighteen-month-old daughter Sádhijiyyih (by his second wife, Mahd-i-'Ulyá) also died during these months and was buried outside the Edirne Gate. Neither of the two houses occupied by Bahá'u'lláh (the houses of Şemsi Beg and Visi Paşa) now exists. Bahá'u'lláh described the city as seat of the 'throne of tyranny', in which the foolish ruled over the wise, and predicted that its 'outward splendour' would soon perish, and its people ('sunk in heedlessness') lament. *BKG* 197–207; *GPB* 156–61; *KA* 52–3 k89; *PDC* 101; *RB2*: 1–6, 55–62, 317–19.

Ives, Howard Colby (1867–1941)

Unitarian minister in New Jersey, who became a Bahá'í after meeting 'Abdu'l-Bahá during his 1912 visit to North America. He subsequently devoted much of his life to TEACHING the Bahá'í Faith, and wrote *Portals to Freedom* (1937), an account of his meetings with 'Abdu'l-Bahá. Shoghi Effendi identified him as an 'outstanding promoter' of the Faith. *BW9*: 608–13; *WEBW* 139–54.

J

Jack, Marion (1866–1954)

Prominent Canadian Bahá'í. She became a Bahá'í in Paris in 1900. In 1908 she taught English to the children of 'Abdu'l-Bahá's household in Akka. In 1919 she and Emogene Hoagg travelled extensively through Alaska and the Yukon to teach the Bahá'í Faith. In 1930 she settled in Bulgaria as a Bahá'í PIONEER, remaining there for the rest of her life despite enormous hardships. Shoghi Effendi described her as an 'immortal heroine' and as a 'shining example' to all Bahá'í pioneers. *BW12*: 674–7.

Jamál Burújirdí

Prominent Iranian Bahá'í who retained his clerical status after becoming a Bahá'í. Enormously respected as a Bahá'í teacher, at one time he insisted on acting as head of the consultative council established by the HANDS OF THE CAUSE in Tehran, although not himself appointed as a Hand. He apparently craved a greater position of leadership, but rapidly lost his following after giving his allegiance to MUḤAMMAD-'ALÍ, and becoming his chief lieutenant in Iran. *GPB* 319; *TCB* 166, 208–15. (*See also* COVENANT-BREAKERS.)

Jamál Effendi (d. 1898)

Pioneer Bahá'í teacher in India, also known as Sulaymán Khán Tunukábuní. He came from a prominent Iranian family in Mázandarán, but spent most of his life as a wandering dervish and, following his conversion, as a Bahá'í teacher. He was first sent to India by Bahá'u'lláh in around 1875 in response to a request from members of the AFNÁN family in Bombay for a Bahá'í teacher. For the next eleven years he travelled widely in the subcontinent, and also visited Sri Lanka and various parts of South East and Central Asia. He taught the Bahá'í Faith extensively during his travels, gaining a number of important converts, most notably Siyyid Mustafa RUMI. *BW4*: 285; *EB* 119–28; *MF* 134–8.

Jamálu'd-dín, Sayyid, 'al-Afghání' (1838/9–97)

Pan-Islamist Muslim reformer and political activist. He published an Arabic-language newspaper (*al-'Urwatu'l-wuthqá*, 'The Sure Handle') in Paris. One of his disciples assassinated NÁṢIRU'D-DÍN SHÁH. He was associated with AZALI freethinkers in Istanbul, and wrote hostile accounts of the Bábís and Bahá'ís in articles in the Egyptian press and an Arabic encyclopedia published in Beirut (Buṭrus al-Bustání's *Dá'ira-tu'l-Ma'árif*). Bahá'u'lláh reproved him both for his writings about the Faith and his political hypocrisy (*TB* 94–6). Keddie, *Sayyid Jamal ad-Din*; *EGBBF* 23–31; *MBBR* 362–3.

Jesus (*c.*6 BCE–29 CE?)

Recognized by Bahá'ís as a MANIFESTATION OF GOD. Bahá'u'lláh emphasized that Jesus' unique station was 'exalted above the imaginings of all that dwell on earth'. At his coming he shed 'the splendour of His glory upon all created things'. At the moment of his death 'the whole creation wept with a great weeping', and by his sacrifice 'a fresh capacity was infused into all created things', the evidences of this 'quickening power' being now manifest in all the world's peoples, including in philosophy, learning, the arts and the potency of statesmanship. He purified the world, and any man who turned to him, 'with a face beaming with light', was blessed (*PDC* 114). 'Abdu'l-Bahá referred to him as the 'essence' of the Holy Spirit; the cause of the spiritual life of humanity; and a ransom for the life of the world. He had brought a 'perfect example of love into the world'; taught a way of life that was 'the highest type of action on earth'; and transformed the lives of his followers. He had been the promised Messiah for the Jews, and had abrogated Mosaic law. Though rejected by most of his own people, he had laid the basis for the eternal glory of the Jews, whose scriptures and prophets had been glorified by Christians throughout the world. Most of the MIRACLES attributed to him were to be interpreted symbolically rather than literally. His RESURRECTION was to be understood as a spiritual rather than physical event. Shoghi Effendi accepted his 'Sonship and Divinity' and the doctrine of the virgin birth (*PDC* 113).

Heggie 100–16; *LG* 489–93; *SAQ* 16–17; Stockman, 'Jesus Christ'. (*See also* CHRISTIANITY.)

Judaism, Jews

Bahá'ís regard Judaism as one of the nine known revealed religions, and include ABRAHAM and MOSES in their list of MANIFESTATIONS OF GOD. The other prophets of Israel are also acknowledged, but mostly as 'Lesser PROPHETS'. The Torah is regarded as divine scripture (*see* BIBLE). Jewish history is seen as indicative of both the power of divine grace to uplift a people and the consequences of human wrongdoing. Thus the Israelites had suffered oppression in Egypt until Moses had delivered them out of their wretchedness and given them divine teachings. On this basis the ancient Jewish state had become a centre of both divine and material civilization. It was subsequently weakened by internal divisions and idolatry, however, such that it was destroyed by the Babylonians and its people made captive. Later returning from exile, the Jews rallied to the reforms introduced by Ezra, but further disobedience towards God, including the rejection and persecution of JESUS, led to a second destruction of Jerusalem, by the Romans (*SDC* 75–81; *PUP* 361–70, 402–10).

Bahá'u'lláh denounced European anti-Semitism as evidence of tyranny, calling for JUSTICE to be exercised under all conditions (*TB* 170). He also stated that the long days of the Jews' abasement were now over: overshadowed by divine bounty, they would progress (*ADJ* 46). Again, in the 1890s, 'Abdu'l-Bahá affirmed that the prophesied 'ingathering' of the Jews to Palestine would occur, and thousands of years of ignominy (since the destruction of Jerusalem in 586 BCE and the beginning of the Babylonian captivity) would be replaced by 'eternal glory', and in the early 1900s stated that this process had now begun (*LG* 499 no. 1677; *SAQ* 65–6; *GPB* 305). But he also warned of future humiliations and, in 1912, referred to the possibility of an uprising against the Jews in Europe (*PUP* 414). Shoghi Effendi regarded Bahá'u'lláh's arrival in Akka as 'ushering in' the Jewish return through its prophetic significance, and the formation of the state of Israel (1948) as adding 'notable impetus' to the development of the BAHÁ'Í WORLD CENTRE (*GPB* 107; *MBW* 13, 19).

Bahá'u'lláh claimed to be the promised one of all religions, including Judaism. He had come to rule on 'the throne of David' (*PDC* 78–9). Bahá'ís interpret many of the verses of the Jewish prophets as referring to him. Specifically, he was the 'Everlasting Father' and 'Prince of Peace' mentioned by Isaiah, and David's 'Lord of Hosts', whilst the Báb was the 'return of Elijah' (*GPB* 58, 94). Bahá'ís also regard Jesus as having been the Jewish Messiah. (Speaking to Jewish congregations in the United States, 'Abdu'l-Bahá was uncompromising in asserting that they should acknowledge the greatness of Jesus, who himself had followed Moses, and whose influence had led to the teachings of Moses becoming known throughout the world (*PUP* 366–9, 407–15).)

A significant number of Iranian Jews became Bahá'ís from the 1870s onwards, including a number of crypto-Jews who had previously been forcibly converted to Islam. Some of these had already been attracted by Bábism, particularly by the eloquence of ṬÁHIRIH; others were affected by the rational proofs offered by Mírzá ABU'L-FAḌL in his *'Epistle to Ayyúb'* (1887/8) addressed specifically to Jews. The Bahá'ís' openness towards the Jews, then a deeply despised minority group in Iran, is also likely to have been a powerful factor in attracting them to the new religion. (ARR 315, 360; *RB3*: 168–71, 260–8; *SBBR* 93–7). Bahá'u'lláh called upon one of his followers of Jewish background to proclaim his Faith to one of the Barons Rothschild, then the effective heads of Western Jewry (*RB3*: 168, 172). A number of eminent Western Bahá'ís have been of Jewish background, including Hippolyte DREYFUS, Lidia ZAMENHOF, Siegfried SCHOPFLOCHER and John FERRABY but, overall, conversions from Western Jewry do not appear to have been numerous. Musa BANANI was one of the most eminent Middle Eastern Bahá'ís of Jewish background. The Bahá'í authorities do not allow Bahá'í TEACHING work to be conducted in Israel.

justice

Bahá'u'lláh decried the injustice, tyranny, corruption and dishonesty that prevail in the world (*TB* 39, 84). He had come as a bringer of justice. The 'best beloved of all things' in the world is justice. It is a divine gift, and those who want to approach God cannot neglect it. Through it they will see and know for themselves and not be dependent on others (*HWa* no. 2). It trains the world (*TB* 27). The tranquillity of humanity depends upon it. Its radiance is beyond comparison (*ADJ* 23). Its purpose is to secure human unity and SOCIAL ORDER (*TB* 67). It is upheld by 'the twin pillars' of REWARD AND PUNISHMENT. If the world's rulers dedicated themselves to the highest interests of humanity as a whole, then the reign of justice would be established and the world sanctified from tyranny and utterly transformed (*TB* 164). The essence of governance is justice (*TB* 166–7). Again, every individual should be just in their dealings with others; this is the 'most fundamental' of human virtues, and a defining quality of being truly human (*ADJ* 21). Lerche, *Toward the Most Great Justice*. (*See also* LAW.)

K

Kappes, Lillian (d. 1920)

American Bahá'í who taught at the Tarbíyat Bahá'í School in Tehran from 1911/12. Shoghi Effendi honoured her as one of the DISCIPLES OF 'ABDU'L-BAHÁ. *Star* 11/19: 324–5.

Karbalá

Iraqi city containing the shrines of the Imám ḤUSAYN and his half-brother 'Abbás, and the site of the battle of Karbalá (10 Muḥarram 61AH/10 October 680) in which Ḥusayn and his companions were killed. The battle became the paradigm for sacrificial MARTYRDOM for Shí'is and also for the Bábís at ṬABARSÍ. The city became a leading centre of Shí'í scholarship, and was the residence of Sayyid KÁẒIM. Mullá 'ALÍ BASṬÁMÍ was sent there by the Báb to proclaim his advent, and the Báb's followers were summoned to gather in the city to await the advent of the MAHDÍ. ṬÁHIRIH made Karbalá her base until expelled by the Ottoman authorities, and Bahá'u'lláh retired there briefly in 1851–2.

Karím Khán Kirmání, Ḥájí (Muḥammad-) (1810–71)

Son of a wealthy Qájár prince who had been city governor of Kirmán, he was one of the leading grandees of his home city, and gradually became the leader of most of the non-Bábí Shaykhís after the death of Sayyid KÁẒIM RASHTÍ. He claimed to possess superior knowledge – his writings being a copy of those of God's eternal book – and emphasized the need for there always to be a 'Perfect Shí'í' (implicitly himself) to guide the people. He was a vehement opponent of the Báb, declaring him to be an infidel, and 'the gate to hell', and writing several books refuting his claims. Opposition to his own claims, combined with a desire not to be categorized with the Bábís as religio-political dissidents, caused him to dissimulate many of his earlier pronouncements in his later public writings (such as his opposition to the powers of the *MUJTAHIDS* of Uṣúlí SHÍ'ISM), but he continued to regard the non-Shaykhí Shí'í majority as heretics. He opposed the spread of Western ideas and educational influences, and declared that anyone who befriended a European was an apostate. Bahá'u'lláh regarded him as superficial, conceited and ignorant of spiritual reality (*KI* 118–22), and addressed him in the 'Tablet of the Veil' (*Lawḥ-i-qiná'*). *ARR* 286–94; Bayat 63–86; MacEoin, 'Early Shaykhí reactions'; *RB1*: 334; *SBBR* 17–18, 179. (*See also* SHAYKHISM.)

Káẓim Rashtí, Sayyid (d. 1843/4)

Shaykhí leader in succession to Shaykh AḤMAD AL-AḤSÁ'Í. Born in the northern

Iranian city of Rasht (*c.*1790s), he joined Shaykh Aḥmad (according to his own account as a result of a visionary dream) whilst the latter was in Yazd, and subsequently became al-Aḥsá'í's most trusted companion and disciple. Appointed as the shaykh's successor, Rashtí established himself in the Iraqi holy city of KARBALÁ, where he remained for the rest of his life, expounding and developing the shaykh's teachings; consolidating the widespread network of Shaykhí followers in Iraq, Iran and Arabia; and becoming one of the major notables of the city. During his leadership opposition to Shaykhí views mounted, and Shaykhism assumed an increasingly sectarian cast. According to Bábí–Bahá'í accounts he taught the near advent of the promised messianic figure of the *QÁ'IM*, and after his death many Shaykhís followed the example of Mullá ḤUSAYN BUSHRÚ'Í, one of the sayyid's leading disciples, and became Bábís. Various dates are given for Rashtí's death, including 31 December 1843 and 1/2 January 1844. (*See also* SHAYKHISM.)

Khadem, Zikrullah (Dhikru'lláh Khádim) (1904–86)

Iranian HAND OF THE CAUSE. He served on the national spiritual ASSEMBLY from 1938 until 1960, and also performed various tasks for Shoghi Effendi, including an extensive series of visits to Bahá'í communities in Iran. He was appointed a Hand of the Cause in February 1952, and subsequently travelled to many Bahá'í communities world-wide. He also translated Bahá'í materials from English into Persian. He moved to the United States in 1960 and, amongst other literary works, compiled some 134 volumes of documentation regarding Bahá'í holy places. Harper 362–71; Khadem.

Khadíjih Bagum (d. 1882)

The Báb's second cousin (her father was an uncle of the Báb's mother) and childhood playmate. She became his first wife (August 1842), and gave birth to a son, Aḥmad, who died in infancy (1843). According to her own later account she recognized her husband's religious station before his 'declaration' of mission to Mullá ḤUSAYN BUSHRÚ'Í (1844). After the execution of the Báb and his uncle (both 1850) she went to live with her sister Zahrá's family, whilst her mother-in-law moved to KARBALÁ. Khadíjih subsequently became a Bahá'í. She and her maid – a devoted African slave-woman named Fiḍḍa, who had served the family since the time of Khadíjih's marriage – both died on 15 September 1882, and were buried in the shrine of Sháh-chirágh in Shíráz. Balyuzi, *Khadíjih Bagum*. (*See also* BÁB, FAMILY OF.)

Khadíjih Khánum

The mother of Bahá'u'lláh, and the second wife of Mírzá 'ABBÁS, whom she married after being widowed (*see* NÚRÍ FAMILY). She had three children by her first marriage, and five by the second, of whom one died. *BKG 13.*

Khammár, 'Údí (d. 1879)

Christian merchant of AKKA. He restored and enlarged the mansion of BAHJÍ. Bahá'u'lláh and his family lived in his house in Akka after their release from the barracks, 'Abdu'l-Bahá later renting Bahjí for his father. 'Údí Khammár's tomb is at Bahjí. Ruhe 201–3.

Kházeh, Jalál (1897–1990)

Iranian HAND OF THE CAUSE born into a Bahá'í family in Tehran. A former colonel in the Iranian army, he was elected onto the national spiritual ASSEMBLY in 1944, but resigned in 1951 to become a full-time itinerant teacher visiting Bahá'ís throughout the country. Shoghi Effendi announced his appointment as a Hand of the Cause on 7

December 1953. He later became one of the custodial Hands in Haifa, and in 1963 moved to Brazil to serve as a focal point for Bahá'í activities in South America. He returned to IRAN in 1969. The upheavals of the Islamic Revolution placed him in special danger, and in 1984 he left the country, eventually settling in Canada. Harper 164–7.

Kheiralla, Ibrahim George
(1849–1929)

Pioneer Bahá'í teacher in the United States. Of Syrian Christian background, he became a Bahá'í in EGYPT in 1889/90, and moved to Chicago in 1893. In 1894 he began a successful spiritual healing practice, at the same time teaching about the Bahá'í Faith to some of those he met. This developed into a systematic endeavour to spread the Bahá'í teachings in America. Initially Kheiralla was extremely successful and, by 1898, some 700 Americans had become Bahá'ís. In 1898–9 he made the pilgrimage to Akka to meet 'Abdu'l-Bahá, who honoured him greatly, describing him as 'Bahá's Peter' and the 'Conqueror of America', and having him assist in laying the foundation stone of the SHRINE OF THE BÁB. On his return to the United States (May 1899) difficulties arose, mostly it would seem because of Kheiralla's wish to be acknowledged as supreme leader of the American Bahá'ís. Failing to gain 'Abdu'l-Bahá's support for this proposal, he turned against him, transferring his allegiance instead to MUḤAMMAD-'ALÍ (1900). A temporary schism among the American Bahá'ís resulted, with a small and declining minority – termed 'Behaists' – supporting Kheiralla. Subsequent efforts to attract new followers were largely unavailing. *BFA1*; Hollinger, 'Kheiralla'; *SBBR* 100–2; Smith, 'American Baha'i community' 88–99. (*See also* EXPANSION; GETSINGER; HEARST.)

Ibrahim George Kheiralla, pioneer Bahá'í teacher to the USA

King and Beloved of Martyrs

Honorific titles bestowed by Bahá'u'lláh on two Bahá'í brothers who were martyred for their faith – publicly beheaded – in Iṣfáhán on 17 March 1879: Mírzá (Muḥammad-)Ḥasan, the King of Martyrs (*Sulṭánu'sh-shuhadá'*), and his elder brother, Mírzá (Muḥammad-)Ḥusayn, the Beloved of Martyrs (*Maḥbúbu'sh-shuhadá'*). Bahá'u'lláh also called them 'the Twin Shining Lights' (*Núrayn-i-nayyirayn*) and eulogized them in a number of his writings. Shoghi Effendi named Mírzá (Sayyid) Ḥasan as one of the APOSTLES OF BAHÁ'U'LLÁH. The brothers were prominent merchants and respected sayyids of Iṣfáhán, and for some years had managed the business affairs of the *imám-jum'a* (leader of the Friday prayers; see *'ULAMÁ*), Mír Muḥammad-Ḥusayn. In so doing they settled debts on his behalf, so that the *imám-jum'a* came to owe them a substantial sum of money. To avoid payment of this sum the *imám-jum'a* conspired with another leading cleric, Shaykh Muḥammad-Báqir (nicknamed the WOLF by Bahá'u'lláh), to have the brothers executed as 'Bábís' (i.e. Bahá'ís). This was accomplished with the connivance of the prince-governor of Iṣfáhán, Sulṭán-Ma'súd Mírzá, the

Mirza Muhammad Hasan and Mirza Muhammad Husayn, prominent Iranian Bahá'í martyrs (the 'King' and 'Beloved' of Martyrs)

ẒILLU'S-SULṬÁN. The killings were significant in that, as was widely recognized at the time, religion was being used to mask financial greed on the part of a leading cleric. They also indicated that, regardless of social prominence, no Bahá'í was safe from attack by those who opposed the Faith. Bahá'u'lláh stigmatized the *imám-jum'a* as the 'She-serpent' (*Raqshá*) and rebuked him in his writings. EB 33–51; MBBR 274–7.

The *imám-jum'a*'s subsequent death (21 June 1881) is regarded by Bahá'ís as an example of specific and highly appropriate DIVINE JUDGEMENT against their oppressors: when others had hesitated to take the lives of the two brothers he had insisted, saying that any wrong committed would be upon 'his neck'. He subsequently contracted a loathsome disease which first infected his neck (possibly scrofula or cancer of the neck) and caused his body to become so malodorous that members of his own family refused to touch him (*GPB* 232–3, *MBBR* 274n).

Bahá'u'lláh also gave both titles, i.e. the king *and* the Beloved of Martyrs, to one man, Sayyid Ismá'íl Zavárihí. See DHABÍḤ.

kings, kingship

Bahá'u'lláh regarded 'the majesty of kingship' as one of the 'signs of God'. Kings manifested God's power and grandeur, and were the 'daysprings of his authority'. Their rank was divinely ordained (*ESW* 89; *KA* 49 k82; *TB* 28, 126, 165). Those kings who were just and not corrupted by 'the vainglory of power' occupied a high spiritual station, and should be supported. They were the shadow of God on earth and nearer to God than others (*PDC* 75; *TB* 65, 164). He instructed the Bahá'ís to pray for kingly justice and love, and serve any king who came to the aid of the Bahá'í community (*TB* 22, 65). Such a king was 'the very eye of mankind' and would receive great blessings (*KA* 50 k84). He favoured constitutional monarchy as a form of GOVERNMENT, because it combined the majesty of kingship with the advantages of democratic government for the common people (*TB* 28). For

'Abdu'l-Bahá just kings had a station second only to the prophets of God (*SDC* 20).

The faults of (absolutist) kings could be great, however, and Bahá'u'lláh condemned their injustice and tyranny, specifically warning several in his proclamation to the RULERS. In *The* PROMISED DAY IS COME Shoghi Effendi interpreted the subsequent decline of monarchy as evidence of DIVINE JUDGEMENT due to the lack of response to this proclamation. Bahá'u'lláh stated that one of the signs of the maturity of the world would be that no one would agree to bear the weight of kingship, with its troubles and dangers, except in order to proclaim God's cause, but also predicted the future emergence of just kings (*PDC* 72–6).

In the *Kitáb-i-*AQDAS Bahá'u'lláh declared himself to be the King of Kings, and the kings of the earth to be but vassals. They should cleanse their hearts from all earthly defilements and ensure that pride did not deter them from recognizing him. He had no wish to seize their kingdoms, but rather to possess the hearts of men (*KA* 48–50 k78–84, 52 k87). The emergence of future Bahá'í monarchs was also predicted. The conversions of (dowager) Queen MARIE of Romania (*c.*1926) and Malietoa TANUMAFILI II of Western Samoa (1968) are consequently regarded by Bahá'ís as highly significant.

Kings, Súra of the

(Ar.: *the Súratu'l-Múluk*)

Arabic tablet of Bahá'u'lláh composed in Edirne in around 1867, and part of his proclamation to the RULERS. In it the 'kings of the earth' were summoned to heed Bahá'u'lláh's call, cast away the things they possessed, and follow God. They were reproved for having neither recognized nor aided the Báb. The reins of government had been committed into their hands that they might rule with JUSTICE, safeguarding the rights of the downtrodden, listening to their appeals, and punishing wrongdoers. If they did not do this they had no right to vaunt themselves amongst men. Again, the poor were their trust for whom they would answer to God. By increasing their expenditures they were laying an unjust burden on their subjects. They should become reconciled among themselves, so that they would no longer need ARMAMENTS except for defence, and thus lessen their outlays. They were called upon to fear God, and warned of his chastisement if they did not heed Bahá'u'lláh's counsels (*see* DIVINE JUDGEMENT). Only by adhering to and enforcing God's laws would they gain glory. In terms of worldly possessions, the earth itself was richer than them. Christian monarchs were separately addressed, and reminded of their obligation to be faithful to Jesus' call to follow the promised 'Spirit of Truth' who had now appeared. Other passages were addressed to Sultan ABDULAZIZ and his ministers, to the people of ISTANBUL and their religious leaders, and to the ambassadors of Iran (ḤUSAYN KHÁN) and France. *GPB* 171–5; *PDC* 20–4; *RB2*: 301–25.

Knights of Bahá'u'lláh

HONORIFIC TITLE given by Shoghi Effendi to PIONEERS who opened new territories during the TEN YEAR CRUSADE (1953–63). It was not possible to open some of the territories during the Crusade itself, and later pioneers to these places were also given the title. Shoghi Effendi prepared a Roll of Honour with the names of the Knights in the form of a scroll, and this was ceremonially interred at the entranceway to the inner Shrine of Bahá'u'lláh at BAHJÍ on 28 May 1992 in the presence of many of the remaining Knights (*BWNS* 1992–3: 98). A partial listing of 246 of the Knights is given in *BW13*: 449–57.

Knobloch, Alma (*c.*1863–1943) and **Fanny** (1859–1949)

Prominent early American Bahá'ís. Alma was a PIONEER Bahá'í teacher in Germany (1907–20), and her sister Fanny in Southern Africa (1923–6, 1928–30). A third sister, Pauline, was married to Joseph HANNEN. *BW9*: 641–3; *BW11*: 473–6.

knowledge

IMPORTANCE

For Bahá'u'lláh knowledge was 'one of the wondrous gifts of God', a ladder for human ascent and a source of gladness. It is incumbent upon everyone to acquire it (*TB* 39, 52). SELF-KNOWLEDGE is of great importance: whatever serves to increase the individual's inner vision and reduce blindness is worthy of consideration (*TB* 35). Knowledge of God is attained through recognition of the MANIFESTATION OF GOD for the present age and observance of his laws (*TB* 50). The technological development of the present age – in which the WEST is preeminent – is of divine origin, reflecting Bahá'u'lláh's own revelation (*TB* 39). Similarly, for 'Abdu'l-Bahá knowledge was the most glorious divine gift and the most noble of human perfections. Opposition to knowledge and SCIENCE is a sign of ignorance and condemnable (*SAQ* 137). There is no limit to knowledge, and individuals could (and should) spend their entire lives learning more. Knowledge should be used for the benefit of others and to promote high ideals, such as the establishment of peace (*PT* 34). (*See also* INTELLECT; REASON.)

EPISTEMOLOGY

'Abdu'l-Bahá identified four bases for human knowledge: sense perceptions; reason; scriptural tradition; and inspiration. Each of these is limited and fallible. Thus sense perceptions do not necessarily represent reality, as in the case of perceptual illusions or seeing a mirage in a desert; reason can lead even the same thinker to different conclusions at different times, as with changing cosmological conceptions; scriptural tradition can only be understood by the use of human reason, itself fallible (above); and inspiration (the inner prompting of the human 'heart' or 'SOUL') can be good or bad. Given this epistemological reality, reliable knowledge is attainable both through 'the bounty of the Holy Spirit' and combined use of the four methods to provide a system of cross-checking (*PUP* 20–2, 253–5; *SAQ* 297–9). (*See also* METAPHYSICS.)

HUMILITY

True knowledge comes from God and brings understanding and love. 'Satanic' knowledge becomes a veil between human beings and their creator and is a source of conceit (*KI* 44–5, 119–21).

Kulluʼṭ-ṭaʻám, Lawḥ-i

See Tablet of 'ALL FOOD'.

L

language

THE POWER OF THE WORD

Bahá'í teachings emphasize the transforming impact of the divine word, but in general stress the importance of understanding more than the sanctity of the actual words: thus, unlike many religions, Bahá'í has no sacred or liturgical language as such (it also encourages LITERACY, EDUCATION and the TRANSLATION of its SCRIPTURES into the various languages of the world). Certain languages do enjoy a special 'canonical' status, however – Arabic, Persian and English. The first two are special because they are the languages of the original writings of the Báb, Bahá'u'lláh and 'Abdu'l-Bahá (there are also a few writings of 'Abdu'l-Bahá in Turkish); English because it was (with Persian) the language used by Shoghi Effendi in his interpretations of the Bahá'í writings, and by the Universal House of Justice in its pronouncements to the Bahá'í world. English has also become the predominant language of international communication among Bahá'ís. Given this special status, many Bahá'ís seek to become fluent in one or more of these languages. Specifically, Persian-speaking Bahá'ís commonly learn some Arabic, as Bahá'u'lláh's Arabic writings have not been translated into Persian, and many of his writings contain passages in both languages. There is an evident emphasis here on 'high' literary forms, found also in the English writings of Shoghi Effendi, which are not easily accessible to those with limited education.

UNIVERSAL LANGUAGE

Bahá'u'lláh instructed the world's parliaments and rulers to choose one language (existing or new) and script to be taught to schoolchildren throughout the world. This would be 'the greatest instrument for promoting harmony and civilization', and one of the signs of the maturity of the HUMAN RACE. It would be a cause of unity, so that the world would be regarded as one country. Ultimately, languages would be reduced to one, and the traveller feel that each city was as his home (*KA* 88 k189, 250 n193; *TB* 22, 68, 89, 127, 165–6; see also *LG* 340 no. 1141; Froughi and Lambden). It was a waste of human effort to have to learn many different languages (*TB* 68). 'Abdu'l-Bahá advised that a committee of experts be appointed to select a suitable language to be adopted as an auxiliary to the native language in all countries (children would learn two languages: their own and the auxiliary), and stated that adoption of such a language was inevitable as divine assistance would aid in its realization. Barriers of language created misunderstandings between nations, but once these had been removed, international education and training, and the transmission of sciences and arts, would become possible. Only with the adoption of a universal language could universal PEACE be established (*PUP* 60–1, 182, 232–3, 300; *SWAB* 32). 'Abdu'l-Bahá also praised the ideal of ESPERANTO, and encouraged Bahá'ís to learn it.

TEACHING

Bahá'u'lláh permitted the learning of foreign languages for the purpose of TEACHING the Bahá'í Faith (*KA* 62 k118); 'Abdu'l-Bahá insisted on its importance (*TDP* 32, 38, 52). Language was a key to the human heart, and the means to explain the divine teachings (*PUP* 60–1). (*See also* PUBLISHING; TRANSLATION; WORD OF GOD.)

law

The Bahá'í writings refer to both sacred and secular law.

SACRED LAW

In Islam sacred law – rooted in the QURAN and the teachings and example of Muḥammad – is seen as providing the ideal pattern for individual human behaviour and the structuring of human society. Emerging out of Islam, the Bábí and Bahá'í religions reflect this emphasis on holy law, both the Báb and Bahá'u'lláh taking the role of sacred law-givers, and revealing books of sacred law, which in part follow the Islamic pattern. *SBBR* 33–5, 80–2, 139–40, 198; Walbridge, *Sacred* 16–29. (*See also* LIBERTY.)

HISTORY

THE EARLY BÁBÍS

They were initially rigorous in their adherence to the Islamic holy law (*sharí'a*), adding to it various practices of a pietistic nature. This changed dramatically in Bábism's later 'radical' phase (*see* BÁBÍ RADICALISM), when the Báb revealed a new Bábí code of law in the *BAYÁN*, which replaced Islamic law. In the confused conditions of the time these new ordinances do not appear to have been widely circulated or practised amongst the Bábís. Instead, a number of Bábís became antinomian in their behaviour: marking their new religious identity and their hostility towards their Shí'í oppressors by deliberately contravening Islamic practice.

BAHÁ'Í LAW

Bábí antinomian tendencies were sharply condemned by Bahá'u'lláh, both in his initial role as a regenerator of Bábism in Baghdad and later as an independent prophet. Eventually, in Akka, and partly in response to the requests of his followers, he revealed his own book of law, the *Kitáb-i-AQDAS* (*c.*1873). This, together with its supplementary texts, the subsequent interpretations of 'Abdu'l-Bahá and Shoghi Effendi, and the legislation of the UNIVERSAL HOUSE OF JUSTICE, constitute the basis for the system of Bahá'í law. Of these the legal writings of Bahá'u'lláh, 'Abdu'l-Bahá and Shoghi Effendi are regarded as fundamental and unchangeable, whilst those of the House of Justice are explicitly identified as subsidiary and subject to alteration or repeal by the House in response to changing circumstances. Bábí law has been abrogated except where specifically reiterated by Bahá'u'lláh. A short codification of Bahá'í laws relating to matters of personal status was prepared in Egypt in the 1930s (*BW*6: 363–79; 8: 493–9). A codification of the laws of the *Aqdas* was published in 1973, and an official English translation of the *Aqdas* in 1992.

ADMINISTRATION

Since the 1890s the practical organizational needs of a growing and increasingly complex network of Bahá'ís has led to the elaboration of the system of Bahá'í ADMINISTRATION. Some Bahá'í national ASSEMBLIES – notably the American – have produced extensive literature detailing organizational procedures that regulate many aspects of communal practice and the relation of the individual Bahá'í and the various administrative bodies. The assemblies are at present the primary bodies concerned with the application of those aspects of Bahá'í law relating to communal membership.

ASPECTS OF BAHÁ'Í LAW

GRADUALISM AND DIVERSITY OF APPLICATION OF BAHÁ'Í LAW

Bahá'u'lláh himself stated that observance of his law should be subject to 'tact and wisdom' so as not to cause 'disturbance and dissension'. Humankind should be guided to 'the ocean of true understanding' in 'a spirit of love and tolerance' (*KA* 6). Seemingly as a result of this principle certain Bahá'í laws (e.g. the limitation on the period of engagement and the payment of dowry) are still only applicable to Middle Eastern Bahá'ís (*MUHJ* 277–9 no. 147), although other Bahá'ís from the 'newer' Bahá'í communities may also practise them if they wish. Similarly, payment of *ḤUQÚQU'LLÁH* was not made universally applicable until 1992. Even quite fundamental social laws – such as the prohibition on drinking ALCOHOL – have only been applied extremely gradually in those countries in which they go against established social patterns and the majority of the Bahá'ís have been very new to the Faith. Shoghi Effendi also made it clear that certain laws (e.g. criminal laws) were only applicable in a future (Bahá'í) society, and that others could not be practised if they came into conflict with the present civil law in certain countries (e.g. the Bahá'í prohibition on embalming the dead: *see* BURIAL.)

INDIVIDUAL CONSCIENCE

Bahá'u'lláh directed his followers to obey his laws for 'the love of My beauty', and warned that those who disobeyed had erred grievously in God's sight (*KA* 20 k2, 4). It is attraction to Bahá'u'lláh, combined with the FEAR OF GOD, that is intended to be the primary motivation for obedience. With the exception of behaviour that is criminal or liable to bring the Bahá'í community into disrepute (punishable by the loss of Bahá'í ADMINISTRATIVE RIGHTS), compliance is a matter of individual CONSCIENCE. There is no equivalent of the Islamic practice of social regulation of prayer, fasting and other individual obligations.

GENERAL PRINCIPLE

Bahá'í law is often presented in the form of general principles which each individual must apply as they best see fit in their own lives. The successive heads of the religion have been reluctant to prescribe detailed codes of behaviour. This is in marked contrast to the detailed provisions found in Islamic law.

GENDER EQUALITY

The Universal House of Justice has established the principle that any Bahá'í law originally defined in relation to one sex should be applied to the other, *mutatis mutandis*, unless this is inappropriate (*MUHJ* 272–3 no. 145; *KA* 7).

CLERICAL CLASS

There is no equivalent to the Islamic *'ULAMÁ* able to elucidate the law authoritatively (*KA* 5).

SECULAR LAW

All should be equal before the law and law itself should be just. 'Abdu'l-Bahá called for the protection of both the rights of the individual and 'all mankind'. In the 19th-century Iranian context capital punishment cases tried by local authorities should be contingent upon confirmation by the central government; litigants should have the right of appeal to higher courts; and uniform codifications of law should replace the often arbitrary pronouncements of individual Islamic jurisconsults (*SDC* 14, 18, 37–8). Shoghi Effendi referred to the need for a future single code of international law with binding authority, and to the development of a world legislature and world court (*WOB* 41, 203). (*See also* HUMAN RIGHTS; JUSTICE.)

lawḥ

(Ar., board, tablet, slate; pl.: *alwáḥ*)

Term used to refer to the writings of Bahá'u'lláh and 'Abdu'l-Bahá, and incorporated as part of the title of many smaller works (e.g. *Lawḥ-i-*AQDAS). The term is traditionally used to refer to various writings, including the tablets of the law brought down by Moses from Mount Sinai and the 'Preserved Tablets' on which, according to Islamic tradition, the doings of humankind have been recorded for all eternity.

Leach, Bernard (1887–1979)

Internationally respected potter and artist who was a Bahá'í. He was honoured by both the British and Japanese governments for his work. His pottery at St Ives in Cornwall attracted students from many parts of the world. He became a Bahá'í in around 1940.

BW18: 669–71; Leach *Beyond East, Drawings*.

League of Nations

See UNITED NATIONS.

'learned'

Many prominent early Bahá'ís belonged to the Islamic learned class, the *'ulamá*, and Bahá'u'lláh specifically blessed them, 'the learned among the people of Bahá'. They were his 'trustees', 'the manifestations' of his commandments, the embodiments of steadfastness, 'the daysprings of Divine Utterance', 'the billows of the Most Mighty Ocean', 'the stars of the firmament of Glory', and 'the standards of triumph [of his cause]' (*KA* 82 k173; *TB* 221). More generally, he praised those servants who dedicated themselves 'to the education of the world' and 'the edification of its peoples'. These brought 'the life-giving water of knowledge' to the peoples of the world, directing them to 'the straight path' and acquainting them with what was conducive 'to human upliftment and exaltation' (*TB* 35). That there would continue to be Bahá'í 'learned' was indicated by Bahá'u'lláh's appointment of certain followers as HANDS OF THE CAUSE, a position later given institutional status as part of the Bahá'í 'Administrative Order', and the establishment of such other 'institutions of the learned' as the AUXILIARY BOARDS and CONTINENTAL BOARDS OF COUNSELLORS. These individuals are accorded high rank, but unlike their Shí'í counterparts are denied executive power (given instead to the elected ASSEMBLIES) or the right to make authoritative interpretations binding on their fellow believers (*MUHJ* 214–17 no. 111). Nor – apart from the Hands – are their appointments for life. Other eminent Bahá'í teachers may also be considered 'learned', but have no administrative rank. (*See also* ADMINISTRATION; *'ULAMÁ*).

Letters of the Living

(*Ḥurúfu'l-ḥayy*)

The first eighteen disciples of the Báb. The list given by the Bahá'í chronicler NABÍL-I-A'ẒAM follows. (Those also listed as Letters by Qatíl al-Karbalá'í (*ARR* 176) are marked *. Qatíl also lists Mullá Muḥammad Mayáma'í.)

(1) *Mullá ḤUSAYN BUSHRÚ'Í, killed at Ṭabarsí
(2) *Muḥammad-Ḥasan Bushrú'í, brother of Mullá Ḥusayn, killed at Ṭabarsí
(3) *Muḥammad-Báqir Bushrú'í, nephew of Mullá Ḥusayn, killed at Ṭabarsí

(4) *Mullá ‘Alí Basṭámí
(5) Mullá Khudá-Bakhsh Qúchání, later known as Mullá ‘Alí
(6) *Mullá Ḥasan Bajistání
(7) *Sayyid Ḥusayn Yazdí, the Báb’s secretary, killed in Tehran (1852)
(8) *Mírzá Muḥammad Rawḍih-Khán Yazdí
(9) (Shaykh?) Sa‘íd Hindí
(10) *Mullá Maḥmúd Khu’í, killed at Ṭabarsí
(11) *Mullá (‘Abdu’l-)Jalíl Urúmí (Urdúbádí), killed at Ṭabarsí
(12) *Mullá Aḥmad-i-Ibdál Marághi’í, killed at Ṭabarsí
(13) *Mullá Báqir Tabrízí, the only one of the Letters to become a Bahá’í. He died in about 1881 in Istanbul, having outlived all his fellows (*RB2* 145–7)
(14) Mullá Yúsuf Ardibílí, killed at Ṭabarsí
(15) Mírzá Hádí Qazvíní, brother of Mírzá Muḥammad-‘Alí Qazvíní
(16) *Mírzá Muḥammad-‘Alí Qazvíní, brother-in-law of Ṭáhirih, killed at Ṭabarsí
(17) Ṭáhirih, killed in Tehran (1852)
(18) *Quddús, killed in Bárfurúsh (1849)

Of Nabíl’s list, six were from Khurasan (nos. 1–6); five from Azerbaiján (nos. 10–14), three from Qazvín (nos. 15–17), two from Yazd (nos. 7–8), and one each from Mazandaran (no. 18) and India (no. 9). Most were of relatively humble social origins, and had been followers of the Shaykhí leader, Sayyid Káẓim. Nine were killed during or immediately following the Shaykh Ṭabarsí conflict.

As a group, the Letters of the Living were given a cosmic role by the Báb, who identified them with the ‘forerunners’ (*sábiqún*), the first members of the human race to respond to God’s pre-eternal covenant and, in Shí‘í tradition, Muḥammad, the Imáms and Fáṭima (*see* return). They were also to have an organizational function as the first ‘unity’ (*wáḥid*) in a proposed hierarchy of nineteen-member groups of believers (*see* numbers). The three most prominent Letters (Mullá Ḥusayn, Ṭáhirih and Quddús) came to exercise an independent charisma and authority, expressed in the attribution of high spiritual stations to them. *ARR* 174–81, 189–93; *GPB* 7–8; MacEoin, ‘Hierarchy’ 104–8, 113–22; *SBBR* 24–5, 41.

liberty

Bahá’u’lláh condemned political and religious tyranny, advocated participatory democracy, and stressed the importance of individual religious freedom. At the same time he regarded unchecked liberty as destructive of social order. The principle of moderation had to apply. Liberty is beneficial in some circumstances but not in others. When carried to excess it exerts a pernicious influence on human beings, leading in the end to sedition, ‘whose flames none can quench’. For human beings, ‘true liberty’ consists in submission to God and his commandments. This protects the individual from both his own ignorance and the bad influences of others. People are like a flock of sheep which need a shepherd for their protection (*KA* 63–4 k122–5; *TB* 169). Similarly, ‘Abdu’l-Bahá referred to the ‘moderate freedom’ that guarantees human welfare and preserves ‘universal relationships’ (*SWAB* 305), and the Universal House of Justice has stressed the need for limits to freedom in order for there to be a balance between the rights of the individual and those of the community (*Individual Rights*). (*See also* human rights.)

literacy

For Bahá’u’lláh it was imperative that every child – boy or girl – learns how to read and write. The responsibility for this rests both with the father and the house of justice (*KA* 37 k48; *TB* 128).

It is the duty of children to exert themselves to acquire these skills, but it is not necessary for all to attain the same level of ability: basic skills are enough for some (*CC1*: 368 no. 771). The importance of EDUCATION in general was also stressed.

The Bahá'ís' response to these teachings has reflected the religion's pattern of EXPANSION. From the late 19th century onwards members of the Iranian Bahá'í community became committed to educational development, and the community as a whole became distinguished for its higher level of education. The contrast was particularly marked in the case of WOMEN, most Iranian Bahá'í women becoming literate by the 1970s at the latest, whilst until very recently most Iranian Muslim women remained illiterate. Western Bahá'ís, by contrast, were generally uninterested in literacy: most were already literate and educated and lived in societies in which education was readily available. With the influx of large numbers of new Bahá'ís in the rural Third World (from the 1950s/60s), many of whom were illiterate, the importance of Bahá'u'lláh's injunction again became evident. Particular attention has been directed to Bahá'í literacy since 1989, when the Universal House of Justice called for systematic action to eliminate illiteracy from the Bahá'í community world-wide, identifying literacy as a 'fundamental right and privilege of every human being', and emphasizing its role in giving the individual access to the 'dynamic influence' of the 'sacred Word' (*see* WORD OF GOD). This encouraged a variety of local literacy projects (186 by 1992). In addition, the Office of Social and Economic Development at the Bahá'í World Centre has embarked on an international literacy campaign, beginning with pilot projects in Cambodia, the Central African Republic and Guyana, and already spreading to other countries (*BWNS* 1992–3: 313; 1994–5: 128).

literature

Bahá'í is an intensely literate religion, which emphasizes the power of the WORD OF GOD and encourages all its adherents to become literate so that they can read its writings for themselves (*see* LITERACY). A large literature has developed, particularly in Persian, Arabic and English. The most important category of Bahá'í literature comprises the religion's CANONICAL TEXTS (the writings of the Báb, Bahá'u'lláh, 'Abdu'l-Bahá, Shoghi Effendi and the Universal House of Justice, together with the authenticated talks of 'Abdu'l-Bahá). There is a large 'secondary literature', comprising the work of individual Bahá'ís and institutions (Collins (*Bibliography* 41–158) lists 2,819 items in English on the Bábí or Bahá'í religions up to 1985, including multiple editions, but excluding materials in Braille (142 items) and PERIODICALS). Braun, *Reader's Guide* provides a review of English-language materials around 1986. (*See also* BÁBÍ AND BAHÁ'Í STUDIES; INTERPRETATION; POETRY; PUBLISHING; TRANSLATION.)

'living the life'

Bahá'ís are exhorted to live lives of virtuous conduct and devoted service to the Bahá'í Cause. This objective is often referred to as 'living the life'. *CC2*: 1–27. (*See also* EXCELLENCE; SPIRITUAL QUALITIES; TEACHING.)

local spiritual assemblies

See ASSEMBLIES.

love

Bahá'u'lláh taught that God created human beings out of his love for them, and so they in turn should love him. His love is their paradise and their safe stronghold (*HWa* nos. 3–9). For 'Abdu'l-Bahá love was 'the ground of all things' (*SWAB* 66). It is a 'living power' which brings life, illumination, hope and gladness to those who are lifeless, cold, hopeless and sorrowful. It is the greatest power in the world of existence. All genuine love is divine (*PT* 192–4). No matter where it is found, love is light and hate is darkness (*SWAB* 3). Love proceeds from God and from human beings. God's love is part of his own essence, and a reflection of himself in the mirror of his creation. His love for his creatures gives them material existence, divine grace and eternal life (*PT* 193). It is 'the Holy Spirit's eternal breath' which vivifies the human soul; the cause of divine revelation; 'the vital bond' inherent in the reality of all created things; the true source of eternal happiness; 'the living link' that unites God and the individual human being; 'heaven's kindly light' that 'guideth in darkness' and assures the progress of every 'illumined soul'. It is the attractive power that binds the material elements together; directs the movements of heavenly bodies; and is the revealer of scientific knowledge. It is the basis for true civilization, and those who turn towards it will be exalted whilst those who turn away from it will fall into despair and be destroyed (*PUP* 255, 268–9; *SWAB* 27–8). Human love is directed towards both God and other human beings. Love of God attracts the individual towards God. It purifies the human heart, preparing it for the revelation of divine grace, and is the source of philanthropy (*PT* 193; *SWAB* 202–3). Through it human beings are transformed, and become self-sacrificing (*PUP* 256–7). Such activities as MUSIC and the quest for KNOWLEDGE become heavenly only when joined with the love of God (*SWAB* 181). True love for other human beings (as opposed to transient attraction) occurs when each see 'the Beauty of God' reflected in the other's soul (*PT* 193–4). A family, a city, a nation, humanity itself, will all progress when their members are bound together in unity and agreement. Correspondingly, they will be destroyed and dispersed if their members are divided by mutual hatred (*PUP* 144–5). Bahá'ís should strive to become the manifestations of divine love. There should be love and 'spiritual communion' among the Bahá'ís (becoming 'as one being and one soul'), but they should also love all human beings of all religions, races and communities, including their enemies (*SWAB* 21, 28, 69, 203, 246). *LG* 403–5. (*See also* HUMAN RACE.)

M

MacNutt, Howard (1858–1926)

Prominent early American Bahá'í. He converted in 1898, and was appointed by Ibrahim KHEIRALLA as Bahá'í teacher for New York. He later travelled widely as a Bahá'í lecturer, and compiled the English translations of 'Abdu'l-Bahá's talks in North America, *The Promulgation of Universal Peace* (1922–5). Shoghi Effendi honoured him as one of the DISCIPLES OF 'ABDU'L-BAHÁ. *BFA1*; *BFA2*; *WEBW* 35–42.

magic

The manipulation of supernatural forces to bring about desired practical consequences (e.g. curing disease, obtaining a good harvest). In general the Bahá'í Faith promotes a rationalistic, 'scientific' understanding of physical and social processes (*see* SCIENCE), and is thus antipathetic towards the magical world-view characteristic of much folk religion. Certain magical and occult practices and beliefs are specifically condemned. The concept of talismanic protection appears to be accepted, however (*see* TALISMANS). Magical elements are sometimes found in Bahá'í 'folk religion', as in the practice of some Persian Bahá'ís of keeping portions of sugar loaf (*nabát*) which have been deliberately placed in the Bahá'í Shrines in Haifa in the belief that they will acquire healing properties – although Shoghi Effendi stressed that the remains of the Prophets have no 'physical significance', but only a spiritual one (*LG* 507). It was a common belief among 19th-century Iranian Muslims that Bahá'ís possessed some magical substance which they added to tea to make people convert to their religion. *SBBR* 38, 84. (*See also* MIRACLES.)

Mahdí (Ar., 'the rightly guided one')

Islamic messianic figure, expected to deliver the world from oppression, establish the rule of justice and restore the purity of Islam. He would fight against the ANTICHRIST, conquer the world, and then reign over a messianic kingdom until the RESURRECTION and the final day of divine judgement. He would come at a time of injustice and decadence, and it was the duty of all true Muslims to hasten to his support. Expectation of the Mahdí is found in both Sunní and Shí'í Islam, but whereas in Sunnism it has been mainly confined to the level of popular religion, in SHÍ'ISM it has become part of the official doctrine, the Hidden Imám – commonly known as the *QÁ'IM* – being equated with the Mahdí. There are various expected 'signs' of his advent and appearance. Numerous individuals have claimed the status of Mahdí over the centuries, and the doctrine possesses considerable religio-political potency.

The Báb claimed to be the Mahdí, and he and his chief disciples consciously sought to fulfil the signs of the Mahdí's coming (the Báb's proclamation at Mecca; the projected gathering of believers at Karbalá; the flying of the BLACK STANDARD; etc.). Browne, *Literary History* 4: 398–400; Momen, *Shi'i Islam* 36, 166–70; Sachedina; *SBBR* 42–3; Smith, 'Millenarianism' 238–9.

Maid of Heaven

In one of his visions in the SÍYÁH-CHÁL prison in Tehran (1852) Bahá'u'lláh saw a maiden (*ḥúrí*) – the 'embodiment' of the remembrance of God's name – who addressed the entire creation to announce his mission, and whose sweet voice imparted such tidings as rejoiced his very being. This figure recurs in a number of Bahá'u'lláh's visionary writings ('The Tablet of the Maiden' (*Lawḥ-i-Ḥúrí*), 'The Tablet of the Deathless Youth' (*Lawḥ-i-Ghulámu'l-khuld*), *The Tablet of the Holy Mariner* (*Lawḥ-i-Malláḥu'l-quds*) and 'The Tablet of the Vision' (*Lawḥ-i- Ru'yá*), the first three all written in Baghdad), luminous, garbed in white, standing in the air before him, consoling him in her embrace, or alluding to his own death. Shoghi Effendi refers to the Maiden as an analogous representation of the divine as the burning bush encountered by Moses, the dove that descended on Jesus, or the Angel Gabriel who appeared to Muḥammad. *GPB* 101; Walbridge, *Sacred* 158–65.

Mákú (Má-Kúh)

Small town in north-western Iran (Azerbaiján) close to the Russian and Turkish borders. Rising above the town is an overhanging rock face at the base of which there is a fortress in which the Báb was imprisoned for nine months (July 1847 – 9 April 1848). The Báb's imprisonment was at first severe, but the attitude of the governor, 'Alí Khán, later changed (reportedly as a result of a vision), and a flow of Bábí visitors was permitted. The local population – Sunní Kurds – were initially hostile, but came to regard the Báb as a holy man whose blessing they sought. The Báb referred to

The fortress of Mákú, near the Turkish and Armenian borders, where the Báb was imprisoned, 1847–8

the place as the 'Open Mountain' (*Jabal-i-Básiṭ*). The town was Ḥájí Mírzá ÁQÁSÍ's birthplace, and was under his control, and it was no doubt for this reason that it was initially chosen as the Báb's place of confinement. Russian security concerns and the governor's leniency prompted the Báb's subsequent transfer to CHIHRÍQ. The Mákú period is significant both as marking the end of any hopes that the Báb might gain the support of the Qájár regime and in its doctrinal developments: the Báb's composition of the *BAYÁN* and the *Dalá'il-i-sab'ih*, and his claim to be the *QÁ'IM*. Balyuzi, *Báb* 128–33; *MBBR* 72; *McS* 16, 82–8; Nabil 242–60.

Manifestations of God

(Pers singular: *maẓhar-i-iláhí*)

For Bahá'ís GOD in essence is unknowable, therefore he sends his messengers – the Manifestations of God – to be his exponents on earth. They are theophanies: mirrors who reflect God's glory and reveal his attributes. They are not incarnations of God: they do not embody the divine essence (*WOB* 112–13). They transmit divine knowledge and infinite grace to humankind (*KI* 63–8). For human beings they represent the divine presence. They are the means of approach to God (*KI* 89–92). They are PROPHETS 'endowed with constancy', who reveal divine LAW; possess the 'Most Great INFALLIBILITY' (*'iṣmah-i-kubrá*); and are protected from sin. They come as a succession of teachers (*see* PROGRESSIVE REVELATION; PROPHECY). There is no definitive list of recognized Manifestations but they include ADAM, ABRAHAM, MOSES, Zoroaster (*see* ZOROASTRIANISM), Krishna (*see* INDIAN RELIGIONS), the Buddha (*see* BUDDHISM), JESUS, MUḤAMMAD, the BÁB and BAHÁ'U'LLÁH. They exercise a spiritual sovereignty over all in heaven and earth (*KI* 69). Each one brings a judgement which separates the faithful (who accept them) from the unbelievers (who reject them) (*KI* 72). They engender a transformation in the lives of their followers, bringing unity to diverse peoples, and giving them peace, courage and certitude (*KI* 72–3, 100). They have a double 'station': of 'essential unity' and 'distinction'. Thus, whilst they share a common role as bringers of divine revelations and proclaim the same faith (*see* RELIGION), each also has his own mission, message and human individuality. Again, as the channels through which human beings approach the divine, they may claim to be the very voice of God, or they may refer to themselves as mere prophets and emphasize the unapproachability of the divine essence (*KI* 97–8, 113–16). Future Manifestations will arise under the 'shadow' of Bahá'u'lláh (*WOB* 111), though none for at least a thousand years (*KA* 32 k37). Cole, *Concept.* (*See also* METAPHYSICS; 'RETURN'.)

Manúchihr Khán, the powerful governor of Iṣfáhán who offered the Báb protection

Manúchihr Khán *Mu'tamadu'd-dawlih* (Ar., 'Trusted of the State'), (d. 1847)

Governor of Iṣfáhán from 1838 until his death. A Georgian eunuch converted to Islam, he was regarded as one of the most capable administrators in mid-19th-century Iran. He gained a reputation as a severe but even-handed ruler of the province, and protected the Jewish and Christian minorities. The Báb gained the *Mu'tamad*'s protection following his escape from Shíráz, and remained for four months in Iṣfáhán. At the governor's request the Báb composed a treatise on the 'special prophethood' of Muḥammad. According to the Bábí–Bahá'í account the governor became a Bábí, and promised the Báb his support in gaining access to MUḤAMMAD SHÁH. Such hopes were cut short by the *Mu'tamad*'s death (21 February 1847). *ARR* 256–8, 381–2n; Balyuzi, *Báb* 108–16; *MBBR* 167–9; Nabil 199–215.

Man-yuẓhiruhu'lláh

See HE WHOM GOD SHALL MAKE MANIFEST.

Maqṣúd, Lawḥ-i-

(PA, *Tablet of Maqṣúd*)

Late Syrian-period tablet of Bahá'u'lláh composed for a Mírzá Maqṣúd. The tablet deals with a range of themes, including the inherent greatness of HUMAN NATURE; JUSTICE; the need for an assemblage of rulers to gather to establish the Lesser PEACE; SERVICE to the human race; MODERATION; WISDOM; and the state of the world. It is written in the form of a letter from Bahá'u'lláh's amanuensis, Mírzá ÁQÁ JÁN. *TB* 159–78.

Marie (1875–1938)

Queen of Romania. She was the granddaughter of Queen VICTORIA of Britain and of Tsar ALEXANDER II of Russia. She married the Romanian crown prince Ferdinand in 1893, and became queen

Queen Marie of Romania

in 1914, and queen dowager after her husband's death in 1927. She learnt of the Bahá'í Faith in 1926 from Martha ROOT, and paid public tribute to the 'wondrous message' of Bahá'u'lláh and 'Abdu'l-Bahá, stating that the Bahá'í teachings represented 'the real spirit of Christ', and brought 'peace to the soul and hope to the heart'. Shoghi Effendi lauded her support. Her daughter Ileana, later an Orthodox nun (the Reverend Mother Alexandra), has denied that her mother ever became a Bahá'í (Miller 304 n41). Elsberry; *GPB* 389–95; *MBBR* 59–62; Rabbani, *Priceless Pearl* 107–17; Zinky and Baram 105–15.

marriage

Bahá'u'lláh bade his followers to marry, both so as to bring forth children and as an 'assistance' to themselves. Marriage is not obligatory, however. True marriage is 'a fortress for well-being and salvation'; a spiritual as well as a physical relationship which will continue through 'all the worlds of God'.

Shoghi Effendi described marriage as the bedrock of the whole structure of human society. It is a divine institution.

REQUIREMENTS OF BAHÁ'Í LAW

The stipulations concerning betrothal, the bridal gift, virginity and travel are at present only applicable for Middle Eastern Bahá'ís.

CONSENT

Marriage is dependent first on the consent of the couple, and then of their parents, this latter permission being required to strengthen ties between family members and to prevent any enmity. Parental permission is required regardless of the age of the parties, and whether or not they have been married before. In cases of adoption it is the permission of the natural parents that is required unless these cannot be located. It is important that the couple thoroughly appraise themselves of each other's characters before marrying: they must be conscious of their commitment to a lifelong relationship rather than being simply attracted by passion. Both partners must have reached 'the age of maturity', i.e. fifteen, and neither can even become engaged before this age.

BETROTHAL

This must not exceed ninety-five days.

THE MARRIAGE CEREMONY

The ceremony itself consists of both partners saying a specific verse ('We will all, verily, abide by the Will of God') in the presence of two witnesses. They may add to this as they wish – for example by the inclusion of prayers and scriptural readings – but the ceremony should remain simple. Any other ceremony, such as a civil marriage in places where the Bahá'í marriage has no legal standing, should take place on the same day as the Bahá'í marriage. Modern Bahá'í marriages take place under the jurisdiction of a spiritual ASSEMBLY, which must ensure that a proper ceremony is held and parental consent obtained.

THE BRIDAL GIFT (*MAHR*)

The marriage is conditional upon the payment of a relatively small amount of money by the husband to the wife. (Bahá'í sources refer to this payment as a 'dowry', giving the term a new meaning: the payment is not brought to the marriage by the bride from her family. In that the payment is not given to the bride's parents, it is not a 'brideprice' either.) This payment is fixed at the equivalent of a minimum of 19 *MITHQÁLS* (69 grams) of precious metal – gold if the husband is a city-dweller and silver if he is a villager – and a maximum of 95 *mithqáls* (346 grams), with the lower rate being preferable. If it is accepted, a husband can instead give his bride a promissory note for the money at the time of the wedding.

VIRGINITY

If a man had supposed that his bride was a virgin, but then at the time of consummating the marriage discovers that she is not, the bride-payment and wedding expenses may be demanded. If the marriage itself had been made conditional on the woman's virginity, then it is thereby invalidated. To conceal the matter is highly meritorious in the sight of God, however.

TRAVEL

If a man embarks on a journey, he must fix a date with his wife for his return. If circumstances prevent his return by the promised date, he must inform her. If she receives no word from him for a period of nine months beyond the appointed date, or she receives reliable report of his death from two witnesses, she can remarry. If his fate is unknown, however, she is encouraged to be patient.

SEXUAL RELATIONSHIPS

Such relationships outside marriage are not permitted (*see* SEX). This includes 'trial' and 'companionate' marriages. Modern Bahá'í practice permits only strict monogamy (cf. POLYGAMY), but if polygamous marriages have been contracted prior to an individual becoming a Bahá'í, then these are accepted.

PROHIBITED RELATIONSHIPS

Bahá'u'lláh forbade men from marrying their father's wives. The Universal House of Justice extends this prohibition, *mutatis mutandis*, to include marriage between a woman and her stepfather, i.e. a man and his stepdaughter. More generally, 'Abdu'l-Bahá stated that the more distant the relationship between the marriage partners the better: this would promote both physical well-being and wider fellowship between peoples. He also encouraged interracial marriages. This contrasts markedly with the common tendency in many Middle Eastern societies to marry close relatives, particularly cousins. The whole question of permitted relationships is left to the future decision of the House of Justice.

INTERRELIGIOUS MARRIAGES

Bahá'ís are free to marry those of other religions, but if they participate in the marriage ceremony of another religion, this should not involve them in any dissimulation of their own faith.

DOMESTIC VIOLENCE

Bahá'í marriage should be based on a relationship of mutual respect and equality. All forms of spousal abuse are therefore condemned. For one partner to use force to compel the other to obey them would contradict the principle of consultation on which the marriage should be based. *CC2*: 458–9. (*See also* FAMILY LIFE.)

KA 7, 41 k63, 42–3 k65–7, 58 k107, 69–70 k139, 105–6 q3–4, 110–11 q13, 115 q26–7, 116 q30, 119 q39, 120 q43, 121 q46–7, 122 q50, 131 q84, 132 q87–8, 133–4 q92, 149–52, 205–10 n88–99, 222–4 n133; *LG* 368–90.

martyrdom

A martyr is one who suffers death in the cause of their religion. They become a 'witness' for their faith. Martyrdom is a major religious motif in Shí'ism, particularly linked to the death of the Imám ḤUSAYN (*see* IMÁMS) at KARBALÁ, and glorifying sacrificial action in the cause of truth. This paradigm was readily appropriated by the Bábís as the tensions between them and the secular and religious authorities increased, the readiness of the Bábís to face martyrdom giving them both courage and religious legitimacy. The struggle at ṬABARSÍ in particular assumed the guise of a re-enactment of Karbalá (*SBBR* 27, 44–5). This motif continued after most of the remaining Bábís had become Bahá'ís, and the readiness of some Bahá'ís to face martyrdom continues to provide powerful validation of their commitment in Iran and elsewhere. Whilst Bahá'u'lláh praised those who had given their lives for God's cause, and eulogized martyrdom as being greater in God's sight than 'the creation of the universe' (*HWa* nos. 45–7), he counselled his followers to be cautious in propagating his faith, and to observe 'WISDOM' (*hikmat*) in identifying themselves as Bahá'ís. They should definitely not seek martyrdom (some Bahá'ís desired to become martyrs, seeing that station as a means of expressing their self-sacrifice and utter dedication, even writing to Bahá'u'lláh asking him to grant them this honour). Instead, they should serve and in particular teach the Bahá'í cause. Those who led lives of self-sacrificial dedication might indeed gain the status of martyr, though they died natural deaths (e.g. IBN-I-AṢDAQ) (*EB* 172; MacEoin, 'From Bábism' 225–7).

The actual number of Bábí martyrs is uncertain. Bahá'í sources commonly refer to a rounded figure of twenty thousand, but a recent estimate places the number at between two and three

These ten women were arrested and subsequently executed in Shíráz in 1983 for engaging in Bahá'í community activities. They refused to save their lives by recanting their faith.

thousand (MacEoin, 'Bahá'í persecutions'; 'From Bábism' 236–7; 'A note on the numbers'). The true figure may lie somewhere between these extremes. The total number of Bahá'ís killed in Iran before the Islamic Revolution of 1979 is again unknown: MacEoin estimates three hundred or so – but, as with the Bábí numbers, we should add probable deaths by starvation of dependants of those killed. Since 1979 over two hundred Bahá'ís have been murdered or executed for their beliefs (*see* IRAN). Outside Iran, whilst there have been many instances of persecution and imprisonment (*see* OPPOSITION), there have been very few cases of Bahá'ís having been martyred, one of the most notable being Duarte VIEIRA (1966), in what was then Portuguese Guinea. Several dedicated individuals who were not killed for their beliefs were given the status of martyrs by Shoghi Effendi (George BENKE; May MAXWELL; Keith RANSOM-KEHLER).

Mashhad (Ar., lit. 'the place of martyrdom') (1868 pop. est. 70,000)

Capital of the north-eastern Iranian province of Khurásán, and the shrine city of the eighth IMÁM, Imám Riḍá. It became Mullá ḤUSAYN BUSHRÚ'Í's centre of operations, and it was from here that he and his companions began their march with the BLACK STANDARD.

Mashriqu'l-Adhkár

(Ar., 'Dawning-place of the remembrances [or mention] of God')

Bahá'í temple or 'House of Worship' and its projected surrounding complex of buildings. The term is also used to refer to designated prayer centres, and to communal dawn prayers. Bahá'u'lláh defined the *Mashriqu'l-Adhkár* as any building that had been erected for the praise of God. Such houses of worship should be built everywhere; they should be 'as perfect as possible', and not be adorned with images. It was a blessing to visit such houses at dawn to listen to the verses of God 'in silence' (*KA* 29 k31, 61 k115). 'Abdu'l-Bahá specified that the central house of worship should be linked to a number of subsidiary buildings, including a hospital, drug dispensary, travellers' hospice, school and university, these philanthropic institutions being open to those of all religions. The house of worship itself should be a focus for communal unity and prayer, and would have a wider impact on the place where it was built. Shoghi Effendi stressed the complementarity between the *Mashriqu'l-Adhkár* and the *Ḥaẓíratu'l-Quds*, and the close interaction between prayer, social service, education and Bahá'í administration embodied in the ideal of the temple complex. *BA* 184–6; *GPB* 339–40; *LG* 605–11; *SWAB* 94–100.

Various meeting places were designated as *Mashriqu'l-Adhkárs* by Bahá'ís in Iran and Asiatic Russia at an early date ('Abdu'l-Bahá stated that every village and hamlet should have a prayer centre, even if it had to be underground to avoid persecution), but it was only in 1902–7 that a proper house of worship was constructed (in Russian Turkistan, see below). A second was begun in the United States in the 1920s, a further three were built as part of the Ten Year Crusade in different continents, and another three under the direction of the Universal House of Justice. Those in the 'Third World' in particular, commonly evoke elements of indigenous design. All are nine-sided (*see* numbers), and have a central auditorium. Some are surrounded by gardens and ornamental pools. To date the temples have been built on a continental basis, being designated as 'mother temples' for their respective regions. Numerous temple sites have been acquired throughout the world for future houses of worship. As yet, few subsidiary buildings have been constructed. Badiee; *SBBR* 161–2; Zohoori 134–40.

The individual houses of worship are as follows:

Ashkhabad, Turkmenistan: The first and most complete Bahá'í temple complex built to date: the main structure of the House of Worship was built between 1902 and 1907, and external decoration completed in 1919. Schools and other satellite institutions were build adjacent to it (*see* Ashkhabad). The project was carried out under the supervision of Ḥájí Mírzá Muḥammad-Taqí, the Afnán, who also provided much of the funding. The building design was by Ustád 'Alí-Akbar Banná. The temple building was confiscated by the Soviet authorities in 1928, and leased back to the Bahá'ís until 1938 when it was fully expropriated and turned into an art gallery. The building suffered earthquake damage in 1948, and was demolished in 1963. *BW14*: 479–81; *GPB* 300–1; Lee, 'Rise'; Momen, 'Bahá'í community'.

Wilmette, Illinois, USA: Inspired by news of the Ashkhabad temple, the Chicago Bahá'ís decided to build a temple of their own (1903), eventually choosing a site in the north shore suburb of Wilmette (1908). A delegate assembly, the Bahai Temple Unity, representative of all the American Bahá'ís, was established in 1909 to collect funds and superintend the project, and 'Abdu'l-Bahá dedicated the site on 1 May 1912, but it was not until 1920 that the design (by Louis Bourgeois) was chosen and preparatory work begun. Financial problems delayed completion of the superstructure until 1931; external ornamentation to 1943; and the interior to 1951 (the total construction costs were over $2.6 million). The temple was finally dedicated for worship on 1 May 1953, and has attracted considerable public attention for its unusual style and the innovative techniques employed in its construction. By 1982 it had received nearly 5 million visitors, and it was

The House of Worship in Ashkhabad, Turkmenistan

The House of Worship in Wilmette, USA

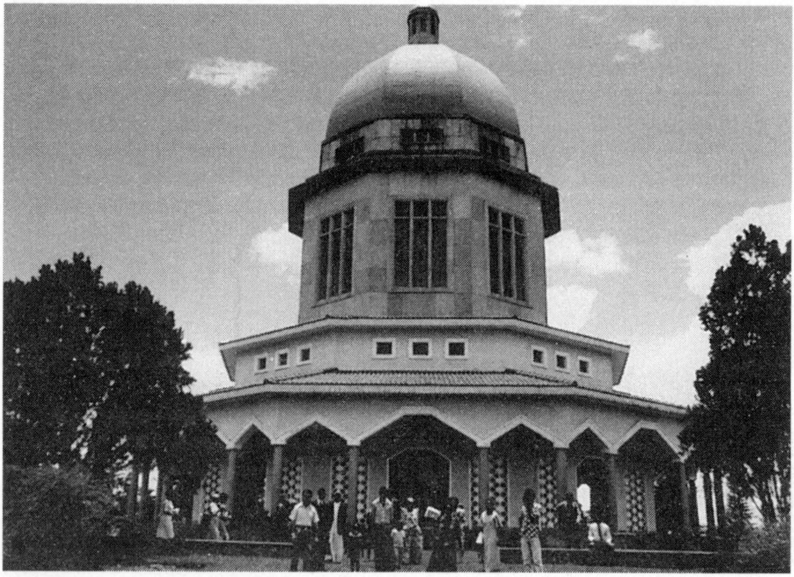

The House of Worship in Kampala, Uganda

The House of Worship in Sydney, Australia

The House of Worship in Frankfurt, Germany

The House of Worship in Panama City, Panama

The House of Worship in Apia, Western Samoa

The House of Worship in New Delhi, India

designated as a national historic place by the American government in 1978. It has a seating capacity of 1,191. The dome ribs rise 164 feet above the floor of the auditorium. The temple's first dependency, a home for the aged, was inaugurated in 1959. *BW13*: 742–8; *17*: 375; *GPB* 348–53; Armstrong-Ingram, *Music, Devotions*; Whitmore.

KAMPALA, UGANDA: Designed by C.M. REMEY, the Foundation stone was laid on 26 January 1958, and the temple was dedicated on 14 January 1961. It has a seating capacity of over 400. *BW13*: 704–19.

SYDNEY, AUSTRALIA: Designed by C.M. Remey: construction work began in 1957, and the temple was dedicated on 15 September 1961. It has a seating capacity of 500. *BW13*: 720–32.

FRANKFURT, GERMANY: Designed by Teuto Rocholl, construction began in 1960 (after a long string of legal delays seemingly caused by church opposition to the project). It was dedicated on 4 July 1964. It has a seating capacity of 450–600. A home for the aged has been built as the first dependency of the temple. *BW13*: 733–41; *14*: 483–4; *18*: 104.

PANAMA CITY, PANAMA: Designed by Peter Tillotson, the foundation stone was laid on 8 October 1967, and construction work began in 1969. It was dedicated on 29 April 1972. It has a seating capacity of 550. *BW14*: 493–4; *15*: 632–49.

APIA, SAMOA: Designed by Husayn Amanat, the foundation stone was laid on 27 January 1979 by Malietoa TANUMAFILI II. It was dedicated on 1 September 1984. The total construction costs came to $6.5m. It has a seating capacity of 500–700. *BW16*: 488–9; 17: 371–4; 18: 104, 585–8.

NEW DELHI, INDIA: Designed by Fariborz Sahba, the foundation stone was laid on 17 October 1977. It was dedicated on 24 December 1986. The construction costs came to approximately $10m. It has a normal seating capacity of 1,200. The building's unusual design – it appears as a giant opening lotus flower – has attracted considerable public interest. *BW16*: 486–7; *17*: 368–70; *18*: 103–4, 571–84.

materialism

For Bahá'ís human beings have both a material and a spiritual existence, both of which need to be recognized and catered for. As long as material progress does not impede spiritual development, it is to be encouraged. Indeed, the 'struggle for existence' is recognized as 'the fountain-head of all calamities' (*SWAB* 302); the ideal society that Bahá'ís regard as the goal of human progress – the future WORLD ORDER – is one in which worldly poverty and injustice will have been eradicated; SOCIO-ECONOMIC DEVELOPMENT (in the spirit of SERVICE) is regarded as an intrinsic part of Bahá'í activity; and whilst the true believer should seek DETACHMENT from the world, ASCETICISM is not the means by which this is to be achieved. This said, the fundamental nature and purpose of human life is spiritual; individual spiritual development through PRAYER, service to others, and the acquisition of SPIRITUAL QUALITIES should be a central goal of human life; and the material elements of CIVILIZATION must be balanced by the spiritual for true human progress to occur. The problem of the present age is the lack of this balance. The material civilization of the WEST has captivated the peoples of the world, such that 'they roved distraught in the wilderness of material causes', oblivious of God, the ultimate Cause (*TB* 144). People have now become 'immersed in the world of nature' (*SWAB* 206). Materialistic civilization absorbs so much of people's energies and interests that they neglect their own spiritual development. The spirit of the present age is irreligious, undermining the foundations of moral and spiritual life. A universal crisis, which is spiritual in nature, is the result (*CC2*: 237–8 no. 1762). Modern-day materialism is 'rampant and brutal' (*ADJ* 39). It is 'all-pervasive', 'pernicious' and 'cancerous'; 'a devouring flame'. Its consequences are moral decline, rising crime, public corruption, the breakdown of marriage, and hedonistic craving (*CF* 124–5). The revival of true RELIGION is essential to rectify this situation. Each individual has the choice of caring for spiritual things or for material things. Whichever they choose they will be drawn nearer to, and further away from its opposite (*CC2*: 235 no. 1754). (*See also* ECONOMIC TEACHINGS; HUMAN NATURE; SECULARISM.)

PHILOSOPHICAL MATERIALISM

This is rejected. Bahá'u'lláh regarded those who clung only to nature 'as it is in itself' as lacking in wisdom (*TB* 144). For 'Abdu'l-Bahá those philosophers who believed that KNOWLEDGE had to be based on sense perception alone ignored the distinctive nature of human rationality and the capacity of human beings to transcend nature, thereby degrading the human reality to that of an animal (*PUP* 177, 355–61; *SAQ* 185–90). Their belief that non-material realities such as the SOUL did not exist was not provable, and their denial of such realities simply indicated a 'blindness' on their part which would be dispelled if they but opened their spiritual eyes (*PT* 91–3). The dominance of this materialistic outlook reflected the obscurantism and disunity of present day religion (*see* RELIGION AND SCIENCE).

maturity, age of

Bahá'u'lláh established fifteen as the age of social and religious maturity at which Bahá'ís were obliged to follow the laws of PRAYER and FASTING, and at which they could marry if they so chose. Engagement or MARRIAGE before this age is not permissible. Use of the BURIAL ring and the special prayer for the dead are also intended only for those who have attained the age of maturity. If inheritors are still children, a trustee has to be appointed to manage the estate until they come of age (*KA* 28 k27, 113 q20, 120 q43, 127 q70, 134 q92, 170 n13). Shoghi Effendi stated that prior to the age of maturity children are under the direction of their parents (and thus need their parents' permission to attend Bahá'í meetings or become Bahá'ís). He also fixed twenty-one as the age of 'administrative' maturity at which Bahá'ís can vote for and be elected to ASSEMBLIES. This is a temporary measure and may change in the future (*BA* 37; *KA* 189 n49; *LG* 153–6).

Maxwell, May Ellis

(née Bolles) (1870–1940)

Prominent early American Bahá'í. She joined the first group of Western pilgrims to visit 'Abdu'l-Bahá, herself reaching Akka in February 1899. She then returned to Paris where she had been living, and established the nucleus of a Bahá'í community. Those introduced to the Faith by her included C.M. REMEY, Thomas BREAKWELL, Hippolyte DREYFUS and Laura Barney (DREYFUS). She married William Sutherland MAXWELL in 1902 and moved with him to Montreal. The couple had one child, Mary (RÚḤIYYIH KHÁNUM). 'Abdu'l-Bahá stayed with the family during his visit to Canada (1912), their home later being accorded the status of a national Bahá'í shrine. Despite poor health, May became extensively involved in Bahá'í teaching and administrative activities in both the United States and Canada, and later in Europe. In 1940 she visited South America to support Bahá'í

May Maxwell, prominent early American Bahá'í

William Sutherland Maxwell, Bahá'í architect and Hand of the Cause

activities in Argentina, but died shortly after reaching Buenos Aires. Shoghi Effendi accorded her the status of a MARTYR. *BW8*: 631–42.

Maxwell, William Sutherland
(1874–1952)

Canadian HAND OF THE CAUSE. He was the husband of May MAXWELL (m. 1902) and father of RÚḤIYYIH KHÁNUM. He became a Bahá'í after meeting 'Abdu'l-Bahá in 1909. Following May's death in 1940 he moved to Haifa. A well-known architect, he designed the superstructure for the SHRINE OF THE BÁB. He was named a Hand in December 1951, shortly before his death. Shoghi Effendi also named one of the doors of the Shrine in his honour. *BW12*: 657–62; Harper 276–86.

Medicine, Tablet of
(PA: *Lawḥ-i-Ṭibb*)

Tablet of Bahá'u'lláh dating from the Akka period addressed to Mírzá Muḥammad Riḍá-yi-Ṭabíb Yazdí, a practitioner of traditional Islamic medicine. The tablet contains advice on healthy eating, and the need for medical treatment, MODERATION and emotional contentment (*see* EMOTIONS); praises medicine as the noblest of the sciences; provides a short healing prayer; and states that if the Bahá'ís had followed his instructions to teach the Cause, then the majority of the world's people would have converted. Fananapazir and Lambden, 'Tablet of Medicine'; EsslemontA 98, 99, 102–3/B 102, 103, 107; PM no. 170; *RB3*: 358–60. (*See also* HEALTH AND HEALING.)

meditation

For Bahá'ís meditation consists primarily of individual contemplation of the WORD OF GOD, particularly when in a state of PRAYER. Its purpose is to deepen the individual's understanding of the Bahá'í revelation and make them more open to the potentially transforming power that Bahá'ís believe their scriptures to have on the human SOUL. It is a form of communion with self, in which the individual abstracts their consciousness from external stimuli and focuses on the divine. In this state, the individual becomes receptive to deeper insights into the nature of things and their spirit is strengthened. There is no formal system of meditation, each individual being free to meditate as they see fit. *CC2*: 226 no. 1724, 234–5 no. 1752, 240–3 nos. 1771, 1774, 1782.

membership

Although some lists of early Bábís were made, there seem to have been no similar listings of early Bahá'ís, and the basis of acceptance into the network of Bahá'í groups is obscure. Ibrahim KHEIRALLA instituted lists of those new American Bahá'ís who received the 'GREATEST NAME', but this practice was not continued after 1900, as more 'inclusivist' conceptions of Bahá'í membership predominated (*SBBR* 109–10). It was not until 1925 that the practice of preparing membership rolls of 'recognized believers' was started in North America – at Shoghi Effendi's instructions – and subsequently became general throughout the Bahá'í world. This raised the 'delicate and complex question' of what exactly the qualifications of a 'true believer' were. Shoghi Effendi listed four 'fundamental' factors which were to be considered: (1) 'full recognition of the station of the Forerunner [the Báb], the Author [Bahá'u'lláh], and the True Exemplar ['Abdu'l-Bahá] of the Bahá'í Cause, as set forth in 'Abdu'l-Bahá's Testament'; (2) 'unreserved acceptance of, and submission to, whatsoever has been revealed by their Pen; (3) 'loyal and steadfast adherence to every clause of our Beloved's ['Abdu'l-Bahá's] sacred Will; and (4) 'close association with the spirit as well as the form of the present day Bahá'í administration throughout the world' (*BA* 90). The assembly was warned to avoid being overly rigid in the implementation of this practice and not to try to further analyse or elucidate these factors. (*See also* CONVERSION; DOGMA.)

All local and national ASSEMBLIES are now expected to keep membership records of their communities. These records include lists of declarations of faith by new Bahá'ís, as well as of births and of those who formally withdraw from the community (*see* APOSTASY). Changes in status (the attainment of the age of spiritual MATURITY at fifteen (*see* YOUTH); the gaining of the right to participate in assembly ELECTIONS at the age of twenty-one; MARRIAGE; the loss or regaining of ADMINISTRATIVE RIGHTS; death) are also recorded. There is considerable variation in the efficiency with which assemblies in different parts of the world are able to compile this data. As in any inclusive religious community, there are considerable variations in commitment amongst Bahá'ís. There are no gradations of membership status on this basis, however. (*See also* COMMUNITY.)

membership in other religious organizations

See BAHÁ'Í FAITH AND OTHER RELIGIONS.

Memorials of the Faithful

(PA: *Tadhkiratu'l-vafá*, lit. 'Memorials of Faithfulness')

Book by 'Abdu'l- Bahá, consisting of his remembrances of over seventy of the early Bahá'ís (and one Bábí, ṬÁHIRIH). The original 'memorials' were delivered as a series of talks to the Bahá'ís in Haifa during the early years of World War I. The Persian transcripts were later corrected by 'Abdu'l-Bahá, and then compiled into a single volume (1915), subsequently published by the Haifa Bahá'í Assembly in 1924. An English translation was published in 1971. The accounts focus on the

SPIRITUAL QUALITIES of the individuals rather than their formal biographies. Banani, 'Writings'.

metaphysics

The study of being and knowing.

THE LIMITS OF HUMAN UNDERSTANDING

Bahá'u'lláh taught that 'no mind nor heart' could ever understand the nature of even the most insignificant of God's creatures, let alone the mystery of GOD himself. All the conceptions of 'the devoutest of mystics' and the most exalted of sages were the product of 'man's finite mind' and were conditioned by its limitations. They were only a reflection of what had been created within themselves (*GWB* 62 no. 26, 316 no. 148). Again, whilst God had endowed the human essence with the 'rational faculty' (the MIND), human beings were unable ever to comprehend this inner reality. Indeed, to acknowledge their own inability was the 'acme of human understanding' (*GWB* 163–5 no. 83). Human beings should seek KNOWLEDGE, but they could never transcend the inherent limitations of their own understanding. (*See also* SCIENCE; REASON.)

RELATIVISM

Shoghi Effendi stated that a 'fundamental principle' of Bahá'u'lláh's teachings was that religious truth was 'not absolute but relative': thus the (seemingly divergent) teachings of the various world religions could be seen as 'facets of one truth' (*Faith* 2). Given the Bahá'í view of the ultimately limited nature of human understanding, divergent views regarding the nature of metaphysical reality may perhaps be reconciled: thus Bahá'u'lláh regarded different understandings of the nature of CREATION as occurring because of divergences in thought (*TB* 140) – 'the comprehension of this matter dependeth upon the observer himself' (*GWB* 162 no. 82), whilst 'Abdu'l-Bahá described theological differences about God as being a product of the imagination: each sect and people created a god in their own thought and worshipped that. God in essence was utterly beyond such conceptions, however (*Bahá'í World Faith* 381–2; *SWAB* 53; see also Momen, 'Relativism'). Much religious disputation can thus be seen as essentially useless, or indeed, when linked to fanaticism and superstition, is to be condemned (*see* RELIGION AND SCIENCE).

GOD AND THE WORLD

For Bahá'ís there is a threefold division of reality. (1) God: the essentially pre-existent cause of existence. The creation is contingent upon him. (2) The logos: this is the realm of God's command and grace; the 'Primal Will', the 'Holy Spirit' and the 'Word of God'. It pervades all created things, and is the ultimate cause of creation (*TB* 140–1). Every thing that can be perceived is an emanation from it, and through its potency it unlocks the human heart (*TB* 173). The MANIFESTATIONS OF GOD are appearances of the logos in the physical world. (3) Creation: the physical universe has always existed. Although subject to change, in temporal terms it has neither beginning nor end. It comprises individual created entities (planets, people) which originate in time. Every created thing in the whole universe is a 'sign' of God's sovereignty, reflects his image, and is dependent upon him (*GWB* 160 no. 82, 165 no. 84). Cole, *Concept*.

Bahá'u'lláh also referred to the many 'worlds of God' (*TB* 187–8), and often used a Neoplatonic cosmological framework which was traditional in certain schools of Islamic metaphysical thought. This distinguishes five realms of existence: (1) *háhút*: the realm of the unknowable, unmanifested essence of God, which even God's Prophets cannot know; (2) *láhút*: the realm in which the divine names and attributes become defined within the divine consciousness as the archetypal forms of all created things. This is the 'All-Glorious Horizon' of the primal will, the active means by which God has created the heavens and the earth; (3) *jabarút*: the realm of the revealed God acting within creation, the 'all-highest Paradise' of divine decrees in which reside the imagery forms of the archangels; (4) *malakút*: the angelic realm, the 'world of similitudes' (*'álam-i-mithál*); (5) *násút*: the physical world, subdivided into animal, vegetable and mineral kingdoms. God is manifested at all of these levels except the first (God's unknowable essence), and the Manifestations of God exist on four of these levels. Human beings exist at the interface between the angelic and physical realms, and are able to choose in which to live. Momen, 'Relativism' 189–4.

TYPES OF SPIRIT

'Abdu'l-Bahá discussed human distinctiveness in terms of a quasi-Aristotelian differentiation between four 'kingdoms' of physical creation (mineral; vegetable; animal; human) and five divisions of spirit (vegative; animal; human; heavenly; the Holy Spirit). Both of these schemata are hierarchical, each level of physical existence being held to encompass the qualities of those below it, whilst also being distinguished by its own particular characteristics which are beyond the attainment of the lower kingdoms. Thus, minerals are held together by atomic attraction; vegetables also have the power of growth; animals also have sense-perception and the power of movement; humans also have the powers of ideation, conscious reflection and discovery, as manifested in science and invention (*PUP* 69–70, 114, 172–3, 189, 268; *SAQ* 143–4, 185–90, 208). Human beings are also distinguished from plants and animals in their spiritual qualities: they possess a non-material entity (the SOUL) which continues to exist after physical death; they are able to recognize and love God, and to be transformed into heavenly beings by the spirit of faith; and they may choose to acquire saintly or satanic qualities. (*See also* EVOLUTION; FREE WILL; HUMAN NATURE.)

Mihdí, Mírzá (1848–70)

Younger son of Bahá'u'lláh by his first wife, NAVVÁB; known as the 'Purest Branch' (*ghuṣn-i-aṭhar*) (*see* AGHṢÁN). Born in Tehran, he remained in the city for several years following the family's departure for Iraq (1853). He accompanied Bahá'u'lláh to Edirne and Akka, serving as one of his father's secretaries. One evening, preoccupied in prayer, he fell through a skylight on the roof of the barracks-prison in Akka, and died the next day (23 June 1870). Bahá'u'lláh gave his death the status of a sacrifice that the Bahá'ís might be 'quickened', 'and all that dwell on earth be united', and linked it to the subsequent ending of

Mírzá Mihdí, younger son of Bahá'u'lláh by Navváb

the exiles' close imprisonment. The boy was buried outside the city wall in the Nabí Ṣáliḥ cemetery. His remains, together with those of his mother, were disinterred by Shoghi Effendi and reburied as one of a group of shrines of family members on the slopes of Mount Carmel in December 1939. *BKG* 310–14; *BW8*: 245–58; *GPB* 188; Rabbani, *Priceless Pearl* 259–63.

Mihdí Dahají, Sayyid

Eminent follower of Bahá'u'lláh, who was honoured by him with the title *Ismu'lláhu'l-Mihdí* ('The Name of God, Mihdí'). He acted as the caretaker of the House of Bahá'u'lláh in Baghdad after the latter's departure for Istanbul. He was enormously respected as a Bahá'í teacher in Iran, but subsequently became a follower of MUḤAMMAD-'ALÍ (*GPB* 319; *see* COVENANT-BREAKERS). He received a number of letters from Bahá'u'lláh, including the *Súriy-i-'Ibád* (*Chapter of the Servants*), written in Edirne (*RB2*: 272–5), and the *Lawḥ-i-Siyyid-i-Mihdíy-i-Dahají*, composed in Akka (*TB* 195–201; *RB4*: 236–8). This latter work refers to Bahá'í TEACHING activity, and to the need for the Bahá'ís to be godly in their deeds and to avoid creating strife.

military service, pacifism

The question of Bahá'ís entering military service was raised by the American and British Bahá'ís during the 1930s. They wished to resolve two potentially conflicting Bahá'í principles: the instruction not to kill (Bahá'u'lláh taught that it was better to be killed than to kill), and the call to be obedient to their governments. Shoghi Effendi's response was: (1) to deny that Bahá'ís could be 'conscientious objectors' (i.e. people who refused to serve in the armed forces on grounds of conscience): Bahá'ís were not 'absolute pacifists' (i.e. the use of force was acceptable under certain circumstances); they rejected the implicit anarchism of pacifism – the individual was important, but social life was based on the subordination of the individual will to that of society; and they did not believe that the refusal to bear arms would of itself establish PEACE – rather a 'spiritual revitalization' of the human heart was necessary; (2) to instruct the Bahá'ís to apply for non-combatant status (ambulance work, air-raid wardens, administration), so that they were not directly involved in the shedding of blood, whilst at the same time they expressed their willingness to obey the authorities unreservedly if called upon to do so. As loyal citizens, it was their duty to serve their country. It was immaterial whether that service placed them in positions of danger. The Universal House of Justice has stated that there is no objection to Bahá'ís enlisting voluntarily in their country's armed forces and pursuing military careers so long as this does not involve combatant service. This is particularly the case if national service includes training in skills valuable to national or professional development such as agriculture. *LG* 406–9. The American national assembly issued a statement on this issue with Shoghi Effendi's approval in 1936 (*BW6*: 202–4).

millenarianism

The belief in a divinely destined future paradise on earth; commonly linked to the acceptance of a particular leader as a messiah; a major motif in Bábí–Bahá'í history. Bábism emerged in the context of Shí'í messianic expectation, and the Báb himself proclaimed that he was the Shí'í messianic figure, the *QÁ'IM*, who had come to usher in the events of the resurrection. Initially at least, many of his followers apparently expected him literally to fulfil the Shí'í prophecies leading to the establishment of a theocratic kingdom. Following the crushing of Bábism (1849–52) further messianic expectations gave hope to the remaining Bábís, and framed Bahá'u'lláh's claim to be HE WHOM GOD SHALL MAKE MANIFEST. Bahá'u'lláh also laid claim to be the promised one of other religions, and prophesied the establishment of the millennial future Most Great PEACE. There were apocalyptic elements in his vision. Through God's assistance the people would perhaps awaken, but the present situation of the world was 'lamentably defective', with injustice, discord and corruption prevalent. The 'signs of impending convulsions and chaos' were evident, and the 'winds of despair' were blowing in every direction (*TB* 171).

The EXPANSION of Bahá'í to the West (from 1894) brought the religion into more immediate contact with the Christian tradition, early American Bahá'ís linking their faith to Christian adventist expectation, and the pioneer (and heterodox) Bahá'í teacher I.G. KHEIRALLA teaching his converts to see 'Abdu'l-Bahá in Christ-like terms and to expect the Great Peace to be established in 1917. In the aftermath of World War I a number of Bahá'ís continued to believe that the Most Great Peace would soon be established. Shoghi Effendi, by contrast, developed a metahistorical schema of the future which combined a millennial vision of the destined but seemingly far-distant future Peace (*see* WORLD ORDER), with apocalyptic warnings of the immediate sufferings (governmental collapse, anarchy, political oppression, racial strife, the burning of cities, etc.) which would be experienced by an as yet unregenerate humanity resisting the impulse towards world unity. Greater Bahá'í TEACHING activity would hasten the advent of peace, and the pressure of events would cause the world's governments to establish the Lesser Peace of their own accord. Strongly apocalyptic themes came to be an important element in the thinking of the dissident Bahá'í C.M. REMEY and his followers. Various Bahá'í writers have sought to present Bahá'u'lláh as the promised messianic figure of all religions, both of the major world religions and local 'tribal' traditions. *SBBR* 42–4, 74–6, 78, 107–8, 140–5; Smith, 'American Bahá'í community', 155–61; Smith, 'Millenarianism'. (*See also* CALAMITY.)

Mills, Mountfort (d. 1949)

Prominent American Bahá'í. He converted in 1906 and made several pilgrimages to visit 'Abdu'l-Bahá. In 1922 he was one of the Bahá'ís consulted by Shoghi Effendi about the future development of the Faith. He was extensively involved in the development of Bahá'í ADMINISTRATION in North America, and served on both the BAHAI TEMPLE UNITY Executive Board and the later national spiritual ASSEMBLY. A lawyer, it was he who prepared the assembly's Declaration of Trust and By-Laws (1927), which became the model for similar documents in other countries. He prepared the legal appeals concerning the House of Bahá'u'lláh in BAGHDAD, and also represented the Bahá'ís at various international gatherings. *BW11*: 509–11.

mind

The entity in an individual responsible for thought, feelings, and speech; intelligence. (*See also* SOUL.)

minorities

The consciousness of division between Bahá'ís on the basis of their racial, religious, national or class background is ultimately alien to the spirit of the Faith. At the same time, however, Bahá'ís should seek to safeguard and nurture minority groups within their communities where these exist. In such circumstances, positive discrimination in favour of the minority might be practised to encourage its participation in community life. Thus, in those cases in which an equal number of ballots had been cast for two or more individuals in an election, or in which there were several equally qualified candidates for an appointed office, the minority group member should be given priority (*ADJ* 29–30). (*See also* INDIGENOUS PEOPLES; PREJUDICE; RACE.)

miracles

'Abdu'l-Bahá taught that all MANIFESTATIONS OF GOD were possessed of supernatural power, but that importance should not be attached to their performance of apparent miracles. Such miracles did not provide a rational proof of their missions (*SAQ* 100–1; cf. *RB1*: 106–7). Miracles were attributed to Bahá'u'lláh and 'Abdu'l-Bahá (and even more to the Báb and some of his leading disciples, such as QUDDÚS (*TJ* 42)), and Bahá'u'lláh himself declared that he had 'such power' that the deadliest of poisons could be transmuted into a panacea and 'a speck of floating dust' caused to generate suns of infinite splendour (*ADJ* 80–1). But neither the Báb nor Bahá'u'lláh generally put much emphasis on the miraculous, other than the greatest of miracles: the revelation of divine verses. The one exception to this was when the performance of miracles was offered as a proof of mission, as in the celebrated instance when Bahá'u'lláh offered to perform a miracle for the *'ulamá* of Iraq on condition that they would afterwards accept his mission – an offer that was not taken up (*SAQ* 29–30). Bahá'u'lláh stated that his followers should not 'debase' his station by reference to what they regarded as miracles on his part (*ESW* 33). SBBR 38, 84–5.

Mishkín-Qalam (1812–1912)

Mírzá (Muḥammad-) Ḥusayn, eminent Iranian calligrapher and Bahá'í. He was renowned for his art and was given the title *Mishqín-Qalam* ('Musk-scented' or 'jet-black pen') by Náṣiru'd-dín Sháh. He developed the technique of drawing with his fingernail ('Nail script', *Khaṭṭ-i-nákhuní*). He was a Sufi of the Ni'matu'lláhí order (*see* SUFISM) and seems to have became a Bahá'í in the 1860s. His Bahá'í CALLIGRAPHY, including his representation of the GREATEST NAME, is well known. He met Bahá'u'lláh in Edirne and was one of the Bahá'ís sent to accompany Ṣubḥ-i-AZAL to Cyprus. He was able to rejoin the companions of Bahá'u'lláh in Akka in 1886. Shoghi Effendi named him as one of the APOSTLES OF BAHÁ'U'LLÁH. EB 270–2.

Mishkín-Qalam, prominent Iranian Bahá'í and calligrapher

mission

Bahá'í advocates the peaceful, non-disputatious propagation of religion, raising such activity to a primary religious duty for the individual (*see* TEACHING; CONVERSION), and organizing systematic PLANS with the objective of enlarging the Bahá'í community world-wide. The Islamic practice of HOLY WAR is explicitly prohibited. (*See also* EXPANSION; PIONEERS.)

Commenting on the Islamic duty of defending God's religion in his *Secret of Divine Civilization*, 'Abdu'l-Bahá held that this involved both the pious observance of religious law and positive measures to promote the Faith amongst non-believers. In this regard the history of Christianity provided vivid examples of successful missionary endeavour: first in the selflessness, SPIRITUAL QUALITIES and devotion (even in the face of MARTYRDOM) that characterized both the disciples and later Christian teachers, who had thus attracted multitudes of followers world-wide; second in the spread of Protestantism, despite the opposition of entrenched Catholic power, on account of the combination of the correctness of Martin Luther's views with the adoption of effective means for their propagation. By contrast, conversion by force – as advocated by some Muslims – was ineffective: those thus converted might outwardly be believers, but inwardly they were apostates who would leave the religion when the threat of compulsion was removed. Again, fanaticism and 'unreasoning religious zeal' would only serve to repel and alienate those so addressed (*SDC* 41–56).

mithqál

Unit of weight used by Bahá'u'lláh. The traditional Middle Eastern equivalence is 1 *mithqál* = 24 *nakhuds* (chick-peas), but in the *Bayán* the Báb changes this to 19 *nakhuds*, and this was subsequently confirmed by Bahá'u'lláh in the *Kitáb-i-Aqdas*. This is equivalent to 3.6417 grams or 0.11708 troy ounces. *KA* 114–15 q23, 200–1 n78, 253.

moderation

Bahá'u'lláh counselled moderation in all things: if something is carried to excess it ceases to exert a beneficial influence and becomes a source of evil. This is the case with LIBERTY and CIVILIZATION (*TB* 169).

monasticism

Bahá'u'lláh praised the pious deeds of Christian monks and priests, but instructed that they should now abandon seclusion and live in the 'open world', working for themselves and to benefit others, and marrying and having children (*ESW* 49; *TB* 24). (*See also* ASCETICISM.)

Moody, Susan (1851–1934)

Early American Bahá'í who became one of the pioneers in the development of health care and education for women in Iran. She became a Bahá'í in Chicago around 1903, and in 1909 moved to Iran to help a group of Bahá'í doctors who were then setting up a hospital in Tehran. Apart from treating her own patients, she trained a group of Iranian women in basic nursing and midwifery, and in 1910 helped to establish the Tarbíyat School for girls (*see* SCHOOLS). She also promoted classes in Bahá'í religious instruction for girls (from 1914). In 1910 she was joined by two more American Bahá'í women: Elizabeth Stewart (d. 1926), a trained nurse, and Dr Sarah Clock (d. 1922). In 1911 a fourth woman, Lillian Kappes (d. 1920), arrived to head the girls school. Political disturbances prompted Moody and Stewart to leave Iran in 1924, but Moody returned in 1928 and remained in Iran until her death. Armstrong-Ingram, 'American Bahá'í women'; *BW6*: 483–6.

Moses (*c.*1300 BCE)

Biblical and Quranic prophet recognized as a MANIFESTATION OF GOD in the Bahá'í teachings and as the originator of JUDAISM as a religion. He is known in Islamic and Bábí–Bahá'í texts as 'He who conversed with God'. Moses' encounter with God on Mount Sinai is a recurring motif in the writings of the Báb and Bahá'u'lláh, both claiming to be 'the voice' of God which spoke to Moses from the burning bush. Both Bahá'u'lláh and 'Abdu'l-Bahá provide allegorical interpretations of various elements of the Moses story. Thus, according to one PILGRIMS' NOTE, 'Abdu'l-Bahá cast doubt on the historicity of Moses' and the Israelites' miraculous crossing and Pharaoh's reported drowning in the Red Sea, interpreting these accounts as their respective success and failure to cross the 'sea' of corruption and iniquity. Heggie 145–7; Lambden, 'Sinaitic mysteries'; *SAQ* 14–15.

mubáhala (Ar., 'mutual cursing')

Islamic religious challenge in which two contenders call upon God to decide between them, with the expectation that some dramatic event will reveal who is speaking the truth and who is in error. Challenges to *mubáhala* were issued by leading Bábís to their clerical opponents on several occasions, but not taken up. Ṣubḥ-i-AZAL's failure to meet Bahá'u'lláh in a *mubáhala* challenge he himself had made in EDIRNE was an important factor in his loss of leadership (*ARR* 245–7, 308, 313; Momen, *Shi'i Islam* 13–14; *RB2*: 291–8). Also of note was Bahá'u'lláh's challenge to the Shí'í *'ulamá* in Iraq to agree on a miracle which he would perform on condition that they would then accept the truth of his claims. The challenge was declined on the grounds that Bahá'u'lláh was a sorcerer who would deceive onlookers (*GPB* 143–4; *PDC* 87–88).

Muhájir, Raḥmatu'lláh (1923–79)

Iranian HAND OF THE CAUSE. Born into an active Bahá'í family, he was involved in Bahá'í committee work as a youth, and delayed his medical studies for two years in order to serve as a Bahá'í pioneer in Ridá'iyyih. He and his wife, Íran, daughter of 'Alí-Akbar FURÚTAN, pioneered to the Mentawai Islands, a poor, backward and disease-ridden area of Indonesia, in 1954, being named as KNIGHTS OF BAHÁ'U'LLÁH. Learning Mentawaian, living with the local people, and bringing them medical care, they began to teach the Bahá'í Faith. The results were rapid and impressive: by 1956 over one thousand Mentawaians had converted, and by 1958 there were some four thousand local Bahá'ís and thirty-three local assemblies. In 1957 Raḥmatu'lláh was elected onto the regional spiritual assembly, and in October named as one of the final group of Hands by Shoghi Effendi. In 1958 the Muhájirs left Indonesia, subsequently travelling extensively throughout the Bahá'í world. Raḥmatu'lláh played a key role in inspiring several Bahá'í communities to begin campaigns of 'mass teaching' to establish Bahá'í communities in the rural areas of the Third World. He also encouraged the establishment of Bahá'í educational and health projects. He died in Ecuador, during an intensive tour of South America. *BW18*: 651–9; Muhájir, *Dr Muhájir*; Harper 455–61.

Muḥammad (*c.*570–632)

Prophet-founder of ISLAM ('the Apostle of God'). Recognized by Bahá'ís as a MANIFESTATION OF GOD and as the recipient of God's revelation in the QURAN. His coming is regarded as having been predicted in the Old and New Testaments, and to have been the object of 'all preceding Dispensations'. Heggie 148–57; *SAQ* 18–24.

Muḥammad, Ḥájí Mírzá Sayyid

A maternal uncle of the Báb (*see* BÁB, FAMILY OF). He became a Bábí after reading Bahá'u'lláh's *Kitáb-i-ÍQÁN*, which had been composed in answer to his questions.

Muḥammad-'Alí, Mírzá

(1853–1937)

Second surviving son of Bahá'u'lláh, born in Baghdad during the first year of his father's exile. His mother was Mahd-i-'Ulyá (*see* Núrí family). In his early teens in Edirne he advanced claims to divine revelation, for which he was chastised by his father. He rose to prominence as a transcriber of Bahá'u'lláh's writings. His father named him *ghuṣn-i-akbar* (the 'Greatest Branch') and in the *Kitáb-i-'Ahd* (*Book of the* Covenant) appointed him to be second in succession after 'Abdu'l-Bahá. Motivated it would seem by an enormous jealousy for 'Abdu'l-Bahá (nine years his senior) he conspired to undermine his elder brother's leadership. Despite the support of Jamál Burújirdí in Iran and Ibrahim Kheiralla in the United States he was unable to gain extensive support amongst the Bahá'ís. He was able to alienate the majority of Bahá'u'lláh's family from 'Abdu'l-Bahá, however. In this he was principally supported by his brother-in-law, Mírzá Majdi'd-dín (d. 1955). He sought unsuccessfully to gain the leadership of the Bahá'í community after 'Abdu'l-Bahá's death. Shoghi Effendi described him as 'the archbreaker of Bahá'u'lláh's Covenant'. *GPB* 246–9; Shoghi Effendi, *Messages to America* 11; *TCB* 125–34, 148. (*See also* Covenant-breakers.)

Muḥammad-'Alí Bárfurúshí, Mullá

See Quddús.

Muḥammad-'Alí Qá'iní, Shaykh (1860/1–1924)

Eminent Iranian Bahá'í. The nephew and close companion of Nabíl-i-Akbar, he became one of the focal points of the Bahá'í community in Ashkhabad. He also visited India. Shoghi Effendi named him as one of the Apostles of Bahá'u'lláh. *EB* 273–4.

Muḥammad-'Alí Zanjání, Mullá

See Ḥujjat.

Muḥammad-'Alí Zunúzí *'Anís'*

(Ar., 'Close Companion'), (d. 1850)

The Báb's disciple who shared martyrdom with him, their remains being impacted together by the force of the bullets. *ARR* 401; Nabil 507–10; *TJ* 297–303.

Muḥammad-Báqir Iṣfáhání, Shaykh

See 'Wolf'.

Muḥammad Iṣfáhání, Sayyid

(d. 1872)

Supporter of Ṣubḥ-i-Azal, regarded by Bahá'ís as the antichrist of the Bahá'í revelation for having encouraged Azal to turn against Bahá'u'lláh and plot against him. He is presented as having been an endless mischief-maker motivated by envy. Azal gave him the Báb's second wife in marriage, an act regarded by others as shameful (*see* Báb, family of). The Ottomans sent him into exile with the Bahá'ís in Akka, presumably to act as a spy. He created numerous difficulties for the exiles, and was one of those murdered by a group of Bahá'ís in the city (January 1872), an action severely condemned by Bahá'u'lláh. *BKG* 128, 158, 184, 227, 248, 252, 317, 322–6, 418; *GPB* 112–13, 125, 164–9, 189–90.

Muḥammad Muṣṭafá al-Baghdádí, Mírzá (1837/8–1910)

Eminent Arab Bahá'í. His father was Shaykh Muḥammad ash-Shibl. He became a devoted follower of Bahá'u'lláh whilst still a boy, and later one of the leading Iraqi Bahá'ís. In the late 1870s he moved to Beirut where he served as Bahá'u'lláh's representative, responsible for the movement of Bahá'í pilgrims. He was also involved in the movement of the Báb's remains to Akka. Shoghi Effendi named him as one of the APOSTLES OF BAHÁ'U'LLÁH. *EB* 270.

Muḥammad-Qulí, Mírzá

(d. 1910)

Bahá'u'lláh's faithful half-brother and companion in exile. He was the only son of his father's third concubine, and greatly devoted to Bahá'u'lláh. After being freed from captivity in Akka he and his family eventually settled near the Sea of Galilee. 'Abdu'l-Bahá referred to him as his 'illustrious uncle' and 'affectionate comforter', and gave his descendants the right to use the family name 'Bahá'í'. Land belonging to his family was exchanged for extra land at BAHJÍ (1952). Ruhe 207–9.

Mírzá Muḥammad-Qulí, half-brother of Bahá'u'lláh

(Muḥammad-)Riḍá Muḥammad-Ábádí, Mullá

(*c.*1814–97)

Eminent Iranian Bahá'í from the province of Yazd. Of clerical background, he was eloquent and outspoken in his defence of the Bahá'í Faith, leading to a number of imprisonments and beatings which he endured with great forbearance (including cleaning his teeth whilst being bastinadoed!). He was one of the Bahá'ís arrested in the aftermath of the assassination of NÁṢIRU'D-DÍN SHÁH, and died subsequently in prison. He appears to have been posthumously named a HAND OF THE CAUSE by 'Abdu'l-Bahá (as 'Shaykh Riḍá Yazdí'). *EB* 98–111; Harper 21–7; *MF* 5; *RB1*: 84–91; *RB4*: 286n.

Muḥammad Sháh (1807–48)

Shah of Iran, 1834–48. Grandson of Fatḥ 'Alí Sháh. The Bábí movement originated during his reign, and the Báb appealed to him to promote his cause, promising him great victories if he did so. The shah appears to have been sympathetic towards the Báb for a while, perhaps in part because of the attitude of MANÚCHIHR KHÁN. He was discouraged by his chief minister and spiritual adviser, Ḥájí Mírzá ÁQÁSÍ, however, and acquiesced in the decisions to imprison the Báb in Azerbaiján and try him in TABRÍZ. The Báb subsequently consigned him to hell. Shoghi Effendi regarded him as bigoted and vacillating (*GPB* 4, 82). Bahá'u'lláh condemned him both for his order of banishment against the Báb and his murder of Mírzá Abu'l-Qásim Faráhán *Qá'im Maqám* (1835), his first chief minister, and friend and patron of Bahá'u'lláh's father, Mírzá 'ABBÁS (*TB* 65). *ARR*. (*See also* IRAN; QÁJÁRS.)

Muḥammad ash-Shibl, Shaykh (d. 1850)

Eminent Arab Bábí, born into a well-known clerical family in Najaf. Sayyid KÁẒIM RASHTÍ's personal representative in Baghdad, he became one of the first Shaykhí leaders to accept the claims of the Báb and one of the chief supporters of Ṭáhirih, accompanying her to Iran. He was the father of Muḥammad Muṣṭafá al-Baghdádí.

Muḥammad-Taqí, Ḥájí Mírzá, *Vakílu'd-dawlih* (1830/1–1909)

Prominent Iranian Bahá'í. He was born in Shíráz. His father was the Báb's maternal uncle, Ḥájí Sayyid Muḥammad. He became a leading merchant in Yazd and the Russian consular agent for the town, thus coming to be known as *Vakílu'd-dawlih* ('Representative of the Government'). In 1909, at 'Abdu'l-Bahá's request, he went to Ashkhabad to supervise the construction of the *Mashriqu'l-Adhkár.* He also provided the major part of the necessary funding. Shoghi Effendi named him as one of the Apostles of Bahá'u'lláh. EB 266–8.

Muḥammad-Taqí Baraghání, Ḥájí Mullá (d. 1847)

Prominent cleric in Qazvín. He was posthumously called the 'Third Martyr' in Shí'í literature. He was the uncle of Ṭáhirih. His accusation that Shaykh Aḥmad's views were un-Islamic (1822) began the process by which Shaykhism came to be regarded as a heterodox Shí'í sect. He was one of the clerics who pressured Fatḥ-'Alí Sháh into the disastrous second Russo-Iranian war (1826–8). Vehement in his opposition to both Shaykhism and Bábism, he encouraged the persecution of both groups, prompting his murder by a Shaykhí with Bábí sympathies in September or October 1847. This event marked a turning point in the history of Bábism. Although the murderer claimed to have been acting alone, the Bábí group in Qazvín as a whole was accused of complicity, and many were arrested, of whom one was executed (Shaykh Ṣáliḥ, regarded as the first Bábí martyr in Iran) and others done to death. Nationally, the Bábís were henceforth seen as dangerous heretics (*see* Bábí radicalism). *ARR* 296–7, 317–23; Momen, *Shi'i Islam* 136, 138; Nabil 273–83; *TJ* 274–81; *TN* 197–8.

Muḥammad-Taqí Iṣfáhání, Shaykh, Áqá Najafí

(the 'Son of the Wolf')

See 'Wolf'.

Muḥammad Zarandí, Mullá

See Nabíl-i-A'ẓam.

Mühlschlegel, Adelbert

(1897–1980)

German Hand of the Cause of Protestant background. He was introduced to the Bahá'í Faith by his mother and became a Bahá'í in 1920. He was active in promoting the Faith in Germany, including translating Bahá'í literature, and serving as a member of the national assembly (1924–37, 1946–59). He was appointed a Hand of the Cause by Shoghi Effendi in February 1952. He later travelled extensively, visiting Bahá'ís in various parts of the world. A medical doctor, he was given the responsibility of preparing the body of Shoghi Effendi for burial (1957). His first wife, Herma Weidle (m. 1926), died in 1964. In 1977 he and his second wife, Ursula Kohler, became Bahá'í pioneers to Greece. He died in Athens. *BW18*: 611–13; Harper 372–83.

mujtahid

High-ranking Shí'í cleric; one who has been recognized as being capable of exercising *ijtihád* (making independent judgments in religious law on the basis of reason and the principles of jurisprudence). This recognition is gained from an established *mujtahid* who issues the new *mujtahid* with a testimonial certificate (*ijáza*). There were relatively few *mujtahids* until the second half of the 19th century. Momen, *Shi'i Islam* 186–8, 202–5. (*See also* 'ulamá.)

Munírih Khánum (1847–1938)

Wife of ʻAbdu'l-Bahá. Originally named Fáṭimih, the name Munírih ('Illumined') was given to her by Bahá'u'lláh. Her father was Mírzá Muḥammad-ʻAlí Nahrí, a member of a prominent Iṣfáhání merchant family and uncle of the KING AND BELOVED OF MARTYRS. According to the Bahá'í account, her parents had been childless until given a portion of the Báb's food to eat. Widowed shortly after her marriage to one of her cousins, she was chosen to marry ʻAbdu'l-Bahá by Bahá'u'lláh, who arranged for her to be brought to Akka. The marriage took place on 8 March 1873. Four children (daughters) survived childhood. She was buried in the Monument Garden close to the Shrine of the Báb (*see* HAIFA). *BKG* 342–8; Munírih Khánum; *RB2*: 202–9.

Munírih Khánum, wife of 'Abdu'l Bahá

Músá, Mírzá (d. 1887)

Also known as Áqáy-i-Kalím, Bahá'u'lláh's younger full brother, aide and companion-in-exile. According to Bahá'u'lláh he was one of only two people who 'were adequately informed' regarding the origins of the Faith. He acted as head of household during Bahá'u'lláh's withdrawal to Kurdistan (1854–6). He was named as one of the APOSTLES OF BAHÁ'U'LLÁH. *BKG*; *GPB* 108.

Mírzá Músá, brother of Bahá'u'lláh

music

In the Islamic world melodious chanting of the Quran is highly regarded, but it is differentiated from music. Music itself commonly occupies an ambiguous role, many devout Muslims regarding it as satanic in nature, and condemning listening to it. By contrast, whilst Bahá'u'lláh praised the chanting of sacred verses, he also made it lawful for his followers to listen to music. He warned them, however, to ensure that listening to it did not cause them 'to overstep the bounds of propriety and dignity'. Expressing a view similar to that of many Sufis, he stated that music should be a ladder for their souls, lifting them up to heavenly realms, and not 'wings to self and passion'. Similarly, ʻAbdu'l-Bahá described singing and music as 'spiritual food' and as a means of uplifting the despondent. Music is a 'praiseworthy science' and should be used as an aspect of prayer to inflame the hearts 'with the fire of the love of God'. Both its promise and its danger lies in its emotional impact: it can increase the existing emotional state, both for good and for ill (*KA* 38 k51, 201 n79; *CC2*: 73–82; *LG* 410–13; Caton, 'Bahá'í influences'). There is no distinctive Bahá'í style of music, but music features prominently in the life of some Bahá'í communities, and, as with the ARTS in general, there have been a number of musicians who as Bahá'ís have found inspiration in their faith. The range of music produced by Bahá'ís is extremely diverse, reflecting different cultural and musical traditions. Amongst the Iranian Bahá'ís there have been a number of well-known musicians and singers, in addition to the general use of traditional chanting styles for Bahá'í prayers and sacred verse. In the West a distinctive Bahá'í hymnody developed in the United States at the beginning of the century, but was abandoned by the 1940s (Armstrong-Ingram, *Music, Devotions*). Music again became an important part of Western Bahá'í life with the large-scale influxes of youth and African-American converts from the late 1960s (*see* EXPANSION). Indigenous musical traditions have been important in the development of a number of 'Third World' Bahá'í communities, including the 'Bahá'í *Bhajans*' of India (Garlington, 'Bahá'í *bhajans*'), and composers and singing groups in several parts of Africa and Andean America. Recently a number of Bahá'í choirs and music groups have been formed in various parts of the world, commonly for the purpose of promoting the Faith. One South American group, El Viento Canta, has become particularly well known amongst Bahá'ís, and has toured widely in Europe, Asia and Africa, as well as in the Americas. In Africa, national or regional Bahá'í music festivals have been held in a number of countries. Some impression of the range of music inspired by the Faith can be gained from the recording of the music at the 1992 Bahá'í World Congress in New York. Of contemporary musicians who are Bahá'ís, the best known was the jazz trumpeter Dizzy GILLESPIE. Others of note include the American pop duo of the 1970s Jimmy Seals and Dash Crofts; the country music performer Dan Seals; the Norwegian contemporary classical composer Lasse Thoresen; the Tajik composer Tolibkhan Shakhidi; and the Iranian singers Ahdieh and Aqilí. *BWNS* 1994–5: 250–1, 262–9.

mysticism

There is no distinctive school of Bahá'í mysticism, but Shoghi Effendi affirmed that the 'core of religious faith' was 'that mystic feeling which unites man with God'. This was a state of 'spiritual communion' – a 'sense of spirituality' – and could be brought about and maintained through MEDITATION and PRAYER. This should have practical effect, coming nearer to God giving the believer greater strength to develop his or her good SPIRITUAL QUALITIES and overcome moral weaknesses. The purpose of religion is to change actions and character and not just thoughts (*CC2*: 238 no. 1762; *LG* 505–7 nos. 1701, 1704, 1709). (*See also* SPIRITUAL PATH; SUFISM.)

N

Nabíl-i-Akbar (1829–92)

Mullá Muḥammad Qá'iní, prominent Iranian Bahá'í. He was born into a clerical family and, in addition to the customary Islamic sciences, he studied with the philosopher Ḥájí Mullá Hádí Sabzivárí (1797/8–1878). He became one of the foremost students of the eminent Shaykh Murtaḍá Anṣárí (1801/2–64/5), and received an *ijázih* from him, giving Qá'iní the rank of *MUJTAHID* (*see* 'ULAMÁ). He became a Bábí in the early 1850s and later a Bahá'í. He was imprisoned a number of times in Iran for his Bahá'í activities and eventually moved to Ashkhabad. He died in Bukhara. He met Bahá'u'lláh on several occasions and was the recipient of the *Lawḥ-i-* ḤIKMAT. 'Abdu'l-Bahá named him posthumously as a HAND OF THE CAUSE and Shoghi Effendi designated him as one of the APOSTLES OF BAHÁ'U'LLÁH. *EB* 112–15; *MF* 1–5.

Nabíl-i-A'ẓam (1831–92)

Mullá Muḥammad Zarandí, prominent Iranian Bahá'í. Of humble origins – he was a shepherd – Nabíl became a Bábí in about 1847, later becoming one of those who transcribed and distributed the Báb's writings. In the early 1850s he put forward claims to leadership of the Bábís on the basis of his receipt of divine inspiration, but withdrew this claim after meeting Bahá'u'lláh in Baghdad and giving him his allegiance. After Bahá'u'lláh moved to Edirne he dispatched Nabíl to visit the Iranian Bábís to announce his open claim to be HE WHOM GOD SHALL MAKE MANIFEST, and also on one occasion to be the first to perform the newly revealed PILGRIMAGE rituals to the House of the Báb in Shíráz and the House of Bahá'u'lláh in Baghdad. He eventually joined the companions of Bahá'u'lláh in Akka. He was so overcome with grief after Bahá'u'lláh's passing that he drowned himself in the

Nabíl-i-Azam, Iranian poet and chronicler

sea. He was renowned as a poet, but is best known to English readers as the author of the historical narrative of the Bábí period which Shoghi Effendi translated as *DAWN-BREAKERS*. Shoghi Effendi named him as one of the APOSTLES OF BAHÁ'U'LLÁH. *EB* 268–70.

Nabíl's Narrative

See DAWN-BREAKERS.

Names, Book of (Ar.: *Kitábu'l-asmá'*)

Late work of the Báb, composed during the period of his imprisonment in CHIHRÍQ. Much of it consists of 'lengthy variations of invocations of the names of God'. Some selected passages have been translated into English (Báb, *Selections* 129–49). *McS* 91–2.

Napoleon III (1808–73)

French emperor, 1852–70. His rule ended following the devastating French defeat in the Franco-Prussian War of 1870–1. Bahá'u'lláh wrote to him twice. The first letter was written towards the end of the stay in Edirne (c.1868). In it Bahá'u'lláh complained of his own sufferings, and praised Napoleon's claims to be the avenger of the oppressed and a succourer of the helpless. The emperor did not reply, but is reported to have flung down the letter, saying: 'If this man [Bahá'u'lláh] is God, I am two gods.' His minister, however, wrote a sympathetic reply to Bahá'u'lláh, offering assistance. Bahá'u'lláh then sent a second letter to the emperor (1869), in which he proclaimed his divine mission and called upon him to arise to serve God and help his cause. Napoleon's sincerity had been found wanting, however, and he had cast Bahá'u'lláh's letter ('the Book of God') behind his back. For this his kingdom would be thrown into confusion and his empire pass from his hands. He could make amends for his actions; only thus would France be spared the commotions that would otherwise seize it. Abasement was hastening after him, and his pomp would not endure. Earthly treasure and dominion would perish, so why should they be made a cause of exultation. The letter was included in the *Súratu'-l-Haykal* (*see* BAHÁ'U'LLÁH, WRITINGS OF), and widely distributed amongst the Bahá'ís of Iran, Napoleon's subsequent unexpected and humiliating downfall being seen as an instance of DIVINE JUDGEMENT. The letter also contains an address to Christian monks (*see* MONASTICISM); counsels to the Bahá'ís regarding TEACHING; and statements regarding Bahá'í HOLY DAYS and FASTING. *ESW* 45–56; *GPB* 173, 207, 225–6; *PDC* 28–30, 50–3; *SAQ* 32–3; *RB3*: 110–15.

Náṣiru'd-dín Sháh (1831–96)

Shah of Iran, 1848–96. He was the son of MUḤAMMAD SHÁH, and crown prince during his father's lifetime. He was appointed governor of Azerbaiján in January 1848 and presided over the Báb's trial in Tabríz. He acceded to the throne following his father's death (September 1848), arriving in Tehran on 19 October. He was assassinated on 1 May 1896 on the eve of the jubilee celebrations to mark fifty (lunar) years of his reign. The assassin was at first suspected of being a 'Bábí', but was then discovered to be a follower of JAMÁLU'D-DÍN 'AL-AFGHÁNÍ'. During his reign the Báb was executed – for Shoghi Effendi, 'the most heinous crime in history' (*PDC* 69); an attempt was made on the shah's life by men linked to AẒÍM's radical Bábí faction (15 August 1852); thousands of Bábís were killed; Bahá'u'lláh imprisoned and exiled; and extensive persecution of Bahá'ís began. Bahá'u'lláh wrote to him in the *Lawḥ-i-SULṬÁN* (Tablet of the King), asking that he treat the Bahá'ís with justice. Persecution continued, however, and Bahá'u'lláh's message-bearer was himself tortured and

Náṣiru'd-din Sháh, Shah of Iran from 1848 until 1896

killed. Bahá'u'lláh subsequently denounced the shah as the 'Prince of Oppressors', who would soon be made 'an object-lesson for the world'. Shoghi Effendi characterized him as a vain and savage despot, whose reign had been one of 'chaos, bankruptcy and oppression' (*GPB* 225; *PDC* 40–3, 66–70). Amanat, *Pivot of the Universe*.

nationalism

Bahá'u'lláh's vision of the future 'Most Great PEACE' is one of WORLD UNITY in which love for the whole world is exalted over that for country. 'Abdu'l-Bahá stated that all national boundaries are artificial human creations, and condemned those nationalistic PREJUDICES that lead to bloodshed between peoples. In reality, the whole earth is one native land, and anyone should be able to live wherever they choose (*SWAB* 300). Shoghi Effendi commented that whilst calling for a wider conception of world citizenship, the Bahá'í Faith is not opposed to an intelligent patriotism in which the individual feels a sense of loyalty and duty towards the nation. It is extremist nationalism which deifies the state and exalts the nation above humanity as a whole that is to be condemned (it is one of the three 'false gods' of SECULARISM). In a world of interdependent parts, particularistic concerns have to be subordinate to the interests of humanity as a whole (*PDC* 117–18, 126–7).

national spiritual assemblies

See ASSEMBLIES.

Navváb (1820–86)

Title of Ásíyih Khánum, first wife of Bahá'u'lláh (m. 1835), named the 'Most Exalted Leaf' by him, and declared to be his 'perpetual consort in all the worlds of God'. She was the daughter of Mírzá Ismá'il-i-Vazír. She gave birth to seven children, three of whom survived childhood: 'ABDU'L-BAHÁ, BAHIYYIH KHÁNUM and Mírzá MIHDÍ. She remained in Akka with 'Abdu'l-Bahá after Bahá'u'lláh moved to BAHJÍ. Initially buried in Akka, her remains were later reinterred close to the Shrine of the Báb by Shoghi Effendi (*see* HAIFA). *GPB* 108, 348; *TCB* 118–21.

Naw-Rúz (Pers., 'New Day')

The Bábí, Bahá'í, Iranian and Zoroastrian New Year. It occurs on the first day of the spring equinox in the northern hemisphere, which is normally 21 March, but may sometimes occur on the twentieth or twenty-second. At present Bahá'ís in the Middle East celebrate it on the equinox, but those elsewhere always celebrate it on the twenty-first. It is the first day of the Bahá'í year from which most other dates in the Bahá'í CALENDAR are set, and also marks the end of the FASTING period. As the first day of the month of Bahá it is specially consecrated, being the day on which 'the breath of life is wafted over all created things' (*KA* 60). It is one of the HOLY DAYS on which work is to be suspended. It is marked by prayers and joyous celebration. Many Bahá'ís exchange greeting cards at this time, whilst those of Iranian background often follow some of the traditional Iranian customs associated with the festival (e.g. growing a dish of sprouting green lentils or beans). These are not official Bahá'í customs, however. *KA* 25 k16, 60 k111, 118 q35, 177–8 n26, 225 n139; Forghani 15–23; Walbridge, *Sacred* 213–16.

Nayríz (1872 pop. est. 3,500)

Small town in southern Iran. It was the site of armed conflict between Bábís under Sayyid Yahyá Darábí (VAḤÍD) and provincial troops. Vaḥíd arrived in Nayríz on 27 May 1850. Himself a local notable and religious leader in the Chinár Súkhtih quarter, he soon converted a large number of the townspeople, perhaps 1,500 in all. Vaḥíd's presence exacerbated existing tensions. An armed struggle developed, in which Vaḥíd and some of his followers withdrew to a nearby fort, where they successfully resisted attacks by forces of the town governor, Ḥájí Zaynu'l-'Ábidín Khán, and by subsequent reinforcements. Responding to a truce offer, Vaḥíd later surrendered to the government forces (17 June), and instructed his followers to abandon their positions. Vaḥíd and many of his companions were then killed, and the 'Bábí quarter' of the town plundered. In revenge, some of the Bábís later killed the governor (26 March 1853), his replacement in turn arresting suspected Bábís and seizing their property. This sparked off a second conflict, with a large group of Bábís retiring to a nearby mountain where they were able to resist troops sent against them until November 1853. A massacre of suspected Bábís followed, and several hundred of the women were enslaved. An active Bahá'í community subsequently developed, itself subject to persecutions. *MBBR* 109–12,147–51, 465, 470; Momen, 'Social basis', 167–9; *McS* 163; Nabil 475–99, 642–5; *TJ* 117–31, 370–1, 415–6; *TN* 183–4, 256–61. (*See also* BÁBÍ RADICALISM.)

newspapers and journalism

Bahá'u'lláh noted the potency of 'swiftly-appearing newspapers'. They are a 'mirror of the world' and possessed of 'hearing, sight and speech'. Journalists should be 'purged from the promptings of evil passions' and be just in what they write, first enquiring into situations as much as possible and ascertaining the facts. Truthfulness and fair speech illumine KNOWLEDGE (*TB* 39–40).

Nicolas, A.L.M. (1864–1939)

French consular official in Iran and orientalist. Born in Iran and a fluent Persian speaker, he made a number of major contributions to the study of the Bábí religion (*see* BÁBÍ AND BAHÁ'Í STUDIES). *MBBR* 36–40.

nineteen day feast

See FEAST, NINETEEN DAY.

Noah

Biblical patriarch and Quranic prophet recognized by Bahá'ís (*KI* 5–6). Shoghi Effendi regarded the story of Noah's Ark and the Flood as symbolic (*LG* 508 no. 1716). Bahá'u'lláh stated that God would soon sail his own Ark on Mount CARMEL, a prophecy seen as foretelling the establishment of the institutions of the BAHÁ'Í WORLD CENTRE.

nuclear power

In what modern Bahá'ís commonly take to be a prophecy of the discovery of nuclear power, Bahá'u'lláh referred to 'astonishing things' which were 'capable of changing the whole atmosphere' and the contamination of which would be lethal (*TB* 69). Similarly, 'Abdu'l-Bahá referred to a stupendous force, as yet undiscovered (1911), which had the capacity to destroy the whole planet if utilized by a materialistic rather than spiritual civilization (Blomfield 183–4). Goodall and Cooper 50–51; Mathews 86–7.

numbers

The Báb emphasized the importance of the 'sciences' of numbers and letters, utilizing the traditional *ABJAD* system of letter–number equivalence to express religious concepts. Thus the importance attached to the ubiquitous number 19, which represented both '[divine] unity' (*wáḥid*) and 'absolute being' (*wujúd*), as well as comprising the number of letters in the Islamic formula, *Bismi'lláh ar-raḥmán ar-raḥím* ('In the name of God, the Merciful, the Compassionate') used before the commencement of any action. Various aspects of the Bábí religion were accordingly structured in units of 19, including the circle of the Báb's first eighteen disciples, the LETTERS OF THE LIVING (*Ḥurúfu'l-Ḥayy*, with *ḥayy* =18), who together with 'the One pervading the numbers' (i.e. the Báb), constituted the first 'unity' (*wáḥid*) of his religion; and the nineteen months of nineteen days of his new CALENDAR, and its cycles of nineteen years. Multiples of 19 were also given significance, particularly 361 (19 × 19, =*kullu-shay'*, 'all things'), and 95 (5 × 19). This emphasis on 19 has been continued into the Bahá'í religion (e.g. in the structure of *ḤUQÚQU'LLÁH* payments), but to a more limited extent. The number 9, equivalent to the word *Bahá*, is also given significance, as in the number of members on each spiritual assembly; the number of sides of a Bahá'í House of Worship (*see* MASHRIQU'L-ADHKÁR); and the number of recognized world RELIGIONS. As the highest single number, 9 is regarded as symbolizing perfection, unity and comprehensiveness. The importance of the number 12 in Judaism, Christianity and Shí'í Islam is noted (twelve tribes, twelve disciples, twelve IMÁMS). The idea that there are lucky or unlucky numbers is explicitly rejected. Browne, *Selections* 225–9; *LG* 414–16; MacEoin, 'Hierarchy' 109–21.

Núrí family

The family of Bahá'u'lláh's father, Mírzá 'ABBÁS NÚRÍ (Mírzá Buzurg; d. 1839), and by extension of Bahá'u'lláh and 'Abdu'l-Bahá. A family tree is given in *BW5* facing p. 205.

THE FAMILY OF 'ABBÁS NÚRÍ

'Abbás had four wives and three concubines, by whom he had a total of fifteen children, twelve of whom survived him. Bahá'u'lláh was the third child by the second wife, Khadíjih; Ṣubḥ-i-AZAL was the only child by the first concubine. Some of the siblings became Bahá'ís, some Azalis, others remained Muslims. Bahá'u'lláh's own siblings also included three children by his mother's first marriage. His companions-in-exile included his younger full brother, Mírzá MÚSÁ, and a half-brother, Mírzá Muḥammad-Qulí. The family was well connected by marriage to other high-ranking members of Iranian society, including Mírzá Áqá Khán Núrí, the second of Naṣiru'd-dín Sháh's chief ministers. *BKG* 9–18; *EB* 339–41.

THE FAMILY OF BAHÁ'U'LLÁH

Bahá'u'lláh married three wives, and had eight children who survived childhood. The first marriage, to Ásíyih Khánum (NAVVÁB) (1820–86), was in 1835, when Bahá'u'lláh was almost eighteen (solar years). Seven children were born of the marriage, but only three survived to adulthood: 'Abbás ('ABDU'L-BAHÁ; 1844–1921), Fáṭimih

(Bahiyyih Khánum; 1846–1932), and Mihdí (1848–70). The second marriage, in 1849, was to Fáṭimih Khánum, '*Mahd-i-'Ulyá*' (1828–1904), one of Bahá'u'lláh's cousins. There were six children, of whom four survived: a daughter, Ṣamadiyyih (b. 1856/7), and three sons, Muḥammad-'Alí (1853/4–1937), Ḍíyá'u'lláh (1864–98) and Badí'u'lláh (1867–1950). The third marriage was to Gawhar Khánum, the sister of Mírzá Mihdí Kashání. The marriage occurred in Baghdad, but the actual date is unknown. Unlike the other wives, Gawhar remained in Baghdad after Bahá'u'lláh's departure, only rejoining him after his exile to Akka. She had only one child, a daughter, Furúghiyyih. Six of the children married – to relatives of prominent Bahá'ís, including in two cases to the offspring of Bahá'u'lláh's brother, Mírzá Musá. There were fifteen grandchildren. Bahiyyih chose to remain unmarried, whilst Mihdí died in his youth. Apart from 'Abdu'l-Bahá's own immediate family, the other family members followed Muḥammad-'Alí in his rejection of 'Abdu'l-Bahá's leadership after Bahá'u'lláh's death, and were declared Covenant-breakers. *TCB* 117–18.

THE FAMILY OF 'ABDU'L-BAHÁ

'Abdu'l-Bahá had one wife, Munírih Khánum, whom he married on 8 March 1873. Nine children were born to the couple, but five died in childhood (two boys and three girls). Four daughters survived. Their husbands and children were as follows:

(1) The eldest, Ḍiyá'iyyih (d. 1951), m. Mírzá Hádí Shírází Afnán (d. 1955) in 1313/1895. Five children (later surnamed Rabbání): Shoghi Effendi (eldest son); Rúḥangíz; Mihranghíz; Ḥusayn; and Riyáḍ.

(2) Ṭúbá (1880–1959), m. Mírzá Muḥsin Afnán (1863–1927). Four children (surnamed Afnán): Rúḥí (1899–1971); Thurayyá; Suhayl; and Fu'ád (d. 1943).

(3) Rúḥá, m. Mírzá Jalál Iṣfáhání, son of Mírzá Muḥammad Ḥasan, the King of Martyrs. Four children (surnamed Shahíd (martyr)): Maryam; Muníb; Zahrá; and Ḥasan.

(4) Munavvar (d. 1971), m. Mírzá Aḥmad, son of Mírzá 'Abdu'r-Raḥím Yazdí. No children.

Six of the children married relatives – following the norms of many upper-class Middle Eastern families. Four of these marriages were with descendants of Bahá'u'lláh's daughter Furúghiyyih who were declared Covenant-breakers, a major factor leading Shoghi Effendi to ultimately expel the majority of his immediate relatives from the Faith.

O

Ode of the Dove
(Ar.: *al-Qaṣída al-Warqá'iyyah*)

Arabic poem of Bahá'u'lláh composed whilst he was in Sulaymániyyih in Iraqi Kurdistan (1854–6). It was composed in the same style as Ibnu'l-Fáriḍ's 'Ode Rhyming in T', the *Tá'iyyah*, a 13th-century Sufi classic. The poem takes the form of a dialogue between Bahá'u'lláh and the MAID OF HEAVEN, in which Bahá'u'lláh refers to his mystical experience in the SÍYÁH-CHÁL, where, having died to his own self, he had ascended to meet God and been entrusted with a divine mission. Cole, 'Bahá'u'lláh and the Naqshbandí Sufis'; *RB1*: 62–4.

Olinga, Enoch (1926–79)

The only black African HAND OF THE CAUSE. Olinga was a Christian Ugandan of the Teso tribe. He became a Bahá'í in 1952 in Kampala, and shortly afterwards returned to his home district to teach the Faith. In 1953 he was the first Bahá'í PIONEER to British Cameroon, and was named as KNIGHT OF BAHA'U'LLAH for that territory. In 1956 he was elected as chairman of the newly formed Regional Spiritual Assembly for North-West Africa, and in 1957 became the first of the new African Bahá'ís to make the pilgrimage to the BAHÁ'Í WORLD CENTRE. Shoghi Effendi named him as 'Father of Victories' (*Abu'l-Futúḥ*) for his services to the Faith, and in October 1957 appointed him as a Hand of the Cause: at thirty-one he was the youngest of those appointed. Extensive world-wide travels followed. He served as a rallying point for the Ugandan Bahá'ís during the troubled 1977–9 period. He, his wife and three of his children were murdered on 16 September 1979 by unknown assailants. *BW18*: 618–35; Harper 462–72.

Enoch Olinga, prominent Ugandan Bahá'í and Hand of the Cause

One Thousand Verses, Tablet of (Pers.: *Lawḥ-i-Hizár Baytí*)

Tablet of 'Abdu'l-Bahá written in 1315/1897–8, and addressed to Jalíl-i-Khú'í. In it, 'Abdu'l-Bahá emphasized the importance of the COVENANT as the means of preserving Bahá'í unity, and described the events during and following the passing of Bahá'u'lláh relating to the emergence of opposition to his own leadership. The tablet includes a condemnation of 'Umar, the second caliph of Islam, whose opposition to the Imám 'Alí 'Abdu'l-Bahá regarded as being the originating cause of both the decline and division of Islam, the sufferings of the IMÁMS and the martyrdom of the Báb. MUḤAMMAD-'ALÍ's actions were compared to those of 'Umar. *TCB* 148–9, 157–8, 215–6, 229.

opposition

Bahá'u'lláh regarded opposition to God's messengers as a recurrent feature of religion, well evidenced by the responses to previous MANIFESTATIONS OF GOD and again in his day. He said that RELIGIOUS LEADERS bore a particular responsibility in this regard, as they often saw a new prophet as a challenge to their established power, or could not reconcile his teachings with their own limited ideas. Opposition to the Bahá'í cause was thus to be expected. The Bahá'ís should not be deterred by it, even when it led to persecution, massacre and banishment. They should put their trust in God, assured of eventual victory. God's purpose could not be thwarted. His signs had encompassed the world. The 'ascendancy of the oppressor' would be temporary and unavailing. God would give those who remained steadfast such power that they would be able to withstand all the forces of the earth. They should teach the Faith with wisdom and tolerance, and if they could, defend it from its opponents in their writings. Those who opposed his Faith were ignorant and heedless (*CC2*: 137–8; *TB* 33, 40–11). 'Abdu'l-Bahá linked opposition to the Faith to its greatness, and predicted that with further progress of the religion in the future opposition to it would increase, whilst Shoghi Effendi maintained that both persecution and criticism by external opponents and the internal attacks mounted by COVENANT-BREAKERS served to strengthen the Bahá'ís' resolve, and separate off the fainthearted (*CC2*: 138–50). (*See also* MARTYRDOM; PERSECUTION.)

organization

See ADMINISTRATION.

Ottomans

Dynastic rulers of what became the most powerful Islamic empire of the modern period. Established in the early 14th century, the empire came to include much of the Middle East, and most of the Balkans and North Africa. The Ottoman rulers were both secular and religious rulers (sultans and caliphs). Their capital, ISTANBUL, became the greatest city of the Muslim world. Although still powerful, the empire was in decay by the 19th century. The impact of the West was by this time considerable, and various attempts at 'reform' and state-strengthening were made, often using Western models. International weakness led to massive losses of territory, however, whilst economic problems, internal political disputes and the rise of nationalist sentiment led to increasing strains. Following the Young Turk Revolution of 1908 a form of constitutional government was adopted. Defeat in World War I led to the loss of the Arab provinces and further war in Turkey itself. The Ottoman empire finally came to an end in 1922 with the abolition of the sultanate (1 November). The CALIPHATE was formally abolished on 3 March 1924. Shaw and Shaw provides a survey of the period.

The sultans during this period were as follows:

ruler	reigned
Abdulmecit I	1839–61
Abdulaziz	1861–76
Murat V	1876
Abdulhamit II	1876–1909
Mehmet V Reşat	1909–18 (first constitutional ruler)
Mehmet VI Vahideddin	1918–22
Abdulmecit II	1922–4 (caliph only)

RELATIONSHIP TO THE BAHÁ'Í FAITH

After his exile to Baghdad Bahá'u'lláh remained in the Ottoman domains for the rest of his life, eventually becoming a Turkish subject. His relations with the Ottoman authorities after his return from Kurdistan (1856) were increasingly cordial, Sultan Abdulmecit I apparently being so impressed by reports he had received about Bahá'u'lláh, that he refused Iranian requests to expel him. The situation changed during the reign of his successor, ABDULAZIZ, with Bahá'u'lláh being first called to Istanbul (1863), and then exiled successively to EDIRNE and AKKA. In various of his writings Bahá'u'lláh reproved Abdulaziz and his ministers, ÂLI PAŞA and FUAT PAŞA, for this action. The situation for the Bahá'ís in Akka varied considerably over the next fifty years, partly depending on the attitude of the local Ottoman authorities. 'Abdu'l-Bahá in particular befriended certain members of the Ottoman elite, including liberal reformers such as Midhat Paşa. Various problems were encountered during the later part of the reign of ABDULHAMIT II, mostly as a consequence of allegations made by MUḤAMMAD-'ALÍ and his associates, and the resultant official commissions of inquiry. This period came to a sudden end following the Young Turk Revolution and the freeing of political prisoners, including 'Abdu'l-Bahá. The World War I period was one of great danger, with the Young Turk leader Cemal Paşa (Jamál Páshá) threatening to have 'Abdu'l-Bahá killed. This danger ceased with the British conquest of Palestine, and the ending of Ottoman rule there in September 1918. Shoghi Effendi regarded the Ottoman rulers as the 'arch-enemy' of the Bahá'í cause, who had inflicted enormous sufferings on both Bahá'u'lláh and 'Abdu'l-Bahá: the survival of the Bahá'í religion in the face of their persecution was remarkable. The calamities ultimately suffered by the empire were seen as evidence of DIVINE JUDGEMENT. *PDC* 63–6; *WOB* 173–8.

P

paradise

See ESCHATOLOGY; HEAVEN.

Parsons, Agnes (1861–1934)

Prominent early American Bahá'í. A member of Washington high society; she became a Bahá'í in 1910 after meeting 'Abdu'l-Bahá in Akka. She did much to support the work of the Persian–American Educational Society (1910) and, at 'Abdu'l-Bahá's suggestion, played the leading role in the succession of race amity conventions which were held in various American cities from 1921 onwards. 'Abdu'l-Bahá stayed in her home during his first visit to Washington, DC. She was a member of both the BAHAI TEMPLE UNITY and new national spiritual assembly for some years. *BW5*: 410–14; Parsons; *WSBR* 76–96.

peace

In his letters to the rulers and elsewhere Bahá'u'lláh appealed for world peace, referring both to a 'Great Peace' (*ṣulḥ-i-akbar*, translated by Shoghi Effendi as the 'Lesser Peace') and a 'Most Great Peace' (*ṣulḥ-i-a'ẓam*). Peace was the chief means for the protection of humanity (*ESW* 30). The Most Great Peace apparently represented the union of all the world's peoples in one common faith. This was the 'sovereign remedy' for the healing of the world, for it was RELIGION that provided the best means for human welfare. This remedy could only be achieved through the power of 'an all-powerful and inspired Physician' (i.e. Bahá'u'lláh). However, as the world's rulers had refused this Most Great Peace (by not accepting Bahá'u'lláh), they should instead strive to establish the 'Lesser Peace', a political peace between nations (*Proclamation* 12–13, 67–8). Conflicts between the nations were the cause of calamity. It was imperative to end them. This would also relieve the people of the world from 'the burden of exorbitant expenditures' (*TB* 89). An 'all-embracing' assembly attended by the world's rulers must be held to establish the foundations of this peace, and the great powers must become reconciled amongst themselves. Thereafter, peace would be upheld by collective security: all other nations acting together in unison against any aggressor nation. This would obviate the need for ARMAMENTS, apart from the limited quantities required to maintain internal order in each country (*ESW* 30–1; *TB* 165). The ministers of the HOUSE OF JUSTICE must also promote this peace (*TB* 89). Those who upheld peace would be greatly blessed (*TB* 23). Ultimately, however, the 'overwhelming corruptions' of the world would only be purged through uniting the peoples of the world in one universal faith and the pursuit of one common aim (*TB* 69).

'Abdu'l-Bahá stated that true civilization would only be established in the world once a number of the world's RULERS had come together 'with firm resolve and clear vision' to establish universal peace. They would have to establish a binding treaty which would delimit all international frontiers, define international relations and restrict the size of each nation's military forces. Breach of this sacred agreement would lead to international intervention against any aggressor nation. Under such circumstances each government would only need a small force in order to maintain internal order, and there would no longer be any need for large stockpiles of armaments or an international arms race. Human energies and resources could instead be devoted to fostering the development and well-being of the world's peoples (*SDC* 64–7). He emphasized that the work towards peace needed to be combined with the achievement of a wider reconstruction of society. Thus, the expansion of democratic forms of government, and in particular the education, enfranchisement and growing political power of WOMEN were of major importance in bringing about international peace (*PUP* 108, 134–5, 167, 375). He also predicted that the excessive costs of military expenditure would ultimately force nations to seek peace; stressed that disarmament should be multilateral (*CC2*: 171, 172); and called on the United States and Canada to take the lead in establishing peace (*PUP* 36–7, 83–4, 318).

Shoghi Effendi reiterated these teachings, distinguishing between the Lesser Peace, to be established by the governments of the world, and the Most Great Peace, to be established by the expansion of the Faith, and characterized by the development of what he termed the 'Bahá'í World Commonwealth' (*see* WORLD ORDER). In 1985 the Universal House of Justice issued its 'peace statement', *The* PROMISE OF WORLD PEACE, a forceful expression of the Bahá'í 'peace programme', addressed to the peoples of the world and widely distributed to world leaders.

CC2: 151–200; *SBBR* 74–7, 140–3; Lee, *Circle of Peace*. (*See also* MILLENARIANISM; UNITED NATIONS; WAR.)

periodicals

A wide range of Bahá'í periodical literature exists. The earliest American periodical was *The Bahai Bulletin* (New York, 1909–10). This was followed by the Chicago-based *Star of the West* (1910–35), which became the premier international journal of Bahá'í news and affairs, until superseded in this role by the American *Bahá'í News* (1924–90). With the development of Bahá'í ADMINISTRATION most national spiritual ASSEMBLIES began to issue their own regular newsletters, generally intended for a specifically Bahá'í readership. Other publications were produced to present Bahá'í views and news to a wider audience, notably the American *World Unity* (1927–35) and *World Order* (1935–49; new series from 1966); the new series of the Australian *Herald of the South* (from 1984); and the BAHÁ'Í INTERNATIONAL COMMUNITY's *One Country* (from 1989). The New York-based *Reality* (1919–29) represented an early and increasingly heterodox endeavour of this type. The main sources of international Bahá'í news are now the *Bahá'í International News Service* (Haifa, from 1967), the *Bahá'í Newsreel* video series (from 1990) and the new series of annual *BAHÁ'Í WORLD* volumes (from 1992). Various local Bahá'í newsletters were produced in Iran at an early date, despite the oppressed conditions under which Bahá'ís often lived. A national newsletter, *Akhbár-i-Amrí*, was also latter produced (from 1922). Following the Islamic revolution (1979) these activities have ceased, but several Persian-language publications have been started in the West, including *Payám-i-Bahá'í* (Paris, from 1979) and *'Andalíb* (Canada, from 1981). Braun, *Reader's Guide* 36–40, 146–8; Collins, *Bibliography* xvii, 164–84; Smith, '*Reality*'.

persecution

Persecution of the Bábí movement began within a year of its inception with the trial of Mullá 'ALÍ BASṬÁMÍ in Baghdad (January 1845) and, by the summer, Bábís had been judicially tortured in Shíráz and the Báb himself arrested and punished. Other attacks on Bábís followed, mostly stemming from the opposition of the Islamic learned ('ULAMÁ), acting as defenders of an Islamic orthodoxy from which the Bábís clearly diverged. The situation changed with the development of BÁBÍ RADICALISM and the armed struggles involving the Bábís, who were thenceforth stigmatized as dangerous revolutionaries whose existence threatened the state, and treated accordingly. Despite Bahá'u'lláh's transformation of the Bábís and his forbidding violent action, persecution of the Bahá'ís of IRAN has continued until the present day. A variety of motivations has been involved, but religious animosity towards the Bahá'ís remains the most constant. Of note has been the emergence of a 'culture of hatred', whereby the Bahá'ís are demonized and dehumanized by their opponents. (*See also* MARTYRDOM; OPPOSITION.)

There have been various instances of persecution of Bahá'ís outside Iran. These include:

THE SOVIET UNION: Following the consolidation of communist power, official persecution of all forms of religion commenced. This included the Bahá'í communities of Soviet Asia (notably ASHKHABAD), which were effectively destroyed in the late 1930s.

NAZI GERMANY: All Bahá'í activities were banned by order of the Gestapo in 1937, largely because of the Faith's 'international and pacifist teachings'.

EGYPT: Bahá'í activities were banned in 1960, largely because of the location of the BAHÁ'Í WORLD CENTRE in what had become Israel (and the consequent suspicion of Zionist links). The ban was extremely influential in the Arab world, and briefly elsewhere. Other instances reflect similar attitudes, as in most of the communist bloc, and with nationalist and totalitarian opposition to independent religious movements. Nowhere has the same 'culture of hatred' developed against the Bahá'ís as in Iran. *SBBR* 173–4, 185.

philosophy

There are few specific references to philosophy in Bahá'í writings, although both Bahá'u'lláh, and more particularly 'Abdu'l-Bahá, addressed philosophical themes, such as the nature of KNOWLEDGE and existence (*see* HUMAN NATURE; METAPHYSICS), and proofs for the existence of GOD. Their discussions of social life (*see* ETHICS; POLITICS) are presented as statements of religious truth and not philosophical propositions, however. Both praised certain approaches to philosophy over others. Thus 'Abdu'l-Bahá praised 'deistic philosophers' (including Socrates, Plato and Aristotle in this category) as well as those 'moderate' materialistic philosophers whose work had been of service to humanity (Vader 70–1), but condemned philosophical MATERIALISM in general. Similarly, Bahá'u'lláh stated that WISDOM began in the acknowledgement of divine revelation. True philosophy recognized God's majesty, and philosophers should be careful lest their concern with wisdom debarred them from its source. He also regarded most of contemporary Islamic philosophy as derivative from the past, in particular from the ancient Greeks. The essence of what the Greeks had said was in turn derived from the prophets of Israel (*TB* 144–51). In this, Bahá'u'lláh reflected the views of medieval Muslim writers, whose writings he quoted verbatim (Cole, 'Problems of chronology'). There is as yet little explicitly philosophical work incorporating a Bahá'í perspective, although a number of writers do address philosophical themes in their discussions of Bahá'í topics (e.g. Conow; J. and W. Hatcher; Savi).

pilgrimage

The Báb declared his own house in SHÍRÁZ to be a place of pilgrimage, and Bahá'u'lláh appointed both the Shíráz House and his own former house in BAGHDAD to be places of pilgrimage, prescribing specific rites of visitation in two *Súrihs of Ḥajj*. All male Bahá'ís who were able to should seek to visit one of these two sacred sites. Women were exempted from this obligation (but are allowed to visit these sites if they wish). 'Abdu'l-Bahá declared Bahá'u'lláh's Shrine at BAHJÍ to be a third centre of pilgrimage, and declared visiting it a religious obligation for those who were able. There are no required rituals for such visits.

Pilgrimage to the Baghdad House became impossible following its seizure by local Shí'is in the 1920s, and the Shíráz House was destroyed in the aftermath of the Islamic Revolution in Iran, so that the SHRINES AND HOLY PLACES at the BAHÁ'Í WORLD CENTRE are now the only places of Bahá'í pilgrimage. At present Bahá'ís are able to apply to join organized nine-day pilgrimage groups, during the course of which they visit the Shrines of Bahá'u'lláh and the Báb, and are taken to visit other Bahá'í holy sites. They also commonly attend meetings addressed by members of the Universal House of Justice and International Teaching Centre. The 'pilgrimage season' extends through most of the year except for the summer months, with visits by successive groups of around one hundred Bahá'ís superintended by Bahá'í World Centre staff. Shorter (normally three-day) pilgrimages are also permitted. During the time of 'Abdu'l-Bahá and Shoghi Effendi, the much smaller size of the pilgrimage groups and the extended stays of many of the pilgrims gave these visits a religious intensity which their modern successors perhaps lack. Pilgrimage is still considered to be of enormous importance, however, both as a means of spiritually regenerating the individual pilgrim and providing the Bahá'í World Centre with an additional channel of contact with Bahá'ís from around the world. Shoghi Effendi described the flow of pilgrims as the 'life-blood' of the World Centre (*ADJ* 4). *KA* 30 k32, 109 q10, 115 q25, 116 q29, 191–2 n54–5, 197 n68; *RB1*: 211–12; *2*: 240; Walbridge, *Sacred* 110–18.

'pilgrims' notes'

Unauthenticated notes taken by Bahá'ís of their pilgrimage experiences in the presence of 'Abdu'l-Bahá and Shoghi Effendi, and in particular of the utterances of the two leaders which they heard. They are effectively the Bahá'í equivalent of Islamic *HADÍTHS*. Both 'Abdu'l-Bahá and Shoghi Effendi were insistent that such notes could have no canonical authority – only authenticated texts were authoritative. Nevertheless, numerous accounts of pilgrimage visits to 'Abdu'l-Bahá have been published, and these undoubtedly exert some influence on popular understandings of the Bahá'í teachings. Shoghi Effendi insisted that notes made of his own remarks were only for the personal use of the pilgrim who had heard them. They might be circulated if they were a source of inspiration, but they should not be printed. They were not official pronouncements, and as recorded were sometimes inaccurate and misleading. *LG* 438–40.

pioneers, pioneering

Bahá'ís who have left their own homes and established their residence in another locality or country to propagate the Bahá'í Faith are considered 'pioneers' (the term is Shoghi Effendi's).

In his *Tablets of the Divine Plan* 'Abdu'l-Bahá called on North American Bahá'ís to propagate the Bahá'í teachings throughout the world. A few responded, but it was only during the first American Seven Year Plan (1937–44) that there was a systematic endeavour to establish the Bahá'í Faith outside North America through the dispatch of pioneers to Latin America. The dispatch of pioneers became an important part of several of the national plans that followed over the next few years, and was greatly emphasized during the international Ten Year Crusade (1953–63), the pioneers of that plan being given the honorific title 'Knights of Bahá'u'lláh'. Pioneering has remained an important part of subsequent plans under the Universal House of Justice (since 1963). The House appointed Continental Pioneer Committees in 1965 to help with the placement of the increasing number of pioneers (402 in that year world-wide) (*MUHJ* 47–50 no. 22).

Bahá'u'lláh praised those who had left their homes to teach his Cause. They would be strengthened by the power of the 'Faithful Spirit', and accompanied by '[a] company of our chosen angels'. Such action was 'the prince of all goodly deeds' (*GWB* 333 no. 157; *MUHJ* 177). 'Abdu'l-Bahá praised the blessings of 'homelessness and adversity in the pathway of God'; called on those who propagated the Faith to be fearless, and to have no thought for themselves; and assured them of divine assistance. They should learn the languages of the places they went to, and be filled with the love of God (*LG* 570; *TDP*). Shoghi Effendi stated that pioneering was the most important Bahá'í activity that anyone could perform, particularly when this was to areas where there were as yet no Bahá'ís. Such pioneers should persevere and not abandon their posts until the Faith was well established in that territory (the example of Marion Jack, who stayed in her pioneer post in the face of tremendous hardship, was lauded). He encouraged them not to congregate in a particular locality but to try to disperse so that they would have more contact with the local population. Ideally they should be self-supporting – earning their own living in their new abode. If they were unable to support themselves, however, they could be assisted from the Bahá'í funds, but this should not be regarded as a permanent arrangement: pioneering was not a job. Those who were unable to pioneer might follow Bahá'u'lláh's injunction to deputize (i.e. subsidize) someone else to do so on their behalf. Pioneers should keep in close contact with the relevant Bahá'í administrative body. *ADJ* 55–7; *LG* 570–81; *MUHJ* 90–2 no. 36, 175–7 no. 86, 420 no. 228, 481–4 no. 279. A number of pioneer stories are given in Vreeland.

Pius IX (1792–1878)

Pope, 1846–78, the longest pontificate in history. He proclaimed the doctrines of the Immaculate Conception of the Virgin Mary (1854) and papal infallibility (1870), and was a staunch advocate of the rights of the papacy and an opponent of liberalism. Bahá'u'lláh wrote to him shortly after his own exile to Akka (which began in 1868), announcing that 'the Lord of Lords' had come down from heaven with grace and justice at his side. Christ's promises had been fulfilled. The pope should not let any name debar him from God, nor dispute as the Pharisees had disputed with Jesus. He should leave his palaces to such as desired them, abandon his kingdom to the kings, and arise to promote God's cause, summoning the

kings to justice and selling all his embellished ornaments so as to expend them in the path of God. The Italian occupation of the papal states in September 1870, in the immediate aftermath of the defeat of NAPOLEON III, finally ended the temporal sovereignty of the papacy, and is regarded by Bahá'ís as further evidence of DIVINE JUDGEMENT.
PDC 30–2, 53–6, *GPB* 227.

plans

Organized campaigns to fulfil specific goals, particularly missionary EXPANSION. They are a significant element in modern Bahá'í activity.

The 'charter' for much of this activity is 'Abdu'l-Bahá's *TABLETS OF THE DIVINE PLAN* (1916–17), addressed to the American and Canadian Bahá'ís, in which he called for a systematic endeavour to teach the Faith throughout the world, naming specific territories to which he wanted Bahá'ís to go, and stressing the need for them to learn the languages of the people they taught and produce relevant literature for distribution. Several individuals responded to this appeal, but the results were at first extremely limited. Instead, under Shoghi Effendi's direction, the Bahá'ís during the 1920s focused their attention on domestic TEACHING campaigns, and building up their system of ADMINISTRATION.

NATIONAL PLANS

Shoghi Effendi began to implement the objectives of 'Abdu'l-Bahá's *Plan* with the first North American Seven Year Plan (1937–44). The Americans had already experimented with two 'Plans of Unified Action' (1926–8; 1931–*c*.3) in their campaign to collect enough money to continue building the Bahá'í House of Worship (*see MASHRIQU'L-ADHKÁR*) at Wilmette. The Seven Year Plan was much more extensive in its objectives, Shoghi Effendi calling on the Bahá'ís to form at least one local spiritual assembly (*see* ASSEMBLIES) in every American state and Canadian province; settle resident Bahá'ís in each Latin American and Caribbean republic; and complete the exterior ornamentation of the Wilmette temple. The success of the plan indicated the value of this approach, and a series of plans was eventually implemented by the other national assemblies extant or newly formed.

INDIA AND BURMA: Six Year (1938–44), Four-and-a-Half Year (January 1946–June 1950) and Nineteen Month (September 1951–April 1953) Plans

BRITISH ISLES: Six (1944–50) and Two (1951–3) Year Plans

UNITED STATES AND CANADA: A second Seven Year Plan (1946–53)

IRAN: Forty-five Month Plan (October 1946–July 1950)

AUSTRALIA AND NEW ZEALAND: Six Year Plan (1947–53)

IRAQ: Three Year Plan (1947–50)

EGYPT AND THE SUDAN: Five Year Plan (1948–53)

GERMANY AND AUSTRIA: Five Year Plan (1948–53)

CANADA: Five Year Plan (1948–53)

CENTRAL AMERICA: One Year Plan (1952–3)

These plans introduced the concept of working to achieve domestic goals to all the national Bahá'í communities, and began the process of establishment of Bahá'í groups and local assemblies in several countries and territories in Europe, South East Asia and Africa. The two-year 'Africa campaign' (1951–3) was of special note, in that it involved collaboration between several national assemblies, and was thus the forerunner of the international plans to come. Also of particular significance was a four-year plan specifically for Iranian Bahá'í women, aimed at helping them to further their education and attain equality with men in Bahá'í administrative work (*BW12*: 65).

INTERNATIONAL PLANS

The culmination of these national endeavours was the Ten Year Crusade (1953–63), an elaborate and ambitious project which aimed to settle Bahá'ís in every significant territory and island group throughout the world; enormously increase the total number of national and local assemblies, Bahá'í centres and range of languages in which there was Bahá'í literature; and secure such 'international' goals as completion of the codification of the *Kitáb-i-Aqdas* and the establishment of a Bahá'í court in Israel as a preliminary to the emergence of the Universal House of Justice. All twelve national spiritual assemblies formed by 1953 participated. The results surpassed expectations, with the beginning of massive growth in a number of communities (*see* EXPANSION). Since its establishment the Universal House of Justice has continued the pattern set by the Ten Year Crusade, with a total of six international plans to date: the Nine (1964–73), Five (1974–9), Seven (1979–86), Six (1986–92), Three (1993–6), and current Four (1996–2000) Year Plans. There has also been a subsidiary two-year plan (1990–2), set to co-ordinate Bahá'í activity in Eastern Europe and the former Soviet Union under the new conditions of religious freedom that followed the collapse of the communist regimes there. The plans have included a wide range of 'expansion goals' (increasing the number of assemblies, localities in which Bahá'ís reside, languages, publishing trusts, properties, etc.; dispatching PIONEERS and travel teachers); PROCLAMATION and the attempt to secure greater PUBLIC RECOGNITION (increasing use of mass media, presenting Bahá'í literature to prominent people and the general public); the organization of international CONFERENCES (to increase the sense of global community amongst the Bahá'ís); the construction of Bahá'í Houses of Worship; the development of qualitative aspects of Bahá'í community life (enhancing the role of WOMEN, fostering Bahá'í FAMILY LIFE, EDUCATION and LITERACY; and increasing the administrative efficiency of assemblies and committees); and BAHÁ'Í WORLD CENTRE goals (institutional developments, new translations of scriptures). Details of the plan goals and achievements are given in the *BAHÁ'Í WORLD* volumes. SBBR 157–62.

poetry

The Bábí leader ṬÁHIRIH remains renowned as a poet, both in Iran and the Indian subcontinent. Among early Bahá'ís who were also well known as poets, we may list Mírzá 'Alí-Muḥammad VARQÁ, ANDALÍB, NABÍL-I-A'ZAM, Áqá Ṣidq-'Alí, Áqá Muḥammad-Ibráhím, Ustád 'Alí-Akbar, and Mírzá Áqá, 'Jináb-i-Muníb'. Of Western Bahá'ís, Izabella GRINEVSKAYA was noted in her day, whilst more recently the American Robert HAYDEN achieved considerable international repute (*BWNS* 1994–5: 246). There have also been many amateur poets, inspired by Bahá'í themes, some of whose work has appeared in *Bahá'í World* and other publications. The best known of these was Roger White (1929–93), several volumes of whose work were published (*Bahá'í Studies Review* 7 (1997): 147–52).

It is a common popular Bahá'í belief that poets such as Shelley (1792–1822) and Wordsworth (1770–1850) were influenced by the spiritual force that came to be embodied in the Bahá'í Faith, and that much 19th-century poetry reflects this emergent 'spirit of the age' (e.g. Townshend, *Christ and Bahá'u'lláh* 56–63).

politics

Bahá'u'lláh and 'Abdu'l-Bahá commented on the ideal nature of GOVERNMENT, and instructed the Bahá'ís to be loyal to established governments (*see* GOVERNMENT, BAHÁ'Í ATTITUDE TOWARDS). Shoghi Effendi insisted that Bahá'ís avoid all involvement in political affairs, including membership in political parties and the making of public comments on current political disputes and personalities. Such involvement is divisive. The Faith is 'non-political', 'supra-national', 'rigidly non-partisan', and 'entirely dissociated' from nationalist and sectional interests. Bahá'ís should love the world's peoples as a whole, and whilst seeking to promote the best interests of their own government and nation should be conscious that in a world of interdependent peoples and nations, 'the advantage of the part' was best reached by 'the advantage of the whole'. They can vote according to the dictates of their own consciences, as long as this does not involve becoming identified with a particular party. The Universal House of Justice has commented that Bahá'ís can become members of neighbourhood councils and the like as long as they neither campaign for office nor become involved in partisanship (*see* Bahá'í ELECTIONS). If a country is a one-party state and party membership is compulsory by law, Bahá'ís can join, but not accept any party offices. They can hold administrative office in government service if this does not entail political involvement. *MUHJ* 125–8 no. 55, 162–6 no. 77, 330–5 no. 173; *LG* 441–51; *WOB* 64–7, 198–9.

Politics, Treatise on

(Per.: *Risáliy-i-Siyásiyyih*)

Essay on GOVERNMENT written by 'Abdu'l-Bahá in 1892/3 and published in Bombay the following year. There is as yet no published English translation. For 'Abdu'l-Bahá government and religion had separate and reciprocal roles. SOCIAL ORDER required effective and just governance, but also the moral discipline provided by religion. The role of religion was to promote morality and not to govern. RELIGIOUS LEADERS should clarify holy law as it related to legislation, but they should not intervene directly in politics. The consequences of such intervention in the past had been disastrous. The authority and legitimacy of secular government should be accepted. The work should be seen in the context of the growing political turmoil in Iran during the 1890s.

polygamy

Under Islamic law a man may marry up to four wives, and in addition may take other women into his household as concubines. In the *Kitáb-i-AQDAS* Bahá'u'lláh restricts the total possible number of wives to two, but adds that having only one wife would be the cause of tranquility for both partners. 'Abdu'l-Bahá states that, as having a second wife is conditional upon treating both wives with justice and equality (cf. Quran 4:3), multiple marriages are not possible in practice. Bahá'í law thus prescribes monogamy. Concubinage and the Shí'í practice of temporary marriage (*mut'a*) are forbidden. Female servants are permitted in a household without the husband having to marry them or having any rights of sexual access. If a new Bahá'í already has more than one marriage partner, then they are not required to divorce them. *KA* 41 k63, 116 q30, 205–7 n89–90.

Given the Bahá'í commitment to gender equality (*see* WOMEN), some Western writers have expressed surprise at examples of early Bahá'í polygyny (e.g. Wilson, *Bahaism*). Thus BAHÁ'U'LLÁH himself had three wives, the BÁB took a second wife when he was in Iṣfáhán, and many of the early Iranian Bahá'ís were also polygamous. Such multiple marriages were in full accord with Islamic law and reflected the social mores of the time, polygyny being common amongst upper-class men in 19th-century Iran (Bahá'u'lláh's father, Mírzá 'Abbás, had four wives and three concubines (*see* NÚRÍ FAMILY)). The *Aqdas* limitation on the number of wives (*c*.1873) and the Bahá'í teachings on gender equality both post-date Bahá'u'lláh's marriages, which were contracted whilst he was in Iran and Iraq. Modern Bahá'ís understand the present Bahá'í insistence on monogamy as being evolutionary in nature, 'Abdu'l-Bahá leading the Bahá'ís away from what had hitherto been a deeply rooted cultural practice. 'Abdu'l-Bahá himself had only one wife, despite the urgings of a number of Bahá'ís for him to take a second (and hence presumably legitimize the practice). (*See also* MARRIAGE.)

prayer

OBLIGATORY PRAYER (*ṢALÁT*)

In the *Kitáb-i-Aqdas*, Bahá'u'lláh prescribes daily ritual prayer as a primary religious obligation for Bahá'ís from the age of fifteen (the 'age of maturity') upwards. Those who are weak from illness or age (over seventy) are exempt. So too are menstruating women, who may instead repeat a specific verse ('Glorified be God, the Lord of Splendour and Beauty') ninety-five times during each twenty-four hour period. The believer may choose each day to say one of three obligatory prayers, two of which are to be said at specific times of the day (a short prayer between noon and sunset; a 'medium' prayer three times: between dawn and noon, noon and sunset, and sunset and two hours after sunset). The third (long) prayer may be said at any time, ideally when in 'a state of humbleness and longing adoration'. Prayer is to be preceded by ritual ABLUTIONS, and made in the direction of the tomb of Bahá'u'lláh at BAHJÍ, which is the Bahá'í *QIBLAH*. Two of the prayers involve ritual movement and prostration (*rak'a*). Prostration may be made on any clean surface. In conditions of insecurity, such as travel, prayer may be omitted, and each missed prayer later compensated for by the repetition of certain verses. The time of prayer may be established by clocks, particularly in high latitudes. Some elements of Bahá'í ritual prayer resemble Islamic *ṣalát*, but the form is distinctively different. So too is the lack of a congregational context: Bahá'í prayer is to be said individually. Together with FASTING obligatory prayer is regarded as a means for the believer to draw closer to God, and as a pillar of divine LAW. It is conducive to humility. *KA* 21 k6, 22–4 k8–10, 12–14, 26 k18, 92–101, 113–14 q21, 124–6 q58–67, 130–1 q81–3, 134 q93, 145–8, 166–74 n3–n22, 176 n25; *LG* 464–8; *PM* nos. 181–3.

Shoghi Effendi encouraged Bahá'ís to avoid rigidity and ritual in their prayers. Such rituals as there are are few, and should be regarded as symbolic: thus the worshipper turning towards the *qiblah* is a physical symbol of turning to Bahá'u'lláh, and the ritual gestures incorporated in two of the obligatory prayers are symbolic of an inner attitude on the part of the worshipper. Those who are uncomfortable making these genuflections should instead use the short prayer in which there are no gestures. *CC2*: 237 no. 1759, 242–3 no. 1780.

PRAYER IN GENERAL

In addition to daily obligatory prayer Bahá'ís are encouraged to pray frequently, both as an individual act of turning to God and in their meetings. There are no set forms for such prayers. The purpose of these prayers is to bring people closer to God and Bahá'u'lláh, to help them to purify their own conduct, and allow them to request divine assistance. They express the individual's love for God and at the same time affect their inner spiritual state. MEDITATION and action are linked to prayer. The more detached the worshipper becomes, the purer and more acceptable are their prayers. Prayer does not have to be necessarily prolonged, but the spirit in which it is offered is important. Individual prayer should be offered in private and when one is free from distractions, such as late at night. Collective prayer – in which individuals usually take it in turn to read, chant, or sing prayers – is encouraged: for example, coming together at dawn for collective prayers, whether as a family or local community (*see* MASHRIQU'L-ADHKAR). Administrative meetings of ASSEMBLIES and committees commonly include prayer, whilst the regular nineteen day FEAST begins with an integral devotional period. *CC2*: 225–43; *LG* 455–63; Hellaby and Hellaby; Walbridge, *Sacred* 45–54.

THE CORPUS OF PRAYERS

There are many prayers in Persian and Arabic, by Bahá'u'lláh and 'Abdu'l-Bahá, and these are widely used. A large number of these have been translated into English. These include prayers to be said on awakening and going to sleep, and during the Bahá'í fast; for travelling, healing, spiritual growth and detachment, protection, forgiveness, assistance and unity; and on behalf of children, parents and spouses. Some of the Báb's prayers have also been translated into English, but as yet few of Shoghi Effendi's. The original words of all these prayers should be used without alteration. Children should be taught to memorize them. Bahá'ís may also use prayers of their own, but these are regarded as less powerful.

PRAYER FOR THE DEAD

Bahá'u'lláh ordained a specific prayer for the dead, based on a similar prayer of the Báb's. This is to be said preceding the interment of any Bahá'í who has reached 'the age of maturity' (fifteen). It is read aloud by one person while the others present stand in silence, and as such is the only Bahá'í congregational prayer. *KA* 22 k8, 23 k12, 101–2, 127 q70, 131 q85, 147–8, 169–70 n10–11, 172–3 n19; *PM* no. 67.

OTHER SPECIAL PRAYERS

Bahá'ís commonly attach importance to three prayers which are regarded as having particular power for those in difficulty or sickness. These are a short prayer of the Báb's, 'The remover of difficulties', and two prayers by Bahá'u'lláh, '*The Tablet of Aḥmad*' and '*The Long Healing Prayer*'. The Islamic 'prayer of the signs', which was said at times of awesome and frightening events (earthquakes, eclipses, etc.) was annulled by Bahá'u'lláh, who substituted in its place a specific verse, the saying of which is optional (*KA* 23 k11, 122 q52, 148, 172 n18).

INVOCATION

Bahá'ís are bidden to recite '*Alláh-u-Abhá*' (God is Most Glorious; *see* GREATEST NAME), ninety-five times each day. *KA* 26 k18, 129 q77, 180 n33.

predestination

See FATE.

prejudice

Bahá'ís are called upon to free themselves of all prejudices in their dealings with those of a different RACE, class or religion. The challenge involved in overcoming such prejudices is great, and higher levels of progress are invariably possible (*ADJ* 18–19). For 'Abdu'l-Bahá the abolition of prejudice was essential for human well-being. Social prejudices – religious, racial, political, economic, patriotic – lead to war and strife. They are a barrier to human progress (*PUP* 181, 316; *SWAB* 299–301). God is not concerned with such ephemeral differences between people, but with the moral worth and spirituality of the individual (*PT* 153–54). Humanity is one race, the world one abode, national barriers arbitrary human creations, and true RELIGION based on love and agreement between people (*PUP* 232, 299–300; *PT* 134, 151–5).

priesthood

The Bahá'í Faith has no priesthood. Its ADMINISTRATION is based on a combination of elected councils (ASSEMBLIES) and individuals who are appointed to provide spiritual guidance and encouragement (Counsellors, Board members) but who are specifically denied any sacramental role or executive power. Bahá'u'lláh praised the pious deeds of Christian priests and monks, but stated that they should now live in the 'open world'; marry and have children if they wished; and be busy with that which would 'profit themselves and others'. The practice of CONFESSION OF SINS to another human being (as to a priest to gain absolution) is forbidden. *KA* 30 k34, 193–4 n58; *TB* 24. (*See also* RELIGIOUS LEADERS.)

principles, Bahá'í

See 'BAHÁ'Í PRINCIPLES'.

proclamation

The endeavour to acquaint all people with the fact and general aims of the Bahá'í Faith. The Universal House of Justice launched a global proclamation campaign in October 1967, following the centenary celebrations of Bahá'u'lláh's proclamatory letters to contemporary RULERS announcing his claims. This campaign involved formal presentations of Bahá'u'lláh's writings to world leaders and other prominent people; large-scale publicity; and a call to Bahá'ís to launch TEACHING programmes designed to reach 'every stratum of human society'. Bahá'ís were counselled to be diligent, wise, dignified and reverent in their proclamation activities. Proclamation has since become a regular part of Bahá'í activities in those countries in which there is religious freedom, with systematic publicity campaigns, and widespread use of mass media. The extensive persecutions suffered by the Bahá'ís in IRAN since 1979, and a second global proclamation campaign started by the House of Justice in 1985 in connection with its statement *The* PROMISE OF WORLD PEACE, have done much to gain the Bahá'ís sympathetic media attention, such that the Faith has now effectively emerged from its former obscurity. *MUHJ* 65 no. 24.22, 106 no. 42.21, 110–11 no. 45, 263 no. 141.9, 487 no. 280.13, 652–4 no. 420.2–3.

progressive revelation

Bahá'í doctrine relating the various recognized world religions as 'different stages in the eternal history and constant evolution of one religion', itself divine and indivisible, and of which the Bahá'í revelation formed an integral part. Bahá'u'lláh's revelation occupied a unique role as it represented the culmination of those of the past (*WOB* 114–19, 166–7). No religion – including the Bahá'í Faith itself – could claim to be the final revelation of God to humanity (*PDC* 112). Revelation was both recurrent and progressive. Each MANIFESTATION OF GOD brought divine teachings appropriate to the spiritual capacity of the people of his day. As such, 'religious truth' is relative to its recipients and not absolute. The prophets proclaimed 'eternal verities' (moral and spiritual truths renewed by each Manifestation), but their message also changed to reflect the particular 'spiritual evolution of human society' at their time of appearance (thus Bahá'u'lláh's message included both eternal moral truths and the call for world unity based on the proclamation of the oneness of humankind; and laws of marriage and criminal punishment varied from one religion to another)

(*Faith* 2–3; *PDC* 112). The cycle of successive divine messengers is like the annual coming of the spring that brings new life to a cold, dead world which has come to neglect the teachings of the previous revelator (*PUP* 106, 115, 126–7, 151, 154, 273–4, 339, 361–70; *SWAB* 51–2). Over time, each religious system has declined as religionists blindly follow tradition rather than the pure teachings of the founder and base their belief on imitation rather than exercising INDEPENDENT INVESTIGATION OF TRUTH (*PUP* 221–2, 443). In the future God will continue to 'send down' his messengers to humanity until 'the end that hath no end', and they will 'unfold' an 'ever-increasing' measure of Divine guidance (*WOB* 116, 118). Bahá'u'lláh was insistent, however, that no further Manifestation would come for at least one thousand years after him (*KA* 32 k37). (*See also* PROPHECY; RELIGIOUS DIVERSITY; SOCIAL EVOLUTION.)

Promise of World Peace

('The Peace Statement')

Statement by the Universal House of Justice dated October 1985 addressed to 'the peoples of the world'. It was issued as part of the Bahá'í activities for the United Nations International Year of World Peace (1986). Formal presentations of the statement were made to world leaders, and hundreds of thousands of copies were distributed worldwide. The House also issued a compilation of Bahá'í writings on PEACE to enable the Bahá'ís to make a more intensive study of the issues involved. The statement insisted on the importance of RELIGION and moral principle in the achievement of peace; appealed to world leaders to convoke the international assembly called for by Bahá'u'lláh; related the establishment of peace to wide-ranging societal changes, including the spread of universal EDUCATION, the emancipation of WOMEN, and the struggle against racism, poverty, and national and religious PREJUDICE; warned of the dangers of materialism, despair and the belief that human beings were intrinsically aggressive; expressed optimism for the long-term future; and noted present 'tentative steps' towards global peace. *MUHJ* 652–4 no. 420, 669 no. 429, 679–80 no. 436, 681–96 no. 438, 700–1 nos. 442–3, 725 no. 456.3.

Promised Day is Come

Book-length letter by Shoghi Effendi addressed to the Bahá'ís of the West, dated 28 March 1941. Composed during the initial period of World War II, the work has an apocalyptic tone. A 'tempest' was sweeping the earth, gaining in power and momentum, sundering the nations, uprooting their institutions, and harrowing the souls of their inhabitants. This 'judgment of God' was both a retributory calamity, punishing the perversity of the human race, and a 'cleansing process', welding the peoples and nations into a single, world-embracing community, and preparing humanity for the future 'Most Great PEACE'. Bahá'u'lláh's proclamation of his mission had for the most part gone unheeded, and the central figures and institutions of the Faith had been persecuted. The world's RULERS and RELIGIOUS LEADERS bore particular responsibility for the world's woes, for it was they to whom Bahá'u'lláh's proclamation had been primarily directed, and at that time their powers had been enormous. They had had the ability to lead their peoples into recognition of God's call, but had disdained to do so. Bahá'u'lláh had therefore prophesied that power would be seized from them, a process described by Shoghi Effendi in this book. People in general also bore responsibility, not only for any failure to respond to God's call, but also for turning away from RELIGION, and thus falling prey to the forces of immorality and SECULARISM.

The 'Promise of World Peace' is presented to President Ronald Reagan

proof

See APOLOGETICS.

prophecy

According to Bahá'í belief the MANIFESTATIONS OF GOD constitute a succession of interrelated figures who speak with the same divine voice. Each foretells the coming of his successor, and may also prophesy other future events, notably the promise of a future messianic age which Bahá'ís equate with the future WORLD ORDER of Bahá'u'lláh. Thus careful study of the scripture of the various world religions will reveal a pattern of promise. In the event, the followers of the religions commonly reject the promised one when he comes (as the Jews rejected Jesus and the Christians rejected Muḥammad), in part because they read their scriptures literally and do not understand the spiritual metaphors that are often used in prophecy, in part because they blindly follow ancestral beliefs without thinking for themselves. This had again happened in the present day with the Muslims' rejection of the Báb and Bahá'u'lláh. 'Lesser PROPHETS' also accurately predict the future. (*See also* APOLOGETICS; ÍQÁN.)

Bahá'u'lláh foretold the coming of future Manifestations after him, but was insistent that the next messenger would not appear until the elapse of at least one thousand years (*KA* 32 k37, 195–6 n62). He also made a number of prophetic statements about the world whose fulfilment Bahá'ís regard as evidence for the validity of his claims. These include the downfall of various world leaders (ABDULAZIZ; ÂLI PAŞA; NAPOLEON III; NÁṢIRU'D-DÍN SHÁH); the loss of OTTOMAN territory; political revolution and popular rule in Iran; the twice-repeated sufferings of Germany (*see* WILHELM I); and what is interpreted as a reference to NUCLEAR POWER. 'Abdu'l-Bahá also predicted the outbreak of World War I (originating in a Balkan conflict), and of a further global conflict in the future; the rise of COMMUNISM; and racial conflict in the United States. Matthews.

prophets

Bahá'ís distinguish between two categories of divine messengers: the MANIFESTATIONS OF GOD, who are independent divine intermediaries, and the 'lesser prophets', who are the followers of the Manifestations, and reflect their light. The Manifestations are the bearers of divine revelation and the founders of the world's great religions. They are prophets 'endowed with constancy'. The contrast is most clearly seen in relationship to Judaism, with ABRAHAM and MOSES both being regarded as Manifestations, whilst Solomon, David, Isaiah, Jeremiah, Ezekiel and the rest are seen as lesser prophets (*SAQ* 164–5). There is no definitive listing of lesser prophets in the Bahá'í writings, nor is the concept discussed in detail, but it is clear that the possibilities of divine guidance and inspiration are not restricted to the recognized Manifestations of God, and would include the Shí'í IMÁMS, amongst others. Some Bahá'ís thus regard figures such as the Native American prophets Viracocha (Inca), Quetzalcoátl (Toltec) and Deganawida (Iroquois) as divine messengers. These views are necessarily speculative in terms of Bahá'í prophetology (which is canonically limited to the prophets mentioned in the Bible, Quran and Bábí-Bahá'í writings (*LG* 503 no. 1696)), but express the Bahá'í belief in the universality of divine guidance to humanity, as well as representing an important 'bridge' in Bahá'í missionary endeavour amongst indigenous peoples. Buck, 'Native messengers'; Shearer; *SBBR* 144–5; Willoya and Brown. (*See also* INDIGENOUS RELIGIONS; for the distinction between 'prophet' (*nabí*) and 'messenger' (*rasúl*) *see* ISLAM.)

Prosperity of Humankind

Statement issued by the BAHÁ'Í INTERNATIONAL COMMUNITY's Office of Public Information at the direction of the Universal House of Justice in 1995. It proposed a global development strategy based on the principles of the oneness of the human race, social JUSTICE, HUMAN RIGHTS, the acceptance of cultural diversity, CONSULTATION, the empowerment of ordinary people through the expansion of scientific and technological knowledge and their involvement in the system of decision making, the development of a new work ethic, and a commitment to WOMEN's equality with men. It called for the abandonment of purely materialistic conceptions of development; asserted the necessity for moral and spiritual change for effective development to occur; and stressed the complementarity of the insights of SCIENCE and RELIGION.

psychic powers

Beliefs in 'psychic powers' were quite common amongst some early Western Bahá'ís. 'Abdu'l-Bahá and Shoghi Effendi regarded spiritualism and other psychic experiences negatively, however, although they treated psychically oriented Bahá'ís with love and consideration: the visions of a medium in a trance have no more material reality than a dream. Communications from the dead are sheer imagination. Automatic writing comes from the writer's own unconscious and not from disembodied spirits. Table writing and other 'psychic dabbling' should be avoided. Artistic creativity is the consequence of innate ability, practice and study, and not of psychic influences. Inner voices might be psychic in nature, but they might also be the product of the subconscious mind. They should not be accorded importance. The existence of genuine 'psychic powers' is possible, but they are not to be used in this present life. Even if an individual sincerely wishes to use such powers to help others, they should leave them dormant. Children who are inclined to be psychic should be discouraged from developing these powers. Psychic powers are not understood, and there is no way to distinguish the true from the false. Neither are such powers consistent or reliable. For individuals to grope around 'in the darkness of their imagination' in these matters is in fact dangerous, weakening their spiritual capacities and ultimately leading to the destruction of their character. If God wants to vouchsafe a spiritual experience to someone, then it will be given, it does not have to be sought. There are also certain psychic powers which are generally a sign of deep psychological disturbance. More generally, individuals imbued with spiritualist ideas find it difficult to accept the Faith unreservedly. If they become Bahá'ís they conceive Bahá'í ideas in spiritualist terms and their pretence to psychic powers causes problems within the Bahá'í community. This had happened in many places, and it is better for Bahá'ís to concentrate their teaching endeavours elsewhere. *LG* 513–19. (*See also* DREAMS AND VISIONS.)

public recognition

The Bahá'í Faith is seen by its followers as an independent world religion, comparable in essence to Buddhism, Christianity, Islam and the rest. This self-understanding is implicit in Bahá'u'lláh's claim to be a MANIFESTATION OF GOD, notwithstanding the reality of his situation as an imprisoned exile with a comparatively small number of followers, the great majority of whom were Iranians of Shí'í Muslim background, and the deliberate caution by which most Bahá'ís at that time avoided being publicly identified as Bahá'ís to avoid persecution (*see* WISDOM). It was scarcely surprising in this context that most outside observers (E.G. BROWNE was an obvious exception) perceived the early Bahá'ís as members of a Muslim sect. This perception remained common even after the EXPANSION of the Faith had led to the establishment of Bahá'í groups in the West and elsewhere.

Shoghi Effendi was determined that the public image of the Faith should change as part of the development of the Faith (*see* BAHÁ'Í FAITH). He therefore encouraged Bahá'ís to seek legal and governmental recognition of their religion, both to increase its public visibility and emphasize its status as an independent world religion, and to enable Bahá'í institutions to hold title to property. 'Negative' recognition could also be of value, most famously as illustrated by the 1925 judgment of a provincial Egyptian court which led to the declaration that the Bahá'ís were not Muslims (*GPB* 364–69). With the onset of systematic PLANS the achievement of public recognition (as by gaining official approval of school or work absences on Bahá'í HOLY DAYS) became an integral goal. An Office of Public Information was established in Haifa in 1985 to better promote public knowledge of the Faith.

In terms of coverage in the news media, the emergence of the Bahá'í Faith from obscurity in many parts of the world occurred as a result of the Iranian persecutions which began in 1979. As in previous instances of persecution, the Bahá'ís embarked on a campaign to publicize the sufferings of their Iranian co-religionists and to garner support from governments and other bodies. To a much greater extent than previously, widespread coverage in newspapers, magazines, radio and television resulted. This continued for several years, and a definite change in public visibility occurred. Having become recognized by the media as a topic of interest the Bahá'ís were subsequently able to gain coverage for their activities far more easily than in the past, particularly as these were now far more diverse than in the past. For an account of recent coverage see *BWNS* 1994–5: 151–66.

publishing

Bahá'ís give great importance to the written word, emphasizing in particular the transforming impact of reading SCRIPTURE. Within the Bahá'í community LITERACY is strongly encouraged, and the use of written material plays an important part in Bahá'í TEACHING activity. Publishing has therefore come to have considerable importance. Amongst 19th-century Middle Eastern Bahá'ís multiple copies of manuscripts were made by hand. This was enormously time-consuming, and some form of publishing was evidently preferable. However, given the opposition to the Faith in Iran and Bahá'u'lláh's status as an Ottoman prisoner, the earliest published materials were made in the safety of British India. The first published works (by lithography) appear to have been Bahá'u'lláh's *Kitáb-i-ÍQÁN* and 'Abdu'l-Bahá's *SECRET OF DIVINE CIVILIZATION* (the latter at least in 1882). Other works followed, both in Bombay and Cairo. The growth of the American Bahá'í community from the 1890s created a new and politically free market for Bahá'í literature. In 1900 the Chicago 'Behais Supply and Publishing Board' was established, and in 1902 it was legally incorporated as the 'Bahai Publishing Society', the precursor of the present American Bahá'í Publishing Trust. Other materials were published independently both in the United States and Europe, and a considerable body of English-language literature was soon available (over one hundred items by 1917 (*SBBR* 103–4); Collins' *Bibliography* lists some 3,700 items up to 1985, including multiple editions, but excluding periodicals and braille literature). From the 1920s onwards translations of Bahá'í literature were published in an increasing range of European and Asian languages, and more recently also in African and Oceanian languages. To provide structure to these burgeoning publication activities Bahá'í publishing trusts have been established in various countries. The first of these was in Britain (est. 1937), and by 1994 there were a total of thirty: twelve in Europe (Belgium, Germany, Italy, Netherlands, Norway, Poland, Portugal, Romania, Russian Federation, Spain, Sweden, United Kingdom); three in the Americas (Argentina, Brazil, United States); four in Africa (Côte d'Ivoire, Kenya, Nigeria, Uganda); one in the Middle East (Lebanon); two in South Asia (India, Pakistan); six in East and South East Asia (Hong Kong, Japan, Korea, Taiwan, Malaysia, Philippines); and two in Australasia (Australia, Fiji) (*BWNS* 1994–5: 325–6). The Bahá'í World Centre has had its own publishing arm since 1963. Many national spiritual ASSEMBLIES also publish Bahá'í literature, as do a number of small independent Bahá'í publishers (in English, notably George Ronald and Oneworld in Oxford (first est. 1947 and 1985 respectively) and Kalimát Press (est. 1979) in Los Angeles). Ironically, Persian Bahá'í literature has become much more readily available since the Islamic Revolution of 1979: the Pahlaví regime (1925–79) had tacitly allowed the Bahá'ís to lithograph small quantities of literature for their own use, but this concession ended with the Revolution, and Persian Bahá'í literature came to be produced in increasing quantities in countries such as Germany and Canada. The Bahá'í World Centre seeks to obtain copies of all published materials relating to the Bahá'í Faith. Collins, *Bibliography* xix–xxii. (*See also* LITERATURE; REVIEW; TRANSLATION.

Purest Branch

See MIHDÍ, MÍRZÁ.

purity

The concept of ritual purity is an important one in Islam, particularly in Shí'ism, but it was de-emphasized by the

Báb, who instead stressed the importance of CLEANLINESS and inner spiritual purity. Bahá'u'lláh went further, abolishing all forms of ritual impurity, both of people and things (menstruating women are exempt from ritual PRAYER and FASTING, but this is voluntary, and the condition of menstruation is not regarded as ritually impure, as in Islam). Ritual ABLUTIONS are required before prayer, however. *KA* 46 k74, 47 k75, 173 n20, 212 n103, n106; Walbridge, *Sacred* 59–67.

Bahá'u'lláh also stressed the importance of purity of heart, and identified payment of both *ḤUQÚQU'LLÁH* and *ZAKÁT* as a means of purifying one's possessions (*KA* 55 k97, 72 k146).

In 19th-century IRAN the Bahá'ís' acceptance of members of non-Muslim minority groups (Jews and Zoroastrians) contrasted sharply with the Shí'í treatment of these people as being ritually impure, and was a factor in attracting them to the Bahá'í Faith.

Q

Qá'im (Ar., 'the one who will arise' (from the family of Muḥammad))

Shí'í term for the MAHDÍ and one of the titles of the Hidden Imám (*see* SHÍ'ISM). According to Bábí and Bahá'í belief the Báb was the *Qá'im*/Mahdí.

Qájárs

The ruling Iranian dynasty from the 1790s until 1925, comprising seven monarchs:

(1) Ághá Muḥammad Sháh, r. 1795–7
(2) Fatḥ-'Alí Sháh, r. 1797–1834; nephew of Ághá Muḥammad Sháh.
(3) Muḥammad Sháh, r. 1834–48; grandson of Fatḥ-'Alí Sháh.
(4) Náṣiru'd-dín Sháh, r. 1848–96; son of Muḥammad Sháh.
(5) Muẓaffari'd-dín Sháh, r. 1896–1907; son of Náṣiru'd-dín Sháh.
(6) Muḥammad-'Alí Sháh, r. 1907–9 (d. 1925); son of Muẓaffari'd-dín Sháh.
(7) Aḥmad Sháh, r. 1909–25 (d. 1930); son of Muḥammad-'Alí Sháh.

The Shaykhí movement (*see* SHAYKHISM) developed during the reign of Fatḥ-'Alí Sháh and the Bábí movement during that of his successor, MUḤAMMAD SHÁH. The extirpation of Bábism and the early development of the Bahá'í Faith occurred during the reign of NÁṢIRU'D-DÍN SHÁH, who remained hostile towards the new religion throughout his reign. The attitude of the last three Qájárs towards the Bahá'ís appears to have varied between indifference and a certain measure of sympathy; individuals known to be Bahá'ís were appointed to public office (e.g. ALI-KULI KHAN). Persecution of Bahá'ís continued, however, due both to the lack of central control over provincial authorities and the struggles for power in what was a complex and unstable political situation. Shoghi Effendi rejoiced in the downfall of 'this blood-stained dynasty' responsible for so much of the persecution of the Bábís and Bahá'ís (*WOB* 173). They had usurped the throne and brought disaster to Iran (*PDC* 67–71). (*See also* IRAN.)

Qaṣída al-Warqá'iyyih

See ODE OF THE DOVE.

Qaṣṣábchí, Ḥájí Maḥmúd (d. 1947)

Prominent Iraqi Bahá'í. He converted in 1911 after reading accounts of 'Abdu'l-Bahá's journeys in the West. He made major financial contributions to various Bahá'í construction projects. After World War I he started restoration work on the House of Bahá'u'lláh in BAGHDAD. He subsequently supported the legal work required to try to regain possession of the House from the Shí'is who had seized it, and played a leading role in the establishment of the Baghdad and national Iraqi *ḤAẒÍRATU'L-QUDS*.

He also financed the extension work to the inner SHRINE OF THE BÁB, and was honoured by Shoghi Effendi by having one of the doors of the Shrine named after him. BW11: 502–3.

Qayyúmu'l-asmá'

Also known as the *Aḥsanu'l-qiṣaṣ* ('The best of stories'). It is the earliest work of the Báb's ministry, composed over a period of forty days, beginning on the night of his declaration of mission to Mullá Ḥusayn (22 May 1844) (Nabil 63, but cf. *TJ* 39), and subsequently extensively copied and widely distributed by his disciples, such that it came to be regarded as the 'Quran' of the Bábís. Written in Arabic, the book is quite lengthy (111 chapters; over 9,300 verses). Although it takes the form of a commentary on the Quranic *súra* of Joseph (*Súra* 12), each chapter except the first dealing with a verse in that *súra*, it is not a commentary in any conventional sense, but rather a reworking of Quranic material to present the Báb's own doctrinal concerns. Central is the Báb's own claim to authority. Though his own exact status is enigmatic – he refers to himself as the exalted or greatest 'Remembrance [of God]' (*dhikr*) and as the 'Gate' (*báb*) of God or of the Hidden IMÁM (*see* QÁ'IM) – the book also includes passages in which the 'speaker' is the Imám, or that claim divine revelation: these were 'new verses from God'; they were 'the essence of the Quran'; God had inspired the Báb as he had in the past inspired Muḥammad and other prophets. Moreover, the book's style and format mirrored those of the Quran, paraphrasing its wording; replicating its 'rhyming, rhythmical cadences' (*McR* 35); employing the same chapter-and-verse divisions and prefatory 'disconnected letters'; and making the same claims to inimitability. All human beings – including the 'rulers of the Earth' and the Islamic learned (*'ULAMÁ*) – were summoned to believe in the Remembrance. Those who rejected him were consigned to hell-fire.

Bahá'u'lláh described the *Qayyúmu'l-asmá'* as the 'greatest' and 'mightiest' of the Báb's works, and Bahá'ís believe its 'fundamental purpose' to have been to forecast what 'the true Joseph' (Bahá'u'lláh) would endure at the hands of his brother (Ṣubḥ-i-AZAL) (*GPB* 23). A few selected passages have been translated into English (Báb, *Selections* 41–74), but the book as a whole remains untranslated. *ARR* 173, 201–6; Browne, *Selections* 210–15; *GPB* 23–4; Lawson, 'Interpretation', 'Qur'án Commentary', 'Remembrance'; *McS* 55–7; Momen, 'Trial'.

Qazvín (1868 pop. est. 25,000)

Northern Iranian city. It was an important centre of Bábí activity, the birthplace of ṬÁHIRIH and the site of the murder of her uncle, MUḤAMMAD-TAQÍ BARAGHÁNÍ.

qiblah (Ar.)

The 'point of adoration' to which believers turn in prayer. For Muslims this is the Ka'ba in Mecca. In the *Arabic BAYÁN* the Báb changed it to HE WHOM GOD SHALL MAKE MANIFEST, stating that it would move as he moved. Bahá'u'lláh confirmed this change in the *Kitáb-i-AQDAS*, identifying his own 'Most Holy Presence' with 'the Centre round which circle the Concourse on High'. After his death the *qiblah* became his tomb at BAHJÍ. Bahá'ís are directed to face the *qiblah* when they perform their daily obligatory PRAYER (*ṣalát*), but all other prayers may be said facing any direction ('Whichever way ye turn, there is the face of God': Qurán 2:115). In practice, the prayer of visitation for Bahá'u'lláh is also commonly said facing the *qiblah*. The bodies of the dead should be buried so that they 'face' the *qiblah*, i.e. have their feet pointing towards it. *KA* 21 k6, 68 k137, 111 q14, 126 q67, 131 q85, 145–6, 168–9 n7–8; *CC1*: 13 no. 42; *LG* 196 no. 646.

Quddús (Ar.: 'the Most Holy')

Title of the Bábí leader Mullá Muḥammad-'Alí Bárfurúshí (*c.*1819/20–49), the last of the Báb's inner circle of disciples, the LETTERS OF THE LIVING. The son of a poor rice farmer from the northern Iranian province of Mázandarán, he became a servant in the house of the local Shaykhí leader, Mullá Muḥammad-Ḥamza Sharí'at-madár, and subsequently trained as a cleric in Mashhad and then in Karbalá under Sayyid KÁẒIM RASHTÍ. Meeting the Báb in Shíráz, he was chosen as the prophet's companion on the pilgrimage to Mecca (1844–5), and was one of those savagely punished for creating religious disorder on his return to Shíráz. He then travelled to Kirmán, where he delivered a proclamatory message from the Báb to the Shaykhí leader KARÍM KHÁN, subsequently returning to Bárfurúsh, where he became embroiled in the sectarian tensions that divided the town. Following the Báb's imprisonment in Azerbaiján and consequent inaccessibility, Quddús came to be regarded by many Bábís as *QÁ'IM*, fulfilling the Báb's role in his stead. He also identified himself with Jesus (in Islamic belief, one of those who would accompany the Mahdí). He attended the conference of BADASHT, initially opposing ṬÁHIRIH's radicalism. He was subsequently placed under house arrest in the northern town of Sárí, until released by the Bábís of ṬABARSÍ, whose struggle he thenceforth directed. Following the Bábí surrender he was delivered into the hands of his chief clerical opponent in Bárfurúsh, the *Sa'ídu'l-'ulamá*, who personally superintended his torture and killing. According to the Bábí–Bahá'í account the dismembered parts of his body miraculously refused to burn, and were later collected together and buried. He wrote extensively – including many thousands of verses in commentary on just one letter in a Quranic verse – but little of this output has survived. The Báb referred to him as 'the last name of God' (*ismu'lláhu'l-ákhir*), and Bahá'u'lláh identified him with one of the divine messengers mentioned in the Quran, calling him 'the Last Point' (*nuqṭi-yi-ukhrá*), the Báb having been the 'Primal Point' (of divine revelation). *ARR* 177–88, 241, 287–8, 325–8; *GPB* 49; MacEoin, 'Hierarchy' 106–11; *McS* 105–7; Nabil 69–72, 142–7, 179–83, 261–7, 288–300, 349–68, 379–82, 384–415; *TJ* 39–40, 43–4, 57–93, 97, 281–2, 336, 355–6, 359–68, *TN* 306–9.

Quran (Ar.: *Qur'án*)

The holy book of Islam, regarded as divine revelation delivered to MUḤAMMAD over the course of his twenty-two-year mission through the intermediary of the angel Gabriel. It consists of 114 chapters (*SÚRAS*), each representing a separate revelation. Bahá'ís regard it as sacred scripture, Bahá'u'lláh referring to it as 'the Way of God' unto all who are in heaven or on earth (*GWB* 44), and as God's 'unfailing testimony' to both the East and the West (*KI* 134). Shoghi Effendi described it as the only work of scripture, apart from the Bábí and Bahá'í writings, that was 'an absolutely authenticated Repository of the Word of God' (*ADJ* 41). It contained a fuller expression of God's purpose and guidance than any preceding scripture, and its 'thorough study' was 'absolutely indispensable' for an adequate understanding and intelligent reading of Bahá'u'lláh's writings (*LG* 497 no. 1670, 561 no. 1904). Bahá'ís should study it over and again (*LG* 496 no. 1666). Several of the Báb's most important works – notably the *QAYYÚMU'L-ASMÁ'* – take the form of commentaries on particular Quranic *súras*. Heggie 186–93. (*See also* ISLAM.)

Qurratu'l-'Ayn

See ṬÁHIRIH.

R

race

Bahá'u'lláh proclaimed the unity and wholeness of the human race. 'Abdu'l-Bahá compared the various races of the world to the different-coloured flowers found in a beautiful garden; racial divisions are a human creation and in reality are imaginary. God makes no distinction between people on the basis of race or colour: all are equally created in his image (*ADJ* 31–2, 45). Bahá'ís regard racist doctrines, which seek to subordinate one group to another on the basis of race, as evil, Shoghi Effendi describing racism as one of the three 'false gods' of SECULARISM (*PDC* 117–18). The Universal House of Justice describes racism as an 'outrageous violation of the dignity of human beings'. It blights human progress, corrupting its perpetrators whilst retarding the progress of its victims. It is a major barrier to world peace. It should not be countenanced under any pretext, and should be countered by 'appropriate legal measures' and the promotion of human solidarity (*MUHJ* 688).

THE UNITED STATES

'Abdu'l-Bahá was keenly conscious of the racial tensions in the United States and sought to promote racial harmony amongst the Bahá'ís, as well as to the wider public, during his North American tour (1912). In what were extremely radical gestures for the time he encouraged interracial marriage, and placed the leading black Bahá'í in the seat of honour at a formal luncheon held in Washington, DC (*see* ALI-KULI KHAN; Louis C. GREGORY). He warned that, if not checked, American racism would lead to bloodshed. The races should therefore seek the points of partnership and agreement that existed between them. If they worked together to achieve mutual advancement, this would attract divine blessings and foster love and unity. Shoghi Effendi repeatedly reminded the American Bahá'ís of their need to respond to this summons of 'Abdu'l-Bahá. Racial prejudice was a corrosive force (a 'cancerous growth', *CF* 154) which had damaged the whole structure of American society, and overcoming it was 'the most vital and challenging issue' facing the American Bahá'ís. Their future progress as a community depended to a significant degree on the extent to which they overcame the historic divisions between the races. They should show genuine love for all, wisdom and uncompromising courage to combat injustice. Enormous effort was required on both sides. All sense of racial superiority and division should be cast away, and subconscious prejudices examined and corrected. Whites should convince the blacks of the sincerity of their friendship, be patient with those who over such a long period of time had received 'such grievous and slow-healing wounds', and avoid being patronizing. Blacks should respond warmly, forget the past, and overcome their suspicions (*ADJ* 28–34). There needed to be a revolutionary change in the attitude of the average white American towards his black fellow citizens (*CF* 126).

The American Bahá'í community was multiracial almost from its inception, and a number of black Bahá'ís soon attained prominence within the community – notably Louis Gregory. Race-related Bahá'í activities have included the race amity conventions of the 1920s, and an annual Race Amity (later Race Unity) Day (started in 1957). Over the years a variety of local parades, picnics, concerts, arts festivals, dance-dramas, exhibitions and seminars have been held. A children's conference ('Calling All Colors') promoting the abandonment of prejudice was originated by a nine-year-old Bahá'í in South Carolina in 1992 and has since been widely emulated. Since the large-scale influx of new Bahá'ís from the rural south (from *c.*1970) blacks have constituted the demographic majority of the American Bahá'í community. *SBBR* 150–1, 187; Morrison; Rutstein, *To Be One*; Thomas, 'A long and thorny path'; Thomas, *Racial Unity*.

ELSEWHERE

Bahá'ís have also become involved in the public debate about racism in various other countries, including Bermuda, South Africa and Switzerland, issuing statements such as the South African Bahá'ís' *Overcoming Racial Prejudice* (1994) which was widely distributed to government officials, newspaper editors and the general public. Bahá'ís have supported ratification of the UN Convention on the Elimination of All Forms of Racial Discrimination (*BWNS* 1994–5: 98–104).

ETHNIC AND NATIONAL DIVISIONS

The Bahá'í teachings also apply to situations where other forms of division disrupt social relations. Thus, in reference to the former Yugoslavia, the Universal House of Justice has appealed to Bahá'ís to demonstrate the ability of the Faith to overcome ethnic divisions and create a peaceful and harmonious society. Again, in India, the Bahá'ís issued a booklet on *Communal Harmony*, referring to the need to overcome the complex of religious, linguistic and caste-based tensions found in that country, and describing this as 'India's greatest challenge'. The statement was later praised and extensively quoted by the Indian Supreme Court (*BWNS* 1994–5: 36, 130–1). (*See also* INDIGENOUS PEOPLES.)

radio; radio stations

Recent years have seen increasing use of radio by Baha'is, particularly in the Americas. Interest in using radio as a means of proclaiming the existence and teachings of the Bahá'í Faith dates back at least to the 1920s. The American Bahá'ís considered establishing their own radio station during the 1940s, but were discouraged on the grounds of cost. Radio assumed much greater potential importance with the large-scale influxes of new rural and often illiterate Bahá'ís in the 'Third World' from the 1960s onwards (*see* EXPANSION). Radio was the ideal medium to reach this constituency. Particular success was gained in Ecuador, where Bahá'í broadcasts in the main indigenous language gained an increasing audience of Bahá'ís and others (from 1973). A Bahá'í-owned radio station was finally opened there in 1977 – the first in the world. Programmes included local news, music, socio-economic and community development topics, and 'cultural education' emphasizing the indigenous language and culture. Bahá'í materials were presented both to deepen the Bahá'ís and introduce the Bahá'í message to others. Community service and local participation were stressed. The Ecuadorian model inspired similar stations in Peru (1981), Bolivia (1984), Panama (1985) and Chile (1986). Other stations have also been established in the United States (in South Carolina, an area with a large rural population of Bahá'ís), and briefly in Liberia, prior to the civil war. Hein; *CC2*: 281–3.

Ra'ís, Tablets of

Two tablets of Bahá'u'lláh named after *ra'ís* (the chief), i.e. Âli Paşa ('Alí Páshá), the Ottoman grand vizier, who is addressed in both tablets. Both are sometimes referred to as the *Lawḥ-i-Ra'ís*.

THE *SÚRATU'L-RA'ÍS*

This tablet, in Arabic, was revealed en route to Gallipoli from Edirne for Ḥájí Muḥammad-Ismá'íl Káshání Dhabíḥ; Bahá'u'lláh summoned Âli Paşa to hearken to the voice of God, and reproved him for having joined with the Iranian ambassador, Mírzá Ḥusayn Khán, in opposition. As in the past, opposition to God's cause would be unavailing, and would merit divine vengeance. Upheavals in the Ottoman domains were predicted, including the loss of Edirne. The tablet also recounted the sufferings of the Bahá'ís in Edirne and the greatness of Bahá'u'lláh's cause, and discussed the nature of the human soul. Elsewhere Bahá'u'lláh stated that the world had not been at peace since the revelation of this tablet: the 'true Physician' (i.e. Bahá'u'lláh) had been prevented from administering the remedy the world needed, and thus its tribulations increased from day to day. Browne, *Selections* 266–9; *GPB* 172, 174; *RB2*: 411–18.

THE *LAWḤ-I-RA'ÍS*

This tablet, in Persian, was composed shortly after Bahá'u'lláh's arrival in Akka (1868); Bahá'u'lláh recounted the sufferings of his companions since their arrival in the prison city and censured Âli Paşa for having inflicted such cruelties on innocent people. He was one of those who in every age had opposed the messengers of God, seeing them as disrupters of the established order. God's 'wrathful anger' would seize him, and the Ottoman domains would be disrupted. *GPB* 208; *RB3*: 33–8.

Randall, William Henry ('Harry') (1863–1929)

Prominent American Bahá'í. Like his father he was a leading Boston businessman. He met 'Abdu'l-Bahá during his American tour (1912). He became a Bahá'í in 1913, at the same time becoming involved with the administration of Green Acre. He served on the Executive Board of the Bahai Temple Unity from 1914 until 1924, often as its president or treasurer. Shoghi Effendi designated him as one of the Disciples of 'Abdu'l-Bahá, describing him as an 'eloquent upholder of the Bahá'í Cause in America' (*BW4*: 119). Winckler and Garis.

Ransom-Kehler, Keith (1876–1933)

Prominent American Bahá'í. She became a Bahá'í in 1921, and after the death of her second husband in 1923 became increasingly active as a Bahá'í speaker and teacher. In 1929 she travelled to the Caribbean, and in 1930 began an extensive world tour to promote the Faith. Shoghi Effendi invited her to Haifa in 1932, and gave her a special mission to go to Iran on behalf of the American national spiritual assembly to petition the shah to ease or lift the restrictions on the Bahá'ís. She stayed in Iran for over a year, but her efforts were unavailing. Exhausted and in poor health she eventually succumbed to smallpox, and was buried in Iṣfáhán near to the graves of the King and

Keith Ransom-Kehler, prominent American Bahá'í

BELOVED OF MARTYRS. Shoghi Effendi named her posthumously as a HAND OF THE CAUSE, and as the first American to have the spiritual station of a MARTYR. *BW5*: 23–7, 93, 389–410; Harper 99–109.

Rashtí, Sayyid Káẓim

See KÁẒIM RASHTÍ.

reason

The faculty of rational argument, deduction and judgement, the use of the INTELLECT. 'Abdu'l-Bahá taught that God had endowed human beings with reason so that they could perceive what was true. To oppose reason in the name of RELIGION is superstition (*PUP* 63, 287). As with all other bases of human KNOWLEDGE, reason is fallible.

regional Bahá'í councils

Institution formally established by the Universal House of Justice in May 1997 as an intermediate level of administration between national and local spiritual ASSEMBLIES. The councils provide a means of decentralized decision-making in those national communities in which this is desirable (e.g. because of size). Whilst possessing considerable autonomy the councils remain subordinate to their national spiritual assemblies. The councils can either be elected (by the members of all local assemblies in their region) or appointed by the national assembly on the basis of a confidential list of nominees proposed by regional electors and AUXILIARY BOARD members. Individual national assemblies can only form such councils following consultations and with the permission of the Universal House of Justice. This development was presaged by a number of national assemblies experimenting with similar bodies, notably the Indian 'State Bahá'í Councils' (from 1986). *American Baha'i* 28/5 (24 June 1997): 1, 12–13.

reincarnation

Bahá'í teachings reject the concept of reincarnation. Instead, the SOUL is believed to come into existence at the moment of conception and to continue in some form of non-material existence after DEATH. It does not return to earth. Accounts by individuals of their 'former lives' are not real memories, but merely indicate the capacity of the human mind to believe firmly in whatever it imagines. *SAQ* 282–9; *LG* 537 no. 1820, 538 nos. 1826–7; *SWAB* 183–5. (*See also* 'RETURN'.)

religion

PURPOSE

For Bahá'u'lláh and 'Abdu'l-Bahá, religion was 'the light of the world', and obedience to divine law the source of human progress, happiness and CIVILIZATION (*SDC* 71). The MANIFESTATIONS OF GOD were sent to promote the knowledge of God and 'unity and fellowship' amongst human beings, and to bring forth 'Mystic Gems' from the people (*ESW* 12, 13). True religion consists of divine teachings, which constitute 'the very life of humankind', leading to refinement of character, higher thoughts and human honour. It is not a mere set of beliefs and customs. It is a channel of love and mercy from God to all the world's peoples (*SWAB* 36, 52–3, 283). Its purpose is to bring fellowship, love and unity, eternal life, and moral excellence to people; to make them joyful, educate them, and free them from prejudice; and to establish universal PEACE (*PUP* 97–8; *SWAB* 28, 51–3).

SOCIAL STABILITY

Religion is the chief means for the establishment of social order (it inculcates morality and the FEAR OF GOD). The more it declines, the greater is the waywardness of the ungodly, leading ultimately to chaos and confusion. The world's rulers and the HOUSE(S) OF JUSTICE should therefore uphold religion (*TB* 63–4, 125, 129–30). The world's religious leaders should consult together with its rulers on the needs of a 'diseased and sorely-afflicted world' and work to rehabilitate it (*TB* 168). Criminal justice might prevent manifest crime, but religion inculcates a moral force which also prevents covert wrongdoing (*SWAB* 302–3). War and hatred can only be overcome through the power of the holy spirit (*SWAB* 53). Secularists, such as Voltaire, erred in denouncing religion, when what was to be condemned were those religious hypocrites who had brought disgrace to religion (*SDC* 71–5). (*See also* SECULARISM.)

HUMAN UNITY

The purpose of religion is to establish unity amongst the peoples of the world, it should not be made a cause of dissension (*TB* 129, 168). God's messengers came to promote unity amongst human beings. Animosity on the basis of religious differences is against the divine purpose. Such hatreds veil people from God; they are a fire that devours the world. It is the duty of the Bahá'ís to strive to still these dissensions (*ESW* 12–14). If religion becomes a source of strife and hatred it is of no value whatsoever, and it would be better not to have it. It is intended as the remedy for human problems, and not their cause (*PUP* 117, 170, 181, 394; *SWAB* 249, 299). God's religion is one. The divine religions are all based on the same reality, and as such are like branches of a single tree. The antagonisms between the followers of different religions and the sectarian divisions within them are the result of human limitations (*PUP* 198). Bigotry and ignorant fanaticism contradict the true purpose of religion. (*See also* RELIGION AND SCIENCE; TOLERANCE.)

religion and science

'Abdu'l-Bahá condemned the antagonism towards SCIENCE held by some religious people. KNOWLEDGE is the gift of God to humanity, and divine religion promotes truth. How then can religion oppose science? To do so is ignorance and a denial of human intelligence. It is ignorance, not science, that threatens the foundations of religion (*SAQ* 137): dogmatism and irrationality are the cause of irreligion and the growth of SECULARISM (*PUP* 374). Religion should be in conformity with science and REASON. Thus its foundation will be solid, and it will be able to influence the human heart. It needs to be based on investigation and not mere imitation (*SWAB* 299, 303). Religion that is not in accordance with science is superstition and a human invention. It should be discarded. The maintenance of irrational beliefs engenders vacillation and is ultimately untenable. Both science and true religion are based on reason and should 'bear its test'. Together they fortify each other: science protects religion from becoming superstition; religion protects science from becoming a barren materialism. *PT* 133, 145–50; *PUP* 63, 107, 128, 170, 175–6, 181, 231, 287, 298–9, 316, 373–4, 394, 434, 455.

religious diversity

The Bahá'í Faith upholds the divine origin and 'God-given authority' of the prophetic religions of the past, recognizing the 'fundamental unity' of all the MANIFESTATIONS OF GOD (*Faith* 2; *PDC* 111; *WOB* 114). Thus Bahá'u'lláh stated that the various divine religions are 'rays of one Light', and proceed from the same source. That they differ from each other is due to the 'varying requirements of the ages in which they were promulgated' (*ESW* 13) (*see* PROGRESSIVE REVELATION). Nine divinely revealed religions – SABEANISM, Hinduism (*see* INDIAN RELIGIONS), BUDDHISM, ZOROASTRIANISM, JUDAISM, CHRISTIANITY, ISLAM, Bábism and the BAHÁ'Í FAITH – each with its own prophet, are recognized, of which the Bahá'í Faith is the latest and fullest (*LG* 414–15 nos. 1373–5). As God is believed to have guided all the world's peoples, the existence of other religions and revelators is assumed, but there is no definitive list of these (*see* PROPHETS).

Belief in the unity of the fundamental principles of these religions raises the problem of explaining their evident diversity. At present this is accomplished by essentially subsuming them all under a single Bahá'í standard: each is held to have proclaimed the same single religion of God; their aims and basic principles are one; their sacred books are correlative in nature; and most have left prophetic witness of the future coming of Bahá'u'lláh. Now, Bahá'u'lláh has restated their eternal verities, and also reconciled and co-ordinated the formerly separate faiths, distinguishing their essential and authentic elements from spurious and 'priest-prompted superstitions' by restoring the 'pristine purity of their teachings'. On this basis both their teachings and their followers will be ultimately reconciled (*Faith* 2; *PDC* 111–12; *WOB* 114). Bahá'í apologists have attempted various reconciliations with regard to several religious traditions (e.g. cf. Fozdar's and Momen's work on Buddhism). (*See also* INTERFAITH DIALOGUE.)

religious leaders

For Bahá'u'lláh there were two types of religious leader. Those divines (of any religion) who were truly knowledgeable, upright, just and godly were like eyes to the people, a head and spirit to the body of the world. They were blessed sources of guidance and divine bounty, whose merit and position should be recognized. If they had not allowed their own learning to separate them from God's messenger, their station was such that the radiance of their light was shed over all in earth and heaven, and 'the inmates of Paradise' sought the blessing of their breath. Such 'righteous men of learning' were 'exponents of celestial power' and 'oceans of heavenly wisdom', and it was 'essential to treat them with deference' (*ESW* 16–17; *PDC* 115; *TB* 97, 171). By contrast (referring specifically to the Islamic learned (*'ULAMÁ*)), he rebuked those who outwardly attired themselves 'with the raiment of knowledge', but inwardly were 'deprived therefrom'. These were like wolves who gave themselves the guise of shepherds, or 'clear but bitter water' (*ESW* 15–16). Such leaders of religion had in every age hindered their followers from recognizing the next MANIFESTATION OF GOD, whether because of a love of leadership or through their own ignorance (*KI* 10–11, 105–7). They became sources of tyranny and the cause of persecution of God's messengers. They weighed 'the book of God' by their own standards.

They were summoned to fear God and set aside the veils that kept them from recognizing Bahá'u'lláh (*KA* 56–7 k99–102; *PDC* 81–7).

Bahá'u'lláh's proclamation of his claims to the secular RULERS was paralleled by addresses to the world's religious leaders, specific letters being dispatched to Pope PIUS IX and to various Shí'í clerics. The leaders and followers of all religions were summoned, however (*PDC* 78–80).

religious tolerance

See TOLERANCE.

Remey, Charles Mason

(1874–1974)

American HAND OF THE CAUSE and, finally, COVENANT-BREAKER. Remey was the son of Admiral George Collier Remey. He became a Bahá'í in Paris in 1899 and became one of the most travelled of the early Western Bahá'ís, visiting Iran and Central Asia with another Bahá'í in 1908 and, in 1909–10, completing the first round-the-world tour of Bahá'í communities. He also became prominent in the American Bahá'í community as an author, public speaker and administrator (*BFA2*: 151–2, 289–95, 333–4, 348–512). He was appointed to the first INTERNATIONAL BAHÁ'Í COUNCIL by Shoghi Effendi in 1950, and named as a Hand in the following year. He designed the Houses of Worship in Kampala and Sydney (*see* *MASHRIQU'L-ADHKÁR*), as well as the future temple on Mount CARMEL. After the death of Shoghi Effendi (1957) Remey joined his fellow Hands in the first conclave and their declaration that there was no designated successor as Guardian. He was chosen as one of the Custodial Hands. He later came to believe that the GUARDIANSHIP had to be continued, however, and that he himself was the second Guardian by dint of having been appointed president of the International Council (itself the precursor of the Universal House of Justice over which the Guardian would preside). He issued a proclamation to this effect in April 1960, but only succeeded in gaining the support of a small number of Bahá'ís world-wide. He and his followers were subsequently declared Covenant-breakers by the Hands, who reasoned that his claim was unsupported by any formal appointment by Shoghi Effendi, and that according to 'Abdu'l-Bahá's *WILL AND TESTAMENT* the line of Guardians was confined to the male descendants of Bahá'u'lláh (*AGHṢÁN*).

Harper 287–306; *SBBR* 130–1; *TCB* 385–91, 429–32; UHJ, *Ministry of the Custodians*. (*See also* REMEYITE GROUPS.

Remeyite groups and organizations

Mason REMEY gained the support of a small but widespread group of Bahá'ís for his claim to be the second Guardian of the Faith (1960). Most of his long-term followers were Americans. The history of these 'Bahá'ís under the Hereditary Guardianship' or 'Orthodox Bahá'ís' is highly complex, with Remey making confused and contradictory appointments as he grew older, and the subsequent emergence of a number of contending claimants to leadership: (1) Donald Harvey (d. 1991), appointed by Remey as his successor as 'third Guardian' in 1967; (2) Joel Marangella, president of the short-lived 'Second International Council' appointed by Remey (1964–6), who in 1969 claimed to have been secretly appointed as Guardian some years previously; (3) Reginald (Rex) King (d. 1977), elected secretary of a Remeyite American national spiritual ASSEMBLY in New Mexico (1963–4), who claimed to be 'Regent' for the Cause in the absence of a living Guardian; and (4) Leland Jensen (d. 1996), who made a variety of religious claims (including being the return of Jesus), and established himself as the head of an apocalyptic cult based in Missoula, Montana. Remey himself had been firmly convinced that there would be a great global catastrophe before the end of the century, and Jensen gained widespread publicity for his claim that the world would end in 1980. Collins, *Bibliography* 295; *SBBR* 131; UHJ, 'Mason Remey'; Balch et al.

repentance

Attachment to the world leads the individual SOUL into disobedience to God and his laws (*see* SIN). To overcome sin, genuine repentance of wrongdoing is required. Bahá'ís are bidden to turn towards God, praying that through his LOVE and grace they may seek to develop SPIRITUAL QUALITIES within themselves; return to obedience to him; and thus draw nearer to the HEAVEN of divine perfection. Many Bahá'í prayers remind the reader of his own imperfection, and give voice to the desire for God's forgiveness and mercy. The individual is bidden to 'bring thyself to account each day' ere death intervenes and it becomes necessary 'to give account of thy deeds' before God (*HWa* no. 31). They should beg for God's forgiveness. The CONFESSION OF SINS to others as a religious rite is regarded as demeaning and is forbidden.

resurrection

In Christianity and Islam it is believed that there will be a final Day of Judgement at which the dead will rise and receive divine judgement, the righteous being assigned to HEAVEN and the sinners to Hell. For Bahá'ís the proclamation of his cause by each MANIFESTATION OF GOD represents a 'resurrection', which separates those who accepted his call from those who rejected it: metaphorically the 'living' and the 'dead'. Báb, *Selections* 78–9, 106–8; *KI* 73–8, 92–7, 109.

Christians traditionally believe that Jesus was physically resurrected from the dead after his crucifixion. 'Abdu'l-Bahá taught that the resurrection account symbolized the rebirth of faith in the hearts of Christ's disciples after the shock of Christ's martyrdom. His followers became animated by the Holy Spirit and they arose to promulgate his cause. It was a spiritual rather than material reality that was described, just as Christ was said to have come 'down from heaven' (though he had been born from a mother), and whilst still alive was 'in heaven' (John 3:13, 6:38). The return to life of a dead body was scientifically impossible. *SAQ* 103–5.

'return' (Ar.: *raj'a*)

Shí'í doctrine, according to which the appearance of the MAHDÍ (the Hidden Imám) would be accompanied by the return of IMÁMS and their followers. In Bábí–Bahá'í belief it has become a more general concept, whereby more or less the same *dramatis personae* reappear in each religious dispensation to re-enact the same roles: the MANIFESTATION OF GOD; his forerunners who announce his coming; and his chief disciples and opponents. Thus for the Báb – as Mahdí – the Prophet Muḥammad, his daughter Fáṭima, the Imáms and their 'Gates' (*abwáb*), together with those who believed in them, had all now returned, and were identified with the LETTERS OF THE LIVING (Mullá ḤUSAYN as Muḥammad; Mullá 'ALÍ BASṬÁMÍ as the Imám 'Alí; etc.). Each was the return of the reality of the former personage. Similarly, for his followers the Bábí struggle at ṬABARSÍ was a re-enactment of KARBALÁ. Again, Bahá'u'lláh claimed that he was the Báb 'arrayed in his new attire' (*TB* 182), and noted that each Manifestation could claim that he was the 'return' of all former prophets, and that those who were first to accept his call were the return of those who had been similarly distinguished in previous dispensations (as with the Bábís who embodied the same qualities of determination, constancy and renunciation of the world as the early Muslims) (*KI* 99, 102). Similarly, 'Abdu'l-Bahá explained the Christian identification of John the Baptist with the Jewish prophet Elijah (Elias) as an expression of the return of the same qualities and perfections (*SAQ* 132–4). 'Return' referred to inner perfections and not to the REINCARNATION of individual souls, a belief he regarded as absurd (*SWAB* 183). This strong rejection of metempsychosis contrasts with the views of some of the more extreme Bábís (*TJ* 338). Browne, *Selections* 322–5; MacEoin, 'Hierarchy' 101–9; Momen, *Shi'i Islam* 166; *SBBR* 43; *TJ* 334–9, 380n. References by Bahá'u'lláh include *ESW* 121–2; *KI* 95–103; *TB* 183–7.

revelation

Bahá'ís regard the MANIFESTATIONS OF GOD as intermediaries between God and humanity. As such, their teachings represent a unique revelation of the divine will, and may be referred to as the 'WORD OF GOD'. Not everything that an individual Manifestation says is to be regarded as revelation, and moments of revelation appear to be marked off from everyday life, as in MOSES' encounter with the Burning Bush and his receipt of Ten Commandments, or MUḤAMMAD's encounters with the angel Gabriel. In the case of Muḥammad, 'revelation' consisted in the utterance of verses which together make up the successive *SÚRAS* of the QURAN. In like manner the Báb and Bahá'u'lláh revealed verses, and regarded this act as a primary proof of their divine mission. Only God could produce such verses (*SBBR* 32, 39–40, 62–3; *TB* 74). Their greater output – each producing hundreds of thousands of verses, as compared with 6,236 in the Quran – indicated the potency of the present era.

The actual process of revelation remains obscure. It is regarded as distinct from human inspiration. Whilst it may involve visionary experiences (as in Bahá'u'lláh's visions of the MAID OF HEAVEN) it is not confined to such experiences. Accounts of the Báb and Bahá'u'lláh indicate that periods of revelation often had a powerful effect on onlookers, with the speed of composition, the melody and vibrancy of the Prophet's voice, and the sound of the reed pen on the paper all exercising a hypnotic attraction. For Bahá'ís Bahá'u'lláh seemed transformed at such times: surrounded by an aura of great vibrancy and power. The verses themselves would be uttered without apparent forethought and with great rapidity, such that Bahá'u'lláh's amanuensis, Mírzá ÁQÁ JÁN, had to develop a special form of speed-writing ('revelation writing') in order to take them down. In the space of one hour, a thousand verses might be revealed in this way. During the early period of his mission (presumably up to the time he was poisoned in Edirne) Bahá'u'lláh might continue in this fashion for lengthy periods, day and night (*see Kitáb-i-Íqán*), but later he was only able to continue for an hour or so. During this period his body would be in a very energetic state, and this would continue for some time afterwards such that he would be unable to eat (*RB1*: 23–5, 28–9, 35–7; *4*: 219). Sometimes he also chanted in what was regarded as a special heavenly language (*BKG* 113–14). Bahá'u'lláh denied having received any formal learning, and stated that whenever he wanted to quote others, then a tablet would appear before his face giving all that had been revealed in past holy books (*TB* 149).

reverence

Bahá'ís are encouraged to be reverent towards the sacred as expressed in the holy places, holy personages and scripture of all religions. The actual manner of showing reverence is recognized as varying between cultures: reverence is an

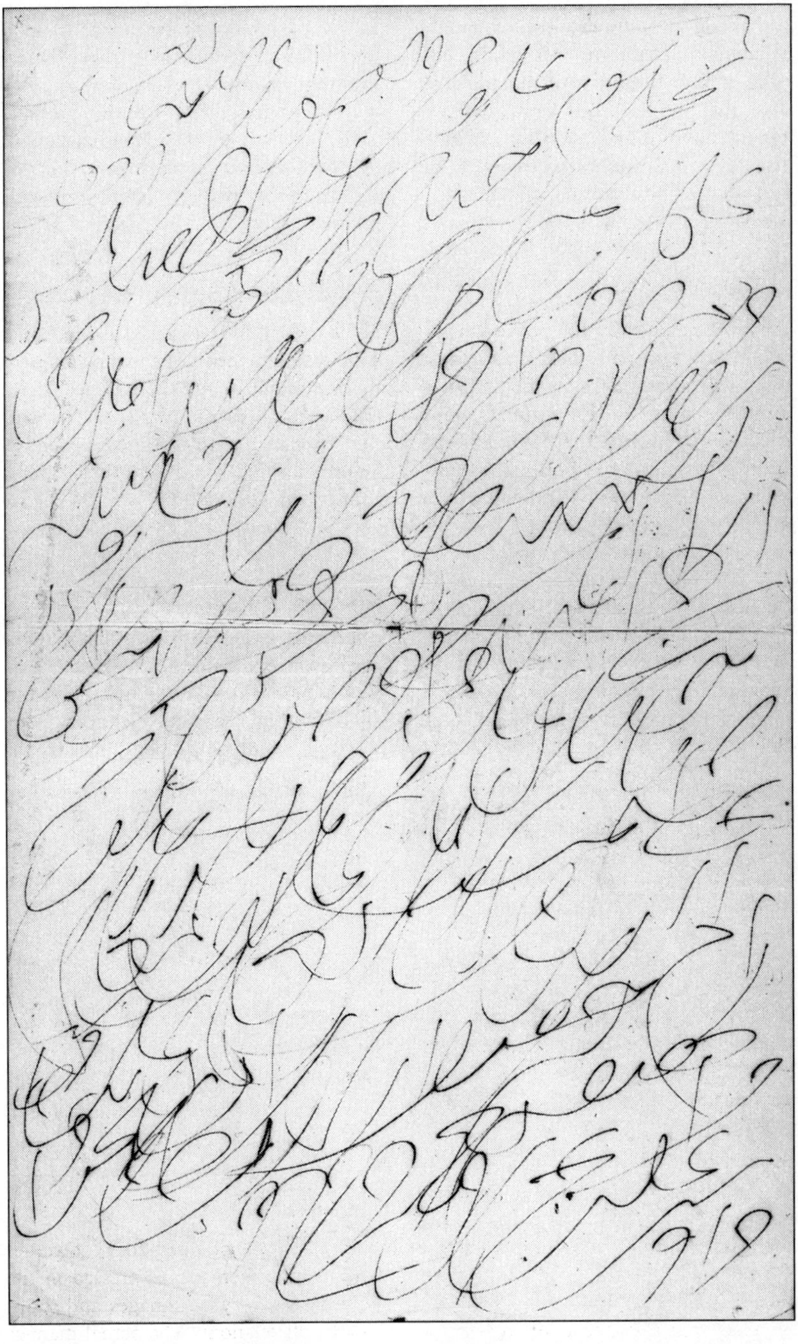

'Revelation writing' in the hand of Mirza Áqá Ján, Bahá'u'lláh's amanuensis

expression of attitude, not of specific behaviours. There are thus few specific rules of behaviour in this regard, other than the non-portrayal of any of the MANIFESTATIONS OF GOD in films or other artistic works, and restrictions on the use of the GREATEST NAME. ITC letter to Counsellors, 1 October 1996.

review

'Abdu'l-Bahá initiated a policy of pre-publication approval of Bahá'í TRANSLATIONS by ASSEMBLIES, and this was formalized by Shoghi Effendi, who directed that, whilst the Faith was still 'in its infancy', all Bahá'í publications – including magazine articles – should be supervised by the relevant local or national assembly, to provide for 'a dignified and accurate' presentation of the Faith (*BA* 23, 38; *LG* 101 no. 349). Literature review was temporary and would be abolished in the future (*WOB* 9). The Universal House of Justice has continued this policy, extending it to all forms of media presentation (books, poems, radio scripts, films), and directing that national assemblies appoint reviewing committees for this purpose (*MUHJ* 185–9 no. 94). Their concern is to guard against 'misrepresentation' of the Faith by Bahá'ís when it is still relatively unknown (*LG* 102 no. 353).

reward and punishment

For Bahá'u'lláh justice and social order were upheld by the hope for reward and the fear of punishment (*TB* 27, 66, 129). One of the purposes of EDUCATION was that children would learn 'the Promise and the Threat', so that they would avoid wrongdoing (*TB* 68. (*See also* FEAR OF GOD.)

Riḍván (PA, 'Paradise')

The name given by Bahá'u'lláh to two gardens: the Najíbiyyih Garden in BAGHDAD, in which Bahá'u'lláh first announced his prophetic claims to some

The Riḍván garden near Akka

of his close companions in 1863, and a garden on the Na'mayn river near AKKA, which Bahá'u'lláh often visited during the closing years of his exile. The Na'mayn Garden is a recognized Bahá'í holy place, but the Najíbiyyih Garden has never been in Bahá'í ownership. The garden has long since been built over, and is now the site of a large modern teaching hospital.

Although the details of Bahá'u'lláh's declaration in the Najíbiyyih Garden are obscure, the period of his stay in the garden is regarded by Bahá'ís as being of immense significance. Bahá'u'lláh himself refers to the first day of Riḍván as being the day on which the splendours of the divine names and attributes were shed upon the whole of creation, and all things were purified. The whole period of Bahá'u'lláh's sojourn in the garden (21 April–2 May) is now commemorated as a sacred festival (the Riḍvan festival), but three particular days are marked off as HOLY DAYS on which Bahá'ís should suspend work: the first, ninth, and twelfth days (21, 29 April, 2 May). These commemorate respectively the arrival of Bahá'u'lláh at the Garden, the arrival of his family, and his final departure. The celebration of the first day of Riḍván should be in the late afternoon, marking the time of Bahá'u'lláh's arrival.

Apart from celebratory meetings, the Riḍván period is also the time of most Bahá'í elections, a practice begun during the ministry of 'Abdu'l-Bahá. Local spiritual ASSEMBLIES are normally elected on the first day of Riḍván. Elections for national assemblies and the Universal House of Justice are also normally held during the Riḍván period. Both Shoghi Effendi and the Universal House of Justice have frequently sent special Riḍván messages to the Bahá'ís at this time. *GPB* 151–5; *KA* 47 k75, 59 k110, 60 k112, 105 q1, 212–13 n107; *RB1*: 259–63, 273–82; Forghani 25–43; Walbridge, *Sacred* 232–41.

ritual

Religious rituals comprise any procedures or ceremonies that form an established part of religious practice. They include both those rites that have been formally prescribed and those that have developed informally as part of popular religion. Bahá'í practice includes a number of formal rites (obligatory PRAYER preceded by ritual ABLUTIONS; the daily recital of the GREATEST NAME; rites of PILGRIMAGE to the houses of the Báb and Bahá'u'lláh; and ceremonies for MARRIAGE and funerals (*see* BURIAL) (*McR* 37–69)), but Shoghi Effendi was insistent both that prescribed practices should remain simple and that the Bahá'ís should not introduce rituals of their own into Bahá'í practice (*LG* 138). He also encouraged flexibility in 'secondary matters', such that Bahá'í weddings and nineteen day FEASTS, for example, retain a universal basic pattern, whilst varying greatly, reflecting individual and cultural preferences. Even at a popular level ritualism is extremely limited in its extent, and commonly consists of practices carried over from the environing cultural tradition, as with some Iranian Bahá'ís who observe the Islamic practice of having a commemoration forty days after a death, or those Western Bahá'ís who incorporate elements of the traditional Christian/Western secular wedding ceremony.

Bahá'ís are allowed to participate in the religious ceremonies of other religions (e.g. the baptism of one's child in a mixed Bahá'í–non-Bahá'í marriage) as long as this does not entail making any vow or commitment that is contrary to Bahá'í principles (*LG* 138–40).

Robarts, John Aldham

(1901–91)

Canadian HAND OF THE CAUSE. He and his wife, Audrey, became Bahá'ís in 1938, having first learned about the

Faith from John's aunt, Grace Ober. Their enormous dedication provided significant support for the growth of the then still minuscule Canadian Bahá'í community: teaching the Faith, helping to establish spiritual assemblies, and serving on committees. In 1948 a separate Canadian national spiritual assembly was formed, with John as its chairman. In 1953 the Robartses and their two youngest children pioneered to Mafeking, then capital of Bechuanaland (modern Botswana), subsequently moving to Southern Rhodesia (now Zimbabwe). In 1956 John was elected onto the newly formed regional assembly for South and West Africa, and in October 1957 was appointed as one of the final group of Hands. In 1966 the Robartses returned to Canada. They continued to travel extensively, visiting Bahá'ís in various parts of the world, despite their advancing age and John's increasing frailty. Harper 473–95.

Martha Root, eminent early international Bahá'í teacher

Root, Martha (1872–1939)

Prominent American Bahá'í itinerant teacher and writer. A journalist and former school teacher, she became a Bahá'í in Pittsburgh in 1909. In 1915 she made a lengthy visit to various Bahá'í communities in Asia and elsewhere, supporting herself by publishing articles in the United States. In 1919, in response to 'Abdu'l-Bahá's appeal in the TABLETS OF THE DIVINE PLAN, she began what was to become her life's work with an extended visit to promote the Faith in several countries of Latin America. Travelling from city to city she gave talks – often to Theosophist and Esperanto groups – wrote articles for newspapers and magazines, put Bahá'í books in libraries, and contacted government officials, educators and others. Other lengthy tours followed: between 1923 and 1930 she visited the Far East, Australasia, Europe, the Middle East and India. Then after a year in the United States and Canada she went again to Europe (1932–6) and then to East Asia, Ceylon, India and Australasia (1937–9). She died in Honolulu on the return leg of her journey. Disregarding her own health and living much of the time in poverty, she pushed herself to seize every opportunity to promote the Faith, making myriads of new contacts, including her meetings with Queen MARIE of Romania. She was the first person to make a radio broadcast about the Bahá'í Faith (in Perth, Australia in 1924). In Europe she helped set up the INTERNATIONAL BAHÁ'Í BUREAU, and enormously expanded Bahá'í links with the ESPERANTO movement. Shoghi Effendi posthumously named her HAND OF THE CAUSE and described her as a Bahá'í immortal. *BW8*: 643–8; Garis; Harper 112–22; Zinky and Baram.

Rosen, Baron Victor
(1849–1908)

Russian orientalist. He was Professor of Oriental Languages at the University of St Petersburg from 1885; founder and president of the Oriental Section of the Imperial Russian Archaeological Society and editor of its journal from 1886. He published descriptions, texts and translations of a number of Bábí and Bahá'í texts. *MBBR* 40–2.

Rosenberg, Ethel Jenner
(1858–1930)

Prominent British Bahá'í. She was introduced to the Faith in 1899 by Mary Thornburgh-Cropper and worked to promote it in both London and Paris. She published two small booklets on Bahá'í and presented a paper on the Faith at the third International Congress for the History of Religions (1908). She assisted Laura Clifford Barney (*see* Dreyfus) in the compilation of *Some Answered Questions* and Lady Blomfield in the production of *Paris Talks*. She also began to learn Persian with the aim of translating Bahá'í writings into English, and later assisted Shoghi Effendi in his translation of Bahá'u'lláh's *Hidden Words*. She was amongst the group of prominent Western Bahá'ís with whom Shoghi Effendi consulted in 1922 regarding the future of the Faith, and was subsequently a member of the newly established British national spiritual assembly. In 1926–7 – now almost seventy – she briefly served as Shoghi Effendi's English-language secretary in Haifa. Shoghi Effendi described her as 'England's pioneer worker', and she is listed among the Disciples of 'Abdu'l-Baha. *BW4*: 262–3; *WEBW* 55–64; Weinberg.

Rúḥí Afnán (1899–1971)

Shoghi Effendi's cousin and personal secretary during the early years of his ministry. He married his cousin Zahrá, daughter of 'Abdu'l-Bahá's daughter Rúḥá (*see* Núrí family). His consent to the marriage of his sister Thurayyá to a Covenant-breaker relative led to the entire family being expelled from the Faith by Shoghi Effendi in 1941. Sohrab, *Abdul Baha's Grandson*; *TCB* 359–64.

Rúḥiyyih Khánum, *Amatu'l-Bahá* (Rúḥiyyih Rabbání, born Mary Maxwell, 1910)

American-Canadian wife of Shoghi Effendi and Hand of the Cause. Her parents were William Sutherland and May Maxwell. Involved in Bahá'í youth activities in North America, she moved to Europe in 1935 to support Bahá'í activities there. She married Shoghi Effendi on 24 March 1937, seemingly without much in the way of courtship. She served also for many years as his personal secretary. Shoghi Effendi appointed her as a member of the International Bahá'í Council in 1951 to act as liaison between him and the Council. She was appointed as a Hand of the Cause on 26 March 1952

Ruhiyyih Khánum, wife of Shoghi Effendi and later Hand of the Cause

following the death of her father. She acted as the rallying point for her fellow Hands after Shoghi Effendi's death and was one of the custodial Hands. Her travels have taken her to almost all parts of the Bahá'í world, including many remote rural areas. The honorific *Amatu'l-Bahá* means maidservant or handmaiden of Bahá. Harper 168–82.

rulers, proclamation to

Beginning during the period of his exile in European Turkey, Bahá'u'lláh addressed a number of world rulers, proclaiming his status as divine messenger and calling upon them to assist him. This proclamation – amounting to some two thousand verses (*PDC* 28) – included both letters sent to specific leaders (the Ottoman sultan ABDULAZIZ, NÁṢIRU'DÍN SHÁH of Iran, NAPOLEON III of France, VICTORIA of Britain, ALEXANDER II of Russia and Pope PIUS IX) and general addresses to the rulers, notably in the *Súra of the* KINGS. Other world leaders were referred to in the *Kitáb-i-*AQDAS (WILHELM I of Germany, FRANZ-JOSEPH of Austria-Hungary, the rulers of the AMERICAS, world parliamentarians) and elsewhere. Two of Abdulaziz's ministers (ÂLI PAŞA and FUAT PAŞA) were also specifically addressed in particular tablets. Bahá'u'lláh's proclamation followed the pattern set by the Prophet Muḥammad, who is supposed to have dispatched a similar series of messages to the rulers of his day. In several cases the proclamation included specific warnings to those rulers whom Bahá'u'lláh judged to have opposed him or been insincere (*see* PROPHECY), the subsequent downfall of those rulers being regarded as evidence of DIVINE JUDGEMENT.

Shoghi Effendi focused on Bahá'u'lláh's proclamation in *THE PROMISED DAY IS COME* (1941), regarding it as a continuation of the Báb's address to the world's rulers included in the first chapter of the *QAYYÚMU'L-ASMÁ'*. Bahá'u'lláh had addressed the rulers and religious leaders of his day because in the 19th century the ordinary people, for the most part, did not have the freedom to investigate the divine message, such was the prevalence of absolutist monarchy and ecclesiastical power. By the same token these leaders bore great responsibility, and their generally negative response had engendered catastrophic consequences, both for the specific monarchies addressed and for their institutions in general. Thus, Bahá'u'lláh had prophesied that God would seize power from the 'kings and ecclesiastics'. This process began on the night of the Báb's declaration and received visible expression in Bahá'u'lláh's prophecies in his letters to the rulers, widely circulated in the *Súratu'l-Haykal*, even before the downfall of Napoleon III and Pope Pius. It subsequently gained momentum with the collapse of the Russian, Austrian and German monarchies during World War I (1914–18), and the ending of OTTOMAN and QÁJÁR rule shortly thereafter. It continued to the present day, representing an unprecedented cataclysm in the fortunes of royalty. A similar process could be noted involving the world's RELIGIOUS LEADERS. (*See also* KINGS, KINGSHIP; SECULARIZATION.)

The Universal House of Justice marked the centenary of Bahá'u'lláh's composition of the *Súra of the Kings* in September 1967, initiating a period of PROCLAMATION (until 1973), in which a specially prepared compilation of Bahá'u'lláh's addresses to the rulers (*The Proclamation of Bahá'u'lláh*) was presented to contemporary heads of state (142 in all), and the generality of the Bahá'ís called upon to work to acquaint 'every stratum of human society' with Bahá'u'lláh's 'healing message'. The original rejection of that message had led to appalling results, but there were now new rulers and peoples who might respond, and thus avoid or mitigate 'the severity of impending catastrophe' (*Proclamation* xiii). The House made a second proclamation to world leaders with the presentation of its statement *The* PROMISE OF WORLD PEACE (October 1985). *MUHJ* 63–5 no. 24.14–22, 104–6 no. 42.15–21, 110–11 no. 45, 238 no. 128.8; *BW14*: 204–20.

Rumi, Siyyid Mustafa

(d. 1942, 1944 or 1945)

Prominent early Bahá'í in India and Burma. His family was from Baghdad but had settled in Madras, and it was there that he came into contact with JAMÁL EFFENDI (1876) and became a Bahá'í. He accompanied Jamál during his travels through India and South East Asia (from 1878), eventually settling in Rangoon, where he married into an Indo-Burman trading family. Learned and active, he was able to build on the work started by Jamál and consolidate several Bahá'í communities in Burma, including an entire village (Daidanaw). In 1899 he was one of those who took the marble casket made by the Bahá'ís of Mandalay for the Báb's remains to 'Abdu'l-Bahá. He worked extensively to further the Bahá'í Faith in Burma and India, including writing and translating Bahá'í literature in Burmese and supervising the publication of various materials in Urdu. He was murdered during the chaotic conditions that prevailed in Burma during World War II. He was then almost ninety-nine years old. Shoghi Effendi posthumously honoured him as a HAND OF THE CAUSE. *BW10*: 517–20; Harper 123–8; Shoghi Effendi, *Messages . . . to the Indian Subcontinent* 430–7.

S

Sabeanism

Ancient Middle Eastern religious tradition or traditions said to have flourished in Chaldea. It is accepted by Bahá'ís as one of nine known revealed religions, although knowledge of its founder and teachings are utterly obscure. *CC1*: 20 nos. 54–7.

sacrifice

The ancient belief that the death of a holy figure has redemptive power was upheld by Bahá'u'lláh, who referred to Abraham's intended sacrifice of his son as a demonstration of DETACHMENT and steadfastness in God's faith; and to Jesus Christ's crucifixion and the death of the Imám ḤUSAYN at KARBALÁ as ransoms 'for the sins and iniquities of all the peoples of the earth'. In the case of Jesus, his sacrifice of himself infused a 'fresh capacity' and 'quickening power' into all created things, the evidences of which were still manifest in learning, the arts and politics (*GWB* 75, 85). Similarly, the death of Bahá'u'lláh's son, Mírzá MIHDÍ, was regarded as a 'ransom' for the regeneration of the world and the unification of its peoples (*GPB* 188, 348).

More generally, self-sacrifice as renunciation of desire; detachment from worldly things; the expenditure of time, energy and resources in service to humanity and to advance the Bahá'í Faith (giving to the Bahá'í FUNDS; TEACHING) are all extolled, and seen as exerting a spiritual influence on the world. So too, to an even greater degree, is acceptance of MARTYRDOM in God's path, though Bahá'u'lláh also taught his followers not to seek confrontation and martyrdom.

Sa'd, 'Abdu'l-Jalíl Bey (d. 1942)

Prominent Egyptian Bahá'í. He became a Bahá'í after coming into contact with Mírzá ABU'L-FAḌL. As a civil court judge in the 1920s he was instrumental in widening the legal basis for freedom of religion in Egypt, and later defended the Bahá'í Faith in newspaper articles from attacks on it (1934). Transferred to a remote area of the country as a result of this publicity, he devoted himself to translating the *DAWN-BREAKERS* and other materials into Arabic, securing permission to publish and distribute these in the face of considerable opposition. He was also able to gain permission for the Bahá'ís to build the national *ḤAẒÍRATU'L-QUDS* in Cairo (1941). He was president of the national spiritual ASSEMBLY of Egypt and Sudan for many years. Shoghi Effendi posthumously honoured him as a HAND OF THE CAUSE. *BW9*: 597–9; Harper 57–9.

Ṣádiq Khurásání, Mullá (d. 1889)

Eminent Bábí and early Bahá'í. Born in Mashhad, the son of a cleric, He furthered his own clerical studies in KARBALÁ under the Shaykhí leader Sayyid KÁẒIM Rashtí, eventually gaining the rank of *mujtahid*, and becoming known by the honorific title *Muqaddas* ('the holy one'). Accepting the Báb, he moved to Shíráz where he became a leader of the congregational prayers, and in that capacity added the Báb's name to the call to prayer (June 1845). This occasioned uproar, and Ṣádiq, together with QUDDÚS and another Bábí, were arrested, scourged, mutilated, and expelled from the city. Ṣádiq subsequently travelled to Yazd and Kirmán, where he publicly proclaimed the Báb's advent. He joined Mullá ḤUSAYN BUSHRÚ'Í, and participated in the struggle at ṬABARSÍ, of which he was one of the few survivors. He met Bahá'u'lláh in Baghdad in around 1861, later becoming one of the foremost promoters of the Faith in Iran, and suffering further persecution and imprisonment. Bahá'u'lláh gave him the title *Ismu'lláhu'l-Aṣdaq* ('the name of God, the most truthful'). 'Abdu'l-Bahá posthumously named him a HAND OF THE CAUSE. His son, IBN-I-AṢDAQ, was one of the Hands appointed by Bahá'u'lláh. *EB* 7–23; Harper 32–41; *MBBR* 69–70; *MF* 5–8.

Ṣáliḥ

Quranic prophet referred to by Bahá'u'lláh (*KI* 7).

Salmán, Shaykh (Shaykh Khanjar)

A devoted Bahá'í who served as Bahá'u'lláh's and later 'Abdu'l-Bahá's messenger to the Iranian Bahá'ís, delivering and receiving letters for a period of some forty years, and travelling thousands of miles on foot between Bahá'u'lláh's various places of exile and throughout Iran. Bahá'u'lláh wrote many tablets in his honour. *RB1*: 109–13.

salvation

For Bahá'ís salvation is dependent on two things: faith in the current MANIFESTATION OF GOD (at the present time Bahá'u'lláh) and good deeds (i.e. seeking to acquire SPIRITUAL QUALITIES; *see* FREE WILL). They also hope for God's mercy (*LG* 209 no. 705). Spiritual progress is potentially limitless, however, and 'heaven' consists of nearness to God. This implies levels or continua of salvation. The faithful are warned never to despise the seemingly sinful, for no one knows what their own end might be: the sinner at the hour of death may attain the essence of faith, whilst the devout believer can abandon it (*KI* 124). (*See also* DEATH; HEAVEN; SOUL.)

Samandar, Shaykh (Muḥammad-)Káẓim (1844–1918)

Eminent Iranian Bahá'í. He was born into a prominent merchant family in Qazvín. His father, known as Shaykh Muḥammad, was a devoted Shaykhí who became an active Bábí and was persecuted for his beliefs. Shaykh Káẓim became a staunch follower of Bahá'u'lláh and opposed the influence of a group of AZALIS who were active in Qazvín for a time. He received many letters from Bahá'u'lláh, who gave him the title *Samandar* ('Phoenix'). He visited Akka a number of times and his daughter Thurayya married Bahá'u'lláh's son Ḍíyá'u'lláh. Shoghi Effendi named him as one of the APOSTLES OF BAHÁ'U'LLÁH. *EB* 191–215.

Samandarí, Ṭarázu'lláh (1875–1968)

Iranian HAND OF THE CAUSE. He was born into a Bahá'í family in Qazvin; his father was Shaykh Káẓim SAMANDAR. He spent much of his long life travelling to promote the Faith and fulfilled various missions on behalf of 'Abdu'l-Bahá and Shoghi Effendi in Iran and elsewhere. Shoghi Effendi appointed him a Hand of the Cause in December 1951. In old age he was among the last to recall meetings with Bahá'u'lláh (in 1891–2), thus giving Bahá'ís in many parts of the world a sense of living history. He long remained active and was a powerful speaker. He was also a skilled calligrapher. He died in Haifa. *BW15*: 410–16; Harper 307–16.

satan

Bahá'ís do not believe in any malevolent superhuman entity such as a devil or satan. Human beings have FREE WILL either to turn towards God and develop SPIRITUAL QUALITIES, or to become immersed in their own selfish desires and commit wrongdoing. If they choose the latter then their actions are sometimes described as 'satanic', but this a metaphorical usage. Both the Báb and Bahá'u'lláh on occasion referred to certain opponents as 'satanic'. (*See also* EVIL.)

scholarship

Advanced study of a subject; the qualities and attainments of a scholar.

THE NEED

For Shoghi Effendi and the Universal House of Justice the development of Bahá'í scholarship was of great importance. Shoghi Effendi noted in the 1940s that the thinking world had already 'caught up' with the universal 'BAHÁ'Í PRINCIPLES' enunciated by Bahá'u'lláh, and that these no longer seemed new. Yet he reiterated that the Faith had the answer to the world's problems. What was needed was individuals able to present the Bahá'í teachings to intelligent people. There was a need for more Bahá'í scholars, and for 'a more profound and co-ordinated Bahá'í scholarship'. The Bahá'ís need both to know the Bahá'í teachings in depth, and to be well educated in general, having a sound knowledge of history, religious history, economics, sociology, science and the like. Thus they should be able to correlate the thinking of modern thinkers and progressive movements with the Bahá'í teachings. Again, the House of Justice has referred to the potential importance of Bahá'í scholarship in the CONSOLIDATION of the Bahá'í community as it becomes better known in the wider world; to the need for intelligent analysis of current issues of social concern from a Bahá'í perspective; and the vital role of scholars in defending the Faith from its detractors. *CC1*: 227–31 nos. 501, 506, 510–11, 515; *Baha'i Scholarship* 3–8, 11, 15, 42, 44; *MUHJ* 387 no. 217.1, 720 no. 453.13.

GENERAL PRINCIPLES

For the House of Justice: (1) There is no conflict between 'true' SCIENCE and 'true' religion: both are sources of knowledge about reality. Bahá'í scholars should combine 'profound faith' with 'freedom of thought'. They should both be loyal to Bahá'u'lláh and his teachings, and study their religion searchingly and intelligently, following the principle of 'an unfettered search after truth'. (2) All human understanding is limited (*see* KNOWLEDGE), including Bahá'ís' understanding of their own scriptures and the scientific theories of a particular period in human history. Thus there is no one 'correct' view of the history and teachings of the Faith. (3) Bahá'ís should not accept uncritically the materialistic theories of much modern thinking just because these are fashionable. (4) The harmony of the Bahá'í community is important. Bahá'ís should avoid the antagonisms that have divided other religious groups into those who blindly hold to the letter of their scriptures and those who question everything (i.e. the 'fundamentalist'/'liberal' divide). Both extremes are destructive. Bahá'í scholars should therefore phrase their findings with tact, moderation, humility and wisdom, whilst the general community – in particular those who hold positions of responsibility in the Bahá'í administration – should be tolerant of the views of others, accept a diversity of opinions, and avoid the censoriousness that could stifle the development of scholarship. (5) REVIEW remains an important means of protecting the Faith at what is still an early stage in its development, when it is both severely persecuted in IRAN and not widely understood. *Baha'i Scholarship* 9–28; UHJRD, *Scholarship*. (*See also* BÁBÍ AND BAHÁ'Í STUDIES.)

schools

The Bahá'í teachings place a high value on EDUCATION, and this has led to the establishment of Bahá'í schools in various parts of the world.

EARLY SCHOOLS

The earliest Bahá'í schools were started in the 1890s in ASHKHABAD and Iran.

ASHKHABAD

A boys' school was founded in 1894 and a girls' school in 1907. Later, kindergartens were also established. These were all closed in 1929, as part of the Soviet authorities' campaign against organized religion.

IRAN

Schools were started by Bahá'ís in several towns and villages towards the end of the 19th century. The most well known of these were the Tarbíyat schools in Tehran: a boys' school opened in 1898, and a girls' school in 1910. The schools gained a reputation for excellence, and began to attract students from many high-ranking non-Bahá'í families, including for a time the children of Reza Sháh. (As with other Bahá'í schools, children of any religion were allowed entry.) They also received support from American Bahá'ís (Susan MOODY, Lillian KAPPES, Genevieve Coy, Adelaide SHARPE), particularly at the girls' school. The provision of schooling for girls was of particular significance, flying in the face of contemporary social convention, and making an important contribution to the emergence of the first generation of educated professional women in Iran. The schools faced considerable opposition from conservative Muslims, and eventually from the government. They were closed, together with all other Bahá'í schools in the country, by order of the ministry of education in 1934. No Bahá'í schools have been allowed to operate in Iran since that date. Armstrong-Ingram, 'American Baha'i Women'; Banani, *Modernization* 95–7; *BW6*: 25–31; *MBBR* 475–9.

OTHER

A Bahá'í village school was started in Daidanaw in Burma by Siyyid Mustafa RUMI at an early date; the Bahá'ís of Kenosha, Wisconsin operated an industrial school for girls during the early years of the century; and there seems to have been some Bahá'í involvement in Henderson Business College in Memphis, Tennessee, which provided schooling for black students.

LATER SCHOOLS

NEW ERA HIGH SCHOOL

The first of the current generation of Bahá'í schools. Located in Panchgani, Maharashtra state, India, it originated in 1945 as an educational hostel, mostly for Iranian Bahá'ís. It expanded and transferred to its present site in 1953, becoming a fully fledged school open to all. With further expansion it has built up a reputation for educational excellence. It attracts both Indian students (regardless of caste or religion) and a considerable number of students

(Bahá'ís and others) from various parts of the world (*BW16*: 320–6).

THIRD WORLD

With the EXPANSION of the Bahá'í Faith from the late 1950s onwards Bahá'í schools were founded in a number of countries, including initially Uganda, Bolivia, and various of the islands of the South Pacific. The subsequent fortunes of these schools have varied widely. Some have flourished, gaining government recognition and expanding to include schooling for a wide age range. Others have remained small in scale and limited in scope. Some have been forced to close. The overall pattern is one of considerable expansion, with schools in an increasing number of countries: in 1946, there were perhaps four Bahá'í schools world-wide; by 1979 this had increased to ten, and by 1992 to one hundred and seventy-eight, including sixty-two kindergartens. Nearly all of these were in the Third World (*BW18*: 207–38; *NS* 1992–3: 313).

OTHER

Recent developments of note have been the establishment of Maxwell International Bahá'í School in Canada (1988); the holding of an international networking conference for Bahá'í schools at Maxwell in 1992; and an agreement between the local authorities and the Bahá'ís of the Marshall Islands, whereby a number of elementary schools were handed over to the Bahá'ís to administer (1993) (*BWNS* 1993–4: 101).

'TUTORIAL SCHOOLS'

In addition to formal academic schools, the Bahá'ís in many poorer countries have established an increasing number of 'tutorial schools' (488 by 1992). These are non-formal village schools designed to provide basic educational skills (such as LITERACY) to children and adults using local resources (*BW18*: 208–9, 213).

Schopflocher, Siegfried ('Fred') (1877–1953)

Canadian HAND OF THE CAUSE of German Jewish background. He became a Bahá'í in 1921. A successful businessman, he made a number of major financial contributions to Bahá'í projects, including the Wilmette temple (*MASHRIQU'L-ADHKAR*) and the GREEN ACRE Bahá'í school. He travelled extensively and served on both the joint American–Canadian and separate Canadian national spiritual assemblies. He was appointed a Hand of the Cause by Shoghi Effendi in February 1952. His wife, Florence Eveline ('Lorol') (1896–1970), was one of the most widely travelled of the early Western Bahá'ís, visiting Bahá'ís in many parts of the world, and trying to help alleviate the persecutions of the Iranian Bahá'ís. *BW12*: 664–6; *15*: 488–9; Harper 384–90.

Schwarz, (Consul) Albert (1871–1931) and Alice (1875–1965)

Prominent early German Bahá'í couple who first learned of the Faith in 1911. Of high social position (Albert was a banker and Norwegian consul in Stuttgart), their conversion was a significant development. In 1919 a Bahá'í office was established in their home and Albert was able to represent the newly formed German Bahá'í Association at a League of Nations conference. In March 1922 they were among the small group of Western Bahá'ís called to Haifa by SHOGHI EFFENDI to discuss the development of the Faith. Alice founded the German Bahá'í magazine *Sonne der Wahrheit* (Sun of Truth). Albert was honoured by Shoghi Effendi as one of the DISCIPLES OF 'ABDU'L-BAHÁ. *BW4*: 264–6; *14*: 377–8.

science

The Bahá'í teachings stress the importance of REASON and the INTELLECT, and praise the quest for KNOWLEDGE. Scientific study and investigation is encouraged, especially when it leads to human advancement (e.g. ending disease; raising the standard of health; improving the functioning of the brain; prolonging the life-span; increasing productivity; exploiting 'the unused and unsuspected resources of the planet'; and stimulating the intellectual, moral and spiritual life 'of the entire human race' (*WOB* 204)). Bahá'u'lláh disparaged those areas of learning that 'begin with words and end with words' – the Islamic scholasticism studied by the Iranian *'ULAMÁ* – as fruitless and unworthy of study (*ESW* 19; *KI* 119–21; *TB* 52, 169). 'Abdu'l-Bahá regarded the conformity of religion with science and reason as a basic Bahá'í principle (*see* RELIGION AND SCIENCE), and the diligent acquisition of scientific knowledge as a form of worship (*SWAB* 144–5, 299). He stressed, however, that scientific knowledge only represents 'droplets of reality', and that the pursuit of knowledge should also draw from divine inspiration (*SWAB* 110); all branches of learning are worthy of praise if they are combined with the love of God, but if they are not, they are barren (*CC1*: 469 no. 1040). Similarly, he condemned purely materialistic CIVILIZATION, which, despite its technological brilliance, engenders such moral monstrosities as war.

scripture

Bahá'ís regard the writings of the Báb and Bahá'u'lláh as divine REVELATION. These, together with the writings and authenticated transcripts of talks of 'Abdu'l-Bahá, are recognized as sacred scripture. This includes both their own writings and those written at their dictation by secretaries. Transcripts of 'Abdu'l-Bahá's talks in the original language are also included. The original teachings of previous MANIFESTATIONS OF GOD (the Buddha, Moses, Jesus, Muḥammad, etc.) are also regarded as having been divine revelations, but doubt is expressed as to the detailed authenticity of the present-day scriptures of BUDDHISM, Hinduism (*see* INDIAN RELIGIONS) and ZOROASTRIANISM. By contrast, the QURAN is recognized as fully authoritative, and the Judaeo-Christian BIBLE as substantially authentic. Although frequently cited in Bahá'í scripture, the Islamic traditions (*HADÍTH*) are not regarded as scriptural. Many Bahá'ís read the scriptures of the past for religious enlightenment, but even in the case of the Bible and Quran, these are not regarded as binding on Bahá'ís in matters of religious belief and practice: each Manifestation brings the laws and teachings appropriate for his time, and explains divine truth in terms appropriate for the understanding of his hearers (*see* PROGRESSIVE REVELATION). All three of the Bahá'í 'Central Figures' (the Báb, Bahá'u'lláh, and 'Abdu'l-Bahá) wrote commentaries on Quranic verses. Bahá'u'lláh and 'Abdu'l-Bahá also commented on biblical verses. (*See also* CANONICAL TEXTS.)

Sears, William (1911–92)

American HAND OF THE CAUSE of Irish Catholic background. He first learnt of the Bahá'í Faith in 1936 from his future wife, Marguerite Reimer, and converted in 1940. In 1953 the Sears moved to South Africa as Bahá'í PIONEERS. William was appointed to the AUXILIARY BOARD for Africa in 1954 and was elected as chairman of the new national spiritual ASSEMBLY for South and West Africa in 1956. He was appointed a Hand of the Cause by Shoghi Effendi in October 1957. The Sears returned to the United States in 1959, and subsequently travelled extensively, visiting Bahá'ís in various parts of the world. Sears was a radio and television writer, performer, commentator and humorist. He was involved with the production of a

William Sears, American pioneer to South Africa and later Hand of the Cause

number of Bahá'í radio programmes, and in 1973 worked with Robert Quigley to prepare the first Bahá'í television series (in Hawaii). His books include a number of popular Bahá'í histories, a Bahá'í account of the fulfilment of biblical prophecy (*Thief in the Night*), and the autobiographical *God Loves Laughter*. Harper 496–506.

Secret of Divine Civilization

(Ar.: *Asrár al-qaybiyya li asbáb al-madaniyya*)

Treatise by 'Abdu'l-Bahá on Iranian 'modernization'. It is commonly referred to in Persian as *Risáli-yi-madaniyyih* ('The Treatise on Civilization'). Written in 1875, the work was lithographed in Bombay in 1882 and received wide circulation in Iran. It was published anonymously and not identified as a specifically Bahá'í work – presumably to avoid prejudicing readers against its contents. The first English translation was published in 1910 in London as *The Mysterious Forces of Civilization*.

The main thrust of 'Abdu'l-Bahá's argument is the urgent need for IRAN to adopt reform measures on Western models. Ancient Iran had been a powerful empire, honoured for its culture and civilization. By contrast, the country was now in a wretched and degenerate state, pitied by others for its backwardness. Injustice and misgovernment had led to its decline. The Iranians should arise out of their torpor and resolve to transform their country and its institutions: promoting EDUCATION (regarded as being of particular importance), industry, commerce, technology, arts and sciences; establishing just laws and protecting the rights of individuals equally before the law; ending corruption and the absolute powers of local governors, particularly their power to administer the death penalty; strengthening relations with other countries, including the great powers and friendly governments; increasing trade linkages and developing national resources and infrastructure; and strengthening the army, such that its soldiers were well housed and fed, its officers well trained and its armaments up to date. Other nations had once been as Iran was now, but through adopting such measures they had progressed. Some Iranians objected that such reforms involved copying the practices of non-Muslims and were hence un-Islamic. This was not valid. There were many Islamic precedents for the adoption of foreign practices, and many elements of European civilization were in any case derived from Islamic roots during the medieval period. Again, reforms such as the introduction of assemblies of consultation could be given Quranic justification. Those who opposed reform would be answerable to God. The rapid progress of Japan and the continuing backwardness and weakness of China indicated the contrast between those nations that modernized and those that did not. In the context of 19th-century reformism in the Middle East the book is unusual in advocating borrowing from the WEST whilst at the same time emphasizing the fundamental role of RELIGION. Both religious bigotry and Western secularism were rejected. 'Abdu'l-Bahá also stressed the importance of SPIRITUAL QUALITIES; outlined the characteristics required of RELIGIOUS LEADERS; and commented on CIVILIZATION, GOVERNMENT, LAW, MISSION, PEACE and wealth.

A proper assessment of how the work was received amongst contemporary Iranian reformers has yet to be made. The book was written at a time when genuine reform of Iran seemed possible – Mírzá ḤUSAYN KHÁN was still politically influential and NÁṢIRU'D-DÍN SHÁH had just made his first visit to Europe (1873). The reform process effectively petered out in the late 1870s, however, and 'Abdu'l-Bahá evidently decided not to pursue his original intention of writing other books on related themes – specifically education (*SDC* 69, 106). Apart from its specifically Iranian context the treatise can be seen as a general Bahá'í prescription for developmental reform in any society.

secret societies

Bahá'ís are not allowed to be members of secret societies such as Masonic lodges, even if the principles of such organizations are in general accord with Bahá'í teachings. This ban is effectively an extension of the ban on Bahá'í political involvement (*see* POLITICS), these organizations being subject to possible politicization. *LG* 54 nos. 192, 421–3.

secularism

Bahá'u'lláh had warned that 'the vitality of men's belief in God' was 'dying out in every land', and 'the corrosion of ungodliness ... [was] eating into the vitals of human society'. Nothing short of his own spiritual 'medicine' could revive it. Shoghi Effendi noted that the world's religions were now being assailed by the forces of secularism (specifically communism, militant nationalism and 'the prevailing spirit of modernism with its emphasis on a purely materialistic philosophy'). The religious institutions of CHRISTIANITY and ISLAM had already been profoundly affected by this process. Given the importance of RELIGION as a bulwark of SOCIAL ORDER, there was now an appreciable decline in morality, with a rising incidence of crime, family breakdown and hedonistic selfishness. The arts and literature had become decadent (*PDC* 119; *WOB* 180–8). God had been 'dethroned from the hearts of men', and in his place the 'false gods' of nationalism, racism and communism were worshipped by nations and peoples throughout the world. These 'crooked doctrines' were but the creations of idle fancies which engendered war and conflict, and would sooner or later incur divine chastisement for those who believed in them (*PDC* 117–18). For 'Abdu'l-Bahá, secularism flourished because people denied religion, and materialism advanced. This denial was itself the consequence of religious division and animosity, blind adherence to forms and imitations of ancestral beliefs, and superstitious practices (*PUP* 161, 179, 374).

self-defence

'Abdu'l-Bahá, Shoghi Effendi and the Universal House of Justice all indicated that in cases of civil disorder, or when there was no legal force at hand to appeal to, Bahá'ís were justified in defending their own lives, for example against attack by robbers and highwaymen. They should ensure that such defence did not deteriorate into retaliation, however. 'Abdu'l-Bahá condemned retaliation, regarding it as being as reprehensible as the act to which it was a response: individually, Bahá'ís should follow Jesus' instruction to 'turn the other cheek' and forgive the aggressor.

At the same time, defence of the community and of others was also essential, even if this involved violence against the aggressor. However, in cases in which there was an organized religious attack on the Bahá'ís, self-defence should never turn into any kind of warfare. (*See also* HOLY WAR.) *MUHJ* 148 no. 69; *SAQ* 269–71.

WEAPONS

Echoing Bábí law, Bahá'u'lláh forbade the Bahá'ís to carry weapons 'unless essential', presumably in situations such as threats of banditry. Weapons may also be legitimately used by people who hunt for the basic necessities of life and in sports such as archery or marksmanship. The House of Justice has discouraged American Bahá'ís from owning guns in the context of present rising urban crime rates in North America. *KA* 76 k159, 240–1 n173; *MUHJ* 148 no. 69.

self-knowledge

Each person should know their own self, and recognize that which led to loftiness or abasement, to wealth or poverty. Inner vision acts as a guide for true knowledge and wisdom. Its power is increased as individuals discover the purpose for which God has called them into being (*TB* 35). They should turn to 'the treasuries latent within their own beings' (*TB* 72). True loss is utter ignorance of one's own self (*TB* 156). (*See also* HUMAN LIFE, PURPOSE OF.)

service to humanity

A Bahá'í ideal. Bahá'u'lláh taught that the individual should turn away from his or her own interests and 'cleave unto that which will profit mankind' (*TB* 64). All should seek to promote security and peace among the peoples of the world (*TB* 171).

Seven Candles of Unity

See WORLD UNITY.

Seven Martyrs of Tehran

Seven Bábís executed for their beliefs in 1850 (19/20 February). A Bábí plot against the life of the chief minister, AMÍR KABÍR, was alleged (but not widely believed), and a group of suspected Bábís arrested. Most chose to avoid identifying themselves as Bábís and were released, but seven remained resolute and were beheaded. As European envoys noted, the execution was in public, and replaced the earlier practice of private executions in the presence of the shah. The seven killed were all men of high social status, and their execution attracted considerable attention. They were: (1) Ḥájí Mírzá Sayyid 'Alí, the Báb's maternal uncle and guardian, a leading merchant of Shíráz; (2) Mírzá Qurbán-'Alí of Bárfurúsh, a prominent spiritual guide (*murshid*) in the Ni'matu'lláhí Sufi order; two clerics, (3) Ḥájí Mullá Ismá'il Qumí and (4) Áqá Sayyid Ḥusayn Turshízí, a *MUJTAHID*; two more merchants, (5) Ḥájí Muḥammad-Taqí Kirmání and (6) Sayyid Murtaḍá Zanjání; and a government official, (7) Muḥammad-Ḥusayn Marágh'í. The Báb referred to them as the 'seven goats' of Islamic tradition who would walk before the promised *QÁ'IM* on the Day of Judgement. Balyuzi, *Báb* 182–5, 206–8; *GPB* 47–8; *MBBR* 100–5; Nabil 441–58, 462–3; *TJ* 249–68, 369–70; *TN* 211–17. (*See also* MARTYRDOM.)

Other groups of seven martyrs are lauded in Bahá'í history, notably the 'Seven Martyrs of Yazd' (1891) and the 'Seven Martyrs of Hurmuzak' (1955). Labib; *MBBR* 301–5.

Seven Proofs (PA: *Dalá'il-i-sab'ih*)

Apologetic work of the Báb composed in MÁKÚ (1847–8), after the *BAYÁN*. There are two books of the same name: a longer Persian and shorter Arabic version. Copies were distributed to a number of Iranian princes and state officials. There is a French translation of the entire text of the Persian work by

Nicolas, and a few selected passages have been translated into English (Báb, *Selections* 117–26). *ARR* 384; Browne, *Selections* 218–19; *GPB* 26.

Seven Valleys (Pers.: *Haft Vádí*)

Well-known treatise by Bahá'u'lláh, described by Shoghi Effendi as his greatest mystical work (*GPB* 140). It was composed in Baghdad some time after Bahá'u'lláh's return from Kurdistan (1856) in reply to a letter by Shaykh Muḥiyu'd-dín, a Qádirí Sufi and sometime religious judge (*qáḍí*) in the town of Khániqín. It describes the seven stages ('valleys') of the journey of the seeker's soul towards God, using the framework established by the great 12th/13th-century mystical poet Shaykh Farídu'd-dín 'Aṭṭár in his *Conference of the Birds* (*Manṭiqu'ṭ-ṭayr*). The valleys are those of: (1) search (*ṭalab*), characterized by patient quest for the divine beloved; (2) love (*'ishq*), with its passion of pain and ecstasy; (3) knowledge (*ma'rifat*), with its certitude and understanding of inner truth; (4) unity (*tawḥíd*), in which the seeker transcends the world of limitation, and is able to see the reality of things as they really are; (5) contentment (*istighná'*), in which the mystic sees the beauty of God in everything, and has burnt away all other veils; (6) wonderment (*ḥayrat*), with its bewilderment with the myriad of divine truths that can now be understood; and (7) 'true poverty' (*faqr-i-ḥaqíqí*) and 'absolute nothingness' (*faná-yi-aṣlí*), characterized by a dying from self and a living in God. *SV* 1–43; *RB1*: 96–101; Walbridge, *Sacred* 150–7. (*See also* GOD.)

sex

The value of the sex impulse is recognized, and regarded as the natural right of every individual: sex is not regarded as evil as it is in some cultures, and should not be suppressed. It must be regulated, however, and can only be legitimately expressed in MARRIAGE. All forms of pre- and extra-marital sexual relationships are thus forbidden (*see* ADULTERY AND FORNICATION; HOMOSEXUALITY). Outside of marriage the relationships of Bahá'ís should be characterized by spiritual comradeship. Present society is seen as permissive and as overemphasizing sex; Bahá'ís should follow a different path, and act and think in such a way that they do not arouse appetites that cannot be legitimately expressed (i.e. exercise self-control outside marriage). Early marriage is commended. *LG* 358–68. (*See also* BIRTH CONTROL; CHASTITY.)

Bahá'í ASSEMBLIES should be loving and compassionate in their response to those Bahá'ís who breach these moral regulations: people's behaviour often falls short of the ideal. An assembly should give counsel and encouragement. However, if immoral behaviour is flagrant and a cause of public scandal, and the individuals involved give no sign that they are willing to change, then the assembly should consider depriving them of their Bahá'í ADMINISTRATIVE RIGHTS.

Shahmírzádí, Mullá 'Alí-Akbar

See ÁKHÚND, ḤÁJÍ.

Sharpe, Adelaide (1896–1976)

American Bahá'í who became a prominent member of the Iranian Bahá'í community. She accepted the post of principal of the Tarbíyat school for girls (*see* SCHOOLS), and accompanied Dr Susan MOODY on her return to Iran in 1929. After the school's closure in 1934 she remained in Iran at Shoghi Effendi's request, and contributed to the development of child education within the Bahá'í community, as well as translating Bahá'í writings. She played a prominent role in Iranian Bahá'í administration, and in 1954, when Shoghi Effendi first permitted women to be elected on to Bahá'í assemblies in Iran, she became the first woman to be elected onto the Iranian national spiritual ASSEMBLY, serving as its foreign correspondent for fourteen years. *BW17*: 418–20.

Shaykhism

School of Shí'í thought which centres on the teachings of Shaykh AḤMAD AL-AḤSÁ'Í and his successors. Shaykh Aḥmad attracted a large and influential following, but his ideas were controversial and his immediate successor, Sayyid KÁẒIM RASHTÍ, faced considerable opposition from some groups within the clerical establishment (see *'ULAMÁ*). After his death there was a period of division in which various prominent disciples sought leadership. A significant number of Shaykhís accepted the Báb, forming the core of the new Bábí movement. Eventually most of the non-Bábí Shaykhís turned to Ḥájí Muḥammad KARÍM KHÁN KIRMÁNÍ and his successor-descendants, and the movement lost much of its earlier heterodoxy, in part it would seem to distance itself from Bábism. Bábí–Bahá'í accounts accord Shaykh Aḥmad and Sayyid Káẓim the status of precursors and heralds of their religion, and there are some doctrinal continuities with early Shaykhism. Karím Khán and other later Shaykhí leaders were prominent opponents of Bábism.

Early Shaykhí doctrine is complex and under-researched. Some aspects seem deliberately obscure (presumably to conceal heterodox elements), and others are subject to varying interpretations. A key element is the belief in the unknowability and transcendence of God. Human beings therefore must approach the divine through the prophets and IMÁMS. These personages were regarded as eternal spiritual realities and manifestations of God's primal will. This viewpoint led the Shaykhís' opponents to accuse them of attributing God's attributes to another (the heresy of *tafwíḍ*). It also led the Shaykhís to extreme veneration of the Imáms. Another crucial doctrine was of the existence of an interworld of archetypal images (*'álamu'l- mithál*), the *Húrqalyá*, which contains counterparts of all that exists in the physical world. This is the world in which the Shí'í eschatological figure of the hidden Twelfth Imám resides; in which the believer can encounter the Imáms; in which Muḥammad made his miraculous night ascent to heaven; and in which the resurrection of the individual occurs. Again, the early Shaykhís believed that there would always be a 'Perfect Shí'í' alive in the world who would act as an intermediary between the Imám and the faithful (this was the doctrine of the 'Fourth Support' which, together with belief in divine unity, prophethood and imamate, constituted the fundamental elements of religion). By implication Shaykh Aḥmad and Sayyid Káẓim occupied this role, Shaykh Aḥmad himself stressing that his own authority derived from intuitive knowledge which he derived directly from inspiration from the Imáms. Bábí and Bahá'í accounts also identify a major emphasis on messianic expectation. *ARR* 48–69; Bayat 37–86; Balyuzi, *Báb* 1–6; Corbin, vol. 4: 205–301 (reflecting later Shaykhí views); MacEoin, 'Early Shaykhí reactions'; 'From Shaykhism'; Momen, *Shi'i Islam* 225–31; 'Works of Shaykh Aḥmad'; Nabil 1–46 (the standard Bahá'í account); Nicolas, *Essai* (an older work); Rafati 'Development'; *SBBR* 8–13; Scholl.

Shí'ism

ISLAM is divided into two main branches: the Sunnís, who comprise the majority of the world's Muslims, and the Shí'ís, who predominate in Iran and Azerbaiján, and comprise important minorities in a number of other countries. Distinctive features of Shí'ism include: (1) Imáms: the Shí'ís recognize 'Alí ibn Abí-Ṭálib,

Muḥammad's cousin and son-in-law, as the Prophet's rightful successor and as the first in a series of IMÁMS. Different Shí'í groups recognize different series of Imáms. The largest group is that of the 'Twelvers' (*Ithná-'asharí*), who follow a succession of twelve Imáms – this is the branch that predominates in Iran, and from which the Bábí–Bahá'í tradition emerged. The Ismá'ilís are another important division of Shí'ism. (2) Law: the Twelvers recognize the teachings of the Imáms as an important supplementary authority to the Quran and the Traditions ascribed to Muḥammad. There are a number of differences in religious practice. Most of these are relatively minor, but *khums* – the 'one-fifth' tax – and the institution of temporary marriage (*mut'a*) are peculiar to Shí'ism. (3) Shí'ism's minority status and its periodic persecution has led to an emphasis on MARTYRDOM as a religious motif (particularly as represented by the death of the Imám ḤUSAYN at KARBALÁ (680 CE), which is commemorated with much emotional fervour during the month of Muḥarram). Dissimulation of religious belief (*taqiyya*) is regarded as a legitimate means of avoiding persecution. (4) Twelver Shí'ism is also characterized by a strong messianic motif centring on the mysterious disappearance ('Occultation') of the Twelfth Imám (260 AH/874 CE), and his expected return at the RESURRECTION as the *QÁ'IM*/MAHDÍ. Following his disappearance, a series of four men claimed to act as his intermediaries as *Bábs* ('Gates') until 329 AH/941 CE. (5) Twelver Shí'ism is also distinctive in the degree of authority and autonomy from government control gained by its 'learned' (*'ULAMÁ*), and the emergence of a definite clerical establishment. Clerical arguments about the role of the *'ulamá* during the 17th and 18th centuries led to an important division between the Uṣúlís, who asserted the centrality of the *MUJTAHIDS*, senior clerics who had gained a licence to exercise independent judgement (*ijtihád*) on matters of religious law, and the Akhbárís, who opposed them. The Uṣúlís eventually dominated, and a clerical hierarchy emerged during the 19th century. (6) Speculative thought in Shí'ism has been influenced by the acceptance of early Islamic Mu'tazilite rationalism and the development of the *Ishráqí* theosophical 'Illuminationist' tradition, of which SHAYKHISM forms a part. Momen, *Shi'i Islam*, provides the best general introduction. See also Mottahedeh; Ṭabáṭabá'í.

THE BAHÁ'Í FAITH AND SHÍ'ISM

The Bábí and Bahá'í religions were rooted in Iranian Shí'ism. The Bahá'í Faith ultimately developed into a world religion (*see* EXPANSION), however, and whilst the Bahá'í teachings incorporate many elements of the Shí'í view of Islamic history (notably the legitimacy of 'Alí and the imamate) and some aspects of Shí'í practice and belief, Bahá'í is quite distinct from its religion of origin, and its incorporation of Shí'í elements is often quite subtle and complex.

Although most of the Bábí leaders and many of the prominent early Bahá'ís were clerics, the Shí'í *'ulamá* were the main force opposing the expansion of the two religions, and were often instrumental in fostering PERSECUTION. Correspondingly, Bahá'ís have condemned the Shí'í *'ulamá* and blamed them for what they see as the decline of Shí'ism's former 'pristine brilliancy'. Shoghi Effendi welcomed moves by Reza Sháh (*See also* IRAN) to reduce the power of the *'ulamá*, seeing this as a direct consequence of their opposition to the Bábís and Bahá'ís. *GPB* 228–9; *PDC* 87–98; *WOB* 172–3, 179. (*See also* RELIGIOUS LEADERS.)

Shíráz (1868 pop. est. 25,000)

Capital of the southern Iranian province of Fárs. Birthplace of the Báb and the site of his initial declaration of mission.

The destruction of the House of the Báb, Shíráz, Iran, 1979

Shíráz: the House of the Báb

The Báb's house, where he first declared his mission in 1844. He later identified it as the new 'House of God' in succession to the Ka'ba at Mecca, and made it a place of PILGRIMAGE for his followers. Bahá'u'lláh named it as one of two sacred houses and as a place of pilgrimage. It later came into the possession of the Bahá'ís and was restored at 'Abdu'l-Bahá's instructions in 1903, becoming a major centre of pilgrimage for Bahá'ís in Iran (*GPB* 300). It also became a focus for anti-Bahá'í zealots, being damaged in an arson attack in 1942, almost destroyed by an anti-Bahá'í mob in 1955, and finally thoroughly demolished by Islamic revolutionaries in September 1979. A road and public square were later built over the site. *KA* 66 k133, 117 q32, 230–1 n154.

Shírází, Mírzá-yi (1815–95)

Ḥájí Mírzá Sayyid Muḥammad-Ḥasan, eminent Shí'í cleric, resident in Iraq. He became recognized as the sole *marja'at-taqlíd* ('centre of imitation', *see* 'ULAMÁ) for the entire Shí'í world in about 1872. Otherwise apolitical, he intervened decisively in 1891 to oppose the granting of the tobacco monopoly by the Iranian government. He was a paternal cousin of the Báb, and is said to have been a secret believer in both the Báb and Bahá'u'lláh, and to have sought to mitigate the persecutions of the Bahá'ís in Iran. Balyuzi, *Báb* 33; *BKG* 403–4; *EB* 251–60; Momen, *Shi'i Islam* 140, 321.

Shoghi Effendi Rabbání

(1897–1957)

First and only Guardian of the Bahá'í Faith (*see* GUARDIANSHIP). He was the leader in succession to 'Abdu'l-Bahá from 1922 until his own death. He was succeeded by the HANDS OF THE CAUSE acting as 'CUSTODIANS' of the Faith until the election of the Universal House of Justice (1963).

EARLY LIFE

Shoghi Effendi was the eldest son of 'Abdu'l-Bahá's daughter Ḍiyá'iyyih Khánum (d. 1951) and Mírzá Hádí Shírází Afnán (d. 1955). He was born in Akka on 1 March 1897, the eldest of 'Abdu'l-Bahá's grandsons, and named in the latter's will as his successor when he was still a child. Educated at first at home with the other children of the household, he was later sent to Catholic schools in Haifa and Beirut and then to the Syrian Protestant College (the predecessor of the American University) in Beirut, spending his summer holidays as one of his grandfather's assistants. He gained an arts degree from the college in 1918, and became 'Abdu'l-Bahá's chief secretary. Then, in 1920, he went to Oxford University (Balliol College), where he studied political science and economics, and also sought to perfect his English so as to be better able to translate Bahá'í literature into that language. He was still in the midst of his studies when summoned to return to Haifa at the news of his grandfather's death.

APPOINTMENT AND SUCCESSION

Shortly after Shoghi Effendi's return to Haifa (29 December 1921) the terms of 'Abdu'l-Bahá's *WILL AND TESTAMENT* were announced. These were explicit. Shoghi Effendi was to be 'Guardian of the Cause of God' (*Valí amru'lláh*, a title immediately reminiscent of the Shí'í IMÁMS). He was the Centre of the Cause and the 'sign of God' on earth. All should show 'their obedience, submissiveness and subordination' to him. He was also to be the head of the as yet unelected UNIVERSAL HOUSE OF JUSTICE, and with them was under the unerring guidance and protection of Bahá'u'lláh and the Báb. The great majority of Bahá'ís rallied round Shoghi Effendi as a new focal centre. Given the force of his appointment by 'Abdu'l-Bahá there was little direct challenge to his leadership, other than from MUḤAMMAD-'ALÍ and his partisans and later from Ruth WHITE and a small group of others who questioned the authenticity of 'Abdu'l-Bahá's will, a claim regarded as ludicrous by Eastern Bahá'ís familiar with 'Abdu'l-Bahá's writings. Potentially more serious challenges came from two prominent veteran Iranian Bahá'ís – ÁVÁRIH in Iran and Ahmad SOHRAB in the United States – who, apparently seeking positions of leadership, made light of Shoghi Effendi's leadership, implying a lack of maturity on his part. All such challenges had been overcome by the 1930s.

SHOGHI EFFENDI'S LEADERSHIP

Although initially traumatized by his appointment and workload (several times during the 1920s he felt himself unable to cope with the burdens of office and took sudden and lengthy breaks to recuperate), Shoghi Effendi had from the outset a clear vision of the future

'Abdu'l Bahá and Shoghi Effendi in Haifa

progress of the Cause, and successfully communicated this to the Bahá'ís of the world through thousands of letters and his meetings with pilgrims. During the 1920s a major focus of his work was the systematization and extension of the Bahá'í ADMINISTRATION throughout the existing Bahá'í communities. During the 1930s he presented the Bahá'ís with his ideas of the future WORLD ORDER, and completed a number of major translation projects (*see* SHOGHI EFFENDI, WRITINGS OF). From 1937 onwards a major focus was the development of the system of systematic planning (*see* PLANS), with the aim of eventually establishing Bahá'í communities in every country of the world. In the late 1940s and 1950s he began a series of major developments at the BAHÁ'Í WORLD CENTRE (construction of the superstructure of the SHRINE OF THE BÁB and the INTERNATIONAL ARCHIVES Building; extension and beautification of the gardens at BAHJÍ). During the 1950s he again turned to matters of administration: establishing the INTERNATIONAL BAHÁ'Í COUNCIL (1950) as a precursor of the Universal House of Justice, and AUXILIARY BOARDS (1954); and appointing Hands of the Cause (1951–7). Throughout his ministry he was concerned to define matters of Bahá'í belief and practice (such that much of the modern understanding of what is involved in being a Bahá'í comes from Shoghi Effendi), and periodically had to deal with persecution of the Bahá'ís in Iran and elsewhere.

LEADERSHIP STYLE

Shoghi Effendi was a young man of twenty-four when he became Guardian. Western educated and, apart from a black fez which he normally wore, Western in dress, his style of leadership was very different from the venerable, patriarchal figure of 'Abdu'l-Bahá (leading to criticism from some members of his family). He signed his letters to the Bahá'ís 'your true brother', and referred to the institution of the guardianship rather than to his own personal role. Whilst 'Abdu'l-Bahá had acted as a local notable, even attending the mosque, Shoghi Effendi distanced himself from the local Palestinian notability and concentrated his energies on the world-wide direction of the Faith. Unlike 'Abdu'l-Bahá he never journeyed to visit the Bahá'ís overseas, his primary contacts with the Bahá'ís being through his extensive correspondence. He met all visiting Bahá'ís during their pilgrimages to Haifa, teaching and inspiring them, and in many instances using them as emissaries to reinforce his instructions to the Bahá'ís in the various national communities.

PERSONAL LIFE

This was generally uneventful, and was largely subordinated to his work as Guardian. The problem of securing sufficient secretarial support to help

The resting place of Shoghi Effendi in London, England

with the ever-growing mass of correspondence was only really resolved in the 1950s, by which time Shoghi Effendi had long since adjusted to a pattern of unremitting hard work when in Haifa, interspersing this with summer breaks during which he might visit Europe – normally in the early years the Swiss Alps – or (on two occasions) traverse Africa from south to north (1929, 1940). In 1937 he married Mary Maxwell (b. 1910), the only daughter of two North American Bahá'ís. The couple had no children, but RÚḤIYYIH KHÁNUM, as she was called, became his helpmate and constant companion until his passing. During the 1940s a conflict developed between Shoghi Effendi and many members of his extended family (his brother, sisters, cousins and aunts), partly because of their contacts, including marriage, with Covenant-breaking members of Bahá'u'lláh's extended family. All were eventually excommunicated by him (*see* COVENANT-BREAKERS; NÚRÍ FAMILY). He died unexpectedly during a visit to London on 4 November 1957 following a bout of influenza and was buried there. Bach; Giachery; Rabbani, *Priceless Pearl*; *SBBR* 115–28, 136–7; *BFSH* 101–12.

Shoghi Effendi, Writings of

Shoghi Effendi wrote extensively in both English and Persian. As he himself emphasized, 'Abdu'l-Bahá had conferred upon the guardianship the function of interpreter of the word of God (*WOB* 148, 150–1). As such, the Guardians were empowered 'to reveal the purport and disclose the implications of the utterances of Bahá'u'lláh and of 'Abdu'l-Bahá' (*WOB* 151). These interpretations were authoritative and binding. In this manner, his writings have been a primary element in the shaping of modern Bahá'í belief (*SBBR* 136–7). George TOWNSHEND served as Shoghi Effendi's literary adviser, reading and commenting on a number of his manuscripts. Bergsmo; Collins, *Bibliography* 31–7; Giachery 29–48; Malouf; Rabbani, *Priceless Pearl* 196–227.

LETTERS

The vast majority of his writings are letters (over 17,500 letters by him or written on his behalf by a secretary have been collected so far). These range from routine correspondence dealing with the activities of Bahá'ís in various parts of the world to lengthy monographs addressing specific themes. To date, fourteen volumes of the English-language letters have been published: collections of more or less routine letters to the American, Canadian, Alaskan, British, German, Indian, Australian and New Zealand Bahá'ís, together with monograph letters on the *WORLD ORDER OF BAHÁ'U'LLÁH*; teaching the Bahá'í Faith (*ADVENT OF DIVINE JUSTICE*, 1938); and Bahá'u'lláh's proclamation to the rulers (*PROMISED DAY IS COME*, 1941). Published copies of other letters are found in various compilations. The letters cover a variety of themes: encouragement to the Bahá'ís to teach and 'live the life' of true Bahá'ís; reports of Bahá'í activities in various parts of the world, commonly pointing to the wider significance of particular events; summons to Bahá'ís to achieve specific goals such as the settlement of pioneers, the establishment of assemblies, the translation of Bahá'í literature, and the acquisition of Bahá'í centres and other properties; analysis of particular developments within Bahá'í history; statements regarding Bahá'í beliefs, morality, social principles, law and administration; and obituaries of outstanding Bahá'ís. Some of the letters to the Iranian Bahá'ís have also been published in the original, but these are generally difficult to obtain, and few have been translated.

BOOKS

Shoghi Effendi wrote one book in English, an interpretive history of the first century of Bábí–Bahá'í history, GOD

Passes By (1944). He also wrote a shorter, Persian-language, version, the *Lawḥ-i-Qarn*, and was extensively involved in editing work for the *Bahá'í World* volumes.

TRANSLATIONS

Of Shoghi Effendi's translations, a few smaller pieces appeared in print in the 1920s, together with a collaborative rendering of Bahá'u'lláh's *Hidden Words* (1929). Later he published a further four volumes of Bahá'u'lláh's writings (*The Kitáb-i-Íqán* (1931); *Gleanings from the Writings of Bahá'u'lláh* (1935); *Prayers and Meditations by Bahá'u'lláh* (1938); and *Epistle to the Son of the Wolf* (1941)), and a translation of Nabíl-i-A'ẓam (Zarandí)'s history of the Bábís, which appeared in English under the title *Dawn-Breakers* (1932). Many other translated passages from Bahá'í scripture appeared in his letters.

OTHER WORKS

Shoghi Effendi prepared several compilations of Bahá'í statistics and other materials, as well as a number of historical maps.

Shrine of the Báb

The Bahá'ís' second-holiest shrine. Located in Haifa and one of the focal points of the Bahá'í World Centre, it is also a major Haifa landmark. *AB* 126–30; Giachery 61–118; *GPB* 274–7; Rabbani, *Priceless Pearl* 234–47.

THE SHRINE

The site for the Shrine was indicated by Bahá'u'lláh to 'Abdu'l-Bahá in 1891 during a visit to Mount Carmel. In 1898 'Abdu'l-Bahá gave instructions for the Báb's remains to be transported from their place of concealment in Tehran, the remains arriving secretly in Akka on 31 January 1899 (fifty lunar years after the Báb's execution). The foundation stone was then laid and, after some months, construction work began. A marble sarcophagus was also received from the Bahá'ís of Burma to serve as the eventual resting place of the remains. The project proceeded slowly in the face of a succession of difficulties regarding the acquisition of land and building permission. The building was completed by 1907, but it was not until March 1909, on the evening following the first *Naw-Rúz* after the ending of his own confinement in Akka, that 'Abdu'l-Bahá finally placed the remains of the Báb and his executed companion inside the sarcophagus which had been placed in a vault beneath what is now the central room of the Shrine. When 'Abdu'l-Bahá died in 1921 he was buried beneath another room of the Shrine, giving the building an increased religious significance.

The Shrine constructed by 'Abdu'l-Bahá consisted of a six-room masonry structure on what was then a relatively isolated site on the northern slope of Mount Carmel some distance above the German Temple Society colony. The Báb's remains were deposited beneath the central of the three southern rooms next to the mountainside and those of 'Abdu'l-Bahá beneath the central of the three northern rooms facing the sea. In 1928–29/30 Shoghi Effendi had extensive excavations made into the side of the mountain and an additional three rooms constructed to the south to form a square with the room of the Báb's remains at the centre. 'Abdu'l-Bahá had intended that a more elaborate outer Shrine would eventually be constructed. In 1942 Shoghi Effendi asked William Sutherland Maxwell (his father-in-law and then resident in Haifa) to begin work on the design of the superstructure, and the final form of this was approved in 1944. Actual construction was delayed until after the end of World War II and preparations finally began in 1947 amidst the turbulent period mark-

Exterior of the Shrine of the Báb

The Shrine of the Báb showing the doors

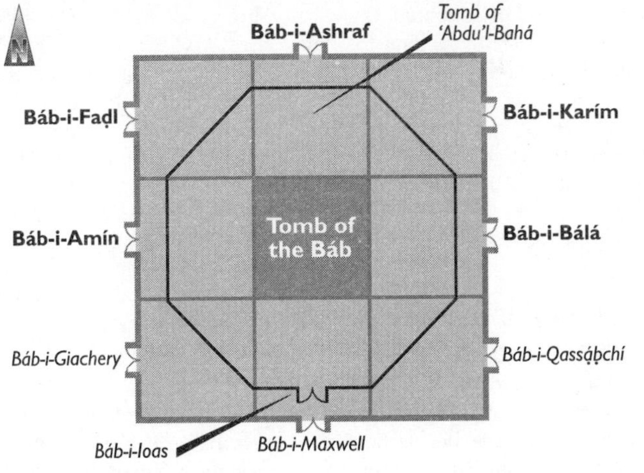

Names given by 'Abdu'l-Bahá in bold

Names given by Shoghi Effendi, to parts he added after 'Abdu'l-Bahá's death in italic

Doors
Ground floor
Upper floor – Octagon

ing the birth of the state of Israel. The work proceeded in stages, with first the construction of a colonnaded arcade surrounding the original Shrine building, topped by a balustrade (completed in May 1950); then a windowed central octagon, topped by a second balustrade with minaret-like pinnacles at each corner; an 11-metre-high drum-like clerestory with eighteen lancet windows; and finally a dome covered in gilded tiles and topped with a lantern and finial. The work was completed in September 1953 at a total cost of three-quarters of a million dollars. Much of the work was completed in Italy, including that on the granite and marble used in the construction. The Shrine is illuminated at night.

THE DOORS

'Abdu'l-Bahá had named the five doors of the original Shrine after two eminent Iranian Bahá'ís (Ḥájí Amín and Mírzá Abu'l-Faḍl) and three of the Bahá'í masons who had contributed to the Shrine's construction (Ustád Áqá 'Alí-Ashraf, Ustád Áqá Bálá, and Ustád 'Abdu'l-Karím). Shoghi Effendi named the doors of the three extra rooms he had built after Ḥájí Maḥmúd Qaṣṣábchí (who provided the funding for the construction of the rooms), W.S. Maxwell (the architect of the superstructure), and Ugo Giachery (who acted as liaison with the various Italian companies involved). The door to the octagon was named after Leroy Ioas, who oversaw much of the final work (Giachery 214–16).

THE GARDENS AND TERRACES

The Shrine is now surrounded by extensive ornamental gardens. Most of these were constructed by Shoghi Effendi, beginning in the 1920s, but particularly in the 1950s. Shoghi Effendi also constructed a series of nine terraces leading up from the foot of the mountain to the Shrine, prophesying that in the future Bahá'í kings and rulers would ascend this pathway to visit the Shrine. In 1987, the Universal House of Justice initiated a massive project involving the reconstruction of these terraces, the construction of a further nine terraces above the Shrine, and extensions to the gardens. This project is now well advanced. Its architect is Fariborz Sahba, the designer of the Indian Bahá'í temple.

Shoghi Effendi described the Shrine as a 'focal center of Divine illumination and power', and the Báb's sacred remains as the spiritual centre of a series of concentric circles which ultimately embraced the entire planet. The Shrine also constituted an institution that would play a major role in the future unfoldment of the Bahá'í world administrative centre (*GPB* 277; *CF* 95–6).

Shrine of Bahá'u'lláh

See Bahjí.

shrines and holy places

Various sites associated with the Báb, Bahá'u'lláh and 'Abdu'l-Bahá are considered holy by Bahá'ís, in particular the Shrines of the Báb and Bahá'u'lláh at the Bahá'í World Centre, the House of the Báb in Shíráz, and the House of Bahá'u'lláh in Baghdad. These last two were accorded special status by Bahá'u'lláh and were designated by him as places of pilgrimage. 'Abdu'l-Bahá added the 'Most Holy Shrine' of Bahá'u'lláh as a place of pilgrimage. The graves of some other prominent Bábís and Bahá'ís – including those of some martyrs – have also acquired the status of holy places.

The importance of holy places lies in their association with particular holy personages and in the faith of those who visit them. Apart from the three designated places of pilgrimage there is no obligation on Bahá'ís to visit any holy site. They may if they wish, however, and if a person draws closer to God as a result of visiting such sites, then their actions are meritorious. Except for the pilgrimages to the Shíráz and Baghdad houses there are no designated rituals for those visiting Bahá'í holy places, apart from a general injunction to observe reverence, both physically and in one's own heart. In practice this involves being quiet in manner and dignified in dress, and in the case of the Bahá'í Shrines the removal of one's shoes. When large groups of Bahá'ís visit the Shrines there is often a prearranged programme of PRAYERS and other writings which are recited or chanted by individuals within the group. On some special occasions large groups of Bahá'ís circumambulate Bahá'u'lláh's Shrine at Bahjí or that of the Báb in Haifa. Individuals who visit holy places on their own will commonly pray (in whatever manner they wish: standing,

Entrance to the Shrine of Bahá'u'lláh at Bahjí

kneeling, sitting), and many will prostrate themselves, particularly at the 'holy thresholds' of the Shrines.

Wherever possible the Bahá'ís have worked to restore and beautify those holy places under their ownership. Internal decorations convey a sense of dignity and beauty. Externally there are often flower gardens. At the Bahá'í World Centre there has been extensive landscaping around the Shrines. In the 1940s, at Shoghi Effendi's instruction, the Iranian Bahá'ís established a committee responsible to locate and wherever possible purchase holy places and historical sites linked to the Faith.

IRAN

The holiest site in Iran for Bahá'ís is that of the House of the Báb in Shíráz. The second holiest site is that of the Síyáh-Chál prison in Tehran. Other sites include the fortress prisons of the Báb in Mákú and Chihríq, the house of Bahá'u'lláh in Tehran (the *bayt-i-mubárak*, 'blessed house'), Bahá'u'lláh's ancestral home in the village of Tákúr, the Shaykh Ṭabarsí shrine, and the grave of Quddús. Almost all Bahá'í holy sites in Iran were seized by the authorities in the aftermath of the Islamic Revolution of 1979.

THE BAHÁ'Í WORLD CENTRE

There are numerous holy sites in the Haifa–Akka area, most importantly the Shrines of the Báb and Bahá'u'lláh. In Akka the main sites are the cell in the Citadel in which Bahá'u'lláh was confined, the combined houses of 'Abbúd and 'Údí Khammár, in which Bahá'u'lláh lived from 1871 until 1873, and the house of 'Abdu'lláh Páshá, in which 'Abdu'l-Bahá lived from 1896 until 1910. In the surrounding area the most important site is Bahjí. In Haifa, apart from the combined Shrine of the Báb and 'Abdu'l-Bahá, the most important site is the House of 'Abdu'l-Bahá.

OTHER

In Iraq there is the House of Bahá'u'lláh in Baghdad and the Riḍván (Najíbiyyih) Garden. In Turkey one of the houses Bahá'u'lláh occupied in Edirne (the house of Riḍá Big) and a nearby orchard rented by Bahá'u'lláh are now in Bahá'í ownership. Other houses he occupied there and in Istanbul are no longer standing. In Canada the Maxwell home in which 'Abdu'l-Bahá stayed when he visited Montreal has the status of a national Bahá'í shrine. In Britain there is the grave of Shoghi Effendi in London, and in Burma the grave of Siyyid Mustafa Rumi.

sin

Disobedience to God and his laws. It results from the soul's attachment to the material world, and reflects the 'animal' elements and demands of human nature. Sin hinders the soul from attaining its destined potential. Though absolute perfection is never to be obtained, seeking to perfect the soul by acquiring spiritual qualities leads the individual towards God (*see* heaven), but a sinful life separates him or her from God. As a person draws nearer to God, their understanding of what God expects of them increases, such that 'the good deeds of the righteous are the sins of the Near Ones [to God]' (*SAQ* 126). God's mercy and love for his creatures are so great that all sins can be forgiven, but genuine repentance is necessary. The fear of God and the development of conscience help the individual to avoid wrongdoing. Specific sins include anger, jealousy, disputatiousness, lust, pride, lying, hypocrisy, fraud, worldliness, self-love, covetousness, avarice, ignorance, prejudice, hatred, pride and tyranny (*SAQ* 92, 119). The Christian doctrine of original sin is rejected: babies are born sinless, it is a person's subsequent behaviour and worldly attachments that separate them from God (*SAQ* 119–26).

The MANIFESTATIONS OF GOD are regarded as free from sin. (*See also* EVIL.)

Singh, Pritam (1881–1959)

Prominent early Indian Bahá'í. The first Bahá'í of Sikh background, he came from a prominent family – his father was a High Court judge in Lahore. He became a Bahá'í shortly after completing his first degree (1904), and subsequently became a university professor of economics, as well as one of the leading Bahá'í speakers and writers in India. His proclamation of the Bahá'í Faith to Sikh princes, ministers and priests engendered considerable opposition. In 1927 he resigned from his profession in order to devote himself full time to Bahá'í activity, travelling and lecturing extensively. He was also a member of the national spiritual assembly for many years. *BW13*: 874–6; Khianra 109–30.

Síyáh-Chál (Pers., lit. 'Black Pit')

The underground dungeon in Tehran in which Bahá'u'lláh and other Bábís were imprisoned following the assassination attempt on the life of NÁṢIRU'D-DÍN SHÁH in 1852. It was a disused cistern which was reached along a narrow corridor and down three steep flights of steps, and into which as many as one hundred and fifty prisoners might be held, in conditions of appalling discomfort. The Bábís were chained together and many were taken away for execution, but they retained their spirit, chanting verses of scripture with such fervour that apparently they could be heard in the royal palace nearby. Bahá'u'lláh was weighed down with the infamous chains '*Qara-Guhar*' (51 kg in weight) and '*Salásil*'. It was here that he experienced the initiatory visions that marked the beginning of his mission (*ESW* 21–2). The Pit was later closed. Shoghi Effendi described it as the second holiest Bahá'í site in Iran (*MBW* 80). It was in Bahá'í ownership from 1954 until the Islamic Revolution of 1979.

Siyásiyyih, Risáliy-i

See POLITICS, TREATISE ON.

slave trade, slavery

In his tablet to Queen VCTORIA, Bahá'u'lláh praised the British abolition of the slave trade, and in the *Kitáb-i-AQDAS* prohibited the buying and selling of slaves, stating also that every individual was a bondslave of God, and that none should exalt himself over another. Shoghi Effendi appears to have interpreted this as a prohibition of slavery itself (in the 19th century the two issues were distinct, the British declaring the slave trade illegal in 1807, and subsequently leading a campaign against the international slave trade from 1811 onwards, but only abolishing slavery in their own colonies at later dates). *Proclamation* 33–4; *KA* 45 k72; *GPB* 214; Huddleston, *Search* 84–92.

smoking

Tobacco smoking is discouraged but not forbidden, 'Abdu'l-Bahá noting that it is a habit that is unclean, progressively injurious to health and expensive. Bahá'ís are advised to be courteous and considerate to all, whether they be smokers or non-smokers. Thus, whilst ASSEMBLIES might decide to prohibit smoking at Bahá'í devotional and administrative meetings for the sake of non-smokers, they should also make provision for any smokers. Smoking other DRUGS (such as marijuana) is completely forbidden. *LG* 354–6.

The Báb forbade the use of tobacco altogether, and one of the distinguishing characteristics of the early Bábís was their abstention from smoking.

social evolution

For Shoghi Effendi Bahá'u'lláh's mission was to achieve the 'organic and spiritual unity of the whole body of nations'. This will mark humanity's 'coming of age', a mystic process of maturation analogous to that of the individual, and the furthermost limits of possible societal organization (*see* WORLD ORDER). Individual progress within such a society will continue indefinitely (*WOB* 163–6). The present age of transition (*see* TIME) represents the adolescent stage in humanity's 'slow and painful evolution' – characterized by impetuosity, self-assurance and rebelliousness. Previous stages in this process have seen the progressive unification of the family, tribe, city-state and nation. The PROGRESSIVE REVELATION of divine truth corresponds to the possibilities of human receptiveness at each stage of social evolution. Thus Bahá'u'lláh's emphasis on the unity of the human race was only possible in an age in which there was knowledge of the whole world and unification was an actual possibility. *PDC* 122–6; *WOB* 43, 202.

social order

Bahá'u'lláh emphasized the importance of social order. The maintenance of social order is based on JUSTICE, and this in turn is based on the hope for REWARD and the fear of punishment (*TB* 66). RELIGION, the FEAR OF GOD and TOLERANCE for other peoples are other important means of securing social order. Those who are poor, downtrodden or captive should be protected (*TB* 70); the individual's social station respected; and craftsmen praised and not disdained as in the past (*TB* 38). Actions that lead to disorder (conflict, contention, theft, entering the house of another without permission, bloodshed) are condemned (*ESW* 23–25).

socio-economic development

For Bahá'ís the development of both spiritual and material CIVILIZATION is important. Bahá'u'lláh and 'Abdu'l-Bahá referred to an idyllic future (the Most Great PEACE), whilst at the same time advocating more immediate measures of societal change. Thus their emphasis on the importance of political and legal reform (HUMAN RIGHTS); care for the poor; limitations on ARMAMENTS (arms spending itself being regarded as a major factor in keeping ordinary people poor); WORK; AGRICULTURE; EDUCATION and LITERACY; and later on the emancipation of WOMEN. Many of these themes are brought together in 'Abdu'l-Bahá's treatise *The* SECRET OF DIVINE CIVILIZATION, which urges the adoption of a wide-ranging policy of social and economic development and state strengthening in Iran. Some of these ideals – notably those to do with education, work and the role of women – had a cumulative effect within the Iranian Bahá'í community, leading to a progressive process of internal socio-economic development which firmly linked the Bahá'ís with 'modernization'.

Development issues assumed increasing importance with the large-scale EXPANSION of the Bahá'í Faith into the poor countries of the 'Third World', particularly from the 1960s onwards. SCHOOLS were established, and in the 1970s a number of rural development programmes were started, including the first in a series of community-oriented RADIO stations. This trend was given focus and impetus by the Universal House of Justice in October 1983, when they called for the more systematic application of Bahá'í principles 'to upraising the quality of human life' and announced the establishment of an Office of Social and Economic Development in Haifa to 'promote and coordinate' Bahá'í development activities world-wide (*MUHJ* 601–4 no. 379; see also 576 no. 358.6, 613 no. 385.6, 723 no. 453.18, 725 no. 456.2). The number of projects rocketed as a result: from 127 in 1979 to 1,344 in 1986 (*BWNS* 1992–3: 238). The largest number of these were educational (488 'tutorial schools' and 178 academic schools). There were also 186 projects concerned with literacy, 56 with health, 52 with conservation and the environment, 52 with women and youth and 21 with agriculture. The largest number were in Asia (532), followed by the Americas (379) and Africa (286) (*BWNS* 1994–5: 319–20). Most were small in scale. A variety of agencies and institutes have been established in a number of countries to promote development. Some of these are agencies of the particular Bahá'í national spiritual ASSEMBLY, and others are separate non-governmental organizations. A considerable body of experience is being built up. Some of the projects have evidently been highly successful, and several have gained government backing and the support of international donor agencies such as the Canadian International Development Agency (CIDA) and the Norwegian Agency for International Development Co-operation (NORAD). There have been a number of national and international conferences for Bahá'ís interested in development issues, where they can share ideas and develop perspectives. *BWNS* 1992–3: 229–45; 1994–5: 126–8. (*See also* BAHÁ'Í-UNIFEM PROJECT; BAHÁ'Í VOCATIONAL INSTITUTE FOR RURAL WOMEN.

Elements of a developing Bahá'í perspective on development include the importance of grassroots initiatives and knowledge, reinforced by local CONSULTATION and empowerment; the essential need for wider social and moral issues to form part of development process (notably female emancipation and the fostering of TRUSTWORTHINESS); a stress on self-reliance, the development of 'human resources', and an ethos of community service (Bahá'í projects are non-sectarian in their focus, and not confined to the Bahá'ís); and a valuing of local minority cultures. Momen, *Baha'i Focus on Development*; Vick.

Sohrab, Ahmad (*c.*1893–1958)

One-time secretary and English-language interpreter of 'Abdu'l- Bahá, who settled in the United States after World War I. In 1929, with the help of Julie (Lewis Stuyvesant) Chanler (1882–1961), he established the New History Society in New York City to propagate the Bahá'í teachings. When he refused to place this venture under the control of the local Bahá'í ASSEMBLY, a confrontation with the national spiritual assembly ensued, and Sohrab and Chanler were excommunicated (1930). A youth organization, the Caravan of East and West, was also started (1930), which developed into a world-wide pen-pal club. Whilst accepting the legitimacy of Shoghi Effendi's appointment as Guardian, Sohrab was highly critical of his leadership, and in particular of the Bahá'í ADMINISTRATION he had built up. Chanler; *SBBR* 124–5; Sohrab, *Broken Silence*; *TCB* 343–7. (*See also* COVENANT-BREAKERS.)

Some Answered Questions

A compilation of talks delivered by 'Abdu'l-Bahá in Akka between 1904 and 1906 in response to questions posed by Laura Clifford DREYFUS-BARNEY, an American Bahá'í. A secretary recorded the talks in Persian, and these transcripts were later checked by 'Abdu'l-Bahá. An English translation was published in London in 1908 (this has been revised in subsequent editions). The topics discussed include Christian subjects, and a range of metaphysical and social issues.

soul

The essential inner reality of each human being.

For Bahá'ís every human being possesses both a physical body and a non-material, rational soul (or human spirit). The nature of this essence is mysterious and beyond human understanding (*GWB* 158 no. 82, 164–5 no. 83). The soul is both a spiritual and an intellectual reality. It is the first among created things to recognize and love God. It is one of the 'signs of God'; the 'harbinger' which proclaims the reality of all of God's worlds (*GWB* 158–60 no. 82). It is a divine bounty; an emanation from God; an intermediary between the heavenly and lower worlds; the medium for spiritual life (Savi 146). If faithful, it reflects the divine light and eventually returns to God. If faithless, it becomes a victim of 'self and passion', and will 'sink in their depths' (*GWB* 158–60 no. 82) (*see* FREE WILL; HUMAN NATURE). The powers of the 'rational faculty', the 'mind' (imagination; conceptualization; reflection; comprehension; memory) are also an expression of the soul (*GWB* 163–4 no. 83; *SAQ* 208–11). The progress of the soul involves pursuit of the SPIRITUAL PATH and the acquisition of SPIRITUAL QUALITIES. The purpose of the PROPHETS is to educate human beings so that at the time of death they will be so detached from the world that they will ascend 'to the throne of the Most High' (*GWB* 156 no. 81).

SOUL AND BODY

The body is subject to physical limitations (it occupies a particular space; it is subject to disease) and it decomposes at death, but the soul is unlimited and immortal (*SAQ* 229, 242). The soul is independent of physical and mental infirmities. These might prevent the soul from revealing its inherent power – like clouds preventing the receipt of the sun's rays – but they do not of themselves affect it (*GWB* 153–4 no. 80). The soul comes into existence and its light becomes reflected in the 'mirror' of the body at the time of conception (*SAQ* 151, 239–40). At that moment all souls are pure and equal to each other. It is subsequent life events and decisions that lead to different levels of spiritual development, some souls reaching a higher and others a lower station. After death the body decomposes, but the soul enters a new existence, freed from the constraints of its former attachment to the body (*SWAB* 170–1).

THE AFTERLIFE

The soul is immortal. After the death of the body it continues to progress until it attains God's presence and manifests divine attributes. That progress is without limit (*LG* 204–9). Those souls that are sanctified from the world, living in accordance with the divine will, are blessed, and will converse with the prophets of God, and the dwellers of the highest heaven will circle around them. Those that have walked humbly with God will be 'invested with the honour and glory of all goodly names and stations' (*GWB* 155–6 no. 81, 159 no. 82). After death each soul will recognize the worth of its own deeds and understand the consequences of its actions. Those who have turned to God will experience inexpressible joy and gladness. Those who have lived in error will be filled with fear and consternation. Those who have rejected God will become aware of the good things that had escaped them and bemoan their plight, humbling themselves before him. Souls will recognize the accomplishments of other souls that have attained the same level as themselves, but they will not understand those that are higher in rank (*GWB* 169–70 no. 86). If a murderer has already been punished for his crime in this life he will not be punished anew in the next (*SWAB* 179). (*See also* DEATH.)

spiritual assemblies

See ASSEMBLIES.

spiritual path

In writings such as the *SEVEN VALLEYS* and *FOUR VALLEYS* Bahá'u'lláh outlined the various stages of the mystical path, and in his *Kitáb-i-ÍQÁN* he referred to the path of the 'true seeker' after God. To follow this path the seeker needs first to 'cleanse and purify' his or her heart from the 'obscuring dust' of 'acquired knowledge', and from those emotions that would divert him from the truth. Then, trusting in God, and with utter detachment, he should seek to acquire moral and SPIRITUAL QUALITIES (humility; patience; refraining from idle speech and BACKBITING; contentment with little; companionship with those who have renounced the world and avoidance of fellowship with the ungodly; daily communing with God at dawn; perseverance in the quest; succouring the dispossessed, the destitute and animals; preparedness to offer up his life for God; faithfulness in promises; observance of the GOLDEN RULE; forgiveness and prayer for the sinful; mindfulness of his own nothingness before God and the unknown nature of his own spiritual fate). Next, with 'earnest striving', 'passionate devotion', 'rapture' and the like, divine love will be wafted over his soul, and 'the lights of knowledge and certitude envelop his being', such that he can see the evidences of divine revelation wherever he goes, and distinguish truth from falsehood as easily as the sun from shadow (*KI* 122–6). The link between spirituality and moral behaviour is constantly stressed. The Bahá'í writings also emphasize the importance of PRAYER, MEDITATION, CLEANLINESS and steadfastness in the COVENANT in the attainment of spirituality (*LG* 540–3). The Universal House of Justice has given a list of six 'essential requisites' for spiritual growth: daily obligatory prayer with pure-hearted devotion; reverential and thoughtful reading of scripture at least every morning and evening; prayerful meditation on the Bahá'í teachings; daily effort to model one's behaviour on the Bahá'í ideals; TEACHING the Faith to others; and 'selfless service' both to the Faith and in one's WORK (*LG* 540). The concept of spirituality is discussed in W. Hatcher, *Concept*, and McLean, *Dimensions in Spirituality*. (*See also* DEVOTIONALISM; HIDDEN WORDS; HUMAN NATURE; SUFISM.)

spiritual qualities

The Bahá'í writings abound with references to various spiritual and moral qualities which the individual should seek to acquire. Although primarily addressed to Bahá'ís, such injunctions are also specifically identified as necessary for those who occupy positions of political or religious leadership in any society. The attributes of good character include the FEAR OF GOD; reverence; piety; obedience to religious law; love for God expressed in love for humanity; prayerfulness; compassion; consideration for others; courtesy; philanthropy; service to others; industriousness; selflessness; forbearance and calm; meekness; amiability; a lack of malice; loyalty; courage; magnanimity; generosity; energy and zeal; a sense of honour and regard for the rights of others; high-mindedness; DETACHMENT from material things; submissiveness to the will of God; humility; control of the passions; temperance; purity; CHASTITY; JUSTICE (including equity and fair-mindedness); honesty (including TRUTHFULNESS, candour and financial probity); TRUSTWORTHINESS (including reliability); faithfulness; integrity; sincerity; WISDOM; and moderation. Purity of motivation is crucial (*CC2*: 1). Such virtues are conducive to human dignity and honour, and the attainment of 'man's true station' (*CC2*: 330, 333). Only those who are adorned with these virtues can be reckoned among 'the true servants of God'. Each individual should 'strive diligently' to acquire them (*CC2*: 332). Moral and religious qualities are also to be balanced by reason and knowledge (*SDC* 60). Bahá'ís should be distinguished by their moral qualities (*SWAB* 71). They should promote freedom (*CC2*: 341). The 'sword' of upright conduct is 'sharper than blades of steel'. It is the means by which 'the citadels of men's hearts' will be subdued (*CC2*: 331; *see* TEACHING). If the Bahá'ís succeed in exemplifying divine virtues then they will become both completely united amongst themselves and a magnet for others, who will want to discover the source of their radiance and joy. Each individual is responsible for their own life, and should seek to perfect their own character (and avoid BACKBITING about others) (*CC2*: 3). (*See also* SPIRITUAL PATH.)

sterilization

Permanent sterilization is forbidden as a form of BIRTH CONTROL, but is permitted for medical reasons.

Ṣubḥ-i-Azal

See AZAL, ṢUBḤ-I-.

suffering

'Abdu'l-Bahá and Shoghi Effendi regarded suffering as having various causes: (1) Some is a consequence of the individual's own actions, e.g. they ruin their digestion through overeating; they become poor because they gamble. Obedience to God's laws would end many of these sources of suffering. (2) God tests those who want to draw nearer to him. Suffering is a means of perfecting the individual, those who suffer most attaining the greatest perfection. It causes people to turn to God, when in happiness they might forget him. It proves the sincerity of those who claim to have dedicated their lives to God. (3) The material world is, by its very nature, transient and unsatisfactory. Suffering alerts people to this reality. They should learn that the only true happiness is to be found in the world of the spirit. (4) Some suffering is a result of fear of the unknown, particularly of DEATH – whereas if people know the nature of the afterlife, they would not fear what is a superior form of existence (*LG* 601–4; *PT* 41–3, 110–13, 191; *PUP* 46–8; Savi 130–2; *SWAB* 81, 200, 239). (5) For those who have truly turned to God, separation from him is the greatest suffering. For the development of the SOUL, ignorance and bad deeds (lying, cruelty, treachery, etc.) are a torment (*SAQ* 224, 265).

In response to suffering people should develop the spiritual qualities of fortitude and patience (*RB1*: 269–71), as with those prophets and saints who found contentment in the midst of ordeal. The fortitude displayed by the sufferer might also have a profound effect on others. This does not imply fatalism, however. Through a combination of PRAYER and determined and continued effort, even seemingly insuperable hindrances can be overcome (*CC1*: 477–8 no. 1060, 479 no. 1067; *LG* 280 nos. 943–4). Again, Bahá'ís should work to overcome such causes of human distress as poverty and disease. If someone is ill, they should seek help from competent physicians (*see* HEALTH AND HEALING).

Sufism

Islamic mysticism, expressed in a diverse range of beliefs, practices and organizations. Bahá'u'lláh evidently sympathized with some aspects of Sufism, but was critical of others. In Kurdistan he lived the life of a solitary dervish, later moving to the Khálidiyya Sufi centre in Sulaymániyya at the invitation of Shaykh Ismá'íl, its local shaykh. He also gained the respect of the leaders of the regional Naqshabandí and Qádirí orders. During his stay, at the request of his hosts, he commented on Ibnu'l-'Arabí's '*Meccan Revelations*' (*Al-futúḥát al-makkiyya*), and composed his ODE OF THE DOVE in the ecstatic style of Ibnu'l-Fáriḍ. Returning to Baghdad he remained in contact with Kurdish Sufis, receiving them as visitors, and writing the *SEVEN VALLEYS* and the *FOUR VALLEYS* in response to Sufi correspondents (*GPB* 121–4, 128–9). Several of his followers were Sufis, notably Ṣidq-'Alí, in whose honour he dedicated an annual night for the remembrance of God (*dhikr*) (*MF* 36–8). In sharp distinction to the beliefs of many Sufis, Bahá'u'lláh absolutely rejected any form of pantheism: GOD in essence is beyond any human attribute or physical location. No human being has ever known him (*SV* 22–3; *TB* 60). He also criticized those expressions of Sufism that involve seclusion from the everyday world and extreme ASCETICISM; or which encourage idleness and drug-taking, their followers believing themselves to be above the constraints of religious LAW. The true Sufi was one who was both severed from all else but God and constant in worship and obedience to holy law (*MF* 36–8; *TB* 60).

suicide

Suicide is forbidden, and is regarded as endangering the soul. Life is a gift of God. The individual is not responsible for acts committed when he or she is mentally deranged, however, and under such circumstances would not suffer from spiritual consequences. *LG* 357 nos. 1199–200.

Sulaymán Khán Tunukábuní

See JAMÁL EFFENDI.

sultanate

An institution of Islamic kingship, most particularly the dynasty of OTTOMAN rulers, who combined secular power with the religious leadership of the Sunní Muslim world by their claims to the CALIPHATE. The sultanate was abolished by the new Turkish republic on 1 November 1922, and the caliphate in 1924. These twin institutions were regarded by Shoghi Effendi as the 'arch-enemy' of the Bahá'í cause, and their collapse cited as an instance of DIVINE JUDGEMENT.

Sulṭán, Lawḥ-i-

(PA, 'Tablet of the King')

Bahá'u'lláh's tablet to NÁṢIRU'D-DÍN SHÁH. Written in a mixture of Arabic and Persian, it is the lengthiest of the letters to the RULERS. Composed in Edirne, it was not sent to the shah until after Bahá'u'lláh had arrived in Akka, the young messenger, BADÍ', who delivered the tablet, being put to death for his pains. The tablet includes an appeal to the shah to grant religious toleration to the Bahá'ís as they were loyal and obedient subjects. Bahá'u'lláh himself had consistently opposed violence, and had summoned the Bábís to lay down the sword and eschew sedition. The clerics were those who were primarily to blame for the persecution of the Bábís and, if the shah wished, Bahá'u'lláh would return to Iran to confront the *'ULAMÁ* and establish the truth of his cause (presumably in *MUBÁHALA*). If the shah would respond to Bahá'u'lláh's call he would attain a great spiritual station. He was reminded that kingship was itself transitory: the skeletal remains of a king and a pauper in their graves were the same, and numerous rulers and countless great men had come and gone without leaving a trace of their existence. Various autobiographical details of Bahá'u'lláh's life were also given. Browne, *Selections* 260–6; *RB2*: 337–40, 346–51, 355–7.

'summer schools'

Courses of learning intended to foster Bahá'í DEEPENING and spiritual and social life. Commonly, summer schools are held for a week or more during the holiday season, and provide Bahá'ís with an opportunity to meet and study their religion. Winter and other seasonal schools are also held, as are shorter-duration weekend schools, all with a similar purpose. Given that in many countries the local Bahá'í groups are small and scattered, these schools offer an experience of Bahá'í community life. As a Bahá'í activity they can be traced back to the GREEN ACRE summer conferences in New England in the early 1900s. These were copied in newly established Bahá'í conference centres, as in other parts of the United States (Geyserville, California, 1927; Louhelen, Michigan, 1931), Germany (1931) and Australia (1937/8), or in temporarily hired premises, as in Britain (from 1936) and India (from 1938). Such schools have since proliferated and have become a common part of Bahá'í life world-wide. Shoghi Effendi stressed the value of attendance; encouraged the study of such topics as Bahá'í scripture and history, Islam, comparative religion, interracial amity, ethics, Bahá'í administration, the COVENANT and public speaking; emphasized the importance of maintaining a high spiritual and intellectual standard, and of linking the schools to the TEACHING campaigns; noted the value of having study classes and discussion groups as well as lectures; and expressed the hope that the schools would eventually evolve into Bahá'í universities. *CC1*: 26–42; *GPB* 340–1; *LG* 558–63.

súra (Ar.)/***súrih*** (Pers.)

The name given to the various 'chapters' of the QURAN. Several of Bahá'u'lláh's writings are also referred to as *súras*, including the *Súra of the* KINGS and the *Súra of the* BRANCH.

T

Ṭabarsí, Shaykh

Small shrine of Shaykh Aḥmad ibn Abí Ṭálib Ṭabarsí about 14 miles south-east of Bárfurúsh. It became a Bábí stronghold and was the site of the most famous of the conflicts between them and their opponents. Mullá Ḥusayn Bushrú'í had led a growing band of armed Bábís westward from Mashhad carrying the messianic symbol of the Black Standard. On entering Bárfurúsh (10 October 1848) they were attacked. Responding, they killed several of their adversaries. Attacked again, they retired to Ṭabarsí (12 October), which they fortified. Other Bábís later joined them, including Quddús, their total numbers rising to perhaps six hundred. Fighting in what they came to see as a re-enactment of Karbalá, the Bábís held out against large numbers of professional troops until, weakened by attrition and starvation, they responded to a false truce and most were massacred (10 May 1849). Nine of the Letters of the Living were killed at Ṭabarsí or in its immediate aftermath. *ARR* 358–9; Browne, *Selections* 141–2; *MBBR* 91–9; Momen, 'Social basis' 160–7; Nabil 324–429; *SBBR* 26–7; *TJ* 44–110, 360–8; *TN* 35–9, 177–9, 189–90. (*See also* Bábí radicalism.)

Tablets of the Divine Plan

Series of fourteen letters by 'Abdu'l-Bahá on the importance of teaching the Bahá'í Faith. They were addressed to the Bahá'ís of the United States and Canada during World War I. The first eight letters were composed in 1916 (26 March–22 April), and five of these had been received and published before communications between Palestine and America were severed because of the war. A further six letters were composed in 1917 (2 February–8 March). Letters were addressed to the North American Bahá'ís as a whole as well as by region (Canada, the North-eastern, Southern, Central and Western United States). The complete set was ceremonially 'unveiled' to the Bahá'ís at a special convention in New York in April 1919. 'Abdu'l-Bahá's instructions were that Bahá'ís should systematically teach the Faith in those American states and Canadian provinces in which there were as yet few or no Bahá'ís; establish it throughout Latin America; and propagate it throughout the rest of the world 'as far as the islands of the Pacific'. Long lists of territories and islands where the Bahá'ís should go were given. The American continent was where God's light would be revealed, and if the North American Bahá'ís responded to his call, waves of spiritual power would emanate, and the Bahá'ís become 'established upon the throne of an everlasting dominion'. Particular significance was attached to teaching the Eskimos and other indigenous Americans, and to establishing the Faith in Alaska, Greenland, Mexico, Panama and the Brazilian city of Bahia (Salvador). The teachers should seek to become 'Apostles of Bahá'u'lláh'. (This required three conditions: to be firm in the COVENANT; fellowship and love amongst the Bahá'ís; and that the teachers were dedicated and severed from the world, continually travelling, sanctified, and like a shining torch in God's love.) Those who travelled to foreign countries should learn the local languages. Bahá'í literature needed to be translated or composed in the world's various languages. The war had made the peoples of the world yearn for peace and become receptive to the Bahá'í message. Specific prayers were given for the teachers to use. AB 420–5; TDP.

'Abdu'l-Bahá had written that 'this is the time' for teaching, but at first only a few Bahá'ís responded to his appeal (these included Martha ROOT, who travelled to Latin America, John and Clara Hyde-DUNN, who settled in Australia, and Leonora ARMSTRONG, who settled in Brazil). Only from 1937 onwards did Shoghi Effendi direct the Bahá'ís to undertake a series of systematic teaching PLANS intended to fulfil the objectives of 'Abdu'l-Bahá's letters. He referred to the fulfilment of 'Abdu'l-Bahá's Divine Plan as passing through a series of stages (*see* TIME).

Tabríz (1868 pop. est. 110,000)

Capital of the north-western Iranian province of Azerbaiján (Ádhirbáyján). A major international trading centre, it was the most populous city in Iran by the 1860s. Unlike the rest of Iran the province is largely Azeri Turkish-speaking. There are also important Kurdish Sunní and Assyrian Christian minorities. It was the site of the Báb's trial (late July 1848) and execution (8/9 July 1850).

Ṭáhirih (PA, the 'Pure')

Title of the Bábí leader Fáṭimih Baraghání (1814–52), given her by the Báb. She was also known as Umm Salamih, Zarrín-Táj ('Crown of Gold'), and Qurratu'l-'Ayn ('Solace of the Eye'). She was born into a prominent clerical family in the northern Iranian city of Qazvín. Her father, Mullá Muḥammad Ṣáliḥ, was a respected and powerful *MUJTAHID*, as was his brother, Mullá MUḤAMMAD-TAQÍ BARAGHÁNÍ. Unusually for a woman in 19th-century Iran she was allowed to undertake higher Islamic studies, and eventually gained a considerable reputation for scholarship. When she was fourteen she was married to her uncle's son, Muḥammad, by whom she had three sons and one daughter (her husband later became leader of the Friday prayers (*imám jum'a*) in Qazvín, and was in turn succeeded by the eldest son). Whilst Muḥammad-Taqí, her elder uncle, was one of the most vehement opponents of SHAYKHISM, several of her relatives became Shaykhís, including a maternal cousin, Mullá Javád Valiyání, and her younger paternal uncle, Mullá 'Alí. Fáṭimih followed suit, and entered into secret correspondence with Sayyid KÁẒIM RASHTÍ, who called her *Qurratu'l-'Ayn*. Her younger sister, Marḍiyyih, married to Mullá Muḥammad-'Alí (like Ṭáhirih a future LETTER OF THE LIVING), a son of the Qazvín Shaykhí leader Mullá 'Abdu'l-Vahháb, also became a Shaykhí. The religious differences within the family exacerbated tensions between Fáṭimih and her husband and, late in 1843, she separated from him and proceeded to Karbalá with her sister, arriving there shortly after Sayyid Káẓim's death. At some point she also sent a message of recognition to the as yet unidentified Báb in Shíráz, being enrolled by him as a Letter of the Living, and rapidly becoming one of his most renowned followers. Residing in Rashtí's house, and with the support of his widow, she energetically promulgated Bábism, attracting many of the Shaykhís in Karbalá. This leadership on the part of a woman, together with her increasingly radical understanding of Bábism as a messianic new age – reflected in her disregard for Islamic convention – generated opposition from more conservative Bábís as well as other Shaykhís. The Báb supported her, however, and in response to allegations of immorality (caused by her apparently appearing unveiled before her disciples on at least one occasion) named her 'the Pure' (*Ṭáhirih*). Mounting opposition finally caused her to leave Karbalá for Baghdad, where she resided for some time in the house of the chief mufti (the head of the Sunní hierarchy in Iraq), Shaykh Maḥmúd Álúsí, who was favourably impressed by her intellect and devotion. Then, in March 1847, on instructions from the Ottoman government, she was deported. Travelling slowly through western Iran with a large group of supporters, she openly proclaimed Bábism to Shí'is, sectarian Ahl-i-Ḥaqq and Jews. She returned to Qazvín in July. Regarding her husband as an infidel, she refused to live with him, staying instead with her brother. Ṭáhirih's arrival exacerbated existing tensions, already made worse by the growth of a Bábí group in the town. Denying involvement in her uncle's subsequent murder (August/September 1847), she escaped to Tehran. She was later one of the principals at the conference of BADASHT (June–July 1848), where she advocated a radical break with Islam. After this she went into hiding. Discovered in January 1850, she was arrested and transferred to Tehran. She remained in confinement until her execution (strangled or choked to death) in September 1852, in the aftermath of the attempt on the life of NÁṢIRU'D-DÍN SHÁH.

Ṭáhirih's role in the development of Bábism was crucial, particularly in its 'radicalization'. She was a charismatic figure who attracted attention, in part because she sought to transcend the restrictions placed on her as a woman in a traditionalistic society. Her own immediate followers regarded her as the 'RETURN' of the Prophet Muḥammad's daughter, Fáṭima. She wrote extensively, including apologetic works and a large correspondence dealing with Bábí matters. Little of this has survived apart from her poems, however. Her poetry, and poetry attributed to her is still widely regarded internationally in the Persian cultural world. Accounts of her life came to inspire later generations of feminists. *ARR* 295–331; Browne, *Materials* 343–52; *GPB* 72–7; *McS* 56, 107–16, 177; *MF* 190–203; Nabil 81–4, 268–73, 283–7, 621–9; *TJ* 269–84, 355–6, 421, 434–41; *TN* 309–16.

Tajallíyát (PA, *Effulgences*)

Tablet of Bahá'u'lláh composed in about 1885–6 in honour of Ustád 'Alí-Akbar Banná, a master builder in Yazd, who was the recipient of twenty-seven tablets from Bahá'u'lláh, and later prepared the initial plans for the Bahá'í House of Worship at ASHKHABAD. He was martyred in 1903. The first part of the tablet is in Arabic, and contrasts the blessedness of those who have accepted Bahá'u'lláh with the utter loss of those who have rejected him. Ustád 'Alí is praised. The remainder of the tablet is in Persian, and details four 'effulgences': (1) In this day knowledge of God can only be attained through recognition of Bahá'u'lláh as a MANIFESTATION OF GOD. Complete recognition entails that the believer should also follow his LAW. (2) Steadfastness in God's Cause requires complete FAITH. (3) The importance of KNOWLEDGE is emphasized. (4) Were someone to judge Bahá'u'lláh fairly then they would recognize him as Manifestation of God. *TB* 45–54; *RB4*: 118–44.

talismans

The idea that a physical object can provide the wearer with some form of supernatural protection from danger is a common element in folk religion around the world. The Báb instructed his followers to make and wear talismans, and there are numerous references to these in his writings. Whilst the Bahá'í teachings greatly de-emphasize the esoteric elements of the Bábí tradition (instead stressing rationality), there are some prayers that appear to offer talismanic protection, as with Bahá'u'lláh's 'Long Healing Prayer', in which God is beseeched 'to protect the bearer of this blessed Tablet ... and whoso passeth around the house wherein it is', and to heal by it (the Tablet), 'every sick, diseased and poor one' (*Writings of Bahá'u'lláh* 708–9; cf. *McR* 138–40). Again, 'Abdu'l-Bahá wrote that those who sought 'immunity from the sway of the forces of the contingent world' should hang a copy of the GREATEST NAME in their dwellings, wear Bahá'í rings, place 'Abdu'l-Bahá's picture in their homes, and always recite his prayers (*LG* 520). *McR* 14–24, 48–51, 98–104, 138–53; *McS* 99–101; MacEoin, 'Nineteenth century Babí talismans'.

Tanumafili II, Malietoa

Head of state of Western Samoa and one of its traditional rulers. He became a Bahá'í in 1968, his declaration of faith being made public in 1973. The Samoan capital, Apia, is the site of the first Bahá'í House of Worship (*MASHRIQU'L-ADHKÁR*) of the Pacific Islands. *BW15*: 180–3.

Ṭarázát (PA, *Ornaments*)

Tablet of Bahá'u'lláh composed around 1889. In it Bahá'u'lláh revealed six 'ornaments', concerning: (1) SELF-KNOWLEDGE; (2) TOLERANCE; (3) good character (ETHICS); (4) TRUSTWORTHINESS; (5) respect for craftsmen and acknowledgement of present Western prowess; (6) KNOWLEDGE and NEWSPAPERS. He also referred to the OPPOSITION to his Cause (even in the face of the 'ascendancy of the oppressor' God's purpose could not be thwarted); revealed a prayer asking that God strengthen his followers to serve the Faith; and complained of the injustice and falsity of the present age, and of the largely erroneous reports that had appeared about him in newspapers. The tablet ends with an address to the AZALI Bábí leader, Mírzá HÁDÍ DAWLATÁBÁDÍ, censuring him for his hypocrisy (he had publicly recanted his faith) and asking him to investigate Bahá'u'lláh's Cause without prejudice. *TB* 31–44; *RB4*: 168–76.

Tarbíyat schools

See SCHOOLS.

teaching

The endeavour to attract more people to the Bahá'í Faith is strongly emphasized in the Bahá'í writings, and is commonly referred to as 'teaching'. All Bahá'ís are given the obligation to teach their religion, and there is now no specific group of teachers, although up until at least the early years of the 20th century certain prominent Iranian Bahá'ís were designated as 'teachers' (*mubalighín*). Some Bahá'ís establish themselves in countries or localities in which there are no Bahá'ís in order to spread the Faith to those places (*see* PIONEERS). Many spend often considerable periods of time as 'travel teachers', travelling from one place to another to teach their faith.

Bahá'u'lláh commanded his followers to teach, emphasizing the importance of ethics and wisdom: it is goodly conduct and saintliness that will ensure the triumph of the Faith (*TB* 88, 126, 196). Teaching and the SPIRITUAL PATH were thus linked, as in the *LAWḤ-I-ḤIKMAT*, in which he counsels those who want to serve his cause to forsake all evil; strive to manifest divine virtues and make each day better than the one before; and be unworldly, generous in prosperity, patient in loss, active, chaste, faithful, truthful, enlightened, just, wise, forgiving and merciful. They should be united in thought; love all of humanity; follow what would profit all people, regardless of age or social status; avoid causing dissension or doubt; respect the Bahá'í learned and the rulers; and banish ignorance from the earth (*TB* 138–9). Elsewhere Bahá'u'lláh counselled Bahá'ís to be as 'unrestrained as the wind' in their teaching endeavour, putting their whole trust in God, arraying themselves with 'the robe of virtue', and becoming enkindled with 'the fire of His love'. Thus would their words have an impact on those who heard them, and God render them victorious over those who opposed the Faith (*ADJ* 42, 47). They should be ablaze with 'the fire of the love of God' (*CC2*: 293), and speak with 'penetrating power' (itself based on purity of spirit) (*TB* 198–9). At the same time, however, they should exercise MODERATION, tact, and wisdom in what they say (*TB* 143) and show 'extreme kindliness' and friendliness to those whom they hope to attract to the Faith. They should not exceed the individual's capacity by saying too much, lest they engender opposition. If others reject the teachings they should not protest, but leave them to themselves and turn to God (*CC2*: 293–4; *TB* 129). The teacher should also memorize passages from scripture, as these exert a potent influence on the hearer when quoted (*TB* 200).

'Abdu'l-Bahá also emphasized the importance of Bahá'ís teaching their religion to others (see particularly his TABLETS OF THE DIVINE PLAN, in which he also outlined a global mission of Bahá'í EXPANSION). Thus they would attract 'divine confirmations'. They should be detached, pure in heart, loving, humble, wise and courageous. They should never argue with anyone. Each Bahá'í should teach one new person each year (*CC2*: 298–301).

In *The* ADVENT OF DIVINE JUSTICE Shoghi Effendi outlined the prerequisites and requirements of teaching in the Seven Year PLAN. Elsewhere he appealed to Bahá'ís to make teaching 'the dominating passion of our life' and emphasized the importance of pioneering (*BA* 69). Bahá'ís should place their reliance on God and deepen their knowledge of the Faith and its holy writings. They should teach constructively. There is no one right method of teaching (though informal meetings in homes – FIRESIDES – with discussions and hospitality, had proved particularly effective). Bahá'ís should be sensitive to those they sought to teach. The Bahá'í Faith is for everyone. To teach educated people Bahá'ís should themselves be well informed so that they could discuss contemporary issues intelligently. They should not disdain illiterates or regard them as unintelligent. PRAYER and perseverance are important (*CC2*: 301–26).

The entry of large numbers of new Bahá'ís in various 'Third World' countries from the 1950s onwards dramatically changed the composition of the Bahá'í community world-wide, and also changed conceptions of teaching. The Universal House of Justice has accordingly emphasized the importance of 'teaching the masses' as a means of achieving continued large-scale expansion. Effective CONSOLIDATION is vital, particularly in areas where large numbers of rural illiterates had become Bahá'ís. New Bahá'ís should be made to feel part of the existing Bahá'í community. Bahá'ís should not give the impression that conversion would lead to any material advantage to the people they were teaching (*CC2*: 61–71).The House has also stressed the importance of fostering cordial relations with prominent people (*CC2*: 258–80). (*See also* MISSION; PROCLAMATION.)

Tehran

(Ṭihrán) (1868 pop. est. 85,000)

Iranian capital since the QÁJÁR period. It was the birthplace of Bahá'u'lláh and

'Abdu'l-Bahá (also of Bahiyyih Khánum and Mírzá Mihdí). Bahá'u'lláh eulogized the city as 'the Dayspring of His [God's] light' and the 'source of joy of all mankind'. God's lovingkindness was directed towards it. Power within it would soon pass to the people, and its agitation change into calm. One day it would be ruled by a just king who would protect the Bahá'ís (*KA* 53–4 k91–3).

As capital, it became an early centre of Bábí activity, Bahá'u'lláh himself being one of the earliest converts there (1844). The first persecution of the Bábís in the city was in 1850 (*see* Seven Martyrs of Tehran). This was followed by the bloody aftermath of the botched attempt on the life of Náṣiru'd-dín Sháh (1852), in which large numbers of Bábís were executed, some in grisly public spectacles of torture and dismemberment. Those killed included Aẓím – seemingly the leader of the militant Bábí group responsible for the assassination attempt – as well as others, such as Ṭáhirih, who had been uninvolved (*MBBR* 132–45). It was at this time that Bahá'u'lláh was arrested and placed in the Síyáh-Chál dungeon.

A Bahá'í community emerged in the 1860s, and appears to have grown rapidly, its numbers augmented both by conversions and the movement of Bahá'ís from other parts of Iran, who were fleeing persecution or seeking greater economic opportunity. Persecution in Tehran itself was relatively limited, in part because family connections between Bahá'ís and government officials enabled the local Bahá'ís to receive warnings of possible action directed against them; in part, no doubt, so that the government could avoid the embarrassment of criticism from the powerful foreign embassies located in the capital. Major exceptions were the martyrdoms of Badí' (1869) and of 'Alí-Muḥammad Varqá and his son, Rúḥu'lláh (1896), and the imprisonment of groups of Bahá'ís in 1882–3 and 1891 (*MBBR* 292–5, 355–6). Tehran became the centre for the emerging system of national Bahá'í administration: all four of the Hands of the Cause appointed by Bahá'u'lláh (1887–*c.*1889) were resident in Tehran, and the Tehran spiritual assembly (1899) served as the central administrative body for the whole country. It was also the locale of the well-known Tarbíyat Bahá'í schools (1898, 1910). MMS, 'Tehran'.

THE HOUSE OF BAHÁ'U'LLÁH

Bahá'u'lláh was born in a large, early 19th-century house complex belonging to his father, Mírzá 'Abbás. The house was located in the Pá-Minár (minaret's foot) area of the old Shimrán Gate district, a neighbourhood in which many Qájár courtiers and notables lived. After his father's fall from office (late 1830s) the house was sold, and the family lived in rented property. The house is regarded by Bahá'ís as a sacred site, and was located, purchased and restored by them during the 1940s. It was confiscated by government authorities after the Islamic Revolution (1979).

temple, Bahá'í

See Mashriqu'l-Adhkár.

Temple Society

(German: *Tempelgesellschaft*).

Also called Templers, a German Christian adventist group which established communities in the Holy Land. The first and largest colony was founded in Haifa in 1868–9 under the leadership of David Hardegg. Both Bahá'u'lláh and 'Abdu'l-Bahá had friendly contacts with the Templers during their visits to Haifa. The colony was dispersed by the British in the late 1930s for security reasons, many families being resettled in Australia. The street along which their houses were built leads to the stairway up to the Shrine of the Báb. Ruhe 189–93.

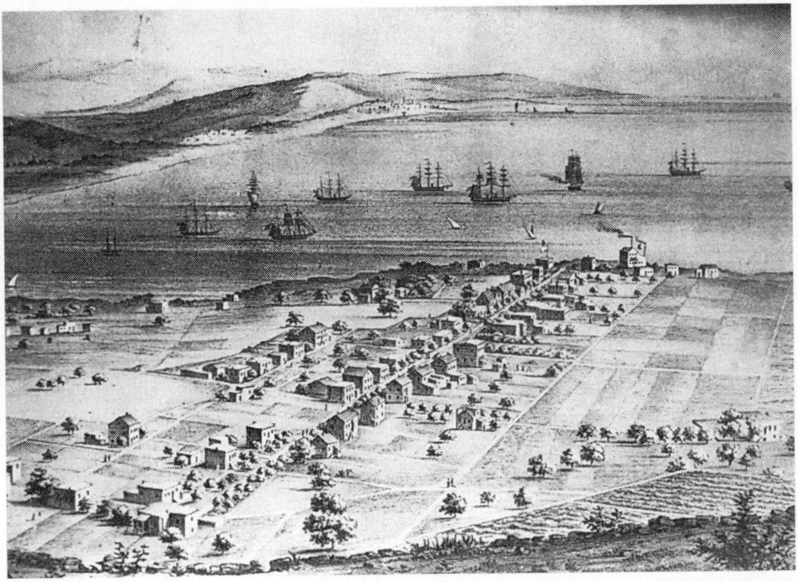

Templer Colony, Haifa

Ten Year Crusade (Plan)
(1953–63)

The first international TEACHING plan (*see* PLANS). It was launched by Shoghi Effendi, and brought to completion by the HANDS OF THE CAUSE. It culminated in 1963 with the first election of the Universal House of Justice, and the holding of the London World Congress (*see* CONFERENCES), at the time the largest gathering of Bahá'ís ever held.

texts

See CANONICAL TEXTS; SCRIPTURE.

Thatcher, Chester Ira (d. 1907)

Early American Bahá'í, from Chicago. Shoghi Effendi honoured him as one of the DISCIPLES OF 'ABDU'L-BAHÁ.

theology

The systematic study of the divine. There is at present little in the way of formal Bahá'í theology. Certain basic theological concepts pervade the Bahá'í writings (notably the unknowability of GOD, the pivotal role of the MANIFESTATIONS OF GOD in the human approach to the divine; the SOUL), but the general thrust of the Bahá'í scriptures and authoritative interpretations most widely available (in English at least) is towards the development of practical spirituality, morality, social change and community functioning, and Bahá'í writers have reflected this emphasis. Inexact translations of some of 'Abdu'l-Bahá's theological texts limit the present possibilities of explicating certain aspects of Bahá'í theology for those reliant on Western language sources. Theological concerns are explored in a few recent publications, including McLean's study of spirituality (*Dimensions in Spirituality*); Savi's examination of the 'Eternal Quest for God'; and the work of the contributors to McLean's *Revisioning the Sacred*, concerned with such topics as INTERFAITH DIALOGUE, liberation theology, and the 'spiritual foundations of science'; see also McLean, 'Prolegomena'. (*See also* METAPHYSICS.)

Thompson, Juliet (1873–1956)

Early American Bahá'í and well-known portrait painter. She became a Bahá'í in Paris in 1901 after meeting May Bolles (MAXWELL). She later returned to the United States. She was greatly devoted to 'Abdu'l-Bahá and was much involved in the work for his visit to New York. During World War I she was a strong advocate of peace (attracting the attention of federal agents). Her memoirs of meetings with 'Abdu'l-Bahá (*The Diary of Juliet Thompson)* are well known. *BW13*: 862–4; *WEBW* 73–85.

Thornburgh-Cropper, Mary Virginia (d. 1938)

Expatriate American who became the first Bahá'í in Britain in 1898 after hearing of the new religion from her friend Phoebe HEARST. She and her mother were among the first group of Western pilgrims to visit 'Abdu'l-Bahá in 1898–9. She was active in the promotion of the Faith in London and was a member of the various Bahá'í administrative bodies established there from 1913 onwards. Shoghi Effendi named her as one of the DISCIPLES OF 'ABDU'L-BAHÁ. *BW8*: 649–51; *WSBR* 17–30.

time

Past, present and future are described according to various frameworks, which structure the whole of religious history on this planet.

DISPENSATIONS AND CYCLES

According to the PROGRESSIVE REVELATION doctrine the impact of each MANIFESTATION OF GOD takes a cyclic form. Each brings a fresh revelation from God which only gradually matures in the form of a new religion and civilization before eventually declining in force, thus necessitating a further revelation. These cycles (often referred to as 'Dispensations') are compared in the Bahá'í writings to the seasonal changes of the year, starting with the 'divine springtime' of each 'appearance' (*ẓuhúr*) of a Manifestation. Collectively these dispensations comprise a 'Universal Cycle' of interrelated PROPHETS, each furthering the spiritual progress of humanity. The present universal cycle centres on Bahá'u'lláh. It consists of two sub-cycles: an approximately six-thousand-year-long cycle of prophecy (the 'Adamic cycle'), which began with the prophet ADAM and ended with the declaration of the Báb (1844), during which successive Manifestations announced the future establishment of a kingdom of God on earth; and a 'Bahá'í cycle', lasting some half-a-million years, during which this kingdom (the 'Most Great PEACE') will be established, and a succession of future Manifestations appear under Bahá'u'lláh's shadow – the first not until the lapse of at least one thousand years. *LG* 474–5, 500; *SAQ* 160–1; *WOB* 102–3.

AGES OF THE FAITH

Shoghi Effendi referred to three evolutionary stages through which the Faith would pass (*CF* 5–7; *GPB* xiii–xiv, 411; *WOB* 98, 156–7):

THE 'HEROIC', 'PRIMITIVE' OR 'APOSTOLIC' AGE (1844–1921)

This is associated with the ministries of the CENTRAL FIGURES of the Faith (the Báb, Bahá'u'lláh and 'Abdu'l-Bahá). This had been a period of unparalleled spiritual fecundity, 'impregnated' with the creative energies of two independent Manifestations of God and the establishment of a COVENANT unique in religious history.

THE PRESENT 'FORMATIVE', 'TRANSITIONAL' OR 'IRON' AGE (FROM 1921)

During this period the Bahá'ís built the 'Administrative Order' (*see* ADMINISTRATION), which would crystallize and shape the spiritual forces of the Heroic Age and which constituted the 'hallmark and glory' of the age. This age was linked to the first via 'Abdu'l-Bahá's *WILL AND TESTAMENT* and BAHIYYIH KHÁNUM, 'the last survivor' of that earlier age. The Age of Transition overlapped with an 'Age of Frustration', which had begun with World War I (1914–18) and the historic changes precipitated by it (*WOB* 171).

THE FUTURE 'GOLDEN' AGE

This would be signalled by the establishment of a 'Bahá'í World Commonwealth' (*see* WORLD ORDER), which would represent the 'fruit' of their present efforts. It would witness the unification of all the world's peoples; the inauguration of the Most Great Peace; and the subsequent birth and efflorescence of a world civilization.

EPOCHS

The first two ages were subdivided into epochs. Those of the Heroic Age merely followed the three successive ministries of the Central Figures (*CF* 5). Those of the Formative Age were as follows:

(1) 1921–44/6

The initial establishment of the Bahá'í administration in all five continents. The first of the systematic national teaching PLANS was also launched during this period.

(2) 1946–63

A series of national teaching plans using the administrative machinery established during the first epoch, followed by the first international plan. Administrative developments including the establishment of the INTERNATIONAL BAHÁ'Í COUNCIL, the HANDS OF THE CAUSE and the AUXILIARY BOARDS, and culminating in the formation of the UNIVERSAL HOUSE OF JUSTICE.

(3) 1963–86

A succession of three international plans under the direction of the Universal House of Justice, characterized by rapid growth, the initiation of SOCIO-ECONOMIC DEVELOPMENT activities and the 'emergence of the Faith from obscurity' (*see* BAHÁ'Í FAITH). Administrative developments included the establishment of the CONTINENTAL BOARDS OF COUNSELLORS and the INTERNATIONAL TEACHING CENTRE. The construction and occupation of the Seat of the House of Justice was the crowning event of this epoch.

(4) FROM 1986

In which, marking the increasing maturity of the Bahá'í administrative institutions, the planning process is becoming localized at the level of national ASSEMBLIES in consultation with the Boards of Counsellors. *CF* 5–6; *MUHJ* 706 no. 447, 710–16 no. 451.

EPOCHS OF THE DIVINE PLAN

Shoghi Effendi also referred to epochs in the fulfilment of 'Abdu'l-Bahá's *TABLETS OF THE DIVINE PLAN*, beginning in 1937 with the initiation of the first systematic teaching plan. The Universal House of Justice has identified two such epochs to date: (1) 1937–63 From the start of the first American Seven Year Plan until the completion of the Ten Year Crusade; (2) After 1963 From the beginning of the Nine Year Plan. There are also stages within these epochs. *MUHJ* 5 no. 1.2, 713 no. 451.7.

Tobey, Mark (1890–1976)

Major modern American artist who was a Bahá'í. His work attracted particular attention in Europe where he lived much of his life. He became a Bahá'í in 1918. *BW17*: 401–4; Dahl, *Mark Tobey*; *World Order* 11/3 (Spring 1977).

tolerance

The Bahá'í Faith advocates cultural and religious tolerance. Bahá'u'lláh instructed his followers to associate with all the peoples of the world with 'joy and

Mark Tobey, modern American artist and Bahá'í

radiance'. This promotes unity, social order and advancement. Tolerance and righteousness are the means of human edification (*TB* 36). Again, the Bahá'ís should 'consort with the followers of all religions in a spirit of friendliness and fellowship' (*TB* 22, 35, 87). Similarly, 'Abdu'l-Bahá advocated 'infinite kindness and forbearance' when speaking with those of a different religion. Fanaticism and 'unreasoning religious zeal' repel others. Shunning others because of their religious beliefs, regarding them as ritually unclean and treating them with discourtesy, are to be condemned (*SDC* 53–5). Even when he strongly disagreed with the religious beliefs of others he avoided directly criticizing them (*SAQ* 282), except when these beliefs engendered social attitudes of which he disapproved, such as racial hatred and religious intolerance. These teachings contrasted strongly with 19th-century Iranian Shí'í practice, in which religious minority groups (Zoroastrians, Jews, Christians) were often severely discriminated against and regarded as ritually unclean. The Bahá'ís' tolerance is very likely to have been a factor in the conversion of members of these groups (*SBBR* 97). (*See also* HUMAN RIGHTS; PREJUDICE.)

Tolstoy, Leo (1828–1910)

Russian novelist and thinker. He made a study of the Bábí and Bahá'í religions, and expressed his intention of writing about them. He was sympathetic to some aspects of the Bahá'í teachings, but critical of others. Ghadirian; Stendardo.

Townshend, George (1876–1957)

Anglo-Irish HAND OF THE CAUSE of Protestant background. He was ordained as an Episcopalian minister in 1906 whilst living in the United States, and resumed a clerical life after he had returned to Ireland, later becoming a Canon at St Patrick's Cathedral, Dublin in 1932 and Archdeacon of Clonfert in 1933. He became a Bahá'í in 1921 and subsequently worked to attract other clergy of the Church of Ireland to his new-found faith. These efforts were completely unavailing. He eventually renounced his orders in 1947. From 1926 onwards he acted as literary adviser to Shoghi Effendi, reading through and editing all of the Guardian's major publications. At Shoghi Effendi's request he wrote the introductions to *The* DAWN-BREAKERS (1932) and GOD PASSES BY (1944). His own writings were extensive, and included *The Old Churches and the New World Faith* (1949), a 'manifesto' to Christians explaining the reasons for leaving the church, and *Christ and Bahá'u'lláh* (1957), presenting Bahá'í as the fulfilment of Christianity. Shoghi Effendi appointed him as a Hand of the Cause in December 1951. *BW13*: 841–6; Hofman.

George Townshend, Anglo–Irish Bahá'í author and Hand of the Cause

translation

Bahá'ís stress the importance of LITERACY and of the individual believer reading the Bahá'í writings for him or herself. The value of reading SCRIPTURE in the original language is appreciated, but with the exception of Persian speakers who read their obligatory PRAYERS and various other writings of Bahá'u'lláh in the original Arabic there is no requirement to do so, even for ritual purposes (i.e. there is no sacred LANGUAGE). Translation of Bahá'í writings, particularly scripture, is therefore given great importance.

The Bahá'í scriptures are mostly in Persian or Arabic, and the EXPANSION of the Bahá'í Faith outside the Middle East necessitated translation of these writings into other languages. Some Bábí and Bahá'í works had been translated into European languages during the 19th and early 20th centuries by orientalists (*see* E.G. BROWNE, J.A. GOBINEAU, A.L.M. NICOLAS, Alexander TUMANSKI), but for the most part translation of texts important to Bahá'ís began with the growth of Bahá'í communities in America and Europe from the 1890s. The work of ALI-KULI KHAN, Laura (DREYFUS-)BARNEY and Ahmad SOHRAB in English and Hippolyte DREYFUS into French were particularly important. With SHOGHI EFFENDI's accession as Guardian (1922) English assumed official status, Shoghi writing extensively in English as well as translating a number of Bahá'í works into that language. Shoghi Effendi's formal style, modelled in part on the English of the King James version of the Bible, has come to be regarded as exemplary for Bahá'í translators in its poetry and beauty. He also established the present system of Bahá'í TRANSLITERATION. The UNIVERSAL HOUSE OF JUSTICE has also sponsored a number of important translation projects.

Translation goals have come to be an important element in Bahá'í expansion PLANS since the 1930s. Whereas in 1928 Bahá'í literature was only available in eight or so languages, by May 1994 literature had been translated into 802 languages (*BWNS* 1994–5: 317). In many cases the literature translated may consist of just a few prayers, but in an increasing number of languages a substantial body of material is now available ('Survey' 75). In the case of scripture these translations are generally made from Shoghi Effendi's English-language translations (this underlines the importance of Shoghi Effendi's role as interpreter). Only in the case of Middle Eastern languages or Urdu are they made directly from the original Persian or Arabic. All translations require pre-publication REVIEW. An increasing number of English translations are now being made from the original texts. These require the approval of the Universal House of Justice before they can be officially published. Translation by committee is encouraged, and the use of informal language is discouraged. The use of simplifications and paraphrases for those who are less educated is permitted, but such work is not to be accorded the status of scripture (*Bahá'í Studies Bulletin* 5/1–2 (January 1991): 90–101; *LG* 106–9 nos. 367–71; *MUHJ* 186 no. 94.3d).

transliteration

In 1923 Shoghi Effendi initiated a policy of having a uniform system of transliteration of Persian and Arabic terms in English, and insisted that it be used in all Bahá'í publications (*BA* 43). The main elements of this system are given in all volumes of the old series of *Bahá'í World* from volume 2 onwards. A modified version of this system is used in the present book (see preface). The system itself is based on one adopted by the Tenth International Congress of Orientalists at Geneva in September 1894. Momen, 'Bahá'í system of transliteration'.

Traveller's Narrative

(Pers.: *Maqáli-yi-shakhṣí sayyáḥ*)

Historical narrative of early Bábí and Bahá'í history by 'Abdu'l-Bahá, composed around 1886. It was first published anonymously in Persian in 1890 in Bombay. A facsimile edition, together with an English translation and detailed – and extremely valuable – notes, was prepared by E.G. BROWNE, and published in 1891. *McS* 169–70.

True, Corinne Knight

(1861–1961)

Prominent early American Bahá'í and HAND OF THE CAUSE. She converted in 1899 in Chicago. She was initially the driving force behind the project to build a Bahá'í temple in the Chicago area, and served on the BAHAI TEMPLE UNITY. She was one of those consulted by Shoghi Effendi about the future development of the Faith in 1922, and was also active as a Bahá'í teacher in the United States, and in the establishment of new Bahá'í groups in Europe after World War II. She was appointed a Hand in February 1952. *BW13*: 846–9; Harper 391–407; Rutstein, *Corinne True*.

trustworthiness

Particularly praised as a human virtue. Bahá'u'lláh described it as 'the sun of the heaven' of his commandments, to which TRUTHFULNESS was the moon. It was 'the greatest portal' leading to human security and tranquillity, and 'the supreme instrument for the prosperity of the world'. 'The stability of every affair' depended upon it, and it was 'the most glorious crown' for the heads of his followers. It was better to be adorned with 'the raiment of trustworthiness' than to visit Bahá'u'lláh as a pilgrim. It protected the individual from harm, and was 'the chief means' of attracting both divine confirmations and prosperity. It was a vital part of economic activity. (No one should deal faithlessly with the wealth of others. Not to settle one's debts if one was in a position to do so was to go against the 'good pleasure' of God.) Bahá'u'lláh referred several times to a vision he had at the Riḍván Garden in AKKA in which he saw trustworthiness personified (*TB* 37–8, 121–2, *ESW* 136–7). 'Abdu'l-Bahá stated that Bahá'ís should be distinguished by their trustworthiness. Piety and the performance of all good deeds were of no value without trustworthiness and honesty. Government officials in particular should strive to be completely trustworthy. *CC2*: 327–53. (*See also* SPIRITUAL QUALITIES.)

truth, independent investigation of

See INDEPENDENT INVESTIGATION OF TRUTH.

truthfulness

Particularly praised as a human virtue. Bahá'u'lláh linked it to TRUSTWORTHINESS, and advised that it was better to be 'of the people of hell-fire' than to be a hypocrite (*CC2*: 337). For 'Abdu'l-Bahá truthfulness was 'the foundation of all human virtues' (*ADJ* 26). It protects the individual from moral afflictions. The evils of falsehood are greater than all other sins (*CC2*: 338). Lying is the worst possible quality – 'the destroyer of all human perfections' and 'the foundation of all evils' (only in the case of a doctor who withholds knowledge of a patient's true condition in the belief that it would help them recover was it considered permissible) (*SAQ* 215–16). (*See also* SPIRITUAL QUALITIES).

Tudor-Pole, Major Wellesley (1884–1968)

Prominent early British Bahá'í. He first heard of Bahá'í in 1908, and visited 'Abdu'l-Bahá in Egypt in 1910. 'Abdu'l-Bahá stayed at his guest house in Clifton during his visits to Bristol in 1911 and 1913. During World War I Tudor-Pole joined British military intelligence in Egypt, and was responsible for initiating British moves to secure 'Abdu'l-Bahá's safety during the invasion of Palestine. He was one of those called to meet Shoghi Effendi to discuss the future of the Faith early in 1922, but subsequently distanced himself from Bahá'í activities, evidently retaining a view of Bahá'í as an inclusive spiritual movement which was incompatible with the more organized form then emerging. A mystic and a clairvoyant, he remained prominent in the milieu of alternative religiosity. He refers to his experiences with 'Abdu'l-Bahá in various of his books, particularly *Writing on the Ground*. *AB* 432–3, 453–4, 477–80; Weinberg 114–18, 142, 168–71, 176, 207–8, 213–14, 286.

Robert Turner, the first black American Bahá'í

Tumanski, Alexander (d. 1920)

Russian soldier (eventually a major-general) and orientalist. He first met Bahá'ís in ASHKHABAD in 1890 and later translated a number of important Bahá'í texts into Russian, including the *Kitáb-i-Aqdas* (1899) – the first translation of that work into a foreign language. *MBBR* 41–3.

Turner, Robert (1855/6–1909)

Butler of Phoebe HEARST. He was probably the first black American to become a Bahá'í (1898), and was among the first group of Western Bahá'í pilgrims to Akka. *BFA1*: 139–40; *WEBW* 15–8.

U

'ulamá

The Islamic 'learned' who have come to constitute a distinctive religious grouping, particularly in SHÍ'ISM, in which they have come to be seen as representatives of the Hidden IMÁM, and as such fulfil his judicial functions, and receive and disburse the religious taxes due to him. To become recognized as 'learned' (and wear distinctive clerical robes and turban and be addressed as 'Mullá') requires a lengthy course of study at a religious college (*madrasa*), typically focusing on the study of Islamic jurisprudence (*fiqh*). By the 19th century a Shí'í clerical hierarchy had developed, headed by those who gained the rank of *MUJTAHID* (possessing the right to make independent legal judgments), and occupied such prestigious posts as leader of the Friday prayers (*imám-jum'a*) at one of the more important mosques, whilst others occupied a variety of subordinate positions. In Iran the more important clerics held enormous power and frequently considerable wealth. Some individuals also saw themselves as upholders of righteous power against ungodly state authorities, and controlled private armies of religious students and street fighters to impose their will. Momen, *Shi'i Islam* 184–205; *SBBR* 6–8.

RELATIONSHIP TO THE BÁBÍ AND BAHÁ'Í MOVEMENTS

The Iranian *'ulamá* were not a homogeneous grouping. Attitudes towards the emerging Bábí and Bahá'í religions varied, with some clerics converting (and then naturally assuming positions of leadership) and some exercising a degree of tolerant reserve, whilst yet others led a vehement campaign of persecution against those whom they regarded as unbelievers (*SBBR* 17, 19–20; *see* OPPOSITION). These were seen by the Bábís and Bahá'ís as their primary opponents, leading the ignorant masses to massacre innocent believers. Bahá'u'lláh declared them to be his main enemies, and stated that were it not for their opposition Iran would have quickly converted to Bábism: their very pulpits lamented at the blasphemies they uttered; because of them the banner of Islam had been hauled down and its throne subverted; they had opposed every person who had truly sought to exalt Islam; ere long they would receive divine punishment, and their glory would become abasement (*PDC* 89–92). Apart from the trial of Mullá 'ALÍ BASṬÁMÍ in Baghdad (1845), Sunní clerics were less immediately involved in Bábí–Bahá'í affairs. Nevertheless, Bahá'u'lláh quietly rebuked the Sunní *'ulamá* of Istanbul for not having enquired about him: they were lovers of names, and had clung to outward things whilst forgetting inner realities. God would no longer accept their devotions or remembrance of him (*PDC* 92–3).

Subsequently Shoghi Effendi welcomed the anti-clerical and secularist policies of the new Turkish Republic (founded 1922) and the Pahlaví government in Iran (from 1925), seeing their restrictions on clerical power as a fulfilment of Bahá'í prophecies, and the just deserts of those who had persecuted God's cause (*PDC* 93–103).

'ABDU'L-BAHÁ'S IDEAL

In his anonymously published *Secret of Divine Civilization* (1875) 'Abdu'l-Bahá held that the truly spiritually learned were 'lamps of guidance among the nations' and a sanctuary for the distressed. Such individuals would be recognized by their SPIRITUAL QUALITIES, intellectual power and enlightened knowledge. They should seek to acquire the attributes of spiritual and material perfection; defend Islam; oppose their own passions; and obey the divine commandments. Only then would they be worthy of emulation (*taqlíd*). Their learning should encompass not only the fundamentals of religion and holy law but also the scriptures of other religions, political science, history and the natural sciences. As to the attributes of perfection, these included 'learning and the cultural attainments of the mind'; justice and selfless impartiality; and dedication to community education. Clerical status of itself was no proof of knowledge and moral continence (*SDC* 34–40, 59). (*See also* 'LEARNED'.)

United Nations, League of Nations

Bahá'u'lláh had called for the creation of an international assembly to establish PEACE between the nations and preserve it through a system of collective security (*ESW* 30–1). The formation of the League of Nations in the aftermath of World War I was therefore welcomed by Bahá'ís as an important step towards this goal, despite its obvious weaknesses and shortcomings from a Bahá'í standpoint: it was seen as incapable of establishing peace because its powers over its constituent nations were slight and it was not representative of all nations (*SWAB* 306–7; *WOB* 191–3). The United Nations is seen as a further step forward towards the Bahá'í goal, albeit still lacking sufficient power. The INTERNATIONAL BAHÁ'Í BUREAU maintained contacts with the League, and the case of the House of Bahá'u'lláh in BAGHDAD became a major issue at the League's Permanent Mandates Commission. Bahá'í contacts with the United Nations have been far more extensive, and are conducted through the BAHÁ'Í INTERNATIONAL COMMUNITY.

unity

Central and recurring concept in the Bahá'í teachings. Bahá'ís refer to 'divine unity' (*tawḥíd*, the 'unity of GOD'); the unity of religions (*see* RELIGION; RELIGIOUS DIVERSITY); the unity of the HUMAN RACE; the eventual establishment of a united world (*see* WORLD UNITY); and the need to preserve unity amongst themselves (*see* COMMUNITY; COVENANT). Bahá'ís do not advocate uniformity, but rather a unity in diversity, 'Abdu'l-Bahá comparing the human race to a flower garden made beautiful by its diversity. Customs, tastes, ideas, and dispositions vary amongst people (*SWAB* 290–2). They can be harmonized to avoid conflict (as in CONSULTATION), but they are a natural part of the pattern of human life. (*See also* MINORITIES; RACE; TOLERANCE.)

unity feast

Gathering of Bahá'ís and their friends resembling the 'nineteen day FEAST', with prayers and fellowship, but without a consultative-administrative period. It may be organized as a means of introducing non-Bahá'ís to Bahá'í devotional practices, or to pray for some particular objective which others outside of the Bahá'í Faith might share. It has no administrative status or function.

Unity, Seven Candles of

See WORLD UNITY.

Universal House of Justice

(Ar.: *bayṭu'l-'adl-i-a'ẓam*)

Supreme ruling body of the Bahá'í Faith, established in 1963.

TEXTUAL BASIS

Bahá'u'lláh referred to the future establishment of a HOUSE OF JUSTICE which would assume authority over his religion, its members taking counsel regarding matters that had not already been determined by Bahá'u'lláh in his writings, and enforcing 'that which is agreeable to them'. The members ('Trustees') were assured of divine inspiration (*TB* 68). They should follow his teachings for the 'training of peoples', the 'upbuilding of nations', and the safeguarding of human honour; have regard for the interests of the people; be 'a shelter for the poor and needy'; promote the Lesser PEACE; safeguard the position of RELIGION; choose a universal LANGUAGE and script; and have charge over Bahá'í charitable endowments in succession to the descendants of Bahá'u'lláh (AGHṢÁN) (*KA* 35 k42; *TB* 70, 89, 125, 127, 128, 130). The House would be able to take appropriate action in response to the changing conditions of the day, and apparently eventually share power with secular rulers (*TB* 27, 93, 128–9; *see* GOVERNMENT). In relationship to Bahá'í LAW it would determine degrees of consanguinity for marriage; the punishments for certain crimes; and aspects of economic policy (*KA* 121–2 q49–50; *TB* 134). 'Abdu'l-Bahá emphasized the authority of the future 'Universal' or 'Supreme' House of Justice. It would be under Bahá'u'lláh's protection, and inspired by the Holy Spirit. Whatever it decided would be 'of God'. It would be 'the source of all good and freed from all error' (*see* INFALLIBILITY). Obedience to it would be obligatory; opposition to it would constitute opposition to God. He also stated that the House was charged with deliberating on such issues as were not determined in Bahá'u'lláh's writings, its legislation having the same authority as scripture. It could later abrogate its own laws in response to changing circumstances. Its decisions could be by majority vote. Its members should be elected by representatives of the various 'national' Bahá'í communities through their 'secondary Houses of Justice' (the present national spiritual ASSEMBLIES). For reasons that would later become apparent its membership was to be confined to men. Its head would be the Guardian of the Faith (*see* GUARDIANSHIP) (*CC1*: 322–8). Shoghi Effendi stressed the common objectives of the guardianship and the then as yet unelected House of Justice (to ensure the continuity of divinely appointed authority; safeguard the unity of the Faith; and maintain the integrity and flexibility of the Bahá'í teachings), and their complementarity of function (*WOB* 148). *CC1*: 319–42.

ESTABLISHMENT

Both 'Abdu'l-Bahá and Shoghi Effendi appear to have considered establishing the Universal House of Justice during their lifetimes, but declined to do so. In Shoghi Effendi's case one reason for this delay seems to have been the perceived weakness of the existing Bahá'í administration. Accordingly, he linked the establishment of well-functioning national assemblies to the future establishment of the House. Finally, in 1950/1 (when there were nine national assemblies, with another two about to be formed), he established an INTERNATIONAL BAHÁ'Í COUNCIL as a precursor to the House of Justice (*MBW* 7–8). After Shoghi Effendi's unexpected death (1957) the HANDS OF THE CAUSE assumed direction of the Faith, announcing that elections for the House would be held in Haifa in April 1963. The electors would be the members of all fifty-six national assemblies then extant. Since then the Universal House of Justice has acted as the supreme Bahá'í administrative body. In the absence of a living Guardian it has also assumed permanent headship of the Faith. Various aspects of its functioning were outlined in its constitution (adopted on 26 November 1972): its membership was to consist of nine men, elected every five years at an international convention of national assembly members (representing 165 assemblies by 1993). The House has no officers, but otherwise conducts its affairs much as the spiritual assemblies do. *SBBR* 126–31; *UHJ Constitution*.

MEMBERSHIP

To date, a total of sixteen men have served as members of the House. The membership has been highly stable, the only changes having occurred as a result of death or retirement. Of the original nine members elected in 1963, three still serve (1998) (see listing below).

By national origins, seven House members have been American (Chance, Gibson, Kavelin, Wolcott, Ruhe, Mitchell, Dunbar), five Iranian (Fathe-Azam, Ḥakím, Nakhjavání, Taherzadeh, Arbab), all resident outside Iran at the

Members of the Universal House of Justice

	PREVIOUS POSITION	YEAR OF ELECTION/YEARS OF SERVICE
Mr Hugh Chance	US	1963–93
Mr Húshmand Fathe-Azam	IN	1963
Mr Amos Gibson	US	1963–82 (d.)
Dr Luṭfu'lláh Ḥakím	IBC	1963–7 (resigned, d. 1968)
Mr David Hofman	Brit	1963–88 (resigned)
Mr H. Borrah Kavelin	IBC	1963–88 (resigned, d. 1988)
Mr 'Alí Nakhjavání	IBC	1963
Mr Ian Semple	IBC	1963
Mr Charles Wolcott	IBC	1963–87 (d.)
Dr David Ruhe	US	1968–93
Mr Glenford Mitchell	US	1982*
Dr Peter Khan	ITC	1987*
Mr Hooper Dunbar	ITC	1988
Mr Adib Taherzadeh	EuC	1988
Dr Farzam Arbab	ITC	1993
Mr Douglas Martin	OPI	1993

**by-election*

Previous position

Brit	British national spiritual assembly
EuC	European Board of Counsellors
IBC	International Bahá'í Council
IN	Indian national spiritual assembly
ITC	International Teaching Centre
OPI	Office of Public Information (BIC)
US	US national spiritual assembly

time of their election; two British (Hofman, Semple), and one each Australian (Khan) and Canadian (Martin). Although greatly respected, the members of the House do not have any special status or authority within the Faith as individuals. It is as a collectivity that the House exercises its leadership. The members clearly cultivate a public ethos of individual self-effacement.

THE RELATIONSHIP BETWEEN THE HOUSE AND THE GUARDIANSHIP

In the *Dispensation of Bahá'u'lláh* (1934) Shoghi Effendi stressed the complementarity of the guardianship and the Universal House of Justice (of which the Guardian would be permanent head) and the essential nature of the guardianship for the integrity of the Faith (*WOB* 148, 150). Shortly after its establishment, however, the House stated that there was no way in which further Guardians could be appointed (October 1963, *MUHJ* 14 no. 5). This announcement raised questions about the manner of the House's functioning in the absence of a Guardian. In response, the House commented that its own authority and infallibility were not dependent on the presence of a Guardian. That there was no successor to Shoghi Effendi as Guardian represented a 'grievous loss', but the continued unity and guidance of the Faith under the direction of the House of Justice, itself receiving divine protection and guidance, was assured. The Covenant was unbroken.
MUHJ 50–8 no. 23, 83–90 no. 35, 156–61 no. 75, 645–6 no. 412.

DEVELOPMENTS IN THE BAHÁ'Í FAITH SINCE 1963

The thirty-five year period of the Universal House of Justice's leadership has seen a number of major developments in terms of the Bahá'í Faith's internal development and 'external relations'.
BFSH 116–28.

PLANS AND EXPANSION

Since 1963 there has been a massive growth in the size of the Bahá'í community world-wide, particularly in the 'Third World'. This expansion has occurred within the framework of systematic planning established by Shoghi Effendi, and continued by the Universal House of Justice. Under its direction there have been five international plans, all in general resembling Shoghi Effendi's Ten Year Crusade. Accomplishments include enormous increases in the number of assemblies, translations and Bahá'í centres, as well as the completion of four new Houses of Worship (*Mashriqu'l-Adhkár*), bringing the global total to seven, and the holding of international conferences and congresses, designed to increase the sense of global solidarity amongst the Bahá'ís.

COMMUNITY DEVELOPMENT

The House has greatly emphasized qualitative change within the Bahá'í community (literacy; education; enhancing the role of women and youth; fostering family life; socio-economic development; communal dawn prayer (*see Mashriqu'l-Adhkár*)). It has also made the Bahá'í law of *Ḥuqúqu'lláh* applicable throughout the Bahá'í world (1992), and published Bahá'u'lláh's book of laws, the *Kitáb-i- Aqdas*.

IRAN

It was necessary to respond to the situation created by the sustained and co-ordinated persecution of the Bahá'ís that followed the Islamic Revolution in Iran (1979): Iranian Bahá'í emigrants and refugees had to be resettled and integrated into their new host communities, and replacement sources of funding found to replace the large donations made by Bahá'ís in Iran (hitherto the main source of international Bahá'í funding). Unprecedented attention from the media was successfully garnered to

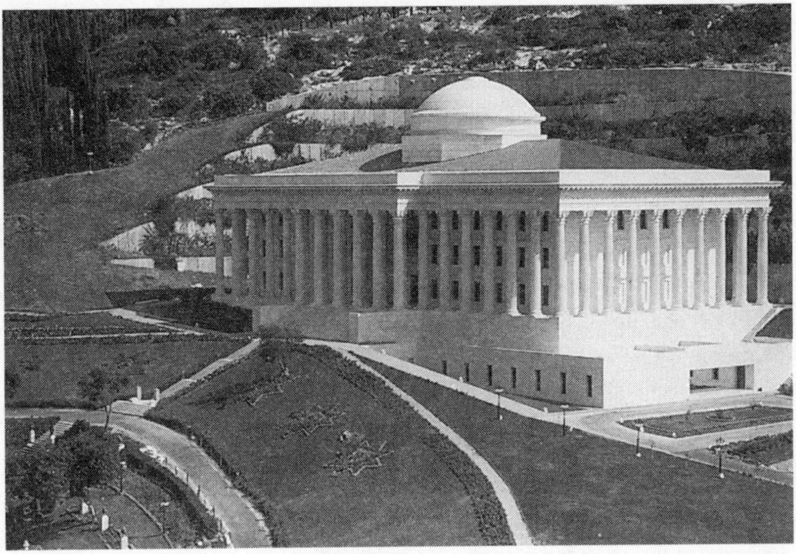

Seat of the Universal House of Justice, Haifa

gain publicity and sympathy for the Bahá'ís world-wide (*see* PUBLIC RECOGNITION).

ADMINISTRATION

The main developments in Bahá'í ADMINISTRATION since 1963 have been the House's ruling that there was no longer a way to appoint further Hands of the Cause (November 1964); and its creation of two new 'institutions of the learned' to continue the Hands' functions into the future – the CONTINENTAL BOARDS OF COUNSELLORS (1968) and an INTERNATIONAL TEACHING CENTRE (1973). The members of the AUXILIARY BOARDS have also been greatly increased in number, and they have been empowered to appoint their own assistants to help them with their work (1973). In several countries, new sub-national REGIONAL BAHÁ'Í COUNCILS have been established.

WORLD CENTRE

Like Shoghi Effendi the House of Justice has worked to secure ownership of sites associated with the central figures of the faith and to extend and beautify the gardens surrounding the Bahá'í Shrines at the BAHÁ'Í WORLD CENTRE. More dramatic has been its construction of a large stately building to serve as its own seat in Haifa (1975–83), and the extensive work on the buildings of the ARC (from 1992) and the terraces of the SHRINE OF THE BÁB. The House has also greatly expanded the number of support staff in Haifa, responding both to the international growth of the Bahá'í community and the increasing range of work that it itself directs or initiates.

PROCLAMATION AND SOCIETAL INVOLVEMENT

The House has launched two global campaigns of PROCLAMATION, the first (1967) centring on the centenary of Bahá'u'lláh's letters to the RULERS, a compilation of which was presented to many world leaders, and the second (1985) on the House's own statement *The PROMISE OF WORLD PEACE*. Bahá'í involvement with the UNITED NATIONS and its agencies has also increased enormously during this period, particularly through the work of the BAHÁ'Í INTERNATIONAL COMMUNITY (permanent UN office, established in 1967). This has reflected the growing numerical strength of the Bahá'í community internationally; its increasing concern with development; and the persecution of Bahá'ís in Iran, and resultant efforts to safeguard their human rights. Bahá'í UN contacts have led to greater collaboration with other non-governmental organizations. There is evident Bahá'í interest in wider societal issues such as PEACE and the ENVIRONMENT.

COVENANT

There have been no significant internal challenges to the leadership of the House from dissident Bahá'ís, albeit some of the REMEYITE GROUPS remain active (*see* COVENANT-BREAKERS).

Universal House of Justice, Constitution of

Declaration of Trust and associated by-laws adopted by the Universal House of Justice on 26 November 1972. The document outlines the House's powers, duties and manner of election and functioning, as well as defining basic elements of Bahá'í ADMINISTRATION. *MUHJ* 229 no. 123; *UHJC*.

Universal House of Justice, Seat of

See ARC.

Universal House of Justice, writings of

Although empowered to legislate on matters not revealed in the Bahá'í scriptures, the Universal House of Justice has as yet been extremely limited in its exercise of this function. Instead it has preferred to provide directive guidance to the Bahá'ís in its role as head of the Faith and to collect and publish a large mass of extracts from the writings of the Báb, Bahá'u'lláh, 'Abdu'l-Bahá and Shoghi Effendi. As with Shoghi Effendi, the House's guidance has taken the form of letters to Bahá'í communities, institutions and individuals, and sometimes to the entire Bahá'í world. Several volumes of these letters are now available, and many other letters are found in Bahá'í periodicals. The letters are regarded as divinely empowered. Compilations of Bahá'í writings on a wide range of subjects have been produced, including various aspects of Bahá'í administration; teaching; prayer; music; education; and family life. Translations of writings by the Báb, Bahá'u'lláh and 'Abdu'l-Bahá have also been commissioned, including Bahá'u'lláh's book of laws, the *Kitáb-i-AQDAS* (1992). In addition to its messages addressed to the Bahá'ís, the House has also published its own CONSTITUTION (1972); prepared a volume of Bahá'u'lláh's letters to the kings for presentation to contemporary heads of state (1967; *see* PROCLAMATION), and issued a call to 'the peoples of the world' to respond to the Bahá'í teachings for the establishment of universal peace (*The PROMISE OF WORLD PEACE*, 1985).

The extent of these endeavours has necessitated the establishment of research and archival departments in Haifa. Of the letters of Bahá'u'lláh, 'Abdu'l-Bahá and Shoghi Effendi, over 60,000 items had already been collected by 1983. An extensive programme of preservation, classification and indexing is in progress. These collected writings give the House a massive data base on which to base its deliberations and an ever-increasing body of published scripture and authoritative interpretation for Bahá'ís in general.

universe

See CREATION; METAPHYSICS.

V

Vafá, Súriy-i- (PA, *Tablet of Vafá*)

Syrian-period tablet of Bahá'u'lláh addressed to Shaykh Muḥammad-Ḥusayn, surnamed *Vafá* (Fidelity) by Bahá'u'lláh, and formerly one of the Bábís in the NAYRÍZ upheaval. In this tablet Bahá'u'lláh praises faithfulness; states that the worlds of God are countless in number; emphasizes the reality of paradise and of divine reward for goodly deeds; and comments on the doctrine of RETURN, himself claiming identity with the Báb (the 'Primal Point') 'arrayed in His new attire', and stating that those Bábís who failed to recognize him had known the Báb only by name, and not through his own self or revelation. *TB* 179–91; *RB4*: 205–13.

Vaḥíd (PA, 'Peerless')

Religious title of the Bábí leader Sayyid Yahyá Darábí (d. 1850). He was a distinguished cleric, and the son of Sayyid Ja'far (known as Kashfí ('discloser') for his skill in the esoteric interpretation of the Quran). Vaḥíd was reportedly delegated by MUḤAMMAD SHÁH to investigate the claims of the Báb whilst the latter was still in Shíráz, converting following the revelation of the Báb's commentary on the Quranic *súra* of Kawthar (autumn 1845). His conversion was significant both because of his social prominence and the fact that he was one of the first non-Shaykhís to accept the Báb. The Báb appointed him his representative to the Shah. He seems to have travelled extensively visiting the Bábís. Early in 1850 he proceeded to YAZD, where his open proclamation of Bábism provoked great controversy, and he became embroiled in an existing local conflict. He then proceeded to the small town of NAYRÍZ, where he already had a local following. A large number of the inhabitants converted, exacerbating tensions with the town governor. An armed struggle developed, which was ended with a truce, broken by the killing of Vaḥíd (29 June 1850) and a number of his companions. Vaḥíd was then aged about forty. *ARR* 278, 350; *GPB* 11–12, 50; *MBBR* 106–12; *McS* 71, 117; Nabil 171–7, 465–99; *SBBR* 28; *TJ* 111–23, 347–8, 400, 411; *TN* 7–8, 45n, 183–4, 253–61.

Vakil, Narayanrao Rangnath Shethji (1866–1943)

Prominent Indian Bahá'í, and the first known Bahá'í of Hindu background. He became a Bahá'í whilst a student in Bombay in 1909, and in 1910 represented the Bahá'ís at the All-India Religious Conference at Allahabad. He helped organize the first Bahá'í Convention of India (1920), and subsequently served as the president of the India and Burma Bahá'í national spiritual ASSEMBLY almost continuously until his death. He was a well-known lawyer. *BW9*: 637–41; Khianra 7–25; Shoghi Effendi, *Messages . . . to the Indian Subcontinent* 438–40.

Varqá, 'Alí-Muḥammad (b. 1912)

Iranian HAND OF THE CAUSE. Son of Valíyu'lláh VARQÁ. He gained a doctorate at the Sorbonne in 1950 (with a thesis on hydrology in Iran), and later became a professor at the universities of Tabriz and Tehran. After his father's death in 1955 he was appointed in his stead as Hand and as Trustee of the *ḤUQÚQU'LLÁH*. As Hand he performed various international missions for the Faith, and was in Europe at the time of the 1979 Islamic Revolution in Iran. He subsequently moved to Canada, later taking up residence in Haifa as one of the Hands at the Bahá'í World Centre. He remains Trustee of *Ḥuqúq*, and has overseen the enormous expansion in its administration in recent years. Harper 183–7.

Varqá ('Dove'), Mírzá 'Alí-Muḥammad (d. 1896)

Prominent Iranian Bahá'í renowned as a poet. He and his young son, Rúḥu'lláh, were killed by one of the Qájár courtiers in the aftermath of the assassination of NÁṢIRU'D-DÍN SHÁH. 'Abdu'l-Bahá named him posthumously as a HAND OF THE CAUSE, and Shoghi Effendi designated him as one of the APOSTLES OF BAHÁ'U'LLÁH. *EB* 75–97; Harper 42–9; *MBBR* 361–2.

Varqá, Valíyu'lláh (1884–1955)

Iranian HAND OF THE CAUSE born in Tabriz. His father was the martyr 'Alí-Muḥammad VARQÁ, but Valíyu'lláh was brought up under the influence of his staunchly Muslim maternal grandmother and it was not until he was in his teens that he was introduced to the Bahá'í teachings and became a Bahá'í. He later worked in the palace of Muḥammad-'Alí Sháh and was able to forward letters from 'Abdu'l-Bahá to the king. In 1912 he travelled to America and later to Europe, acting as 'Abdu'l-Bahá's treasurer and sometimes as his interpreter. He was a member of the Tehran spiritual ASSEMBLY, and later of the national spiritual assembly. Shoghi Effendi appointed him as Trustee of the *ḤUQÚQU'LLÁH* in 1938 following the death of Ghulám-Riḍá, and in December 1951 he was raised to the rank of Hand of the Cause. He travelled to various countries at Shoghi Effendi's direction. After his death (in Germany) his eldest son – another 'Alí-Muḥammad VARQÁ – was appointed a Hand and trustee of the *Ḥuqúq* in his father's stead. *BW13*: 831–4; Harper 329–32.

Victoria (1819–1901)

British Queen, 1837–1901. Constitutional monarch. She was the recipient of a tablet from Bahá'u'lláh (the *Lawḥ-i-Malikih*, 'Tablet of the Queen'), written during his early years in Akka (from 1868), in which Bahá'u'lláh summoned her to accept his claims and praised her for both Britain's prohibition of the SLAVE TRADE (1807) and its system of parliamentary government (the Second Reform Act had been passed in 1867, greatly extending the franchise). The requirements of GOVERNMENT and PEACE were also referred to. Victoria is said to have remarked: 'If this is of God, it will endure'. *ESW* 59–64; *PDC* 26, 34–6, 66; *Proclamation* 12–13, 33–5, 67–8.

Vieira, Eduardo Duarte (1921–66)

Early Bahá'í of Portuguese Guinea (now Guinea-Bissau). He became a Bahá'í in Lisbon, and actively taught the Faith on his return to his homeland, thereby incurring the opposition of the colonial Catholic authorities and losing his prestigious government position. A rising campaign of persecution led to arrests and brutal beatings by the police, culminating in his torture and death in prison. He was first African Bahá'í to be martyred for his faith. *BW14*: 389–90; *16*: 568.

visitation, tablets of

Specific prayers to be said during visits to the shrines of holy men are part of Islamic practice.

The Báb wrote many tablets of visitation. Of particular note is his 'Large Prayer of Visitation' (*Ziyára al-jámi'a al-kabíra*), written before the start of his mission for Muḥammad, Fáṭima and the Shí'í IMÁMS. This expresses great respect for these figures, and states the self-abnegation of the pilgrim to their shrines. There are later tablets of visitation in honour of the Báb's own martyred followers. Browne, *Selections* 202–8; *McS* 45–6, 99, 210.

Bahá'u'lláh and 'Abdu'l-Bahá also wrote many visitation tablets, including for particular Bahá'í martyrs. These commonly take the form of eulogies for the deceased. The *Tablet of Visitation* used by Bahá'ís during visits to the Shrines of the Báb and Bahá'u'lláh and commemorations for HOLY DAYS associated with them comprises passages taken from several tablets of Bahá'u'lláh, compiled by NABÍL-I-A'ẒAM at 'Abdu'l-Bahá's request after Bahá'u'lláh's passing. There is also a tablet of visitation by Bahá'u'lláh for the Imám Ḥusayn, which also allusively refers to the Báb, and which used to be chanted in the Shrine of the Báb on the anniversary of his martyrdom. The tablet used by visitors to the Shrine of 'Abdu'l-Bahá is one of his prayers expressive of humility and selflessness. Walbridge, *Sacred* 119–23.

W

war

Bahá'u'lláh proclaimed that he had come to establish the 'Most Great PEACE'; called for national rulers to work for peace; and decried the destructiveness of war and the use of national resources on ARMAMENTS. 'Abdu'l-Bahá condemned war as the antithesis of true civilization. It brings death and destruction, turns human beings into ferocious animals, and leads to the pointless destruction of life, cities and economic resources (*CC2*: 165). The conquests of arrogant men such as Alexander, Tamerlane and Napoleon served only to spread terror and anguish. Their destructive legacies contrast with the achievements of wise and just rulers. Only the latter achieved true glory. Only when employed to oppose insurrection and aggression, or to bring order and unity in situations of civil strife, can war be justified (*SDC* 67–71).

During his Western tours (1911–13) 'Abdu'l-Bahá warned of the danger of war, comparing Europe to an arsenal filled with explosives waiting for a spark to ignite it (*CC2*: 164; NSA of Canada 48–50). World War I (1914–18) was seen by Bahá'ís as fulfilment of these prophecies, the collapse of Germany and its monarchy being regarded as particularly significant in the light of Bahá'u'lláh's warning parenthetically addressed to WILHELM I. 'Abdu'l-Bahá remained pessimistic at the end of the War, regarding the Paris peace treaties (1919) as a cruel deception which masked 'the fire of unquenched hatreds'. International instability would continue, including continued tensions in the Balkans, agitation by the vanquished powers and the emergence of world-wide political movements. Communism would acquire increasing importance (*WOB* 30). A new war, 'fiercer than the last', would assuredly break out (*SWAB* 307). He also predicted that the increasing chaos in the world would become unbearable, causing people to turn to religion as a stronghold of security (*CC2*: 165).

wealth

See ECONOMIC TEACHINGS.

West

The Western impact on the Middle East during the 19th century was enormous. Iran was less affected than other areas until late in the century, so the Bábí movement developed in a socio-religious context little subject to extraneous influence. Bábí references to the West are correspondingly slight (*SBBR* 35, 53–56). By contrast, Bahá'u'lláh and 'Abdu'l-Bahá came to an Ottoman empire that was strongly and increasingly under Western influence, and in which various Ottoman statesmen and thinkers advanced Western-influenced reform. Some of their writings address these reform issues (*see* GOVERNMENT; *SECRET OF DIVINE CIVILIZATION*; see Cole, 'Iranian millenarianism'). They also referred directly to the West, indicating their knowledge of contemporary developments; their praise for many aspects of Western material advance ('the sun of craftsmanship' was now shining above the horizon of the Occident, and 'the river of arts' flowing out of that region (*TB* 38–9)) and for British-style constitutional government; their advocacy that beneficial aspects of Western civilization should be emulated; and their condemnation of Western MATERIALISM. Regarding the last, Bahá'u'lláh complained that Western civilization had gone beyond the bounds of moderation and become a source of evil: it had 'agitated and alarmed the peoples of the world' (*TB* 69); and that when the people of the East had become captivated by 'the arts and wonders of the West' they had 'roved distraught in the wilderness of material causes', oblivious of God (*TB* 144). More strongly, 'Abdu'l-Bahá described European culture as 'superficial' and 'unsupported by a cultivated morality'. The Europeans were drowning in a 'terrifying sea of passion and desire'. Their lack of morality was indicated by their warlike intentions and destructive conduct. This was only a 'nominal civilization', and quite incapable of bringing about PEACE and human well-being (*SDC* 60–4). In the Iranian context, Bahá'í acceptance of many aspects of Western culture made them distinctive compared to the traditionalism of most Iranians (*SBBR* 78, 177, 196–7).

White, Ruth

American Bahá'í who opposed the developing Bahá'í ADMINISTRATION in North America during the 1920s, insisting that 'Abdu'l-Bahá had said that the Bahá'í religion was an inclusive movement that could not be organized. In 1927 she expanded her critique to deny the validity of 'Abdu'l-Bahá's *WILL AND TESTAMENT* – which she dismissed as a forgery – and hence of Shoghi Effendi's guardianship. Her efforts, which included the publication of several books, were largely unavailing apart from in Germany where a small group of believers under the leadership of Wilhelm Herrigal (d. 1932) formed a 'Bahai World Union' inspired by her ideas. A small group of 'Free Bahais' reorganized after World War II, forming the 'World Union for Universal Religion and Universal Peace'. A polemical attack on '*Political Shoghism*' by Hermann Zimmer, one of the Free Bahais, was translated and published in English in 1973 and widely distributed to libraries throughout the world. White herself eventually become a follower of Meher Baba. Shoghi Effendi's first two WORLD ORDER letters are partly a response to her attacks. Bramson-Lerche, 'Some aspects of the establishment'; *TCB* 347–9.

Wilhelm, Roy C. (1875–1951)

Prominent early American Bahá'í. He was a millionaire businessman in New York City, and head of the family coffee company. His mother, Laurie, became a Bahá'í in 1898, but Roy was not attracted to the Faith until he accompanied his mother on her pilgrimage to Akka in 1907. This experience transformed his life. He was elected to serve on the Executive Board of the BAHAI TEMPLE UNITY in 1909 and, except for one year of illness, remained a member on it, and its successor, the national spiritual assembly, until 1946, often acting as its treasurer. He also helped administer the Bahá'í community in New York, produced Bahá'í literature, and supported the teaching work of Martha ROOT and Louis GREGORY. He

Roy C. Wilhelm, prominent early American Bahá'í

acted as a channel of communication between 'Abdu'l-Bahá and the American Bahá'ís, and was one of those whom Shoghi Effendi consulted about the future development of the Faith in 1922. He died on 24 November 1951, and was posthumously named a HAND OF THE CAUSE by Shoghi Effendi. An annual unity feast is held at the former Wilhelm property at West Englewood, New Jersey, to commemorate a feast held there by 'Abdu'l-Bahá during his visit to America. *BW12*: 662–4; Harper 129–41; *WEBW* 87–99.

Wilhelm I (1797–1888)

German Kaiser, 1871–88. He was addressed by Bahá'u'lláh in his *Kitáb-i-Aqdas*, and warned not to let pride debar him from recognizing Bahá'u'lláh. He should remember the fate of NAPOLEON III, whose power had surpassed his own but who had been overthrown. God brought down conquerors and rulers 'from their palaces to their graves'. The 'banks of the Rhine' were also addressed, Bahá'u'lláh having envisioned them 'covered with gore' when 'the swords of retribution' were drawn against them. They would have 'another turn', and though Berlin was now in 'conspicuous glory' her lamentations would be heard. The subsequent defeat of Germany in World War I, and the abdication and flight of the then Kaiser, Wilhelm II (r. 1888–1918), was regarded by Bahá'ís as a vivid fulfilment of this prophecy, and was regarded as a proof of the Bahá'í Faith by a number of Iranians. *KA* 51 k86, 53 k90, 217–18 n121; *GPB* 226; *PDC* 58–9; *WOB* 171–2.

Will and Testament of 'Abdu'l-Bahá

'Abdu'l-Bahá's *Will* is a lengthy document, written in three parts over a seven-year period (1901–8) during the early period of his ministry. He wrote it in his own hand, and addressed it to SHOGHI EFFENDI. Its contents were not known by the Bahá'ís until after 'Abdu'l-Bahá's death (28 November 1921), and it was apparently not even read to Shoghi Effendi until 'a few days' after his arrival in Haifa (29 December) (Rabbani, *Priceless Pearl* 42). The *Will* identified Shoghi as the 'primal' and 'chosen' branch (*see* AGHṢÁN); appointed him as the first in a projected line of Guardians of the Cause (*see* GUARDIANSHIP) and head of the as yet unelected UNIVERSAL HOUSE OF JUSTICE; and directed all Bahá'ís to turn to him and take the greatest care of him. Both he and the House were assured of divine protection and guidance. All should obey them. Those who disputed with them disputed with God, and would be subject to divine wrath. There would be no excuse for any attack on the COVENANT, such as had been mounted by MUḤAMMAD-'ALÍ and his partisans after the passing of Bahá'u'lláh. The *Will* also stated that Muḥammad-'Alí (the 'Center of Sedition' and 'the focal Center of Hate') had 'passed out from under the shadow of the Cause' and been 'cut off from the Holy Tree' by dint of his

COVENANT-BREAKING (some details of which are given), thus implicitly setting aside the original successorship established by Bahá'u'lláh in his *Book of the* COVENANT. Other provisions include instructions to the Bahá'ís to teach the Cause (*see* TEACHING), manifest SPIRITUAL QUALITIES, lovingly associate with all peoples, be loyal to their rulers, avoid contention, and shun Covenant-breakers; and descriptions of the duties and manner of election of the Universal House of Justice, and the obligations of the HANDS OF THE CAUSE. *Will; AB* 484–93.

The *Will* was first read officially on 3 January 1922, and copies were subsequently sent to Bahá'ís in the East. Shoghi Effendi himself prepared an English-language translation, but copies of the whole *Will* were not widely circulated in the West. The provisions were almost universally accepted by the Bahá'ís with the exception of Ruth WHITE and a few Western followers, who later challenged the *Will*'s authenticity (a charge rebutted by those who read Persian and were familiar with 'Abdu'l-Bahá's handwriting, including opponents of Shoghi Effendi). Shoghi addressed some of the issues raised by this challenge in the first two of his *WORLD ORDER OF BAHÁ'U'LLÁH* letters. Elsewhere he described the *Will* as being the 'Charter' for a new WORLD ORDER (*GPB* 325–6; *WOB* 143–4). Rabbani, *Priceless Pearl* 41–52.

wills

Bahá'ís are instructed each to write a will. The document should be headed by the GREATEST NAME; attest to the oneness of God 'in the Dayspring of His Revelation'; and may make mention 'of that which is praiseworthy' as a testimony for the deceased. The testator is entitled to dispose of their property as he or she wishes, and is encouraged to specify that their BURIAL should follow the requirements of Bahá'í law. In cases of intestacy, a detailed schedule of INHERITANCE was laid out by Bahá'u'lláh. *KA* 59 k109, 224 n136–7; *LG* 192–4.

wine

As in Sufi literature the Bahá'í writings sometimes use 'wine' as a religious metaphor: thus the believer should not turn away from 'the matchless wine of the immortal Beloved', nor 'the celestial wine of unity' (*HW*p nos. 61, 62). Bahá'u'lláh's laws were a 'choice Wine'. He offered the 'Mystic Wine of everlasting life' (*KA* 21 k5, 74 k150, 82 k173). As a form of ALCOHOL, the drinking of wine is prohibited in Bahá'í law, however.

wisdom

In Arabic translations of Greek philosophical texts the terms for wisdom (*sophia*) and prudence (*phronesis*) were conflated under the term *hikmat* (wisdom). This double meaning is seen in Bahá'u'lláh's writings, in which he both praises 'wisdom' (*sophia*) and advocates prudence by the Bahá'ís in the presentation of their religion.

Thus, wisdom is described as a divine quality which educates, protects and strengthens the individual, revealing the loftiness of the human station. It illumines JUSTICE (*TB* 66–7), and is illumined by CONSULTATION and compassion (*TB* 168). Its essence is the FEAR OF GOD (*TB* 155). Its 'pearls' are to be found in the 'ocean' of Bahá'u'lláh's words (*KA* 85 k182). The wise and the truly learned are like eyes to the body of humanity, and one of its greatest gifts (*TB* 171). (*See also* PHILOSOPHY.)

PRUDENCE

In terms of the prudential TEACHING of the Faith, wisdom is expressed in words that are both 'impressive and penetrating', and uttered only for the sake of God and with due regard for the appropriateness of time and place. The

words should be as milk for a babe so as to enlighten the people, and should be expressed with moderation, refinement and detachment. The wrong words might be as poison (*TB* 172–3). Whilst the Shí'í practice of dissimulation of belief (*taqiyyih*) in times of danger is condemned, Bahá'ís should not seek persecution, avoid unnecessary controversialism and be tactful in their speech. They should also be prudent in their observation of Bahá'í law, so as not to cause disturbance. The gradual development and application of the Bahá'í law prohibiting POLYGAMY, and of the public expression of the Bahá'í principle of gender equality in Middle Eastern societies (by women not veiling and being allowed to serve on Bahá'í ASSEMBLIES), are also regarded as expressions of wise prudence (*CC2*: 361–2; *KA* 206 k89).
Maneck, 'Wisdom'.

Wisdom, Tablet of

See Lawḥ-i-Ḥikmat.

'Wolf' and 'the Son of the Wolf'

Derogatory epithets given by Bahá'u'lláh to two prominent Iṣfáhání clerics, Shaykh Muḥammad-Báqir, 'the Wolf' (*Dhi'b*; d. 1883), and his son, Shaykh Muḥammad-Taqí (Áqá Najafí), 'the Son of the Wolf' (*Ibn-i-Dhi'b*; 1846–1914). Both men were responsible for extensive persecution of the Bábís and Bahá'ís in the Iṣfáhán region, including the killing of the KING AND BELOVED OF MARTYRS (1879) and of ASHRAF (1888). The son in particular attained a position of enormous power and wealth, and became a leading opponent of the QÁJÁR rulers. Bahá'u'lláh addressed Muḥammad-Báqir in his *Lawḥ-i-Burhán*, and Áqá Najafí in the *Epistle to the Son of the Wolf*.
Algar 16, 180, 209, 220, 231–2; *GPB* 200–1; *MBBR* 268–88, 364, 376–85, 395, 398–400, 426–9, 434, 513, 514; Momen, *Shi'i Islam* 140, 141.

women

GENDER EQUALITY

The essential equality of men and women is a basic Bahá'í principle. Bahá'u'lláh stated that in the present day God has removed the distinctions that formerly differentiated the 'stations' of men and women (upheld for example in Islamic religious law). They are equal in the sight of God. For both it is the extent of their recognition and devotion to God's cause that determines their real status. Those women who are truly believers are recognized as the 'men' of the past, and excel many men of the present (*CC2*: 358–9, 378–9). Bahá'u'lláh also made it an obligation for parents to educate their daughters as well as their sons (*KA* 38 k48). 'Abdu'l-Bahá was more emphatic, describing gender equality as one of the distinctive teachings of the Faith, and repeatedly emphasizing it in his talks and writings. All human beings are made in the image of God, and God does not differentiate between them on the basis of gender. Both sexes possess the same potentialities of intelligence, virtue and prowess. Yet social inequality between the sexes was general throughout the world, and even in the United States, 'the cradle of women's liberation', women remained unenfranchised (until 1920). This is wrong. Not only is it unjust, but women and men are like the two wings of a bird: only if both wings are strong will the bird of humanity be able to fly, i.e. the success and prosperity of the human race as a whole depends on the advancement of women. Women are held back by lack of education and by the conditions of oppression in which many of them live. This has to change. Both sexes should receive equal educational opportunity (including access to the same curriculum) and be given the same political, social and economic rights. Women should strive to achieve equality but avoid confrontation ('Abdu'l-Bahá expressed his disapproval of the militant methods employed by the British suffragettes, and counselled Iranian Bahá'í women to be patient in their endeavours to attain equality and the desire of some to abandon the use of the veil (*CC2*: 361–2, 400)). Male attitudes of superiority are baseless and have to be abandoned. The achievement of gender equality is a wide-ranging process of societal change which in part reflects a basic shift in social values and the development of a new CIVILIZATION (*CC2*: 359–69; *PT* 169–72, 195–7; *PUP* 74–7, 108, 133–7, 174–5, 233, 280–4, 374–5). There is no evidence for gender equality being a formal Bábí teaching, beyond the Báb's appointment of a woman (ṬÁHIRIH) as one of his chief disciples, but this in itself was a highly significant act in both symbolic and practical terms.

GENDER DIFFERENTIATION

Whilst proclaiming the basic equality of the sexes the Bahá'í Faith also upholds or accepts gender differentiation in certain areas of life. One aspect of this relates to the biological fact of potential motherhood for women. Thus 'Abdu'l-Bahá stated that, if necessary, girls should be given educational priority because as potential mothers they would be their children's first educators. As such, a mother can lead her children to wisdom and morality, but if she is ignorant and illiterate then this would have an adverse effect (*KA* 200 n76; *PT* 170; *PUP* 133–4, 175). Again, the Bahá'í view of FAMILY LIFE accords the mother the right to be supported by the husband, whilst she has the primary (but not exclusive) duty to bring up the child (*CC1*: 414). The differences in the *Kitáb-i-A*QDAS provisions regarding intestate INHERITANCE can be seen in a similar light. 'Abdu'l-Bahá also saw women as being more likely to possess certain spiritual qualities, notably tender-heartedness, intuition and receptivity, and, as mothers, to be a major force in opposing war and establishing PEACE: having raised sons to adulthood, they would oppose their slaughter. Similarly, it would be better if women were not given military training (*PT* 170, 196; *PUP* 75). Gender equality would engender wider social change, but it would also reflect a newly developing civilization, in which the more feminine qualities would be more balanced with masculine force which had until now been dominant (*CC2*: 369).

DIFFERENCES IN BAHÁ'Í ACTIVITY

Ritual differences based on gender are minor: women are exempted from FASTING when they are menstruating, pregnant or nursing. Menstruating women are also exempted from obligatory PRAYER. These exemptions reflect biological differences. They are not compulsory and do not reflect any concept of ritual impurity. All levels of Bahá'í administration except for the all-male UNIVERSAL HOUSE OF JUSTICE are equally open to men and women (*PT* 196–7). No reason is given for this exception, but 'Abdu'l-Bahá stated that the wisdom of it would eventually become clear (*CC2*: 369–70). Referring in particular to the Western Bahá'ís, 'Abdu'l-Bahá noted that women had evinced 'greater boldness' than their male coreligionists in working for the Faith (*ADJ* 57; *CC2*: 398).

THE ADVANCEMENT OF WOMEN

There is as yet no overall study of Bahá'í women's history, and their role in the 19th-century Iranian community has not been researched. Certainly, by the early 1900s both American and Iranian Bahá'í women were active in seeking their own advancement, and were encouraged in this by 'Abdu'l-Bahá. In North America women were quite rapidly able to gain a position of equality with men in Bahá'í administration, despite determined resistance on the part of some men. Thereafter women's issues do not appear to have to have been of major concern until the rise of modern feminism. In Iran the situation was very different, with women remaining largely illiterate and socially disadvantaged. Girls' education classes were started by a number of Bahá'ís, leading in 1910 to the establishment of the Tarbíyat School for girls, which became a key institution in training the first generation of Iranian professional women. Although progress was slow, an increasing number of Bahá'í women of all social classes gained a basic education, such that by the 1970s, when the majority of Iranian women were still illiterate, most Bahá'í women could read and write, and literacy amongst those under forty was almost universal. Health education also became general. Other developments included the formation of a Bahá'í committee for the advancement of women in Tehran (1909). Iranian Bahá'í women became able to participate in the Bahá'í electoral process, but because of caution regarding Muslim reactions they were not allowed to become members of Bahá'í assemblies until 1954 (*MBW* 65).

Outside Iran several Bahá'ís became involved in work for the advancement of women in the wider society, most prominently Laura DREYFUS-BARNEY and Shirin FOZDAR.

Within the Bahá'í community the advancement of women has again become an important issue in recent years, particularly following the large-scale influx of poor Third World villagers into the Faith (many of them illiterate women; *See* EXPANSION), and the debate engendered by the modern feminist movement. Since 1975 (International Women's Year) the Universal House of Justice has repeatedly called for national Bahá'í communities to implement programmes to promote the full and equal participation of women in Bahá'í activities (*CC2*: 403–4), and has sought to sensitize Bahá'ís regarding the implications of the principle of gender equality for Bahá'í community life. One consequence has been an increasing number of women appointed or elected to Bahá'í administrative positions: by 1993, for example, 28 per cent of national spiritual assembly membership world-wide was female (generally higher figures in richer countries and lower figures in much of Africa and Asia). The issuance of a compilation of Bahá'í writings on *Women* in January 1986 (*CC2*: 355–406), and the establishment of a BAHÁ'Í INTERNATIONAL COMMUNITY Office for the Advancement of Women (New York) in 1993, have further stimulated Bahá'í communities in many parts of the world both to lay more stress on gender equality amongst the Bahá'ís and to work more with non-Bahá'í women's organizations and share Bahá'í teachings on the status of women with them. Several communities have now established their own offices for the advancement of women or their equivalent. The European Board of Counsellors has also established a continent-wide Task Force on Women (1992). Activities on this theme include the promotion of girls' education, adult female literacy, rural health care, income-generating skills, and consultation on gender roles in the community (specifically involving men, the change of whose attitudes is seen as essential to any meaningful change in women's status). Two projects that have received particular attention are the BAHÁ'Í VOCATIONAL INSTITUTE FOR RURAL WOMEN in India (founded in 1983), and the BAHÁ'Í-UNIFEM PROJECT (started in 1991). Numerous conferences on the advancement of women and related issues have also been held, and Bahá'í involvement in non-governmental organizations' conferences on women has become increasingly extensive (notably the NGO Forum at the United Nations' Fourth World Conference on Women at Beijing, 1995). *BWNS* 1993–4: 83–9, 237–75; 1994–5: 104–12, 145–7; Armstrong-Ingram, 'American Bahá'í women'; Caton, *Equal Circles;* Maneck, 'Women'; UHJRD compilation on *Women, CC2*: 355–406.

Word of God

In Bahá'í belief the writings and teachings of the MANIFESTATIONS OF GOD are divine REVELATION. They are often described as the 'Word of God' (*KI* 127; *SAQ* 173). As such, they are thought to have a spiritual power capable of changing the hearts of those who hear or read them. Accordingly, there are numerous CONVERSION accounts which attribute the attainment of belief to hearing or reading the writings of the Báb or Bahá'u'lláh. The impact on the pure hearted was such as to draw them to spiritual worlds which could not be expressed in words, and to which worldly and heavenly sovereignty could never be compared (*KA* 61 k116). Believers should therefore recite the divine verses, so that the 'sweetness' of their melody might 'kindle' their own souls 'and attract the hearts of all men'. They might at first be unaware of the impact of what they were saying, but sooner or later it would transform them (Gl. 294 no. 136; *TB* 93–4). They should immerse themselves 'in the ocean' of Bahá'u'lláh's words, and discover 'all the pearls of wisdom' that lay hidden in its depths (*KA* 85 k182). As a specific obligation they should recite 'the verses of God' every morning and evening (*KA* 73 k149; *see* DEVOTIONALISM) and, as a blessing, listen to divine verses read at dawn in the *MASHRIQU'L-ADHKÁR* (*KA* 61 k115).

Words of Paradise

(Pers.: *Kalimát-i-Firdawsiyyih*)

Tablet of Bahá'u'lláh, composed in Persian around 1890 for Ḥájí Mírzá ḤAYDAR-'ALÍ. The bulk of the tablet consists of a listing of some of Bahá'u'lláh's teachings, presented as eleven leaves of 'the Most Exalted Paradise': (1) the FEAR OF GOD as a means of preventing wrongdoing; (2) the importance of RELIGION as a means of securing order in the world; (3) praise for SERVICE TO HUMANITY and humility; a statement of the GOLDEN RULE; (4) praise for just KINGS (and condemnation of MUḤAMMAD SHÁH); (5) WISDOM; (6) JUSTICE; (7) the unity of the HUMAN RACE; (8) the need for moral EDUCATION, and for the choice of a universal LANGUAGE; the duties of the UNIVERSAL HOUSE OF JUSTICE; (9) MODERATION (and a variety of other subjects); (10) the unacceptability of ASCETICISM; and the praiseworthiness of charity; (11) Bahá'ís must not allow themselves to become the cause of strife. The remainder of the tablet deals with a variety of themes, including summoning Bahá'ís to detachment, righteousness and unity; criticism of some aspects of SUFISM; questioning the claims of the Iranian philosopher Ḥájí Mullá Hádí Sabzivárí (d. 1873) and his failure to respond to Bahá'u'lláh's message; commenting on the barriers to acceptance of Bahá'u'lláh's call in IRAN; and challenging Ṣubḥ-i-AZAL to produce a single verse if he wished to prove that he possessed divinely inspired knowledge. *TB* 55–80; *RB4*: 214–26.

Words of Wisdom

(Ar.: *Aṣl-i-Kullu'l-Khayr*)

Late Syrian-period tablet of Bahá'u'lláh in Arabic. It consists of twenty-two aphorisms concerned with various aspects of the spiritual life (trust in God; the essence of wisdom, love, and detachment; the knowledge of God; etc). *TB* 155–7.

work

Bahá'u'lláh instructed his followers that they should each have an occupation, and occupy themselves with that which would benefit themselves and others.

Such work was ranked as worship. Other people's work and CRAFTSMANSHIP should be valued. Idleness and BEGGING were condemned. Every father should educate his sons and daughters in a craft or profession (*CC1*: 1–3; *KA* 30 k33; *TB* 26). 'Abdu'l-Bahá and Shoghi Effendi commented that everyone should have a profession ('Abdu'l-Bahá said that his was mat-making), whether it be manual or literary. This applies to rich and poor and, as far as possible, to the handicapped and elderly. No one should live off others 'like a parasitic plant'. There is no social role for those who have no desire to work. Even those who can afford not to work – for example, through inherited wealth – should work, because work not only has a utilitarian purpose, but also draws the individual closer to God. This is particularly the case when the work is performed in a spirit of service to others, and Bahá'ís should try to work in occupations that are of benefit to society. They should also strive to achieve EXCELLENCE in the work they do, whatever it is. Such action constitutes devotion to God. It is the duty of government to ensure that every individual has the opportunity to gain the skills necessary to work and the means to exercise their talents. The action of work is good, but the individual should not be completely occupied with it: their heart should be attracted towards God, and they should be detached from worldly attachments. The obligation to work applies also to those who want to devote themselves to Bahá'í activity. Bahá'u'lláh had forbidden ASCETICISM, MONASTICISM and PRIESTHOOD in his religion, and there should be no specialized class of people who made Bahá'í service their only lifework. All should be self-supporting, and combine Bahá'í activities with following a profession. Regarding the role of mothers, the Universal House of Justice has stated that 'home-making' and looking after a child itself constitutes an 'honourable and responsible' form of work, and that in such circumstances the woman is not obliged to seek work outside the home: her primary obligation is the care of her child, and financial support of the family that of her husband (*see* FAMILY LIFE). Family situations vary enormously, however, and the work-roles of the two parents are not fixed. *CC1*: 1–7; *KA* 192–3 n56; 235n162; *LG* 623–6; *LG* (1st edn) 88 no. 264; *PUP* 187, 435; *SWAB* 144–6 no. 126–8. (*See also* ECONOMIC TEACHINGS.)

World, Tablet of

(Per.: *Lawḥ-i-Dunyá*)

Tablet of Bahá'u'lláh, composed in Persian in Haifa in 1891 for Mírzá Áqá Sayyid Muḥammad AFNÁN (*Núru'd-dín*). Major themes are:

BAHÁ'U'LLÁH'S MESSAGE

This was for the whole human race, and only when all had been converted would they become truly free. Bahá'u'lláh had 'breathed a new life into every human frame', and the whole world had been regenerated. His teachings were intended to promote human advancement and the reconstruction of the world. They included the importance of establishing the Lesser PEACE, of choosing a common universal LANGUAGE, and of promoting UNITY and AGRICULTURE; the need for universal funding of EDUCATION; and the abrogation of those Islamic and Bábí laws that had been used by the faithless to justify their wrongdoing (killing those regarded as unbelievers, burning books, shunning or exterminating those of other religions).

IRAN

Bahá'u'lláh decried its people, who once had been 'the symbols of mercy' and 'unrivalled in sciences and arts', but had now 'sunk to the lowest level of degradation' and had arisen to destroy both themselves and their friends (i.e. the Bahá'ís) with their own hands. They delighted in cursing people, whilst their nobles gloried in savagery and tyranny (the prince-governor of Yazd, Maḥmúd Mírzá, *Jalálu'd-dawlih*, was specifically condemned). Iran needed laws, which should be approved by the Shah, the *'ULAMÁ* and other dignitaries, who should consult together. They would need fewer regulations if they followed Bahá'u'lláh's exhortations.

THE CONDUCT OF THE BAHÁ'ÍS

Bahá'ís should promote the Bahá'í Cause (*see* TEACHING); be righteous, saintly and courteous in their conduct (*see* ETHICS); and flee from anything that caused strife or mischief (the world was in turmoil, and Bahá'ís should be prudent in their conduct). The actions of the Bahá'ís in ASHKHABAD in interceding on behalf of the convicted Shí'í murderers of a Bahá'í were praised.

Bahá'u'lláh also emphasized the importance of the FEAR OF GOD, commented on the form of GOVERNMENT (praising constitutional monarchy), praised the HANDS OF THE CAUSE, and reproved the political activist Sayyid JAMÁLU'D-DÍN AL-AFGHÁNÍ (1838/9–97). *TB* 81–97; *RB4*: 337–48.

world commonwealth, Bahá'í

See WORLD ORDER.

World Crusade

Another term for the TEN YEAR CRUSADE (*see* PLANS).

world government

See WORLD ORDER.

world language

See LANGUAGE.

World Order

Conceptualization of a future Bahá'í world society outlined by Shoghi Effendi, particularly in some of his letters of the 1930s (*see* *WORLD ORDER OF BAHÁ'U'LLÁH*). For reflections on related themes see Lerche, *Emergence*; Tyson.

THE GOAL

Bahá'u'lláh's promised Most Great PEACE represented a 'New World Order' that would replace the defective world order of the present. It would be established as the 'practical consequence' of the spiritualization of the world and the fusion of its various peoples. It would represent the 'coming of age' of the human race (*see* SOCIAL EVOLUTION); entail the emergence of a world community, a consciousness of world citizenship, and the development of a world civilization and culture; and coincide with the beginnings of the 'Golden Age' of the Faith (*see* TIME). The Administrative Order (*see* ADMINISTRATION) that the Bahá'ís were establishing would be its basis (*WOB* 161–6). It would be characterized by the emergence of a 'world commonwealth', a world federal system with 'unchallengeable authority' permanently uniting all nations, but in which the relative autonomy of these nations would be preserved. There would be a world legislature, executive, police force and adjudicatory tribunal. Force would be the servant of justice. War would be abolished. National, racial and sectarian animosities would cease. The personal freedom and initiative of the individual in each component nation would be 'completely safeguarded'. The press, whilst ceasing to be manipulated by vested interests or promoting nationalist contention, would give 'full scope to the expression of the diversified views and convictions of mankind'. The global economy would be unified and co-ordinated, with a world currency and system of weights and measures. Inordinate class distinctions would be obliterated by the abolition of the extremes of wealth and poverty (*see* ECONOMIC TEACHINGS). There would be a world civilization, LANGUAGE, script and literature. RELIGION AND SCIENCE would be reconciled. Human energies would no longer be devoted to conflict, but instead to scientific research; the increase of productivity; the eradication of disease; the raising of physical health; the prolongation of human life; the development of the human brain; and the stimulation of the intellectual, moral and spiritual life of the human race as a whole. The millennial hopes of past religions would be realized (*WOB* 203–6).

THE PROCESS

The present 'Age of Transition' was witnessing a 'universal fermentation' which was reshaping humanity. There was both an integrative process (in particular represented by the Bahá'í Faith, but including a growing consciousness of global solidarity and acceptance of the principle of collective security) which led towards WORLD UNITY and a destructive one which tore down, 'with increasing violence', those barriers in the way of humanity's 'destined goal'. A titanic spiritual struggle ensued, which saw the 'death-pangs' of the old order and the 'birth-pangs' of the new (*WOB* 166–71, 191–3). DIVINE JUDGEMENT on those institutions that opposed the Faith; the growth of SECULARISM and moral decline; and the breakdown of the existing social and political order were part of this process (*WOB* 171–90). World-wide suffering marked humanity's resistance to Bahá'u'lláh's prophetic call (which alone could solve the world's ills) and, more immediately, the failure of governments to adjust to the political and economic realities of a world of already interdependent parts. The 'fire' of ordeal would forge humanity into a single whole (*WOB* 35–6, 45–6, 210–12).

World Order of Bahá'u'lláh

The 'World Order' letters. It comprises a compilation of seven major letters by Shoghi Effendi addressed to the American and Western Bahá'ís (1929–36).

(1) *The World Order of Bahá'u'lláh* (27 February 1929), partly written in response to Ruth WHITE's activities. It emphasized that the system of Bahá'í ADMINISTRATION was rooted in the Bahá'í writings, particularly in 'Abdu'l-Bahá's *WILL AND TESTAMENT*. The administration was a channel through which Bahá'u'lláh's promised blessings were intended to flow. It was not a substitute for the Faith, however, and the Bahá'ís should ensure that it did not rigidify and fetter the 'liberating forces' released by Bahá'u'lláh.

(2) *The World Order of Bahá'u'lláh: Further Consideration* (21 March 1930) referred to the transforming impact of the Faith on human society; noted that part of the uniqueness of the Bahá'í Faith lay in its divinely appointed 'Administrative Order', which ensured the religion's continuing unity and flexibility; and stated that attacks on the Faith (implicitly referring to those by White and Ahmad SOHRAB) served only to purge it internally and proclaim it to the wider world. Eventually there would be world-wide attacks from the enemies of the Faith, and Bahá'ís should be prepared for this.

(3) *The Goal of a New World Order* (28 November 1931) reviewed the economic and other ills of the world since World War I, and attributed these to the failure of the world's leaders to respond to the imperative needs of the present age, specifically for the creation of a world federation expressive of the essential oneness of the human race. Further war and ordeal would implant the necessary sense of responsibility.

(4) *The Golden Age of the Cause of Bahá'u'lláh* (21 March 1932) extolled the achievements of the Faith, the bravery of the early Bábís, and the contributions the American Bahá'ís had already made to the progress of the Cause; outlined the Bahá'í view of other RELIGIONS and of the station of the BÁB; introduced the principle of Bahá'í non-involvement in POLITICS; and appealed for greater support for the construction of the Wilmette House of Worship.
(5) *America and the Most Great Peace* (21 April 1933) again extolled the achievements of the American Bahá'ís, reviewed their history and summoned them to greater service.
(6) *The DISPENSATION OF BAHÁ'U'LLÁH* (8 February 1934).
(7) *The Unfoldment of World Civilization* (11 March 1936) placed the worsening economic and political situation of the time in the context of Bahá'u'lláh's summons to establish the Most Great Peace, outlining the guiding principles of Bahá'u'lláh's WORLD ORDER and referring to an 'age of transition' in human history heralding the emergence of a new age and a world civilization. *WOB.*

World Parliament of Religions

One of the many conferences held in conjunction with the Columbian Exposition in Chicago in 1893. It generated considerable interest in world religions in the United States, and was a stimulus to the development of the GREEN ACRE conference centre by Sarah FARMER. One session included the first public reference to the Bahá'í Faith in America (23 September). *BFA1*: 31–3; *GPB* 256.

World Peace Day

A special event day begun by the American national spiritual assembly in 1959 to stress the need for international PEACE. It was abandoned in 1985 in favour of the United Nations International Day of Peace (on the third Tuesday in September). W. Momen, *Baha'i Dictionary* 242.

World Religion Day

See INTERFAITH DIALOGUE.

world unity

Bahá'u'lláh saw the world as one country, of which all human beings were the citizens. Glory for the individual lay in love for the whole human race and service to it. In the future 'Most Great PEACE' all people would become as one kindred and family (*see* HUMAN RACE).

'THE SEVEN CANDLES OF UNITY'

In a letter to Mrs J.E. Whyte of Edinburgh in the early 1900s 'Abdu'l-Bahá noted that the present age was distinctive in the development of global communications and of political and economic interdependence between all parts of the world. Self-sufficiency was no longer possible. The 20th century was a 'century of light' in which major advances towards human unity would be made. Eventually, seven 'candles of unity' would illuminate the world's 'darkened horizon': (1) political unity; (2) unity of thought in world undertakings; (3) unity in freedom; (4) religious unity; (5) unity of nations (specifically to be established within the 20th century); (6) unity of races; (7) unity of language (i.e. the choice of a universal LANGUAGE). *AB* 360–2; *WOB* 38–9.

worship

See DEVOTIONALISM; FEAST; *MASHRIQU'L-ADHKÁR*; PRAYER.

Y

Yaḥyá, Mírzá

See AZAL.

Yaḥyá Darábí, Sayyid

See VAḤÍD.

Yamamoto, Kanichi

(1879–1961)

First Japanese Bahá'í. He converted in Hawaii in 1902, and subsequently moved to California. *BW13*: 931–3; *WSBR* 176–86.

Yazd (1868 pop. est. 40,000)

Southern Iranian provincial, commercial and agricultural centre. One of the towns visited by VAHÍD. His proclamation of the Báb's message there led to unrest (*MBBR* 106–8). It later became a major centre of Bahá'í activity (including the conversion of Zoroastrians), as well as the site of a considerable number of martyrdoms, including the 'Seven Martyrs of Yazd' (1891) and the infamous 1903 massacre (*MBBR* 301–5, 357–8, 385–98).

youth

In 19th-century Iran age was respected, and youthful immaturity generally disdained. The youthfulness of the Báb (twenty-four when he made his declaration) and of many of the LETTERS OF THE LIVING is therefore remarkable, and probably contributed to their rejection by the older *'ULAMÁ* whose authority they were challenging. By contrast, with the exception of 'Abdu'l-Bahá, who effectively served as his father's vicegerent during Bahá'u'lláh's lifetime, and – more ambiguously – of his half-brother, MUḤAMMAD-'ALÍ, early Bahá'í leadership was much older. Young Bahá'ís do not seem to have played a major role in Bahá'í activities, though two – BADÍ' and Rúḥu'lláh, the son of Mírza 'Alí-Muḥammad VARQÁ – were esteemed as heroic martyrs. Similarly, most of those who became prominent in the small early Western Bahá'í communities (from the 1890s) were relatively mature in years, with the prominent exception of May Bolles (MAXWELL) and her group in Paris.

The emergence of a distinctive category of 'Bahá'í youth' occurred during Shoghi Effendi's ministry (1922–57). Shoghi Effendi's own accession as Guardian at the age of twenty-four appears to have elicited disdain from a few of the older Bahá'ís, and in letters in the 1920s and 1930s, he emphasized the vital role of the young in Bahá'í TEACHING activity: the future progress of the Faith depended on their energy and devotion. Young people were particularly likely to respond to the Bahá'í message because of their greater openness to new ideas. Young Bahá'ís should prepare themselves for the future by securing a good EDUCATION, by intensively DEEPENING their knowledge of the Bahá'í Faith, and by developing their sense of spirituality. They were also called upon to exemplify the highest standards of Bahá'í conduct and morality (*CC2*: 416–39; see *ADVENT OF DIVINE JUSTICE*). A specific administrative category of 'Bahá'í youth' also emerged during these years to refer to those in the fifteen-to-twenty age group, Bahá'u'lláh having established fifteen as the age of MATURITY for the observance of religious duties (prayer, fasting, etc.), whilst Shoghi Effendi provisionally limited Bahá'í voting rights and ASSEMBLY membership to those aged twenty-one and over (*KA* 113 q20, 134 q93, 189 n49). Specific youth activities for those in their teens and twenties began to be organized. The Bahá'í youth organization in ASHKHABAD was of particular importance, and in the 1920s was seen as a serious rival to the communist *Komsomol* (Kolarz 471). Bahá'í youth groups and committees were established in various countries during the early 1930s, the American national committee being particularly active (*BW5*: 370–87; 6: 426–35). Shoghi Effendi emphasized the desirability of Bahá'í youth participating in Bahá'í administrative work (*ADJ* 58).

The role of youth has been greatly emphasized by the Universal House of Justice, young people being encouraged to spiritualize their lives; study and teach the Faith; prepare themselves for their future careers (careers that are of social benefit or enable youth to pioneer later are of particular value); participate in Bahá'í community life; learn the skill of CONSULTATION; strive after EXCELLENCE; and work for world PEACE. The young have a relative freedom from family and other responsibilities which enables them to be a 'driving force' in Bahá'í expansion. To canalize the energies and enthusiasm of youth, the House introduced the concept of a voluntary 'Youth Year of Service' (1984), Bahá'í youth being encouraged to devote a year of their lives to some aspect of service, such as travel teaching, working at the BAHÁ'Í WORLD CENTRE or participating in SOCIO-ECONOMIC DEVELOPMENT projects. *MUHJ* 92–5 no. 37, 142–3 no. 67, 582 no. 365, 584–5 no. 369, 614–17 no. 386, 641 no. 408, 668–9 no. 428, 670 no. 431, 709 no. 449.

Recent developments have included (1) the American 'Bahá'í Youth Workshops' (Los Angeles, from 1974) which, using contemporary dance styles, music and drama, have sought to convey basic Bahá'í principles, such as peace, racial harmony, gender equality and the need for spiritual awareness. These proved to be both immensely popular among Bahá'í youth, and a highly appealing way of teaching about the Bahá'í Faith to others. By 1994 some seventy workshops had been formed in various parts of the United States, and another thirty in other parts of the world; (2) the European Bahá'í Youth Council (est. 1989), its members appointed directly by the Universal House of Justice, which functions to co-ordinate Bahá'í youth activities in the continent and to foster links with other youth organizations; (3) increasing involvement with other groups and with the wider youth population, such as in the International Youth Consultation on Social Development in Copenhagen (1995), and the Chandigarh Youth Development Institute in India (est. 1991), which aims to provide career counselling, encourage community service, and promote moral education amongst local youth. *BWNS* 1994–5: 167–90.

Z

zakát (Ar., 'tithes')

The Islamic alms-tax used to help the poor and for the promotion of the Faith (Quran 9:60). Bahá'u'lláh instructed that Bahá'í practice should follow the Quranic ordinance, and advised that such payment was a means for believers to purify their wealth. Until the details of such payments have been specified by the Universal House of Justice, Bahá'ís should instead make regular contributions to the Bahá'í FUNDS. *KA* 72 k146, 140 q107, 234–5 n161. (*See also* ḤUQÚQU'LLÁH.)

Lidia Zamenhof, daughter of the founder of Esperanto

Zamenhof, Lidia (1904–42)

Prominent Bahá'í and Esperantist of Polish-Jewish background. She was the daughter of Dr Ludwig Zamenhof, the creator of ESPERANTO. She first learned of the Bahá'í Faith in 1925 from Martha ROOT. She worked energetically to promote Bahá'í and Esperanto, and translated Bahá'í literature into both Esperanto and Polish. She was amongst those murdered in the gas chambers of Treblinka during World War II. *BW10*: 533–38; Heller.

Zanján (1868 pop. est. 20,000)

City in north-western Iran on the road between Tehran and Tabríz. A large Bábí community of at least 3,000 emerged following the conversion of one of the town's religious leaders, Mullá Muḥammad-'Alí Zanjání (ḤUJJAT). This was probably the largest concentration of Bábís in Iran. An altercation between some Bábís and orthodox Shí'ís led to a rapidly escalating dispute between Ḥujjat and the city governor, who finally ordered that the city be physically divided into Bábí and orthodox sectors. Hostilities thereafter erupted (13 May 1850), the Bábís maintaining a sustained resistance against large numbers of regular troops, several thousand of whom were killed. Finally, following the death of Ḥujjat (*c.* 29 December

1850), their own numbers greatly reduced, the remaining Bábís surrendered at the beginning of January 1851, and were massacred by the soldiery. The struggle is noted for the involvement of Bábí women in the defence and, in at least one case, in the actual fighting. Much of the town remained in ruins until at least the late 1860s. A strong Bahá'í community later emerged. *ARR* 358; Browne, 'Personal reminiscences'; *GPB* 44–6; Issawi 28; *MBBR* 114–27; Momen, 'Social basis' 169–70; *McS* 163–4; Nabil 527–80; *TJ* 135–70, 371–3; *TN* 179–81; Walbridge, 'Bábí uprising'. (*See also* BÁBÍ RADICALISM.)

Zaynu'l-Muqarrabín

(1818–1903)

Mullá Zaynu'l-'Ábidín, eminent Iranian Bahá'í. He was born into a clerical family in one of the villages of Najafábád near Iṣfáhán and himself became a *MUJTAHID* and a preacher at one of the mosques. He became a Bábí in 1851, and under his leadership a large local Bábí (later Bahá'í) community developed. In 1864 he moved to Baghdad to escape persecution, and in 1870 was amongst the Bahá'ís who were exiled to Mosul (*see* IRAQ), where he served as their leader. He transcribed copies of Bahá'u'lláh's letters to the Iranian Bahá'ís to ensure their wider distribution. He later moved to Akka. As a qualified Islamic jurist he asked Bahá'u'lláh a series of questions to explicate legal points in the *Kitáb-i-Aqdas*, Bahá'u'lláh's replies together with the original questions forming an appendix to that book. Bahá'u'lláh titled him *Zaynu'l-Muqarrabín* ('the Ornament of the Near Ones') and *Ismu'lláhu'l- Zayn* ('the Name of God, Zayn'). Shoghi Effendi named him as one of the APOSTLES OF BAHÁ'U'LLÁH. *EB* 274–6.

Ẓillu's-sulṭán

(Ar., 'Shadow of the king')

Title of Sulṭán-Ma'súd Mírzá (1850–1918), prince-governor of Iṣfáhán, 1874–1906, and in effective control of most of southern Iran until 1888. He tried unsuccessfully to involve the Bahá'ís in his political schemes. For his personal advantage he sometimes also permitted, or in some instances was directly involved in, persecutions and killings of Bahá'ís. *BKG* 409–10; *MBBR*.

Zoroastrianism

Ancient Persian religion recognized by Bahá'ís as one of the nine known revealed religions. Its founder, Zoroaster, is accorded the status of a MANIFESTATION OF GOD, but its scriptures, the Zend-Avesta, are not accepted as completely authentic or reliable (*CC1*: 18–22). Nevertheless, Zoroastrian prophecies are regarded as foretelling the advent of Islam, the Báb (=the Zoroastrian 'Úshídar Máh'), and Bahá'u'lláh (='Sháh-Bahrám', the world-saver) (*GPB* 58, 94, 95; *WOB* 101–2). Bahá'u'lláh is also believed to be descended from Zoroaster and Yazdigird, the last Zoroastrian king of Iran, a claim used in support of Bahá'í missionary endeavour among Zoroastrians.

By the 19th century the majority of the world's Zoroastrians lived in Bombay, India, where they were known as Parsees. The rest lived as a despised and disadvantaged minority in Iran, mostly around the southern towns of Yazd and Kirmán. A significant number of Yazdí Zoroastrians became Bahá'ís from the 1880s onwards, coming to play an important role in the local Zoroastrian lay council. Conversions were also gained amongst recent Iranian migrants in Bombay, Bahá'ís of Zoroastrian background making a major contribution to the subsequent development of the Bahá'í Faith in India. Khianra; Stiles; *SBBR* 92–7.

Further Reading

For an excellent introduction to the Bahá'í Faith see Momen, *The Bahá'í Faith: A Short Introduction*. See also Smith, *Bahá'í Religion*. The classic introduction from a Bahá'í perspective is Esslemont's *Bahá'u'lláh and the New Era*. More recent works in the same vein include those by Ferraby, and Hatcher and Martin. An overall account of Bábí and Bahá'í history is provided by Smith, *The Babi and Baha'i Religions* (*SBBR*). This work contains a guide to further reading for English-language sources up to 1985. See also my *Bahá'í Faith: A Short History*. Shoghi Effendi's *God Passes By* (1944) places Bábí-Bahá'í history in theological context.

The individual topic entries in this volume give specific references. English-language scholarship on Bábí and Bahá'í Studies is now increasing quite rapidly. Recent works by Amanat (*ARR*) and MacEoin (*McR*; *McS*) are invaluable for an understanding of Bábism. Nabíl's *Dawn-Breakers* remains the standard Bahá'í account of the Bábí period. As yet, no full-length English translations of any of the writings of the Báb have been published, but a selection of extracts is available. On Bahá'u'lláh, we can now refer to the works by H. M. Balyuzi (*BKG*) and Cole (*Modernity and the Millennium*). A substantial body of Bahá'u'lláh's writings have been translated into English. On 'Abdu'l-Bahá, there are a number of works dealing with his Western travels, but only one full-length biography, again by Balyuzi (*AB*). A number of 'Abdu'l-Bahá's major writings have been translated and many of his talks in the West are also available. For Shoghi Effendi, the main source is the biography by Rúḥíyyih Rabbání (*Priceless Pearl*). A substantial body of his English-language writings is now available. A compilation of the major messages of the Universal House of Justice up to 1986 was recent published. There is as yet a general lack of detailed accounts of the expansion of the Bahá'í Faith apart from early North American

Bahá'í history (Hollinger; Stockman; Van den Hoonaard). The successive volumes of the *Bahá'í WWorld* provide an account of major developments from the 1920s onwards. For the period of the custodianship of the Hands of the Cause of God (1957–63) see Universal House of Justice, *Ministry.* There is a large secondary literature (of variable quality) on various aspects of Bahá'í belief and practice.

Bibliography

'Abdu'l-Bahá, *Memorials of the Faithful*, trans. M. Gail. Wilmette, Bahá'í Publishing Trust, 1971

—— *Paris Talks: Addresses Given by 'Abdu'l-Bahá in 1911*, 12th edn. London, Bahá'í Publishing Trust, 1995. (first publ. 1912)

—— *Promulgation of Universal Peace*, comp. H. MacNutt, 2nd edn. Wilmette, Bahá'í Publishing Trust, 1982 (first publ. 1922–5)

—— *The Secret of Divine Civilization*, trans. M. Gail, 3rd edn. Wilmette, Bahá'í Publishing Trust, 1979, (1st edn. 1957)

—— *Selections from the Writings of 'Abdu'l-Bahá*, trans. M. Gail et al. Haifa, Bahá'í World Centre, 1978

—— *Some Answered Questions*. Wilmette, Bahá'í Publishing Trust, 1981, (first publ. 1908)

—— *Tablets of Abdul Baha Abbas*, comp. A.R. Windust, 3 vols. Chicago, Bahai Publishing Society, 1909–16

—— *The Tablets of the Divine Plan*, rev. edn. Wilmette, Bahá'í Publishing Trust, 1977

—— *The Will and Testament of 'Abdu'l-Bahá*. Wilmette, Bahá'í Publishing Committee, 1944

Abu'l-Faḍl Gulpáygání, Mírzá, *The Bahá'í Proofs*, trans. Ali-Kuli Khan, 3rd edn. Wilmette, Bahá'í Publishing Trust, 1983 (1st edn. 1902)

—— *Letters and Essays, 1886–1913*, trans. J.R.I. Cole. Los Angeles, Kalimát Press, 1985

—— *Miracles and Metaphors*, trans. J.R. Cole. Los Angeles, Kalimát Press, 1981

Áfáqí, S., *Proofs from the Holy Qur'án (Regarding the Advent of Bahá'u'lláh)*. New Delhi, Mir'át Publications, 1993

Alexander, A.B., *History of the Baha'i Faith in Japan, 1914–1936*. [Tokyo] Bahá'í Publishing Trust, 1977

—— *Personal Recollections of a Bahai Life in the Hawaiian Islands/Forty Years of the Bahai Cause in Hawaii, 1902–1942*. Honolulu, NSA of the Hawaiian Islands, 1974

Algar, H., *Religion and State in Iran, 1785–1906: The Role of the Ulama in the Qajar Period*. Berkeley and Los Angeles, University of California Press, 1969

Amanat, A., *Pivot of the Universe: Nasir al-Din Shah Qajar and the Iranian Monarchy, 1831–1896*. London, I.B. Tauris, 1997

—— *Resurrection and Renewal: The Making of the Bábí Movement in Iran, 1844–1850*. Ithaca, Cornell University Press, 1989

Armstrong-Ingram, R.J., 'American Bahá'í women and the education of girls in Tehran, 1909–1934', in *In Iran, KSBBH 3*, ed. P. Smith, pp. 181–210. Los Angeles, Kalimát Press, 1986

—— *Music, Devotions, and Mashriqu'l-Adhkár, KSBBH 4*. Los Angeles, Kalimát Press, 1987

Báb, The, *Le Béyân arabe*, trans. A.L.M. Nicolas. Paris, Ernest Leroux, 1905

—— *Le Béyân persan*. trans. A.L.M. Nicolas, 4 vols, Paris, Librairie Paul Geuthner, 1911–14

—— *Le Livre des sept preuves*, trans. A.L.M. Nicolas. Paris, Maisonneuve, 1902

—— *Selections from the Writings of the Báb*, trans. Habib Taherzadeh et al. Haifa, Baha'i World Centre, 1976

Bach, M., *Shoghi Effendi: An Appreciation*. New York, Hawthorne Books, 1958

Backwell, R., *The Christianity of Jesus*. Portlaw, Ireland, Volturna Press, 1972

Badiee, J., *An Earthly Paradise: Bahá'í Houses of Worship Around the World*. Oxford, George Ronald, 1992

Badi'i, H. (comp.), *The True Foundation of All Economics*, 2nd. edn. Saint Vincent, n.p., 1996

Bahá'í International Community, *The Bahá'ís of Iran: A Report on the Persecution of a Religious Minority*, rev. edn. New York, Bahá'í International Community, 1982; supplement: *Major Developments, July 1982–July 1983*

—— *The Prosperity of Humankind*. [Haifa] Office of Public Information, 1995

—— *World Citizenship: A Global Ethic for Sustainable Development*, *BWNS* 1993–4: 295–304

Bahá'í Revelation (comp.), rev. edn. London, Bahá'í Publishing Trust, 1970

Bahá'í Scholarship: A Compilation and Essays. Bahá'í Studies in Australia, Vol. 1. Parksville, VIC, Association for Bahá'í Studies, Australia, 1993

Bahá'í World, vol. 1 (*Bahá'í Yearbook*), vols. 2–12 Wilmette, Bahá'í Publishing Trust, 1980–1 (first publ. 1926–56); vols. 13–18 Haifa, Bahá'í World Centre, 1970–86; NS from 1992/3 Haifa, Bahá'í World Centre

Bahá'í World Faith: Selected Writings of Bahá'u'lláh and 'Abdu'l-Bahá, 2nd edn. Wilmette, Bahá'í Publishing Trust, 1956

Bahá'u'lláh, *Epistle to the Son of the Wolf*, trans. Shoghi Effendi. Wilmette, Bahá'í Publishing Trust, 1962 (1st edn. 1941)

—— *Gleanings from the Writings of Bahá'u'lláh*, trans. Shoghi Effendi, rev. edn. London, Bahá'í Publishing Trust, 1978 (1st edn. (USA) 1935)

—— *The Hidden Words of Bahá'u'lláh*, trans. Shoghi Effendi. London, Bahá'í Publishing Trust, 1966 (1st edn. 1929)

—— *The Kitáb-i-Aqdas: The Most Holy Book*. Haifa, Bahá'í World Centre, 1992

—— *The Kitáb-i-Iqan: The Book of Certitude*, trans. Shoghi Effendi, 3rd edn. London, Bahá'í Publishing Trust, 1982 (1st edn. (USA) 1931)

—— *Prayers and Meditations by Bahá'u'lláh*, comp. and trans. Shoghi Effendi, rev. edn. London, Bahá'í Publishing Trust, 1978 (1st edn. (USA) 1938)

—— *The Proclamation of Bahá'u'lláh to the Kings and Leaders of the World*. Haifa, Bahá'í World Centre, 1967

—— *The Seven Valleys and the Four Valleys*, trans. Ali Kuli Khan and M. Gail, 3rd rev. edn. Wilmette, Bahá'í Publishing Trust, 1978 (1st edn. 1945)

—— *Tablets of Bahá'u'lláh Revealed after the* Kitáb-i-Aqdas, trans. H. Taherzadeh et al. Haifa, Bahá'í World Centre, 1978

—— *Writings of Bahá'u'lláh*. New Delhi, Bahá'í Publishing Trust, 1986

Bakhash, Shaul, *Iran: Monarchy, Bureaucracy and Reform Under the Qajars, 1858–1896*. London, Ithaca Press, for St Antony's College, Oxford, 1978

Balch, R.W., Farnsworth, G., and Wilkins, S., 'When the bombs drop: Reactions to disconfirmed prophecy in a millennial sect', *Sociological Perspectives* 26 (1983): 137–58

Balyuzi, H.M., *'Abdu'l-Bahá: The Centre of the Covenant of Bahá'u'lláh*. London, George Ronald, 1971

—— *The Báb: The Herald of the King of Days*. Oxford, George Ronald, 1973

—— *Bahá'u'lláh The King of Glory*. Oxford, George Ronald, 1980

—— *Edward Granville Browne and the Bahá'í Faith*. Oxford, George Ronald, 1970

—— *Eminent Bahá'ís in the Time of Bahá'u'lláh*. Oxford, George Ronald, 1985

—— *Khadíjih Bagum: The Wife of the Báb*. Oxford, George Ronald, 1981

Banani, A., *The Modernization of Iran, 1921–1941*. Stanford, Stanford University Press, 1961

—— 'The writings of 'Abdu'l-Bahá', *World Order* 6/1 (1971): 67–74

Bayat, M., *Mysticism and Dissent: Socioreligious Thought in Qajar Iran*. Syracuse, Syracuse University Press, 1982

Bergsmo, M. (ed.), *Studying the Writings of Shoghi Effendi*. Oxford, George Ronald, 1991

Bjorling, Joel, *The Bahai Faith: A Historical Bibliography*. New York, Garland, 1985

Blomfield, Lady, *The Chosen Highway*. Wilmette, Bahá'í Publishing Trust, 1967 (first publ. 1940)

Blomfield, Lady and Shoghi Effendi, *The Passing of 'Abdu'l-Bahá*. London, Bahá'í Publishing Trust, n.d. (first publ. Haifa, 1922)

Bramson-Lerche, L., 'The Bahá'í Faith in Nigeria', *Dialogue and Alliance* 6/4 (1992–3): 104–25

—— 'Some aspects of the development of the Bahá'í Administrative Order in America, 1922–1936', in M. Momen (ed.), *Studies in Bábí and Bahá'í History, Vol. 1*, pp. 255–300. Los Angeles, Kalimát Press, 1982

—— 'Some aspects of the establishment of the Guardianship', in *Studies in Honor of the Late Hasan M. Balyuzi, KSBBR 5*, ed. M. Momen, pp. 253–93. Los Angeles, Kalimát Press, 1988

Braun, E., *From Strength to Strength: The First Half Century of the Formative Age of the Bahá'í Era*. Wilmette, Bahá'í Publishing Trust, 1978

—— *A Reader's Guide: The Development of Bahá'í Literature in English*. Oxford, George Ronald, 1986

Brown, R.A., *Memories of 'Abdu'l-Bahá: Recollections of the Early Days of the Bahá'í Faith in California*. Wilmette, Bahá'í Publishing Trust, 1980

Browne, E.G., *A Literary History of Persia*, 4 vols. Cambridge, Cambridge University Press, 1902–24

—— *Selections from the Writings of E.G. Browne on the Bábí and Bahá'í Religions*, ed. M. Momen. Oxford, George Ronald, 1987

—— (ed.), *Kitáb-i-Nuqṭatu'l-Káf*. Leyden, Brill and London, Luzac, 1910

—— (ed. and trans.), *The Táríkh-i-Jadíd, or New History of Mírzá 'Alí Muḥammad the Báb, by Mírzá Ḥusayn of Hamadán*. Cambridge, Cambridge University Press, 1893

—— (ed. and trans.), *A Traveller's Narrative, Written to Illustrate the Episode of the Báb*, 2 vols. Cambridge, Cambridge University Press, 1891

—— (trans.), 'Personal reminiscences of the Bábí insurrection at Zanján in 1850, . . . by Áqá 'Abdu'l-Aḥad-i-Zanjání', *Journal of the Royal Asiatic Society* 29 (1897): 761–827

—— (comp.), *Materials for the Study of the Bábí Religion*. Cambridge, Cambridge University Press, 1918

Buck, C., *Symbol and Secret: Qur'an Commentary in Bahá'u'lláh's Kitáb-i-Íqán, KSBBR 7*. Los Angeles, Kalimát Press, 1995

—— 'Native messengers of God in Canada?: A test case for Bahá'í universalism', *Bahá'í Studies Review* 6 (1996): 97–133

—— 'A unique eschatological interface: Bahá'u'lláh and cross-cultural messianism', In *In Iran. KSBBH 3*, ed. P. Smith, pp. 157–79. Los Angeles, Kalimát Press, 1986

Cambridge History of Iran, vol. 7: *From Nadir Shah to the Islamic Republic*, ed. Peter Avery, Gavin Hambly, and Charles Melville. Cambridge, Cambridge University Press, 1991

Cameron, G. and Momen, W., *A Basic Bahá'í Chronology*. Oxford, George Ronald, 1996

Caton, P., *Equal Circles: Women and Men in the Bahá'í Community*. Los Angeles, Kalimát Press, 1987

—— (ed.), 'Bahá'í influences on Mírzá 'Abdu'lláh, Qájár court musician and master of the *radíf*', in *From Iran East and West, KSBBH* 2, ed. J.R. Cole and M. Momen, pp. 31–64. Los Angeles, Kalimát Press, 1984

Chamberlain, S. (comp.), *Abdul Baha on Divine Philosophy*. Boston, Tudor Press, 1916

Chanler, J., *From Gaslight to Dawn*. New York, New History Society, 1956

Chase, T., *In Galilee*. Chicago, Bahai Publishing Society, 1908; rev. edn. Los Angeles, Kalimát Press, 1985

Chew, P.G.L., *The Chinese Religion and the Bahá'í Faith*. Oxford, George Ronald, 1993

—— 'The first forty years of the Bahá'í Faith in Malaysia and Singapore', rev. edn. mimeographed. Singapore, Singapore Bahá'í Bookshop, 1991

—— 'The Singapore Council of Women and the women's movement', *Journal of Southeast Asian Studies* 25/1 (1994): 112–40

Cheyne, Thomas K. *The Reconciliation of Races and Religions*. London; A&C Black, 1914.

Cole, J.R.I., 'Bahá'u'lláh and the Naqshbandí Sufis in Iraq, 1854–1856', In *From Iran East and West, KSBBH* 2, ed. J.R. Cole and M. Momen, pp. 1–28. Los Angeles, Kalimát Press, 1984

—— 'Bahá'u'lláh's 'Commentary on the Súrah of the Sun'. Introduction and translation', *Bahá'í Studies Bulletin* 4/3–4 (April 1990): 4–27

—— 'Bahá'u'lláh on Hinduism and Zoroastrianism: The tablet to Mírzá Abu'l-Faḍl concerning the questions of Manakji Limji Hatataria, introduction and provisional translation', unpublished paper

—— 'The Concept of Manifestation in the Bahá'í Writings', *Bahá'í Studies* 9 (1982)

—— 'Iranian millenarianism and democratic thought in the 19th century', *International Journal of Middle East Studies* 24 (1992): 1–26

—— *Modernity and the Millennium: The Genesis of the Bahai Faith in the Nineteenth-Century Middle East*. New York, Columbia University Press, 1998

—— 'Problems of chronology in Bahá'u'lláh's Tablet of Wisdom'. *World Order* 13/3 (1979): 24–39

Collins, W.P., *Bibliography of English-Language Works on the Bábí and Bahá'í Faiths, 1844–1985*. Oxford, George Ronald, 1990

—— 'Kenosha, 1893–1912: History of an early Bahá'í community in the United States', in M. Momen (ed.), *Studies in Bábí and Bahá'í History, Vol. 1*, pp. 225–53. Los Angeles, Kalimát Press, 1982

Conow, B.H., *The Bahá'í Teachings: A Resurgent Model of the Universe*. Oxford, George Ronald, 1990

Continental Board of Counsellors in Europe (comp.), *Keenness of Vision*. London, Bahá'í Publishing Trust, 1994

Cooper, R., *The Bahais of Iran*, rev. edn. London: Minority Rights Group, 1985

Corbin, H., *En Islam iranien: Aspects spirituels et philosophiques* 4 vols. Paris, Gallimard, 1971–2

Covenant of Bahá'u'lláh (comp.), 2nd edn. London, Bahá'í Publishing Trust, 1963

Dahl, A.L., *The Eco Principle: Ecology and Economics in Symbiosis*. Oxford, George Ronald and London, Zed Books, 1996

—— 'The world order of nature', in Charles Lerche (ed.), *Emergence: Dimensions of a New World Order*, pp. 161–74. London, Bahá'í Publishing Trust, 1991

—— (ed.) *Mark Tobey: Art and Belief*. Oxford, George Ronald, 1984

Danesh, H.B., 'Remarks to the meeting of fraternal affiliate Associations of Bahá'í Studies, Wednesday, October 6, 1988, Ottawa, Canada', *Bahá'í Studies Bulletin* 4/3–4 (April 1990): 71–80

Ebaugh, H.R.F. and Vaughn, S.L., 'Ideology and recruitment in religious groups', *Review of Religious Research* 26/2 (1984): 148–57

Elsberry, T., *Marie of Romania*. London, Cassell, 1972

Esslemont, J.E., *Bahá'u'lláh and the New Era*. (A=) London, George Allen & Unwin, 1923; (B=) 4th edn. London, Bahá'í Publishing Trust, 1974

Faizi, A.Q., *Milly: A Tribute to the Hand of the Cause, Amelia E. Collins*. Oxford, George Ronald, 1977

Fananapazir, K. and Lambden, S., 'The Tablet of Medicine (*Lawḥ-i-Ṭibb*) of Bahá'u'lláh: A provisional translation with occasional notes', *Bahá'í Studies Bulletin* 6/4–7/2 (October 1992): 18–65

Fazel, S., "Abdu'l-Bahá on Christ and Christianity. In conversation with Pasteur Monnier', *Bahá'í Studies Review* 3/1 (1993): 1–17

—— 'Is the Bahá'í Faith a world religion', *Journal of Bahá'í Studies* 6/1 (1994): 1–16

Ferraby, J. *All Things Made New: A Comprehensive Outline of the Bahá'í Faith*. London, George Allen and Unwin, 1957; rev. edn. London, Bahá'í Publishing Trust, 1975

Fischer, M.M.J., 'Social change and the mirrors of tradition: The Bahá'ís of Yazd', in H. Moayyad (ed.), *The Bahá'í Faith and Islam*, pp. 25–55. Ottawa, Ont.: Bahá'í Studies Publications, 1990

Fitzgerald, M. (ed.), *The Creative Circle: Art, Literature, and Music in Bahá'í Perspective*. Los Angeles, Kalimát Press, 1989

Forghani, B. (comp.), *Days to Remember*. Mona Vale, NSW, Bahá'í Publications Australia, 1983

Fozdar, J.K., *Buddha Maitrya-Amitabha has Appeared*. New Delhi, Bahá'í Publishing Trust, 1976

—— *The God of Buddha*, 3rd edn. Ariccia, Italy, Casa Editrice Bahá'í Srl., 1995

Freeman, D., *From Copper to Gold: The Life of Dorothy Baker*. Oxford, George Ronald, 1984

Froughi, F. and Lambden, S., 'A tablet of Bahá'u'lláh commenting on that verse of the Most Holy Book (*Kitáb-i-Aqdas*) about the need for an international language', *Bahá'í Studies Bulletin* 4/3–4 (April 1990): 28–49

Furútan, A.-A., *Mothers, Fathers, and Children: Practical Advice to Parents*, trans. K. and R. Crerar. Oxford, George Ronald, 1980

—— *Stories of Bahá'u'lláh*, trans. K. and R. Crerar. Oxford, George Ronald, 1986

—— *The Story of my Heart*, trans. M.A. Javid. Oxford, George Ronald, 1984

Gail, M., *Arches of the Years*. Oxford, George Ronald, 1991

—— *Khánum: The Greatest Holy Leaf*. Oxford, George Ronald, 1981

—— *Summon up Remembrance*. Oxford, George Ronald, 1987

—— *The Sheltering Branch*. Oxford, George Ronald, 1959

Garis, M.R., *Martha Root: Lioness at the Threshold*. Wilmette, Bahá'í Publishing Trust, 1983

Garlington, W.N., 'Bahá'í *bhajans*', *World Order* 16/2 (Winter 1982): 43–9

—— 'Bahá'í conversions in Malwa, central India', in *From Iran East and West*, *KSBBH* 2, ed. J.R. Cole and M. Momen, pp. 157–85. Los Angeles, Kalimát Press, 1984

—— 'The Bahai Faith in Malwa', in G.A. Odie (ed.), *Religion in South Asia*, pp. 101–17. London, Curzon Press, 1977

—— 'The Bahai Faith in Malwa: A study of a contemporary religious movement', unpublished Ph.D. dissertation, Australian National University, 1975

Garrigues, S.L., 'The Bahais of Malwa: Identity and change among the urban Bahais of central India', unpublished Ph.D. dissertation, University of Lucknow, 1976

Ghadirian, A.M., 'Count Leo Tolstoy and his appreciation of the Bahá'í Faith', *Bahá'í Studies* 5 (1979): 15–21

Ghanea-Hercock, N., 'A review of secondary literature in English on recent persecutions of Bahá'ís in Iran', *Bahá'í Studies Review* 7 (1991): 1–14

Ghaznavi, A., *The Family Repair and Maintenance Manual*. Oxford, George Ronald, 1989

Giachery, U., *Shoghi Effendi: Recollections*. Oxford, George Ronald, 1973

Goodall, H.S., and Cooper, E., *Daily Lessons Received at 'Akká, January 1908*, rev. edn. Wilmette, Bahá'í Publishing Trust, 1979, (first publ. 1908)

Gottlieb, R. and S. (eds.), *Once to Every Man and Nation: Stories About Becoming a Bahá'í*. Oxford, George Ronald, 1985

Greussing, K., 'The Babí movement in Iran, 1844–52: From merchant protest to peasant revolution', in J.M. Bak and G. Benecke (eds.), *Religion and Rural Revolt*, pp. 256–69. Manchester, Manchester University Press, 1984

Grundy, J.M., *Ten Days in the Light of 'Akká*. Wilmette, Bahá'í Publishing Trust, 1979 (first publ. 1907)

Hammond, E. (comp.), *'Abdu'l-Bahá in London*, rev. edn. London, Bahá'í Publishing Trust, 1982 (1st edn. 1912)

Harper, B.D., *Lights of Fortitude: Glimpses into the Lives of the Hands of the Cause of God*. Oxford, George Ronald, 1997

Hassall, G., 'The Bahá'í Faith in the Asia Pacific: Issues and prospects', *Bahá'í Studies Review* 6 (1996): 1–10

—— 'Outpost of a world religion: The Bahai Faith in Australia, 1920–1947', *Journal of Religious History* 16/3 (1991): 315–38

Hatcher, J.S., *From the Auroral Darkness*. Oxford, George Ronald, 1984

Hatcher, J. and W., *The Law of Love Enshrined*. Oxford, George Ronald, 1996

Hatcher, W.S., 'The Concept of Spirituality', *Bahá'í Studies* 11 (1982); also in J. and W. Hatcher, *The Law of Love*, pp. 189–249

—— *Logic and Logos: Essays on Science, Religion and Philosophy*. Oxford, George Ronald, 1990

Hatcher, W.S. and Martin, J.D. *The Bahá'í Faith: The Emerging Global Religion.* New York and San Francisco, Harper and Row, 1984

Ḥaydar-'Alí, Ḥájí Mírzá, *Stories from the Delight of Hearts*, trans. A.Q. Faizi. Los Angeles, Kalimát Press, 1980

Heggie, J. (comp.), *Bahá'í References to Judaism, Christianity and Islam, with other Materials for the Study of Progressive Revelation.* Oxford, George Ronald, 1986

Hein, K.J., *Radio Bahá'í Ecuador: A Bahá'í Development Project.* Oxford, George Ronald, 1988

Hellaby, M., *Education in the Bahá'í Family.* Oxford, George Ronald, 1987

Hellaby, W. and Hellaby, M., *Prayer: A Bahá'í Approach.* Oxford, George Ronald, 1985

Heller, W., *Lidia: The Life of Lidia Zamenhof, Daughter of Esperanto.* Oxford, George Ronald, 1985

Hofman, D., *George Townshend.* Oxford, George Ronald, 1983

Hollinger, R. (ed.), *Community Histories, KSBBR 6.* Los Angeles, Kalimát Press, 1992

—— 'Ibrahim George Kheiralla and the Bahá'í Faith in America', in *From Iran East and West, KSBBH 2*, ed. J.R. Cole and M. Momen, pp. 94–133. Los Angeles, Kalimát Press, 1984

Honnald, A. (comp.), *Vignettes from the Life of 'Abdu'l-Bahá.* Oxford, George Ronald, 1982

Hornby, H. (comp.), *Lights of Guidance: A Bahá'í Reference File*, 2nd edn. New Delhi, Bahá'í Publishing Trust, 1988 (1st edn. 1983)

Huddleston, J., *The Earth is But One Country.* 2nd edn. London, Bahá'í Publishing Trust, 1980

—— *The Search for a Just Society.* Oxford, George Ronald, 1989

Issawi, C. (ed.), *The Economic History of Iran, 1800–1914.* Chicago, University of Chicago Press, 1971

Ivanov, M.S., *Babidski Vostanii i Irane, 1848–1852.* Moscow, 1939; English-language review by V. Minorski in *Bulletin of the School of Oriental and African Studies* 11 (1946): 878–80

—— 'Babism'; and 'Babi uprisings', *Great Soviet Encyclopedia.* New York, Macmillan, 1973

Ives, H.C., *Portals to Freedom.* London, George Ronald, 1962

Jensen, M.S., 'Religion and family planning in contemporary Iran', In *In Iran. KSBBH 3*, ed. P. Smith, pp. 213–37. Los Angeles, Kalimát Press, 1986

Kazem-Beg, M., 'Bab et les Babis', *Journal Asiatique* (6th series) 7 (1866): 329–84, 457–522; 8 (1866): 196–252, 357–400, 473–507

Keddie, N.R., 'Religion and irreligion in early Iranian nationalism', *Comparative Studies in Society and History* 4/3 (1962): 265–95

Keddie, N.R., *Roots of Revolution: An Interpretive History of Modern Iran.* New Haven, Yale University Press, 1981

—— *Sayyid Jamal ad-Din 'al-Afghani': A Political Biography.* Berkeley and Los Angeles, University of California Press, 1972

Khadem, J., *Zikrullah Khadem, the Itinerant Hand of the Cause.* Wilmette, Bahá'í Publishing Trust, 1990

Khavari, K. and Khavari, S.W., *Creating a Successful Family.* Oxford, Oneworld, 1989

Khianra, D., *Immortals.* New Delhi, Bahá'í Publishing Trust, 1988

Khursheed, A., *The Seven Candles of Unity: The Story of 'Abdu'l-Bahá in Edinburgh.* London, Bahá'í Publishing Trust, 1991

Kolarz, W., *Religion in the Soviet Union*. London, Macmillan, 1961
Kolstoe, J.E., *Consultation: A Universal Light of Guidance*. Oxford, George Ronald, 1985
—— *Developing Genius: Getting the Most Out of Group Decision-Making*. Oxford, George Ronald, 1995
Labib, M., *The Seven Martyrs of Hurmuzak*, trans. M. Momen. Oxford, George Ronald, 1981
Lambden, S., 'An episode in the childhood of the Báb', in *In Iran, KSBBH 3*, ed. P. Smith, pp. 1–31. Los Angeles, Kalimát Press, 1986
—— 'The Sinaitic mysteries: Notes on Moses/Sinai motifs in Bábí and Bahá'í scripture', in *Studies in Honor of the Late Hasan M. Balyuzi, KSBBR 5*, ed. M. Momen, pp. 65–183. Los Angeles, Kalimát Press, 1988; also 'Supplement 1', *Bahá'í Studies Bulletin* 4/3–4 (April 1990): 54–6
—— 'A tablet of Mírzá Ḥusayn 'Alí Bahá'u'lláh of the early Iraq period: The Tablet of All Food', *Bahá'í Studies Bulletin* 3/1 (June 1984): 4–67
Lample, P. (comp.), *The Proofs of Bahá'u'lláh's Mission*. Riviera Beach, Palabra, 1994
Law and International Order, proceedings of the First European Bahá'í Conference on Law and International Order, De Poort, the Netherlands, 8–11 June 1995. London, Bahá'í Publishing Trust, 1996
Lawson, B.T., 'Interpretation as revelation: The Qur'án commentary of Sayyid 'Alí Muḥammad Shírází, the Báb (1819–1850)', in Andrew Rippin (ed.), *Approaches to the History of the Interpretation of the Qur'án*, pp. 223–53, Oxford, Oxford University Press, 1988
—— The Qur'án Commentary of Sayyid 'Alí Muḥammad Shírází, the Báb', Ph.D dissertation, McGill University, 1987
—— 'The terms 'Remembrance' (*dhikr*) and 'Gate' (*báb*) in the Báb's Commentary on the Sura of Joseph', in *Studies in Honor of the Late Hasan M. Balyuzi, KSBBR 5*, ed. Moojan Momen, pp. 1–63. Los Angeles, Kalimát Press, 1988
Leach, B., *Beyond East and West: Memoirs, Portraits and Essays*. London, Faber & Faber, 1960
—— *Drawings, Verse and Belief*, rev. edn. London, Oneworld, 1988
Lee, A.A. (ed.), *Circle of Peace: Reflections on the Bahá'í Teachings*. Los Angeles, Kalimát Press, 1985
—— 'The rise of the Bahá'í community of 'Ishqábád', *Bahá'í Studies* 5 (January 1979): 1–13
Lerche, C. (ed.), *Emergence: Dimensions of a New World Order*. London, Bahá'í Publishing Trust, 1991
—— (ed.), *Toward the Most Great Justice: Elements of Justice in the New World Order*. London, Bahá'í Publishing Trust, 1996
MacEoin, D., 'Aspects of militancy and quietism in Imami Shi'ism', *British Society for Middle Eastern Studies Bulletin* 11 (1984): 18–27
—— 'The Babi concept of holy war', *Religion* 12 (1982): 93–129
—— 'Bahai persecutions', *Encyclopaedia Iranica*
—— 'Changes in charismatic authority in Qajar Shi'ism', in Edmund Bosworth and Carole Hillenbrand (eds.), *Qajar Iran: Political, Social and Cultural Change, 1800–1925*, pp. 148–76. Edinburgh, Edinburgh University Press, 1983
—— 'Early Shaykhí reactions to the Báb and his claims', in M. Momen (ed.), *Studies in Babí and Bahá'í History, Vol. 1*, pp. 1–47. Los Angeles, Kalimát Press, 1982
—— 'From Babism to Bahaism: Problems of militancy, quietism, and conflation in the construction of a religion', *Religion* 13 (1983): 219–55

—— 'From Shaykhism to Babism: A Study in Charismatic Renewal in Shi'i Islam', Ph.D. dissertation, University of Cambridge, 1979
—— 'Hierarchy, authority, and eschatology in early Bábí thought', in *In Iran. KSBBH 3*, ed. P. Smith, pp. 95–155. Los Angeles, Kalimát Press, 1986
—— 'Nineteenth century Babi talismans', *Studia Iranica* 14/1 (1985): 77–98
—— 'A note on the numbers of Bábí and Bahá'í martyrs in Iran', *Bahá'í Studies Bulletin* 2/2 (1983): 84–8
—— 'Orthodoxy and heterodoxy in nineteenth-century Shi'ism: The cases of Shaykhism and Babism', *Journal of the American Oriental Society* 110 (1990): 323–9
—— *Rituals in Babism and Bahaism*. London, I.B. Tauris, British Academic Press, 1994
—— *The Sources for Early Babi Doctrine and History: A Survey*. Leiden, Brill, 1992
McLean, J.A., *Dimensions in Spirituality: Reflections on the Meaning of Spiritual Life and Transformation in Light of the Bahá'í Faith*. Oxford, George Ronald, 1994
—— 'Prolegomena to Bahá'í theology', *Journal of Bahá'í Studies* 5/1 (1992): 25–66
—— (ed.), *Revisioning the Sacred: New Perspectives on a Bahá'í Theology, KSBBR 8*. Los Angeles, Kalimát Press, 1997
Malouf, D.L., *Unveiling the Hidden Words: The Norms Used by Shoghi Effendi in his Translation of the Hidden Words*. Oxford, George Ronald, 1997
Maneck, S.S., 'Wisdom and dissimulation: The use and meaning of *hikmat* in the Bahá'í writings and history', *Bahá'í Studies Review* 6 (1996): 11–23
—— 'Women in the Bahai Faith', in A. Sharma (ed.), *Religion and Women*, Albany, State University of New York Press, 1994
Martin, D., 'The Persecution of the Bahá'ís of Iran, 1844–1984'. *Bahá'í Studies* 12/13, 1984
Martin, J.D., 'The Life and Work of Sarah Jane Farmer, 1847–1916', MA thesis, University of Waterloo (Ontario), 1967
Matthews, G.L., *The Challenge of Bahá'u'lláh*. Oxford, George Ronald, 1993
Maxwell, M., *An Early Pilgrimage*. Oxford, George Ronald, 1953
Mehrabkhani, R., *Mullá Ḥusayn: Disciple at Dawn*. Los Angeles, Kalimát Press, 1987
Metelmann, V.P., *Lua Getsinger: Herald of the Covenant*. Oxford, George Ronald, 1997
Miller, W.M., *The Bahá'í Faith: Its History and Teachings*. South Pasadena, William Carey Library, 1974
Mishra, P.N., *Kalki Avatar*. New Delhi, Bahá'í Publishing Trust, 1977
Moayyad, H. (ed.) *The Bahá'í Faith and Islam*. Ottawa, Association for Bahá'í Studies, 1990
Moffett, R.J., *New Keys to the Book of Revelation*, 2nd edn. New Delhi, Bahá'í Publishing Trust, 1980
Momen, M., "Abdu'l-Bahá's commentary on the Islamic tradition "I was a hidden treasure"', *Bahá'í Studies Bulletin* 3/4 (December 1985): 4–64
—— 'The Bahai community of Ashkhabad: Its social basis and historical importance', in S. Akiner (ed.), *Cultural Change and Continuity in Central Asia*, pp. 278–305. London, Kegan Paul, 1991
—— *The Bahá'í Faith: A Short Introduction*. Oxford, Oneworld, rev. edn. 1999
—— *Bahá'í Focus on Development*. London, Bahá'í Publishing Trust, 1988

—— 'The Bahá'í influence on the reform movements of the Islamic world in the 1860s and 1870s', *Bahá'í Studies Bulletin* 2/2 (1983): 47–65
—— 'The Bahá'í system of transliteration', *Bahá'í Studies Bulletin* 5/1–2 (January 1991): 13–55
—— *Buddhism and the Bahá'í Faith: An Introduction to the Bahá'í Faith for Theravada Buddhists*. Oxford, George Ronald, 1995
—— 'The Cyprus exiles', *Bahá'í Studies Bulletin* 5/3 (June 1991): 84–113
—— 'Early relations between Christian missionaries and the Bábí and Bahá'í communities', in M. Momen (ed.), *Studies in Bábí and Bahá'í History, Vol. 1*, pp. 49–82. Los Angeles, Kalimát Press, 1982
—— *Dr J.E. Esslemont*. London, Bahá'í Publishing Trust, 1975
—— 'Hasan M. Balyuzi (1908–1980): A bio-bibliographical sketch', in M. Momen (ed.), *Studies in Honor of the Late Hasan M. Balyuzi, KSBBR 5*, pp. xi–xx. Los Angeles, Kalimát Press, 1988
—— *Hinduism and the Bahá'í Faith*. Oxford, George Ronald, 1990
—— 'The integration into the British Bahá'í community of recent Iranian Bahá'í migrants', *Bahá'í Studies Bulletin* 4/3–4 (April 1990): 50–3
—— *An Introduction to Shi'i Islam: The History and Doctrines of Twelver Shi'ism*. Oxford, George Ronald, 1985
—— 'Relativism: A basis for Bahá'í metaphysics', in M. Momen (ed.), *Studies in Honor of the Late Hasan M. Balyuzi. KSBBR 5*, pp. 185–217. Los Angeles, Kalimát Press, 1988
—— 'The social basis of the Babi upheavals in Iran (1848–53): A preliminary analysis', *International Journal of Middle East Studies* 15 (1983): 157–83
—— 'The trial of Mullá 'Alí Basṭámí: A combined Sunní–Shí'í *fatwá* against the Báb', *Iran* 20 (1982): 113–43
—— unpublished manuscripts: 'Iran'; 'Tehran'
—— The works of Shaykh Aḥmad al-Aḥsá'í: A bibliography, based upon *Fihirist kutub masháyikh'izám* of Shaykh Abu'l-Qásim Kirmání. *Bahá'í Studies Bulletin Monograph, No.1*. Cyclostyled
—— (ed.), *The Bábí and Bahá'í Religions, 1844–1944: Some Contemporary Western Accounts*. Oxford, George Ronald, 1981
—— (ed.), *Scripture and Revelation*. Oxford, George Ronald, 1997
Momen, W. (ed.), *A Basic Bahá'í Dictionary*. Oxford, George Ronald, 1989
—— 'How close are we to the Lesser Peace?', in *Law and International Order*, pp. 103–50. London, Bahá'í Publishing Trust, 1996
Morrison, G., *To Move the World: Louis G. Gregory and the Advancement of Racial Unity in America*. Wilmette, Bahá'í Publishing Trust, 1982
Mottahedeh, R., *The Mantle of the Prophet: Religion and Politics in Iran*. Harmondsworth, Penguin Books, 1985
Muhájir, Í.F., (ed.), *The Blazing Years: 50th Anniversary of the Bahá'í Faith in the Philippines*. Manila, Philippines Bahá'í Publishing Trust, n.d
—— *Dr Muhájir: Hand of the Cause of God, Knight of Bahá'u'lláh*. London, Bahá'í Publishing Trust, 1992
—— (comp.), *The Mystery of God*, rev. edn. London: Bahá'í Publishing Trust, 1979
Muhammad, K.B.A.M., 'Some new notes on Babism', *Journal of the Royal Asiatic Society* (July 1927): 442–70
Mühlschlegel, P., *Auguste Forel and the Bahá'í Faith*, trans. H. Neri. Oxford, George Ronald, 1978

Munírih Khánum, *Memoirs and Letters*, trans. S.A. Smith. Los Angeles, Kalimát Press, 1986
Muṣṭafá, M., *Bahá'u'lláh: The Great Announcement of the Qur'án*, trans. R. Muṣṭafá, ed. L.M. Herzog. Dhaka, Bahá'í Publishing Trust [1993]
Nabíl (-i-A'zam), *The Dawn-Breakers: Nabíl's Narrative of the Early Days of the Bahá'í Revelation*, trans. Shoghi Effendi. Wilmette, Bahá'í Publishing Trust, 1932
Nakhjavání, B., *When We Grow Up*. Oxford, George Ronald, 1979
National Spiritual Assembly of the Bahá'ís of Canada (comp.), *'Abdu'l-Bahá in Canada*. Forest, Ontario, Forest Free Press, 1962
National Spiritual Assembly of the Bahá'ís of South Africa, *A Pictorial History of the Bahá'í Faith in South Africa, 1911 to 1989*. Johannesburg, 1989
National Spiritual Assembly of the Bahá'ís of the United Kingdom (comp.), *Principles of Bahá'í Administration*, 4th edn. London: Bahá'í Publishing Trust, 1976
Nerenberg, A. *Love and Estrangement in the Bahá'í Community*. Los Angeles, Kalimát Press, n.d
Nicolas, A.L.M., *Essai sur le Chéikhisme*, 4 vols. Paris, Geunther & Leroux, 1910–14
—— *Massacres de Babis en Perse*. Paris, Adrien-Maisonneuve, Libraire d'Amérique et d'Orient, 1936
Nikjoo, H. and Vickers, S. *Distinctive Aspects of Bahá'í Education*. London, Bahá'í Publishing Trust, 1993
Osei, A., 'African traditional religion: A Bahá'í perspective'. *Herald of the South* 23 (April–June 1990): 35–9
Parsons, A., *'Abdu'l-Bahá in America: Agnes Parson's Diary, April 11, 1912–November 11, 1912*, ed. Richard Hollinger. Los Angeles, Kalimát Press, 1996
Perkins, M., *Hour of the Dawn*. Oxford, George Ronald, 1987
Phelps, M.H., *The Life and Teachings of Abbas Effendi*. New York, G.P. Putnams, 1904; rev. and abridged edn. *The Master in 'Akká*. Los Angeles, Kalimát Press, 1985
Rabbani, R., *The Desire of the World: Material for the Contemplation of God and his Manifestation for this Day*. Oxford, George Ronald, 1982
—— *The Priceless Pearl*. London, Bahá'í Publishing Trust, 1969
Rafati, V., 'The Bahai community of Iran', *Encyclopaedia Iranica*
—— 'The Development of Shaykhi Thought in Shi'i Islam', Ph.D. dissertation, University of California at Los Angeles, 1979
Richardson, R.P., 'The rise and fall of the Parliament of Religions at Greenacre', *Open Court* 46/3 (March 1931): 129–66
Riggs, R.F., *The Apocalypse Unsealed*. New York, Philosophical Library, 1981
Rost, H.T.D., *The Brilliant Stars: The Bahá'í Faith and the Education of Children*. Oxford, George Ronald, 1979
—— *The Golden Rule: A Universal Ethic*. Oxford, George Ronald, 1986
Ruhe, D.S., *Door of Hope: A Century of the Bahá'í Faith in the Holy Land*. Oxford, George Ronald, 1983
Rutstein, N., *Corinne True: Faithful Handmaid of 'Abdu'l-Bahá*. Oxford, George Ronald, 1987
—— *To Be One: A Battle Against Racism*. Oxford, George Ronald, 1988
Sabet, H., *The Heavens are Cleft Asunder*. Oxford, George Ronald, 1975
Sachedina, A.A., *Islamic Messianism: The Idea of the Mahdi in Twelver Shi'ism*. Albany, State University of New York Press, 1981
Saint-Blancat, C., 'Nation et religion chez les immigrés iraniens en Italie', *Archives science social des religions* 68/1 (1989): 27–37

Salmání, U.M-'A., *My Memories of Bahá'u'lláh*, trans. M. Gail. Los Angeles, Kalimát Press, 1982

Savi, J., *The Eternal Quest for God: An Introduction to the Divine Philosophy of 'Abdu'l- Bahá*. Oxford, George Ronald, 1989

Scholl, S., 'Shaykhíyah', in *The Encyclopedia of Religion*, ed. M. Eliade. New York, Macmillan, 1987

Sears, W., *God Loves Laughter*. London, George Ronald, 1960

—— *Release the Sun*. Wilmette, Bahá'í Publishing Trust, 1975

—— *Thief in the Night, or the Strange Case of the Missing Millennium*. London, George Ronald, 1961

—— *The Wine of Astonishment*. London, George Ronald, 1963

Sears, W. and Quigley, R., *The Flame*. Oxford, George Ronald, 1972

Seow, J.E.H., *The Pure in Heart: The Historical Development of the Bahai Faith in China, Southeast Asia and Far East*. Mona Vale, NSW, Bahai Publications Australia, 1991

Shaw, S.J. and E.K., *History of the Ottoman Empire and Modern Turkey*, 2 vols. Cambridge, Cambridge University Press, 1976–7

Shearer, T., *Lord of the Dawn: Quetzalcoátl, the Plumed Serpent of Mexico*. Healdsburg CA, Naturegraph, 1971

Shoghi Effendi, *The Advent of Divine Justice*, rev. edn. Wilmette, Bahá'í Publishing Trust, 1963

—— *Arohanui: Letters from Shoghi Effendi to New Zealand*. Suva, Bahá'í Publishing Trust, 1982

—— *Bahá'í Administration*, 5th edn. Wilmette, Bahá'í Publishing Trust, 1945

—— *Citadel of Faith: Messages to America, 1947–1957*. Wilmette, Bahá'í Publishing Trust, 1965

—— *The Faith of Bahá'u'lláh, A World Religion*. Wilmette, Bahá'í Publishing Committee, 1947; republished in National Spiritual Assembly of the Bahá'ís of the United Kingdom, in *Guidance for Today and Tomorrow*. London, Bahá'í Publishing Trust, 1953, pp. 1–10

—— *God Passes By*, rev. edn. Wilmette, Bahá'í Publishing Trust, 1974

—— *High Endeavours: Messages to Alaska*. [Anchorage] National Spiritual Assembly of the Bahá'ís of Alaska, 1976

—— *Letters from the Guardian to Australia and New Zealand, 1923–1957*. Sydney, NSW, National Spiritual Assembly of the Bahá'ís of Australia, 1970

—— *The Light of Divine Guidance: The Messages of the Guardian of the Bahá'í Faith to the Bahá'ís of Germany and Austria*, 2 vols. Langenhain, Bahá'í-Verlag, 1982–5

—— *Messages to America: Selected Letters and Cablegrams Addressed to the Bahá'ís of North America, 1932–1946*. Wilmette, Bahá'í Publishing Trust, 1947

—— *Messages to the Antipodes: Communications from Shoghi Effendi to the Bahá'í Communities of Australasia*, ed. Graham Hassall. Mona Vale, Bahá'í Publications Australia, 1997

—— *Messages to the Bahá'í World, 1950–1957*, 2nd edn. Wilmette, Bahá'í Publishing Trust, 1971

—— *Messages to Canada*. [Toronto, Ont.] National Spiritual Assembly of the Bahá'ís of Canada, 1965

—— *Messages of Shoghi Effendi to the Indian Subcontinent, 1923–1957*, comp. I.F. Muhajir. New Delhi, Bahá'í Publishing Trust, 1995

—— *The Promised Day is Come*, rev. edn. Wilmette, Bahá'í Publishing Trust, 1980

—— *The Unfolding Destiny of the British Bahá'í Community.* London, Bahá'í Publishing Trust, 1981
—— *The World Order of Bahá'u'lláh*, rev. edn. Wilmette, Bahá'í Publishing Trust, 1965
—— (comp.), *The Bahá'í Faith, 1844–1952: Information Statistical and Comparative.* London, Bahá'í Publishing Trust [1953]
Sims, B.R. (comp.), *Japan Will Turn Ablaze! Tablets of 'Abdu'l-Bahá, Letters of Shoghi Effendi, and Historical Notes About Japan.* [Tokyo] Bahá'í Publishing Trust, Japan, 1974
—— (comp.), *Traces that Remain: A Pictorial History of the Early Days of the Bahai Faith Among the Japanese.* [Tokyo] Bahai Publishing Trust, 1989
Smith, P., 'The American Bahá'í community, 1894–1917: A preliminary survey', in M. Momen (ed.), *Studies in Bábí and Bahá'í History, Vol. 1*, pp. 85–223. Los Angeles, Kalimát Press, 1982
—— *The Bábí and Bahá'í Religions: From Messianic Shí'ism to a World Religion.* Cambridge, Cambridge University Press, 1987
—— 'The Bahai communities', *Encyclopaedia Iranica*
—— *The Bahá'í Faith: A Short History.* Oxford, Oneworld, 1996
—— 'The Bahá'í Faith in the West: History and social composition', in P. Smith (ed.), *The Bahá'í Faith in the West.* Los Angeles, Kalimát Press, forthcoming
—— *The Bahá'í Religion: A Short Introduction to its History and Teachings.* Oxford, George Ronald, 1988
—— 'Millenarianism in the Babi and Baha'i religions', in Roy Wallis (ed.), *Millennialism and Charisma*, pp. 231–83. Belfast, Queen's University, 1982
—— 'A note on Babi and Bahá'í numbers in Iran', *Iranian Studies* 17/2–3 (1984): 295–301
—— '*Reality* magazine: Editorship and ownership of an American Bahá'í periodical', in *From Iran East and West, KSBBH 2*, ed. J.R. Cole and M. Momen, pp. 135–55. Los Angeles, Kalimát Press, 1984
Smith, P. and Momen, M., 'The Bábí movement: A resource mobilization perspective', in *In Iran, KSBBH 3*, ed. P. Smith, pp. 33–93. Los Angeles, Kalimát Press, 1986
—— 'The Bahai Faith 1957–1988: A survey of contemporary developments', *Religion* 19 (1989): 63–91
Smith, P.R., 'The development and influence of the Bahá'í Administrative Order in Great Britain, 1914–50', in *Community Histories, KSBBR 6*, ed. R. Hollinger, pp. 153–215. Los Angeles, Kalimát Press, 1992
—— 'What was a Bahá'í? Concerns of British Bahá'ís, 1900–1920', in *Studies in Honor of the Late Hasan M. Balyuzi, KSBBR 5*, ed. M. Momen, pp. 219–51. Los Angeles, Kalimát Press, 1988
Sohrab, M.A., *Abdul Baha in Egypt.* New York, J.H. Sears for New History Foundation, 1929
—— *Abdul Baha's Grandson: Story of a Twentieth Century Excommunication.* New York, Universal Publishing Co. for the New History Foundation, 1943
—— *Broken Silence: The Story of Today's Struggle for Religious Freedom.* New York, Universal Publishing Co. for the New History Society, 1942
—— *The Will and Testament of Abdul Baha: An Analysis.* New York, Universal Publishing Co. for the New History Society, 1944
Sours, M., *A Study of Bahá'u'lláh's Tablet to the Christians.* Oxford, Oneworld, 1990

—— *The Prophecies of Jesus*. Oxford, Oneworld, 1991
—— *Understanding Biblical Evidence*. Oxford, Oneworld, 1990
—— *Understanding Christian Beliefs*. Oxford, Oneworld, 1991
Sprague, S., *A Year with the Bahais of India and Burma*. London, Priory Press, 1908
Star of the West, vol. 1 (*Bahai News*), vol. 2–14. Chicago; Reprinted Oxford, George Ronald, 1978
Stendardo, L., *Leo Tolstoy and the Bahá'í Faith*, trans. J. Fox. Oxford, George Ronald, 1985
Stephens, K.D., *So Great A Cause! A Surprising New Look at the Latter Day Saints*. Healdsburg, Naturegraph, 1973
Stiles, S., 'Early Zoroastrian conversions to the Bahá'í Faith in Yazd, Iran', in *From Iran East and West, KSBBH* 2, ed. J.R. Cole and M. Momen, pp. 67–93. Los Angeles, Kalimát Press, 1984
Stockman, R.H., *The Bahá'í Faith in America*, 2 vols to date, vol. 1: *Origins, 1892–1900*. Wilmette, Bahá'í Publishing Trust, 1985; vol. 2: *Early Expansion, 1900–1912*. Oxford, George Ronald, 1995
—— 'Jesus Christ in the Bahá'í Writings', *Bahá'í Studies Review* 2/1 (1992): 33–41
Szanto-Felbermann, R., *Rebirth*. London, Bahá'í Publishing Trust, 1980
Ṭabáṭabá'í, A.S.M.H., *Shi'ite Islam*, trans. S.H. Naṣr. London Allen & Unwin, 1975
Taherzadeh, A., *The Covenant of Bahá'u'lláh*. Oxford, George Ronald, 1992
—— *The Revelation of Bahá'u'lláh*, 4 vols. Oxford, George Ronald, 1974–87
Thomas, R.W., 'A long and thorny path: Race relations in the American Bahá'í community', in Anthony A. Lee (ed), *Circle of Unity: Bahá'í Approaches to Current Social Issues*, pp. 37–65. Los Angeles, Kalimát Press, 1984
—— *Racial Unity: An Imperative for Progress*. Wilmette, NSA of the United States, 1992
Thompson, J., *The Diary of Juliet Thompson*. Los Angeles, Kalimát Press, 1983
Townshend, G., *Christ and Bahá'u'lláh*. London, George Ronald, 1957
—— *The Heart of the Gospel*, rev. edn. London, George Ronald, 1951 (first published 1939)
Tudor-Pole, W., *Writing on the Ground*. London, Neville Spearman, 1968
Tyson, J., *World Peace and World Government: From Vision to Reality. A Bahá'í Approach*. Oxford, George Ronald, 1986
Ullman, C., *The Transformed Self: The Psychology of Religious Conversion*. New York, Plenum Press, 1989
Universal House of Justice, *Compilation of Compilations*. 2 vols. Mona Vale, NSW Bahá'í Publications Australia, 1991
—— *The Constitution of the Universal House of Justice*. Haifa, Bahá'í World Centre, 1972
—— *The Four Year Plan*. Riviera Beach, Palabra, 1996
—— *Individual Rights and Freedoms in the World Order of Bahá'u'lláh*. Wilmette, Bahá'í Publishing Trust, 1989
—— 'Mason Remey and Those Who Followed Him'. Cyclostyled MS
—— *Messages from the Universal House of Justice, 1963–1986: The Third Epoch of the Formative Age*, comp. G.W. Marks. Wilmette, Bahá'í Publishing Trust, 1996
—— *The Ministry of the Custodians: An Account of the Stewardship of the Hands of the Cause*. Haifa, Bahá'í World Centre, 1992
—— *The Promise of World Peace*. Haifa, Bahá'í World Centre, 1985
—— *The Six Year Plan, 1986–1992: Summary of Achievements*. [Haifa] Bahá'í World Centre, n.d

—— *A Synopsis and Codification of the Kitáb-i-Aqdas, the Most Holy Book of Bahá'u'lláh*. Haifa, Bahá'í World Centre, 1973
—— *A Wider Horizon: Selected Messages of the Universal House of Justice, 1983–1992*. Riviera Beach, Palabra, 1992
—— Department of Statistics. Memorandum, 15 May 1988, unpublished
—— Department of Statistics. 'Statistical Table, Six Year Plan Final Figures, 20 April 1992', mimeographed
—— Research Department, *Scholarship*. Mona Vale, NSW, Bahá'í Publications Australia, 1995
—— Research Department (comp.), *Bahíyyih Khánum: The Greatest Holy Leaf*. Haifa, Bahá'í World Centre, 1982
Vader, J.P., *For the Good of Mankind: August Forel and the Bahá'í Faith*. Oxford, George Ronald, 1984
Van den Hoonaard, W., 'The development and decline of an early Bahá'í community: Saint John, New Brunswick, Canada, 1910–1925', In *Community Histories, KSBBR* 6, ed. R. Hollinger, pp. 217–39. Los Angeles, Kalimát Press, 1992
—— *The Origins of the Bahá'í Community of Canada, 1898–1948*. Waterloo, Ont., Wilfrid Laurier University Press, 1996
Vick, H.H., *Social and Economic Development: A Bahá'í Approach*. Oxford, George Ronald, 1989
Vreeland, C. (comp.), *And the Trees Clapped their Hands: Stories of Bahá'í Pioneers*. Oxford, George Ronald, 1994
Walbridge, J., 'The Babí uprising in Zanjan: Causes and issues', *Iranian Studies* 29/3–4 (1996): 339–62
—— *Sacred Acts; Sacred Space; Sacred Time. Bahá'í Studies, Vol. 1*. Oxford, George Ronald, 1996
Warburg, M., 'Economic rituals: The structure and meaning of donations in the Bahai religion', *Social Compass* 40 (1993): 25–31
—— 'Growth patterns of new religions: The case of Bahai, in Robert Towler (ed.), *New Religions and the New Europe*, pp. 177–93. Aarhus, Aarhus University Press, 1995
—— *Iranske dokumenter: Forfølgelsen af bahá'íerne i Iran*. Copenhagen, Rhodos, 1985
Ward, A.L., *239 Days: 'Abdu'l-Bahá's Journey in America*. Wilmette, Bahá'í Publishing Trust, 1979
Weinberg, R., *Ethel Jenner Rosenberg: The Life and Times of England's Pioneer Worker*. Oxford, George Ronald, 1995
Weixelman, J., 'The traditional Navajo religion and the Bahá'í Faith', *World Order* 20/1 (fall 1985): 31–51
Whitehead, O.Z., *Some Bahá'ís to Remember*. Oxford, George Ronald, 1983
—— *Some Early Bahá'ís of the West*. Oxford, George Ronald, 1976
Whitmore, B.W., *The Dawning Place: The Building of a Temple, the Forging of the North American Bahá'í Community*. Wilmette, Bahá'í Publishing Trust, 1984
Wilcox, P., *Bahá'í Families: Perspectives, Principles, Practice*. Oxford, George Ronald, 1991
Wilhelm, R., Cobb, S. and Coy, G.L., *In His Presence: Visits to 'Abdu'l-Bahá*. Los Angeles, Kalimát Press, 1989
Williams, J.A. (comp.), *Highlights of Bahá'í Activities in Africa, 1987–1995*. n.p., 1996

Willoya, W. and Brown, V., *Warriors of the Rainbow: Strange and Prophetic Dreams of the Indian Peoples*. Healdsburg, Naturegraph Publishers, 1962

Wilson, S.G., *Bahaism and its Claims*. New York, Fleming Revell, 1915; repr. New York, AMS Press, 1970

—— 'The Bayan of the Bab', *Princeton Theological Review* 13 (1915): 633–54

Winckler, B.R., *My Pilgrimage to Haifa, November 1919*. Wilmette, Bahá'í Publishing Trust, 1996

Winckler, B.R. and Garis, M.R., *William Henry Randall: Disciple of 'Abdu'l- Bahá*. Oxford, Oneworld, 1996

Zinky, K. and Baram, A. (comp. and ed.), *Martha Root: Herald of the Kingdom*. New Delhi, Bahá'í Publishing Trust, 1983

Zohoori, E., *Names and Numbers: A Bahai History Reference Guide*. Caribbean Printers, Jamaica, 1990

Thematic Index

The Principal Figures and Periods of Bábí–Bahá'í History

Aspects of Bahá'í belief and practice

Naw Rúz
regional Bahá'í councils
review
Riḍván
'summer schools'
unity feast
Universal House of Justice
youth
zakát

The arts:

architecture
art
calligraphy
cinema and film
craftsmanship
drama and dance
iconography
music
poetry

The Bahá'í Faith and other religions:

Abraham
Adam
Bahá'í Faith and other religions
baptism
Bible
Buddhism
caliphate
Chinese religion
Christianity
confession of sins
hadíth
holy war
Húd
Ḥusayn
Imáms
Indian religions
indigenous religions
interfaith dialogue
Islam
Jesus
Judaism, Jews
Mahdí
monasticism
Moses
Muḥammad
mujtahid
Noah
priesthood
Quran
religious diversity
religious leaders
Sabeanism
Ṣáliḥ
Shaykhism
Shi'ism
sufism
tolerance
'ulamá
World Parliament of Religions
Zoroastrianism

The Covenant:

Azalís
Covenant
Covenant-breakers
Remeyite groups and organizations

Doctrines and religious teachings:

action and merit
angels
antichrist
astrology
badá
Bahá'í Faith
'Bahá'í principles'
calamity
'Central Figures'
conscience
creation
death and the afterlife
detachment
dispensation
divine judgement
dogma
dreams and visions
emotions
eschatology
esotericism

Expansion and 'teaching':

Literature:

canonical texts
lawḥ
language
literature
periodicals
'pilgrims' notes'
publishing
review
scripture
Shoghi Effendi, writings of
súra
translation
transliteration
Universal House of Justice, writings of
Word of God

Practice and law:

ablutions
abortion
adultery and fornication
alcohol
animals
artificial fertilization
ascetism
backbiting
begging
birth control
burial
charity
chastity
circumcision
cleanliness
confession of sins
cremation
dancing
devotionalism
diet
divorce
dress
drugs
excellence
fear of God
gambling
government, Bahá'í attitude towards
homosexuality
inheritance
law
'living the life'
marriage
Mashriqu'l-Adhkár
military service, pacificism
moderation
meditation
pilgrimage
politics
polygamy
prayer
prejudice
purity
qiblah
reverence
secret societies
self-defence
service to humanity
sex
slave trade, slavery
smoking
spiritual path
spiritual qualities
sterilization
suicide
talismans
trustworthiness
truthfulness
wills
work
World Peace Day
zakát

Social teachings:

agriculture
armaments
Bahá'í International Community (BIC)
Bahá'í–UNIFEM project
Bahá'í Vocational Institute for Rural Women, Indore
civilization
communism

People and places

People:

Custodians
Dayyán
Dhabíḥ
Disciples of 'Abdu'l-Bahá
Dodge, Arthur P.
Dolgorukov, Prince Dmitri Ivanovitch
Dreyfus-Barney, Hippolyte
Dreyfus-Barney, Laura
Dunn, Clara
Dunn, John Hyde
Esslemont, John E.
Fáḍil (Fazel) Mázandarání, Mírzá Asadu'lláh
Faizí, Abu'l-Qásim
Farmer, Sarah
Featherstone, Collis
Ferraby, John
Forel, August
Fozdar, Shirin
Franz-Joseph
Fuat Paşa
Furúghí, Mírzá Maḥmúd
Furútan, Alí-Akbar
Getsinger, Edward and Louisa ('Lua') Aurora Moore
Giachery, Ugo
Gillespie, Dizzy
Gobineau, Joseph Arthur, Comte de
Goodall, Helen S.
Greenleaf, Charles and Elizabeth
Gregory, Louis C.
Grinevskaya, Izabella Arkadevna
Grossman, Hermann
Hádí Dawlatábádí, Mírzá
Hands of the Cause of God
Haney, Paul E.
Hannen, Joseph and Pauline
Ḥaydar-'Alí Iṣfahání, Hájí Mírzá
Hayden, Robert E.
Hearst, Pheobe
Hoar, William H.
Holley, Horace
Ḥujjat
Ḥusayn Bushrú'í, Mullá
Ḥusayn Khán, Mírzá, *Mushíru'd-dawlih*
Ibn-i-Abhar
Ibn-i-Aṣdaq
Imbrie, Robert
Ioas, Leroy
Iṣfahání, Muḥammad-Taqí
Ishráq-Khávarí, Abdu'l-Ḥamíd
Ives, Howard Colby
Jack, Marion
Jamál Burújirdí
Jamál Effendi
Jamálu'd-dín, Sayyid, 'al-Afghání'
Kappes, Lillian
Karím Khán Kirmání, Ḥájí (Muḥammad-)
Kázim Rashtí, Sayyid
Khadem, Zikrullah
Khadíjih Bagum
Khadíjih Khánum
Khammár, 'Udí
Khâzeh, Jalál
Kheiralla, Ibrahim George
King and Beloved of Martyrs
Knights of Bahá'u'lláh
Knobloch, Alma and Fanny
Leach, Bernard
MacNutt, Howard
Manúchihr Khán
Marie
Maxwell, May Ellis
Maxwell, William Sutherland
Mihdí, Mírzá
Mihdí Dahají, Sayyid
Mills, Mountfort
Mishkín-Qalam
Moody, Susan
Muhájir, Raḥmatu'lláh
Muḥammad, Ḥájí Mírzá Sayyid
Muḥammad-'Alí, Mírzá
Muḥammad-'Alí Qá'iní, Shaykh
Muḥammad-'Alí Zunúzí
Muḥammad Iṣfahání, Sayyid
Muḥammad Muṣṭafá al-Baghdádí, Mírzá

Bahá'í holy places and other places of significance:

Chihríq
Edirne
Egypt
Green Acre
Haifa
International Archives
International Baha'i Library
Iran
Iraq
Isfáhán
Istanbul
Karbalá
Mákú
Mashhad
Mashriqu'l-Adhkár
Nayríz
Qazvín
Shíráz
Shíráz: the House of the Báb
shrines and holy places
Shrine of the Báb
Síyáh-Chál
Ṭabarsí, Shaykh
Tabríz
Tehran
Yazd
Zanján